# B1205

*Body List*

# EASTERN COACH WORKS

# Series 2

# 1001 - 5000

PUBLISHED BY

THE PSV CIRCLE

MARCH 2015

# FOREWORD

The draft for this publication was prepared by Maurice Doggett, making extensive use of ECW official records. In particular, East Yorkshire and Western Welsh body numbers have been corrected from previously published information.

The assistance of David Corke, Richard Gadsby, Tony Holdsworth, Colin Martin, Ron Maybray, Peter Tulloch and Fred Ward is gratefully acknowledged.

This publication lists all known information to March 2015.

The main section of this publication is presented in eight columns as follows:-

1. Vehicle body number
2. * if the vehicle has notes associated with it
3. Original vehicle registration mark
4. Chassis manufacturer and model
5. Chassis number
6. Seating arrangement following standard PSV Circle codes
7. Date the body was new – where known this is the date of effective first licensing or entry into service.
8. First operator / county code / fleet number (if used)

Photographs were taken or supplied by John Cockshott, A Cross, Maurice Doggett, Roy Marshall, John May, G Mead, Geoffrey Morant, Omnibus Society and Photobus. The assistance of Mike Eyre in preparing the photographs for printing is gratefully acknowledged.

Contents:

Note:

This is one of a wide range of publications produced by the PSV Circle primarily as a service to its members. The information contained herein has been taken from the content of PSV Circle monthly News Sheets and also includes information provided from other reliable sources. Considerable time and effort is taken to ensure that the content of this publication is as complete and accurate as possible, but no responsibility can be accepted for any errors or omissions. However, please tell us if you discover any!

Any general comments, updates or corrections to this publication may be sent to the Publications Manager, PSV Circle, Unit GK, Leroy House, 436 Essex Road, London N1 3QP or via email to publications.manager@psv-circle.org.uk.

Details of how to join The PSV Circle and a list of all our publications can be obtained (and ordered) from The PSV Circle website - www.psv-circle.org.uk or from the PSV Circle, Unit GK, Leroy House, 436 Essex Road, London, N1 3QP.

ISBN: 978-1-908953- 55-1

Published by the PSV Circle.
© The PSV Circle March 2015

# Introduction

The origins of the Lowestoft factory date back to 1919 when Mr E B Hutchinson (who started United Automobile Services Ltd) acquired an area of land in Laundry Lane on which buildings were erected which not only served as a garage and workshop for the Lowestoft area fleet but also as a bodybuilding workshop. During the 1920's, the Lowestoft premises, which became known as 'The Coach Factory', were enlarged to accommodate the increase in the Company's bodybuilding activities which came to embrace bodies for other operators as well as for their own fleet.

In 1929 and after seeing his Company become one of the major players in the 1920's bus and coach industry, Mr. Hutchinson sold United to the Tilling & British Automobile Traction Group jointly with the London & North Eastern Railway. The construction of new bodies by United continued as before, but as the result of the desire of the TBAT Group to rationalise the activities of its operating subsidiaries in East Anglia, a new company, the Eastern Counties Omnibus Co Ltd was registered on 14th July 1931 to take over the operations and assets of the Eastern Counties Road Car Co Ltd of Ipswich, the Ortona Motor Co Ltd of Cambridge, the Peterborough Electric Traction Co Ltd and the East Anglian area services of United. The new company came under the control of the TBAT Group and was managed by Tilling.

Included in the merger was United's bodybuilding factory at Lowestoft and Eastern Counties continued the construction of bodies as a separate activity from its main core business, but in mid-1933, negotiations began to sell the bodybuilding side. The suitor was Charles Roberts of Wakefield, but the deal fell through and the coach building business continued as before. By mid-1936, an average of nine single-deck bodies and one double-deck body per week were being constructed and it was decided to form a separate company to run that side of Eastern Counties' activities. Consequently, Eastern Coach Works Ltd. came into being on 1st July 1936 as a Tilling and BAT subsidiary, although the whole of the share capital of £100,000 was, at that time, owned by Eastern Counties.

The premises were further enlarged up to the outbreak of the Second World War on 3rd September 1939 to allow for increased production which continued until 28th May 1940, the effective date of an order to close the premises in the light of the evacuation of the British Expeditionary Force from France and the threat of a German invasion along the East Coast. However, alternative premises were quickly found at Irthlingborough in Northamptonshire, in buildings formerly occupied by the United Counties Omnibus Co Ltd as a garage and here the Company built a comparatively small number of new bodies, but undertook a large amount of refurbishment, repair and overhaul of existing bodies, mainly for the Tilling Group operators. In the meantime, ECW was allowed to gradually resume activities at its Lowestoft premises so that by the end of 1945, both factories were fully committed. However, it was not until 22nd February 1946 that the first post-war body to the new standard design on a Bristol K-type chassis was delivered, to be added to the Crosville fleet.

In the Grouping division of September 1942 whereby the major regional bus operators became controlled either by the Tilling Group or the BET Group, Eastern Coach Works came under the control of the former, therefore becoming responsible for most of the body requirements of the Tilling Group operators. Whilst The Coach Factory had supplied a large number of new bodies to BET Group subsidiary companies, most single decks to the standard BEF design, during the 1930s and early 1940s, as well as to a few municipal operators, these two sectors of the industry continued to place orders for bodies in the second half of the 1940s. However, this aspect was to be short-lived because effectively from the 1st January 1948, ECW came under the control of The British Transport Commission. This meant that ECW could no longer supply their products to non-nationalised operators although the company was allowed to complete orders from BET Group and municipal operators which had already been placed. Another change of control took place on 1st January 1963 when the Transport Holding Company took over from the BTC and in July 1965, the Leyland Motor Corporation procured a 25 per cent, interest in both Bristol Commercial Vehicles Ltd. (the successor to the chassis manufacturing side of the Bristol Tramways & Carriage Co. Ltd) and Eastern Coach Works Ltd. which paved the way for both manufacturers to sell their products on the open market. In all this time, ECW's factory at Lowestoft continued production without any noticeable changes but the premises at Irthlingborough were closed in May 1952 following the completion of almost 550 single deck bodies built during the preceding six years.

## Body Numbers

Post-war production of new bodies started a new series, known as Series 2, commencing at 1001 and continued up to 26600. Another new series was started, this time in 1951, for work involving major repairs, conversions and various modifications, including repaints, commencing at 501 with an 'R' prefix and which eventually reached R1557. These numbers were allocated mainly to existing ECW bodies but several bodies of other makes were included. In addition, ECW utilised three other separate sequences of numbers in the ' B', 'SA' and 'W' series for various types of work to existing bodies but full details of these are not available.

## Body List

| 1001 | FFM 432 | Bristol K6A | W3.033 | L27/28R | 3/46 | Crosville MS, Chester (CH) MB251 |
|------|---------|-------------|--------|---------|------|----------------------------------|
| 1002 | FFM 433 | Bristol K6A | W3.040 | L27/28R | 5/46 | Crosville MS, Chester (CH) MB252 |
| 1003 | FFM 434 | Bristol K6A | W3.041 | L27/28R | 3/46 | Crosville MS, Chester (CH) MB253 |
| 1004 | FFM 435 | Bristol K6A | W3.042 | L27/28R | 3/46 | Crosville MS, Chester (CH) MB254 |
| 1005 | FFM 436 | Bristol K6A | W3.043 | L27/28R | 3/46 | Crosville MS, Chester (CH) MB255 |
| 1006 | FFM 437 | Bristol K6A | W3.044 | L27/28R | 3/46 | Crosville MS, Chester (CH) MB256 |
| 1007 | FFM 438 | Bristol K6A | W3.045 | L27/28R | 3/46 | Crosville MS, Chester (CH) MB257 |
| 1008 | FFM 439 | Bristol K6A | W3.046 | L27/28R | 3/46 | Crosville MS, Chester (CH) MB258 |
| 1009 | KHK 513 | Bristol K5G | W3.049 | L27/28R | 3/46 | Eastern National, Chelmsford (EX) 3889 |
| 1010 | KHK 514 | Bristol K5G | W3.050 | L27/28R | 3/46 | Eastern National, Chelmsford (EX) 3890 |
| 1011 | FNG 810 | Bristol K5G | W3.051 | L27/28R | 3/46 | Eastern Counties, Norwich (NK) LK13 |
| 1012 | FNG 811 | Bristol K5G | W3.052 | L27/28R | 3/46 | Eastern Counties, Norwich (NK) LK14 |
| 1013 | HHN 42 | Bristol K5G | W3.055 | L27/28R | 5/46 | United AS, Darlington (DM) BDO42 |
| 1014 | HHN 43 | Bristol K5G | W3.056 | L27/28R | 5/46 | United AS, Darlington (DM) BDO43 |
| 1015 | HHN 44 | Bristol K5G | W3.057 | L27/28R | 5/46 | United AS, Darlington (DM) BDO44 |
| 1016 | HTT 970 | Bristol K5G | W3.058 | L27/28R | 5/46 | Western National, Exeter (DN) 356 |
| 1017 | HTT 971 | Bristol K5G | W3.059 | L27/28R | 5/46 | Western National, Exeter (DN) 800 |
| 1018 | DMR 836 | Bristol K5G | W3.065 | L27/28R | 3/46 | Wilts & Dorset, Salisbury (WI) 264 |
| 1019 | EWY 401 | Bristol K5G | W3.067 | L27/28R | 3/46 | West Yorkshire RCC, Harrogate (WR) 712 |
| 1020 | EWY 402 | Bristol K5G | W3.068 | L27/28R | 3/46 | West Yorkshire RCC, Harrogate (WR) 713 |
| 1021 | EWY 403 | Bristol K5G | W3.069 | L27/28R | 3/46 | West Yorkshire RCC, Harrogate (WR) 714 |
| 1022 | DMR 837 | Bristol K5G | W3.066 | L27/28R | 3/46 | Wilts & Dorset, Salisbury (WI) 265 |
| 1023 | FNG 812 | Bristol K5G | W3.074 | L27/28R | 4/46 | Eastern Counties, Norwich (NK) LK15 |
| 1024 | FNG 813 | Bristol K5G | W3.075 | L27/28R | 4/46 | Eastern Counties, Norwich (NK) LK16 |
| 1025 | FRU 824 | Bristol K5G | W3.073 | L27/28R | 4/46 | Hants & Dorset, Bournemouth (HA) TD779 |
| 1026 | JHT 801 | Bristol K5G | W3.150 | H30/26R | 8/46 | Bristol Tramways (GL) C3385 |
| 1027 | JHT 802 | Bristol K5G | W3.151 | H30/26R | 8/46 | Bristol Tramways (GL) C3386 |
| 1028 | JHT 803 | Bristol K5G | W3.152 | H30/26R | 8/46 | Bristol Tramways (GL) C3387 |
| 1029 | JHT 804 | Bristol K5G | W3.153 | H30/26R | 8/46 | Bristol Tramways (GL) C3388 |
| 1030 | JHT 805 | Bristol K5G | W3.154 | H30/26R | 8/46 | Bristol Tramways (GL) C3389 |
| 1031 | JHT 806 | Bristol K5G | W3.155 | H30/26R | 8/46 | Bristol Tramways (GL) C3390 |
| 1032 | JHT 807 | Bristol K5G | W3.156 | H30/26R | 8/46 | Bristol Tramways (GL) C3391 |
| 1033 | JHT 808 | Bristol K5G | W3.157 | H30/26R | 8/46 | Bristol Tramways (GL) C3392 |
| 1034 | EWY 412 | Bristol K5G | W3.162 | H30/26R | 7/46 | York-West Yorkshire, Harrogate (WR) Y723 |
| 1035 | EWY 413 | Bristol K5G | W3.163 | H30/26R | 7/46 | York-West Yorkshire, Harrogate (WR) Y724 |
| 1036 | EWY 414 | Bristol K5G | W3.164 | H30/26R | 7/46 | York-West Yorkshire, Harrogate (WR) Y725 |
| 1037 | CPN 1 | Bristol K5G | W3.165 | H30/26R | 7/46 | Brighton, Hove & District (ES) 6376 |
| 1038 | CPN 2 | Bristol K5G | W3.166 | H30/26R | 7/46 | Brighton, Hove & District (ES) 6377 |
| 1039 | CPN 3 | Bristol K5G | W3.167 | H30/26R | 7/46 | Brighton, Hove & District (ES) 6378 |
| 1040 | DBE 185 | Bristol K6A | W3.171 | H30/26R | 7/46 | Lincolnshire RCC, Bracebridge Heath (KN) 659 |
| 1041 | DBE 186 | Bristol K6A | W3.172 | H30/26R | 7/46 | Lincolnshire RCC, Bracebridge Heath (KN) 660 |
| 1042 | DBE 187 | Bristol K6A | W3.173 | H30/26R | 7/46 | Lincolnshire RCC, Bracebridge Heath (KN) 661 |
| 1043 | DBE 188 | Bristol K6A | W3.174 | H30/26R | 7/46 | Lincolnshire RCC, Bracebridge Heath (KN) 662 |
| 1044 | DBE 189 | Bristol K6A | W3.175 | H30/26R | 7/46 | Lincolnshire RCC, Bracebridge Heath (KN) 663 |
| 1045 | DBE 190 | Bristol K6A | W3.176 | H30/26R | 7/46 | Lincolnshire RCC, Bracebridge Heath (KN) 664 |
| 1046 | FNG 819 | Bristol K5G | W3.181 | H30/26R | 8/46 | Eastern Counties, Norwich (NK) LKH7 |
| 1047 | FNG 820 | Bristol K5G | W3.182 | H30/26R | 8/46 | Eastern Counties, Norwich (NK) LKH8 |
| 1048 | FNG 821 | Bristol K5G | W3.192 | H30/26R | 8/46 | Eastern Counties, Norwich (NK) LKH9 |
| 1049 | JHT 809 | Bristol K5G | W3.195 | H30/26R | 8/46 | Bristol Tramways (GL) C3393 |
| 1050 | JHT 810 | Bristol K5G | W3.196 | H30/26R | 8/46 | Bristol Tramways (GL) C3394 |
| 1051 | FFM 470 | Bristol L6A | W4.003 | B35R | 7/46 | Crosville MS, Chester (CH) KB2 |
| 1052 | FFM 471 | Bristol L6A | W4.004 | B35R | 7/46 | Crosville MS, Chester (CH) KB3 |
| 1053 | GHN 943 | Bristol L5G | W4.005 | B35R | 7/46 | United AS, Darlington (DM) BLO143 |
| 1054 | GHN 944 | Bristol L5G | W4.006 | B35R | 7/46 | United AS, Darlington (DM) BLO144 |
| 1055 | KNO 599 | Bristol L5G | W4.008 | B35R | 7/46 | Eastern National, Chelmsford (EX) 3896 |
| 1056 | KNO 600 | Bristol L5G | W4.013 | B35R | 7/46 | Eastern National, Chelmsford (EX) 3897 |
| 1057 | JHT 824 | Bristol L5G | W4.009 | B35R | 8/46 | Bristol Tramways (GL) 2169 |
| 1058 | JHT 825 | Bristol L5G | W4.010 | B35R | 8/46 | Bristol Tramways (GL) 2170 |
| 1059 | KNO 601 | Bristol L5G | W4.014 | B35R | 7/46 | Eastern National, Chelmsford (EX) 3898 |
| 1060 | KNO 602 | Bristol L5G | W4.015 | B35R | 7/46 | Eastern National, Chelmsford (EX) 3899 |
| 1061 | KNO 603 | Bristol L5G | W4.007 | B35R | 7/46 | Eastern National, Chelmsford (EX) 3900 |
| 1062 | KNO 604 | Bristol L5G | W4.018 | B35R | 7/46 | Eastern National, Chelmsford (EX) 3901 |

| | | | | | | |
|---|---|---|---|---|---|---|
| 1063 | KNO 605 | Bristol L5G | W4.019 | B35R | 7/46 | Eastern National, Chelmsford (EX) 3902 |
| 1064 | KNO 606 | Bristol L5G | W4.020 | B35R | 8/46 | Eastern National, Chelmsford (EX) 3903 |
| 1065 | JHT 826 | Bristol L5G | W4.027 | B35R | 8/46 | Bristol Tramways (GL) 2173 |
| 1066 | JHT 827 | Bristol L5G | W4.028 | B35R | 8/46 | Bristol Tramways (GL) 2174 |
| 1067 | JHT 828 | Bristol L5G | W4.029 | B35R | 8/46 | Bristol Tramways (GL) 2175 |
| 1068 | GHN 945 | Bristol L5G | W4.034 | B35R | 8/46 | United AS, Darlington (DM) BLO145 |
| 1069 | GHN 946 | Bristol L5G | W4.035 | B35R | 8/46 | United AS, Darlington (DM) BLO146 |
| 1070 | GHN 947 | Bristol L5G | W4.036 | B35R | 8/46 | United AS, Darlington (DM) BLO147 |
| 1071 | GHN 948 | Bristol L5G | W4.037 | B35R | 9/46 | United AS, Darlington (DM) BLO148 |
| 1072 | GHN 949 | Bristol L5G | W4.038 | B35R | 9/46 | United AS, Darlington (DM) BLO149 |
| 1073 | FFM 472 | Bristol L6A | W4.039 | B35R | 8/46 | Crosville MS, Chester (CH) KB4 |
| 1074 | FFM 473 | Bristol L6A | W4.040 | B35R | 8/46 | Crosville MS, Chester (CH) KB5 |
| 1075 * | FPW 501 | Bristol L5G | W4.047 | B35R | 9/46 | Eastern Counties, Norwich (NK) LL130 |
| 1076 | FPW 502 | Bristol L5G | W4.048 | B35R | 9/46 | Eastern Counties, Norwich (NK) LL131 |
| 1077 | FFM 474 | Bristol L6A | W4.050 | B35R | 8/46 | Crosville MS, Chester (CH) KB6 |
| 1078 | FFM 475 | Bristol L6A | 61.001 | B35R | 8/46 | Crosville MS, Chester (CH) KB7 |
| 1079 | FFM 476 | Bristol L6A | 61.013 | B35R | 9/46 | Crosville MS, Chester (CH) KB8 |
| 1080 | EWY 417 | Bristol L5G | 61.003 | B35R | 9/46 | West Yorkshire RCC, Harrogate (WR) 206 |
| 1081 | EWY 418 | Bristol L5G | 61.004 | B35R | 9/46 | West Yorkshire RCC, Harrogate (WR) 207 |
| 1082 | GSM 120 | Bristol L5G | 61.005 | B35R | 9/46 | Caledonian OC, Dumfries (DF) 313 |
| 1083 | FTX 476 | Bristol L6A | W4.025 | B35R | 9/46 | Aberdare UDC (GG) 27 |
| 1084 | FTX 477 | Bristol L6A | W4.026 | B35R | 9/46 | Aberdare UDC (GG) 28 |
| 1085 | JHT 829 | Bristol L5G | 61.012 | B35R | 10/46 | Bristol Tramways (GL) 2176 |
| 1086 | KNO 607 | Bristol L5G | 61.011 | B35R | 9/46 | Eastern National, Chelmsford (EX) 3904 |
| 1087 | GHN 950 | Bristol L5G | 61.014 | B35R | 10/46 | United AS, Darlington (DM) BLO150 |
| 1088 | GHN 951 | Bristol L5G | 61.015 | B35R | 10/46 | United AS, Darlington (DM) BLO151 |
| 1089 | GHN 952 | Bristol L5G | 61.016 | B35R | 10/46 | United AS, Darlington (DM) BLO152 |
| 1090 | FFM 477 | Bristol L6A | 61.020 | B35R | 10/46 | Crosville MS, Chester (CH) KB9 |
| 1091 | HHN 49 | Bristol K5G | W3.115 | L27/28R | 6/46 | United AS, Darlington (DM) BDO49 |
| 1092 | FFM 441 | Bristol K6A | W3.079 | L27/28R | 4/46 | Crosville MS, Chester (CH) MB260 |
| 1093 | FNG 814 | Bristol K5G | W3.080 | L27/28R | 5/46 | Eastern Counties, Norwich (NK) LK17 |
| 1094 | HTT 992 | Bristol K5G | W3.081 | L27/28R | 5/46 | Southern National, Exeter (DN) 364 |
| 1095 | EWY 406 | Bristol K5G | W3.082 | L27/28R | 3/46 | Keighley-West Yorkshire, Harrogate (WR) K717 |
| 1096 | EWY 407 | Bristol K5G | W3.083 | L27/28R | 3/46 | Keighley-West Yorkshire, Harrogate (WR) K718 |
| 1097 | EWY 408 | Bristol K5G | W3.086 | L27/28R | 3/46 | Keighley-West Yorkshire, Harrogate (WR) K719 |
| 1098 | HHN 47 | Bristol K5G | W3.113 | L27/28R | 6/46 | United AS, Darlington (DM) BDO47 |
| 1099 | FFM 442 | Bristol K6A | W3.089 | L27/28R | 4/46 | Crosville MS, Chester (CH) MB261 |
| 1100 | FFM 443 | Bristol K6A | W3.094 | L27/28R | 4/46 | Crosville MS, Chester (CH) MB262 |
| 1101 | FFM 444 | Bristol K6A | W3.095 | L27/28R | 4/46 | Crosville MS, Chester (CH) MB263 |
| 1102 | FFM 445 | Bristol K6A | W3.096 | L27/28R | 4/46 | Crosville MS, Chester (CH) MB264 |
| 1103 | FFM 446 | Bristol K6A | W3.097 | L27/28R | 5/46 | Crosville MS, Chester (CH) MB265 |
| 1104 | FFM 447 | Bristol K6A | W3.098 | L27/28R | 5/46 | Crosville MS, Chester (CH) MB266 |
| 1105 | HTT 972 | Bristol K5G | W3.099 | L27/28R | 6/46 | Western National, Exeter (DN) 801 |
| 1106 | FFM 448 | Bristol K6A | W3.107 | L27/28R | 5/46 | Crosville MS, Chester (CH) MB267 |
| 1107 | FFM 449 | Bristol K6A | W3.108 | L27/28R | 5/46 | Crosville MS, Chester (CH) MB268 |
| 1108 | DDL 985 | Bristol K5G | W3.109 | L27/28R | 4/46 | Southern Vectis, Newport (IW) 710 |
| 1109 | DDL 986 | Bristol K5G | W3.110 | L27/28R | 4/46 | Southern Vectis, Newport (IW) 711 |
| 1110 | CRX 549 | Bristol K6A | W3.112 | L27/28R | 5/46 | Thames Valley, Reading (BE) 440 |
| 1111 | CRX 548 | Bristol K6A | W3.111 | L27/28R | 5/46 | Thames Valley, Reading (BE) 439 |
| 1112 | HHN 45 | Bristol K5G | W3.088 | L27/28R | 5/46 | United AS, Darlington (DM) BDO45 |
| 1113 | HHN 46 | Bristol K5G | W3.087 | L27/28R | 6/46 | United AS, Darlington (DM) BDO46 |
| 1114 | HHN 48 | Bristol K5G | W3.114 | L27/28R | 6/46 | United AS, Darlington (DM) BDO48 |
| 1115 | BJN 111 | Bristol K5G | W3.116 | L27/28R | 5/46 | Westcliff-on-Sea MS (EX) |
| 1116 | BJN 113 | Bristol K5G | W3.118 | L27/28R | 5/46 | Westcliff-on-Sea MS (EX) |
| 1117 | BJN 112 | Bristol K5G | W3.117 | L27/28R | 5/46 | Westcliff-on-Sea MS (EX) |
| 1118 | KNO 442 | Bristol K5G | W3.119 | L27/28R | 5/46 | Eastern National, Chelmsford (EX) 3891 |
| 1119 | KNO 443 | Bristol K5G | W3.120 | L27/28R | 5/46 | Eastern National, Chelmsford (EX) 3892 |
| 1120 | FRU 825 | Bristol K5G | W3.122 | L27/28R | 5/46 | Hants & Dorset, Bournemouth (HA) TD780 |
| 1121 | FRU 826 | Bristol K5G | W3.123 | L27/28R | 5/46 | Hants & Dorset, Bournemouth (HA) TD781 |
| 1122 * | FRU 827 | Bristol K5G | W3.121 | L27/28R | 5/46 | Hants & Dorset, Bournemouth (HA) TD782 |
| 1123 | DMR 838 | Bristol K5G | W3.129 | L27/28R | 5/46 | Wilts & Dorset, Salisbury (WI) 266 |
| 1124 | DMR 839 | Bristol K5G | W3.130 | L27/28R | 5/46 | Wilts & Dorset, Salisbury (WI) 267 |
| 1125 | DMR 840 | Bristol K5G | W3.131 | L27/28R | 6/46 | Wilts & Dorset, Salisbury (WI) 268 |
| 1126 | CRX 551 | Bristol K6A | W3.133 | L27/28R | 6/46 | Thames Valley, Reading (BE) 442 |

| | | | | | | | |
|---|---|---|---|---|---|---|---|
| 1127 | CRX 550 | Bristol K6A | W3.132 | L27/28R | 6/46 | Thames Valley, Reading (BE) 441 |
| 1128 | FFM 440 | Bristol K6B | W3.078 | L27/28R | 5/46 | Crosville MS, Chester (CH) MB259 |
| 1129 | FFM 450 | Bristol K6A | W3.135 | L27/28R | 5/46 | Crosville MS, Chester (CH) MB269 |
| 1130 | FFM 451 | Bristol K6A | W3.136 | L27/28R | 5/46 | Crosville MS, Chester (CH) MB270 |
| 1131 | FFM 452 | Bristol K6A | W3.137 | L27/28R | 5/46 | Crosville MS, Chester (CH) MB271 |
| 1132 | FFM 453 | Bristol K6A | W3.138 | L27/28R | 6/46 | Crosville MS, Chester (CH) MB272 |
| 1133 | FFM 454 | Bristol K6A | W3.139 | L27/28R | 6/46 | Crosville MS, Chester (CH) MB273 |
| 1134 | HTT 994 | Bristol K5G | W3.147 | L27/28R | 7/46 | Southern National, Exeter (DN) 822 |
| 1135 | HTT 995 | Bristol K5G | W3.148 | L27/28R | 7/46 | Southern National, Exeter (DN) 823 |
| 1136 | HTT 993 | Bristol K5G | W3.146 | L27/28R | 7/46 | Southern National, Exeter (DN) 821 |
| 1137 * | HTT 974 | Bristol K5G | W3.149 | L27/28R | 8/46 | Western National, Exeter (DN) 803 |
| 1138 | HTT 973 | Bristol K5G | W3.100 | L27/28R | 6/46 | Western National, Exeter (DN) 802 |
| 1139 | FFM 455 | Bristol K6B | W3.134 | L27/28R | 4/46 | Crosville MS, Chester (CH) MB274 |
| 1140 * | FRU 828 | Bristol K5G | W3.072 | L27/28R | 6/46 | Hants & Dorset, Bournemouth (HA) TD783 |
| 1141 | FNG 822 | Bristol K6B | 62.030 | H30/26R | 1/47 | Eastern Counties, Norwich (NK) LKH60 |
| 1142 | FNG 823 | Bristol K6B | 62.073 | H30/26R | 3/47 | Eastern Counties, Norwich (NK) LKH61 |
| 1143 | CPN  4 | Bristol K5G | 62.003 | H30/26R | 9/46 | Brighton, Hove & District (ES) 6379 |
| 1144 | CPN  5 | Bristol K5G | 62.004 | H30/26R | 9/46 | Brighton, Hove & District (ES) 6380 |
| 1145 | CPN  6 | Bristol K6B | 62.002 | H30/26R | 10/46 | Brighton, Hove & District (ES) 6381 |
| 1146 | JHT 811 | Bristol K5G | 62.022 | H30/26R | 10/46 | Bristol Tramways (GL) C3395 |
| 1147 | JHT 812 | Bristol K5G | 62.023 | H30/26R | 10/46 | Bristol Tramways (GL) C3396 |
| 1148 | JHT 813 | Bristol K5G | 62.024 | H30/26R | 10/46 | Bristol Tramways (GL) C3397 |
| 1149 | JHT 814 | Bristol K5G | 62.048 | H30/26R | 11/46 | Bristol Tramways (GL) C3398 |
| 1150 | JHT 815 | Bristol K5G | 62.049 | H30/26R | 11/46 | Bristol Tramways (GL) C3399 |
| 1151 | JHT 816 | Bristol K5G | 62.050 | H30/26R | 11/46 | Bristol Tramways (GL) C3400 |
| 1152 | JHT 817 | Bristol K5G | 62.065 | H30/26R | 1/47 | Bristol Tramways (GL) C3401 |
| 1153 | JHT 818 | Bristol K5G | 62.066 | H30/26R | 1/47 | Bristol Tramways (GL) C3402 |
| 1154 | FNG 824 | Bristol K6B | 62.074 | H30/26R | 3/47 | Eastern Counties, Norwich (NK) LKH62 |
| 1155 | EWY 415 | Bristol K5G | 62.096 | H30/26R | 3/47 | York-West Yorkshire, Harrogate (WR) Y726 |
| 1156 | EWY 416 | Bristol K5G | 62.110 | H30/26R | 3/47 | York-West Yorkshire, Harrogate (WR) Y727 |
| 1157 | FNG 825 | Bristol K5G | 62.103 | H30/26R | 5/47 | Eastern Counties, Norwich (NK) LKH63 |
| 1158 | FNG 826 | Bristol K5G | 62.104 | H30/26R | 5/47 | Eastern Counties, Norwich (NK) LKH64 |
| 1159 | CPN  7 | Bristol K5G | 62.077 | H30/26R | 3/47 | Brighton, Hove & District (ES) 6382 |
| 1160 | CPN  8 | Bristol K5G | 62.078 | H30/26R | 3/47 | Brighton, Hove & District (ES) 6383 |
| 1161 | CPN  9 | Bristol K6B | 62.086 | H30/26R | 3/47 | Brighton, Hove & District (ES) 6384 |
| 1162 | JHT 820 | Bristol K5G | 62.088 | H30/26R | 4/47 | Bristol Tramways (GL) 3682 |
| 1163 | JHT 822 | Bristol K5G | 62.106 | H30/26R | 4/47 | Bristol Tramways (GL) 3683 |
| 1164 | CPN 10 | Bristol K6B | 62.099 | H30/26R | 5/47 | Brighton, Hove & District (ES) 6385 |
| 1165 | JHT 823 | Bristol K5G | 62.107 | H30/26R | 5/47 | Bristol Tramways (GL) 3685 |
| 1166 | JHT 819 | Bristol K6B | 62.087 | H30/26R | 5/47 | Bristol Tramways (GL) 3684 |
| 1167 | JHT 821 | Bristol K6B | 62.100 | H30/26R | 5/47 | Bristol Tramways (GL) 3686 |
| 1168 | DBL 151 | Bristol K6A | 62.005 | L27/28R | 9/46 | Thames Valley, Reading (BE) 443 |
| 1169 | HTT 976 | Bristol K5G | W3.200 | L27/28R | 9/46 | Western National, Exeter (DN) 805 |
| 1170 | HTT 996 | Bristol K5G | 62.001 | L27/28R | 9/46 | Southern National, Exeter (DN) 824 |
| 1171 | HTT 975 | Bristol K5G | W3.199 | L27/28R | 9/46 | Western National, Exeter (DN) 804 |
| 1172 | DBL 152 | Bristol K6A | 62.006 | L27/28R | 9/46 | Thames Valley, Reading (BE) 444 |
| 1173 | DBL 153 | Bristol K6A | 62.007 | L27/28R | 9/46 | Thames Valley, Reading (BE) 445 |
| 1174 | HTT 977 | Bristol K5G | 62.008 | L27/28R | 9/46 | Western National, Exeter (DN) 806 |
| 1175 | HTT 978 | Bristol K5G | 62.009 | L27/28R | 10/46 | Western National, Exeter (DN) 807 |
| 1176 | HTT 979 | Bristol K5G | 62.010 | L27/28R | 10/46 | Western National, Exeter (DN) 808 |
| 1177 | KNO 596 | Bristol K5G | 62.011 | L27/28R | 9/46 | Eastern National, Chelmsford (EX) 3893 |
| 1178 | KNO 597 | Bristol K5G | 62.012 | L27/28R | 9/46 | Eastern National, Chelmsford (EX) 3894 |
| 1179 | KNO 598 | Bristol K5G | 62.013 | L27/28R | 9/46 | Eastern National, Chelmsford (EX) 3895 |
| 1180 | DBL 154 | Bristol K6A | 62.014 | L27/28R | 10/46 | Thames Valley, Reading (BE) 446 |
| 1181 | DBL 155 | Bristol K6A | 62.015 | L27/28R | 10/46 | Thames Valley, Reading (BE) 447 |
| 1182 | FFM 536 | Bristol K6A | 62.016 | L27/28R | 9/46 | Crosville MS, Chester (CH) MB275 |
| 1183 | HTT 980 | Bristol K5G | 62.019 | L27/28R | 10/46 | Western National, Exeter (DN) 809 |
| 1184 | HTT 981 | Bristol K5G | 62.020 | L27/28R | 10/46 | Western National, Exeter (DN) 810 |
| 1185 | BJN 114 | Bristol K5G | 62.021 | L27/28R | 10/46 | Westcliff-on-Sea MS (EX) |
| 1186 | DBL 156 | Bristol K6A | 62.028 | L27/28R | 11/46 | Thames Valley, Reading (BE) 448 |
| 1187 | HHN 50 | Bristol K5G | 62.034 | L27/28R | 12/46 | United AS, Darlington (DM) BDO50 |
| 1188 | HHN 51 | Bristol K5G | 62.035 | L27/28R | 12/46 | United AS, Darlington (DM) BDO51 |
| 1189 | DBL 157 | Bristol K6A | 62.041 | L27/28R | 12/46 | Thames Valley, Reading (BE) 449 |
| 1190 | DBL 158 | Bristol K6A | 62.042 | L27/28R | 12/46 | Thames Valley, Reading (BE) 450 |

| | | | | | | |
|---|---|---|---|---|---|---|
| 1191 | FFM 537 | Bristol K6A | 62.043 | L27/28R | 11/46 | Crosville MS, Chester (CH) MB276 |
| 1192 | DBL 159 | Bristol K6A | 62.044 | L27/28R | 12/46 | Thames Valley, Reading (BE) 451 |
| 1193 | DBL 160 | Bristol K6A | 62.045 | L27/28R | 12/46 | Thames Valley, Reading (BE) 452 |
| 1194 | HHN 52 | Bristol K5G | 62.046 | L27/28R | 12/46 | United AS, Darlington (DM) BDO52 |
| 1195 | HHN 53 | Bristol K5G | 62.047 | L27/28R | 12/46 | United AS, Darlington (DM) BDO53 |
| 1196 | DBL 161 | Bristol K6B | 62.051 | L27/28R | 1/47 | Thames Valley, Reading (BE) 453 |
| 1197 | DBL 162 | Bristol K6B | 62.057 | L27/28R | 4/47 | Thames Valley, Reading (BE) 454 |
| 1198 | HTT 982 | Bristol K5G | 62.058 | L27/28R | 12/46 | Western National, Exeter (DN) 811 |
| 1199 | HTT 983 | Bristol K5G | 62.059 | L27/28R | 12/46 | Western National, Exeter (DN) 812 |
| 1200 | GLJ 362 | Bristol K5G | 62.060 | L27/28R | 12/46 | Hants & Dorset, Bournemouth (HA) TD784 |
| 1201 | GLJ 363 | Bristol K5G | 62.061 | L27/28R | 1/47 | Hants & Dorset, Bournemouth (HA) TD785 |
| 1202 | GLJ 364 | Bristol K5G | 62.062 | L27/28R | 1/47 | Hants & Dorset, Bournemouth (HA) TD786 |
| 1203 | FFM 538 | Bristol K6A | 62.029 | L27/28R | 2/47 | Crosville MS, Chester (CH) MB277 |
| 1204 | EWY 409 | Bristol K5G | 62.072 | L27/28R | 3/47 | Keighley-West Yorkshire, Harrogate (WR) K720 |
| 1205 | HTT 984 | Bristol K5G | 62.075 | L27/28R | 2/47 | Western National, Exeter (DN) 813 |
| 1206 | HTT 985 | Bristol K5G | 62.076 | L27/28R | 4/47 | Western National, Exeter (DN) 814 |
| 1207 | HTT 986 | Bristol K5G | 62.080 | L27/28R | 4/47 | Western National, Exeter (DN) 815 |
| 1208 | HTT 987 | Bristol K5G | 62.098 | L27/28R | 4/47 | Western National, Exeter (DN) 816 |
| 1209 | HTT 997 | Bristol K5G | 62.081 | L27/28R | 4/47 | Southern National, Exeter (DN) 825 |
| 1210 | HTT 998 | Bristol K5G | 62.082 | L27/28R | 5/47 | Southern National, Exeter (DN) 826 |
| 1211 | EAM 613 | Bristol K5G | 62.084 | L27/28R | 4/47 | Wilts & Dorset, Salisbury (WI) 270 |
| 1212 | EAM 612 | Bristol K6B | 62.083 | L27/28R | 4/47 | Wilts & Dorset, Salisbury (WI) 269 |
| 1213 | HTT 999 | Bristol K5G | 62.085 | L27/28R | 5/47 | Southern National, Exeter (DN) 827 |
| 1214 | FFM 539 | Bristol K6B | 62.101 | L27/28R | 5/47 | Crosville MS, Chester (CH) MB278 |
| 1215 | HHN 54 | Bristol K5G | 62.090 | L27/28R | 6/47 | United AS, Darlington (DM) BDO54 |
| 1216 | HHN 55 | Bristol K5G | 62.091 | L27/28R | 6/47 | United AS, Darlington (DM) BDO55 |
| 1217 | HHN 56 | Bristol K5G | 62.092 | L27/28R | 6/47 | United AS, Darlington (DM) BDO56 |
| 1218 | HHN 57 | Bristol K5G | 62.093 | L27/28R | 6/47 | United AS, Darlington (DM) BDO57 |
| 1219 | EWY 410 | Bristol K5G | 62.094 | L27/28R | 5/47 | Keighley-West Yorkshire, Harrogate (WR) K721 |
| 1220 | EWY 411 | Bristol K5G | 62.095 | L27/28R | 5/47 | Keighley-West Yorkshire, Harrogate (WR) K722 |
| 1221 | EWY 404 | Bristol K5G | 62.031 | L27/28R | 5/47 | West Yorkshire RCC, Harrogate (WR) 715 |
| 1222 | HTT 988 | Bristol K6B | 62.079 | L27/28R | 5/47 | Western National, Exeter (DN) 817 |
| 1223 | HTT 989 | Bristol K5G | 62.112 | L27/28R | 5/47 | Western National, Exeter (DN) 818 |
| 1224 | FFM 540 | Bristol K6B | 62.089 | L27/28R | 5/47 | Crosville MS, Chester (CH) MB279 |
| 1225 | FFM 541 | Bristol K6B | 62.102 | L27/28R | 5/47 | Crosville MS, Chester (CH) MB280 |
| 1226 | FNG 815 | Bristol K5G | W3.193 | L27/28R | 8/46 | Eastern Counties, Norwich (NK) LK18 |
| 1227 | FNG 816 | Bristol K5G | W3.194 | L27/28R | 8/46 | Eastern Counties, Norwich (NK) LK19 |
| 1228 | EAM 614 | Bristol K6B | 62.105 | L27/28R | 6/47 | Wilts & Dorset, Salisbury (WI) 271 |
| 1229 | FNG 817 | Bristol K5G | 62.109 | L27/28R | 6/47 | Eastern Counties, Norwich (NK) LK50 |
| 1230 | HAH 230 | Bristol K6B | 62.108 | L27/28R | 7/47 | Eastern Counties, Norwich (NK) LK30 |
| 1231 | EWY 405 | Bristol K5G | 62.071 | L27/28R | 5/47 | West Yorkshire RCC, Harrogate (WR) 716 |
| 1232 | HTT 990 | Bristol K6B | 62.097 | L27/28R | 5/47 | Western National, Exeter (DN) 819 |
| 1233 | JTT 996 | Bristol K6A | 62.136 | L27/28R | 6/47 | Western National, Exeter (DN) 828 |
| 1234 | FFM 542 | Bristol K6B | 62.113 | L27/28R | 6/47 | Crosville MS, Chester (CH) MB281 |
| 1235 | FFM 543 | Bristol K6B | 62.114 | L27/28R | 6/47 | Crosville MS, Chester (CH) MB282 |
| 1236 | FFM 478 | Bristol L6A | 61.021 | B35R | 10/46 | Crosville MS, Chester (CH) KB10 |
| 1237 | FPW 503 | Bristol L5G | 61.019 | B35R | 10/46 | Eastern Counties, Norwich (NK) LL132 |
| 1238 | GHN 953 | Bristol L5G | 61.017 | B35R | 10/46 | United AS, Darlington (DM) BLO153 |
| 1239 | GHN 954 | Bristol L5G | 61.022 | B35R | 11/46 | United AS, Darlington (DM) BLO154 |
| 1240 * | EDL 14 | Bristol L5G | 61.026 | B35R | 4/46 | Southern Vectis, Newport (IW) 829 |
| 1241 * | EDL 15 | Bristol L5G | 61.027 | B35R | 4/46 | Southern Vectis, Newport (IW) 830 |
| 1242 * | EDL 16 | Bristol L5G | 61.028 | B35R | 4/46 | Southern Vectis, Newport (IW) 831 |
| 1243 | GHN 955 | Bristol L5G | 61.029 | B35R | 11/46 | United AS, Darlington (DM) BLO155 |
| 1244 | JHT 830 | Bristol L5G | 61.037 | B35R | 10/46 | Bristol Tramways (GL) 2177 |
| 1245 | JHT 831 | Bristol L5G | 61.038 | B35R | 10/46 | Bristol Tramways (GL) 2178 |
| 1246 | FFM 479 | Bristol L6A | 61.039 | B35R | 10/46 | Crosville MS, Chester (CH) KB11 |
| 1247 | JHT 832 | Bristol L5G | 61.044 | B35R | 11/46 | Bristol Tramways (GL) 2179 |
| 1248 | FFM 480 | Bristol L6A | 61.045 | B35R | 10/46 | Crosville MS, Chester (CH) KB12 |
| 1249 | FFM 481 | Bristol L6A | 61.046 | B35R | 11/46 | Crosville MS, Chester (CH) KB13 |
| 1250 | FTX 478 | Bristol L6A | 61.036 | B35R | 11/46 | Aberdare UDC (GG) 25 |
| 1251 | GHN 956 | Bristol L5G | 61.055 | B35R | 12/46 | United AS, Darlington (DM) BLO156 |
| 1252 | GHN 957 | Bristol L5G | 61.056 | B35R | 12/46 | United AS, Darlington (DM) BLO157 |
| 1253 | GHN 958 | Bristol L5G | 61.058 | B35R | 12/46 | United AS, Darlington (DM) BLO158 |
| 1254 | GHN 959 | Bristol L5G | 61.057 | B35R | 12/46 | United AS, Darlington (DM) BLO159 |

| | | | | | | |
|---|---|---|---|---|---|---|
| 1255 | FFM 482 | Bristol L6A | 61.059 | B35R | 11/46 | Crosville MS, Chester (CH) KB14 |
| 1256 | FFM 483 | Bristol L6A | 61.060 | B35R | 11/46 | Crosville MS, Chester (CH) KB15 |
| 1257 | FPW 504 | Bristol L5G | 61.061 | B35R | 12/46 | Eastern Counties, Norwich (NK) LL133 |
| 1258 | FPW 505 | Bristol L5G | 61.062 | B35R | 12/46 | Eastern Counties, Norwich (NK) LL134 |
| 1259 | FPW 506 | Bristol L5G | 61.063 | B35R | 12/46 | Eastern Counties, Norwich (NK) LL135 |
| 1260 | KNO 608 | Bristol L5G | 61.064 | B35R | 12/46 | Eastern National, Chelmsford (EX) 3905 |
| 1261 | KNO 609 | Bristol L5G | 61.065 | B35R | 12/46 | Eastern National, Chelmsford (EX) 3906 |
| 1262 | DBL 163 | Bristol L6A | 61.066 | B35R | 1/47 | Thames Valley, Reading (BE) 455 |
| 1263 | EWY 419 | Bristol L5G | 61.067 | B35R | 1/47 | West Yorkshire RCC, Harrogate (WR) 208 |
| 1264 | EWY 420 | Bristol L5G | 61.068 | B35R | 1/47 | West Yorkshire RCC, Harrogate (WR) 209 |
| 1265 | EWY 421 | Bristol L5G | 61.069 | B35R | 1/47 | West Yorkshire RCC, Harrogate (WR) 210 |
| 1266 | JHT 833 | Bristol L6A | 61.070 | B35R | 12/46 | Bristol Tramways (GL) 2180 |
| 1267 | FPW 507 | Bristol L5G | 61.074 | B35R | 1/47 | Eastern Counties, Norwich (NK) LL136 |
| 1268 | FPW 508 | Bristol L5G | 61.075 | B35R | 1/47 | Eastern Counties, Norwich (NK) LL137 |
| 1269 | KNO 610 | Bristol L5G | 61.077 | B35R | 12/46 | Eastern National, Chelmsford (EX) 3907 |
| 1270 | KNO 611 | Bristol L5G | 61.076 | B35R | 12/46 | Eastern National, Chelmsford (EX) 3908 |
| 1271 | DBL 164 | Bristol L6A | 61.085 | B35R | 1/47 | Thames Valley, Reading (BE) 456 |
| 1272 | DBL 165 | Bristol L6A | 61.086 | B35R | 1/47 | Thames Valley, Reading (BE) 457 |
| 1273 | GHN 961 | Bristol L5G | 61.104 | B35R | 1/47 | United AS, Darlington (DM) BLO161 |
| 1274 | FFM 484 | Bristol L6A | 61.091 | B35R | 12/46 | Crosville MS, Chester (CH) KB16 |
| 1275 | FFM 485 | Bristol L6A | 61.092 | B35R | 12/46 | Crosville MS, Chester (CH) KB17 |
| 1276 | EWY 422 | Bristol L5G | 61.106 | B35R | 3/47 | West Yorkshire RCC, Harrogate (WR) 211 |
| 1277 | EWY 423 | Bristol L5G | 61.107 | B35R | 3/47 | West Yorkshire RCC, Harrogate (WR) 212 |
| 1278 | FFM 512 | Bristol L6A | 61.099 | B35R | 2/47 | Crosville MS, Chester (CH) KB18 |
| 1279 | DBL 166 | Bristol L6A | 61.103 | B35R | 1/47 | Thames Valley, Reading (BE) 458 |
| 1280 | GHN 962 | Bristol L5G | 61.105 | B35R | 2/47 | United AS, Darlington (DM) BLO162 |
| 1281 | HB 6260 | Bristol L5G | 61.094 | B35R | -/47 | Merthyr Tydfil Corporation (GG) 1 |
| 1282 | HB 6261 | Bristol L5G | 61.095 | B35R | -/47 | Merthyr Tydfil Corporation (GG) 6 |
| 1283 | HB 6262 | Bristol L5G | 61.114 | B35R | -/47 | Merthyr Tydfil Corporation (GG) 10 |
| 1284 | GHN 965 | Bristol L5G | 61.125 | B35R | 2/47 | United AS, Darlington (DM) BLO165 |
| 1285 | GHN 960 | Bristol L5G | 61.123 | B35R | 7/47 | United AS, Darlington (DM) BLO160 |
| 1286 * | GHN 997 | Bristol L5G | 63.108 | B35R | 7/47 | United AS, Darlington (DM) BLO197 |
| 1287 | JHT 834 | Bristol L6A | 61.108 | B35R | 1/47 | Bristol Tramways (GL) 2181 |
| 1288 | JHT 835 | Bristol L6A | 61.109 | B35R | 1/47 | Bristol Tramways (GL) 2182 |
| 1289 | JHT 836 | Bristol L6A | 61.110 | B35R | 5/47 | Bristol Tramways (GL) 2183 |
| 1290 | KNO 612 | Bristol L5G | 61.112 | B35R | 1/47 | Eastern National, Chelmsford (EX) 3909 |
| 1291 | KNO 613 | Bristol L5G | 61.113 | B35R | 1/47 | Eastern National, Chelmsford (EX) 3910 |
| 1292 | FFM 513 | Bristol L6A | 61.117 | B35R | 2/47 | Crosville MS, Chester (CH) KB19 |
| 1293 | FFM 514 | Bristol L6A | 61.118 | B35R | 2/47 | Crosville MS, Chester (CH) KB20 |
| 1294 | FFM 515 | Bristol L6A | 61.119 | B35R | 4/47 | Crosville MS, Chester (CH) KB21 |
| 1295 | FPW 509 | Bristol L5G | 61.120 | B35R | 3/47 | Eastern Counties, Norwich (NK) LL638 |
| 1296 | FPW 510 | Bristol L5G | 61.122 | B35R | 3/47 | Eastern Counties, Norwich (NK) LL639 |
| 1297 | FPW 511 | Bristol L5G | 61.121 | B35R | 3/47 | Eastern Counties, Norwich (NK) LL640 |
| 1298 * | GHN 998 | Bristol L5G | 63.109 | B35R | 7/47 | United AS, Darlington (DM) BLO198 |
| 1299 * | GHN 999 | Bristol L5G | 63.111 | B35R | 7/47 | United AS, Darlington (DM) BLO199 |
| 1300 * | HHN 200 | Bristol L5G | 63.129 | B35R | 7/47 | United AS, Darlington (DM) BLO200 |
| 1301 | JHT 837 | Bristol L6A | 61.127 | B35R | 3/47 | Bristol Tramways (GL) 2184 |
| 1302 | JHT 838 | Bristol L6A | 61.128 | B35R | 3/47 | Bristol Tramways (GL) 2185 |
| 1303 | KNO 614 | Bristol L5G | 61.131 | B35R | 4/47 | Eastern National, Chelmsford (EX) 3911 |
| 1304 | KNO 615 | Bristol L5G | 61.132 | B35R | 4/47 | Eastern National, Chelmsford (EX) 3912 |
| 1305 | EWY 424 | Bristol L5G | 61.129 | B35R | 3/47 | West Yorkshire RCC, Harrogate (WR) 213 |
| 1306 | EWY 425 | Bristol L5G | 61.135 | B35R | 3/47 | West Yorkshire RCC, Harrogate (WR) 214 |
| 1307 | EWY 426 | Bristol L5G | 61.136 | B35R | 3/47 | West Yorkshire RCC, Harrogate (WR) 215 |
| 1308 | GSM 121 | Bristol L5G | 61.142 | B35R | 3/47 | Caledonian OC, Dumfries (DF) 314 |
| 1309 | GSM 122 | Bristol L5G | 61.143 | B35R | 3/47 | Caledonian OC, Dumfries (DF) 315 |
| 1310 * | HHN 201 | Bristol L5G | 63.130 | B35R | 7/47 | United AS, Darlington (DM) BLO201 |
| 1311 * | HHN 205 | Bristol L5G | 63.086 | B35R | 7/47 | United AS, Darlington (DM) BLO205 |
| 1312 | FFM 516 | Bristol L6A | 61.148 | B35R | 4/47 | Crosville MS, Chester (CH) KB22 |
| 1313 | FFM 517 | Bristol L6A | 61.149 | B35R | 4/47 | Crosville MS, Chester (CH) KB23 |
| 1314 | FFM 518 | Bristol L6A | 61.150 | B35R | 4/47 | Crosville MS, Chester (CH) KB24 |
| 1315 | FPW 512 | Bristol L5G | 61.130 | B35R | 5/47 | Eastern Counties, Norwich (NK) LL641 |
| 1316 | FPW 513 | Bristol L5G | 63.004 | B35R | 5/47 | Eastern Counties, Norwich (NK) LL642 |
| 1317 | FPW 514 | Bristol L5G | 63.005 | B35R | 5/47 | Eastern Counties, Norwich (NK) LL643 |
| 1318 * | GHN 963 | Bristol L5G | 61.087 | B35R | 2/47 | United AS, Darlington (DM) BLO163 |

| | | | | | | |
|---|---|---|---|---|---|---|
| 1319 | KNO 616 | Bristol L5G | 63.010 | B35R | 4/47 | Eastern National, Chelmsford (EX) 3913 |
| 1320 | FTX 479 | Bristol L6A | 61.126 | B35R | 2/47 | Aberdare UDC (GG) 26 |
| 1321 | KNO 617 | Bristol L5G | 63.011 | B35R | 4/47 | Eastern National, Chelmsford (EX) 3914 |
| 1322 * | GHN 964 | Bristol L5G | 61.124 | B35R | 2/47 | United AS, Darlington (DM) BLO164 |
| 1323 * | GHN 969 | Bristol L5G | 61.138 | B35R | 3/47 | United AS, Darlington (DM) BLO169 |
| 1324 * | GHN 970 | Bristol L5G | 61.139 | B35R | 3/47 | United AS, Darlington (DM) BLO170 |
| 1325 | JHT 839 | Bristol L6A | 61.146 | B35R | 4/47 | Bristol Tramways (GL) 1270 |
| 1326 | JHT 840 | Bristol L6A | 61.147 | B35R | 5/47 | Bristol Tramways (GL) 1271 |
| 1327 | GSM 123 | Bristol L5G | 63.019 | B35R | 5/47 | Caledonian OC, Dumfries (DF) 316 |
| 1328 | GSM 124 | Bristol L5G | 63.020 | B35R | 5/47 | Caledonian OC, Dumfries (DF) 317 |
| 1329 | FPW 515 | Bristol L5G | 63.021 | B35R | 5/47 | Eastern Counties, Norwich (NK) LL644 |
| 1330 | FPW 516 | Bristol L5G | 63.022 | B35R | 6/47 | Eastern Counties, Norwich (NK) LL645 |
| 1331 | DBL 167 | Bristol L6A | 63.026 | B35R | 5/47 | Thames Valley, Reading (BE) 459 |
| 1332 * | GHN 971 | Bristol L5G | 61.140 | B35R | 3/47 | United AS, Darlington (DM) BLO171 |
| 1333 * | HHN 206 | Bristol L5G | 63.089 | B35R | 7/47 | United AS, Darlington (DM) BLO206 |
| 1334 | JHT 841 | Bristol L6A | 63.017 | B35R | 5/47 | Bristol Tramways (GL) 2188 |
| 1335 | JHT 842 | Bristol L5G | 63.018 | B35R | 5/47 | Bristol Tramways (GL) 2189 |
| 1336 | EWY 427 | Bristol L5G | 61.137 | B35R | 5/47 | West Yorkshire RCC, Harrogate (WR) 216 |
| 1337 * | HHN 207 | Bristol L5G | 63.094 | B35R | 7/47 | United AS, Darlington (DM) BLO207 |
| 1338 * | HHN 210 | Bristol L5G | 63.097 | B35R | 8/47 | United AS, Darlington (DM) BLO210 |
| 1339 * | HHN 202 | Bristol L5G | 63.001 | B35R | 8/47 | United AS, Darlington (DM) BLO202 |
| 1340 | GSM 125 | Bristol L5G | 63.045 | B35R | 6/47 | Caledonian OC, Dumfries (DF) 318 |
| 1341 | GSM 126 | Bristol L5G | 63.046 | B35R | 6/47 | Caledonian OC, Dumfries (DF) 319 |
| 1342 | FFM 519 | Bristol L6A | 63.032 | B35R | 6/47 | Crosville MS, Chester (CH) KB25 |
| 1343 | FFM 520 | Bristol L6A | 63.033 | B35R | 5/47 | Crosville MS, Chester (CH) KB26 |
| 1344 | FFM 521 | Bristol L6A | 63.048 | B35R | 6/47 | Crosville MS, Chester (CH) KB27 |
| 1345 * | HHN 203 | Bristol L5G | 63.002 | B35R | 8/47 | United AS, Darlington (DM) BLO203 |
| 1346 * | HHN 204 | Bristol L5G | 63.003 | B35R | 8/47 | United AS, Darlington (DM) BLO204 |
| 1347 * | HHN 215 | Bristol L5G | 63.131 | B35R | 8/47 | United AS, Darlington (DM) BLO215 |
| 1348 * | HHN 208 | Bristol L5G | 63.095 | B35R | 8/47 | United AS, Darlington (DM) BLO208 |
| 1349 * | HHN 209 | Bristol L5G | 63.096 | B35R | 8/47 | United AS, Darlington (DM) BLO209 |
| 1350 | EWY 428 | Bristol L5G | 63.042 | B35R | 5/47 | West Yorkshire RCC, Harrogate (WR) 217 |
| 1351 | EWY 429 | Bristol L5G | 63.043 | B35R | 6/47 | West Yorkshire RCC, Harrogate (WR) 218 |
| 1352 | JHT 843 | Bristol L5G | 63.060 | B35R | 5/47 | Bristol Tramways (GL) 2190 |
| 1353 | JHT 844 | Bristol L5G | 63.061 | B35R | 6/47 | Bristol Tramways (GL) 2191 |
| 1354 | JHT 845 | Bristol L5G | 63.062 | B35R | 5/47 | Bristol Tramways (GL) 2192 |
| 1355 | FFM 522 | Bristol L6A | 63.047 | B35R | 6/47 | Crosville MS, Chester (CH) KB28 |
| 1356 | FFM 523 | Bristol L6A | 63.049 | B35R | 6/47 | Crosville MS, Chester (CH) KB29 |
| 1357 | FFM 524 | Bristol L6A | 63.063 | B35R | 5/47 | Crosville MS, Chester (CH) KB30 |
| 1358 | FPW 517 | Bristol L5G | 63.066 | B35R | 6/47 | Eastern Counties, Norwich (NK) LL646 |
| 1359 | FPW 518 | Bristol L5G | 63.067 | B35R | 6/47 | Eastern Counties, Norwich (NK) LL647 |
| 1360 | FPW 519 | Bristol L5G | 63.068 | B35R | 6/47 | Eastern Counties, Norwich (NK) LL648 |
| 1361 * | HHN 211 | Bristol L5G | 63.107 | B35R | 8/47 | United AS, Darlington (DM) BLO211 |
| 1362 * | HHN 212 | Bristol L5G | 63.110 | B35R | 8/47 | United AS, Darlington (DM) BLO212 |
| 1363 | EWY 430 | Bristol L5G | 63.044 | B35R | 6/47 | West Yorkshire RCC, Harrogate (WR) 219 |
| 1364 | FFM 525 | Bristol L6A | 63.064 | B35R | 5/47 | Crosville MS, Chester (CH) KB31 |
| 1365 | FFM 526 | Bristol L6A | 63.065 | B35R | 5/47 | Crosville MS, Chester (CH) KB32 |
| 1366 | GSM 127 | Bristol L5G | 63.077 | B35R | 6/47 | Caledonian OC, Dumfries (DF) 320 |
| 1367 | GSM 128 | Bristol L5G | 63.078 | B35R | 6/47 | Caledonian OC, Dumfries (DF) 321 |
| 1368 | FFM 527 | Bristol L6A | 63.079 | B35R | 6/47 | Crosville MS, Chester (CH) KB33 |
| 1369 | KNO 618 | Bristol L5G | 63.080 | B35R | 6/47 | Eastern National, Chelmsford (EX) 3915 |
| 1370 | KNO 619 | Bristol L5G | 63.081 | B35R | 6/47 | Eastern National, Chelmsford (EX) 3916 |
| 1371 * | HHN 213 | Bristol L5G | 63.112 | B35R | 8/47 | United AS, Darlington (DM) BLO213 |
| 1372 * | HHN 214 | Bristol L5G | 63.128 | B35R | 8/47 | United AS, Darlington (DM) BLO214 |
| 1373 * | HHN 216 | Bristol L5G | 63.140 | B35R | 8/47 | United AS, Darlington (DM) BLO216 |
| 1374 * | HHN 217 | Bristol L5G | 63.141 | B35R | 8/47 | United AS, Darlington (DM) BLO217 |
| 1375 | EWY 431 | Bristol L5G | 63.098 | B35R | 6/47 | West Yorkshire RCC, Harrogate (WR) 220 |
| 1376 | KNO 620 | Bristol L5G | 63.090 | B35R | 6/47 | Eastern National, Chelmsford (EX) 3917 |
| 1377 | FFM 528 | Bristol L6A | 63.119 | B35R | 6/47 | Crosville MS, Chester (CH) KB34 |
| 1378 * | HHN 218 | Bristol L5G | 63.142 | B35R | 8/47 | United AS, Darlington (DM) BLO218 |
| 1379 * | HHN 219 | Bristol L5G | 63.150 | B35R | 8/47 | United AS, Darlington (DM) BLO219 |
| 1380 * | HHN 220 | Bristol L5G | 63.151 | B35R | 8/47 | United AS, Darlington (DM) BLO220 |
| 1381 * | HHN 221 | Bristol L5G | 63.152 | B35R | 8/47 | United AS, Darlington (DM) BLO221 |
| 1382 * | HHN 222 | Bristol L5G | 63.153 | B35R | 8/47 | United AS, Darlington (DM) BLO222 |

| | | | | | | | |
|---|---|---|---|---|---|---|---|
| 1383 | EWY 432 | Bristol L5G | 63.099 | B35R | 6/47 | West Yorkshire RCC, Harrogate (WR) 221 |
| 1384 | EWY 433 | Bristol L5G | 63.100 | B35R | 7/47 | West Yorkshire RCC, Harrogate (WR) 222 |
| 1385 | GSM 129 | Bristol L5G | 63.101 | B35R | 7/47 | Caledonian OC, Dumfries (DF) 322 |
| 1386 | FPW 520 | Bristol L5G | 63.102 | B35R | 7/47 | Eastern Counties, Norwich (NK) LL649 |
| 1387 | FPW 521 | Bristol L5G | 63.103 | B35R | 7/47 | Eastern Counties, Norwich (NK) LL650 |
| 1388 | FPW 522 | Bristol L5G | 63.114 | B35R | 7/47 | Eastern Counties, Norwich (NK) LL651 |
| 1389 | EWY 434 | Bristol L5G | 63.113 | B35R | 7/47 | West Yorkshire RCC, Harrogate (WR) 223 |
| 1390 | KNO 621 | Bristol L5G | 63.091 | B35R | 6/47 | Eastern National, Chelmsford (EX) 3918 |
| 1391 | KNO 622 | Bristol L5G | 63.116 | B35R | 6/47 | Eastern National, Chelmsford (EX) 3919 |
| 1392 | KNO 623 | Bristol L5G | 63.117 | B35R | 6/47 | Eastern National, Chelmsford (EX) 3920 |
| 1393 | KNO 624 | Bristol L5G | 63.118 | B35R | 6/47 | Eastern National, Chelmsford (EX) 3921 |
| 1394 | FPW 523 | Bristol L5G | 63.115 | B35R | 7/47 | Eastern Counties, Norwich (NK) LL652 |
| 1395 | FFM 529 | Bristol L6A | 63.136 | B35R | 6/47 | Crosville MS, Chester (CH) KB35 |
| 1396 | FFM 530 | Bristol L6A | 63.137 | B35R | 6/47 | Crosville MS, Chester (CH) KB36 |
| 1397 | FFM 531 | Bristol L6A | 63.146 | B35R | 6/47 | Crosville MS, Chester (CH) KB37 |
| 1398 | FFM 532 | Bristol L6A | 63.147 | B35R | 6/47 | Crosville MS, Chester (CH) KB38 |
| 1399 | FFM 533 | Bristol L6A | 63.148 | B35R | 7/47 | Crosville MS, Chester (CH) KB39 |
| 1400 | FFM 534 | Bristol L6A | 63.161 | B35R | 6/47 | Crosville MS, Chester (CH) KB40 |
| 1401 | FFM 535 | Bristol L6A | 63.162 | B35R | 6/47 | Crosville MS, Chester (CH) KB41 |
| 1402 | KNO 625 | Bristol L5G | 63.138 | B35R | 7/47 | Eastern National, Chelmsford (EX) 3922 |
| 1403 | EWY 435 | Bristol L5G | 63.143 | B35R | 7/47 | West Yorkshire RCC, Harrogate (WR) 224 |
| 1404 | EWY 436 | Bristol L5G | 63.154 | B35R | 7/47 | West Yorkshire RCC, Harrogate (WR) 225 |
| 1405 | FPW 524 | Bristol L5G | 63.195 | B35R | 7/47 | Eastern Counties, Norwich (NK) LL653 |
| 1406 | FPW 525 | Bristol L5G | 63.196 | B35R | 7/47 | Eastern Counties, Norwich (NK) LL654 |
| 1407 | FPW 526 | Bristol L5G | 63.197 | B35R | 7/47 | Eastern Counties, Norwich (NK) LL655 |
| 1408 | FPW 527 | Bristol L5G | 63.198 | B35R | 7/47 | Eastern Counties, Norwich (NK) LL656 |
| 1409 | EDL 17 | Bristol K5G | 62.124 | L27/28R | 3/47 | Southern Vectis, Newport (IW) 713 |
| 1410 | EDL 18 | Bristol K5G | 62.125 | L27/28R | 3/47 | Southern Vectis, Newport (IW) 714 |
| 1411 | EDL 19 | Bristol K5G | 62.126 | L27/28R | 3/47 | Southern Vectis, Newport (IW) 715 |
| 1412 | EDL 20 | Bristol K5G | 62.127 | L27/28R | 5/47 | Southern Vectis, Newport (IW) 716 |
| 1413 | EDL 21 | Bristol K5G | 62.128 | L27/28R | 5/47 | Southern Vectis, Newport (IW) 717 |
| 1414 | EDL 22 | Bristol K5G | 62.129 | L27/28R | 5/47 | Southern Vectis, Newport (IW) 718 |
| 1415 | EDL 23 | Bristol K5G | 62.130 | L27/28R | 5/47 | Southern Vectis, Newport (IW) 719 |
| 1416 | JHT 846 | Bristol L5G | 63.075 | B33D | 6/47 | Bristol Tramways (GL) C2711 |
| 1417 | JHT 847 | Bristol L5G | 63.076 | B33D | 7/47 | Bristol Tramways (GL) C2712 |
| 1418 | JHT 852 | Bristol L5G | 63.144 | B33D | 7/47 | Bristol Tramways (GL) C2717 |
| 1419 | JHT 853 | Bristol L5G | 63.145 | B33D | 8/47 | Bristol Tramways (GL) C2718 |
| 1420 | JHT 854 | Bristol L5G | 63.155 | B33D | 8/47 | Bristol Tramways (GL) C2719 |
| 1421 | JHT 856 | Bristol L5G | 63.157 | B33D | 7/47 | Bristol Tramways (GL) C2721 |
| 1422 | JHT 848 | Bristol L5G | 63.132 | B33D | 7/47 | Bristol Tramways (GL) C2713 |
| 1423 | JHT 849 | Bristol L5G | 63.133 | B33D | 7/47 | Bristol Tramways (GL) C2714 |
| 1424 | JHT 850 | Bristol L5G | 63.134 | B33D | 8/47 | Bristol Tramways (GL) C2715 |
| 1425 | JHT 851 | Bristol L5G | 63.135 | B33D | 8/47 | Bristol Tramways (GL) C2716 |
| 1426 | JHT 855 | Bristol L5G | 63.156 | B33D | 7/47 | Bristol Tramways (GL) C2720 |
| 1427 | JHT 857 | Bristol L5G | 63.158 | B33D | 7/47 | Bristol Tramways (GL) C2722 |
| 1428 | JHT 858 | Bristol L5G | 63.159 | B33D | 8/47 | Bristol Tramways (GL) C2723 |
| 1429 | JHT 859 | Bristol L5G | 63.160 | B33D | 8/47 | Bristol Tramways (GL) C2724 |
| 1430 | JHT 860 | Bristol L5G | 63.167 | B33D | 8/47 | Bristol Tramways (GL) C2725 |
| 1431 | JHT 861 | Bristol L5G | 63.168 | B33D | 8/47 | Bristol Tramways (GL) C2726 |
| 1432 | JHT 862 | Bristol L5G | 63.169 | B33D | 8/47 | Bristol Tramways (GL) C2727 |
| 1433 | JHT 863 | Bristol L5G | 63.170 | B33D | 8/47 | Bristol Tramways (GL) C2728 |
| 1434 | JHT 864 | Bristol L5G | 63.171 | B33D | 8/47 | Bristol Tramways (GL) C2729 |
| 1435 | JHT 865 | Bristol L5G | 63.172 | B33D | 8/47 | Bristol Tramways (GL) C2730 |
| 1436 * | GHN 966 | Bristol L5G | 61.141 | B35R | 3/47 | United AS, Darlington (DM) BLO166 |
| 1437 * | GHN 967 | Bristol L5G | 61.144 | B35R | 3/47 | United AS, Darlington (DM) BLO167 |
| 1438 * | GHN 968 | Bristol L5G | 61.145 | B35R | 5/47 | United AS, Darlington (DM) BLO168 |
| 1439 * | GHN 972 | Bristol L5G | 63.009 | B35R | 5/47 | United AS, Darlington (DM) BLO172 |
| 1440 * | GHN 973 | Bristol L5G | 63.014 | B35R | 5/47 | United AS, Darlington (DM) BLO173 |
| 1441 * | GHN 974 | Bristol L5G | 63.015 | B35R | 5/47 | United AS, Darlington (DM) BLO174 |
| 1442 * | GHN 975 | Bristol L5G | 63.016 | B35R | 5/47 | United AS, Darlington (DM) BLO175 |
| 1443 * | GHN 976 | Bristol L5G | 63.027 | B35R | 5/47 | United AS, Darlington (DM) BLO176 |
| 1444 * | GHN 977 | Bristol L5G | 63.028 | B35R | 5/47 | United AS, Darlington (DM) BLO177 |
| 1445 * | GHN 978 | Bristol L5G | 63.029 | B35R | 5/47 | United AS, Darlington (DM) BLO178 |
| 1446 * | GHN 979 | Bristol L5G | 63.037 | B35R | 5/47 | United AS, Darlington (DM) BLO179 |

| | | | | | | | |
|---|---|---|---|---|---|---|---|
| 1447 * | GHN 980 | Bristol L5G | 63.038 | B35R | 5/47 | United AS, Darlington (DM) | BLO180 |
| 1448 * | GHN 981 | Bristol L5G | 63.039 | B35R | 6/47 | United AS, Darlington (DM) | BLO181 |
| 1449 * | GHN 982 | Bristol L5G | 63.040 | B35R | 6/47 | United AS, Darlington (DM) | BLO182 |
| 1450 * | GHN 983 | Bristol L5G | 63.041 | B35R | 6/47 | United AS, Darlington (DM) | BLO183 |
| 1451 * | GHN 984 | Bristol L5G | 63.055 | B35R | 6/47 | United AS, Darlington (DM) | BLO184 |
| 1452 * | GHN 985 | Bristol L5G | 63.056 | B35R | 6/47 | United AS, Darlington (DM) | BLO185 |
| 1453 * | GHN 986 | Bristol L5G | 63.057 | B35R | 6/47 | United AS, Darlington (DM) | BLO186 |
| 1454 * | GHN 987 | Bristol L5G | 63.058 | B35R | 6/47 | United AS, Darlington (DM) | BLO187 |
| 1455 * | GHN 988 | Bristol L5G | 63.059 | B35R | 6/47 | United AS, Darlington (DM) | BLO188 |
| 1456 * | GHN 989 | Bristol L5G | 63.072 | B35R | 6/47 | United AS, Darlington (DM) | BLO189 |
| 1457 * | GHN 990 | Bristol L5G | 63.073 | B35R | 6/47 | United AS, Darlington (DM) | BLO190 |
| 1458 * | GHN 991 | Bristol L5G | 63.074 | B35R | 6/47 | United AS, Darlington (DM) | BLO191 |
| 1459 * | GHN 992 | Bristol L5G | 63.085 | B35R | 7/47 | United AS, Darlington (DM) | BLO192 |
| 1460 * | GHN 993 | Bristol L5G | 63.088 | B35R | 7/47 | United AS, Darlington (DM) | BLO193 |
| 1461 * | GHN 994 | Bristol L5G | 63.087 | B35R | 7/47 | United AS, Darlington (DM) | BLO194 |
| 1462 * | GHN 995 | Bristol L5G | 63.092 | B35R | 7/47 | United AS, Darlington (DM) | BLO195 |
| 1463 * | GHN 996 | Bristol L5G | 63.093 | B35R | 7/47 | United AS, Darlington (DM) | BLO196 |
| 1464 | BJA 436 | Bristol L5G | 61.049 | B35R | 12/46 | North Western RCC, Stockport (CH) | 136 |
| 1465 | BJA 437 | Bristol L5G | 61.050 | B35R | 12/46 | North Western RCC, Stockport (CH) | 137 |
| 1466 | BJA 438 | Bristol L5G | 61.051 | B35R | 12/46 | North Western RCC, Stockport (CH) | 138 |
| 1467 | BJA 439 | Bristol L5G | 61.052 | B35R | 12/46 | North Western RCC, Stockport (CH) | 139 |
| 1468 | BJA 440 | Bristol L5G | 61.053 | B35R | 12/46 | North Western RCC, Stockport (CH) | 140 |
| 1469 | BJA 441 | Bristol L5G | 63.034 | B35R | 5/47 | North Western RCC, Stockport (CH) | 141 |
| 1470 | BJA 442 | Bristol L5G | 63.035 | B35R | 5/47 | North Western RCC, Stockport (CH) | 142 |
| 1471 | BJA 443 | Bristol L5G | 63.036 | B35R | 5/47 | North Western RCC, Stockport (CH) | 143 |
| 1472 | BJA 444 | Bristol L5G | 63.050 | B35R | 5/47 | North Western RCC, Stockport (CH) | 144 |
| 1473 | BJA 445 | Bristol L5G | 63.051 | B35R | 5/47 | North Western RCC, Stockport (CH) | 145 |
| 1474 | BJA 446 | Bristol L5G | 63.052 | B35R | 5/47 | North Western RCC, Stockport (CH) | 146 |
| 1475 | BJA 449 | Bristol L5G | 63.069 | B35R | 5/47 | North Western RCC, Stockport (CH) | 149 |
| 1476 | BJA 450 | Bristol L5G | 63.070 | B35R | 5/47 | North Western RCC, Stockport (CH) | 150 |
| 1477 | CDB 151 | Bristol L5G | 63.071 | B35R | 5/47 | North Western RCC, Stockport (CH) | 151 |
| 1478 | CDB 152 | Bristol L5G | 63.082 | B35R | 5/46 | North Western RCC, Stockport (CH) | 152 |
| 1479 | CDB 153 | Bristol L5G | 63.083 | B35R | 6/47 | North Western RCC, Stockport (CH) | 153 |
| 1480 | CDB 154 | Bristol L5G | 63.084 | B35R | 6/47 | North Western RCC, Stockport (CH) | 154 |
| 1481 | BJA 447 | Bristol L5G | 63.053 | B35R | 6/47 | North Western RCC, Stockport (CH) | 147 |
| 1482 | BJA 448 | Bristol L5G | 63.054 | B35R | 6/47 | North Western RCC, Stockport (CH) | 148 |
| 1483 | CDB 155 | Bristol L5G | 63.104 | B35R | 6/47 | North Western RCC, Stockport (CH) | 155 |
| 1484 | CDB 156 | Bristol L5G | 63.105 | B35R | 6/47 | North Western RCC, Stockport (CH) | 156 |
| 1485 | CDB 157 | Bristol L5G | 63.106 | B35R | 6/47 | North Western RCC, Stockport (CH) | 157 |
| 1486 | CDB 158 | Bristol L5G | 63.123 | B35R | 6/47 | North Western RCC, Stockport (CH) | 158 |
| 1487 | CDB 159 | Bristol L5G | 63.124 | B35R | 9/47 | North Western RCC, Stockport (CH) | 159 |
| 1488 | CDB 160 | Bristol L5G | 63.139 | B35R | 9/47 | North Western RCC, Stockport (CH) | 160 |
| 1489 | JTT 997 | Bristol K6A | 62.137 | L27/28R | 6/47 | Western National, Exeter (DN) | 829 |
| 1490 | JTT 998 | Bristol K6A | 62.138 | L27/28R | 6/47 | Western National, Exeter (DN) | 830 |
| 1491 | JTT 999 | Bristol K6A | 62.139 | L27/28R | 6/47 | Western National, Exeter (DN) | 831 |
| 1492 | HTT 991 | Bristol K6B | 62.111 | L27/28R | 7/47 | Western National, Exeter (DN) | 820 |
| 1493 | CUH 798 | Leyland PS1 | 460565 | B35R | 10/46 | Western Welsh, Cardiff (GG) | 798 |
| 1494 | CUH 799 | Leyland PS1 | 461040 | B35R | 10/46 | Western Welsh, Cardiff (GG) | 799 |
| 1495 | CUH 800 | Leyland PS1 | 461052 | B35R | 11/46 | Western Welsh, Cardiff (GG) | 800 |
| 1496 | CUH 801 | Leyland PS1 | 461053 | B35R | 11/46 | Western Welsh, Cardiff (GG) | 801 |
| 1497 | CUH 802 | Leyland PS1 | 461064 | B35R | 10/46 | Western Welsh, Cardiff (GG) | 802 |
| 1498 | CUH 803 | Leyland PS1 | 461107 | B35R | 10/46 | Western Welsh, Cardiff (GG) | 803 |
| 1499 | CUH 804 | Leyland PS1 | 461108 | B35R | 11/46 | Western Welsh, Cardiff (GG) | 804 |
| 1500 | CUH 805 | Leyland PS1 | 461120 | B35R | 11/46 | Western Welsh, Cardiff (GG) | 805 |
| 1501 | CUH 806 | Leyland PS1 | 461132 | B35R | 11/46 | Western Welsh, Cardiff (GG) | 806 |
| 1502 | CUH 807 | Leyland PS1 | 461137 | B35R | 11/46 | Western Welsh, Cardiff (GG) | 807 |
| 1503 | CUH 808 | Leyland PS1 | 461138 | B35R | 11/46 | Western Welsh, Cardiff (GG) | 808 |
| 1504 | CUH 809 | Leyland PS1 | 461139 | B35R | 11/46 | Western Welsh, Cardiff (GG) | 809 |
| 1505 | CUH 810 | Leyland PS1 | 461140 | B35R | 11/46 | Western Welsh, Cardiff (GG) | 810 |
| 1506 | CUH 811 | Leyland PS1 | 461141 | B35R | 11/46 | Western Welsh, Cardiff (GG) | 811 |
| 1507 | CUH 812 | Leyland PS1 | 461146 | B35R | 12/46 | Western Welsh, Cardiff (GG) | 812 |
| 1508 | CUH 813 | Leyland PS1 | 461147 | B35R | 12/46 | Western Welsh, Cardiff (GG) | 813 |
| 1509 | CUH 814 | Leyland PS1 | 461148 | B35R | 12/46 | Western Welsh, Cardiff (GG) | 814 |
| 1510 | CUH 815 | Leyland PS1 | 460564 | B35R | 12/46 | Western Welsh, Cardiff (GG) | 815 |

| 1511 | CUH 816 | Leyland PS1 | 462379 | B35R | 1/47 | Western Welsh, Cardiff (GG) 816 |
|------|---------|-------------|--------|------|------|--------------------------------|
| 1512 | CUH 817 | Leyland PS1 | 462380 | B35R | 1/47 | Western Welsh, Cardiff (GG) 817 |
| 1513 | CUH 818 | Leyland PS1 | 462384 | B35R | 1/47 | Western Welsh, Cardiff (GG) 818 |
| 1514 | CUH 819 | Leyland PS1 | 462447 | B35R | 1/47 | Western Welsh, Cardiff (GG) 819 |
| 1515 | CUH 820 | Leyland PS1 | 462448 | B35R | 2/47 | Western Welsh, Cardiff (GG) 820 |
| 1516 | CUH 822 | Leyland PS1 | 462673 | B35R | 2/47 | Western Welsh, Cardiff (GG) 822 |
| 1517 | CUH 823 | Leyland PS1 | 462674 | B35R | 2/47 | Western Welsh, Cardiff (GG) 823 |
| 1518 | CUH 830 | Leyland PS1 | 462701 | B35R | 2/47 | Western Welsh, Cardiff (GG) 830 |
| 1519 | CUH 821 | Leyland PS1 | 462672 | B35R | 2/47 | Western Welsh, Cardiff (GG) 821 |
| 1520 | CUH 828 | Leyland PS1 | 462697 | B35R | 2/47 | Western Welsh, Cardiff (GG) 828 |
| 1521 | CUH 825 | Leyland PS1 | 462676 | B35R | 3/47 | Western Welsh, Cardiff (GG) 825 |
| 1522 | CUH 826 | Leyland PS1 | 462677 | B35R | 3/47 | Western Welsh, Cardiff (GG) 826 |
| 1523 | CUH 824 | Leyland PS1 | 462675 | B35R | 3/47 | Western Welsh, Cardiff (GG) 824 |
| 1524 | CUH 829 | Leyland PS1 | 462700 | B35R | 3/47 | Western Welsh, Cardiff (GG) 829 |
| 1525 | CUH 827 | Leyland PS1 | 462696 | B35R | 3/47 | Western Welsh, Cardiff (GG) 827 |
| 1526 | CUH 831 | Leyland PS1 | 462702 | B35R | 4/47 | Western Welsh, Cardiff (GG) 831 |
| 1527 | CUH 833 | Leyland PS1 | 462750 | B35R | 5/47 | Western Welsh, Cardiff (GG) 833 |
| 1528 | CUH 832 | Leyland PS1 | 462678 | B35R | 4/47 | Western Welsh, Cardiff (GG) 832 |
| 1529 | CUH 834 | Leyland PS1 | 462749 | B35R | 5/47 | Western Welsh, Cardiff (GG) 834 |
| 1530 | CUH 835 | Leyland PS1 | 462764 | B35R | 5/47 | Western Welsh, Cardiff (GG) 835 |
| 1531 | CUH 836 | Leyland PS1 | 462822 | B35R | 5/47 | Western Welsh, Cardiff (GG) 836 |
| 1532 | CUH 837 | Leyland PS1 | 462829 | B35R | 5/47 | Western Welsh, Cardiff (GG) 837 |
| 1533 | CUH 839 | Leyland PS1 | 463047 | B35R | 5/47 | Western Welsh, Cardiff (GG) 839 |
| 1534 | CUH 838 | Leyland PS1 | 463046 | B35R | 5/47 | Western Welsh, Cardiff (GG) 838 |
| 1535 | CUH 840 | Leyland PS1 | 470417 | B35R | 6/47 | Western Welsh, Cardiff (GG) 840 |
| 1536 | CUH 841 | Leyland PS1 | 470418 | B35R | 6/47 | Western Welsh, Cardiff (GG) 841 |
| 1537 | CUH 842 | Leyland PS1 | 470496 | B35R | 6/47 | Western Welsh, Cardiff (GG) 842 |
| 1538 | CUH 843 | Leyland PS1 | 470589 | B35R | 6/47 | Western Welsh, Cardiff (GG) 843 |
| 1539 | CUH 844 | Leyland PS1 | 470587 | B35R | 7/47 | Western Welsh, Cardiff (GG) 844 |
| 1540 | CUH 845 | Leyland PS1 | 470588 | B35R | 7/47 | Western Welsh, Cardiff (GG) 845 |
| 1541 | CUH 846 | Leyland PS1 | 470590 | B35R | 8/47 | Western Welsh, Cardiff (GG) 846 |
| 1542 | CUH 847 | Leyland PS1 | 470663 | B35R | 8/47 | Western Welsh, Cardiff (GG) 847 |
| 1543 | CUH 848 | Leyland PS1 | 470664 | B35R | 7/47 | Western Welsh, Cardiff (GG) 848 |
| 1544 | CUH 849 | Leyland PS1 | 470698 | B35R | 8/47 | Western Welsh, Cardiff (GG) 849 |
| 1545 | CUH 850 | Leyland PS1 | 470927 | B35R | 8/47 | Western Welsh, Cardiff (GG) 850 |
| 1546 | CUH 851 | Leyland PS1 | 470928 | B35R | 8/47 | Western Welsh, Cardiff (GG) 851 |
| 1547 | CUH 852 | Leyland PS1 | 471129 | B35R | 8/47 | Western Welsh, Cardiff (GG) 852 |
| 1548 | CUH 853 | Leyland PS1 | 471131 | B35R | 8/47 | Western Welsh, Cardiff (GG) 853 |
| 1549 | CUH 854 | Leyland PS1 | 471132 | B35R | 8/47 | Western Welsh, Cardiff (GG) 854 |
| 1550 | CUH 855 | Leyland PS1 | 471130 | B35R | 9/47 | Western Welsh, Cardiff (GG) 855 |
| 1551 | CUH 856 | Leyland PS1 | 471209 | B35R | 8/47 | Western Welsh, Cardiff (GG) 856 |
| 1552 | CUH 857 | Leyland PS1 | 471210 | B35R | 9/47 | Western Welsh, Cardiff (GG) 857 |
| 1553 | CUH 858 | Leyland PS1 | 471211 | B35R | 9/47 | Western Welsh, Cardiff (GG) 858 |
| 1554 | CUH 859 | Leyland PS1 | 471208 | B35R | 10/47 | Western Welsh, Cardiff (GG) 859 |
| 1555 | CUH 867 | Leyland PS1 | 471313 | B35R | 9/47 | Western Welsh, Cardiff (GG) 867 |
| 1556 | CUH 860 | Leyland PS1 | 471314 | B35R | 10/47 | Western Welsh, Cardiff (GG) 860 |
| 1557 | CUH 861 | Leyland PS1 | 471315 | B35R | 10/47 | Western Welsh, Cardiff (GG) 861 |
| 1558 | CUH 862 | Leyland PS1 | 471316 | B35R | 10/47 | Western Welsh, Cardiff (GG) 862 |
| 1559 | CUH 863 | Leyland PS1 | 471363 | B35R | 10/47 | Western Welsh, Cardiff (GG) 863 |
| 1560 | CUH 864 | Leyland PS1 | 471364 | B35R | 10/47 | Western Welsh, Cardiff (GG) 864 |
| 1561 | CUH 865 | Leyland PS1 | 471365 | B35R | 10/47 | Western Welsh, Cardiff (GG) 865 |
| 1562 | CUH 866 | Leyland PS1 | 471366 | B35R | 10/47 | Western Welsh, Cardiff (GG) 866 |
| 1563 | CUH 869 | Leyland PS1 | 471368 | B35R | 11/47 | Western Welsh, Cardiff (GG) 869 |
| 1564 | CUH 871 | Leyland PS1 | 471446 | B35R | 10/47 | Western Welsh, Cardiff (GG) 871 |
| 1565 | CUH 872 | Leyland PS1 | 471457 | B35R | 11/47 | Western Welsh, Cardiff (GG) 872 |
| 1566 | CUH 873 | Leyland PS1 | 471458 | B35R | 11/47 | Western Welsh, Cardiff (GG) 873 |
| 1567 | CUH 868 | Leyland PS1 | 471367 | B35R | 11/47 | Western Welsh, Cardiff (GG) 868 |
| 1568 | CUH 870 | Leyland PS1 | 471445 | B35R | 10/47 | Western Welsh, Cardiff (GG) 870 |
| 1569 | CUH 874 | Leyland PS1 | 471456 | B35R | 12/47 | Western Welsh, Cardiff (GG) 874 |
| 1570 | CUH 875 | Leyland PS1 | 471681 | B35R | 12/47 | Western Welsh, Cardiff (GG) 875 |
| 1571 | CUH 876 | Leyland PS1 | 471682 | B35R | 12/47 | Western Welsh, Cardiff (GG) 876 |
| 1572 | CUH 877 | Leyland PS1 | 471683 | B35R | 12/47 | Western Welsh, Cardiff (GG) 877 |
| 1573 * | HUW 780 | Leyland PS1 | 461045 | B35R | 10/46 | Birch Bros, London NW5 (LN) K80 |
| 1574 * | HUW 781 | Leyland PS1 | 462416 | B35R | 3/47 | Birch Bros, London NW5 (LN) K81 |

| | | | | | | |
|---|---|---|---|---|---|---|
| 1575 * | HUW 782 | Leyland PS1 | 462459 | B35R | 3/47 | Birch Bros, London NW5 (LN) K82 |
| 1576 * | HUW 783 | Leyland PS1 | 462664 | B35R | 3/47 | Birch Bros, London NW5 (LN) K83 |
| 1577 * | HUW 784 | Leyland PS1 | 462985 | B35R | 5/47 | Birch Bros, London NW5 (LN) K84 |
| 1578 * | HUW 785 | Leyland PS1 | 463043 | B35R | 5/47 | Birch Bros, London NW5 (LN) K85 |
| 1579 | GBJ 190 | AEC Regent II | O6617943 | H30/26R | 1/47 | Lowestoft Corporation (EK) 19 |
| 1580 | GBJ 191 | AEC Regent II | O6617944 | H30/26R | 1/47 | Lowestoft Corporation (EK) 20 |
| 1581 | GBJ 192 | AEC Regent II | O6617945 | H30/26R | 1/47 | Lowestoft Corporation (EK) 21 |
| 1582 | GBJ 193 | AEC Regent II | O6617946 | H30/26R | 1/47 | Lowestoft Corporation (EK) 22 |
| 1583 | GBJ 194 | AEC Regent II | O6617947 | H30/26R | 1/47 | Lowestoft Corporation (EK) 23 |
| 1584 | GBJ 195 | AEC Regent II | O6617948 | H30/26R | 1/47 | Lowestoft Corporation (EK) 24 |
| 1585 | GBJ 196 | AEC Regent II | O6617949 | H30/26R | 1/47 | Lowestoft Corporation (EK) 25 |
| 1586 | GBJ 197 | AEC Regent II | O6617951 | H30/26R | 2/47 | Lowestoft Corporation (EK) 26 |
| 1587 | GBJ 198 | AEC Regent II | O6617950 | H30/26R | 3/47 | Lowestoft Corporation (EK) 27 |
| 1588 | HAL 841 | AEC Regent II | O6617820 | H30/26R | 1/47 | Ebor Bus Co Ltd, Mansfield (NG) 21 |
| 1589 | KHU 621 | Bristol K6A | 64.025 | L27/28R | 8/47 | Bristol Tramways (GL) L4100 |
| 1590 | KHU 623 | Bristol K5G | 64.027 | L27/28R | 9/47 | Bristol Tramways (GL) L4102 |
| 1591 | KHU 624 | Bristol K5G | 64.028 | L27/28R | 9/47 | Bristol Tramways (GL) L4103 |
| 1592 | KHU 622 | Bristol K5G | 64.026 | L27/28R | 8/47 | Bristol Tramways (GL) L4101 |
| 1593 | KHU 605 | Bristol K6A | 64.029 | L27/28R | 9/47 | Bristol Tramways (GL) L4108 |
| 1594 | KHU 606 | Bristol K6A | 64.030 | L27/28R | 9/47 | Bristol Tramways (GL) L4109 |
| 1595 | KHU 607 | Bristol K6A | 64.031 | L27/28R | 9/47 | Bristol Tramways (GL) L4110 |
| 1596 | KHU 602 | Bristol K6A | 64.002 | L27/28R | 9/47 | Bristol Tramways (GL) L4105 |
| 1597 | KHU 601 | Bristol K6B | 62.121 | L27/28R | 9/47 | Bristol Tramways (GL) L4104 |
| 1598 | KHU 603 | Bristol K6B | 64.005 | L27/28R | 9/47 | Bristol Tramways (GL) L4106 |
| 1599 | KHU 604 | Bristol K6B | 64.006 | L27/28R | 9/47 | Bath Tramways Motor Co (SO) L3900 |
| 1600 | KHU 608 | Bristol K5G | 64.056 | L27/28R | 1/48 | Bristol Tramways (GL) L4107 |
| 1601 | KHU 609 | Bristol K5G | 64.057 | L27/28R | 10/47 | Bristol Tramways (GL) L4111 |
| 1602 | KHU 610 | Bristol K5G | 64.058 | L27/28R | 10/47 | Bristol Tramways (GL) L4112 |
| 1603 | KHU 611 | Bristol K5G | 64.059 | L27/28R | 10/47 | Bristol Tramways (GL) L4113 |
| 1604 | KHU 612 | Bristol K5G | 64.060 | L27/28R | 10/47 | Bristol Tramways (GL) L4114 |
| 1605 | KHW 633 | Bristol K5G | 64.071 | L27/28R | 11/47 | Bath Tramways Motor Co (SO) L3901 |
| 1606 | KHW 635 | Bristol K5G | 64.126 | L27/28R | 1/48 | Bristol Tramways (GL) L4115 |
| 1607 | KHW 636 | Bristol K5G | 64.127 | L27/28R | 2/48 | Bristol Tramways (GL) L4116 |
| 1608 | KHW 637 | Bristol K5G | 64.128 | L27/28R | 2/48 | Bristol Tramways (GL) L4117 |
| 1609 | KHW 638 | Bristol K5G | 64.129 | L27/28R | 1/48 | Bath Tramways Motor Co (SO) L3902 |
| 1610 | KHW 639 | Bristol K5G | 64.130 | L27/28R | 1/48 | Bath Tramways Motor Co (SO) L3903 |
| 1611 | MPU 1 | Bristol K5G | 64.012 | L27/28R | 8/47 | Eastern National, Chelmsford (EX) 3940 |
| 1612 | MPU 2 | Bristol K5G | 64.013 | L27/28R | 9/47 | Eastern National, Chelmsford (EX) 3941 |
| 1613 | MPU 3 | Bristol K5G | 64.035 | L27/28R | 9/47 | Eastern National, Chelmsford (EX) 3942 |
| 1614 | MPU 4 | Bristol K5G | 64.037 | L27/28R | 10/47 | Eastern National, Chelmsford (EX) 3943 |
| 1615 | MPU 5 | Bristol K5G | 64.036 | L27/28R | 11/47 | Eastern National, Chelmsford (EX) 3944 |
| 1616 | MPU 6 | Bristol K5G | 64.045 | L27/28R | 11/47 | Eastern National, Chelmsford (EX) 3945 |
| 1617 | MPU 7 | Bristol K5G | 64.081 | L27/28R | 11/47 | Eastern National, Chelmsford (EX) 3946 |
| 1618 | MPU 8 | Bristol K5G | 64.113 | L27/28R | 11/47 | Eastern National, Chelmsford (EX) 3947 |
| 1619 | MPU 9 | Bristol K5G | 64.132 | L27/28R | 12/47 | Eastern National, Chelmsford (EX) 3948 |
| 1620 | MPU 10 | Bristol K5G | 64.191 | L27/28R | 2/48 | Eastern National, Chelmsford (EX) 3949 |
| 1621 | MPU 11 | Bristol K5G | 64.192 | L27/28R | 2/48 | Eastern National, Chelmsford (EX) 3950 |
| 1622 | MPU 12 | Bristol K5G | 64.193 | L27/28R | 2/48 | Eastern National, Chelmsford (EX) 3951 |
| 1623 | MPU 13 | Bristol K5G | 66.017 | L27/28R | 2/48 | Eastern National, Chelmsford (EX) 3952 |
| 1624 | MPU 14 | Bristol K5G | 66.018 | L27/28R | 2/48 | Eastern National, Chelmsford (EX) 3953 |
| 1625 | MPU 16 | Bristol K5G | 66.054 | L27/28R | 2/48 | Eastern National, Chelmsford (EX) 3955 |
| 1626 | MPU 15 | Bristol K5G | 66.053 | L27/28R | 3/48 | Eastern National, Chelmsford (EX) 3954 |
| 1627 | MPU 17 | Bristol K5G | 66.055 | L27/28R | 3/48 | Eastern National, Chelmsford (EX) 3956 |
| 1628 | MPU 18 | Bristol K5G | 66.108 | L27/28R | 3/48 | Eastern National, Chelmsford (EX) 3957 |
| 1629 | MPU 19 | Bristol K5G | 66.109 | L27/28R | 3/48 | Eastern National, Chelmsford (EX) 3958 |
| 1630 | MPU 20 | Bristol K6B | 66.084 | L27/28R | 6/48 | Eastern National, Chelmsford (EX) 3959 |
| 1631 | MPU 21 | Bristol K6B | 66.085 | L27/28R | 6/48 | Eastern National, Chelmsford (EX) 3960 |
| 1632 | MPU 22 | Bristol K6B | 66.086 | L27/28R | 6/48 | Eastern National, Chelmsford (EX) 3961 |
| 1633 | MPU 23 | Bristol K6B | 66.156 | L27/28R | 6/48 | Eastern National, Chelmsford (EX) 3962 |
| 1634 | MPU 24 | Bristol K6B | 66.122 | L27/28R | 6/48 | Eastern National, Chelmsford (EX) 3963 |
| 1635 | MPU 25 | Bristol K6B | 66.155 | L27/28R | 6/48 | Eastern National, Chelmsford (EX) 3964 |
| 1636 | GUF 738 | Leyland PS1/1 | 462038 | C31R | 2/47 | Southdown, Brighton (ES) 1238 |
| 1637 | GUF 743 | Leyland PS1/1 | 462061 | C31R | 2/47 | Southdown, Brighton (ES) 1243 |
| 1638 | GUF 744 | Leyland PS1/1 | 462063 | C31R | 2/47 | Southdown, Brighton (ES) 1244 |

| | | | | | | |
|---|---|---|---|---|---|---|
| 1639 | GUF 745 | Leyland PS1/1 | 462064 | C31R | 3/47 | Southdown, Brighton (ES) 1245 |
| 1640 | GUF 746 | Leyland PS1/1 | 462131 | C31R | 3/47 | Southdown, Brighton (ES) 1246 |
| 1641 | GUF 735 | Leyland PS1/1 | 461218 | C31R | 3/47 | Southdown, Brighton (ES) 1235 |
| 1642 | HCD 447 | Leyland PS1/1 | 462424 | C31R | 3/47 | Southdown, Brighton (ES) 1247 |
| 1643 | HCD 448 | Leyland PS1/1 | 462425 | C31R | 3/47 | Southdown, Brighton (ES) 1248 |
| 1644 | HCD 449 | Leyland PS1/1 | 462467 | C31R | 3/47 | Southdown, Brighton (ES) 1249 |
| 1645 | HCD 450 | Leyland PS1/1 | 462468 | C31R | 3/47 | Southdown, Brighton (ES) 1250 |
| 1646 | HCD 451 | Leyland PS1/1 | 462469 | C31R | 3/47 | Southdown, Brighton (ES) 1251 |
| 1647 | GUF 731 | Leyland PS1/1 | 461173 | C31R | 3/47 | Southdown, Brighton (ES) 1231 |
| 1648 | GUF 740 | Leyland PS1/1 | 462040 | C31R | 5/47 | Southdown, Brighton (ES) 1240 |
| 1649 | GUF 732 | Leyland PS1/1 | 461174 | C31R | 3/47 | Southdown, Brighton (ES) 1232 |
| 1650 | GUF 741 | Leyland PS1/1 | 462041 | C31R | 4/47 | Southdown, Brighton (ES) 1241 |
| 1651 | GUF 742 | Leyland PS1/1 | 462062 | C31R | 4/47 | Southdown, Brighton (ES) 1242 |
| 1652 | GUF 730 | Leyland PS1/1 | 461121 | C31R | 4/47 | Southdown, Brighton (ES) 1230 |
| 1653 | GUF 737 | Leyland PS1/1 | 462037 | C31R | 4/47 | Southdown, Brighton (ES) 1237 |
| 1654 | GUF 727 | Leyland PS1/1 | 461056 | C31R | 4/47 | Southdown, Brighton (ES) 1227 |
| 1655 | GUF 728 | Leyland PS1/1 | 461065 | C31R | 4/47 | Southdown, Brighton (ES) 1228 |
| 1656 | GUF 729 | Leyland PS1/1 | 461071 | C31R | 4/47 | Southdown, Brighton (ES) 1229 |
| 1657 | GUF 736 | Leyland PS1/1 | 461217 | C31R | 4/47 | Southdown, Brighton (ES) 1236 |
| 1658 | GUF 734 | Leyland PS1/1 | 461214 | C31R | 5/47 | Southdown, Brighton (ES) 1234 |
| 1659 | GUF 733 | Leyland PS1/1 | 461216 | C31R | 5/47 | Southdown, Brighton (ES) 1233 |
| 1660 | GUF 739 | Leyland PS1/1 | 462039 | C31R | 5/47 | Southdown, Brighton (ES) 1239 |
| 1661 | GFM 891 | Bristol K6A | 62.145 | L27/28R | 8/47 | Crosville MS, Chester (CH) MB283 |
| 1662 | GFM 892 | Bristol K6A | 62.146 | L27/28R | 8/47 | Crosville MS, Chester (CH) MB284 |
| 1663 | GFM 894 | Bristol K6A | 64.032 | L27/28R | 10/47 | Crosville MS, Chester (CH) MB286 |
| 1664 | GFM 893 | Bristol K6A | 64.009 | L27/28R | 12/47 | Crosville MS, Chester (CH) MB285 |
| 1665 | GFM 895 | Bristol K6A | 64.033 | L27/28R | 12/47 | Crosville MS, Chester (CH) MB287 |
| 1666 | GFM 896 | Bristol K6A | 64.034 | L27/28R | 12/47 | Crosville MS, Chester (CH) MB288 |
| 1667 | GFM 897 | Bristol K6A | 64.088 | L27/28R | 12/47 | Crosville MS, Chester (CH) MB289 |
| 1668 | GFM 898 | Bristol K6A | 64.112 | L27/28R | 2/48 | Crosville MS, Chester (CH) MB290 |
| 1669 | GFM 899 | Bristol K6A | 64.131 | L27/28R | 2/48 | Crosville MS, Chester (CH) MB291 |
| 1670 | GFM 900 | Bristol K6A | 64.139 | L27/28R | 2/48 | Crosville MS, Chester (CH) MB292 |
| 1671 | GFM 901 | Bristol K6A | 64.140 | L27/28R | 4/48 | Crosville MS, Chester (CH) MB293 |
| 1672 | GFM 902 | Bristol K6A | 64.141 | L27/28R | 4/48 | Crosville MS, Chester (CH) MB294 |
| 1673 | GFM 903 | Bristol K6A | 66.098 | L27/28R | 4/48 | Crosville MS, Chester (CH) MB295 |
| 1674 | GFM 904 | Bristol K6A | 66.097 | L27/28R | 4/48 | Crosville MS, Chester (CH) MB296 |
| 1675 | GFM 905 | Bristol K6A | 66.099 | L27/28R | 4/48 | Crosville MS, Chester (CH) MB297 |
| 1676 | GLJ 964 | Bristol K5G | 62.143 | L27/28R | 8/47 | Hants & Dorset, Bournemouth (HA) TD787 |
| 1677 | GLJ 965 | Bristol K5G | 64.001 | L27/28R | 8/47 | Hants & Dorset, Bournemouth (HA) TD788 |
| 1678 | GLJ 966 | Bristol K5G | 64.046 | L27/28R | 9/47 | Hants & Dorset, Bournemouth (HA) TD789 |
| 1679 | GLJ 967 | Bristol K5G | 64.047 | L27/28R | 9/47 | Hants & Dorset, Bournemouth (HA) TD790 |
| 1680 | GLJ 968 | Bristol K5G | 64.048 | L27/28R | 9/47 | Hants & Dorset, Bournemouth (HA) TD791 |
| 1681 | GLJ 969 | Bristol K5G | 64.061 | L27/28R | 10/47 | Hants & Dorset, Bournemouth (HA) TD792 |
| 1682 | GLJ 971 | Bristol K5G | 64.083 | L27/28R | 10/47 | Hants & Dorset, Bournemouth (HA) TD794 |
| 1683 | GLJ 972 | Bristol K5G | 64.084 | L27/28R | 11/47 | Hants & Dorset, Bournemouth (HA) TD795 |
| 1684 | GLJ 973 | Bristol K5G | 64.085 | L27/28R | 11/47 | Hants & Dorset, Bournemouth (HA) TD796 |
| 1685 | GLJ 970 | Bristol K5G | 64.082 | L27/28R | 11/47 | Hants & Dorset, Bournemouth (HA) TD793 |
| 1686 | GLJ 974 | Bristol K5G | 64.089 | L27/28R | 11/47 | Hants & Dorset, Bournemouth (HA) TD797 |
| 1687 | GLJ 975 | Bristol K5G | 64.100 | L27/28R | 11/47 | Hants & Dorset, Bournemouth (HA) TD798 |
| 1688 | GLJ 976 | Bristol K5G | 64.114 | L27/28R | 11/47 | Hants & Dorset, Bournemouth (HA) TD799 |
| 1689 | GLJ 977 | Bristol K5G | 64.115 | L27/28R | 11/47 | Hants & Dorset, Bournemouth (HA) TD800 |
| 1690 | GLJ 978 | Bristol K5G | 64.152 | L27/28R | 11/47 | Hants & Dorset, Bournemouth (HA) TD850 |
| 1691 | GLJ 979 | Bristol K5G | 64.153 | L27/28R | 11/47 | Hants & Dorset, Bournemouth (HA) TD851 |
| 1692 | GLJ 980 | Bristol K5G | 64.154 | L27/28R | 11/47 | Hants & Dorset, Bournemouth (HA) TD852 |
| 1693 | GLJ 981 | Bristol K5G | 64.133 | L27/28R | 12/47 | Hants & Dorset, Bournemouth (HA) TD853 |
| 1694 | GLJ 982 | Bristol K5G | 64.189 | L27/28R | 12/47 | Hants & Dorset, Bournemouth (HA) TD854 |
| 1695 | GLJ 983 | Bristol K5G | 64.194 | L27/28R | 1/48 | Hants & Dorset, Bournemouth (HA) TD855 |
| 1696 | GLJ 986 | Bristol K5G | 66.021 | L27/28R | 2/48 | Hants & Dorset, Bournemouth (HA) TD858 |
| 1697 | GLJ 984 | Bristol K5G | 66.019 | L27/28R | 2/48 | Hants & Dorset, Bournemouth (HA) TD856 |
| 1698 | GLJ 985 | Bristol K5G | 66.020 | L27/28R | 2/48 | Hants & Dorset, Bournemouth (HA) TD857 |
| 1699 | GLJ 987 | Bristol K5G | 66.022 | L27/28R | 2/48 | Hants & Dorset, Bournemouth (HA) TD859 |
| 1700 | GLJ 988 | Bristol K6A | 66.056 | L27/28R | 5/48 | Hants & Dorset, Bournemouth (HA) TD860 |
| 1701 | GLJ 989 | Bristol K6A | 66.100 | L27/28R | 5/48 | Hants & Dorset, Bournemouth (HA) TD861 |
| 1702 | GLJ 990 | Bristol K6A | 66.101 | L27/28R | 5/48 | Hants & Dorset, Bournemouth (HA) TD862 |

| 1703 | GLJ 991 | Bristol K6A | 66.123 | L27/28R | 5/48 | Hants & Dorset, Bournemouth (HA) TD863 |
| 1704 | GLJ 992 | Bristol K6A | 66.140 | L27/28R | 5/48 | Hants & Dorset, Bournemouth (HA) TD864 |
| 1705 | GLJ 993 | Bristol K6A | 66.157 | L27/28R | 5/48 | Hants & Dorset, Bournemouth (HA) TD865 |
| 1706 | JUO 963 | Bristol K6A | 64.044 | L27/28R | 9/47 | Southern National, Exeter (DN) 859 |
| 1707 | JUO 964 | Bristol K6A | 64.043 | L27/28R | 9/47 | Southern National, Exeter (DN) 860 |
| 1708 | JUO 965 | Bristol K6A | 64.078 | L27/28R | 9/47 | Southern National, Exeter (DN) 861 |
| 1709 | JUO 966 | Bristol K6A | 64.079 | L27/28R | 11/47 | Southern National, Exeter (DN) 862 |
| 1710 | JUO 967 | Bristol K6A | 64.080 | L27/28R | 11/47 | Southern National, Exeter (DN) 863 |
| 1711 | JUO 968 | Bristol K5G | 64.158 | L27/28R | 12/47 | Southern National, Exeter (DN) 864 |
| 1712 | JUO 969 | Bristol K5G | 64.159 | L27/28R | 12/47 | Southern National, Exeter (DN) 865 |
| 1713 | JUO 970 | Bristol K5G | 64.160 | L27/28R | 12/47 | Southern National, Exeter (DN) 866 |
| 1714 | JUO 971 | Bristol K5G | 64.190 | L27/28R | 2/48 | Southern National, Exeter (DN) 867 |
| 1715 | JUO 972 | Bristol K5G | 66.006 | L27/28R | 4/48 | Southern National, Exeter (DN) 868 |
| 1716 | JUO 973 | Bristol K5G | 66.007 | L27/28R | 4/48 | Southern National, Exeter (DN) 869 |
| 1717 | JUO 974 | Bristol K5G | 66.079 | L27/28R | 3/48 | Southern National, Exeter (DN) 870 |
| 1718 | JUO 975 | Bristol K5G | 66.080 | L27/28R | 3/48 | Southern National, Exeter (DN) 871 |
| 1719 | JUO 976 | Bristol K5G | 66.124 | L27/28R | 6/48 | Southern National, Exeter (DN) 872 |
| 1720 | JUO 977 | Bristol K5G | 66.125 | L27/28R | 6/48 | Southern National, Exeter (DN) 873 |
| 1721 | EDL 656 | Bristol K5G | 64.049 | L27/28R | 9/47 | Southern Vectis, Newport (IW) 720 |
| 1722 | EDL 657 | Bristol K5G | 64.050 | L27/28R | 9/47 | Southern Vectis, Newport (IW) 721 |
| 1723 | EDL 658 | Bristol K5G | 64.086 | L27/28R | 12/47 | Southern Vectis, Newport (IW) 722 |
| 1724 | EDL 659 | Bristol K5G | 64.094 | L27/28R | 12/47 | Southern Vectis, Newport (IW) 723 |
| 1725 | DMO 670 | Bristol K6A | 64.067 | L27/28R | 11/47 | Thames Valley, Reading (BE) 466 |
| 1726 | DMO 671 | Bristol K6A | 64.068 | L27/28R | 12/47 | Thames Valley, Reading (BE) 467 |
| 1727 | DMO 672 | Bristol K6B | 64.155 | L27/28R | 3/48 | Thames Valley, Reading (BE) 468 |
| 1728 | DMO 673 | Bristol K6B | 64.156 | L27/28R | 3/48 | Thames Valley, Reading (BE) 469 |
| 1729 | DMO 674 | Bristol K6B | 64.195 | L27/28R | 4/48 | Thames Valley, Reading (BE) 470 |
| 1730 | DMO 675 | Bristol K6B | 64.196 | L27/28R | 4/48 | Thames Valley, Reading (BE) 471 |
| 1731 | JHN 458 | Bristol K6B | 64.076 | L27/28R | 1/48 | United AS, Darlington (DM) BDO58 |
| 1732 | JHN 459 | Bristol K6B | 64.077 | L27/28R | 1/48 | United AS, Darlington (DM) BDO59 |
| 1733 | JHN 460 | Bristol K6B | 64.121 | L27/28R | 3/48 | United AS, Darlington (DM) BDO60 |
| 1734 | JHN 461 | Bristol K6B | 64.122 | L27/28R | 3/48 | United AS, Darlington (DM) BDO61 |
| 1735 | JHN 462 | Bristol K6B | 64.123 | L27/28R | 3/48 | United AS, Darlington (DM) BDO62 |
| 1736 | JHN 463 | Bristol K6B | 64.124 | L27/28R | 3/48 | United AS, Darlington (DM) BDO63 |
| 1737 * | JHN 464 | Bristol K6B | 64.125 | L27/28R | 5/48 | United AS, Darlington (DM) BDO64 |
| 1738 | JHN 465 | Bristol K6B | 66.026 | L27/28R | 5/48 | United AS, Darlington (DM) BDO65 |
| 1739 | JHN 466 | Bristol K6B | 66.027 | L27/28R | 5/48 | United AS, Darlington (DM) BDO66 |
| 1740 | JHN 467 | Bristol K6B | 66.028 | L27/28R | 6/48 | United AS, Darlington (DM) BDO67 |
| 1741 | DBD 980 | Bristol K5G | 64.101 | L27/28R | 11/47 | United Counties, Northampton (NO) 639 |
| 1742 | DBD 981 | Bristol K5G | 64.102 | L27/28R | 11/47 | United Counties, Northampton (NO) 640 |
| 1743 | DBD 982 | Bristol K5G | 64.157 | L27/28R | 11/47 | United Counties, Northampton (NO) 641 |
| 1744 | DBD 983 | Bristol K5G | 64.197 | L27/28R | 1/48 | United Counties, Northampton (NO) 642 |
| 1745 | DBD 985 | Bristol K5G | 66.117 | L27/28R | 4/48 | United Counties, Northampton (NO) 644 |
| 1746 | DBD 984 | Bristol K5G | 66.116 | L27/28R | 4/48 | United Counties, Northampton (NO) 643 |
| 1747 | DBD 986 | Bristol K6B | 66.057 | L27/28R | 5/48 | United Counties, Northampton (NO) 645 |
| 1748 | DBD 987 | Bristol K6B | 66.058 | L27/28R | 5/48 | United Counties, Northampton (NO) 646 |
| 1749 | FWX 831 | Bristol K6B | 64.069 | L27/28R | 1/48 | Keighley-West Yorkshire, Harrogate (WR) K738 |
| 1750 | FWX 832 | Bristol K6B | 64.070 | L27/28R | 1/48 | Keighley-West Yorkshire, Harrogate (WR) K739 |
| 1751 | FWX 833 | Bristol K6B | 64.095 | L27/28R | 1/48 | Keighley-West Yorkshire, Harrogate (WR) K740 |
| 1752 | FWX 834 | Bristol K6B | 64.103 | L27/28R | 3/48 | Keighley-West Yorkshire, Harrogate (WR) K741 |
| 1753 | FWX 835 | Bristol K6B | 64.104 | L27/28R | 3/48 | Keighley-West Yorkshire, Harrogate (WR) K742 |
| 1754 | FWX 836 | Bristol K6B | 64.137 | L27/28R | 3/48 | Keighley-West Yorkshire, Harrogate (WR) K743 |
| 1755 | FWX 821 | Bristol K6B | 64.149 | L27/28R | 3/48 | West Yorkshire RCC, Harrogate (WR) 728 |
| 1756 | FWX 822 | Bristol K6B | 64.150 | L27/28R | 3/48 | West Yorkshire RCC, Harrogate (WR) 729 |
| 1757 | FWX 823 | Bristol K6B | 64.151 | L27/28R | 3/48 | West Yorkshire RCC, Harrogate (WR) 730 |
| 1758 | FWX 824 | Bristol K6B | 66.064 | L27/28R | 5/48 | West Yorkshire RCC, Harrogate (WR) 731 |
| 1759 | FWX 825 | Bristol K6B | 66.065 | L27/28R | 5/48 | West Yorkshire RCC, Harrogate (WR) 732 |
| 1760 | FWX 826 | Bristol K6B | 66.066 | L27/28R | 5/48 | West Yorkshire RCC, Harrogate (WR) 733 |
| 1761 | FWX 827 | Bristol K5G | 66.118 | L27/28R | 7/48 | West Yorkshire RCC, Harrogate (WR) 734 |
| 1762 | FWX 828 | Bristol K6B | 66.119 | L27/28R | 6/48 | West Yorkshire RCC, Harrogate (WR) 735 |
| 1763 | FWX 829 | Bristol K6B | 66.120 | L27/28R | 7/48 | West Yorkshire RCC, Harrogate (WR) 736 |
| 1764 | FWX 830 | Bristol K6B | 66.121 | L27/28R | 6/48 | West Yorkshire RCC, Harrogate (WR) 737 |
| 1765 | JUO 905 | Bristol K6A | 64.015 | L27/28R | 8/47 | Western National, Exeter (DN) 832 |
| 1766 | JUO 906 | Bristol K6A | 64.014 | L27/28R | 9/47 | Western National, Exeter (DN) 833 |

| 1767 | JUO 908 | Bristol K6A | 64.017 | L27/28R | 9/47 | Western National, Exeter (DN) 835 |
|------|---------|-------------|--------|---------|------|------------------------------------|
| 1768 | JUO 907 | Bristol K6A | 64.016 | L27/28R | 9/47 | Western National, Exeter (DN) 834 |
| 1769 | JUO 909 | Bristol K6A | 64.062 | L27/28R | 10/47 | Western National, Exeter (DN) 836 |
| 1770 | JUO 910 | Bristol K6A | 64.063 | L27/28R | 10/47 | Western National, Exeter (DN) 837 |
| 1771 | JUO 911 | Bristol K6A | 64.064 | L27/28R | 10/47 | Western National, Exeter (DN) 838 |
| 1772 | JUO 912 | Bristol K6A | 64.105 | L27/28R | 10/47 | Western National, Exeter (DN) 839 |
| 1773 | JUO 913 | Bristol K6A | 64.106 | L27/28R | 10/47 | Western National, Exeter (DN) 840 |
| 1774 | JUO 914 | Bristol K6A | 64.107 | L27/28R | 10/47 | Western National, Exeter (DN) 841 |
| 1775 | JUO 915 | Bristol K5G | 64.164 | L27/28R | 12/47 | Western National, Exeter (DN) 842 |
| 1776 | JUO 916 | Bristol K5G | 64.165 | L27/28R | 12/47 | Western National, Exeter (DN) 843 |
| 1777 | JUO 917 | Bristol K5G | 64.166 | L27/28R | 12/47 | Western National, Exeter (DN) 844 |
| 1778 | JUO 918 | Bristol K5G | 64.167 | L27/28R | 12/47 | Western National, Exeter (DN) 845 |
| 1779 | JUO 919 | Bristol K5G | 64.198 | L27/28R | 2/48 | Western National, Exeter (DN) 846 |
| 1780 | JUO 920 | Bristol K5G | 64.199 | L27/28R | 2/48 | Western National, Exeter (DN) 847 |
| 1781 | JUO 921 | Bristol K5G | 64.200 | L27/28R | 2/48 | Western National, Exeter (DN) 848 |
| 1782 | JUO 922 | Bristol K5G | 66.013 | L27/28R | 2/48 | Western National, Exeter (DN) 849 |
| 1783 | JUO 923 | Bristol K5G | 66.015 | L27/28R | 2/48 | Western National, Exeter (DN) 850 |
| 1784 | JUO 924 | Bristol K5G | 66.014 | L27/28R | 2/48 | Western National, Exeter (DN) 851 |
| 1785 | JUO 925 | Bristol K5G | 66.016 | L27/28R | 4/48 | Western National, Exeter (DN) 852 |
| 1786 | JUO 926 | Bristol K5G | 66.110 | L27/28R | 4/48 | Western National, Exeter (DN) 853 |
| 1787 | JUO 927 | Bristol K5G | 66.111 | L27/28R | 4/48 | Western National, Exeter (DN) 854 |
| 1788 | JUO 928 | Bristol K5G | 66.126 | L27/28R | 6/48 | Western National, Exeter (DN) 855 |
| 1789 | JUO 929 | Bristol K5G | 66.127 | L27/28R | 6/48 | Western National, Exeter (DN) 856 |
| 1790 | JUO 930 | Bristol K5G | 66.160 | L27/28R | 7/48 | Western National, Exeter (DN) 857 |
| 1791 | JUO 931 | Bristol K5G | 66.161 | L27/28R | 7/48 | Western National, Exeter (DN) 858 |
| 1792 | CHJ 250 | Bristol K5G | 64.096 | L27/28R | 11/47 | Westcliff-on-Sea MS (EX) |
| 1793 | CHJ 251 | Bristol K5G | 64.097 | L27/28R | 11/47 | Westcliff-on-Sea MS (EX) |
| 1794 | CHJ 252 | Bristol K5G | 64.170 | L27/28R | 12/47 | Westcliff-on-Sea MS (EX) |
| 1795 | CHJ 253 | Bristol K5G | 64.171 | L27/28R | 12/47 | Westcliff-on-Sea MS (EX) |
| 1796 | CHJ 254 | Bristol K5G | 66.048 | L27/28R | 3/48 | Westcliff-on-Sea MS (EX) |
| 1797 | CHJ 255 | Bristol K6B | 66.087 | L27/28R | 5/48 | Westcliff-on-Sea MS (EX) |
| 1798 | CHJ 256 | Bristol K6B | 66.088 | L27/28R | 6/48 | Westcliff-on-Sea MS (EX) |
| 1799 | EMW 181 | Bristol K5G | 64.108 | L27/28R | 11/47 | Wilts & Dorset, Salisbury (WI) 272 |
| 1800 | EMW 182 | Bristol K5G | 64.109 | L27/28R | 11/47 | Wilts & Dorset, Salisbury (WI) 273 |
| 1801 | EMW 285 | Bristol K5G | 64.180 | L27/28R | 12/47 | Wilts & Dorset, Salisbury (WI) 280 |
| 1802 | EMW 286 | Bristol K5G | 64.181 | L27/28R | 12/47 | Wilts & Dorset, Salisbury (WI) 281 |
| 1803 | EMW 287 | Bristol K5G | 66.069 | L27/28R | 3/48 | Wilts & Dorset, Salisbury (WI) 282 |
| 1804 | EMW 288 | Bristol K5G | 66.070 | L27/28R | 3/48 | Wilts & Dorset, Salisbury (WI) 283 |
| 1805 | KHT 519 | Bristol K5G | 62.131 | H30/26R | 6/47 | Bristol Tramways (GL) C3403 |
| 1806 | KHT 520 | Bristol K5G | 62.132 | H30/26R | 12/47 | Bristol Tramways (GL) C3404 |
| 1807 | KHT 521 | Bristol K5G | 62.133 | H30/26R | 12/47 | Bristol Tramways (GL) C3405 |
| 1808 | KHT 522 | Bristol K5G | 62.134 | H30/26R | 7/37 | Bristol Tramways (GL) 3687 |
| 1809 | KHU 613 | Bristol K5G | 62.135 | H30/26R | 8/47 | Bristol Tramways (GL) 3688 |
| 1810 | KHU 614 | Bristol K5G | 62.140 | H30/26R | 8/47 | Bristol Tramways (GL) 3689 |
| 1811 | KHU 615 | Bristol K5G | 62.141 | H30/26R | 8/47 | Bristol Tramways (GL) 3690 |
| 1812 | KHU 616 | Bristol K5G | 62.142 | H30/26R | 8/47 | Bristol Tramways (GL) 3691 |
| 1813 | KHT 513 | Bristol K6B | 62.117 | H30/26R | 11/47 | Bristol Tramways (GL) C3406 |
| 1814 | KHT 514 | Bristol K6B | 62.118 | H30/26R | 11/47 | Bristol Tramways (GL) C3408 |
| 1815 | KHT 515 | Bristol K6B | 62.119 | H30/26R | 11/47 | Bristol Tramways (GL) C3409 |
| 1816 | KHT 512 | Bristol K6B | 62.116 | H30/26R | 8/47 | Bristol Tramways (GL) 3692 |
| 1817 | KHT 517 | Bristol K6B | 62.122 | H30/26R | 8/47 | Bristol Tramways (GL) C3407 |
| 1818 | KHT 511 | Bristol K6B | 62.115 | H30/26R | 8/47 | Bristol Tramways (GL) 3693 |
| 1819 | KHT 516 | Bristol K6B | 62.120 | H30/26R | 8/47 | Bristol Tramways (GL) 3694 |
| 1820 | KHT 518 | Bristol K6B | 62.123 | H30/26R | 8/47 | Bristol Tramways (GL) 3695 |
| 1821 | KHU 617 | Bristol K6A | 64.003 | H30/26R | 8/47 | Bristol Tramways (GL) 3700 |
| 1822 | KHU 618 | Bristol K6A | 64.004 | H30/26R | 9/47 | Bristol Tramways (GL) 3696 |
| 1823 | KHU 619 | Bristol K6A | 64.023 | H30/26R | 6/47 | Bristol Tramways (GL) 3697 |
| 1824 | KHU 620 | Bristol K6A | 64.024 | H30/26R | 9/47 | Bristol Tramways (GL) 3701 |
| 1825 | KHW 634 | Bristol K5G | 64.072 | H30/26R | 2/48 | Bristol Tramways (GL) 3698 |
| 1826 | KHY 384 | Bristol K6B | 64.073 | H30/26R | 2/48 | Bristol Tramways (GL) 3702 |
| 1827 | KHY 385 | Bristol K5G | 64.184 | H30/26R | 2/48 | Bristol Tramways (GL) 3699 |
| 1828 | KHY 386 | Bristol K5G | 64.185 | H30/26R | 2/48 | Bristol Tramways (GL) 3703 |
| 1829 | KHY 387 | Bristol K6B | 64.110 | H30/26R | 2/48 | Bristol Tramways (GL) 3704 |
| 1830 | KHY 388 | Bristol K6B | 64.111 | H30/26R | 2/48 | Bristol Tramways (GL) 3705 |

| 1831 | KHY 389 | Bristol K6B | 64.138 | H30/26R | 2/48 | Bath Electric Tramways (SO) 3838 |
|---|---|---|---|---|---|---|
| 1832 | KHY 390 | Bristol K5G | 66.049 | H30/26R | 2/48 | Bristol Tramways (GL) 3707 |
| 1833 | KHY 741 | Bristol K6B | 64.161 | H30/26R | 2/48 | Bath Electric Tramways (SO) 3839 |
| 1834 | KHY 742 | Bristol K6B | 64.162 | H30/26R | 2/48 | Bristol Tramways (GL) 1511 |
| 1835 | KHY 743 | Bristol K6B | 64.163 | H30/26R | 2/48 | Bristol Tramways (GL) 1512 |
| 1836 | KHY 744 | Bristol K6B | 64.172 | H30/26R | 2/48 | Bristol Tramways (GL) 1513 |
| 1837 | KHY 745 | Bristol K6B | 64.173 | H30/26R | 2/48 | Bristol Tramways (GL) 1514 |
| 1838 | KHY 746 | Bristol K6B | 64.174 | H30/26R | 3/48 | Bristol Tramways (GL) 3706 |
| 1839 | KHY 747 | Bristol K6B | 64.175 | H30/26R | 3/48 | Bristol Tramways (GL) 3708 |
| 1840 | KHY 748 | Bristol K6B | 64.176 | H30/26R | 3/48 | Bristol Tramways (GL) 3709 |
| 1841 | KHY 749 | Bristol K6A | 66.001 | H30/26R | 3/48 | Bristol Tramways (GL) 3710 |
| 1842 | KHY 750 | Bristol K6A | 66.002 | H30/26R | 3/48 | Bristol Tramways (GL) 3711 |
| 1843 | LAE 19 | Bristol K6A | 66.003 | H30/26R | 3/48 | Bristol Tramways (GL) 3712 |
| 1844 | LAE 20 | Bristol K6A | 66.004 | H30/26R | 3/48 | Bristol Tramways (GL) 3713 |
| 1845 | LAE 21 | Bristol K6A | 66.005 | H30/26R | 3/48 | Bristol Tramways (GL) 3714 |
| 1846 | LAE 22 | Bristol K6A | 66.008 | H30/26R | 3/48 | Bristol Tramways (GL) 3715 |
| 1847 | LAE 24 | Bristol K6A | 66.010 | H30/26R | 5/48 | Bristol Tramways (GL) 3717 |
| 1848 | LAE 27 | Bristol K6A | 66.039 | H30/26R | 5/48 | Bristol Tramways (GL) 3720 |
| 1849 | LAE 28 | Bristol K6A | 66.040 | H30/26R | 5/48 | Bristol Tramways (GL) 3721 |
| 1850 | LAE 23 | Bristol K6A | 66.009 | H30/26R | 3/48 | Bristol Tramways (GL) 3716 |
| 1851 | LAE 25 | Bristol K6A | 66.011 | H30/26R | 5/48 | Bristol Tramways (GL) 3718 |
| 1852 | LAE 26 | Bristol K6A | 66.012 | H30/26R | 5/48 | Bristol Tramways (GL) 3719 |
| 1853 | LAE 29 | Bristol K6B | 66.041 | H30/26R | 5/48 | Bristol Tramways (GL) 3722 |
| 1854 | LAE 30 | Bristol K6B | 66.042 | H30/26R | 5/48 | Bristol Tramways (GL) 3723 |
| 1855 | LAE 303 | Bristol K6B | 66.068 | H30/26R | 6/48 | Bristol Tramways (GL) 3726 |
| 1856 | LAE 301 | Bristol K6B | 66.043 | H30/26R | 6/48 | Bristol Tramways (GL) 3724 |
| 1857 | LAE 302 | Bristol K6B | 66.067 | H30/26R | 5/48 | Bristol Tramways (GL) 3725 |
| 1858 | LAE 304 | Bristol K6B | 66.071 | H30/26R | 6/48 | Bristol Tramways (GL) 3727 |
| 1859 | LAE 305 | Bristol K6B | 66.072 | H30/26R | 5/48 | Bristol Tramways (GL) 3728 |
| 1860 | LAE 306 | Bristol K6B | 66.073 | H30/26R | 5/48 | Bristol Tramways (GL) 3729 |
| 1861 | LAE 307 | Bristol K6B | 66.074 | H30/26R | 5/48 | Bristol Tramways (GL) 3730 |
| 1862 | LAE 308 | Bristol K6B | 66.075 | H30/26R | 6/48 | Bristol Tramways (GL) 3731 |
| 1863 | LAE 309 | Bristol K6B | 66.081 | H30/26R | 5/48 | Bristol Tramways (GL) 3732 |
| 1864 | LAE 310 | Bristol K6B | 66.082 | H30/26R | 5/48 | Bristol Tramways (GL) 3733 |
| 1865 | LAE 312 | Bristol K6B | 66.089 | H30/26R | 6/48 | Bristol Tramways (GL) 3735 |
| 1866 | LAE 313 | Bristol K6B | 66.090 | H30/26R | 6/48 | Bristol Tramways (GL) 3736 |
| 1867 | LAE 311 | Bristol K6B | 66.083 | H30/26R | 6/48 | Bristol Tramways (GL) 3734 |
| 1868 | LAE 314 | Bristol K6B | 66.091 | H30/26R | 5/48 | Bristol Tramways (GL) 3737 |
| 1869 | LAE 315 | Bristol K6B | 66.092 | H30/26R | 6/48 | Bristol Tramways (GL) 3738 |
| 1870 | LAE 319 | Bristol K5G | 66.103 | H30/26R | 10/48 | Bristol Tramways (GL) C3415 |
| 1871 | LAE 320 | Bristol K5G | 66.104 | H30/26R | 6/48 | Bristol Tramways (GL) 3739 |
| 1872 | LAE 702 | Bristol K5G | 66.105 | H30/26R | 6/48 | Bristol Tramways (GL) 3740 |
| 1873 | LAE 703 | Bristol K5G | 66.106 | H30/26R | 10/48 | Bristol Tramways (GL) C3418 |
| 1874 | LAE 704 | Bristol K5G | 66.107 | H30/26R | 6/48 | Bristol Tramways (GL) 3742 |
| 1875 | LAE 316 | Bristol K6B | 66.093 | H30/26R | 6/48 | Bristol Tramways (GL) 3741 |
| 1876 | LAE 317 | Bristol K6B | 66.094 | H30/26R | 7/48 | Bristol Tramways (GL) 3743 |
| 1877 | LAE 701 | Bristol K6B | 64.074 | H30/26R | 7/48 | Bristol Tramways (GL) C3410 |
| 1878 | LAE 318 | Bristol K6B | 66.096 | H30/26R | 7/48 | Bristol Tramways (GL) 3745 |
| 1879 | LAE 705 | Bristol K5G | 66.128 | H30/26R | 7/48 | Bristol Tramways (GL) 3746 |
| 1880 | LAE 706 | Bristol K5G | 66.129 | H30/26R | 7/48 | Bristol Tramways (GL) 3747 |
| 1881 | LAE 707 | Bristol K5G | 66.130 | H30/26R | 7/48 | Bristol Tramways (GL) 3748 |
| 1882 | LAE 708 | Bristol K5G | 66.131 | H30/26R | 7/48 | Bristol Tramways (GL) 3749 |
| 1883 | LAE 709 | Bristol K5G | 66.132 | H30/26R | 8/48 | Bristol Tramways (GL) 3750 |
| 1884 | LAE 712 | Bristol K5G | 66.135 | H30/26R | 7/48 | Bristol Tramways (GL) 3753 |
| 1885 | LAE 713 | Bristol K5G | 66.136 | H30/26R | 7/48 | Bristol Tramways (GL) 3754 |
| 1886 | LAE 714 | Bristol K5G | 66.137 | H30/26R | 8/48 | Bristol Tramways (GL) 3755 |
| 1887 | LAE 715 | Bristol K5G | 66.138 | H30/26R | 8/48 | Bristol Tramways (GL) 3756 |
| 1888 | LAE 716 | Bristol K5G | 66.139 | H30/26R | 8/48 | Bristol Tramways (GL) 3757 |
| 1889 | LAE 717 | Bristol K5G | 66.153 | H30/26R | 8/48 | Bristol Tramways (GL) 3761 |
| 1890 | LAE 710 | Bristol K6B | 66.133 | H30/26R | 8/48 | Bristol Tramways (GL) 3751 |
| 1891 | LAE 711 | Bristol K6B | 66.134 | H30/26R | 10/48 | Bristol Tramways (GL) 3752 |
| 1892 | LAE 718 | Bristol K5G | 66.185 | H30/26R | 10/48 | Bristol Tramways (GL) 3744 |
| 1893 | LAE 719 | Bristol K5G | 66.150 | H30/26R | 8/48 | Bristol Tramways (GL) 3758 |
| 1894 | LAE 720 | Bristol K5G | 66.151 | H30/26R | 8/48 | Bristol Tramways (GL) 3759 |

| 1895 | LHT 901 | Bristol K5G | 66.152 | H30/26R | 8/48 | Bristol Tramways (GL) 3760 |
|------|---------|-------------|--------|---------|------|----------------------------|
| 1896 | DNJ 995 | Bristol K6B | 64.087 | H30/26R | 4/48 | Brighton, Hove & District (ES) 6386 |
| 1897 | DNJ 996 | Bristol K6B | 64.098 | H30/26R | 4/48 | Brighton, Hove & District (ES) 6387 |
| 1898 | DNJ 997 | Bristol K6B | 64.099 | H30/26R | 4/48 | Brighton, Hove & District (ES) 6388 |
| 1899 | DNJ 998 | Bristol K6B | 64.182 | H30/26R | 4/48 | Brighton, Hove & District (ES) 6389 |
| 1900 | DNJ 999 | Bristol K6B | 64.183 | H30/26R | 4/48 | Brighton, Hove & District (ES) 6390 |
| 1901 | GVF 65 | Bristol K5G | 64.007 | H30/26R | 10/47 | Eastern Counties, Norwich (NK) LKH65 |
| 1902 | GVF 66 | Bristol K5G | 64.008 | H30/26R | 9/47 | Eastern Counties, Norwich (NK) LKH66 |
| 1903 | GVF 67 | Bristol K5G | 64.143 | H30/26R | 12/47 | Eastern Counties, Norwich (NK) LKH67 |
| 1904 | GVF 68 | Bristol K6B | 64.142 | H30/26R | 2/48 | Eastern Counties, Norwich (NK) LKH68 |
| 1905 | GVF 69 | Bristol K6B | 64.186 | H30/26R | 5/48 | Eastern Counties, Norwich (NK) LKH69 |
| 1906 | GVF 70 | Bristol K6B | 64.187 | H30/26R | 6/48 | Eastern Counties, Norwich (NK) LKH70 |
| 1907 | GVF 71 | Bristol K6B | 64.188 | H30/26R | 6/48 | Eastern Counties, Norwich (NK) LKH71 |
| 1908 | GVF 72 | Bristol K6B | 66.046 | H30/26R | 5/48 | Eastern Counties, Norwich (NK) LKH72 |
| 1909 | GVF 73 | Bristol K6B | 66.047 | H30/26R | 6/48 | Eastern Counties, Norwich (NK) LKH73 |
| 1910 | GVF 74 | Bristol K6B | 66.052 | H30/26R | 6/48 | Eastern Counties, Norwich (NK) LKH74 |
| 1911 | DFW 353 | Bristol K6A | 64.065 | H30/26R | 10/47 | Lincolnshire RCC, Bracebridge Heath (KN) 681 |
| 1912 | DFW 354 | Bristol K6A | 64.066 | H30/26R | 10/47 | Lincolnshire RCC, Bracebridge Heath (KN) 682 |
| 1913 | DFW 355 | Bristol K6A | 64.168 | H30/26R | 12/47 | Lincolnshire RCC, Bracebridge Heath (KN) 683 |
| 1914 | DFW 356 | Bristol K6A | 64.169 | H30/26R | 11/47 | Lincolnshire RCC, Bracebridge Heath (KN) 684 |
| 1915 * | GFM 852 | Bristol L6A | 63.194 | B35R | 9/47 | Crosville MS, Chester (CH) KB43 |
| 1916 * | GFM 851 | Bristol L6A | 63.193 | B35R | 9/47 | Crosville MS, Chester (CH) KB42 |
| 1917 * | GFM 853 | Bristol L6A | 65.028 | B35R | 10/47 | Crosville MS, Chester (CH) KB44 |
| 1918 * | GFM 854 | Bristol L6A | 63.180 | B35R | 10/47 | Crosville MS, Chester (CH) KB45 |
| 1919 * | GFM 855 | Bristol L6A | 65.064 | B35R | 10/47 | Crosville MS, Chester (CH) KB46 |
| 1920 * | GFM 856 | Bristol L6A | 65.065 | B35R | 10/47 | Crosville MS, Chester (CH) KB47 |
| 1921 * | GFM 857 | Bristol L6A | 65.074 | B35R | 10/47 | Crosville MS, Chester (CH) KB48 |
| 1922 * | GFM 858 | Bristol L6A | 65.090 | B35R | 10/47 | Crosville MS, Chester (CH) KB49 |
| 1923 * | GFM 859 | Bristol L6A | 65.091 | B35R | 10/47 | Crosville MS, Chester (CH) KB50 |
| 1924 | GFM 860 | Bristol L6A | 65.095 | B35R | 10/47 | Crosville MS, Chester (CH) KB51 |
| 1925 | GFM 861 | Bristol L6A | 65.096 | B35R | 10/47 | Crosville MS, Chester (CH) KB52 |
| 1926 | GFM 862 | Bristol L6A | 65.159 | B35R | 10/47 | Crosville MS, Chester (CH) KB53 |
| 1927 | GFM 863 | Bristol L6A | 65.160 | B35R | 11/47 | Crosville MS, Chester (CH) KB54 |
| 1928 | GFM 864 | Bristol L6A | 65.192 | B35R | 1/48 | Crosville MS, Chester (CH) KB55 |
| 1929 | GFM 865 | Bristol L6A | 65.193 | B35R | 11/47 | Crosville MS, Chester (CH) KB56 |
| 1930 | GFM 866 | Bristol L6A | 65.187 | B35R | 11/47 | Crosville MS, Chester (CH) KB57 |
| 1931 | GFM 867 | Bristol L6A | 65.188 | B35R | 1/48 | Crosville MS, Chester (CH) KB58 |
| 1932 | GFM 868 | Bristol L6A | 65.189 | B35R | 1/48 | Crosville MS, Chester (CH) KB59 |
| 1933 | GFM 869 | Bristol L6A | 65.194 | B35R | 1/48 | Crosville MS, Chester (CH) KB60 |
| 1934 | GFM 870 | Bristol L6A | 65.195 | B35R | 1/48 | Crosville MS, Chester (CH) KB61 |
| 1935 | GFM 871 | Bristol L6A | 67.059 | B35R | 2/48 | Crosville MS, Chester (CH) KB62 |
| 1936 | GFM 872 | Bristol L6A | 67.015 | B35R | 2/48 | Crosville MS, Chester (CH) KB63 |
| 1937 | GFM 873 | Bristol L6A | 67.060 | B35R | 2/48 | Crosville MS, Chester (CH) KB64 |
| 1938 | GFM 874 | Bristol L6A | 67.016 | B35R | 2/48 | Crosville MS, Chester (CH) KB65 |
| 1939 | GFM 875 | Bristol L6A | 67.038 | B35R | 2/48 | Crosville MS, Chester (CH) KB66 |
| 1940 | GFM 876 | Bristol L6A | 67.039 | B35R | 2/48 | Crosville MS, Chester (CH) KB67 |
| 1941 | GFM 877 | Bristol L6A | 67.070 | B35R | 3/48 | Crosville MS, Chester (CH) KB68 |
| 1942 | GFM 878 | Bristol L6A | 67.071 | B35R | 3/48 | Crosville MS, Chester (CH) KB69 |
| 1943 | GFM 879 | Bristol L6B | 65.181 | B35R | 3/48 | Crosville MS, Chester (CH) KB70 |
| 1944 | GFM 880 | Bristol L6B | 65.182 | B35R | 3/48 | Crosville MS, Chester (CH) KB71 |
| 1945 | GFM 881 | Bristol L6A | 67.103 | B35R | 3/48 | Crosville MS, Chester (CH) KB72 |
| 1946 | GFM 882 | Bristol L6A | 67.115 | B35R | 4/48 | Crosville MS, Chester (CH) KB73 |
| 1947 | GFM 883 | Bristol L6A | 67.131 | B35R | 4/48 | Crosville MS, Chester (CH) KB74 |
| 1948 | GFM 884 | Bristol L6A | 67.116 | B35R | 4/48 | Crosville MS, Chester (CH) KB75 |
| 1949 * | GFM 885 | Bristol L6A | 67.104 | B35R | 4/48 | Crosville MS, Chester (CH) KB76 |
| 1950 * | GFM 886 | Bristol L6A | 67.105 | B35R | 6/48 | Crosville MS, Chester (CH) KB77 |
| 1951 * | GFM 887 | Bristol L6A | 67.106 | B35R | 5/48 | Crosville MS, Chester (CH) KB78 |
| 1952 * | GFM 888 | Bristol L6A | 67.132 | B35R | 4/48 | Crosville MS, Chester (CH) KB79 |
| 1953 * | GFM 889 | Bristol L6A | 67.152 | B35R | 5/48 | Crosville MS, Chester (CH) KB80 |
| 1954 * | GFM 890 | Bristol L6A | 67.151 | B35R | 5/48 | Crosville MS, Chester (CH) KB81 |
| 1955 | GPW 657 | Bristol L5G | 65.099 | B35R | 11/47 | Eastern Counties, Norwich (NK) LL657 |
| 1956 | GPW 658 | Bristol L5G | 65.100 | B35R | 1/48 | Eastern Counties, Norwich (NK) LL658 |
| 1957 | GPW 659 | Bristol L5G | 65.134 | B35R | 12/47 | Eastern Counties, Norwich (NK) LL659 |
| 1958 | GPW 660 | Bristol L5G | 65.135 | B35R | 12/47 | Eastern Counties, Norwich (NK) LL660 |

| | | | | | | | |
|---|---|---|---|---|---|---|---|
| 1959 | GPW 661 | Bristol L5G | 65.136 | B35R | 1/48 | Eastern Counties, Norwich (NK) | LL661 |
| 1960 | GPW 662 | Bristol L5G | 65.161 | B35R | 1/48 | Eastern Counties, Norwich (NK) | LL662 |
| 1961 | GPW 663 | Bristol L5G | 65.162 | B35R | 1/48 | Eastern Counties, Norwich (NK) | LL663 |
| 1962 | GPW 664 | Bristol L5G | 65.167 | B35R | 2/48 | Eastern Counties, Norwich (NK) | LL664 |
| 1963 | GPW 665 | Bristol L5G | 65.168 | B35R | 2/48 | Eastern Counties, Norwich (NK) | LL665 |
| 1964 | GPW 666 | Bristol L5G | 65.169 | B35R | 2/48 | Eastern Counties, Norwich (NK) | LL666 |
| 1965 | GPW 667 | Bristol L5G | 65.175 | B35R | 2/48 | Eastern Counties, Norwich (NK) | LL667 |
| 1966 | GPW 668 | Bristol L5G | 65.185 | B35R | 2/48 | Eastern Counties, Norwich (NK) | LL668 |
| 1967 | GPW 669 | Bristol L5G | 65.186 | B35R | 2/48 | Eastern Counties, Norwich (NK) | LL669 |
| 1968 | GPW 670 | Bristol L5G | 67.001 | B35R | 2/48 | Eastern Counties, Norwich (NK) | LL670 |
| 1969 | GPW 671 | Bristol L5G | 67.002 | B35R | 3/48 | Eastern Counties, Norwich (NK) | LL671 |
| 1970 | GPW 672 | Bristol L5G | 67.003 | B35R | 3/48 | Eastern Counties, Norwich (NK) | LL672 |
| 1971 | GPW 673 | Bristol L5G | 67.009 | B35R | 3/48 | Eastern Counties, Norwich (NK) | LL673 |
| 1972 | GPW 674 | Bristol L5G | 67.010 | B35R | 3/48 | Eastern Counties, Norwich (NK) | LL674 |
| 1973 | GPW 675 | Bristol L5G | 67.026 | B35R | 3/48 | Eastern Counties, Norwich (NK) | LL675 |
| 1974 | GPW 676 | Bristol L5G | 67.027 | B35R | 3/48 | Eastern Counties, Norwich (NK) | LL676 |
| 1975 | GPW 677 | Bristol L5G | 67.028 | B35R | 3/48 | Eastern Counties, Norwich (NK) | LL677 |
| 1976 | GPW 678 | Bristol L5G | 67.008 | B35R | 3/48 | Eastern Counties, Norwich (NK) | LL678 |
| 1977 | GPW 679 | Bristol L5G | 67.050 | B35R | 3/48 | Eastern Counties, Norwich (NK) | LL679 |
| 1978 | GPW 680 | Bristol L5G | 67.051 | B35R | 3/48 | Eastern Counties, Norwich (NK) | LL680 |
| 1979 | GPW 681 | Bristol L5G | 67.052 | B35R | 3/48 | Eastern Counties, Norwich (NK) | LL681 |
| 1980 | GPW 682 | Bristol L5G | 67.100 | B35R | 3/48 | Eastern Counties, Norwich (NK) | LL682 |
| 1981 * | GPW 683 | Bristol L5G | 67.119 | B35R | 4/48 | Eastern Counties, Norwich (NK) | LL683 |
| 1982 * | GPW 684 | Bristol L5G | 67.117 | B35R | 4/48 | Eastern Counties, Norwich (NK) | LL684 |
| 1983 * | GPW 685 | Bristol L5G | 67.118 | B35R | 6/48 | Eastern Counties, Norwich (NK) | LL685 |
| 1984 * | GPW 686 | Bristol L5G | 67.107 | B35R | 6/48 | Eastern Counties, Norwich (NK) | LL686 |
| 1985 * | GPW 687 | Bristol L5G | 67.108 | B35R | 6/48 | Eastern Counties, Norwich (NK) | LL687 |
| 1986 * | GPW 688 | Bristol L5G | 67.111 | B35R | 6/48 | Eastern Counties, Norwich (NK) | LL688 |
| 1987 * | GPW 689 | Bristol L5G | 67.137 | B35R | 7/48 | Eastern Counties, Norwich (NK) | LL689 |
| 1988 * | GPW 690 | Bristol L5G | 67.138 | B35R | 7/48 | Eastern Counties, Norwich (NK) | LL690 |
| 1989 * | GPW 691 | Bristol L5G | 67.139 | B35R | 7/48 | Eastern Counties, Norwich (NK) | LL691 |
| 1990 * | GPW 692 | Bristol L5G | 67.140 | B35R | 8/48 | Eastern Counties, Norwich (NK) | LL692 |
| 1991 * | GPW 693 | Bristol L5G | 67.141 | B35R | 8/48 | Eastern Counties, Norwich (NK) | LL693 |
| 1992 * | GPW 694 | Bristol L5G | 67.155 | B35R | 7/48 | Eastern Counties, Norwich (NK) | LL694 |
| 1993 * | GPW 695 | Bristol L5G | 67.154 | B35R | 8/48 | Eastern Counties, Norwich (NK) | LL695 |
| 1994 * | GPW 696 | Bristol L5G | 67.153 | B35R | 9/48 | Eastern Counties, Norwich (NK) | LL696 |
| 1995 | GLJ 994 | Bristol L5G | 65.103 | B35R | 10/47 | Hants & Dorset, Bournemouth (HA) | TS816 |
| 1996 | GLJ 995 | Bristol L5G | 65.183 | B35R | 1/48 | Hants & Dorset, Bournemouth (HA) | TS817 |
| 1997 | GLJ 996 | Bristol L5G | 65.184 | B35R | 1/48 | Hants & Dorset, Bournemouth (HA) | TS818 |
| 1998 | GLJ 997 | Bristol L5G | 67.011 | B35R | 2/48 | Hants & Dorset, Bournemouth (HA) | TS819 |
| 1999 | GLJ 998 | Bristol L5G | 67.012 | B35R | 2/48 | Hants & Dorset, Bournemouth (HA) | TS820 |
| 2000 | GLJ 999 | Bristol L5G | 67.029 | B35R | 2/48 | Hants & Dorset, Bournemouth (HA) | TS821 |
| 2001 | DMO 676 | Bristol L6A | 65.198 | DP31R | 1/48 | Thames Valley, Reading (BE) | 472 |
| 2002 | DMO 677 | Bristol L6A | 65.199 | DP31R | 1/48 | Thames Valley, Reading (BE) | 473 |
| 2003 | DMO 678 | Bristol L6A | 67.020 | DP31R | 1/48 | Thames Valley, Reading (BE) | 474 |
| 2004 | DMO 679 | Bristol L6A | 67.021 | DP31R | 1/48 | Thames Valley, Reading (BE) | 475 |
| 2005 | DMO 680 | Bristol L6A | 67.063 | DP31R | 1/48 | Thames Valley, Reading (BE) | 476 |
| 2006 | DMO 681 | Bristol L6A | 67.064 | DP31R | 1/48 | Thames Valley, Reading (BE) | 477 |
| 2007 | DMO 682 | Bristol L6A | 67.079 | DP31R | 3/48 | Thames Valley, Reading (BE) | 478 |
| 2008 | DMO 683 | Bristol L6A | 67.080 | DP31R | 3/48 | Thames Valley, Reading (BE) | 479 |
| 2009 | DMO 684 | Bristol L6A | 67.081 | DP31R | 3/48 | Thames Valley, Reading (BE) | 480 |
| 2010 | DMO 685 | Bristol L6A | 67.093 | DP31R | 3/48 | Thames Valley, Reading (BE) | 481 |
| 2011 | DMO 686 | Bristol L6A | 67.094 | DP31R | 3/48 | Thames Valley, Reading (BE) | 482 |
| 2012 | DMO 687 | Bristol L6A | 67.109 | DP31R | 3/48 | Thames Valley, Reading (BE) | 483 |
| 2013 | DMO 688 | Bristol L6A | 67.110 | DP31R | 3/48 | Thames Valley, Reading (BE) | 484 |
| 2014 | DMO 689 | Bristol L6A | 67.163 | DP31R | 4/48 | Thames Valley, Reading (BE) | 485 |
| 2015 | DMO 690 | Bristol L6A | 67.164 | DP31R | 5/48 | Thames Valley, Reading (BE) | 486 |
| 2016 * | JHN 324 | Bristol L5G | 63.199 | B35R | 9/47 | United AS, Darlington (DM) | BLO224 |
| 2017 * | JHN 325 | Bristol L5G | 63.200 | B35R | 9/47 | United AS, Darlington (DM) | BLO225 |
| 2018 * | JHN 326 | Bristol L5G | 63.182 | B35R | 9/47 | United AS, Darlington (DM) | BLO226 |
| 2019 * | JHN 327 | Bristol L5G | 63.183 | B35R | 9/47 | United AS, Darlington (DM) | BLO227 |
| 2020 * | JHN 328 | Bristol L5G | 65.007 | B35R | 9/47 | United AS, Darlington (DM) | BLO228 |
| 2021 * | JHN 329 | Bristol L5G | 65.006 | B35R | 9/47 | United AS, Darlington (DM) | BLO229 |
| 2022 * | JHN 330 | Bristol L5G | 65.034 | B35R | 9/47 | United AS, Darlington (DM) | BLO230 |

| | | | | | | | |
|---|---|---|---|---|---|---|---|
| 2023 * | JHN 331 | Bristol L5G | 65.035 | B35R | 10/47 | United AS, Darlington (DM) | BLO231 |
| 2024 * | JHN 332 | Bristol L5G | 65.036 | B35R | 10/47 | United AS, Darlington (DM) | BLO232 |
| 2025 * | JHN 333 | Bristol L5G | 65.050 | B35R | 10/47 | United AS, Darlington (DM) | BLO233 |
| 2026 * | JHN 334 | Bristol L5G | 65.051 | B35R | 10/47 | United AS, Darlington (DM) | BLO234 |
| 2027 * | JHN 335 | Bristol L5G | 65.072 | B35R | 10/47 | United AS, Darlington (DM) | BLO235 |
| 2028 * | JHN 336 | Bristol L5G | 65.075 | B35R | 10/47 | United AS, Darlington (DM) | BLO236 |
| 2029 * | JHN 337 | Bristol L5G | 65.076 | B35R | 11/47 | United AS, Darlington (DM) | BLO237 |
| 2030 * | JHN 338 | Bristol L5G | 65.077 | B35R | 11/47 | United AS, Darlington (DM) | BLO238 |
| 2031 * | JHN 339 | Bristol L5G | 65.086 | B35R | 11/47 | United AS, Darlington (DM) | BLO239 |
| 2032 * | JHN 340 | Bristol L5G | 65.094 | B35R | 11/47 | United AS, Darlington (DM) | BLO240 |
| 2033 * | JHN 341 | Bristol L5G | 65.097 | B35R | 11/47 | United AS, Darlington (DM) | BLO241 |
| 2034 * | JHN 342 | Bristol L5G | 65.098 | B35R | 11/47 | United AS, Darlington (DM) | BLO242 |
| 2035 * | JHN 343 | Bristol L5G | 65.114 | B35R | 12/47 | United AS, Darlington (DM) | BLO243 |
| 2036 * | JHN 344 | Bristol L5G | 65.115 | B35R | 12/47 | United AS, Darlington (DM) | BLO244 |
| 2037 * | JHN 345 | Bristol L5G | 65.116 | B35R | 12/47 | United AS, Darlington (DM) | BLO245 |
| 2038 * | JHN 346 | Bristol L5G | 65.122 | B35R | 12/47 | United AS, Darlington (DM) | BLO246 |
| 2039 * | JHN 347 | Bristol L5G | 65.123 | B35R | 12/47 | United AS, Darlington (DM) | BLO247 |
| 2040 * | JHN 348 | Bristol L5G | 65.130 | B35R | 12/47 | United AS, Darlington (DM) | BLO248 |
| 2041 * | JHN 349 | Bristol L5G | 65.131 | B35R | 12/47 | United AS, Darlington (DM) | BLO249 |
| 2042 * | JHN 350 | Bristol L5G | 65.132 | B35R | 12/47 | United AS, Darlington (DM) | BLO250 |
| 2043 * | JHN 351 | Bristol L5G | 65.133 | B35R | 12/47 | United AS, Darlington (DM) | BLO251 |
| 2044 * | JHN 352 | Bristol L5G | 65.140 | B35R | 12/47 | United AS, Darlington (DM) | BLO252 |
| 2045 * | JHN 353 | Bristol L5G | 65.148 | B35R | 12/47 | United AS, Darlington (DM) | BLO253 |
| 2046 * | JHN 354 | Bristol L5G | 65.149 | B35R | 12/47 | United AS, Darlington (DM) | BLO254 |
| 2047 * | JHN 356 | Bristol L5G | 65.151 | B35R | 12/47 | United AS, Darlington (DM) | BLO256 |
| 2048 * | JHN 357 | Bristol L5G | 65.152 | B35R | 12/47 | United AS, Darlington (DM) | BLO257 |
| 2049 * | JHN 359 | Bristol L5G | 65.154 | B35R | 12/47 | United AS, Darlington (DM) | BLO259 |
| 2050 * | JHN 363 | Bristol L5G | 65.158 | B35R | 12/47 | United AS, Darlington (DM) | BLO263 |
| 2051 * | JHN 366 | Bristol L5G | 65.165 | B35R | 3/48 | United AS, Darlington (DM) | BLO266 |
| 2052 * | JHN 355 | Bristol L5G | 65.150 | B35R | 3/48 | United AS, Darlington (DM) | BLO255 |
| 2053 * | JHN 358 | Bristol L5G | 65.153 | B35R | 3/48 | United AS, Darlington (DM) | BLO258 |
| 2054 * | JHN 360 | Bristol L5G | 65.155 | B35R | 3/48 | United AS, Darlington (DM) | BLO260 |
| 2055 * | JHN 361 | Bristol L5G | 65.156 | B35R | 3/48 | United AS, Darlington (DM) | BLO261 |
| 2056 * | JHN 362 | Bristol L5G | 65.157 | B35R | 3/48 | United AS, Darlington (DM) | BLO262 |
| 2057 * | JHN 364 | Bristol L5G | 65.163 | B35R | 3/48 | United AS, Darlington (DM) | BLO264 |
| 2058 * | JHN 365 | Bristol L5G | 65.164 | B35R | 3/48 | United AS, Darlington (DM) | BLO265 |
| 2059 * | JHN 367 | Bristol L5G | 65.166 | B35R | 3/48 | United AS, Darlington (DM) | BLO267 |
| 2060 * | JHN 368 | Bristol L5G | 65.170 | B35R | 3/48 | United AS, Darlington (DM) | BLO268 |
| 2061 * | JHN 369 | Bristol L5G | 65.171 | B35R | 3/48 | United AS, Darlington (DM) | BLO269 |
| 2062 * | JHN 370 | Bristol L5G | 65.172 | B35R | 3/48 | United AS, Darlington (DM) | BLO270 |
| 2063 * | JHN 371 | Bristol L5G | 65.177 | B35R | 3/48 | United AS, Darlington (DM) | BLO271 |
| 2064 * | JHN 372 | Bristol L5G | 65.178 | B35R | 3/48 | United AS, Darlington (DM) | BLO272 |
| 2065 * | JHN 373 | Bristol L5G | 67.004 | B35R | 3/48 | United AS, Darlington (DM) | BLO273 |
| 2066 * | JHN 374 | Bristol L5G | 67.005 | B35R | 3/48 | United AS, Darlington (DM) | BLO274 |
| 2067 * | JHN 375 | Bristol L5G | 67.006 | B35R | 5/48 | United AS, Darlington (DM) | BLO275 |
| 2068 * | JHN 376 | Bristol L5G | 67.018 | B35R | 5/48 | United AS, Darlington (DM) | BLO276 |
| 2069 * | JHN 377 | Bristol L5G | 67.019 | B35R | 5/48 | United AS, Darlington (DM) | BLO277 |
| 2070 * | JHN 378 | Bristol L5G | 67.007 | B35R | 5/48 | United AS, Darlington (DM) | BLO278 |
| 2071 * | JHN 379 | Bristol L5G | 67.022 | B35R | 5/48 | United AS, Darlington (DM) | BLO279 |
| 2072 * | JHN 380 | Bristol L5G | 67.023 | B35R | 5/48 | United AS, Darlington (DM) | BLO280 |
| 2073 * | JHN 381 | Bristol L5G | 67.024 | B35R | 5/48 | United AS, Darlington (DM) | BLO281 |
| 2074 * | JHN 382 | Bristol L5G | 67.025 | B35R | 5/48 | United AS, Darlington (DM) | BLO282 |
| 2075 * | JHN 383 | Bristol L5G | 67.030 | B35R | 5/48 | United AS, Darlington (DM) | BLO283 |
| 2076 * | JHN 384 | Bristol L5G | 67.033 | B35R | 5/48 | United AS, Darlington (DM) | BLO284 |
| 2077 * | JHN 385 | Bristol L5G | 67.031 | B35R | 5/48 | United AS, Darlington (DM) | BLO285 |
| 2078 * | JHN 386 | Bristol L5G | 67.032 | B35R | 5/48 | United AS, Darlington (DM) | BLO286 |
| 2079 * | JHN 387 | Bristol L5G | 67.056 | B35R | 5/48 | United AS, Darlington (DM) | BLO287 |
| 2080 * | JHN 388 | Bristol L5G | 67.057 | B35R | 6/48 | United AS, Darlington (DM) | BLO288 |
| 2081 * | JHN 389 | Bristol L5G | 67.058 | B35R | 6/48 | United AS, Darlington (DM) | BLO289 |
| 2082 * | JHN 390 | Bristol L5G | 67.061 | B35R | 6/48 | United AS, Darlington (DM) | BLO290 |
| 2083 * | JHN 391 | Bristol L5G | 67.062 | B35R | 6/48 | United AS, Darlington (DM) | BLO291 |
| 2084 * | JHN 392 | Bristol L5G | 67.065 | B35R | 6/48 | United AS, Darlington (DM) | BLO292 |
| 2085 * | JHN 393 | Bristol L5G | 67.066 | B35R | 6/48 | United AS, Darlington (DM) | BLO293 |
| 2086 * | JHN 394 | Bristol L5G | 67.072 | B35R | 6/48 | United AS, Darlington (DM) | BLO294 |

| | | | | | | | |
|---|---|---|---|---|---|---|---|
| 2087 * | JHN 395 | Bristol L5G | 67.073 | B35R | 6/48 | United AS, Darlington (DM) | BLO295 |
| 2088 * | JHN 396 | Bristol L5G | 67.089 | B35R | 6/48 | United AS, Darlington (DM) | BLO296 |
| 2089 * | JHN 397 | Bristol L5G | 67.090 | B35R | 6/48 | United AS, Darlington (DM) | BLO297 |
| 2090 * | JHN 398 | Bristol L6B | 65.190 | DP31R | 6/48 | United AS, Darlington (DM) | BLO298 |
| 2091 * | JHN 399 | Bristol L6B | 65.191 | DP31R | 6/48 | United AS, Darlington (DM) | BLO299 |
| 2092 * | JHN 400 | Bristol L5G | 67.088 | B35R | 6/48 | United AS, Darlington (DM) | BLO300 |
| 2093 * | JHN 401 | Bristol L5G | 67.102 | B35R | 6/48 | United AS, Darlington (DM) | BLO301 |
| 2094 * | JHN 402 | Bristol L5G | 65.124 | B35R | 6/48 | United AS, Darlington (DM) | BLO302 |
| 2095 * | JHN 403 | Bristol L5G | 67.112 | B35R | 6/48 | United AS, Darlington (DM) | BLO303 |
| 2096 * | JHN 404 | Bristol L5G | 67.113 | B35R | 7/48 | United AS, Darlington (DM) | BLO304 |
| 2097 * | JHN 405 | Bristol L5G | 67.114 | B35R | 7/48 | United AS, Darlington (DM) | BLO305 |
| 2098 * | JHN 406 | Bristol L5G | 67.133 | DP31R | 6/48 | United AS, Darlington (DM) | BLO306 |
| 2099 * | JHN 407 | Bristol L5G | 67.134 | DP31R | 7/48 | United AS, Darlington (DM) | BLO307 |
| 2100 * | JHN 408 | Bristol L5G | 67.135 | DP31R | 7/48 | United AS, Darlington (DM) | BLO308 |
| 2101 * | JHN 409 | Bristol L5G | 67.136 | DP31R | 7/48 | United AS, Darlington (DM) | BLO309 |
| 2102 * | JHN 410 | Bristol L6B | 67.042 | DP31R | 7/48 | United AS, Darlington (DM) | BLO310 |
| 2103 * | JHN 411 | Bristol L6B | 67.043 | DP31R | 8/48 | United AS, Darlington (DM) | BLO311 |
| 2104 * | JHN 412 | Bristol L6B | 67.044 | DP31R | 8/48 | United AS, Darlington (DM) | BLO312 |
| 2105 * | JHN 413 | Bristol L5G | 67.145 | DP31R | 8/48 | United AS, Darlington (DM) | BLO313 |
| 2106 * | JHN 414 | Bristol L5G | 67.146 | DP31R | 7/48 | United AS, Darlington (DM) | BLO314 |
| 2107 * | JHN 415 | Bristol L5G | 67.147 | DP31R | 8/48 | United AS, Darlington (DM) | BLO315 |
| 2108 * | JHN 416 | Bristol L6B | 67.045 | DP31R | 8/48 | United AS, Darlington (DM) | BLO316 |
| 2109 * | JHN 417 | Bristol L5G | 67.158 | DP31R | 8/48 | United AS, Darlington (DM) | BLO317 |
| 2110 * | JHN 418 | Bristol L6B | 67.122 | DP31R | 8/48 | United AS, Darlington (DM) | BLO318 |
| 2111 * | JHN 419 | Bristol L6B | 67.123 | DP31R | 8/48 | United AS, Darlington (DM) | BLO319 |
| 2112 * | JHN 420 | Bristol L6B | 67.013 | DP31R | 8/48 | United AS, Darlington (DM) | BLO320 |
| 2113 * | JHN 421 | Bristol L6B | 67.014 | DP31R | 9/48 | United AS, Darlington (DM) | BLO321 |
| 2114 * | JHN 422 | Bristol L6B | 67.156 | DP31R | 8/48 | United AS, Darlington (DM) | BLO322 |
| 2115 * | JHN 423 | Bristol L5G | 67.157 | DP31R | 6/49 | United AS, Darlington (DM) | BLO323 |
| 2116 | FWX 811 | Bristol L5G | 65.040 | B35R | 9/47 | York-West Yorkshire, Harrogate (WR) | Y236 |
| 2117 | FWX 812 | Bristol L5G | 65.041 | B35R | 10/47 | York-West Yorkshire, Harrogate (WR) | Y237 |
| 2118 | FWX 813 | Bristol L5G | 65.042 | B35R | 10/47 | York-West Yorkshire, Harrogate (WR) | Y238 |
| 2119 | FWX 814 | Bristol L5G | 65.143 | B35R | 1/48 | York-West Yorkshire, Harrogate (WR) | Y239 |
| 2120 | FWX 815 | Bristol L5G | 65.144 | B35R | 1/48 | York-West Yorkshire, Harrogate (WR) | Y240 |
| 2121 | FWX 816 | Bristol L5G | 65.179 | B35R | 2/48 | York-West Yorkshire, Harrogate (WR) | Y241 |
| 2122 | FWX 817 | Bristol L5G | 65.180 | B35R | 1/48 | York-West Yorkshire, Harrogate (WR) | Y242 |
| 2123 | FWX 818 | Bristol L5G | 65.197 | B35R | 2/48 | York-West Yorkshire, Harrogate (WR) | Y243 |
| 2124 | FWX 819 | Bristol L5G | 65.200 | B35R | 3/48 | York-West Yorkshire, Harrogate (WR) | Y244 |
| 2125 | FWX 820 | Bristol L5G | 67.067 | B35R | 3/48 | York-West Yorkshire, Harrogate (WR) | Y245 |
| 2126 | FWX 801 | Bristol L6B | 65.196 | DP31R | 6/48 | West Yorkshire RCC, Harrogate (WR) | 226 |
| 2127 | FWX 802 | Bristol L6B | 67.068 | DP31R | 6/48 | West Yorkshire RCC, Harrogate (WR) | 227 |
| 2128 | FWX 803 | Bristol L6B | 67.091 | DP31R | 6/48 | West Yorkshire RCC, Harrogate (WR) | 228 |
| 2129 | FWX 804 | Bristol L6B | 67.069 | DP31R | 6/48 | West Yorkshire RCC, Harrogate (WR) | 229 |
| 2130 | FWX 805 | Bristol L6B | 67.092 | DP31R | 6/48 | West Yorkshire RCC, Harrogate (WR) | 230 |
| 2131 | FWX 806 | Bristol L6B | 67.095 | DP31R | 7/48 | West Yorkshire RCC, Harrogate (WR) | 231 |
| 2132 | FWX 807 | Bristol L6B | 67.148 | DP31R | 7/48 | West Yorkshire RCC, Harrogate (WR) | 232 |
| 2133 | FWX 808 | Bristol L6B | 67.149 | DP31R | 7/48 | West Yorkshire RCC, Harrogate (WR) | 233 |
| 2134 | FWX 809 | Bristol L6B | 67.159 | DP31R | 7/48 | West Yorkshire RCC, Harrogate (WR) | 234 |
| 2135 | FWX 810 | Bristol L6B | 67.150 | DP31R | 7/48 | West Yorkshire RCC, Harrogate (WR) | 235 |
| 2136 | CDB 161 | Bristol L5G | 63.185 | B35R | 8/47 | North Western RCC, Stockport (CH) | 161 |
| 2137 | CDB 162 | Bristol L5G | 63.186 | B35R | 8/47 | North Western RCC, Stockport (CH) | 162 |
| 2138 | CDB 163 | Bristol L5G | 65.029 | B35R | 8/47 | North Western RCC, Stockport (CH) | 163 |
| 2139 | CDB 164 | Bristol L5G | 65.030 | B35R | 8/47 | North Western RCC, Stockport (CH) | 164 |
| 2140 | CDB 165 | Bristol L5G | 65.031 | B35R | 8/47 | North Western RCC, Stockport (CH) | 165 |
| 2141 | CDB 166 | Bristol L5G | 65.032 | B35R | 8/47 | North Western RCC, Stockport (CH) | 166 |
| 2142 | CDB 167 | Bristol L5G | 65.033 | B35R | 8/47 | North Western RCC, Stockport (CH) | 167 |
| 2143 | CDB 168 | Bristol L5G | 65.037 | B35R | 9/47 | North Western RCC, Stockport (CH) | 168 |
| 2144 | CDB 169 | Bristol L5G | 65.052 | B35R | 9/47 | North Western RCC, Stockport (CH) | 169 |
| 2145 | CDB 170 | Bristol L5G | 65.053 | B35R | 9/47 | North Western RCC, Stockport (CH) | 170 |
| 2146 | CDB 171 | Bristol L5G | 65.054 | B35R | 9/47 | North Western RCC, Stockport (CH) | 171 |
| 2147 | CDB 172 | Bristol L5G | 65.055 | B35R | 9/47 | North Western RCC, Stockport (CH) | 172 |
| 2148 | CDB 173 | Bristol L5G | 65.062 | B35R | 9/47 | North Western RCC, Stockport (CH) | 173 |
| 2149 | CDB 174 | Bristol L5G | 65.063 | B35R | 9/47 | North Western RCC, Stockport (CH) | 174 |
| 2150 | CDB 175 | Bristol L5G | 65.066 | B35R | 9/47 | North Western RCC, Stockport (CH) | 175 |

| | | | | | | |
|---|---|---|---|---|---|---|
| 2151 | CDB 176 | Bristol L5G | 65.083 | B35R | 9/47 | North Western RCC, Stockport (CH) 176 |
| 2152 | CDB 177 | Bristol L5G | 65.084 | B35R | 10/47 | North Western RCC, Stockport (CH) 177 |
| 2153 | CDB 178 | Bristol L5G | 65.085 | B35R | 10/47 | North Western RCC, Stockport (CH) 178 |
| 2154 | CDB 179 | Bristol L5G | 65.104 | B35R | 10/47 | North Western RCC, Stockport (CH) 179 |
| 2155 | CDB 180 | Bristol L5G | 65.105 | B35R | 3/48 | North Western RCC, Stockport (CH) 180 |
| 2156 | CDB 181 | Bristol L5G | 65.106 | B35R | 10/47 | North Western RCC, Stockport (CH) 181 |
| 2157 | CDB 182 | Bristol L5G | 65.117 | B35R | 3/48 | North Western RCC, Stockport (CH) 182 |
| 2158 | CDB 183 | Bristol L5G | 65.118 | B35R | 3/48 | North Western RCC, Stockport (CH) 183 |
| 2159 | CDB 184 | Bristol L5G | 65.119 | B35R | 3/48 | North Western RCC, Stockport (CH) 184 |
| 2160 | CDB 185 | Bristol L5G | 65.125 | B35R | 3/48 | North Western RCC, Stockport (CH) 185 |
| 2161 | CDB 186 | Bristol L5G | 65.126 | B35R | 3/48 | North Western RCC, Stockport (CH) 186 |
| 2162 | CDB 187 | Bristol L5G | 65.127 | B35R | 3/48 | North Western RCC, Stockport (CH) 187 |
| 2163 | CDB 188 | Bristol L5G | 65.128 | B35R | 1/48 | North Western RCC, Stockport (CH) 188 |
| 2164 | CDB 189 | Bristol L5G | 65.129 | B35R | 1/48 | North Western RCC, Stockport (CH) 189 |
| 2165 | CDB 190 | Bristol L5G | 65.137 | B35R | 3/48 | North Western RCC, Stockport (CH) 190 |
| 2166 | CDB 191 | Bristol L5G | 65.138 | B35R | 3/48 | North Western RCC, Stockport (CH) 191 |
| 2167 | CDB 192 | Bristol L5G | 65.139 | B35R | 3/48 | North Western RCC, Stockport (CH) 192 |
| 2168 | KHW 640 | Bristol L6B | 65.003 | DP31R | 3/48 | Bristol Tramways (GL) 2191 |
| 2169 | KHW 641 | Bristol L6B | 65.004 | DP31R | 3/48 | Bristol Tramways (GL) 2192 |
| 2170 | KHW 642 | Bristol L6B | 65.005 | DP31R | 3/48 | Bristol Tramways (GL) 2377 |
| 2171 | KHW 643 | Bristol L6B | 65.010 | DP31R | 3/48 | Bristol Tramways (GL) 2378 |
| 2172 | KHW 644 | Bristol L6B | 65.011 | DP31R | 3/48 | Bristol Tramways (GL) 2379 |
| 2173 | KHY 381 | Bristol L6B | 65.012 | DP31R | 3/48 | Bristol Tramways (GL) 2380 |
| 2174 | KHY 382 | Bristol L6B | 65.013 | DP31R | 3/48 | Bristol Tramways (GL) 2381 |
| 2175 | KHY 383 | Bristol L6B | 65.014 | DP31R | 3/48 | Bristol Tramways (GL) 2382 |
| 2176 * | LHT 902 | Bristol L6B | 67.096 | DP31R | 7/48 | Bristol Tramways (GL) 2384 |
| 2177 * | LHT 903 | Bristol L6B | 67.097 | DP31R | 7/48 | Bristol Tramways (GL) 2385 |
| 2178 * | LHT 904 | Bristol L6B | 67.098 | DP31R | 7/48 | Bristol Tramways (GL) 2386 |
| 2179 * | LHT 905 | Bristol L6B | 67.099 | DP31R | 7/48 | Bristol Tramways (GL) 2383 |
| 2180 * | LHT 906 | Bristol L6B | 67.085 | B35R | 7/48 | Bath Tramways Motor Co (SO) 2267 |
| 2181 * | LHT 907 | Bristol L6B | 67.124 | B35R | 7/48 | Bath Tramways Motor Co (SO) 2268 |
| 2182 * | LHT 908 | Bristol L6B | 67.125 | B35R | 8/48 | Bath Tramways Motor Co (SO) 2269 |
| 2183 * | LHT 909 | Bristol L6B | 67.126 | B35R | 8/48 | Bath Tramways Motor Co (SO) 2270 |
| 2184 * | LHT 910 | Bristol L6B | 67.127 | B35R | 9/48 | Bristol Tramways (GL) 2387 |
| 2185 * | LHT 911 | Bristol L6B | 67.128 | B35R | 9/48 | Bristol Tramways (GL) 2388 |
| 2186 * | LHT 912 | Bristol L6B | 67.129 | B35R | 10/48 | Bristol Tramways (GL) 2389 |
| 2187 * | LHT 913 | Bristol L6B | 67.130 | B35R | 9/48 | Bristol Tramways (GL) 2390 |
| 2188 * | LHT 914 | Bristol L6B | 67.160 | B35R | 9/48 | Bristol Tramways (GL) 2391 |
| 2189 * | LHT 915 | Bristol L6B | 67.161 | B35R | 10/48 | Bath Tramways Motor Co (SO) 2271 |
| 2190 | MPU 26 | Bristol L5G | 65.019 | DP31R | 10/47 | Eastern National, Chelmsford (EX) 3965 |
| 2191 | MPU 27 | Bristol L5G | 65.082 | DP31R | 10/47 | Eastern National, Chelmsford (EX) 3966 |
| 2192 | MPU 28 | Bristol L5G | 65.092 | DP31R | 10/47 | Eastern National, Chelmsford (EX) 3967 |
| 2193 | MPU 29 | Bristol L5G | 65.101 | DP31R | 10/47 | Eastern National, Chelmsford (EX) 3968 |
| 2194 | MPU 30 | Bristol L5G | 65.102 | DP31R | 11/47 | Eastern National, Chelmsford (EX) 3969 |
| 2195 | MPU 31 | Bristol L5G | 65.145 | B35R | 3/48 | Eastern National, Chelmsford (EX) 3970 |
| 2196 | MPU 32 | Bristol L5G | 65.146 | B35R | 1/48 | Eastern National, Chelmsford (EX) 3971 |
| 2197 | MPU 33 | Bristol L5G | 65.147 | DP31R | 3/48 | Eastern National, Chelmsford (EX) 3972 |
| 2198 | MPU 34 | Bristol L5G | 65.176 | DP31R | 3/48 | Eastern National, Chelmsford (EX) 3973 |
| 2199 | MPU 35 | Bristol L5G | 67.101 | DP31R | 5/48 | Eastern National, Chelmsford (EX) 3974 |
| 2200 | DFW 357 | Bristol L6B | 63.164 | DP31R | 9/47 | Lincolnshire RCC, Bracebridge Heath (KN) 685 |
| 2201 | DFW 358 | Bristol L6B | 65.049 | DP31R | 11/47 | Lincolnshire RCC, Bracebridge Heath (KN) 686 |
| 2202 | DFW 359 | Bristol L6B | 65.024 | DP31R | 11/47 | Lincolnshire RCC, Bracebridge Heath (KN) 687 |
| 2203 | DFW 360 | Bristol L6B | 65.048 | DP31R | 2/48 | Lincolnshire RCC, Bracebridge Heath (KN) 688 |
| 2204 * | DOD 505 | Bristol K5G | 55.006 | L27/26R | -/47 | Western National, Exeter (DN) 316 |
| 2205 * | GTG 863 | Bristol K6A | 64.051 | H30/26R | 12/47 | Aberdare UDC (GG) 42 |
| 2206 * | GTG 864 | Bristol K6A | 64.052 | H30/26R | 12/47 | Aberdare UDC (GG) 43 |
| 2207 * | GTG 865 | Bristol K6A | 64.053 | H30/26R | 11/47 | Aberdare UDC (GG) 1 |
| 2208 * | GTG 866 | Bristol K6A | 64.054 | H30/26R | 12/47 | Aberdare UDC (GG) 44 |
| 2209 * | GTG 867 | Bristol K6A | 64.055 | H30/26R | 11/47 | Aberdare UDC (GG) 9 |
| 2210 | GTG 868 | Bristol L6A | 65.110 | B35R | 12/47 | Aberdare UDC (GG) 29 |
| 2211 | GTG 869 | Bristol L6A | 65.111 | B35R | 12/47 | Aberdare UDC (GG) 30 |
| 2212 | GTG 870 | Bristol L6A | 65.112 | B35R | 12/47 | Aberdare UDC (GG) 32 |
| 2213 | GTG 871 | Bristol L6A | 65.113 | B35R | 12/47 | Aberdare UDC (GG) 33 |
| 2214 | GFM 906 | Leyland PD1A | 470460 | L27/26R | 6/47 | Crosville MS, Chester (CH) M521 |

| 2215 | GFM 907 | Leyland PD1A | 470461 | L27/26R | 6/47 | Crosville MS, Chester (CH) M522 |
|------|---------|--------------|--------|---------|------|--------------------------------|
| 2216 | GFM 908 | Leyland PD1A | 470473 | L27/26R | 6/47 | Crosville MS, Chester (CH) M523 |
| 2217 | GFM 909 | Leyland PD1A | 470474 | L27/26R | 6/47 | Crosville MS, Chester (CH) M524 |
| 2218 | GFM 910 | Leyland PD1A | 470475 | L27/26R | 6/47 | Crosville MS, Chester (CH) M525 |
| 2219 | GFM 911 | Leyland PD1A | 470518 | L27/26R | 3/47 | Crosville MS, Chester (CH) M526 |
| 2220 | GFM 912 | Leyland PD1A | 470519 | L27/26R | 3/47 | Crosville MS, Chester (CH) M527 |
| 2221 | GFM 913 | Leyland PD1A | 470520 | L27/26R | 3/47 | Crosville MS, Chester (CH) M528 |
| 2222 | GFM 914 | Leyland PD1A | 470543 | L27/26R | 3/47 | Crosville MS, Chester (CH) M529 |
| 2223 | GFM 915 | Leyland PD1A | 470544 | L27/26R | 3/47 | Crosville MS, Chester (CH) M530 |
| 2224 | GFM 916 | Leyland PD1A | 470558 | L27/26R | 3/47 | Crosville MS, Chester (CH) M531 |
| 2225 | GFM 917 | Leyland PD1A | 470559 | L27/26R | 3/47 | Crosville MS, Chester (CH) M532 |
| 2226 | GFM 918 | Leyland PD1A | 470560 | L27/26R | 3/47 | Crosville MS, Chester (CH) M533 |
| 2227 | GFM 919 | Leyland PD1A | 470561 | L27/26R | 3/47 | Crosville MS, Chester (CH) M534 |
| 2228 | GFM 920 | Leyland PD1A | 470592 | L27/26R | 3/47 | Crosville MS, Chester (CH) M535 |
| 2229 | GFM 921 | Leyland PD1A | 470603 | L27/26R | 4/47 | Crosville MS, Chester (CH) M536 |
| 2230 | GFM 922 | Leyland PD1A | 470604 | L27/26R | 4/47 | Crosville MS, Chester (CH) M537 |
| 2231 | GFM 923 | Leyland PD1A | 470605 | L27/26R | 4/47 | Crosville MS, Chester (CH) M538 |
| 2232 | GFM 924 | Leyland PD1A | 470606 | L27/26R | 4/47 | Crosville MS, Chester (CH) M539 |
| 2233 | GFM 925 | Leyland PD1A | 470607 | L27/26R | 4/47 | Crosville MS, Chester (CH) M540 |
| 2234 | GPW 347 | Leyland PD1A | 470801 | L27/26R | 4/47 | Eastern Counties, Norwich (NK) AP347 |
| 2235 | GPW 348 | Leyland PD1A | 470802 | L27/26R | 4/47 | Eastern Counties, Norwich (NK) AP348 |
| 2236 | GPW 349 | Leyland PD1A | 470803 | L27/26R | 4/47 | Eastern Counties, Norwich (NK) AP349 |
| 2237 | GPW 350 | Leyland PD1A | 470804 | L27/26R | 4/47 | Eastern Counties, Norwich (NK) AP350 |
| 2238 | GPW 346 | Leyland PD1A | 470800 | L27/26R | 4/47 | Eastern Counties, Norwich (NK) AP346 |
| 2239 | GPW 351 | Leyland PD1A | 470940 | L27/26R | 5/47 | Eastern Counties, Norwich (NK) AP351 |
| 2240 | GPW 352 | Leyland PD1A | 470939 | L27/26R | 5/47 | Eastern Counties, Norwich (NK) AP352 |
| 2241 | GPW 353 | Leyland PD1A | 471062 | L27/26R | 5/47 | Eastern Counties, Norwich (NK) AP353 |
| 2242 | GPW 354 | Leyland PD1A | 471063 | L27/26R | 5/47 | Eastern Counties, Norwich (NK) AP354 |
| 2243 | GPW 355 | Leyland PD1A | 471059 | L27/26R | 5/47 | Eastern Counties, Norwich (NK) AP355 |
| 2244 | GPW 356 | Leyland PD1A | 471060 | L27/26R | 5/47 | Eastern Counties, Norwich (NK) AP356 |
| 2245 | GPW 357 | Leyland PD1A | 471061 | L27/26R | 5/47 | Eastern Counties, Norwich (NK) AP357 |
| 2246 | GPW 358 | Leyland PD1A | 471163 | L27/26R | 5/47 | Eastern Counties, Norwich (NK) AP358 |
| 2247 | GPW 359 | Leyland PD1A | 471164 | L27/26R | 5/47 | Eastern Counties, Norwich (NK) AP359 |
| 2248 | GPW 360 | Leyland PD1A | 471165 | L27/26R | 5/47 | Eastern Counties, Norwich (NK) AP360 |
| 2249 | MPU 36 | Leyland PD1A | 470813 | L27/26R | 4/47 | Eastern National, Chelmsford (EX) 3975 |
| 2250 | MPU 38 | Leyland PD1A | 470815 | L27/26R | 4/47 | Eastern National, Chelmsford (EX) 3977 |
| 2251 | MPU 40 | Leyland PD1A | 470817 | L27/26R | 4/47 | Eastern National, Chelmsford (EX) 3979 |
| 2252 | MPU 37 | Leyland PD1A | 470814 | L27/26R | 4/47 | Eastern National, Chelmsford (EX) 3976 |
| 2253 | MPU 39 | Leyland PD1A | 470816 | L27/26R | 4/47 | Eastern National, Chelmsford (EX) 3978 |
| 2254 | MPU 41 | Leyland PD1A | 470941 | L27/26R | 4/47 | Eastern National, Chelmsford (EX) 3980 |
| 2255 | MPU 42 | Leyland PD1A | 470942 | L27/26R | 4/47 | Eastern National, Chelmsford (EX) 3981 |
| 2256 | MPU 43 | Leyland PD1A | 470968 | L27/26R | 4/47 | Eastern National, Chelmsford (EX) 3982 |
| 2257 | MPU 45 | Leyland PD1A | 470970 | L27/26R | 5/47 | Eastern National, Chelmsford (EX) 3984 |
| 2258 | MPU 44 | Leyland PD1A | 470969 | L27/26R | 5/47 | Eastern National, Chelmsford (EX) 3983 |
| 2259 | MPU 46 | Leyland PD1A | 471267 | L27/26R | 6/47 | Eastern National, Chelmsford (EX) 3985 |
| 2260 | MPU 47 | Leyland PD1A | 471268 | L27/26R | 6/47 | Eastern National, Chelmsford (EX) 3986 |
| 2261 | MPU 48 | Leyland PD1A | 471269 | L27/26R | 6/47 | Eastern National, Chelmsford (EX) 3987 |
| 2262 | JUO 945 | Leyland PD1A | 470823 | L27/26R | 4/47 | Western National, Exeter (DN) 2918 |
| 2263 | JUO 946 | Leyland PD1A | 470824 | L27/26R | 4/47 | Western National, Exeter (DN) 2919 |
| 2264 | JUO 947 | Leyland PD1A | 470825 | L27/26R | 4/47 | Western National, Exeter (DN) 2920 |
| 2265 | JUO 948 | Leyland PD1A | 470841 | L27/26R | 4/47 | Western National, Exeter (DN) 2921 |
| 2266 | JUO 949 | Leyland PD1A | 470971 | L27/26R | 5/47 | Western National, Exeter (DN) 2922 |
| 2267 | JUO 950 | Leyland PD1A | 470983 | L27/26R | 5/47 | Western National, Exeter (DN) 2923 |
| 2268 | JUO 951 | Leyland PD1A | 470985 | L27/26R | 5/47 | Western National, Exeter (DN) 2924 |
| 2269 | JUO 952 | Leyland PD1A | 471058 | L27/26R | 5/47 | Western National, Exeter (DN) 2925 |
| 2270 | JUO 953 | Leyland PD1A | 471270 | L27/26R | 6/47 | Western National, Exeter (DN) 2926 |
| 2271 | JUO 954 | Leyland PD1A | 472302 | L27/26R | 9/47 | Western National, Exeter (DN) 2927 |
| 2272 | JUO 955 | Leyland PD1A | 472303 | L27/26R | 9/47 | Western National, Exeter (DN) 2928 |
| 2273 | JUO 956 | Leyland PD1A | 472304 | L27/26R | 9/47 | Western National, Exeter (DN) 2929 |
| 2274 | HFM 63 | Leyland PD1A | 471403 | L27/26R | 7/47 | Crosville MS, Chester (CH) M541 |
| 2275 | HFM 64 | Leyland PD1A | 471404 | L27/26R | 7/47 | Crosville MS, Chester (CH) M542 |
| 2276 | HFM 65 | Leyland PD1A | 471590 | L27/26R | 7/47 | Crosville MS, Chester (CH) M543 |
| 2277 | HFM 66 | Leyland PD1A | 471592 | L27/26R | 7/47 | Crosville MS, Chester (CH) M544 |
| 2278 | HFM 67 | Leyland PD1A | 472227 | L27/26R | 9/47 | Crosville MS, Chester (CH) M545 |

| 2279 | HFM 68 | Leyland PD1A | 472228 | L27/26R | 9/47 | Crosville MS, Chester (CH) M546 |
|------|--------|--------------|--------|---------|------|--------------------------------|
| 2280 | HFM 69 | Leyland PD1A | 472784 | L27/26R | 12/47 | Crosville MS, Chester (CH) M547 |
| 2281 | HFM 71 | Leyland PD1A | 472786 | L27/26R | 12/47 | Crosville MS, Chester (CH) M549 |
| 2282 | HFM 70 | Leyland PD1A | 472785 | L27/26R | 12/47 | Crosville MS, Chester (CH) M548 |
| 2283 | HFM 72 | Leyland PD1A | 472787 | L27/26R | 12/47 | Crosville MS, Chester (CH) M550 |
| 2284 | HFM 73 | Leyland PD1A | 473145 | L27/26R | 12/47 | Crosville MS, Chester (CH) M551 |
| 2285 | HFM 74 | Leyland PD1A | 473248 | L27/26R | 12/47 | Crosville MS, Chester (CH) M552 |
| 2286 | HFM 75 | Leyland PD1A | 473299 | L27/26R | 12/47 | Crosville MS, Chester (CH) M553 |
| 2287 | HFM 76 | Leyland PD1A | 473300 | L27/26R | 12/47 | Crosville MS, Chester (CH) M554 |
| 2288 | HFM 77 | Leyland PD1A | 473142 | L27/26R | 12/47 | Crosville MS, Chester (CH) M555 |
| 2289 | GPW 361 | Leyland PD1A | 472022 | L27/26R | 8/47 | Eastern Counties, Norwich (NK) AP361 |
| 2290 | GPW 362 | Leyland PD1A | 472023 | L27/26R | 8/47 | Eastern Counties, Norwich (NK) AP362 |
| 2291 | GPW 363 | Leyland PD1A | 472229 | L27/26R | 9/47 | Eastern Counties, Norwich (NK) AP363 |
| 2292 | GPW 364 | Leyland PD1A | 472230 | L27/26R | 9/47 | Eastern Counties, Norwich (NK) AP364 |
| 2293 | GPW 365 | Leyland PD1A | 472231 | L27/26R | 9/47 | Eastern Counties, Norwich (NK) AP365 |
| 2294 | MPU 49 | Leyland PD1A | 472024 | L27/26R | 8/47 | Eastern National, Chelmsford (EX) 3988 |
| 2295 | MPU 50 | Leyland PD1A | 472099 | L27/26R | 8/47 | Eastern National, Chelmsford (EX) 3989 |
| 2296 | MPU 51 | Leyland PD1A | 472105 | L27/26R | 8/47 | Eastern National, Chelmsford (EX) 3990 |
| 2297 | MPU 52 | Leyland PD1A | 472154 | L27/26R | 9/47 | Eastern National, Chelmsford (EX) 3991 |
| 2298 | MPU 53 | Leyland PD1A | 472155 | L27/26R | 9/47 | Eastern National, Chelmsford (EX) 3992 |
| 2299 | JUO 990 | Leyland PD1A | 470826 | L27/26R | 4/47 | Southern National, Exeter (DN) 2930 |
| 2300 | JUO 991 | Leyland PD1A | 470984 | L27/26R | 5/47 | Southern National, Exeter (DN) 2931 |
| 2301 | JUO 992 | Leyland PD1A | 471271 | L27/26R | 6/47 | Southern National, Exeter (DN) 2932 |
| 2302 | JUO 993 | Leyland PD1A | 472305 | L27/26R | 9/47 | Southern National, Exeter (DN) 2933 |
| 2303 | DFW 566 | Leyland PD1A | 472306 | L27/26R | 3/48 | Lincolnshire RCC, Bracebridge Heath (KN) 689 |
| 2304 | DFW 567 | Leyland PD1A | 472307 | L27/26R | 1/48 | Lincolnshire RCC, Bracebridge Heath (KN) 690 |
| 2305 | DFW 568 | Leyland PD1A | 472324 | L27/26R | 4/48 | Lincolnshire RCC, Bracebridge Heath (KN) 691 |
| 2306 | DFW 569 | Leyland PD1A | 472325 | L27/26R | 5/48 | Lincolnshire RCC, Bracebridge Heath (KN) 692 |
| 2307 | GLJ 957 | Leyland PD1A | 472326 | L27/26R | 9/47 | Hants & Dorset, Bournemouth (HA) PD959 |
| 2308 | GLJ 958 | Leyland PD1A | 472327 | L27/26R | 9/47 | Hants & Dorset, Bournemouth (HA) PD960 |
| 2309 | GLJ 959 | Leyland PD1A | 472328 | L27/26R | 9/47 | Hants & Dorset, Bournemouth (HA) PD961 |
| 2310 | GLJ 960 | Leyland PD1A | 472329 | L27/26R | 9/47 | Hants & Dorset, Bournemouth (HA) PD962 |
| 2311 | GLJ 961 | Leyland PD1A | 472330 | L27/26R | 10/47 | Hants & Dorset, Bournemouth (HA) PD963 |
| 2312 | GLJ 962 | Leyland PD1A | 472633 | L27/26R | 12/47 | Hants & Dorset, Bournemouth (HA) PD964 |
| 2313 | GLJ 963 | Leyland PD1A | 472632 | L27/26R | 12/47 | Hants & Dorset, Bournemouth (HA) PD965 |
| 2314 | KHW 623 | Leyland PD1A | 471159 | H30/26R | 11/47 | Bristol Tramways (GL) C4012 |
| 2315 | KHW 627 | Leyland PD1A | 471609 | H30/26R | 10/47 | Bristol Tramways (GL) C4016 |
| 2316 | KHW 628 | Leyland PD1A | 471401 | H30/26R | 10/47 | Bristol Tramways (GL) C4017 |
| 2317 | KHW 626 | Leyland PD1A | 471402 | H30/26R | 11/47 | Bristol Tramways (GL) C4015 |
| 2318 | KHW 624 | Leyland PD1A | 471274 | H30/26R | 1/48 | Bristol Tramways (GL) C4013 |
| 2319 | KHW 625 | Leyland PD1A | 471275 | H30/26R | 1/48 | Bristol Tramways (GL) C4014 |
| 2320 | KHW 630 | Leyland PD1A | 471610 | H30/26R | 1/48 | Bristol Tramways (GL) C4019 |
| 2321 | KHW 629 | Leyland PD1A | 471694 | H30/26R | 1/48 | Bristol Tramways (GL) C4018 |
| 2322 | KHW 631 | Leyland PD1A | 471695 | H30/26R | 3/48 | Bristol Tramways (GL) C4020 |
| 2323 | KHW 632 | Leyland PD1A | 472096 | H30/26R | 2/48 | Bristol Tramways (GL) C4021 |
| 2324 | KHY 395 | Leyland PD1A | 472148 | H30/26R | 3/48 | Bristol Tramways (GL) C4026 |
| 2325 | LAE 7 | Leyland PD1A | 472628 | H30/26R | 3/48 | Bristol Tramways (GL) C4038 |
| 2326 | LAE 5 | Leyland PD1A | 472351 | H30/26R | 3/48 | Bristol Tramways (GL) C4036 |
| 2327 | LAE 6 | Leyland PD1A | 472564 | H30/26R | 3/48 | Bristol Tramways (GL) C4037 |
| 2328 | LAE 11 | Leyland PD1A | 472631 | H30/26R | 3/48 | Bristol Tramways (GL) C4042 |
| 2329 | LAE 15 | Leyland PD1A | 472863 | H30/26R | 3/48 | Bristol Tramways (GL) C4046 |
| 2330 | LAE 8 | Leyland PD1A | 472565 | H30/26R | 3/48 | Bristol Tramways (GL) C4039 |
| 2331 | LAE 13 | Leyland PD1A | 472861 | H30/26R | 3/48 | Bristol Tramways (GL) C4044 |
| 2332 | LAE 14 | Leyland PD1A | 472862 | H30/26R | 5/48 | Bristol Tramways (GL) C4045 |
| 2333 | LAE 4 | Leyland PD1A | 472350 | H30/26R | 5/48 | Bristol Tramways (GL) C4035 |
| 2334 | LAE 12 | Leyland PD1A | 472849 | H30/26R | 3/48 | Bristol Tramways (GL) C4043 |
| 2335 | LAE 18 | Leyland PD1A | 473247 | H30/26R | 5/48 | Bristol Tramways (GL) C4049 |
| 2336 | KHY 399 | Leyland PD1A | 472234 | H30/26R | 7/48 | Bristol Tramways (GL) C4030 |
| 2337 | LAE 1 | Leyland PD1A | 472308 | H30/26R | 7/48 | Bristol Tramways (GL) C4032 |
| 2338 | LAE 3 | Leyland PD1A | 472310 | H30/26R | 7/48 | Bristol Tramways (GL) C4034 |
| 2339 | CDB 213 | Leyland PD1A | 472331 | L27/26R | 11/47 | North Western RCC, Stockport (CH) 213 |
| 2340 | CDB 214 | Leyland PD1A | 472332 | L27/26R | 11/47 | North Western RCC, Stockport (CH) 214 |
| 2341 | CDB 216 | Leyland PD1A | 472343 | L27/26R | 11/47 | North Western RCC, Stockport (CH) 216 |
| 2342 | CDB 215 | Leyland PD1A | 472333 | L27/26R | 11/47 | North Western RCC, Stockport (CH) 215 |

| | | | | | | |
|---|---|---|---|---|---|---|
| 2343 | CDB 218 | Leyland PD1A | 472345 | L27/26R | 11/47 | North Western RCC, Stockport (CH) 218 |
| 2344 | CDB 217 | Leyland PD1A | 472344 | L27/26R | 11/47 | North Western RCC, Stockport (CH) 217 |
| 2345 | CDB 220 | Leyland PD1A | 472347 | L27/26R | 12/47 | North Western RCC, Stockport (CH) 220 |
| 2346 | CDB 222 | Leyland PD1A | 472349 | L27/26R | 12/47 | North Western RCC, Stockport (CH) 222 |
| 2347 | CDB 221 | Leyland PD1A | 472348 | L27/26R | 12/47 | North Western RCC, Stockport (CH) 221 |
| 2348 | CDB 219 | Leyland PD1A | 472346 | L27/26R | 12/47 | North Western RCC, Stockport (CH) 219 |
| 2349 | JAT 618 | Leyland PS1/1 | 472049 | DP31R | 3/48 | East Yorkshire, Kingston upon Hull (ER) 499 |
| 2350 | JAT 620 | Leyland PS1/1 | 472051 | DP31R | 5/48 | East Yorkshire, Kingston upon Hull (ER) 501 |
| 2351 | JAT 619 | Leyland PS1/1 | 472082 | DP31R | 4/48 | East Yorkshire, Kingston upon Hull (ER) 500 |
| 2352 | HMN 787 | Leyland PS1/1 | 462354 | B35R | 4/48 | Isle of Man RS, Douglas (IM) 34 |
| 2353 | HMN 788 | Leyland PS1/1 | 462355 | B35R | 4/48 | Isle of Man RS, Douglas (IM) 52 |
| 2354 | HMN 789 | Leyland PS1/1 | 462356 | B35R | 4/48 | Isle of Man RS, Douglas (IM) 57 |
| 2355 | HMN 790 | Leyland PS1/1 | 462357 | B35R | 4/48 | Isle of Man RS, Douglas (IM) 58 |
| 2356 | IH 6242 | AEC Regal III | O682232 | B35R | 9/48 | Londonderry & Lough Swilly Railway Co (LY) 53 |
| 2357 | IH 6243 | AEC Regal III | O682233 | B35R | 8/48 | Londonderry & Lough Swilly Railway Co (LY) 54 |
| 2358 | IH 6244 | AEC Regal III | O682234 | B35R | 9/48 | Londonderry & Lough Swilly Railway Co (LY) 55 |
| 2359 | IH 6245 | AEC Regal III | O682235 | B35R | 8/48 | Londonderry & Lough Swilly Railway Co (LY) 56 |
| 2360 * | ? | Bristol LWL6G | 67.162 | B39F | -/48 | Greyhound Bus Lines (Pty) Ltd, Johannesburg (O-ZA) |
| 2361 * | TG 10024 | Bristol LWL6G | 67.165 | B39F | -/48 | Germiston Municipality (O-ZA) 36 |
| 2362 * | TA 763 | Bristol LWL6G | 67.166 | B39F | 8/48 | Benoni Municipality (O-ZA) 1 |
| 2363 * | TA 810 | Bristol LWL6G | 67.167 | B39F | 8/48 | Benoni Municipality (O-ZA) 11 |
| 2364 * | TG 12363 | Bristol LWL6G | 67.184 | B39F | -/48 | Germiston Municipality (O-ZA) 41 |
| 2365 * | TG 10025 | Bristol LWL6G | 77.001 | B39F | -/48 | Germiston Municipality (O-ZA) 37 |
| 2366 * | TG 10022 | Bristol LWL6G | 77.002 | B39F | -/48 | Germiston Municipality (O-ZA) 22 |
| 2367 * | TA 795 | Bristol LWL6G | 77.003 | B39F | 8/48 | Benoni Municipality (O-ZA) 6 |
| 2368 * | TA 817 | Bristol LWL6G | 77.005 | B39F | 9/48 | Benoni Municipality (O-ZA) 13 |
| 2369 * | TG 10023 | Bristol LWL6G | 77.006 | B39F | -/48 | Germiston Municipality (O-ZA) 26 |
| 2370 * | TA 865 | Bristol LWL6G | 77.009 | B39F | 9/48 | Benoni Municipality (O-ZA) 15 |
| 2371 * | TA 869 | Bristol LWL6G | 77.010 | B39F | 9/48 | Benoni Municipality (O-ZA) 19 |
| 2372 * | TS 3014 | Bristol LWL6G | 77.004 | B39F | 3/49 | Springs Municipality (O-ZA) 30 |
| 2373 * | ? | Bristol LWL6G | 77.007 | B46F | -/48 | Vaal Bus Service (Pty) Ltd, Vereengiging (O-ZA) |
| 2374 * | ? | Bristol LWL6G | 77.008 | B46F | -/48 | Vaal Bus Service (Pty) Ltd, Vereengiging (O-ZA) |
| 2375 * | ? | Bristol LWL6G | 77.011 | B46F | -/48 | Vaal Bus Service (Pty) Ltd, Vereengiging (O-ZA) |
| 2376 * | ? | Bristol LWL6G | 77.012 | B46F | -/48 | Vaal Bus Service (Pty) Ltd, Vereengiging (O-ZA) |
| 2377 * | ? | Bristol LWL6G | 77.013 | B46F | -/48 | Vaal Bus Service (Pty) Ltd, Vereengiging (O-ZA) |
| 2378 * | TV 2053 or TVB 2053 | Bristol LWL6G | 77.014 | B39F | -/48 | Vaal Bus Service (Pty) Ltd, Vereengiging (O-ZA) ?27? |
| 2379 * | TS 3624 | Bristol LWL6G | 77.016 | B39F | 2/49 | Springs Municipality (O-ZA) 31 |
| 2380 * | TG 10047 | Bristol LWL6G | 77.017 | B39F | -/48 | Germiston Municipality (O-ZA) 33 |
| 2381 * | TS 3595 | Bristol LWL6G | 77.021 | B39F | 2/49 | Springs Municipality (O-ZA) 44 |
| 2382 * | TA 8216 | Bristol LWL6G | 77.015 | B39F | 12/48 | Benoni Municipality (O-ZA) 30 |
| 2383 * | TA 8215 | Bristol LWL6G | 77.018 | B39F | 12/48 | Benoni Municipality (O-ZA) 28 |
| 2384 * | TS 718 | Bristol LWL6G | 77.019 | B39F | 10/50 | Springs Municipality (O-ZA) 28 |
| 2385 * | TS 165 | Bristol LWL6G | 77.024 | B39F | 10/50 | Springs Municipality (O-ZA) 6 |
| 2386 * | TG 12362 | Bristol LWL6G | 77.025 | B39F | -/48 | Germiston Municipality (O-ZA) 40 |
| 2387 * | TA 8217 | Bristol LWL6G | 77.026 | B39F | 12/48 | Benoni Municipality (O-ZA) 31 |
| 2388 * | ? | Bristol LWL6G | 77.028 | B39F | -/48 | Greyhound Bus Lines (O-ZA) |
| 2389 * | TU 6048 | Bristol LWL6G | 77.029 | B39F | -/49 | Roodepoort Municipality (O-ZA) 7 |
| 2390 * | TS 875 | Bristol LWL6G | 77.033 | B39F | 10/50 | Springs Municipality (O-ZA) 9 |
| 2391 * | TS 924 | Bristol LWL6G | 77.027 | B39F | 10/50 | Springs Municipality (O-ZA) 8 |
| 2392 * | TS 4902 | Bristol LWL6G | 77.030 | B39F | 2/49 | Springs Municipality (O-ZA) 45 |
| 2393 * | TA 8214 | Bristol LWL6G | 77.031 | B39F | 12/48 | Benoni Municipality (O-ZA) 26 |
| 2394 * | TU 6047 | Bristol LWL6G | 77.032 | B39F | 5/49 | Roodepoort Municipality (O-ZA) 6 |
| 2395 * | TS 585 | Bristol LWL6G | 77.034 | B39F | 10/50 | Springs Municipality (O-ZA) 7 |

| | | | | | | |
|---|---|---|---|---|---|---|
| 2396 * | OJB 108 | Bristol LWL6G | 77.035 | B39F | -/48 | Electric Supply Commission (Vaal Generating Station) (O-ZA) |
| 2397 * | TA 8213 | Bristol LWL6G | 77.036 | B39F | 12/48 | Benoni Municipality (O-ZA) 8 |
| 2398 * | TS 876 | Bristol LWL6G | 77.037 | B39F | 10/50 | Springs Municipality (O-ZA) 29 |
| 2399 * | TA 7076 | Bristol LWL6G | 77.042 | B39F | 12/48 | Benoni Municipality (O-ZA) 27 |
| 2400 * | TS 8195 | Bristol LWL6G | 77.043 | B39F | 2/49 | Springs Municipality (O-ZA) 3 |
| 2401 * | ? | Bristol LWL6G | 77.044 | B39F | -/48 | Greyhound Bus Lines (Pty) Ltd, Johannesburg (O-ZA) |
| 2402 * | TA 7068 | Bristol LWL6G | 77.045 | B39F | 7/49 | Benoni Municipality (O-ZA) 17 |
| 2403 * | ? | Bristol LWL6G | 77.046 | B39F | -/48 | Greyhound Bus Lines (Pty) Ltd, Johannesburg (O-ZA) |
| 2404 * | TA 7079 | Bristol LWL6G | 77.038 | B39F | 12/48 | Benoni Municipality (O-ZA) 40 |
| 2405 * | TS 8196 | Bristol LWL6G | 77.041 | B39F | 2/49 | Springs Municipality (O-ZA) 4 |
| 2406 * | ? | Bristol LWL6G | 77.040 | B39F | -/48 | Greyhound Bus Lines (Pty) Ltd, Johannesburg (O-ZA) |
| 2407 * | OKC 4464 | Bristol LWL6G | 77.039 | B39F | -/48 | Anglo-American Corporation (Welkom Township Co) (O-ZA) |
| 2408 * | ? | Bristol LWL6G | 77.047 | B39F | -/48 | Greyhound Bus Lines (Pty) Ltd, Johannesburg (O-ZA) |
| 2409 * | TA 8212 | Bristol LWL6G | 77.056 | B39F | 12/48 | Benoni Municipality (O-ZA) 2 |
| 2410 * | JG 7017 | Leyland TD4 | 9502 | L27/28R | 6/48 | East Kent, Canterbury (KT) |
| 2411 * | JG 8202 | Leyland TD4 | 11598 | L27/28R | 7/48 | East Kent, Canterbury (KT) |
| 2412 * | JG 9917 | Leyland TD5 | 16045 | L27/28R | 6/48 | East Kent, Canterbury (KT) |
| 2413 * | JG 9928 | Leyland TD5 | 16046 | L27/28R | 6/48 | East Kent, Canterbury (KT) |
| 2414 * | JG 9922 | Leyland TD5 | 16036 | L27/28R | 6/48 | East Kent, Canterbury (KT) |
| 2415 * | JG 9929 | Leyland TD5 | 16048 | L27/28R | 6/48 | East Kent, Canterbury (KT) |
| 2416 * | JG 7015 | Leyland TD4 | 9500 | L27/28R | 6/48 | East Kent, Canterbury (KT) |
| 2417 * | JG 7022 | Leyland TD4 | 9525 | L27/28R | 6/48 | East Kent, Canterbury (KT) |
| 2418 * | JG 8204 | Leyland TD4 | 11600 | L27/28R | 7/48 | East Kent, Canterbury (KT) |
| 2419 * | JG 8229 | Leyland TD4 | 12196 | L27/28R | 6/48 | East Kent, Canterbury (KT) |
| 2420 * | JG 8231 | Leyland TD4 | 12198 | L27/28R | 6/48 | East Kent, Canterbury (KT) |
| 2421 * | JG 8243 | Leyland TD4 | 12210 | L27/28R | 6/48 | East Kent, Canterbury (KT) |
| 2422 * | JG 8230 | Leyland TD4 | 12197 | L27/28R | 6/48 | East Kent, Canterbury (KT) |
| 2423 * | JG 8244 | Leyland TD4 | 12211 | L27/28R | 6/48 | East Kent, Canterbury (KT) |
| 2424 * | JG 8248 | Leyland TD4 | 12566 | L27/28R | 6/48 | East Kent, Canterbury (KT) |
| 2425 * | JG 7018 | Leyland TD4 | 9503 | L27/28R | 7/48 | East Kent, Canterbury (KT) |
| 2426 * | JG 8201 | Leyland TD4 | 11597 | L27/28R | 7/48 | East Kent, Canterbury (KT) |
| 2427 * | JG 8240 | Leyland TD4 | 12207 | L27/28R | 7/48 | East Kent, Canterbury (KT) |
| 2428 * | JG 7011 | Leyland TD4 | 9496 | L27/28R | 7/48 | East Kent, Canterbury (KT) |
| 2429 * | JG 7024 | Leyland TD4 | 9527 | L27/28R | 7/48 | East Kent, Canterbury (KT) |
| 2430 * | JG 8226 | Leyland TD4 | 12193 | L27/28R | 7/48 | East Kent, Canterbury (KT) |
| 2431 * | JG 8228 | Leyland TD4 | 12195 | L27/28R | 6/48 | East Kent, Canterbury (KT) |
| 2432 * | JG 8238 | Leyland TD4 | 12205 | L27/28R | 7/48 | East Kent, Canterbury (KT) |
| 2433 * | JG 8227 | Leyland TD4 | 12194 | L27/28R | 7/48 | East Kent, Canterbury (KT) |
| 2434 * | RN 8186 | Leyland TD5 | 15860 | L27/26R | 6/48 | Ribble MS, Preston (LA) 1802 |
| 2435 * | RN 8187 | Leyland TD5 | 15861 | L27/26R | 6/48 | Ribble MS, Preston (LA) 1803 |
| 2436 * | RN 8177 | Leyland TD5 | 15840 | L27/26R | 6/48 | Ribble MS, Preston (LA) 1793 |
| 2437 * | RN 8314 | Leyland TD5 | 16487 | L27/26R | 6/48 | Ribble MS, Preston (LA) 1920 |
| 2438 * | RN 8183 | Leyland TD5 | 15853 | L27/26R | 6/48 | Ribble MS, Preston (LA) 1799 |
| 2439 * | RN 8174 | Leyland TD5 | 15836 | L27/26R | 6/48 | Ribble MS, Preston (LA) 1790 |
| 2440 * | RN 8181 | Leyland TD5 | 15848 | L27/26R | 6/48 | Ribble MS, Preston (LA) 1797 |
| 2441 * | RN 8165 | Leyland TD5 | 15856 | L27/26R | 6/48 | Ribble MS, Preston (LA) 1781 |
| 2442 * | RN 8322 | Leyland TD5 | 16504 | L27/26R | 6/48 | Ribble MS, Preston (LA) 1928 |
| 2443 * | RN 8156 | Leyland TD5 | 15837 | L27/26R | 6/48 | Ribble MS, Preston (LA) 1772 |
| 2444 * | RN 8297 | Leyland TD5 | 16485 | L27/26R | 6/48 | Ribble MS, Preston (LA) 1903 |
| 2445 * | RN 8182 | Leyland TD5 | 15852 | L27/26R | 6/48 | Ribble MS, Preston (LA) 1798 |
| 2446 * | RN 8157 | Leyland TD5 | 15841 | L27/26R | 7/48 | Ribble MS, Preston (LA) 1773 |
| 2447 * | RN 8311 | Leyland TD5 | 16481 | L27/26R | 6/48 | Ribble MS, Preston (LA) 1917 |
| 2448 * | RN 8306 | Leyland TD5 | 16503 | L27/26R | 7/48 | Ribble MS, Preston (LA) 1912 |
| 2449 * | RN 8189 | Leyland TD5 | 15866 | L27/26R | 7/48 | Ribble MS, Preston (LA) 1805 |
| 2450 * | RN 8319 | Leyland TD5 | 16495 | L27/26R | 7/48 | Ribble MS, Preston (LA) 1925 |
| 2451 * | RN 8313 | Leyland TD5 | 16486 | L27/26R | 7/48 | Ribble MS, Preston (LA) 1919 |
| 2452 * | RN 8317 | Leyland TD5 | 16493 | L27/26R | 7/48 | Ribble MS, Preston (LA) 1923 |
| 2453 * | RN 8176 | Leyland TD5 | 15839 | L27/26R | 7/48 | Ribble MS, Preston (LA) 1792 |

| | | | | | | | |
|---|---|---|---|---|---|---|---|
| 2454 * | RN 8190 | Leyland TD5 | 15867 | L27/26R | 7/48 | Ribble MS, Preston (LA) | 1806 |
| 2455 * | RN 8301 | Leyland TD5 | 16497 | L27/26R | 7/48 | Ribble MS, Preston (LA) | 1907 |
| 2456 * | RN 8184 | Leyland TD5 | 15854 | L27/26R | 7/48 | Ribble MS, Preston (LA) | 1800 |
| 2457 * | RN 8188 | Leyland TD5 | 15862 | L27/26R | 7/48 | Ribble MS, Preston (LA) | 1804 |
| 2458 * | RN 8316 | Leyland TD5 | 16492 | L27/26R | 7/48 | Ribble MS, Preston (LA) | 1922 |
| 2459 * | DKH 466 | Leyland TD5 | 16199 | H28/26R | 10/48 | East Yorkshire, Kingston upon Hull (ER) | 358 |
| 2460 * | ERH 359 | Leyland TD5 | 301124 | H28/26R | 10/48 | East Yorkshire, Kingston upon Hull (ER) | 365 |
| 2461 * | ERH 362 | Leyland TD5 | 301127 | H28/26R | 10/48 | East Yorkshire, Kingston upon Hull (ER) | 368 |
| 2462 * | ERH 360 | Leyland TD5 | 301125 | H28/26R | 10/48 | East Yorkshire, Kingston upon Hull (ER) | 366 |
| 2463 * | ERH 366 | Leyland TD5 | 301131 | H28/26R | 10/48 | East Yorkshire, Kingston upon Hull (ER) | 372 |
| 2464 * | GAT 60 | Leyland TD5 | 303730 | H28/26R | 10/48 | East Yorkshire, Kingston upon Hull (ER) | 374 |
| 2465 * | GAT 62 | Leyland TD5 | 303732 | H28/26R | 11/48 | East Yorkshire, Kingston upon Hull (ER) | 376 |
| 2466 * | GAT 61 | Leyland TD5 | 303731 | H28/26R | 11/48 | East Yorkshire, Kingston upon Hull (ER) | 375 |
| 2467 * | GAT 66 | Leyland TD5 | 303736 | H28/26R | 11/48 | East Yorkshire, Kingston upon Hull (ER) | 380 |
| 2468 * | GAT 63 | Leyland TD5 | 303733 | H28/26R | 11/48 | East Yorkshire, Kingston upon Hull (ER) | 377 |
| 2469 * | GAT 69 | Leyland TD5 | 303739 | H28/26R | 11/48 | East Yorkshire, Kingston upon Hull (ER) | 383 |
| 2470 * | GAT 64 | Leyland TD5 | 303734 | H28/26R | 11/48 | East Yorkshire, Kingston upon Hull (ER) | 378 |
| 2471 * | GAT 70 | Leyland TD5 | 303740 | H28/26R | 11/48 | East Yorkshire, Kingston upon Hull (ER) | 384 |
| 2472 * | GAT 67 | Leyland TD5 | 303737 | H28/26R | 11/48 | East Yorkshire, Kingston upon Hull (ER) | 381 |
| 2473 * | GAT 68 | Leyland TD5 | 303738 | H28/26R | 11/48 | East Yorkshire, Kingston upon Hull (ER) | 382 |
| 2474 * | GR 5075 | Leyland TD5 | 17626 | H29/26R | 10/48 | Northern General, Gateshead (DM) | 852 |
| 2475 * | GR 5077 | Leyland TD5 | 17628 | H29/26R | 10/48 | Northern General, Gateshead (DM) | 854 |
| 2476 * | GR 5078 | Leyland TD5 | 17629 | H29/26R | 10/48 | Northern General, Gateshead (DM) | 855 |
| 2477 * | GR 5076 | Leyland TD5 | 17627 | H29/26R | 10/48 | Northern General, Gateshead (DM) | 853 |
| 2478 * | GR 5079 | Leyland TD5 | 17630 | H29/26R | 12/48 | Northern General, Gateshead (DM) | 856 |
| 2479 | LHU 511 | Bristol K6B | 66.095 | L27/28R | 9/48 | Bristol Tramways (GL) | L4118 |
| 2480 | LHU 512 | Bristol K6A | 68.002 | L27/28R | 9/48 | Bristol Tramways (GL) | L4119 |
| 2481 | LHU 515 | Bristol K5G | 68.017 | L27/28R | 10/48 | Bristol Tramways (GL) | L4125 |
| 2482 | LHU 516 | Bristol K5G | 68.018 | L27/28R | 9/48 | Bristol Tramways (GL) | L4120 |
| 2483 | LHU 517 | Bristol K5G | 68.019 | L27/28R | 9/48 | Bristol Tramways (GL) | L4121 |
| 2484 | LHU 518 | Bristol K5G | 68.020 | L27/28R | 10/48 | Bristol Tramways (GL) | L4122 |
| 2485 | LHU 513 | Bristol K6A | 68.012 | L27/28R | 10/48 | Bristol Tramways (GL) | L4123 |
| 2486 | LHU 514 | Bristol K6A | 68.013 | L27/28R | 10/48 | Bristol Tramways (GL) | L4124 |
| 2487 | LHU 519 | Bristol K6B | 68.032 | L27/28R | 10/48 | Bristol Tramways (GL) | L4126 |
| 2488 | HSM 642 | Bristol K6B | 68.021 | L27/28R | 10/48 | Caledonian OC, Dumfries (DF) | 323 |
| 2489 | HSM 643 | Bristol K6B | 68.022 | L27/28R | 10/48 | Caledonian OC, Dumfries (DF) | 324 |
| 2490 * | HSM 644 | Bristol K5G | 72.041 | L27/28R | 1/49 | Caledonian OC, Dumfries (DF) | 325 |
| 2491 * | HSM 645 | Bristol K5G | 74.054 | L27/28R | 3/49 | Caledonian OC, Dumfries (DF) | 326 |
| 2492 | JFM 51 | Bristol K6A | 66.179 | L27/28R | 8/48 | Crosville MS, Chester (CH) | MB298 |
| 2493 | JFM 52 | Bristol K6A | 66.180 | L27/28R | 9/48 | Crosville MS, Chester (CH) | MB299 |
| 2494 | JFM 53 | Bristol K6A | 66.181 | L27/28R | 9/48 | Crosville MS, Chester (CH) | MB300 |
| 2495 | JFM 54 | Bristol K6A | 66.182 | L27/28R | 9/48 | Crosville MS, Chester (CH) | MB301 |
| 2496 | JFM 55 | Bristol K6A | 66.183 | L27/28R | 9/48 | Crosville MS, Chester (CH) | MB302 |
| 2497 | JFM 56 | Bristol K6A | 68.034 | L27/28R | 9/48 | Crosville MS, Chester (CH) | MB303 |
| 2498 | JFM 57 | Bristol K6A | 68.035 | L27/28R | 10/48 | Crosville MS, Chester (CH) | MB304 |
| 2499 | JFM 58 | Bristol K6A | 68.037 | L27/28R | 10/48 | Crosville MS, Chester (CH) | MB305 |
| 2500 | JFM 59 | Bristol K6A | 68.038 | L27/28R | 11/48 | Crosville MS, Chester (CH) | MB306 |
| 2501 | JFM 60 | Bristol K6A | 68.036 | L27/28R | 12/48 | Crosville MS, Chester (CH) | MB307 |
| 2502 | JFM 61 | Bristol K6A | 68.102 | L27/28R | 11/48 | Crosville MS, Chester (CH) | MB308 |
| 2503 | JFM 62 | Bristol K6A | 68.103 | L27/28R | 11/48 | Crosville MS, Chester (CH) | MB309 |
| 2504 | JFM 63 | Bristol K6B | 68.127 | L27/28R | 11/48 | Crosville MS, Chester (CH) | MB310 |
| 2505 | JFM 64 | Bristol K6B | 68.128 | L27/28R | 12/48 | Crosville MS, Chester (CH) | MB311 |
| 2506 | JFM 65 | Bristol K6B | 68.129 | L27/28R | 12/48 | Crosville MS, Chester (CH) | MB312 |
| 2507 | JFM 66 | Bristol K6B | 68.130 | L27/28R | 12/48 | Crosville MS, Chester (CH) | MB313 |
| 2508 | JFM 67 | Bristol K6B | 68.139 | L27/28R | 12/48 | Crosville MS, Chester (CH) | MB314 |
| 2509 | JFM 68 | Bristol K6B | 68.142 | L27/28R | 12/48 | Crosville MS, Chester (CH) | MB315 |
| 2510 | JFM 69 | Bristol K6B | 68.140 | L27/28R | 12/48 | Crosville MS, Chester (CH) | MB316 |
| 2511 | JFM 70 | Bristol K6B | 68.141 | L27/28R | 12/48 | Crosville MS, Chester (CH) | MB317 |
| 2512 | JFM 71 | Bristol K6B | 68.171 | L27/28R | 12/48 | Crosville MS, Chester (CH) | MB318 |
| 2513 * | JFM 72 | Bristol K6A | 68.168 | L27/28R | 12/48 | Crosville MS, Chester (CH) | MB319 |
| 2514 * | JFM 73 | Bristol K6B | 68.170 | L27/28R | 3/49 | Crosville MS, Chester (CH) | MB320 |
| 2515 * | JFM 74 | Bristol K6A | 68.169 | L27/28R | 12/48 | Crosville MS, Chester (CH) | MB321 |
| 2516 | JFM 75 | Bristol K6B | 68.172 | L27/28R | 3/49 | Crosville MS, Chester (CH) | MB322 |
| 2517 * | JFM 76 | Bristol K6A | 72.011 | L27/28R | 1/49 | Crosville MS, Chester (CH) | MB323 |

| 2518 * | JFM 77 | Bristol K6A | 72.012 | L27/28R | 1/49 | Crosville MS, Chester (CH) MB324 |
|---|---|---|---|---|---|---|
| 2519 * | JFM 78 | Bristol K6A | 72.065 | L27/28R | 3/49 | Crosville MS, Chester (CH) MB325 |
| 2520 * | JFM 79 | Bristol K6A | 72.098 | L27/28R | 3/49 | Crosville MS, Chester (CH) MB326 |
| 2521 * | JFM 80 | Bristol K6A | 72.097 | L27/28R | 3/49 | Crosville MS, Chester (CH) MB327 |
| 2522 * | JFM 81 | Bristol K6A | 74.029 | L27/28R | 3/49 | Crosville MS, Chester (CH) MB328 |
| 2523 * | JFM 82 | Bristol K6A | 74.055 | L27/28R | 3/49 | Crosville MS, Chester (CH) MB329 |
| 2524 * | JFM 83 | Bristol K6A | 74.050 | L27/28R | 3/49 | Crosville MS, Chester (CH) MB330 |
| 2525 * | JFM 84 | Bristol K6A | 74.056 | L27/28R | 3/49 | Crosville MS, Chester (CH) MB331 |
| 2526 * | JFM 85 | Bristol K6A | 74.057 | L27/28R | 3/49 | Crosville MS, Chester (CH) MB332 |
| 2527 * | JFM 86 | Bristol K6A | 74.058 | L27/28R | 4/49 | Crosville MS, Chester (CH) MB333 |
| 2528 * | JFM 87 | Bristol K6A | 74.064 | L27/28R | 4/49 | Crosville MS, Chester (CH) MB334 |
| 2529 * | JFM 88 | Bristol K6A | 74.109 | L27/28R | 4/49 | Crosville MS, Chester (CH) MB335 |
| 2530 * | JFM 89 | Bristol K6A | 74.107 | L27/28R | 4/49 | Crosville MS, Chester (CH) MB336 |
| 2531 * | JFM 90 | Bristol K6A | 74.108 | L27/28R | 4/49 | Crosville MS, Chester (CH) MB337 |
| 2532 * | JFM 91 | Bristol K6A | 74.110 | L27/28R | 4/49 | Crosville MS, Chester (CH) MB338 |
| 2533 * | JFM 92 | Bristol K6A | 74.138 | L27/28R | 4/49 | Crosville MS, Chester (CH) MB339 |
| 2534 * | JFM 93 | Bristol K6A | 74.139 | L27/28R | 4/49 | Crosville MS, Chester (CH) MB340 |
| 2535 * | JFM 94 | Bristol K6A | 74.001 | L27/28R | 5/49 | Crosville MS, Chester (CH) MB341 |
| 2536 * | JFM 95 | Bristol K6A | 74.002 | L27/28R | 5/49 | Crosville MS, Chester (CH) MB342 |
| 2537 * | JFM 96 | Bristol K6A | 74.018 | L27/28R | 5/49 | Crosville MS, Chester (CH) MB343 |
| 2538 * | JFM 97 | Bristol K6A | 74.021 | L27/28R | 5/49 | Crosville MS, Chester (CH) MB344 |
| 2539 * | JFM 98 | Bristol K6A | 74.019 | L27/28R | 5/49 | Crosville MS, Chester (CH) MB345 |
| 2540 * | JFM 99 | Bristol K6A | 74.020 | L27/28R | 5/49 | Crosville MS, Chester (CH) MB346 |
| 2541 * | JFM 100 | Bristol K6A | 74.017 | L27/28R | 5/49 | Crosville MS, Chester (CH) MB347 |
| 2542 * | JFM 101 | Bristol K6A | 74.027 | L27/28R | 5/49 | Crosville MS, Chester (CH) MB348 |
| 2543 * | JFM 102 | Bristol K6A | 74.028 | L27/28R | 5/49 | Crosville MS, Chester (CH) MB349 |
| 2544 * | JFM 103 | Bristol K6A | 74.194 | L27/28R | 5/49 | Crosville MS, Chester (CH) MB350 |
| 2545 * | JFM 104 | Bristol K6A | 74.195 | L27/28R | 5/49 | Crosville MS, Chester (CH) MB351 |
| 2546 * | JFM 105 | Bristol K6A | 74.196 | L27/28R | 5/49 | Crosville MS, Chester (CH) MB352 |
| 2547 * | JFM 106 | Bristol K6A | 74.197 | L27/28R | 5/49 | Crosville MS, Chester (CH) MB353 |
| 2548 * | JFM 107 | Bristol K6A | 74.198 | L27/28R | 5/49 | Crosville MS, Chester (CH) MB354 |
| 2549 * | JFM 108 | Bristol K6A | 74.003 | L27/28R | 5/49 | Crosville MS, Chester (CH) MB355 |
| 2550 * | JFM 109 | Bristol K6A | 74.004 | L27/28R | 5/49 | Crosville MS, Chester (CH) MB356 |
| 2551 * | JFM 110 | Bristol K6A | 76.062 | L27/28R | 5/49 | Crosville MS, Chester (CH) MB357 |
| 2552 | NNO 96 | Bristol K5G | 68.084 | L27/28R | 11/48 | Eastern National, Chelmsford (EX) 3996 |
| 2553 | NNO 97 | Bristol K5G | 68.085 | L27/28R | 10/48 | Eastern National, Chelmsford (EX) 3997 |
| 2554 | NNO 93 | Bristol K5G | 68.081 | L27/28R | 11/48 | Eastern National, Chelmsford (EX) 3993 |
| 2555 | NNO 94 | Bristol K5G | 68.082 | L27/28R | 11/48 | Eastern National, Chelmsford (EX) 3994 |
| 2556 | NNO 95 | Bristol K5G | 68.083 | L27/28R | 11/48 | Eastern National, Chelmsford (EX) 3995 |
| 2557 | NNO 98 | Bristol K5G | 68.131 | L27/28R | 11/48 | Eastern National, Chelmsford (EX) 3998 |
| 2558 | NNO 99 | Bristol K5G | 68.132 | L27/28R | 12/48 | Eastern National, Chelmsford (EX) 3999 |
| 2559 * | NNO 100 | Bristol K5G | 68.133 | L27/28R | 12/48 | Eastern National, Chelmsford (EX) 4000 |
| 2560 * | NNO 101 | Bristol K5G | 68.134 | L27/28R | 12/48 | Eastern National, Chelmsford (EX) 4001 |
| 2561 * | NNO 102 | Bristol K5G | 68.135 | L27/28R | 12/48 | Eastern National, Chelmsford (EX) 4002 |
| 2562 * | NNO 103 | Bristol K5G | 74.086 | L27/28R | 3/49 | Eastern National, Chelmsford (EX) 4003 |
| 2563 * | NNO 104 | Bristol K5G | 74.087 | L27/28R | 3/49 | Eastern National, Chelmsford (EX) 4004 |
| 2564 * | NNO 105 | Bristol K5G | 74.090 | L27/28R | 3/49 | Eastern National, Chelmsford (EX) 4005 |
| 2565 * | NNO 106 | Bristol K5G | 74.088 | L27/28R | 3/49 | Eastern National, Chelmsford (EX) 4006 |
| 2566 * | NNO 107 | Bristol K5G | 74.089 | L27/28R | 3/49 | Eastern National, Chelmsford (EX) 4007 |
| 2567 | HLJ 15 | Bristol K6A | 68.039 | L27/28R | 9/48 | Hants & Dorset, Bournemouth (HA) TD866 |
| 2568 | HLJ 16 | Bristol K6A | 68.040 | L27/28R | 9/48 | Hants & Dorset, Bournemouth (HA) TD867 |
| 2569 | HLJ 17 | Bristol K6A | 68.041 | L27/28R | 9/48 | Hants & Dorset, Bournemouth (HA) TD868 |
| 2570 | HLJ 18 | Bristol K6A | 68.042 | L27/28R | 9/48 | Hants & Dorset, Bournemouth (HA) TD869 |
| 2571 | HLJ 19 | Bristol K6A | 68.043 | L27/28R | 10/48 | Hants & Dorset, Bournemouth (HA) TD870 |
| 2572 | HLJ 20 | Bristol K6A | 68.104 | L27/28R | 10/48 | Hants & Dorset, Bournemouth (HA) TD871 |
| 2573 * | HLJ 21 | Bristol K6A | 68.105 | L27/28R | 11/48 | Hants & Dorset, Bournemouth (HA) TD872 |
| 2574 | HLJ 22 | Bristol K6A | 68.106 | L27/28R | 11/48 | Hants & Dorset, Bournemouth (HA) TD873 |
| 2575 | HLJ 23 | Bristol K6A | 68.107 | L27/28R | 11/48 | Hants & Dorset, Bournemouth (HA) TD874 |
| 2576 | HLJ 24 | Bristol K6A | 68.108 | L27/28R | 11/48 | Hants & Dorset, Bournemouth (HA) TD875 |
| 2577 * | HLJ 25 | Bristol K6A | 68.155 | L27/28R | 12/48 | Hants & Dorset, Bournemouth (HA) TD876 |
| 2578 * | HLJ 27 | Bristol K6A | 68.157 | L27/28R | 12/48 | Hants & Dorset, Bournemouth (HA) TD878 |
| 2579 * | HLJ 26 | Bristol K6A | 68.156 | L27/28R | 12/48 | Hants & Dorset, Bournemouth (HA) TD877 |
| 2580 * | HLJ 28 | Bristol K6A | 68.158 | L27/28R | 12/48 | Hants & Dorset, Bournemouth (HA) TD879 |
| 2581 * | HLJ 29 | Bristol K6A | 68.188 | L27/28R | 12/48 | Hants & Dorset, Bournemouth (HA) TD880 |

| | | | | | | |
|---|---|---|---|---|---|---|
| 2582 * | HLJ 30 | Bristol K6A | 72.013 | L27/28R | 12/48 | Hants & Dorset, Bournemouth (HA) TD881 |
| 2583 * | HLJ 31 | Bristol K6A | 72.014 | L27/28R | 12/48 | Hants & Dorset, Bournemouth (HA) TD882 |
| 2584 * | HLJ 32 | Bristol K6A | 72.015 | L27/28R | 12/48 | Hants & Dorset, Bournemouth (HA) TD883 |
| 2585 * | HLJ 33 | Bristol K6A | 72.016 | L27/28R | 12/48 | Hants & Dorset, Bournemouth (HA) TD884 |
| 2586 * | HLJ 34 | Bristol K6A | 72.023 | L27/28R | 12/48 | Hants & Dorset, Bournemouth (HA) TD885 |
| 2587 * | HLJ 35 | Bristol K6A | 72.024 | L27/28R | 12/48 | Hants & Dorset, Bournemouth (HA) TD886 |
| 2588 * | HLJ 36 | Bristol K6A | 72.025 | L27/28R | 12/48 | Hants & Dorset, Bournemouth (HA) TD887 |
| 2589 * | HLJ 37 | Bristol K6A | 72.026 | L27/28R | 12/48 | Hants & Dorset, Bournemouth (HA) TD888 |
| 2590 * | HLJ 38 | Bristol K6A | 72.027 | L27/28R | 12/48 | Hants & Dorset, Bournemouth (HA) TD889 |
| 2591 * | HLJ 39 | Bristol K6A | 72.059 | L27/28R | 2/49 | Hants & Dorset, Bournemouth (HA) TD890 |
| 2592 * | HLJ 40 | Bristol K6A | 72.057 | L27/28R | 2/49 | Hants & Dorset, Bournemouth (HA) TD891 |
| 2593 * | HLJ 41 | Bristol K6A | 72.058 | L27/28R | 2/49 | Hants & Dorset, Bournemouth (HA) TD892 |
| 2594 * | HLJ 42 | Bristol K6A | 72.078 | L27/28R | 2/49 | Hants & Dorset, Bournemouth (HA) TD893 |
| 2595 * | HLJ 43 | Bristol K6A | 72.079 | L27/28R | 2/49 | Hants & Dorset, Bournemouth (HA) TD894 |
| 2596 * | HLJ 44 | Bristol K6A | 72.080 | L27/28R | 2/49 | Hants & Dorset, Bournemouth (HA) TD895 |
| 2597 * | HRU 844 | Bristol K6A | 74.006 | L27/28R | 2/49 | Hants & Dorset, Bournemouth (HA) TD896 |
| 2598 * | HRU 845 | Bristol K6A | 74.033 | L27/28R | 2/49 | Hants & Dorset, Bournemouth (HA) TD897 |
| 2599 * | HRU 846 | Bristol K6A | 74.039 | L27/28R | 2/49 | Hants & Dorset, Bournemouth (HA) TD898 |
| 2600 * | HRU 847 | Bristol K6A | 74.040 | L27/28R | 3/49 | Hants & Dorset, Bournemouth (HA) TD899 |
| 2601 * | HRU 848 | Bristol K6A | 74.038 | L27/28R | 3/49 | Hants & Dorset, Bournemouth (HA) TD900 |
| 2602 * | HRU 849 | Bristol K5G | 74.079 | L27/28R | 3/49 | Hants & Dorset, Bournemouth (HA) TD901 |
| 2603 * | HRU 850 | Bristol K6A | 74.081 | L27/28R | 3/49 | Hants & Dorset, Bournemouth (HA) TD902 |
| 2604 * | HRU 851 | Bristol K6A | 74.082 | L27/28R | 3/49 | Hants & Dorset, Bournemouth (HA) TD903 |
| 2605 * | HRU 852 | Bristol K6A | 74.007 | L27/28R | 3/49 | Hants & Dorset, Bournemouth (HA) TD904 |
| 2606 * | HRU 853 | Bristol K6A | 74.080 | L27/28R | 3/49 | Hants & Dorset, Bournemouth (HA) TD905 |
| 2607 * | HRU 854 | Bristol K6B | 74.091 | L27/28R | 3/49 | Hants & Dorset, Bournemouth (HA) TD906 |
| 2608 * | HRU 855 | Bristol K6A | 74.121 | L27/28R | 4/49 | Hants & Dorset, Bournemouth (HA) TD907 |
| 2609 * | HRU 856 | Bristol K6A | 74.132 | L27/28R | 4/49 | Hants & Dorset, Bournemouth (HA) TD908 |
| 2610 * | HRU 857 | Bristol K6A | 74.119 | L27/28R | 4/49 | Hants & Dorset, Bournemouth (HA) TD909 |
| 2611 * | HRU 858 | Bristol K6A | 74.120 | L27/28R | 4/49 | Hants & Dorset, Bournemouth (HA) TD910 |
| 2612 * | HRU 859 | Bristol K6A | 74.122 | L27/28R | 4/49 | Hants & Dorset, Bournemouth (HA) TD911 |
| 2613 * | HRU 860 | Bristol K6A | 74.131 | L27/28R | 4/49 | Hants & Dorset, Bournemouth (HA) TD912 |
| 2614 * | HRU 861 | Bristol K6A | 74.133 | L27/28R | 4/49 | Hants & Dorset, Bournemouth (HA) TD913 |
| 2615 * | HRU 862 | Bristol K6A | 74.148 | L27/28R | 4/49 | Hants & Dorset, Bournemouth (HA) TD914 |
| 2616 | HRU 863 | Bristol K6A | 74.149 | L27/28R | 6/49 | Hants & Dorset, Bournemouth (HA) TD915 |
| 2617 | HRU 864 | Bristol K6A | 74.150 | L27/28R | 6/49 | Hants & Dorset, Bournemouth (HA) TD916 |
| 2618 | HRU 865 | Bristol K6A | 74.157 | L27/28R | 6/49 | Hants & Dorset, Bournemouth (HA) TD917 |
| 2619 | HRU 866 | Bristol K6A | 74.155 | L27/28R | 6/49 | Hants & Dorset, Bournemouth (HA) TD918 |
| 2620 | HRU 867 | Bristol K6A | 74.156 | L27/28R | 6/49 | Hants & Dorset, Bournemouth (HA) TD919 |
| 2621 | HRU 868 | Bristol K6A | 74.151 | L27/28R | 6/49 | Hants & Dorset, Bournemouth (HA) TD920 |
| 2622 | HOD 84 | Bristol K6A | 68.054 | L27/28R | 10/48 | Southern National, Exeter (DN) 900 |
| 2623 | HOD 85 | Bristol K6A | 68.055 | L27/28R | 10/48 | Southern National, Exeter (DN) 901 |
| 2624 | HOD 86 | Bristol K6A | 68.101 | L27/28R | 11/48 | Southern National, Exeter (DN) 902 |
| 2625 | HOD 87 | Bristol K6A | 68.099 | L27/28R | 12/48 | Southern National, Exeter (DN) 903 |
| 2626 | HOD 88 | Bristol K6A | 68.098 | L27/28R | 12/48 | Southern National, Exeter (DN) 904 |
| 2627 | HOD 89 | Bristol K6A | 68.100 | L27/28R | 12/48 | Southern National, Exeter (DN) 905 |
| 2628 * | HOD 90 | Bristol K5G | 72.010 | L27/28R | 1/49 | Southern National, Exeter (DN) 906 |
| 2629 * | HOD 91 | Bristol K5G | 72.018 | L27/28R | 1/49 | Southern National, Exeter (DN) 907 |
| 2630 * | HOD 92 | Bristol K5G | 72.017 | L27/28R | 1/49 | Southern National, Exeter (DN) 908 |
| 2631 * | HOD 93 | Bristol K6A | 74.012 | L27/28R | 3/49 | Southern National, Exeter (DN) 909 |
| 2632 * | HOD 94 | Bristol K5G | 74.052 | L27/28R | 3/49 | Southern National, Exeter (DN) 910 |
| 2633 * | HOD 95 | Bristol K5G | 74.053 | L27/28R | 3/49 | Southern National, Exeter (DN) 911 |
| 2634 * | HOD 96 | Bristol K6A | 74.105 | L27/28R | 4/49 | Southern National, Exeter (DN) 912 |
| 2635 * | HOD 97 | Bristol K6A | 74.106 | L27/28R | 4/49 | Southern National, Exeter (DN) 913 |
| 2636 | FDL 292 | Bristol K5G | 66.173 | L27/28R | 9/49 | Southern Vectis, Newport (IW) 724 |
| 2637 | FDL 293 | Bristol K5G | 66.174 | L27/28R | 9/49 | Southern Vectis, Newport (IW) 725 |
| 2638 | FDL 294 | Bristol K5G | 66.175 | L27/28R | 9/49 | Southern Vectis, Newport (IW) 726 |
| 2639 | FDL 295 | Bristol K5G | 66.176 | L27/28R | 9/49 | Southern Vectis, Newport (IW) 727 |
| 2640 | FDL 296 | Bristol K5G | 66.177 | L27/28R | 9/49 | Southern Vectis, Newport (IW) 728 |
| 2641 * | FDL 297 | Bristol K5G | 72.038 | L27/28R | 2/49 | Southern Vectis, Newport (IW) 729 |
| 2642 * | FDL 298 | Bristol K5G | 74.059 | L27/28R | 3/49 | Southern Vectis, Newport (IW) 730 |
| 2643 | EJB 214 | Bristol K6B | 68.091 | L27/28R | 11/48 | Thames Valley, Reading (BE) 492 |
| 2644 | EJB 215 | Bristol K6B | 68.092 | L27/28R | 12/48 | Thames Valley, Reading (BE) 493 |
| 2645 | EJB 216 | Bristol K6B | 68.093 | L27/28R | 12/48 | Thames Valley, Reading (BE) 494 |

| | | | | | | | |
|---|---|---|---|---|---|---|---|
| 2646 | EJB 217 | Bristol K6B | 68.094 | L27/28R | 12/48 | Thames Valley, Reading (BE) | 495 |
| 2647 | EJB 218 | Bristol K6B | 68.095 | L27/28R | 12/48 | Thames Valley, Reading (BE) | 496 |
| 2648 | EJB 219 | Bristol K6B | 68.162 | L27/28R | 1/49 | Thames Valley, Reading (BE) | 497 |
| 2649 | EJB 220 | Bristol K6B | 68.163 | L27/28R | 1/49 | Thames Valley, Reading (BE) | 498 |
| 2650 | EJB 221 | Bristol K6B | 68.164 | L27/28R | 12/48 | Thames Valley, Reading (BE) | 499 |
| 2651 | EJB 222 | Bristol K6B | 68.165 | L27/28R | 1/49 | Thames Valley, Reading (BE) | 500 |
| 2652 | EJB 223 | Bristol K6B | 68.166 | L27/28R | 1/49 | Thames Valley, Reading (BE) | 501 |
| 2653 | EJB 224 | Bristol K6B | 72.004 | L27/28R | 1/49 | Thames Valley, Reading (BE) | 502 |
| 2654 | EJB 225 | Bristol K6B | 72.005 | L27/28R | 1/49 | Thames Valley, Reading (BE) | 503 |
| 2655 | EJB 226 | Bristol K6B | 72.006 | L27/28R | 1/49 | Thames Valley, Reading (BE) | 504 |
| 2656 | EJB 227 | Bristol K6B | 72.007 | L27/28R | 1/49 | Thames Valley, Reading (BE) | 505 |
| 2657 | EJB 228 | Bristol K6B | 72.008 | L27/28R | 1/49 | Thames Valley, Reading (BE) | 506 |
| 2658 | EJB 229 | Bristol K6B | 72.092 | L27/28R | 7/49 | Thames Valley, Reading (BE) | 507 |
| 2659 | EJB 230 | Bristol K6B | 72.093 | L27/28R | 7/49 | Thames Valley, Reading (BE) | 508 |
| 2660 | EJB 231 | Bristol K6B | 72.094 | L27/28R | 7/49 | Thames Valley, Reading (BE) | 509 |
| 2661 | EJB 235 | Bristol K6B | 74.092 | L27/28R | 7/49 | Thames Valley, Reading (BE) | 513 |
| 2662 | EJB 236 | Bristol K6B | 74.093 | L27/28R | 8/49 | Thames Valley, Reading (BE) | 514 |
| 2663 | EJB 237 | Bristol K6B | 74.116 | L27/28R | 8/49 | Thames Valley, Reading (BE) | 515 |
| 2664 | EJB 239 | Bristol K6B | 74.118 | L27/28R | 8/49 | Thames Valley, Reading (BE) | 517 |
| 2665 | EJB 238 | Bristol K6B | 74.117 | L27/28R | 8/49 | Thames Valley, Reading (BE) | 516 |
| 2666 | EJB 240 | Bristol K6B | 74.161 | L27/28R | 8/49 | Thames Valley, Reading (BE) | 518 |
| 2667 | EJB 241 | Bristol K6B | 74.162 | L27/28R | 8/49 | Thames Valley, Reading (BE) | 519 |
| 2668 | KHN 368 | Bristol K6B | 66.172 | L27/28R | 10/48 | United AS, Darlington (DM) | BDO68 |
| 2669 | KHN 369 | Bristol K6B | 66.199 | L27/28R | 10/48 | United AS, Darlington (DM) | BDO69 |
| 2670 | KHN 370 | Bristol K6B | 66.198 | L27/28R | 10/48 | United AS, Darlington (DM) | BDO70 |
| 2671 | KHN 371 | Bristol K6B | 66.200 | L27/28R | 10/48 | United AS, Darlington (DM) | BDO71 |
| 2672 | KHN 372 | Bristol K6B | 68.047 | L27/28R | 11/48 | United AS, Darlington (DM) | BDO72 |
| 2673 | KHN 373 | Bristol K6B | 68.048 | L27/28R | 11/48 | United AS, Darlington (DM) | BDO73 |
| 2674 | KHN 374 | Bristol K6B | 68.049 | L27/28R | 11/48 | United AS, Darlington (DM) | BDO74 |
| 2675 | KHN 375 | Bristol K6B | 68.050 | L27/28R | 11/48 | United AS, Darlington (DM) | BDO75 |
| 2676 | KHN 376 | Bristol K6B | 68.051 | L27/28R | 11/48 | United AS, Darlington (DM) | BDO76 |
| 2677 | KHN 377 | Bristol K6B | 68.109 | L27/28R | 11/48 | United AS, Darlington (DM) | BDO77 |
| 2678 | KHN 378 | Bristol K6B | 68.110 | L27/28R | 11/48 | United AS, Darlington (DM) | BDO78 |
| 2679 | KHN 379 | Bristol K6B | 68.111 | L27/28R | 12/48 | United AS, Darlington (DM) | BDO79 |
| 2680 | KHN 380 | Bristol K6B | 68.121 | L27/28R | 12/48 | United AS, Darlington (DM) | BDO80 |
| 2681 | KHN 381 | Bristol K6B | 68.122 | L27/28R | 12/48 | United AS, Darlington (DM) | BDO81 |
| 2682 | KHN 382 | Bristol K6B | 68.112 | L27/28R | 12/48 | United AS, Darlington (DM) | BDO82 |
| 2683 | KHN 383 | Bristol K6B | 68.181 | L27/28R | 7/49 | United AS, Darlington (DM) | BDO83 |
| 2684 | KHN 384 | Bristol K6B | 68.182 | L27/28R | 8/49 | United AS, Darlington (DM) | BDO84 |
| 2685 | KHN 385 | Bristol K6B | 68.183 | L27/28R | 8/49 | United AS, Darlington (DM) | BDO85 |
| 2686 | KHN 386 | Bristol K6B | 72.030 | L27/28R | 8/49 | United AS, Darlington (DM) | BDO86 |
| 2687 | KHN 387 | Bristol K6B | 72.031 | L27/28R | 8/49 | United AS, Darlington (DM) | BDO87 |
| 2688 | KHN 388 | Bristol K6B | 72.032 | L27/28R | 8/49 | United AS, Darlington (DM) | BDO88 |
| 2689 | KHN 389 | Bristol K6B | 66.178 | L27/28R | 8/49 | United AS, Darlington (DM) | BDO89 |
| 2690 | KHN 390 | Bristol K6B | 72.028 | L27/28R | 8/49 | United AS, Darlington (DM) | BDO90 |
| 2691 | KHN 391 | Bristol K6B | 72.029 | L27/28R | 8/49 | United AS, Darlington (DM) | BDO91 |
| 2692 * | KHN 392 | Bristol K5G | 72.070 | L27/28R | 5/49 | United AS, Darlington (DM) | BDO92 |
| 2693 * | KHN 493 | Bristol K5G | 72.096 | L27/28R | 5/49 | United AS, Darlington (DM) | BDO93 |
| 2694 * | KHN 494 | Bristol K5G | 72.100 | L27/28R | 5/49 | United AS, Darlington (DM) | BDO94 |
| 2695 * | KHN 495 | Bristol K5G | 74.022 | L27/28R | 5/49 | United AS, Darlington (DM) | BDO95 |
| 2696 * | KHN 496 | Bristol K5G | 74.023 | L27/28R | 5/49 | United AS, Darlington (DM) | BDO96 |
| 2697 * | KHN 497 | Bristol K5G | 74.025 | L27/28R | 5/49 | United AS, Darlington (DM) | BDO97 |
| 2698 * | KHN 498 | Bristol K5G | 74.024 | L27/28R | 5/49 | United AS, Darlington (DM) | BDO98 |
| 2699 * | KHN 499 | Bristol K5G | 74.026 | L27/28R | 5/49 | United AS, Darlington (DM) | BDO99 |
| 2700 * | KHN 500 | Bristol K5G | 74.031 | L27/28R | 5/49 | United AS, Darlington (DM) | BDO100 |
| 2701 * | LHN 101 | Bristol K5G | 74.094 | L27/28R | 5/49 | United AS, Darlington (DM) | BDO101 |
| 2702 * | LHN 102 | Bristol K5G | 74.123 | L27/28R | 5/49 | United AS, Darlington (DM) | BDO102 |
| 2703 * | LHN 103 | Bristol K5G | 74.030 | L27/28R | 5/49 | United AS, Darlington (DM) | BDO103 |
| 2704 * | LHN 104 | Bristol K5G | 74.100 | L27/28R | 5/49 | United AS, Darlington (DM) | BDO104 |
| 2705 * | LHN 305 | Bristol K5G | 74.158 | L27/28R | 5/49 | United AS, Darlington (DM) | BDO105 |
| 2706 * | LHN 306 | Bristol K5G | 74.159 | L27/28R | 5/49 | United AS, Darlington (DM) | BDO106 |
| 2707 * | LHN 307 | Bristol K5G | 74.124 | L27/28R | 5/49 | United AS, Darlington (DM) | BDO107 |
| 2708 * | LHN 308 | Bristol K5G | 74.125 | L27/28R | 5/49 | United AS, Darlington (DM) | BDO108 |
| 2709 * | LHN 309 | Bristol K5G | 74.160 | L27/28R | 6/49 | United AS, Darlington (DM) | BDO109 |

| 2710 | LHN 310 | Bristol K6B | 72.039 | L27/28R | 8/49 | United AS, Darlington (DM) BDO110 |
|------|---------|-------------|--------|---------|------|------------------------------------|
| 2711 | LHN 311 | Bristol K6B | 72.086 | L27/28R | 8/49 | United AS, Darlington (DM) BDO111 |
| 2712 | LHN 312 | Bristol K6B | 72.087 | L27/28R | 8/49 | United AS, Darlington (DM) BDO112 |
| 2713 | EBD 216 | Bristol K5G | 66.168 | L27/28R | 8/48 | United Counties, Northampton (NO) 647 |
| 2714 | EBD 217 | Bristol K5G | 66.169 | L27/28R | 8/48 | United Counties, Northampton (NO) 648 |
| 2715 | EBD 218 | Bristol K5G | 66.170 | L27/28R | 8/48 | United Counties, Northampton (NO) 649 |
| 2716 | EBD 219 | Bristol K5G | 66.171 | L27/28R | 8/48 | United Counties, Northampton (NO) 650 |
| 2717 * | EBD 220 | Bristol K5G | 68.189 | L27/28R | 12/48 | United Counties, Northampton (NO) 651 |
| 2718 * | EBD 221 | Bristol K5G | 68.184 | L27/28R | 12/48 | United Counties, Northampton (NO) 652 |
| 2719 * | EBD 222 | Bristol K5G | 68.185 | L27/28R | 12/48 | United Counties, Northampton (NO) 653 |
| 2720 * | EBD 223 | Bristol K5G | 68.186 | L27/28R | 12/48 | United Counties, Northampton (NO) 654 |
| 2721 * | EBD 244 | Bristol K5G | 72.040 | L27/28R | 1/49 | United Counties, Northampton (NO) 655 |
| 2722 * | EBD 225 | Bristol K5G | 72.045 | L27/28R | 1/49 | United Counties, Northampton (NO) 656 |
| 2723 * | EBD 226 | Bristol K5G | 72.055 | L27/28R | 2/49 | United Counties, Northampton (NO) 657 |
| 2724 * | EBD 227 | Bristol K5G | 74.060 | L27/28R | 2/49 | United Counties, Northampton (NO) 658 |
| 2725 | EBD 228 | Bristol K6B | 74.102 | L27/28R | 5/49 | United Counties, Northampton (NO) 659 |
| 2726 | EBD 229 | Bristol K6B | 74.101 | L27/28R | 5/49 | United Counties, Northampton (NO) 660 |
| 2727 | EBD 230 | Bristol K6B | 74.135 | L27/28R | 7/49 | United Counties, Northampton (NO) 661 |
| 2728 | EBD 231 | Bristol K6B | 74.136 | L27/28R | 6/49 | United Counties, Northampton (NO) 662 |
| 2729 | EBD 232 | Bristol K6B | 74.137 | L27/28R | 9/49 | United Counties, Northampton (NO) 663 |
| 2730 | EBD 233 | Bristol K6B | 74.163 | L27/28R | 9/49 | United Counties, Northampton (NO) 664 |
| 2731 | GWX 101 | Bristol K6B | 68.005 | L27/28R | 10/48 | West Yorkshire RCC, Harrogate (WR) 744 |
| 2732 | GWX 102 | Bristol K6B | 68.006 | L27/28R | 10/48 | West Yorkshire RCC, Harrogate (WR) 745 |
| 2733 | GWX 103 | Bristol K6B | 68.007 | L27/28R | 10/48 | West Yorkshire RCC, Harrogate (WR) 746 |
| 2734 | GWX 104 | Bristol K6B | 68.008 | L27/28R | 11/48 | West Yorkshire RCC, Harrogate (WR) 747 |
| 2735 | GWX 105 | Bristol K6B | 68.009 | L27/28R | 11/48 | West Yorkshire RCC, Harrogate (WR) 748 |
| 2736 | GWX 106 | Bristol K6B | 68.063 | L27/28R | 11/48 | West Yorkshire RCC, Harrogate (WR) 749 |
| 2737 | GWX 107 | Bristol K6B | 68.064 | L27/28R | 11/48 | West Yorkshire RCC, Harrogate (WR) 750 |
| 2738 | GWX 108 | Bristol K6B | 74.061 | L27/28R | 7/49 | West Yorkshire RCC, Harrogate (WR) 751 |
| 2739 | GWX 109 | Bristol K6B | 74.062 | L27/28R | 7/49 | West Yorkshire RCC, Harrogate (WR) 752 |
| 2740 | GWX 110 | Bristol K6B | 74.063 | L27/28R | 7/49 | West Yorkshire RCC, Harrogate (WR) 753 |
| 2741 | GWX 121 | Bristol K6B | 68.175 | L27/28R | 12/48 | Keighley-West Yorkshire, Harrogate (WR) K764 |
| 2742 | GWX 122 | Bristol K6B | 68.176 | L27/28R | 7/49 | Keighley-West Yorkshire, Harrogate (WR) K765 |
| 2743 | GWX 123 | Bristol K6B | 68.191 | L27/28R | 7/49 | Keighley-West Yorkshire, Harrogate (WR) K766 |
| 2744 | GWX 124 | Bristol K6B | 68.190 | L27/28R | 7/49 | Keighley-West Yorkshire, Harrogate (WR) K767 |
| 2745 | GWX 125 | Bristol K6B | 72.046 | L27/28R | 7/49 | Keighley-West Yorkshire, Harrogate (WR) K768 |
| 2746 | GWX 126 | Bristol K6B | 72.047 | L27/28R | 7/49 | Keighley-West Yorkshire, Harrogate (WR) K769 |
| 2747 | GWX 127 | Bristol K6B | 72.048 | L27/28R | 7/49 | Keighley-West Yorkshire, Harrogate (WR) K770 |
| 2748 | GWX 128 | Bristol K6B | 74.084 | L27/28R | 10/49 | Keighley-West Yorkshire, Harrogate (WR) K771 |
| 2749 | GWX 129 | Bristol K6B | 74.085 | L27/28R | 10/49 | Keighley-West Yorkshire, Harrogate (WR) K772 |
| 2750 | GWX 130 | Bristol K6B | 74.083 | L27/28R | 10/49 | Keighley-West Yorkshire, Harrogate (WR) K773 |
| 2751 | HOD 2 | Bristol K6A | 68.052 | L27/28R | 10/48 | Western National, Exeter (DN) 875 |
| 2752 | HOD 1 | Bristol K6A | 68.053 | L27/28R | 10/48 | Western National, Exeter (DN) 874 |
| 2753 | HOD 3 | Bristol K6A | 68.097 | L27/28R | 10/48 | Western National, Exeter (DN) 876 |
| 2754 | HOD 4 | Bristol K6A | 68.096 | L27/28R | 11/48 | Western National, Exeter (DN) 877 |
| 2755 * | HOD 5 | Bristol K6A | 68.123 | L27/28R | 12/48 | Western National, Exeter (DN) 878 |
| 2756 * | HOD 6 | Bristol K6A | 68.124 | L27/28R | 12/48 | Western National, Exeter (DN) 879 |
| 2757 * | HOD 7 | Bristol K6A | 68.192 | L27/28R | 12/48 | Western National, Exeter (DN) 880 |
| 2758 * | HOD 8 | Bristol K6A | 72.003 | L27/28R | 12/48 | Western National, Exeter (DN) 881 |
| 2759 * | HOD 9 | Bristol K5G | 72.009 | L27/28R | 1/49 | Western National, Exeter (DN) 882 |
| 2760 * | HOD 10 | Bristol K5G | 72.090 | L27/28R | 1/49 | Western National, Exeter (DN) 883 |
| 2761 * | HOD 11 | Bristol K5G | 72.091 | L27/28R | 2/49 | Western National, Exeter (DN) 884 |
| 2762 * | HOD 12 | Bristol K5G | 72.060 | L27/28R | 2/49 | Western National, Exeter (DN) 885 |
| 2763 * | HOD 13 | Bristol K5G | 72.063 | L27/28R | 2/49 | Western National, Exeter (DN) 886 |
| 2764 * | HOD 14 | Bristol K5G | 72.061 | L27/28R | 2/49 | Western National, Exeter (DN) 887 |
| 2765 * | HOD 15 | Bristol K5G | 72.062 | L27/28R | 2/49 | Western National, Exeter (DN) 888 |
| 2766 * | HOD 16 | Bristol K5G | 72.064 | L27/28R | 2/49 | Western National, Exeter (DN) 889 |
| 2767 * | HOD 17 | Bristol K5G | 74.008 | L27/28R | 3/49 | Western National, Exeter (DN) 890 |
| 2768 * | HOD 18 | Bristol K5G | 74.009 | L27/28R | 3/49 | Western National, Exeter (DN) 891 |
| 2769 * | HOD 19 | Bristol K5G | 74.010 | L27/28R | 3/49 | Western National, Exeter (DN) 892 |
| 2770 * | HOD 20 | Bristol K5G | 74.051 | L27/28R | 3/49 | Western National, Exeter (DN) 893 |
| 2771 * | HOD 21 | Bristol K5G | 74.011 | L27/28R | 3/49 | Western National, Exeter (DN) 894 |
| 2772 * | HOD 22 | Bristol K6A | 74.096 | L27/28R | 3/49 | Western National, Exeter (DN) 895 |
| 2773 * | HOD 23 | Bristol K6A | 74.095 | L27/28R | 4/49 | Western National, Exeter (DN) 896 |

| | | | | | | | |
|---|---|---|---|---|---|---|---|
| 2774 * | HOD 24 | Bristol K6A | 74.097 | L27/28R | 4/49 | Western National, Exeter (DN) 897 |
| 2775 * | HOD 25 | Bristol K6A | 74.103 | L27/28R | 4/49 | Western National, Exeter (DN) 898 |
| 2776 * | HOD 26 | Bristol K6A | 74.104 | L27/28R | 4/49 | Western National, Exeter (DN) 899 |
| 2777 | DHJ 21 | Bristol K5G | 68.138 | L27/28R | 11/48 | Westcliff-on-Sea MS (EX) |
| 2778 | CJN 321 | Bristol K5G | 68.136 | L27/28R | 11/48 | Westcliff-on-Sea MS (EX) |
| 2779 | CJN 322 | Bristol K5G | 68.137 | L27/28R | 11/48 | Westcliff-on-Sea MS (EX) |
| 2780 | CJN 323 | Bristol K6B | 68.187 | L27/28R | 7/49 | Westcliff-on-Sea MS (EX) |
| 2781 * | CJN 324 | Bristol K5G | 72.056 | L27/28R | 2/49 | Westcliff-on-Sea MS (EX) |
| 2782 * | CJN 325 | Bristol K5G | 74.044 | L27/28R | 3/49 | Westcliff-on-Sea MS (EX) |
| 2783 * | CJN 326 | Bristol K5G | 74.045 | L27/28R | 3/49 | Westcliff-on-Sea MS (EX) |
| 2784 | CJN 327 | Bristol K6B | 74.071 | L27/28R | 7/49 | Westcliff-on-Sea MS (EX) |
| 2785 | CJN 328 | Bristol K6B | 74.072 | L27/28R | 7/49 | Westcliff-on-Sea MS (EX) |
| 2786 | FAM 4 | Bristol K6B | 68.152 | L27/28R | 12/48 | Wilts & Dorset, Salisbury (WI) 287 |
| 2787 | FAM 5 | Bristol K6B | 68.153 | L27/28R | 12/48 | Wilts & Dorset, Salisbury (WI) 288 |
| 2788 | FAM 6 | Bristol K6B | 68.154 | L27/28R | 12/48 | Wilts & Dorset, Salisbury (WI) 289 |
| 2789 | FMW 652 | Bristol K6B | 72.071 | L27/28R | 9/49 | Wilts & Dorset, Salisbury (WI) 290 |
| 2790 | FMW 653 | Bristol K6B | 72.072 | L27/28R | 9/49 | Wilts & Dorset, Salisbury (WI) 291 |
| 2791 | FMW 827 | Bristol K6B | 74.073 | L27/28R | 9/49 | Wilts & Dorset, Salisbury (WI) 292 |
| 2792 | LHU 521 | Bristol K6B | 68.033 | H30/26R | 10/48 | Bristol Tramways (GL) C3412 |
| 2793 | LHU 522 | Bristol K6B | 68.044 | H30/26R | 10/48 | Bristol Tramways (GL) C3413 |
| 2794 | LHU 524 | Bristol K6B | 68.046 | H30/26R | 10/48 | Bristol Tramways (GL) C3416 |
| 2795 | LHU 525 | Bristol K5G | 68.056 | H30/26R | 10/48 | Bristol Tramways (GL) C3417 |
| 2796 | LHU 528 | Bristol K6B | 68.059 | H30/26R | 10/48 | Bristol Tramways (GL) C3421 |
| 2797 | LHU 529 | Bristol K6B | 68.060 | H30/26R | 10/48 | Bristol Tramways (GL) C3422 |
| 2798 | LHU 520 | Bristol K5G | 66.184 | H30/26R | 10/48 | Bristol Tramways (GL) C3411 |
| 2799 | LHU 523 | Bristol K6B | 68.045 | H30/26R | 10/48 | Bristol Tramways (GL) C3414 |
| 2800 | LHU 526 | Bristol K5G | 68.057 | H30/26R | 10/48 | Bristol Tramways (GL) C3419 |
| 2801 | LHU 527 | Bristol K5G | 68.058 | H30/26R | 10/48 | Bristol Tramways (GL) C3420 |
| 2802 | LHU 530 | Bristol K6B | 68.061 | H30/26R | 10/48 | Bristol Tramways (GL) C3423 |
| 2803 | LHU 531 | Bristol K6B | 68.068 | H31/28R | 11/48 | Bristol Tramways (GL) C3424 |
| 2804 | LHU 972 | Bristol K6B | 68.069 | H30/26R | 11/48 | Bristol Tramways (GL) C3425 |
| 2805 | LHU 974 | Bristol K6B | 68.076 | H30/26R | 11/48 | Bristol Tramways (GL) C3427 |
| 2806 | LHU 975 | Bristol K6B | 68.077 | H30/26R | 11/48 | Bristol Tramways (GL) C3428 |
| 2807 | LHU 973 | Bristol K6B | 68.070 | H30/26R | 11/48 | Bristol Tramways (GL) C3426 |
| 2808 | LHU 976 | Bristol K6B | 68.078 | H30/26R | 11/48 | Bristol Tramways (GL) C3429 |
| 2809 | LHU 977 | Bristol K6B | 68.079 | H30/26R | 11/48 | Bristol Tramways (GL) C3430 |
| 2810 | LHU 971 | Bristol K6B | 68.065 | H30/26R | 12/48 | Bristol Tramways (GL) 3762 |
| 2811 | LHU 978 | Bristol K6B | 68.080 | H30/26R | 11/48 | Bristol Tramways (GL) C3431 |
| 2812 | LHU 979 | Bristol K6B | 68.090 | H30/26R | 11/48 | Bristol Tramways (GL) C3432 |
| 2813 | LHU 980 | Bristol K6B | 68.113 | H30/26R | 11/48 | Bristol Tramways (GL) C3433 |
| 2814 | LHU 981 | Bristol K6B | 68.116 | H30/26R | 11/48 | Bristol Tramways (GL) C3434 |
| 2815 | LHU 982 | Bristol K6B | 68.117 | H30/26R | 11/48 | Bristol Tramways (GL) C3435 |
| 2816 | LHU 983 | Bristol K6B | 68.125 | H30/26R | 12/48 | Bristol Tramways (GL) 3763 |
| 2817 | LHU 984 | Bristol K5G | 68.126 | H30/26R | 2/49 | Bristol Tramways (GL) 3764 |
| 2818 | LHU 985 | Bristol K6B | 72.082 | H30/26R | 1/49 | Bath Electric Tramways (SO) 3841 |
| 2819 | LHU 986 | Bristol K6B | 72.083 | H30/26R | 1/49 | Bath Electric Tramways (SO) 3842 |
| 2820 | LHU 987 | Bristol K6B | 72.081 | H31/28R | 6/49 | Bristol Tramways (GL) 3766 |
| 2821 | LHU 988 | Bristol K6B | 74.032 | H31/28R | 6/49 | Bristol Tramways (GL) 3765 |
| 2822 | LHU 989 | Bristol K6B | 74.048 | H31/28R | 6/49 | Bristol Tramways (GL) 3767 |
| 2823 | LHU 990 | Bristol K6B | 74.049 | H31/28R | 6/49 | Bristol Tramways (GL) 3768 |
| 2824 | LHU 991 | Bristol K6B | 74.013 | H31/28R | 6/49 | Bristol Tramways (GL) 3769 |
| 2825 | LHU 992 | Bristol K6B | 74.014 | H31/28R | 6/49 | Bristol Tramways (GL) 3770 |
| 2826 | LHU 993 | Bristol K6B | 74.015 | H31/28R | 6/49 | Bristol Tramways (GL) 3771 |
| 2827 | LHU 994 | Bristol K6B | 74.016 | H31/28R | 6/49 | Bristol Tramways (GL) 3772 |
| 2828 | EAP 2 | Bristol K5G | 66.162 | H30/26R | 7/48 | Brighton, Hove & District (ES) 6394 |
| 2829 | EAP 3 | Bristol K5G | 66.163 | H30/26R | 7/48 | Brighton, Hove & District (ES) 6395 |
| 2830 | EAP 4 | Bristol K5G | 68.010 | H30/26R | 10/48 | Brighton, Hove & District (ES) 6396 |
| 2831 | EAP 5 | Bristol K5G | 68.011 | H30/26R | 10/48 | Brighton, Hove & District (ES) 6397 |
| 2832 | EAP 6 | Bristol K5G | 68.114 | H30/26R | 11/48 | Brighton, Hove & District (ES) 6398 |
| 2833 | EAP 7 | Bristol K5G | 68.115 | H30/26R | 11/48 | Brighton, Hove & District (ES) 6399 |
| 2834 * | EAP 8 | Bristol K6A | 68.161 | H30/26R | 1/49 | Brighton, Hove & District (ES) 6400 |
| 2835 * | EAP 9 | Bristol K6B | 68.167 | H30/26R | 1/49 | Brighton, Hove & District (ES) 6401 |
| 2836 * | EAP 10 | Bristol K5G | 72.085 | H30/26R | 1/49 | Brighton, Hove & District (ES) 6402 |
| 2837 * | EAP 11 | Bristol K5G | 72.084 | H30/26R | 1/49 | Brighton, Hove & District (ES) 6403 |

| | | | | | | | |
|---|---|---|---|---|---|---|---|
| 2838 | HPW 75 | Bristol K5G | 66.186 | H30/26R | 10/48 | Eastern Counties, Norwich (NK) | LKH75 |
| 2839 | HPW 76 | Bristol K5G | 66.187 | H30/26R | 10/48 | Eastern Counties, Norwich (NK) | LKH76 |
| 2840 | HPW 77 | Bristol K5G | 66.188 | H30/26R | 10/48 | Eastern Counties, Norwich (NK) | LKH77 |
| 2841 | HPW 78 | Bristol K5G | 66.189 | H30/26R | 10/48 | Eastern Counties, Norwich (NK) | LKH78 |
| 2842 | HPW 79 | Bristol K5G | 66.190 | H30/26R | 10/48 | Eastern Counties, Norwich (NK) | LKH79 |
| 2843 | HPW 80 | Bristol K5G | 68.023 | H30/26R | 10/48 | Eastern Counties, Norwich (NK) | LKH80 |
| 2844 | HPW 81 | Bristol K5G | 68.024 | H30/26R | 10/48 | Eastern Counties, Norwich (NK) | LKH81 |
| 2845 | HPW 82 | Bristol K5G | 68.025 | H30/26R | 10/48 | Eastern Counties, Norwich (NK) | LKH82 |
| 2846 | HPW 83 | Bristol K5G | 68.026 | H30/26R | 10/48 | Eastern Counties, Norwich (NK) | LKH83 |
| 2847 | HPW 84 | Bristol K5G | 68.027 | H30/26R | 10/48 | Eastern Counties, Norwich (NK) | LKH84 |
| 2848 | HPW 85 | Bristol K5G | 68.071 | H30/26R | 11/48 | Eastern Counties, Norwich (NK) | LKH85 |
| 2849 | HPW 86 | Bristol K5G | 68.072 | H30/26R | 11/48 | Eastern Counties, Norwich (NK) | LKH86 |
| 2850 | HPW 87 | Bristol K5G | 68.073 | H30/26R | 11/48 | Eastern Counties, Norwich (NK) | LKH87 |
| 2851 | HPW 88 | Bristol K5G | 68.074 | H30/26R | 11/48 | Eastern Counties, Norwich (NK) | LKH88 |
| 2852 | HPW 89 | Bristol K5G | 68.075 | H30/26R | 11/48 | Eastern Counties, Norwich (NK) | LKH89 |
| 2853 | HPW 90 | Bristol K5G | 68.118 | H30/26R | 11/48 | Eastern Counties, Norwich (NK) | LKH90 |
| 2854 | HPW 91 | Bristol K5G | 68.119 | H30/26R | 12/48 | Eastern Counties, Norwich (NK) | LKH91 |
| 2855 | HPW 92 | Bristol K5G | 68.120 | H30/26R | 12/48 | Eastern Counties, Norwich (NK) | LKH92 |
| 2856 | HPW 93 | Bristol K5G | 68.173 | H30/26R | 11/48 | Eastern Counties, Norwich (NK) | LKH93 |
| 2857 * | HPW 94 | Bristol K5G | 68.179 | H30/26R | 1/49 | Eastern Counties, Norwich (NK) | LKH94 |
| 2858 * | HPW 95 | Bristol K5G | 68.174 | H30/26R | 1/49 | Eastern Counties, Norwich (NK) | LKH95 |
| 2859 * | HPW 96 | Bristol K5G | 68.177 | H30/26R | 1/49 | Eastern Counties, Norwich (NK) | LKH96 |
| 2860 * | HPW 97 | Bristol K5G | 68.178 | H30/26R | 1/49 | Eastern Counties, Norwich (NK) | LKH97 |
| 2861 * | HPW 98 | Bristol K5G | 68.180 | H30/26R | 1/49 | Eastern Counties, Norwich (NK) | LKH98 |
| 2862 * | HPW 99 | Bristol K5G | 68.198 | H30/26R | 1/49 | Eastern Counties, Norwich (NK) | LKH99 |
| 2863 | HPW 100 | Bristol K6B | 68.193 | H30/26R | 6/49 | Eastern Counties, Norwich (NK) | LKH100 |
| 2864 | HPW 101 | Bristol K6B | 68.194 | H30/26R | 6/49 | Eastern Counties, Norwich (NK) | LKH101 |
| 2865 * | HPW 102 | Bristol K6B | 68.195 | H30/26R | 8/49 | Eastern Counties, Norwich (NK) | LKH102 |
| 2866 * | HPW 103 | Bristol K6B | 68.196 | H30/26R | 8/49 | Eastern Counties, Norwich (NK) | LKH103 |
| 2867 * | HPW 104 | Bristol K6B | 68.197 | H30/26R | 9/49 | Eastern Counties, Norwich (NK) | LKH104 |
| 2868 * | HPW 105 | Bristol K6B | 72.019 | H30/26R | 9/49 | Eastern Counties, Norwich (NK) | LKH105 |
| 2869 * | HPW 106 | Bristol K6B | 72.021 | H30/26R | 9/49 | Eastern Counties, Norwich (NK) | LKH106 |
| 2870 * | HPW 107 | Bristol K5G | 72.088 | H30/26R | 1/49 | Eastern Counties, Norwich (NK) | LKH107 |
| 2871 * | HPW 108 | Bristol K5G | 72.089 | H30/26R | 1/49 | Eastern Counties, Norwich (NK) | LKH108 |
| 2872 * | HPW 109 | Bristol K5G | 72.074 | H30/26R | 1/49 | Eastern Counties, Norwich (NK) | LKH109 |
| 2873 * | HPW 110 | Bristol K5G | 72.066 | H30/26R | 1/49 | Eastern Counties, Norwich (NK) | LKH110 |
| 2874 * | HPW 111 | Bristol K5G | 72.075 | H30/26R | 1/49 | Eastern Counties, Norwich (NK) | LKH111 |
| 2875 * | HPW 112 | Bristol K5G | 72.073 | H30/26R | 1/49 | Eastern Counties, Norwich (NK) | LKH112 |
| 2876 * | HPW 113 | Bristol K5G | 72.076 | H30/26R | 1/49 | Eastern Counties, Norwich (NK) | LKH113 |
| 2877 * | HPW 114 | Bristol K5G | 72.077 | H30/26R | 1/49 | Eastern Counties, Norwich (NK) | LKH114 |
| 2878 * | HPW 115 | Bristol K5G | 74.066 | H30/26R | 2/49 | Eastern Counties, Norwich (NK) | LKH115 |
| 2879 * | HPW 116 | Bristol K5G | 74.067 | H30/26R | 2/49 | Eastern Counties, Norwich (NK) | LKH116 |
| 2880 * | HPW 117 | Bristol K5G | 74.074 | H30/26R | 2/49 | Eastern Counties, Norwich (NK) | LKH117 |
| 2881 * | HPW 118 | Bristol K5G | 74.065 | H30/26R | 2/49 | Eastern Counties, Norwich (NK) | LKH118 |
| 2882 * | HPW 119 | Bristol K5G | 74.075 | H30/26R | 2/49 | Eastern Counties, Norwich (NK) | LKH119 |
| 2883 * | HPW 120 | Bristol K5G | 74.076 | H30/26R | 2/49 | Eastern Counties, Norwich (NK) | LKH120 |
| 2884 * | HPW 121 | Bristol K5G | 74.077 | H30/26R | 2/49 | Eastern Counties, Norwich (NK) | LKH121 |
| 2885 * | HPW 122 | Bristol K5G | 74.078 | H30/26R | 2/49 | Eastern Counties, Norwich (NK) | LKH122 |
| 2886 * | HPW 123 | Bristol K5G | 74.099 | H30/26R | 2/49 | Eastern Counties, Norwich (NK) | LKH123 |
| 2887 * | HPW 124 | Bristol K5G | 74.098 | H30/26R | 5/49 | Eastern Counties, Norwich (NK) | LKH124 |
| 2888 * | HPW 125 | Bristol K5G | 74.115 | H30/26R | 5/49 | Eastern Counties, Norwich (NK) | LKH125 |
| 2889 * | HPW 126 | Bristol K5G | 74.111 | H30/26R | 5/49 | Eastern Counties, Norwich (NK) | LKH126 |
| 2890 * | HPW 127 | Bristol K5G | 74.112 | H30/26R | 5/49 | Eastern Counties, Norwich (NK) | LKH127 |
| 2891 * | HPW 128 | Bristol K5G | 74.113 | H30/26R | 5/49 | Eastern Counties, Norwich (NK) | LKH128 |
| 2892 * | HPW 129 | Bristol K5G | 74.114 | H30/26R | 5/49 | Eastern Counties, Norwich (NK) | LKH129 |
| 2893 * | HPW 131 | Bristol K5G | 74.145 | H30/26R | 5/49 | Eastern Counties, Norwich (NK) | LKH131 |
| 2894 * | HPW 130 | Bristol K5G | 74.146 | H30/26R | 5/49 | Eastern Counties, Norwich (NK) | LKH130 |
| 2895 * | HPW 132 | Bristol K5G | 74.147 | H30/26R | 5/49 | Eastern Counties, Norwich (NK) | LKH132 |
| 2896 * | HPW 133 | Bristol K5G | 74.152 | H30/26R | 5/49 | Eastern Counties, Norwich (NK) | LKH133 |
| 2897 * | HPW 134 | Bristol K5G | 74.153 | H30/26R | 5/49 | Eastern Counties, Norwich (NK) | LKH134 |
| 2898 * | HPW 135 | Bristol K5G | 74.154 | H30/26R | 5/49 | Eastern Counties, Norwich (NK) | LKH135 |
| 2899 * | HPW 136 | Bristol K5G | 74.167 | H30/26R | 5/49 | Eastern Counties, Norwich (NK) | LKH136 |
| 2900 * | HPW 137 | Bristol K5G | 74.168 | H30/26R | 5/49 | Eastern Counties, Norwich (NK) | LKH137 |
| 2901 * | HPW 138 | Bristol K5G | 74.169 | H30/26R | 5/49 | Eastern Counties, Norwich (NK) | LKH138 |

| 2902 * | HPW 139 | Bristol K6B | 72.033 | H30/26R | 9/49 | Eastern Counties, Norwich (NK) LKH139 |
|---|---|---|---|---|---|---|
| 2903 * | HPW 140 | Bristol K6B | 72.020 | H30/26R | 9/49 | Eastern Counties, Norwich (NK) LKH140 |
| 2904 * | HPW 141 | Bristol K6B | 72.052 | H30/26R | 9/49 | Eastern Counties, Norwich (NK) LKH141 |
| 2905 * | HPW 142 | Bristol K6B | 72.053 | H30/26R | 9/49 | Eastern Counties, Norwich (NK) LKH142 |
| 2906 | FBE 321 | Bristol K6A | 68.003 | H30/26R | 9/48 | Lincolnshire RCC, Bracebridge Heath (KN) 717 |
| 2907 | FBE 322 | Bristol K6A | 68.004 | H30/26R | 9/48 | Lincolnshire RCC, Bracebridge Heath (KN) 718 |
| 2908 | FBE 323 | Bristol K6B | 68.062 | H30/26R | 11/48 | Lincolnshire RCC, Bracebridge Heath (KN) 719 |
| 2909 | GWX 111 | Bristol K6B | 68.066 | H30/26R | 10/48 | York-West Yorkshire, Harrogate (WR) Y754 |
| 2910 | GWX 112 | Bristol K6B | 68.067 | H30/26R | 10/48 | York-West Yorkshire, Harrogate (WR) Y755 |
| 2911 | GWX 114 | Bristol K6B | 68.148 | H30/26R | 12/48 | York-West Yorkshire, Harrogate (WR) Y757 |
| 2912 | GWX 116 | Bristol K6B | 68.150 | H30/26R | 12/48 | York-West Yorkshire, Harrogate (WR) Y759 |
| 2913 | GWX 113 | Bristol K6B | 68.147 | H30/26R | 12/48 | York-West Yorkshire, Harrogate (WR) Y756 |
| 2914 | GWX 115 | Bristol K6B | 68.149 | H30/26R | 12/48 | York-West Yorkshire, Harrogate (WR) Y758 |
| 2915 | GWX 117 | Bristol K6B | 68.151 | H30/26R | 12/48 | York-West Yorkshire, Harrogate (WR) Y760 |
| 2916 | GWX 118 | Bristol K6B | 74.142 | H30/26R | 6/49 | York-West Yorkshire, Harrogate (WR) Y761 |
| 2917 | GWX 119 | Bristol K6B | 74.143 | H30/26R | 6/49 | York-West Yorkshire, Harrogate (WR) Y762 |
| 2918 * | GWX 120 | Bristol K6B | 74.144 | H30/26R | 9/49 | York-West Yorkshire, Harrogate (WR) Y763 |
| 2919 * | LHT 916 | Bristol L6A | 67.193 | B35R | 10/48 | Bath Tramways Motor Co (SO) 2272 |
| 2920 * | LHT 917 | Bristol L6A | 67.194 | B35R | 10/48 | Bath Tramways Motor Co (SO) 2273 |
| 2921 * | LHT 918 | Bristol L6A | 67.196 | B35R | 11/48 | Bristol Tramways (GL) 2392 |
| 2922 * | LHT 919 | Bristol L6A | 67.197 | B35R | 11/48 | Bristol Tramways (GL) 2393 |
| 2923 * | LHT 920 | Bristol L6A | 67.198 | B35R | 11/48 | Bath Tramways Motor Co (SO) 2274 |
| 2924 * | LHU 501 | Bristol L6B | 71.005 | B35R | 11/48 | Bath Tramways Motor Co (SO) 2275 |
| 2925 * | LHU 502 | Bristol L6B | 71.006 | B35R | 12/48 | Bristol Tramways (GL) 2394 |
| 2926 * | LHU 503 | Bristol L6B | 71.007 | B35R | 12/48 | Bristol Tramways (GL) 2395 |
| 2927 * | LHU 504 | Bristol L6B | 71.012 | B35R | 1/49 | Bristol Tramways (GL) 2396 |
| 2928 * | LHW 902 | Bristol L5G | 71.058 | B35R | 1/49 | Bristol Tramways (GL) 2399 |
| 2929 * | LHW 903 | Bristol L5G | 71.059 | B35R | 1/49 | Bristol Tramways (GL) 2400 |
| 2930 * | LHW 905 | Bristol L6B | 71.061 | B35R | 1/49 | Bristol Tramways (GL) 2402 |
| 2931 * | LHW 917 | Bristol L6B | 71.073 | B35R | 2/49 | Bath Tramways Motor Co (SO) 2281 |
| 2932 * | LHW 920 | Bristol L5G | 71.076 | B35R | 2/49 | Bath Tramways Motor Co (SO) 2282 |
| 2933 * | LHW 922 | Bristol L6A | 71.078 | B35R | 2/49 | Bath Tramways Motor Co (SO) 2283 |
| 2934 | JFM 112 | Bristol L6A | 67.170 | B35R | 6/48 | Crosville MS, Chester (CH) KB83 |
| 2935 | JFM 114 | Bristol L6A | 67.171 | B35R | 6/48 | Crosville MS, Chester (CH) KB85 |
| 2936 | JFM 113 | Bristol L6A | 67.172 | B35R | 6/48 | Crosville MS, Chester (CH) KB84 |
| 2937 | JFM 111 | Bristol L6A | 67.173 | B35R | 5/48 | Crosville MS, Chester (CH) KB82 |
| 2938 | JFM 115 | Bristol L6A | 67.174 | B35R | 6/48 | Crosville MS, Chester (CH) KB86 |
| 2939 * | JFM 116 | Bristol L6A | 71.021 | B35R | 9/48 | Crosville MS, Chester (CH) KB87 |
| 2940 * | JFM 117 | Bristol L6A | 71.022 | B35R | 9/48 | Crosville MS, Chester (CH) KB88 |
| 2941 * | JFM 118 | Bristol L6A | 71.027 | B35R | 9/48 | Crosville MS, Chester (CH) KB89 |
| 2942 * | NNO 108 | Bristol L5G | 71.014 | B35R | 8/48 | Eastern National, Chelmsford (EX) 4008 |
| 2943 * | NNO 109 | Bristol L5G | 71.015 | B35R | 9/48 | Eastern National, Chelmsford (EX) 4009 |
| 2944 * | NNO 110 | Bristol L5G | 71.016 | B35R | 9/48 | Eastern National, Chelmsford (EX) 4010 |
| 2945 | HLJ 45 | Bristol L6A | 67.181 | B35R | 6/48 | Hants & Dorset, Bournemouth (HA) TS840 |
| 2946 | HLJ 46 | Bristol L6A | 67.182 | B35R | 7/48 | Hants & Dorset, Bournemouth (HA) TS841 |
| 2947 | HLJ 47 | Bristol L6A | 67.183 | B35R | 7/48 | Hants & Dorset, Bournemouth (HA) TS842 |
| 2948 * | HLJ 48 | Bristol L6A | 67.195 | B35R | 8/48 | Hants & Dorset, Bournemouth (HA) TS843 |
| 2949 * | FBE 324 | Bristol L6B | 67.199 | B35R | 8/48 | Lincolnshire RCC, Bracebridge Heath (KN) 720 |
| 2950 * | FBE 325 | Bristol L6B | 67.200 | B35R | 8/48 | Lincolnshire RCC, Bracebridge Heath (KN) 721 |
| 2951 * | KHN 424 | Bristol L6B | 71.036 | B35R | 11/48 | United AS, Darlington (DM) BLO324 |
| 2952 * | KHN 425 | Bristol L6B | 71.037 | B35R | 11/48 | United AS, Darlington (DM) BLO325 |
| 2953 * | KHN 426 | Bristol L6B | 71.040 | B35R | 11/48 | United AS, Darlington (DM) BLO326 |
| 2954 * | KHN 427 | Bristol L5G | 71.031 | B35R | 11/48 | United AS, Darlington (DM) BLO327 |
| 2955 * | KHN 428 | Bristol L5G | 71.032 | B35R | 11/48 | United AS, Darlington (DM) BLO328 |
| 2956 * | KHN 429 | Bristol L6B | 71.041 | B35R | 1/49 | United AS, Darlington (DM) BLO329 |
| 2957 * | KHN 430 | Bristol L6B | 71.042 | B35R | 1/49 | United AS, Darlington (DM) BLO330 |
| 2958 * | KHN 431 | Bristol L6B | 71.046 | B35R | 5/49 | United AS, Darlington (DM) BLO331 |
| 2959 * | KHN 432 | Bristol L6B | 71.047 | B35R | 5/49 | United AS, Darlington (DM) BLO332 |
| 2960 * | KHN 433 | Bristol L6B | 71.048 | B35R | 5/49 | United AS, Darlington (DM) BLO333 |
| 2961 * | KHN 434 | Bristol L6B | 71.049 | B35R | 5/49 | United AS, Darlington (DM) BLO334 |
| 2962 * | KHN 435 | Bristol L6B | 71.050 | DP31R | 6/49 | United AS, Darlington (DM) BLO335 |
| 2963 | EBD 234 | Bristol L6B | 71.023 | DP31R | 8/48 | United Counties, Northampton (NO) 107 |
| 2964 | EBD 235 | Bristol L6B | 71.024 | DP31R | 9/48 | United Counties, Northampton (NO) 108 |
| 2965 * | GWX 131 | Bristol L5G | 71.043 | B35R | 10/48 | West Yorkshire RCC, Harrogate (WR) 246 |

| | | | | | | |
|---|---|---|---|---|---|---|
| 2966 * | GWX 133 | Bristol L5G | 71.045 | B35R | 10/48 | West Yorkshire RCC, Harrogate (WR) 248 |
| 2967 * | GWX 132 | Bristol L5G | 71.044 | B35R | 10/48 | West Yorkshire RCC, Harrogate (WR) 247 |
| 2968 * | HRU 32 | Bristol L6A | 71.025 | B35R | 9/48 | Hants & Dorset, Bournemouth (HA) TS844 |
| 2969 * | HRU 33 | Bristol L6A | 71.026 | B35R | 9/48 | Hants & Dorset, Bournemouth (HA) TS845 |
| 2970 | | | | | | Not Built |
| 2971 | | | | | | Not Built |
| 2972 | | | | | | Not Built |
| 2973 * | FT 4497 | Leyland TD5 | 16710 | H30/26R | 10/48 | Tynemouth & District (ND) T97 |
| 2974 * | FT 4500 | Leyland TD5 | 16713 | H30/26R | 10/48 | Tynemouth & District (ND) T100 |
| 2975 * | FT 4498 | Leyland TD5 | 16711 | H30/26R | 10/48 | Tynemouth & District (ND) T98 |
| 2976 * | FT 4502 | Leyland TD5 | 16715 | H30/26R | 10/48 | Tynemouth & District (ND) T102 |
| 2977 * | FT 4499 | Leyland TD5 | 16712 | H30/26R | 12/48 | Tynemouth & District (ND) T99 |
| 2978 * | FT 4496 | Leyland TD5 | 16709 | H30/26R | 12/48 | Tynemouth & District (ND) T96 |
| 2979 * | FT 4501 | Leyland TD5 | 16714 | H30/26R | 12/48 | Tynemouth & District (ND) T101 |
| 2980 * | FT 4503 | Leyland TD5 | 16716 | H30/26R | 12/48 | Tynemouth & District (ND) T103 |
| 2981 | GWO 882 | Albion CX19 | 60037E | L27/28R | 7/48 | Red & White, Chepstow (MH) 882 |
| 2982 | FCY 405 | Albion CX19 | 60037H | L27/28R | 7/48 | United Welsh, Swansea (GG) 944 |
| 2983 | GWO 883 | Albion CX19 | 60037J | L27/28R | 7/48 | Red & White, Chepstow (MH) 883 |
| 2984 | FCY 406 | Albion CX19 | 60037K | L27/28R | 7/48 | United Welsh, Swansea (GG) 945 |
| 2985 | GWO 884 | Albion CX19 | 60037D | L27/28R | 7/48 | Red & White, Chepstow (MH) 884 |
| 2986 | FCY 407 | Albion CX19 | 60038A | L27/28R | 7/48 | United Welsh, Swansea (GG) 946 |
| 2987 | GWO 885 | Albion CX19 | 60038E | L27/28R | 7/48 | Red & White, Chepstow (MH) 885 |
| 2988 | FCY 408 | Albion CX19 | 60038B | L27/28R | 7/48 | United Welsh, Swansea (GG) 947 |
| 2989 | GWO 886 | Albion CX19 | 60038D | L27/28R | 7/48 | Red & White, Chepstow (MH) 886 |
| 2990 | FCY 409 | Albion CX19 | 60038C | L27/28R | 7/48 | United Welsh, Swansea (GG) 948 |
| 2991 | GWO 887 | Albion CX19 | 60039D | L27/28R | 7/48 | Red & White, Chepstow (MH) 887 |
| 2992 | GWO 916 | Albion CX19 | 60041F | L27/28R | 8/48 | Red & White, Chepstow (MH) 889 |
| 2993 | GWO 917 | Albion CX19 | 60041J | L27/28R | 8/48 | Red & White, Chepstow (MH) 890 |
| 2994 | FCY 412 | Albion CX19 | 60041H | L27/28R | 9/48 | United Welsh, Swansea (GG) 951 |
| 2995 | GWO 918 | Albion CX19 | 60041K | L27/28R | 8/48 | Red & White, Chepstow (MH) 891 |
| 2996 | FCY 410 | Albion CX19 | 60040J | L27/28R | 9/48 | United Welsh, Swansea (GG) 949 |
| 2997 | GWO 888 | Albion CX19 | 60040K | L27/28R | 8/48 | Red & White, Chepstow (MH) 888 |
| 2998 | FCY 411 | Albion CX19 | 60041E | L27/28R | 9/48 | United Welsh, Swansea (GG) 950 |
| 2999 | GWO 921 | Albion CX19 | 60042E | L27/28R | 8/48 | Red & White, Chepstow (MH) 894 |
| 3000 | GWO 925 | Albion CX19 | 60043B | L27/28R | 8/48 | Red & White, Chepstow (MH) 898 |
| 3001 | GWO 919 | Albion CX19 | 60041L | L27/28R | 8/48 | Red & White, Chepstow (MH) 892 |
| 3002 | GWO 920 | Albion CX19 | 60042C | L27/28R | 8/48 | Red & White, Chepstow (MH) 893 |
| 3003 | GWO 922 | Albion CX19 | 60042F | L27/28R | 8/48 | Red & White, Chepstow (MH) 895 |
| 3004 | GWO 923 | Albion CX19 | 60042H | L27/28R | 8/48 | Red & White, Chepstow (MH) 896 |
| 3005 | GWO 924 | Albion CX19 | 60042K | L27/28R | 8/48 | Red & White, Chepstow (MH) 897 |
| 3006 | ADC 654 | Leyland PD1/3 | 490963 | H30/26R | 3/49 | Middlesbrough Corporation (NR) 54 |
| 3007 | ADC 653 | Leyland PD1/3 | 490962 | H30/26R | 5/49 | Middlesbrough Corporation (NR) 53 |
| 3008 | ADC 655 | Leyland PD1/3 | 490964 | H30/26R | 5/49 | Middlesbrough Corporation (NR) 55 |
| 3009 | ADC 656 | Leyland PD1/3 | 491057 | H30/26R | 6/49 | Middlesbrough Corporation (NR) 56 |
| 3010 | ADC 657 | Leyland PD1/3 | 491058 | H30/26R | 6/49 | Middlesbrough Corporation (NR) 57 |
| 3011 | ADC 658 | Leyland PD1/3 | 491059 | H30/26R | 6/49 | Middlesbrough Corporation (NR) 58 |
| 3012 | ADC 659 | Leyland PD1/3 | 491060 | H30/26R | 6/49 | Middlesbrough Corporation (NR) 59 |
| 3013 | ADC 660 | Leyland PD1/3 | 491061 | H30/26R | 6/49 | Middlesbrough Corporation (NR) 60 |
| 3014 | ADC 661 | Leyland PD1/3 | 491591 | H30/26R | 7/49 | Middlesbrough Corporation (NR) 61 |
| 3015 | ADC 662 | Leyland PD1/3 | 491590 | H30/26R | 7/49 | Middlesbrough Corporation (NR) 62 |
| 3016 | ADC 663 | Leyland PD1/3 | 492132 | H30/26R | 7/49 | Middlesbrough Corporation (NR) 63 |
| 3017 | ADC 664 | Leyland PD1/3 | 492133 | H30/26R | 7/49 | Middlesbrough Corporation (NR) 64 |
| 3018 | ADC 665 | Leyland PD1/3 | 492167 | H30/26R | 7/49 | Middlesbrough Corporation (NR) 65 |
| 3019 | ADC 666 | Leyland PD1/3 | 492168 | H30/26R | 7/49 | Middlesbrough Corporation (NR) 66 |
| 3020 | ADC 668 | Leyland PD1/3 | 493173 | H30/26R | 9/49 | Middlesbrough Corporation (NR) 68 |
| 3021 | ADC 667 | Leyland PD1/3 | 493172 | H30/26R | 9/49 | Middlesbrough Corporation (NR) 67 |
| 3022 * | JXT 490 | Leyland PS1/1 | 481867 | DP31R | 9/48 | Birch Bros, London NW5 (LN) K90 |
| 3023 * | JXT 492 | Leyland PS1/1 | 482502 | DP31R | 9/48 | Birch Bros, London NW5 (LN) K92 |
| 3024 * | JXT 493 | Leyland PS1/1 | 482621 | DP31R | 10/48 | Birch Bros, London NW5 (LN) K93 |
| 3025 * | JXT 491 | Leyland PS1/1 | 481997 | DP31R | 10/48 | Birch Bros, London NW5 (LN) K91 |
| 3026 * | JXT 494 | Leyland PS1/1 | 482670 | DP31R | 10/48 | Birch Bros, London NW5 (LN) K94 |
| 3027 * | JXT 495 | Leyland PS1/1 | 482671 | DP31R | 10/48 | Birch Bros, London NW5 (LN) K95 |
| 3028 * | BHN 269 | Leyland TS7 | 8892 | B35R | 11/48 | United AS, Darlington (DM) LTO19 |
| 3029 * | AHN 431 | Leyland TS7 | 5608 | B35R | 11/48 | United AS, Darlington (DM) LTO1 |

| 3030 * | BHN 263 | Leyland TS7 | 8338 | B35R | 11/48 | United AS, Darlington (DM) LTO13 |
|---|---|---|---|---|---|---|
| 3031 * | BHN 276 | Leyland TS7 | 8895 | B35R | 11/48 | United AS, Darlington (DM) LTO26 |
| 3032 * | AHN 385 | Leyland TS7 | 5606 | B35R | 12/48 | United AS, Darlington (DM) LTO6 |
| 3033 * | BHN 271 | Leyland TS7 | 8889 | B35R | 12/48 | United AS, Darlington (DM) LTO21 |
| 3034 * | BHN 278 | Leyland TS7 | 8897 | B35R | 12/48 | United AS, Darlington (DM) LTO28 |
| 3035 * | AHN 814 | Leyland TS7 | 7058 | B35R | 12/48 | United AS, Darlington (DM) LTO10 |
| 3036 * | BHN 261 | Leyland TS7 | 8335 | B35R | 12/48 | United AS, Darlington (DM) LTO11 |
| 3037 * | BHN 279 | Leyland TS7 | 8898 | B35R | 12/48 | United AS, Darlington (DM) LTO29 |
| 3038 * | AHN 812 | Leyland TS7 | 7056 | B35R | 12/48 | United AS, Darlington (DM) LTO8 |
| 3039 * | BHN 268 | Leyland TS7 | 8888 | B35R | 12/48 | United AS, Darlington (DM) LTO18 |
| 3040 * | BHN 272 | Leyland TS7 | 8890 | B35R | 12/48 | United AS, Darlington (DM) LTO22 |
| 3041 * | AHN 433 | Leyland TS7 | 5610 | B35R | 12/48 | United AS, Darlington (DM) LTO3 |
| 3042 * | AHN 434 | Leyland TS7 | 7059 | B35R | 1/49 | United AS, Darlington (DM) LTO4 |
| 3043 * | AHN 435 | Leyland TS7 | 7060 | B35R | 1/49 | United AS, Darlington (DM) LTO5 |
| 3044 * | BHN 265 | Leyland TS7 | 8337 | B35R | 1/49 | United AS, Darlington (DM) LTO15 |
| 3045 * | BHN 270 | Leyland TS7 | 8893 | B35R | 1/49 | United AS, Darlington (DM) LTO20 |
| 3046 * | AHN 432 | Leyland TS7 | 5609 | B35R | 1/49 | United AS, Darlington (DM) LTO2 |
| 3047 * | AHN 811 | Leyland TS7 | 5607 | B35R | 1/49 | United AS, Darlington (DM) LTO7 |
| 3048 * | BHN 262 | Leyland TS7 | 8336 | B35R | 2/49 | United AS, Darlington (DM) LTO12 |
| 3049 * | BHN 275 | Leyland TS7 | 8894 | B35R | 2/49 | United AS, Darlington (DM) LTO25 |
| 3050 * | BHN 273 | Leyland TS7 | 8886 | B35R | 2/49 | United AS, Darlington (DM) LTO23 |
| 3051 * | AHN 813 | Leyland TS7 | 7057 | B35R | 2/49 | United AS, Darlington (DM) LTO9 |
| 3052 * | BHN 266 | Leyland TS7 | 8885 | B35R | 2/49 | United AS, Darlington (DM) LTO16 |
| 3053 * | BHN 267 | Leyland TS7 | 8887 | B35R | 2/49 | United AS, Darlington (DM) LTO17 |
| 3054 * | BHN 277 | Leyland TS7 | 8896 | B35R | 2/49 | United AS, Darlington (DM) LTO27 |
| 3055 * | BHN 280 | Leyland TS7 | 8899 | B35R | 3/49 | United AS, Darlington (DM) LTO30 |
| 3056 * | BHN 274 | Leyland TS7 | 8891 | B35R | 3/49 | United AS, Darlington (DM) LTO24 |
| 3057 * | BHN 264 | Leyland TS7 | 8334 | B35R | 3/49 | United AS, Darlington (DM) LTO14 |
| 3058 * | VV 6255 | Bristol JO5G | JO5G.562 | B35R | 12/48 | United Counties, Northampton (NO) 425 |
| 3059 * | NV 6638 | Bristol JO5G | JO5G.136 | B35R | 1/49 | United Counties, Northampton (NO) 423 |
| 3060 * | VV 4564 | Bristol JO5G | JO5G.133 | B35R | 1/49 | United Counties, Northampton (NO) 426 |
| 3061 * | VV 5041 | Bristol JO5G | JO5G.235 | B35R | 1/49 | United Counties, Northampton (NO) 427 |
| 3062 * | VV 5042 | Bristol JO5G | JO5G.236 | B35R | 1/49 | United Counties, Northampton (NO) 428 |
| 3063 * | NV 7496 | Bristol JO5G | JO5G.237 | B35R | 1/49 | United Counties, Northampton (NO) 429 |
| 3064 * | VV 5693 | Bristol JO5G | JO5G.386 | B35R | 1/49 | United Counties, Northampton (NO) 447 |
| 3065 * | NV 7497 | Bristol JO5G | JO5G.238 | B35R | 2/49 | United Counties, Northampton (NO) 430 |
| 3066 * | NV 8666 | Bristol JO5G | JO5G.384 | B35R | 2/49 | United Counties, Northampton (NO) 445 |
| 3067 * | NV 8667 | Bristol JO5G | JO5G.385 | B35R | 3/49 | United Counties, Northampton (NO) 446 |
| 3068 * | VV 5694 | Bristol JO5G | JO5G.387 | B35R | 3/49 | United Counties, Northampton (NO) 448 |
| 3069 * | VV 5695 | Bristol JO5G | JO5G.388 | B35R | 3/49 | United Counties, Northampton (NO) 449 |
| 3070 * | VV 6257 | Bristol JO5G | JO5G.546 | B35R | 4/49 | United Counties, Northampton (NO) 459 |
| 3071 * | VV 6258 | Bristol JO5G | JO5G.547 | B35R | 4/49 | United Counties, Northampton (NO) 460 |
| 3072 * | VV 5696 | Bristol JO5G | JO5G.389 | B35R | 4/49 | United Counties, Northampton (NO) 450 |
| 3073 * | VV 6260 | Bristol JO5G | JO5G.549 | B35R | 4/49 | United Counties, Northampton (NO) 462 |
| 3074 * | WX 2111 | Leyland TD1 | 71098 | L27/26R | 1/49 | Crosville MS, Chester (CH) M247 |
| 3075 * | FM 6415 | Leyland TD1 | 71748 | L27/26R | 1/49 | Crosville MS, Chester (CH) M39 |
| 3076 * | CK 4418 | Leyland TD1 | 71882 | L27/26R | 1/49 | Crosville MS, Chester (CH) M572 |
| 3077 * | FM 6416 | Leyland TD1 | 71749 | L27/26R | 2/49 | Crosville MS, Chester (CH) M40 |
| 3078 * | UF 5644 | Leyland TD1 | 71107 | L27/26R | 8/49 | Crosville MS, Chester (CH) M248 |
| 3079 * | CK 4405 | Leyland TD1 | 71860 | L27/26R | 8/49 | Crosville MS, Chester (CH) M569 |
| 3080 * | CK 4403 | Leyland TD1 | 71858 | L27/26R | 8/49 | Crosville MS, Chester (CH) M575 |
| 3081 * | EK 8106 | Leyland TD1 | 72004 | L27/26R | 8/49 | Crosville MS, Chester (CH) M578 |
| 3082 * | CK 4411 | Leyland TD1 | 71866 | L27/26R | 8/49 | Crosville MS, Chester (CH) M571 |
| 3083 * | CK 4406 | Leyland TD1 | 71861 | L27/26R | 8/49 | Crosville MS, Chester (CH) M570 |
| 3084 * | HL 5339 | Leyland TD2 | 454 | L27/26R | 12/49 | Crosville MS, Chester (CH) M515 |
| 3085 * | HL 5318 | Leyland TD2 | 433 | L27/26R | 1/49 | Crosville MS, Chester (CH) M514 |
| 3086 * | KG 1148 | Leyland TD2 | 1341 | L27/26R | 1/49 | Crosville MS, Chester (CH) M580 |
| 3087 * | KG 1151 | Leyland TD2 | 1344 | L27/26R | 12/48 | Crosville MS, Chester (CH) M581 |
| 3088 * | FM 7467 | Leyland TD2 | 1873 | L27/26R | 1/49 | Crosville MS, Chester (CH) M35 |
| 3089 * | FM 7763 | Leyland TD2 | 2697 | L27/26R | 1/49 | Crosville MS, Chester (CH) M37 |
| 3090 * | FM 7234 | Leyland TD2 | 1391 | L27/26R | 1/49 | Crosville MS, Chester (CH) M27 |
| 3091 * | AG 8246 | Leyland TD2 | 737 | L27/26R | 1/49 | Crosville MS, Chester (CH) M245 |
| 3092 * | FM 6918 | Leyland TD2 | 126 | L27/26R | 3/49 | Crosville MS, Chester (CH) M24 |
| 3093 * | FM 7462 | Leyland TD2 | 2005 | L27/26R | 3/49 | Crosville MS, Chester (CH) M30 |

| | | | | | | |
|---|---|---|---|---|---|---|
| 3094 * | AG 8258 | Leyland TD2 | 749 | L27/26R | 3/49 | Crosville MS, Chester (CH) M246 |
| 3095 * | FM 7461 | Leyland TD2 | 2004 | L27/26R | 3/49 | Crosville MS, Chester (CH) M29 |
| 3096 * | FM 6919 | Leyland TD2 | 127 | L27/26R | 3/49 | Crosville MS, Chester (CH) M25 |
| 3097 * | FM 7466 | Leyland TD2 | 1872 | L27/26R | 3/49 | Crosville MS, Chester (CH) M34 |
| 3098 * | FM 7463 | Leyland TD2 | 2006 | L27/26R | 8/49 | Crosville MS, Chester (CH) M31 |
| 3099 * | FM 6920 | Leyland TD2 | 128 | L27/26R | 8/49 | Crosville MS, Chester (CH) M1 |
| 3100 * | FM 6276 | Leyland TD3 | 3223 | L27/26R | 8/49 | Crosville MS, Chester (CH) M10 |
| 3101 * | GP 6231 | AEC Regent | 6611669 | L27/28R | 11/48 | Crosville MS, Chester (CH) MA601 |
| 3102 * | GP 6238 | AEC Regent | 6611676 | L27/28R | 12/48 | Crosville MS, Chester (CH) MA605 |
| 3103 * | GP 6242 | AEC Regent | 6611680 | L27/28R | 12/48 | Crosville MS, Chester (CH) MA602 |
| 3104 * | GN 6206 | AEC Regent | 6611520 | L27/28R | 12/48 | Crosville MS, Chester (CH) MA603 |
| 3105 * | GW 6255 | AEC Regent | 6611730 | L27/28R | 12/48 | Crosville MS, Chester (CH) MA606 |
| 3106 * | GW 6288 | AEC Regent | 6611791 | L27/28R | 12/48 | Crosville MS, Chester (CH) MA604 |
| 3107 * | FM 8984 | Leyland LT7 | 5900 | B35R | 5/49 | Crosville MS, Chester (CH) JA14 |
| 3108 * | FM 8979 | Leyland LT7 | 5895 | B35R | 5/49 | Crosville MS, Chester (CH) JA9 |
| 3109 * | FM 8988 | Leyland LT7 | 6140 | B35R | 5/49 | Crosville MS, Chester (CH) JA18 |
| 3110 * | FM 8993 | Leyland LT7 | 6145 | B35R | 5/49 | Crosville MS, Chester (CH) JA23 |
| 3111 * | FM 8977 | Leyland LT7 | 5893 | B35R | 5/49 | Crosville MS, Chester (CH) JA7 |
| 3112 * | FM 8996 | Leyland LT7 | 5905 | B35R | 5/49 | Crosville MS, Chester (CH) JA26 |
| 3113 * | FM 8983 | Leyland LT7 | 5899 | B35R | 5/49 | Crosville MS, Chester (CH) JA13 |
| 3114 * | FM 8998 | Leyland LT7 | 5907 | B35R | 5/49 | Crosville MS, Chester (CH) JA28 |
| 3115 * | FM 8994 | Leyland LT7 | 5903 | B35R | 5/49 | Crosville MS, Chester (CH) JA24 |
| 3116 * | FM 8975 | Leyland LT7 | 5891 | B35R | 5/49 | Crosville MS, Chester (CH) JA5 |
| 3117 * | FM 8976 | Leyland LT7 | 5892 | B35R | 5/49 | Crosville MS, Chester (CH) JA6 |
| 3118 * | FM 8985 | Leyland LT7 | 5901 | B35R | 5/49 | Crosville MS, Chester (CH) JA15 |
| 3119 * | FM 8997 | Leyland LT7 | 5906 | B35R | 5/49 | Crosville MS, Chester (CH) JA27 |
| 3120 * | FM 8991 | Leyland LT7 | 6143 | B35R | 5/49 | Crosville MS, Chester (CH) JA221 |
| 3121 * | FM 8978 | Leyland LT7 | 5894 | B35R | 5/49 | Crosville MS, Chester (CH) JA8 |
| 3122 * | FM 7482 | Leyland LT5 | 1953 | B33R | 3/49 | Crosville MS, Chester (CH) FA2 |
| 3123 * | SM 8851 | Leyland LT2 | 51601 | B31R | 2/49 | Caledonian OC, Dumfries (DF) 346 |
| 3124 * | SM 8852 | Leyland LT2 | 51602 | B31R | 2/49 | Caledonian OC, Dumfries (DF) 347 |
| 3125 * | SM 8853 | Leyland LT2 | 51603 | B31R | 2/49 | Caledonian OC, Dumfries (DF) 348 |
| 3126 * | SM 8854 | Leyland LT2 | 51604 | B31R | 2/49 | Caledonian OC, Dumfries (DF) 349 |
| 3127 * | SM 9502 | Leyland LT5 | 1706 | B33R | 2/49 | Caledonian OC, Dumfries (DF) 351 |
| 3128 * | SM 9501 | Leyland LT5 | 1705 | B33R | 3/49 | Caledonian OC, Dumfries (DF) 350 |
| 3129 * | BSM 826 | Dennis Lancet II | 175052 | B35R | 3/49 | Caledonian OC, Dumfries (DF) 352 |
| 3130 * | DSM 453 | Dennis Lancet II | 175486 | B35R | 3/49 | Caledonian OC, Dumfries (DF) 353 |
| 3131 * | ENO 932 | Bristol GO5G | GO5G.187 | L27/28R | 1/49 | Eastern National, Chelmsford (EX) 3654 |
| 3132 * | ENO 933 | Bristol GO5G | GO5G.188 | L27/28R | 1/49 | Eastern National, Chelmsford (EX) 3655 |
| 3133 * | DEV 479 | Bristol GO5G | GO5G.78 | L27/28R | 1/49 | Eastern National, Chelmsford (EX) 3643 |
| 3134 * | DEV 478 | Bristol GO5G | GO5G.77 | L27/28R | 1/49 | Eastern National, Chelmsford (EX) 3642 |
| 3135 * | DEV 477 | Bristol GO5G | GO5G.76 | L27/28R | 1/49 | Eastern National, Chelmsford (EX) 3641 |
| 3136 * | ENO 931 | Bristol GO5G | GO5G.186 | L27/28R | 1/49 | Eastern National, Chelmsford (EX) 3653 |
| 3137 * | DEV 480 | Bristol GO5G | GO5G.79 | L27/28R | 1/49 | Eastern National, Chelmsford (EX) 3644 |
| 3138 * | DEV 470 | Bristol GO5G | GO5G.69 | L27/28R | 1/49 | Eastern National, Chelmsford (EX) 3634 |
| 3139 * | DEV 476 | Bristol GO5G | GO5G.75 | L27/28R | 1/49 | Eastern National, Chelmsford (EX) 3640 |
| 3140 * | BTW 498 | Leyland TD3 | 5731 | L27/28R | 7/49 | Eastern National, Chelmsford (EX) 3559 |
| 3141 * | ENO 937 | Leyland TD4 | 13158 | L27/28R | 6/49 | Eastern National, Chelmsford (EX) 3659 |
| 3142 * | ENO 936 | Leyland TD4 | 13157 | L27/28R | 6/49 | Eastern National, Chelmsford (EX) 3658 |
| 3143 * | ENO 935 | Leyland TD4 | 13156 | L27/28R | 7/49 | Eastern National, Chelmsford (EX) 3657 |
| 3144 * | ENO 939 | Leyland TD4 | 13160 | L27/28R | 2/50 | Eastern National, Chelmsford (EX) 3661 |
| 3145 * | FEV 179 | Leyland TD5 | 14562 | L27/28R | 5/49 | Eastern National, Chelmsford (EX) 3710 |
| 3146 * | FEV 176 | Leyland TD5 | 14436 | L27/28R | 6/49 | Eastern National, Chelmsford (EX) 3707 |
| 3147 * | FEV 180 | Leyland TD5 | 14563 | L27/28R | 8/49 | Eastern National, Chelmsford (EX) 3711 |
| 3148 * | FEV 178 | Leyland TD5 | 14438 | L27/28R | 9/49 | Eastern National, Chelmsford (EX) 3709 |
| 3149 * | FEV 177 | Leyland TD5 | 14437 | L27/28R | 10/49 | Eastern National, Chelmsford (EX) 3708 |
| 3150 * | FEV 182 | Leyland TD5 | 14565 | L27/28R | 12/49 | Eastern National, Chelmsford (EX) 3713 |
| 3151 * | FEV 175 | Leyland TD5 | 14435 | L27/28R | 12/49 | Eastern National, Chelmsford (EX) 3706 |
| 3152 * | FEV 181 | Leyland TD5 | 14564 | L27/28R | 1/50 | Eastern National, Chelmsford (EX) 3712 |
| 3153 * | UH 7175 | Leyland TD1 | 70932 | L27/26R | 1/49 | Southern Vectis, Newport (IW) 709 |
| 3154 * | TF 6821 | Leyland TD1 | 72309 | L27/26R | 1/49 | Southern Vectis, Newport (IW) 708 |
| 3155 * | CHN 101 | Bristol GO5G | GO5G.155 | L27/28R | 6/49 | United AS, Darlington (DM) BDO11 |
| 3156 * | CHN 103 | Bristol GO5G | GO5G.157 | L27/28R | 6/49 | United AS, Darlington (DM) BDO13 |
| 3157 * | CHN 104 | Bristol GO5G | GO5G.158 | L27/28R | 6/49 | United AS, Darlington (DM) BDO14 |

| | | | | | | |
|---|---|---|---|---|---|---|
| 3158 * | CHN 106 | Bristol GO5G | GO5G.160 | L27/28R | 6/49 | United AS, Darlington (DM) BDO16 |
| 3159 * | CHN 102 | Bristol GO5G | GO5G.156 | L27/28R | 6/49 | United AS, Darlington (DM) BDO12 |
| 3160 * | CHN 105 | Bristol GO5G | GO5G.159 | L27/28R | 6/49 | United AS, Darlington (DM) BDO15 |
| 3161 * | HN 9012 | Leyland TD2 | 2566 | L27/28R | 1/49 | United AS, Darlington (DM) LDO78 |
| 3162 * | HN 9013 | Leyland TD2 | 2567 | L27/26R | 1/49 | United AS, Darlington (DM) LDO79 |
| 3163 * | TF 7211 | Leyland TD2 | 129 | L27/26R | 1/49 | United AS, Darlington (DM) LDO71 |
| 3164 * | TF 9947 | Leyland TD2 | 1869 | L27/26R | 4/49 | United AS, Darlington (DM) LDO72 |
| 3165 * | HN 9007 | Leyland TD2 | 2561 | L27/26R | 4/49 | United AS, Darlington (DM) LDO73 |
| 3166 * | HN 9010 | Leyland TD2 | 2564 | L27/26R | 4/49 | United AS, Darlington (DM) LDO76 |
| 3167 * | HN 9014 | Leyland TD2 | 2568 | L27/26R | 3/49 | United AS, Darlington (DM) LDO80 |
| 3168 * | HN 9011 | Leyland TD2 | 2565 | L27/26R | 3/49 | United AS, Darlington (DM) LDO77 |
| 3169 * | HN 9008 | Leyland TD2 | 2562 | L27/26R | 3/49 | United AS, Darlington (DM) LDO74 |
| 3170 * | HN 9009 | Leyland TD2 | 2563 | L27/26R | 3/49 | United AS, Darlington (DM) LDO75 |
| 3171 * | NV 2276 | Leyland TD2 | 2493 | L27/26R | 1/49 | United Counties, Northampton (NO) 277 |
| 3172 * | NV 2270 | Leyland TD2 | 2487 | L27/26R | 1/49 | United Counties, Northampton (NO) 271 |
| 3173 * | NV 2277 | Leyland TD2 | 2494 | L27/26R | 1/49 | United Counties, Northampton (NO) 278 |
| 3174 * | NV 2280 | Leyland TD2 | 2497 | L27/26R | 1/49 | United Counties, Northampton (NO) 281 |
| 3175 * | NV 2272 | Leyland TD2 | 2489 | L27/26R | 1/49 | United Counties, Northampton (NO) 273 |
| 3176 * | NV 2268 | Leyland TD2 | 2485 | L27/26R | 4/49 | United Counties, Northampton (NO) 269 |
| 3177 * | NV 2271 | Leyland TD2 | 2488 | L27/26R | 8/49 | United Counties, Northampton (NO) 272 |
| 3178 * | NV 2278 | Leyland TD2 | 2495 | L27/26R | 8/49 | United Counties, Northampton (NO) 279 |
| 3179 * | BWY 984 | Bristol K5G | 42.34 | L27/28R | 2/49 | West Yorkshire RCC, Harrogate (WR) 352 |
| 3180 * | BWY 988 | Bristol K5G | 42.38 | L27/28R | 2/49 | West Yorkshire RCC, Harrogate (WR) 356 |
| 3181 * | BWY 982 | Bristol K5G | 42.32 | L27/28R | 2/49 | West Yorkshire RCC, Harrogate (WR) 350 |
| 3182 * | BWY 987 | Bristol K5G | 42.37 | L27/28R | 3/49 | West Yorkshire RCC, Harrogate (WR) 355 |
| 3183 * | BWY 981 | Bristol K5G | 42.31 | L27/28R | 3/49 | West Yorkshire RCC, Harrogate (WR) 349 |
| 3184 * | BWY 992 | Bristol K5G | 42.42 | L27/28R | 3/49 | West Yorkshire RCC, Harrogate (WR) 360 |
| 3185 * | BWY 990 | Bristol K5G | 42.40 | L27/28R | 3/49 | West Yorkshire RCC, Harrogate (WR) 358 |
| 3186 * | BWY 991 | Bristol K5G | 42.41 | L27/28R | 6/49 | West Yorkshire RCC, Harrogate (WR) 359 |
| 3187 * | BWY 983 | Bristol K5G | 42.33 | L27/28R | 6/49 | West Yorkshire RCC, Harrogate (WR) 351 |
| 3188 * | BWY 986 | Bristol K5G | 42.36 | L27/28R | 7/49 | West Yorkshire RCC, Harrogate (WR) 354 |
| 3189 * | BWY 985 | Bristol K5G | 42.35 | L27/28R | 7/49 | West Yorkshire RCC, Harrogate (WR) 353 |
| 3190 * | BWY 979 | Bristol K5G | 42.29 | L27/28R | 7/49 | West Yorkshire RCC, Harrogate (WR) 347 |
| 3191 * | BWY 989 | Bristol K5G | 42.39 | L27/28R | 7/49 | West Yorkshire RCC, Harrogate (WR) 357 |
| 3192 * | BWY 993 | Bristol K5G | 42.43 | L27/28R | 7/49 | West Yorkshire RCC, Harrogate (WR) 361 |
| 3193 * | BWY 980 | Bristol K5G | 42.30 | L27/28R | 8/49 | West Yorkshire RCC, Harrogate (WR) 348 |
| 3194 * | BWY 996 | Bristol K5G | 42.46 | L27/28R | 3/49 | Keighley-West Yorkshire, Harrogate (WR) K364 |
| 3195 * | CWX 667 | Bristol K5G | 47.8 | L27/28R | 3/49 | Keighley-West Yorkshire, Harrogate (WR) K379 |
| 3196 * | BWY 997 | Bristol K5G | 42.47 | L27/28R | 6/49 | Keighley-West Yorkshire, Harrogate (WR) K365 |
| 3197 * | BWY 999 | Bristol K5G | 42.49 | L27/28R | 7/49 | Keighley-West Yorkshire, Harrogate (WR) K367 |
| 3198 * | BWY 995 | Bristol K5G | 42.45 | L27/28R | 7/49 | Keighley-West Yorkshire, Harrogate (WR) K363 |
| 3199 * | CWX 668 | Bristol K5G | 47.9 | L27/28R | 7/49 | Keighley-West Yorkshire, Harrogate (WR) K380 |
| 3200 * | JN 4745 | AEC Regent | 6612888 | L27/28R | 7/49 | Westcliff-on-Sea MS (EX) |
| 3201 * | JN 4294 | AEC Regent | 6612730 | L27/28R | 9/49 | Westcliff-on-Sea MS (EX) |
| 3202 * | JN 6892 | Bristol GO5G | GO5G.104 | L27/28R | 1/49 | Westcliff-on-Sea MS (EX) |
| 3203 * | JN 6893 | Bristol GO5G | GO5G.105 | L27/28R | 1/49 | Westcliff-on-Sea MS (EX) |
| 3204 * | JN 6896 | Bristol GO5G | GO5G.108 | L27/28R | 2/49 | Westcliff-on-Sea MS (EX) |
| 3205 * | JN 6894 | Bristol GO5G | GO5G.106 | L27/28R | 5/49 | Westcliff-on-Sea MS (EX) |
| 3206 * | BFJ 158 | Bristol GO5G | GO5G.32 | H30/26R | 11/48 | Bristol Tramways (GL) 3666 |
| 3207 * | AHW 953 | Bristol GO5G | GO5G.29 | H30/26R | 11/48 | Bristol Tramways (GL) 3667 |
| 3208 * | BFJ 156 | Bristol GO5G | GO5G.34 | H30/26R | 11/48 | Bristol Tramways (GL) 3664 |
| 3209 * | BFJ 157 | Bristol GO5G | GO5G.33 | H30/26R | 11/48 | Bristol Tramways (GL) 3665 |
| 3210 * | DKN 45 | Bristol GO5G | GO5G.145 | H30/26R | 11/48 | Bath Electric Tramways (SO) 3828 |
| 3211 * | DKN 42 | Bristol GO5G | GO5G.154 | H30/26R | 12/48 | Bath Electric Tramways (SO) 3825 |
| 3212 * | BFJ 155 | Bristol GO5G | GO5G.31 | H30/26R | 11/48 | Bristol Tramways (GL) 3663 |
| 3213 * | DHT 943 | Bristol GO5G | GO5G.163 | H30/26R | 11/48 | Bristol Tramways (GL) C3061 |
| 3214 * | EAE 281 | Bristol GO5G | GO5G.204 | H30/26R | 11/48 | Bristol Tramways (GL) 3071 |
| 3215 * | EAE 596 | Bristol GO5G | GO5G.203 | H30/26R | 12/48 | Bristol Tramways (GL) 3070 |
| 3216 * | BHT 530 | Bristol G.JW | G105 | H30/26R | 12/48 | Bristol Tramways (GL) C3007 |
| 3217 * | DKN 40 | Bristol GO5G | GO5G.152 | H30/26R | 12/48 | Bath Electric Tramways (SO) 3823 |
| 3218 * | BHT 531 | Bristol G.JW | G106 | H30/26R | 12/48 | Bristol Tramways (GL) C3008 |
| 3219 * | DKN 32 | Bristol GO5G | GO5G.139 | H30/26R | 12/48 | Bath Electric Tramways (SO) 3815 |
| 3220 * | DHU 349 | Bristol GO5G | GO5G.168 | H30/26R | 12/48 | Bristol Tramways (GL) C3066 |
| 3221 * | CHW 45 | Bristol GO5G | GO5G.88 | H30/26R | 1/49 | Bristol Tramways (GL) 3034 |

| | | | | | | |
|---|---|---|---|---|---|---|
| 3222 * | EAE 285 | Bristol GO5G | GO5G.208 | H30/26R | 1/49 | Bristol Tramways (GL) 3075 |
| 3223 * | DHU 350 | Bristol GO5G | GO5G.164 | H30/26R | 1/49 | Bristol Tramways (GL) C3062 |
| 3224 * | HY 3629 | Bristol G.JW | G103 | H30/26R | 1/49 | Bristol Tramways (GL) C3001 |
| 3225 * | CHY 116 | Bristol GO5G | GO5G.119 | H30/26R | 1/49 | Bristol Tramways (GL) 3039 |
| 3226 * | EAE 288 | Bristol GO5G | GO5G.212 | H30/26R | 1/49 | Bristol Tramways (GL) 3079 |
| 3227 * | EAE 289 | Bristol GO5G | GO5G.213 | H30/26R | 9/49 | Bristol Tramways (GL) 3080 |
| 3228 * | AHW 74 | Bristol G.JW | G104 | H30/26R | 2/49 | Bristol Tramways (GL) C3006 |
| 3229 * | BHT 533 | Bristol G.JW | G108 | H30/26R | 2/49 | Bristol Tramways (GL) C3010 |
| 3230 * | DKN 37 | Bristol GO5G | GO5G.149 | H30/26R | 2/49 | Bath Electric Tramways (SO) 3820 |
| 3231 * | BHY 694 | Bristol G.JW | G131 | H30/26R | 2/49 | Bristol Tramways (GL) 3014 |
| 3232 * | DKN 38 | Bristol GO5G | GO5G.150 | H30/26R | 2/49 | Bath Electric Tramways (SO) 3821 |
| 3233 * | CHY 119 | Bristol GO5G | GO5G.123 | H30/26R | 2/49 | Bristol Tramways (GL) 3042 |
| 3234 * | EAE 282 | Bristol GO5G | GO5G.205 | H30/26R | 3/49 | Bristol Tramways (GL) 3072 |
| 3235 * | EAE 283 | Bristol GO5G | GO5G.206 | H30/26R | 3/49 | Bristol Tramways (GL) 3073 |
| 3236 * | EAE 287 | Bristol GO5G | GO5G.211 | H30/26R | 3/49 | Bristol Tramways (GL) 3078 |
| 3237 * | DKN 33 | Bristol GO5G | GO5G.140 | H30/26R | 3/49 | Bath Electric Tramways (SO) 3816 |
| 3238 * | DKN 34 | Bristol GO5G | GO5G.141 | H30/26R | 3/49 | Bath Electric Tramways (SO) 3817 |
| 3239 * | BHT 534 | Bristol G.JW | G109 | H30/26R | 3/49 | Bristol Tramways (GL) C3011 |
| 3240 * | DKN 43 | Bristol GO5G | GO5G.147 | H30/26R | 4/49 | Bath Electric Tramways (SO) 3826 |
| 3241 * | DKN 39 | Bristol GO5G | GO5G.151 | H30/26R | 4/49 | Bath Electric Tramways (SO) 3822 |
| 3242 * | CHW 47 | Bristol GO5G | GO5G.90 | H31/28R | 6/49 | Bristol Tramways (GL) C3036 |
| 3243 * | DKN 36 | Bristol GO5G | GO5G.143 | H31/28R | 6/49 | Bath Electric Tramways (SO) 3819 |
| 3244 * | DAE 374 | Bristol GO5G | GO5G.132 | H31/28R | 7/49 | Bristol Tramways (GL) C3053 |
| 3245 * | CHW 46 | Bristol GO5G | GO5G.89 | H31/28R | 7/49 | Bristol Tramways (GL) C3035 |
| 3246 * | DAE 369 | Bristol GO5G | GO5G.137 | H31/28R | 7/49 | Bristol Tramways (GL) C3058 |
| 3247 * | BHU 975 | Bristol GO5G | GO5G.28 | H31/28R | 7/49 | Bristol Tramways (GL) C3023 |
| 3248 * | BHY 693 | Bristol G.JW | G130 | H31/28R | 8/49 | Bristol Tramways (GL) C3013 |
| 3249 * | DAE 377 | Bristol GO5G | GO5G.129 | H31/28R | 7/49 | Bristol Tramways (GL) C3050 |
| 3250 * | CHY 118 | Bristol GO5G | GO5G.122 | H31/28R | 8/49 | Bristol Tramways (GL) 3041 |
| 3251 * | EAE 284 | Bristol GO5G | GO5G.207 | H31/28R | 8/49 | Bristol Tramways (GL) 3074 |
| 3252 * | CHY 120 | Bristol GO5G | GO5G.125 | H31/28R | 8/49 | Bristol Tramways (GL) 3043 |
| 3253 * | CHW 43 | Bristol GO5G | GO5G.83 | H31/28R | 8/49 | Bristol Tramways (GL) C3032 |
| 3254 | LHU 510 | Bristol L6B | 71.039 | B35R | 10/48 | Bristol Tramways (GL) 2404 |
| 3255 | LHU 509 | Bristol L6B | 71.038 | B35R | 11/48 | Bath Tramways Motor Co (SO) 2277 |
| 3256 | LHU 508 | Bristol L6B | 71.029 | B35R | 12/48 | Bath Tramways Motor Co (SO) 2279 |
| 3257 | LHU 507 | Bristol L6B | 71.028 | B35R | 11/48 | Bath Tramways Motor Co (SO) 2276 |
| 3258 | LHU 506 | Bristol L6B | 71.020 | B35R | 12/48 | Bath Tramways Motor Co (SO) 2278 |
| 3259 | LHU 505 | Bristol L6B | 71.013 | B35R | 12/48 | Bath Tramways Motor Co (SO) 2280 |
| 3260 | LHU 995 | Bristol L5G | 71.056 | B35R | 1/49 | Bristol Tramways (GL) 2397 |
| 3261 | LHW 901 | Bristol L5G | 71.057 | B35R | 1/49 | Bristol Tramways (GL) 2398 |
| 3262 | LHW 904 | Bristol L6A | 71.060 | B35R | 1/49 | Bristol Tramways (GL) 2401 |
| 3263 * | LHW 907 | Bristol L5G | 71.063 | B35R | 6/49 | Bath Tramways Motor Co (SO) 2284 |
| 3264 * | LHW 908 | Bristol L6B | 71.064 | B35R | 6/49 | Bath Tramways Motor Co (SO) 2285 |
| 3265 * | LHW 909 | Bristol L6B | 71.065 | B35R | 5/49 | Bath Tramways Motor Co (SO) 2286 |
| 3266 * | LHW 906 | Bristol L5G | 71.062 | B35R | 6/49 | Bristol Tramways (GL) 2403 |
| 3267 * | LHW 910 | Bristol L6B | 71.066 | B35R | 6/49 | Bath Tramways Motor Co (SO) 2287 |
| 3268 * | LHW 911 | Bristol L6B | 71.067 | B35R | 6/49 | Bristol Tramways (GL) 2405 |
| 3269 * | LHW 912 | Bristol L5G | 71.068 | B35R | 6/49 | Bristol Tramways (GL) 2406 |
| 3270 * | LHW 913 | Bristol L5G | 71.069 | B35R | 6/49 | Bath Tramways Motor Co (SO) 2288 |
| 3271 | LHW 915 | Bristol L6B | 71.071 | B35R | 6/49 | Bristol Tramways (GL) 2409 |
| 3272 * | LHW 916 | Bristol L6B | 71.072 | B35R | 6/49 | Bristol Tramways (GL) 2407 |
| 3273 * | LHW 914 | Bristol L6B | 71.070 | B35R | 6/49 | Bristol Tramways (GL) 2408 |
| 3274 | LHW 918 | Bristol L5G | 71.074 | B35R | 7/49 | Bristol Tramways (GL) 2410 |
| 3275 * | LHW 919 | Bristol L5G | 71.075 | B35R | 7/49 | Bristol Tramways (GL) 2411 |
| 3276 * | LHW 921 | Bristol L6A | 71.077 | B35R | 7/49 | Bristol Tramways (GL) 2412 |
| 3277 * | LHW 924 | Bristol L5G | 71.080 | B35R | 7/49 | Bristol Tramways (GL) 2414 |
| 3278 * | LHW 923 | Bristol L6B | 71.079 | B35R | 7/49 | Bristol Tramways (GL) 2413 |
| 3279 * | LHW 925 | Bristol L5G | 71.081 | B35R | 8/49 | Bristol Tramways (GL) 2415 |
| 3280 * | LHW 927 | Bristol L6B | 71.083 | B35R | 8/49 | Bristol Tramways (GL) 2417 |
| 3281 * | LHW 926 | Bristol L5G | 71.082 | B35R | 8/49 | Bristol Tramways (GL) 2416 |
| 3282 * | LHW 929 | Bristol L6B | 71.087 | B35R | 8/49 | Bristol Tramways (GL) 2419 |
| 3283 * | LHW 930 | Bristol L6B | 71.088 | B35R | 8/49 | Bristol Tramways (GL) 2428 |
| 3284 * | LHW 931 | Bristol L6B | 71.089 | B35R | 8/49 | Bristol Tramways (GL) 2429 |
| 3285 * | LHW 928 | Bristol L6B | 71.086 | B35R | 8/49 | Bristol Tramways (GL) 2418 |

| 3286 | JFM 119 | Bristol L6A | 71.084 | B35R | 2/49 | Crosville MS, Chester (CH) KB90 |
|------|---------|-------------|--------|------|------|--------------------------------|
| 3287 | JFM 120 | Bristol L6A | 71.085 | B35R | 2/49 | Crosville MS, Chester (CH) KB91 |
| 3288 | JFM 121 | Bristol L6B | 71.090 | B35R | 2/49 | Crosville MS, Chester (CH) KB92 |
| 3289 | JFM 122 | Bristol L6B | 71.098 | B35R | 2/49 | Crosville MS, Chester (CH) KB93 |
| 3290 | JFM 123 | Bristol L6B | 71.099 | B35R | 2/49 | Crosville MS, Chester (CH) KB94 |
| 3291 * | JFM 124 | Bristol L6B | 71.100 | B35R | 3/49 | Crosville MS, Chester (CH) KB95 |
| 3292 * | JFM 125 | Bristol L6A | 71.117 | B35R | 3/49 | Crosville MS, Chester (CH) KB96 |
| 3293 * | JFM 126 | Bristol L6A | 71.118 | B35R | 3/49 | Crosville MS, Chester (CH) KB97 |
| 3294 * | LHN 346 | Bristol L5G | 71.101 | B35R | 5/49 | United AS, Darlington (DM) BLO346 |
| 3295 * | LHN 347 | Bristol L5G | 71.102 | B35R | 5/49 | United AS, Darlington (DM) BLO347 |
| 3296 * | LHN 344 | Bristol L6B | 71.103 | B35R | 5/49 | United AS, Darlington (DM) BLO344 |
| 3297 * | LHN 345 | Bristol L6B | 71.104 | B35R | 5/49 | United AS, Darlington (DM) BLO345 |
| 3298 * | LHN 348 | Bristol L5G | 71.105 | B35R | 5/49 | United AS, Darlington (DM) BLO348 |
| 3299 * | LHN 349 | Bristol L5G | 71.111 | B35R | 6/49 | United AS, Darlington (DM) BLO349 |
| 3300 * | LHN 350 | Bristol L5G | 71.113 | B35R | 5/49 | United AS, Darlington (DM) BLO350 |
| 3301 * | LHN 351 | Bristol L5G | 71.112 | B35R | 6/49 | United AS, Darlington (DM) BLO351 |
| 3302 * | LHN 352 | Bristol L5G | 71.114 | B35R | 6/49 | United AS, Darlington (DM) BLO352 |
| 3303 * | LHN 353 | Bristol L5G | 71.119 | B35R | 6/49 | United AS, Darlington (DM) BLO353 |
| 3304 * | LHN 354 | Bristol L5G | 71.120 | B35R | 6/49 | United AS, Darlington (DM) BLO354 |
| 3305 * | LHN 355 | Bristol L5G | 71.121 | B35R | 6/49 | United AS, Darlington (DM) BLO355 |
| 3306 | LHN 336 | Bristol L6B | 71.106 | B35R | 6/49 | United AS, Darlington (DM) BLO336 |
| 3306 * | JHN 406 | Bristol L5G | 71.106 | DP31R | 6/49 | United AS, Darlington (DM) BLO306 |
| 3307 | LHN 337 | Bristol L6B | 71.107 | B35R | 7/49 | United AS, Darlington (DM) BLO337 |
| 3307 * | JHN 407 | Bristol L5G | 71.107 | DP31R | 7/49 | United AS, Darlington (DM) BLO307 |
| 3308 | LHN 338 | Bristol L6B | 71.108 | B35R | 7/49 | United AS, Darlington (DM) BLO338 |
| 3308 * | JHN 408 | Bristol L5G | 71.108 | DP31R | 7/49 | United AS, Darlington (DM) BLO308 |
| 3309 | LHN 339 | Bristol L6B | 71.109 | B35R | 6/49 | United AS, Darlington (DM) BLO339 |
| 3309 * | JHN 409 | Bristol L5G | 71.109 | DP31R | 6/49 | United AS, Darlington (DM) BLO309 |
| 3310 | LHN 340 | Bristol L6B | 71.110 | B35R | 7/49 | United AS, Darlington (DM) BLO340 |
| 3310 * | JHN 413 | Bristol L5G | 71.110 | DP31R | 7/49 | United AS, Darlington (DM) BLO313 |
| 3311 | LHN 341 | Bristol L6B | 71.115 | B35R | 6/49 | United AS, Darlington (DM) BLO341 |
| 3311 * | JHN 414 | Bristol L5G | 71.115 | DP31R | 6/49 | United AS, Darlington (DM) BLO314 |
| 3312 | LHN 342 | Bristol L6B | 71.116 | B35R | 7/49 | United AS, Darlington (DM) BLO342 |
| 3312 * | JHN 415 | Bristol L5G | 71.116 | DP31R | 7/49 | United AS, Darlington (DM) BLO315 |
| 3313 | LHN 343 | Bristol L6B | 71.122 | B35R | 6/49 | United AS, Darlington (DM) BLO343 |
| 3313 * | JHN 417 | Bristol L5G | 71.122 | DP31R | 6/49 | United AS, Darlington (DM) BLO317 |
| 3314 * | ERU 514 | Bristol L5G | 48.145 | B35R | 3/49 | Hants & Dorset, Bournemouth (HA) TS703 |
| 3315 * | EEL 806 | Bristol L5G | 46.16 | B35R | 3/49 | Hants & Dorset, Bournemouth (HA) TS692 |
| 3316 * | ERU 516 | Bristol L5G | 48.147 | B35R | 4/49 | Hants & Dorset, Bournemouth (HA) TS705 |
| 3317 * | LJ 7095 | Leyland TD2 | 2333 | L27/26R | 2/49 | Hants & Dorset, Bournemouth (HA) M156 |
| 3318 * | LJ 7097 | Leyland TD2 | 2335 | L27/26R | 2/49 | Hants & Dorset, Bournemouth (HA) M166 |
| 3319 * | LJ 7091 | Leyland TD2 | 2329 | L27/26R | 2/49 | Hants & Dorset, Bournemouth (HA) M112 |
| 3320 * | LJ 7092 | Leyland TD2 | 2330 | L27/26R | 3/49 | Hants & Dorset, Bournemouth (HA) M126 |
| 3321 * | TK 8915 | Leyland TD2 | 2327 | L27/26R | 3/49 | Hants & Dorset, Bournemouth (HA) M50 |
| 3322 * | LJ 7094 | Leyland TD2 | 2332 | L27/26R | 3/49 | Hants & Dorset, Bournemouth (HA) M154 |
| 3323 * | TK 8916 | Leyland TD2 | 2328 | L27/26R | 3/49 | Hants & Dorset, Bournemouth (HA) M54 |
| 3324 * | LJ 7096 | Leyland TD2 | 2334 | L27/26R | 3/49 | Hants & Dorset, Bournemouth (HA) M158 |
| 3325 * | FM 6917 | Leyland TD2 | 125 | L27/268 | 8/49 | Crosville MS, Chester (CH) M23 |
| 3326 * | FM 7464 | Leyland TD2 | 1870 | L27/26R | 3/49 | Crosville MS, Chester (CH) M32 |
| 3327 * | CHT 337 | Bristol J.NW | J.NW.93 | B35R | 7/49 | Bristol Tramways (GL) 2158 |
| 3328 * | AHT 972 | Bristol J.JW | J152 | B35R | 7/49 | Bristol Tramways (GL) 2023 |
| 3329 * | BHW 431 | Bristol J.NW | J.NW.67 | B35R | 7/49 | Bristol Tramways (GL) 2197 |
| 3330 * | CHU 563 | Bristol J.JW | J.JW.217 | B35R | 7/49 | Bristol Tramways (GL) 2038 |
| 3331 * | CHU 567 | Bristol J.JW | J.JW.221 | B35R | 7/49 | Bristol Tramways (GL) 2042 |
| 3332 * | CHU 564 | Bristol J.JW | J.JW.218 | B35R | 7/49 | Bristol Tramways (GL) 2039 |
| 3333 * | CHU 565 | Bristol J.JW | J.JW.219 | B35R | 7/49 | Bristol Tramways (GL) 2040 |
| 3334 * | EHT 548 | Bristol JO5G | JO5G.513 | B35R | 9/49 | Bristol Tramways (GL) 2064 |
| 3335 * | BHU 981 | Bristol J.NW | J.NW.66 | B35R | 9/49 | Bristol Tramways (GL) 2195 |
| 3336 * | DHY 666 | Bristol JO5G | JO5G.500 | B35R | 9/49 | Bristol Tramways (GL) 2214 |
| 3337 * | CHT 332 | Bristol J.NW | J.NW.88 | B35R | 9/49 | Bristol Tramways (GL) 2375 |
| 3338 * | BHU 969 | Bristol J.NW | J.NW.60 | B35R | 10/49 | Bristol Tramways (GL) 2374 |
| 3339 * | BHW 432 | Bristol J.NW | J.NW.70 | B35R | 10/49 | Bristol Tramways (GL) 2199 |
| 3340 * | CHW 49 | Bristol J.PW | J.PW.1 | B35R | 10/49 | Bristol Tramways (GL) 2121 |
| 3341 * | CHT 334 | Bristol J.NW | J.NW.90 | B35R | 10/49 | Bristol Tramways (GL) 2159 |

| | | | | | | |
|---|---|---|---|---|---|---|
| 3342 * | CHT 336 | Bristol J.NW | J.NW.92 | B35R | 10/49 | Bristol Tramways (GL) 2160 |
| 3343 * | BHU 637 | Bristol J.JW | J.JW.183 | B35R | 10/49 | Bristol Tramways (GL) 2056 |
| 3344 * | EHT 541 | Bristol JO5G | JO5G.294 | B35R | 11/49 | Bristol Tramways (GL) 2079 |
| 3345 * | AHW 536 | Bristol J.JW | J143 | B35R | 10/49 | Bristol Tramways (GL) 2363 |
| 3346 * | CHU 569 | Bristol J.JW | J.JW.223 | B35R | 10/49 | Bristol Tramways (GL) 2044 |
| 3347 * | CHT 333 | Bristol J.NW | J.NW.89 | B35R | 12/49 | Bristol Tramways (GL) 2376 |
| 3348 * | BHU 978 | Bristol J.NW | J.NW.64 | B35R | 12/49 | Bristol Tramways (GL) 2194 |
| 3349 * | CHY 821 | Bristol JO5G | JO5G.207 | B35R | 12/49 | Bristol Tramways (GL) 2004 |
| 3350 * | BHY 691 | Bristol JO5G | JO5G.15 | B35R | 12/49 | Bristol Tramways (GL) 2002 |
| 3351 * | CHU 413 | Bristol JO6A | JO6A.2 | B35R | 1/50 | Bristol Tramways (GL) 2005 |
| 3352 * | CHU 571 | Bristol J.JW | J.JW.225 | B35R | 12/49 | Bristol Tramways (GL) 2046 |
| 3353 * | BHU 979 | Bristol J.NW | J.NW.68 | B35R | 1/50 | Bristol Tramways (GL) 2196 |
| 3354 * | BHW 430 | Bristol J.NW | J.NW.69 | B35R | 1/50 | Bristol Tramways (GL) 2198 |
| 3355 | LHN 556 | Bristol L6B | 73.133R | B35R | 6/49 | United AS, Darlington (DM) BLO356 |
| 3356 | LHN 557 | Bristol L6B | 73.134R | B35R | 6/49 | United AS, Darlington (DM) BLO357 |
| 3357 | LHN 558 | Bristol L6B | 73.135R | B35R | 6/49 | United AS, Darlington (DM) BLO358 |
| 3358 | LHN 559 | Bristol L6B | 73.136R | B35R | 6/49 | United AS, Darlington (DM) BLO359 |
| 3359 | LHN 560 | Bristol L6B | 73.137R | B35R | 7/49 | United AS, Darlington (DM) BLO360 |
| 3360 | LHN 561 | Bristol L6B | 73.138R | B35R | 7/49 | United AS, Darlington (DM) BLO361 |
| 3361 | LHN 562 | Bristol L6B | 73.139R | B35R | 7/49 | United AS, Darlington (DM) BLO362 |
| 3362 | LHN 565 | Bristol L6B | 73.142R | B35R | 7/49 | United AS, Darlington (DM) BLO365 |
| 3363 | LHN 564 | Bristol L6B | 73.141R | B35R | 7/49 | United AS, Darlington (DM) BLO364 |
| 3364 | LHN 563 | Bristol L6B | 73.140R | B35R | 6/49 | United AS, Darlington (DM) BLO363 |
| 3365 | LHN 566 | Bristol L6B | 73.143R | B35R | 7/49 | United AS, Darlington (DM) BLO366 |
| 3366 | LHN 567 | Bristol L6B | 73.144R | B35R | 7/49 | United AS, Darlington (DM) BLO367 |
| 3367 | LHN 368 | Bristol L5G | 73.145R | B35R | 7/49 | United AS, Darlington (DM) BLO368 |
| 3368 | LHN 369 | Bristol L5G | 73.146R | B35R | 7/49 | United AS, Darlington (DM) BLO369 |
| 3369 | LHN 370 | Bristol L5G | 73.147R | B35R | 7/49 | United AS, Darlington (DM) BLO370 |
| 3370 | LHN 371 | Bristol L5G | 73.148R | B35R | 7/49 | United AS, Darlington (DM) BLO371 |
| 3371 | LHN 372 | Bristol L5G | 73.149R | B35R | 7/49 | United AS, Darlington (DM) BLO372 |
| 3372 | LHN 373 | Bristol L5G | 73.150R | B35R | 7/49 | United AS, Darlington (DM) BLO373 |
| 3373 | LHN 374 | Bristol L5G | 73.151R | B35R | 7/49 | United AS, Darlington (DM) BLO374 |
| 3374 | LHN 375 | Bristol L5G | 73.152R | B35R | 7/49 | United AS, Darlington (DM) BLO375 |
| 3375 | LHN 376 | Bristol L5G | 73.153R | B35R | 7/49 | United AS, Darlington (DM) BLO376 |
| 3376 | LHN 377 | Bristol L5G | 73.154R | B35R | 7/49 | United AS, Darlington (DM) BLO377 |
| 3377 | LHN 578 | Bristol L5G | 73.155R | B35R | 7/49 | United AS, Darlington (DM) BLO378 |
| 3378 | LHN 579 | Bristol L5G | 73.156R | B35R | 8/49 | United AS, Darlington (DM) BLO379 |
| 3379 | LHN 581 | Bristol L5G | 73.158R | B35R | 9/49 | United AS, Darlington (DM) BLO381 |
| 3380 | LHN 582 | Bristol L5G | 73.159R | B35R | 9/49 | United AS, Darlington (DM) BLO382 |
| 3381 | LHN 580 | Bristol L5G | 73.157R | B35R | 9/49 | United AS, Darlington (DM) BLO380 |
| 3382 | LHN 584 | Bristol L5G | 73.161R | B35R | 9/49 | United AS, Darlington (DM) BLO384 |
| 3383 | LHN 583 | Bristol L5G | 73.160R | B35R | 9/49 | United AS, Darlington (DM) BLO383 |
| 3384 | LHN 585 | Bristol L5G | 73.162R | B35R | 9/49 | United AS, Darlington (DM) BLO385 |
| 3385 | LHN 586 | Bristol L5G | 73.163R | B35R | 9/49 | United AS, Darlington (DM) BLO386 |
| 3386 | LHN 587 | Bristol L5G | 73.164R | B35R | 9/49 | United AS, Darlington (DM) BLO387 |
| 3387 | HPW 817 | ECW | CD1 | B32R | 6/50 | Eastern Counties, Norwich (NK) CD832 |
| 3388 | HPW 818 | ECW | CD2 | B32R | 5/50 | Eastern Counties, Norwich (NK) CD833 |
| 3389 | HPW 819 | ECW | CD3 | B32R | 6/50 | Eastern Counties, Norwich (NK) CD834 |
| 3390 | HPW 820 | ECW | CD4 | B32R | 6/50 | Eastern Counties, Norwich (NK) CD835 |
| 3391 | HPW 821 | ECW | CD5 | B32R | 6/50 | Eastern Counties, Norwich (NK) CD836 |
| 3392 | HPW 822 | ECW | CD6 | B32R | 7/50 | Eastern Counties, Norwich (NK) CD837 |
| 3393 | HPW 823 | ECW | CD7 | B32R | 7/50 | Eastern Counties, Norwich (NK) CD838 |
| 3394 | HPW 824 | ECW | CD8 | B32R | 8/50 | Eastern Counties, Norwich (NK) CD839 |
| 3395 | HPW 825 | ECW | CD9 | B32R | 8/50 | Eastern Counties, Norwich (NK) CD840 |
| 3396 | HPW 826 | ECW | CD10 | B32R | 9/50 | Eastern Counties, Norwich (NK) CD841 |
| 3397 | HPW 827 | ECW | CD11 | B32R | 9/50 | Eastern Counties, Norwich (NK) CD842 |
| 3398 | HPW 828 | ECW | CD12 | B32R | 10/50 | Eastern Counties, Norwich (NK) CD843 |
| 3399 | HPW 829 | ECW | CD13 | B32R | 10/50 | Eastern Counties, Norwich (NK) CD844 |
| 3400 | HPW 830 | ECW | CD14 | B32R | 11/50 | Eastern Counties, Norwich (NK) CD845 |
| 3401 | HPW 831 | ECW | CD15 | B32R | 11/50 | Eastern Counties, Norwich (NK) CD846 |
| 3402 | KAH 401 | Bristol L4G | 73.179R | B35R | 7/49 | Eastern Counties, Norwich (NK) LL401 |
| 3403 | KAH 402 | Bristol L4G | 73.180R | B35R | 7/49 | Eastern Counties, Norwich (NK) LL402 |
| 3404 | KAH 403 | Bristol L4G | 73.181R | B35R | 7/49 | Eastern Counties, Norwich (NK) LL403 |
| 3405 | KAH 404 | Bristol L4G | 73.182R | B35R | 7/49 | Eastern Counties, Norwich (NK) LL404 |

| 3406 | KAH 405 | Bristol L4G | 73.183R | B35R | 7/49 | Eastern Counties, Norwich (NK) LL405 |
|---|---|---|---|---|---|---|
| 3407 | KAH 407 | Bristol L4G | 73.185R | B35R | 8/49 | Eastern Counties, Norwich (NK) LL407 |
| 3408 | KAH 409 | Bristol L4G | 73.187R | B35R | 8/49 | Eastern Counties, Norwich (NK) LL409 |
| 3409 | KAH 410 | Bristol L4G | 73.188R | B35R | 8/49 | Eastern Counties, Norwich (NK) LL410 |
| 3410 | KAH 406 | Bristol L4G | 73.184R | B35R | 9/49 | Eastern Counties, Norwich (NK) LL406 |
| 3411 | KAH 408 | Bristol L4G | 73.186R | B35R | 9/49 | Eastern Counties, Norwich (NK) LL408 |
| 3412 * | BTR 312 | Bristol K5G | 45.83 | L27/28R | 6/49 | Hants & Dorset, Bournemouth (HA) TD638 |
| 3413 * | BTR 308 | Bristol K5G | 45.17 | L27/28R | 6/49 | Hants & Dorset, Bournemouth (HA) TD630 |
| 3414 * | BTR 311 | Bristol K5G | 45.82 | L27/28R | 6/49 | Hants & Dorset, Bournemouth (HA) TD636 |
| 3415 * | JT 9355 | Bristol K5G | 45.88 | L27/28R | 6/49 | Hants & Dorset, Bournemouth (HA) TD648 |
| 3416 * | JT 9354 | Bristol K5G | 45.87 | L27/28R | 6/49 | Hants & Dorset, Bournemouth (HA) TD646 |
| 3417 * | JT 9357 | Bristol K5G | 45.90 | L27/28R | 6/49 | Hants & Dorset, Bournemouth (HA) TD652 |
| 3418 * | BTR 306 | Bristol K5G | 45.15 | L27/28R | 8/49 | Hants & Dorset, Bournemouth (HA) TD626 |
| 3419 * | JT 9360 | Bristol K5G | 45.93 | L27/28R | 8/49 | Hants & Dorset, Bournemouth (HA) TD658 |
| 3420 * | BTR 304 | Bristol K5G | 45.13 | L27/28R | 8/49 | Hants & Dorset, Bournemouth (HA) TD622 |
| 3421 * | FLJ 429 | Bristol L5G | 52.002 | B35R | 3/49 | Hants & Dorset, Bournemouth (HA) TS802 |
| 3422 * | FLJ 433 | Bristol L5G | 52.006 | B35R | 3/49 | Hants & Dorset, Bournemouth (HA) TS806 |
| 3423 * | FLJ 435 | Bristol L5G | 52.008 | B35R | 4/49 | Hants & Dorset, Bournemouth (HA) TS808 |
| 3424 * | EEL 801 | Bristol L5G | 46.11 | B35R | 4/49 | Hants & Dorset, Bournemouth (HA) TS682 |
| 3425 * | FLJ 430 | Bristol L5G | 52.003 | B35R | 4/49 | Hants & Dorset, Bournemouth (HA) TS803 |
| 3426 * | FLJ 437 | Bristol L5G | 52.010 | B35R | 5/49 | Hants & Dorset, Bournemouth (HA) TS810 |
| 3427 * | BOW 165 | Bristol L5G | 46.4 | B35R | 5/49 | Hants & Dorset, Bournemouth (HA) TS668 |
| 3428 * | BOW 163 | Bristol L5G | 46.2 | B35R | 5/49 | Hants & Dorset, Bournemouth (HA) TS664 |
| 3429 * | LJ 7093 | Leyland TD2 | 2331 | L27/26R | 3/49 | Hants & Dorset, Bournemouth (HA) M152 |
| 3430 * | TK 8914 | Leyland TD2 | 2326 | L27/26R | 3/49 | Hants & Dorset, Bournemouth (HA) M34 |
| 3431 * | DTA 423 | Bristol GO5G | GO5G.194 | L27/26R | 3/49 | Western National, Exeter (DN) 234 |
| 3432 * | DTA 425 | Bristol GO5G | GO5G.196 | L27/26R | 4/49 | Western National, Exeter (DN) 236 |
| 3433 * | DTA 422 | Bristol GO5G | GO5G.193 | L27/26R | 4/49 | Western National, Exeter (DN) 233 |
| 3434 * | DTA 424 | Bristol GO5G | GO5G.195 | L27/26R | 5/49 | Western National, Exeter (DN) 235 |
| 3435 * | ETA 966 | Bristol GO5G | GO5G.201 | L27/26R | 5/49 | Western National, Exeter (DN) 241 |
| 3436 * | ETA 967 | Bristol GO5G | GO5G.202 | L27/26R | 9/49 | Western National, Exeter (DN) 242 |
| 3437 * | ETA 984 | Bristol GO5G | GO5G.197 | L27/26R | 4/49 | Western National, Exeter (DN) 237 |
| 3438 * | ETA 986 | Bristol GO5G | GO5G.199 | L27/26R | 4/49 | Western National, Exeter (DN) 239 |
| 3439 * | ETA 985 | Bristol GO5G | GO5G.198 | L27/26R | 6/49 | Western National, Exeter (DN) 238 |
| 3440 * | ETA 987 | Bristol GO5G | GO5G.200 | L27/26R | 8/49 | Western National, Exeter (DN) 240 |
| 3441 * | JC 1343 | Leyland TS6 | 2973 | DP32R | 6/49 | Crosville MS, Chester (CH) KA194 |
| 3442 | HPW 832 | ECW | CD16 | B32R | 11/50 | Eastern Counties, Norwich (NK) CD847 |
| 3443 * | FM 7468 | Leyland TS4 | 2051 | DP31R | 4/49 | Crosville MS, Chester (CH) KA189 |
| 3444 * | FM 7469 | Leyland TS4 | 2052 | DP31R | 4/49 | Crosville MS, Chester (CH) KA190 |
| 3445 * | FM 7470 | Leyland TS4 | 2053 | DP31R | 7/49 | Crosville MS, Chester (CH) KA191 |
| 3446 * | FM 7471 | Leyland TS4 | 2054 | DP31R | 7/49 | Crosville MS, Chester (CH) KA192 |
| 3447 * | FM 7472 | Leyland TS4 | 2055 | DP31R | 7/49 | Crosville MS, Chester (CH) KA193 |
| 3448 * | LTA 723 | Bristol K5G | 76.060 | L27/28R | 11/49 | Western National, Exeter (DN) 988 |
| 3449 * | LTA 887 | Bristol K5G | 76.061 | L27/28R | 11/49 | Southern National, Exeter (DN) 987 |
| 3450 | GDL 434 | Bristol K5G | 78.101 | L27/28R | 1/50 | Southern Vectis, Newport (IW) 736 |
| 3451 | GDL 435 | Bristol K5G | 78.177 | L27/28R | 2/50 | Southern Vectis, Newport (IW) 737 |
| 3452 * | KFM 234 | Bristol K6A | 76.063 | L27/28R | 5/49 | Crosville MS, Chester (CH) MB358 |
| 3453 * | KFM 235 | Bristol K6A | 76.064 | L27/28R | 5/49 | Crosville MS, Chester (CH) MB359 |
| 3454 * | KFM 236 | Bristol K6A | 74.005 | L27/28R | 5/49 | Crosville MS, Chester (CH) MB360 |
| 3455 | KFM 237 | Bristol K6B | 72.042 | L27/28R | 9/49 | Crosville MS, Chester (CH) MW361 |
| 3456 | KFM 238 | Bristol K6B | 72.043 | L27/28R | 9/49 | Crosville MS, Chester (CH) MW362 |
| 3457 | KFM 239 | Bristol K6B | 72.044 | L27/28R | 9/49 | Crosville MS, Chester (CH) MW363 |
| 3458 | KFM 240 | Bristol K6B | 72.049 | L27/28R | 9/49 | Crosville MS, Chester (CH) MW364 |
| 3459 | KFM 241 | Bristol K6B | 72.050 | L27/28R | 9/49 | Crosville MS, Chester (CH) MW365 |
| 3460 | KFM 242 | Bristol K6A | 76.065 | L27/28R | 9/49 | Crosville MS, Chester (CH) MB366 |
| 3461 | KFM 243 | Bristol K6A | 76.066 | L27/28R | 9/49 | Crosville MS, Chester (CH) MB367 |
| 3462 | KFM 244 | Bristol K6A | 76.157 | L27/28R | 9/49 | Crosville MS, Chester (CH) MB368 |
| 3463 * | KFM 245 | Bristol K6A | 76.158 | L27/28R | 9/49 | Crosville MS, Chester (CH) MB369 |
| 3464 * | KFM 246 | Bristol K6A | 76.127 | L27/28R | 9/49 | Crosville MS, Chester (CH) MB370 |
| 3465 * | KFM 247 | Bristol K6A | 76.149 | L27/28R | 9/49 | Crosville MS, Chester (CH) MB371 |
| 3466 * | KFM 248 | Bristol K6A | 76.150 | L27/28R | 9/49 | Crosville MS, Chester (CH) MB372 |
| 3467 * | KFM 249 | Bristol K6A | 76.156 | L27/28R | 11/49 | Crosville MS, Chester (CH) MB373 |
| 3468 * | KFM 250 | Bristol K6A | 76.096 | L27/28R | 11/49 | Crosville MS, Chester (CH) MB374 |
| 3469 * | KFM 251 | Bristol K6A | 76.098 | L27/28R | 11/49 | Crosville MS, Chester (CH) MB375 |

| | | | | | | | |
|---|---|---|---|---|---|---|---|
| 3470 * | KFM 252 | Bristol K6A | 76.097 | L27/28R | 11/49 | Crosville MS, Chester (CH) | MB376 |
| 3471 * | KFM 253 | Bristol K6A | 76.125 | L27/28R | 11/49 | Crosville MS, Chester (CH) | MB377 |
| 3472 * | KFM 254 | Bristol K6A | 76.126 | L27/28R | 11/49 | Crosville MS, Chester (CH) | MB378 |
| 3473 | KFM 255 | Bristol K6B | 76.147 | L27/28R | 11/49 | Crosville MS, Chester (CH) | MW379 |
| 3474 | KFM 256 | Bristol K6B | 76.140 | L27/28R | 11/49 | Crosville MS, Chester (CH) | MW380 |
| 3475 | KFM 257 | Bristol K6B | 76.148 | L27/28R | 11/49 | Crosville MS, Chester (CH) | MW381 |
| 3476 | KFM 258 | Bristol K6B | 76.139 | L27/28R | 11/49 | Crosville MS, Chester (CH) | MW382 |
| 3477 | KFM 259 | Bristol K6B | 76.141 | L27/28R | 12/49 | Crosville MS, Chester (CH) | MW383 |
| 3478 | KFM 260 | Bristol K6B | 76.136 | L27/28R | 1/50 | Crosville MS, Chester (CH) | MW384 |
| 3479 | KFM 261 | Bristol K6B | 76.137 | L27/28R | 1/50 | Crosville MS, Chester (CH) | MW385 |
| 3480 | KFM 262 | Bristol K6B | 76.138 | L27/28R | 1/50 | Crosville MS, Chester (CH) | MW386 |
| 3481 | KFM 263 | Bristol K6B | 76.011 | L27/28R | 1/50 | Crosville MS, Chester (CH) | MW387 |
| 3482 | KFM 264 | Bristol K6B | 76.012 | L27/28R | 1/50 | Crosville MS, Chester (CH) | MW388 |
| 3483 | KFM 265 | Bristol K6B | 78.005 | L27/28R | 1/50 | Crosville MS, Chester (CH) | MW389 |
| 3484 | KFM 266 | Bristol K6B | 76.013 | L27/28R | 2/50 | Crosville MS, Chester (CH) | MW390 |
| 3485 | KFM 267 | Bristol K6B | 76.051 | L27/28R | 1/50 | Crosville MS, Chester (CH) | MW391 |
| 3486 | KFM 270 | Bristol K6B | 78.008 | L27/28R | 2/50 | Crosville MS, Chester (CH) | MW394 |
| 3487 | KFM 271 | Bristol K6B | 78.009 | L27/28R | 1/50 | Crosville MS, Chester (CH) | MW395 |
| 3488 | KFM 272 | Bristol K6B | 78.010 | L27/28R | 1/50 | Crosville MS, Chester (CH) | MW396 |
| 3489 | KFM 268 | Bristol K6B | 78.006 | L27/28R | 1/50 | Crosville MS, Chester (CH) | MW392 |
| 3490 | KFM 269 | Bristol K6B | 78.007 | L27/28R | 3/50 | Crosville MS, Chester (CH) | MW393 |
| 3491 | KFM 273 | Bristol K6B | 78.011 | L27/28R | 3/50 | Crosville MS, Chester (CH) | MW397 |
| 3492 | KFM 274 | Bristol K6B | 78.019 | L27/28R | 3/50 | Crosville MS, Chester (CH) | MW398 |
| 3493 | KFM 275 | Bristol K6B | 78.020 | L27/28R | 3/50 | Crosville MS, Chester (CH) | MW399 |
| 3494 | KFM 276 | Bristol K6B | 78.021 | L27/28R | 3/50 | Crosville MS, Chester (CH) | MW400 |
| 3495 | KFM 277 | Bristol K6B | 78.022 | L27/28R | 3/50 | Crosville MS, Chester (CH) | MW401 |
| 3496 | KFM 278 | Bristol K6B | 78.042 | L27/28R | 3/50 | Crosville MS, Chester (CH) | MW402 |
| 3497 | KFM 279 | Bristol K6B | 78.043 | L27/28R | 3/50 | Crosville MS, Chester (CH) | MW403 |
| 3498 | KFM 281 | Bristol K6B | 78.046 | L27/28R | 3/50 | Crosville MS, Chester (CH) | MW405 |
| 3499 | KFM 280 | Bristol K6B | 78.045 | L27/28R | 3/50 | Crosville MS, Chester (CH) | MW404 |
| 3500 | KFM 282 | Bristol K6B | 78.044 | L27/28R | 3/50 | Crosville MS, Chester (CH) | MW406 |
| 3501 | KFM 283 | Bristol K6B | 78.047 | L27/28R | 3/50 | Crosville MS, Chester (CH) | MW407 |
| 3502 | KFM 284 | Bristol K6B | 78.048 | L27/28R | 3/50 | Crosville MS, Chester (CH) | MW408 |
| 3503 | KFM 285 | Bristol K6B | 78.049 | L27/28R | 3/50 | Crosville MS, Chester (CH) | MW409 |
| 3504 | KFM 286 | Bristol K6B | 78.086 | L27/28R | 3/50 | Crosville MS, Chester (CH) | MW410 |
| 3505 | KFM 287 | Bristol K6B | 78.087 | L27/28R | 3/50 | Crosville MS, Chester (CH) | MW411 |
| 3506 | KFM 288 | Bristol K6B | 78.132 | L27/28R | 3/50 | Crosville MS, Chester (CH) | MW412 |
| 3507 | KFM 289 | Bristol K6B | 78.148 | L27/28R | 6/50 | Crosville MS, Chester (CH) | MW413 |
| 3508 | KFM 290 | Bristol K6B | 78.149 | L27/28R | 5/50 | Crosville MS, Chester (CH) | MW414 |
| 3509 | KFM 291 | Bristol K6B | 78.150 | L27/28R | 5/50 | Crosville MS, Chester (CH) | MW415 |
| 3510 | KFM 292 | Bristol K6B | 78.165 | L27/28R | 6/50 | Crosville MS, Chester (CH) | MW416 |
| 3511 | KFM 293 | Bristol K6B | 78.164 | L27/28R | 6/50 | Crosville MS, Chester (CH) | MW417 |
| 3512 * | KNG 366 | Bristol K6B | 72.054 | L27/28R | 9/49 | Eastern Counties, Norwich (NK) | LK366 |
| 3513 | KNG 367 | Bristol K6B | 72.051 | L27/28R | 10/49 | Eastern Counties, Norwich (NK) | LK367 |
| 3514 | KNG 368 | Bristol K6B | 72.022 | L27/28R | 10/49 | Eastern Counties, Norwich (NK) | LK368 |
| 3515 | KNG 370 | Bristol K5G | 74.171 | L27/28R | 10/49 | Eastern Counties, Norwich (NK) | LK370 |
| 3516 | KNG 369 | Bristol K5G | 74.170 | L27/28R | 10/49 | Eastern Counties, Norwich (NK) | LK369 |
| 3517 | KNG 371 | Bristol K6B | 76.036 | L27/28R | 10/49 | Eastern Counties, Norwich (NK) | LK371 |
| 3518 | KNG 372 | Bristol K6B | 76.037 | L27/28R | 10/49 | Eastern Counties, Norwich (NK) | LK372 |
| 3519 | KNG 373 | Bristol K6B | 76.038 | L27/28R | 12/49 | Eastern Counties, Norwich (NK) | LK373 |
| 3520 | KNG 374 | Bristol K6B | 76.039 | L27/28R | 12/49 | Eastern Counties, Norwich (NK) | LK374 |
| 3521 | KNG 375 | Bristol K6B | 76.040 | L27/28R | 12/49 | Eastern Counties, Norwich (NK) | LK375 |
| 3522 | KNG 376 | Bristol K5G | 76.128 | L27/28R | 12/49 | Eastern Counties, Norwich (NK) | LK376 |
| 3523 | KNG 377 | Bristol K5G | 76.129 | L27/28R | 12/49 | Eastern Counties, Norwich (NK) | LK377 |
| 3524 | KNG 378 | Bristol K6B | 76.099 | L27/28R | 12/49 | Eastern Counties, Norwich (NK) | LK378 |
| 3525 | KNG 379 | Bristol K6B | 76.100 | L27/28R | 12/49 | Eastern Counties, Norwich (NK) | LK379 |
| 3526 | KNG 380 | Bristol K6B | 76.101 | L27/28R | 1/50 | Eastern Counties, Norwich (NK) | LK380 |
| 3527 | KNG 381 | Bristol K6B | 76.102 | L27/28R | 1/50 | Eastern Counties, Norwich (NK) | LK381 |
| 3528 | KNG 382 | Bristol K6B | 76.103 | L27/28R | 1/50 | Eastern Counties, Norwich (NK) | LK382 |
| 3529 | KNG 383 | Bristol K5G | 76.131 | L27/28R | 1/50 | Eastern Counties, Norwich (NK) | LK383 |
| 3530 | KNG 384 | Bristol K5G | 76.132 | L27/28R | 2/50 | Eastern Counties, Norwich (NK) | LK384 |
| 3531 | KNG 385 | Bristol K5G | 76.130 | L27/28R | 2/50 | Eastern Counties, Norwich (NK) | LK385 |
| 3532 | KNG 386 | Bristol K5G | 76.160 | L27/28R | 3/50 | Eastern Counties, Norwich (NK) | LK386 |
| 3533 | KNG 387 | Bristol K5G | 76.159 | L27/28R | 3/50 | Eastern Counties, Norwich (NK) | LK387 |

| 3534 | KNG 388 | Bristol K5G | 76.161 | L27/28R | 3/50 | Eastern Counties, Norwich (NK) LK388 |
|---|---|---|---|---|---|---|
| 3535 | KNG 389 | Bristol K5G | 76.162 | L27/28R | 3/50 | Eastern Counties, Norwich (NK) LK389 |
| 3536 | KNG 390 | Bristol K5G | 76.163 | L27/28R | 3/50 | Eastern Counties, Norwich (NK) LK390 |
| 3537 | KNG 391 | Bristol K5G | 76.198 | L27/28R | 3/50 | Eastern Counties, Norwich (NK) LK391 |
| 3538 | KNG 392 | Bristol K5G | 76.199 | L27/28R | 3/50 | Eastern Counties, Norwich (NK) LK392 |
| 3539 | KNG 393 | Bristol K5G | 78.072 | L27/28R | 4/50 | Eastern Counties, Norwich (NK) LK393 |
| 3540 | KNG 394 | Bristol K5G | 78.073 | L27/28R | 4/50 | Eastern Counties, Norwich (NK) LK394 |
| 3541 | KNG 395 | Bristol K5G | 78.074 | L27/28R | 5/50 | Eastern Counties, Norwich (NK) LK395 |
| 3542 * | ONO 51 | Bristol K5G | 74.199 | L27/28R | 6/49 | Eastern National, Chelmsford (EX) 4030 |
| 3543 * | ONO 52 | Bristol K5G | 74.200 | L27/28R | 6/49 | Eastern National, Chelmsford (EX) 4031 |
| 3544 * | ONO 53 | Bristol K5G | 76.001 | L27/28R | 6/49 | Eastern National, Chelmsford (EX) 4032 |
| 3545 * | ONO 54 | Bristol K5G | 76.002 | L27/28R | 6/49 | Eastern National, Chelmsford (EX) 4033 |
| 3546 * | ONO 55 | Bristol K5G | 76.003 | L27/28R | 6/49 | Eastern National, Chelmsford (EX) 4034 |
| 3547 | ONO 56 | Bristol K5G | 76.072 | L27/28R | 10/49 | Eastern National, Chelmsford (EX) 4035 |
| 3548 | ONO 57 | Bristol K5G | 76.074 | L27/28R | 10/49 | Eastern National, Chelmsford (EX) 4036 |
| 3549 | ONO 58 | Bristol K5G | 76.075 | L27/28R | 11/49 | Eastern National, Chelmsford (EX) 4037 |
| 3550 | ONO 59 | Bristol K5G | 76.073 | L27/28R | 11/49 | Eastern National, Chelmsford (EX) 4038 |
| 3551 | ONO 60 | Bristol K5G | 76.076 | L27/28R | 12/49 | Eastern National, Chelmsford (EX) 4039 |
| 3552 | ONO 61 | Bristol K5G | 76.053 | L27/28R | 1/50 | Eastern National, Chelmsford (EX) 4040 |
| 3553 | ONO 62 | Bristol K5G | 76.052 | L27/28R | 1/50 | Eastern National, Chelmsford (EX) 4041 |
| 3554 | ONO 63 | Bristol K5G | 76.010 | L27/28R | 1/50 | Eastern National, Chelmsford (EX) 4042 |
| 3555 | ONO 64 | Bristol K5G | 76.086 | L27/28R | 3/50 | Eastern National, Chelmsford (EX) 4043 |
| 3556 | ONO 65 | Bristol K5G | 76.089 | L27/28R | 3/50 | Eastern National, Chelmsford (EX) 4044 |
| 3557 | ONO 67 | Bristol K5G | 78.054 | L27/28R | 2/50 | Eastern National, Chelmsford (EX) 4046 |
| 3558 | ONO 66 | Bristol K5G | 78.053 | L27/28R | 3/50 | Eastern National, Chelmsford (EX) 4045 |
| 3559 | ONO 68 | Bristol K5G | 78.055 | L27/28R | 3/50 | Eastern National, Chelmsford (EX) 4047 |
| 3560 | ONO 69 | Bristol K5G | 78.056 | L27/28R | 3/50 | Eastern National, Chelmsford (EX) 4048 |
| 3561 | ONO 70 | Bristol K5G | 78.057 | L27/28R | 3/50 | Eastern National, Chelmsford (EX) 4049 |
| 3562 | ONO 71 | Bristol K5G | 78.103 | L27/28R | 3/50 | Eastern National, Chelmsford (EX) 4050 |
| 3563 | ONO 72 | Bristol K5G | 78.104 | L27/28R | 4/50 | Eastern National, Chelmsford (EX) 4051 |
| 3564 | ONO 73 | Bristol K5G | 78.173 | L27/28R | 6/50 | Eastern National, Chelmsford (EX) 4052 |
| 3565 | ONO 74 | Bristol K5G | 78.174 | L27/28R | 7/50 | Eastern National, Chelmsford (EX) 4053 |
| 3566 | ONO 75 | Bristol K5G | 78.175 | L27/28R | 6/50 | Eastern National, Chelmsford (EX) 4054 |
| 3567 | ONO 76 | Bristol K5G | 78.176 | L27/28R | 6/50 | Eastern National, Chelmsford (EX) 4055 |
| 3568 | ONO 77 | Bristol K5G | 78.189 | L27/28R | 7/50 | Eastern National, Chelmsford (EX) 4056 |
| 3569 | ONO 78 | Bristol K5G | 78.190 | L27/28R | 7/50 | Eastern National, Chelmsford (EX) 4057 |
| 3570 | ONO 79 | Bristol K5G | 78.191 | L27/28R | 8/50 | Eastern National, Chelmsford (EX) 4058 |
| 3571 | ONO 80 | Bristol K5G | 78.192 | L27/28R | 8/50 | Eastern National, Chelmsford (EX) 4059 |
| 3572 | JEL 244 | Bristol K6A | 74.177 | L27/28R | 9/49 | Hants & Dorset, Bournemouth (HA) 1225 |
| 3573 | JEL 245 | Bristol K6A | 74.178 | L27/28R | 9/49 | Hants & Dorset, Bournemouth (HA) 1226 |
| 3574 | JEL 247 | Bristol K6A | 74.180 | L27/28R | 9/49 | Hants & Dorset, Bournemouth (HA) 1228 |
| 3575 | JEL 246 | Bristol K6A | 74.179 | L27/28R | 9/49 | Hants & Dorset, Bournemouth (HA) 1227 |
| 3576 | JEL 248 | Bristol K6A | 74.181 | L27/28R | 9/49 | Hants & Dorset, Bournemouth (HA) 1229 |
| 3577 | JEL 249 | Bristol K6B | 76.067 | L27/28R | 9/49 | Hants & Dorset, Bournemouth (HA) 1230 |
| 3578 | JEL 250 | Bristol K6B | 76.068 | L27/28R | 9/49 | Hants & Dorset, Bournemouth (HA) 1231 |
| 3579 | JEL 251 | Bristol K6B | 76.069 | L27/28R | 11/49 | Hants & Dorset, Bournemouth (HA) 1232 |
| 3580 | JEL 252 | Bristol K6B | 76.070 | L27/28R | 11/49 | Hants & Dorset, Bournemouth (HA) 1233 |
| 3581 | JEL 253 | Bristol K5G | 76.142 | L27/28R | 11/49 | Hants & Dorset, Bournemouth (HA) 1234 |
| 3582 | JEL 254 | Bristol K6B | 76.071 | L27/28R | 11/49 | Hants & Dorset, Bournemouth (HA) 1235 |
| 3583 | JEL 255 | Bristol K5G | 76.144 | L27/28R | 11/49 | Hants & Dorset, Bournemouth (HA) 1236 |
| 3584 | JEL 256 | Bristol K5G | 76.146 | L27/28R | 12/49 | Hants & Dorset, Bournemouth (HA) 1237 |
| 3585 | JEL 257 | Bristol K5G | 76.143 | L27/28R | 12/49 | Hants & Dorset, Bournemouth (HA) 1238 |
| 3586 | JEL 258 | Bristol K5G | 76.145 | L27/28R | 12/49 | Hants & Dorset, Bournemouth (HA) 1239 |
| 3587 | JEL 259 | Bristol K5G | 76.026 | L27/28R | 12/49 | Hants & Dorset, Bournemouth (HA) 1240 |
| 3588 | JEL 260 | Bristol K5G | 78.001 | L27/28R | 1/50 | Hants & Dorset, Bournemouth (HA) 1241 |
| 3589 | JEL 261 | Bristol K5G | 78.003 | L27/28R | 1/50 | Hants & Dorset, Bournemouth (HA) 1242 |
| 3590 | JEL 262 | Bristol K5G | 78.004 | L27/28R | 1/50 | Hants & Dorset, Bournemouth (HA) 1243 |
| 3591 | JEL 263 | Bristol K5G | 78.002 | L27/28R | 2/50 | Hants & Dorset, Bournemouth (HA) 1244 |
| 3592 | JEL 264 | Bristol K6B | 76.124 | L27/28R | 2/50 | Hants & Dorset, Bournemouth (HA) 1245 |
| 3593 | JEL 265 | Bristol K6B | 76.123 | L27/28R | 2/50 | Hants & Dorset, Bournemouth (HA) 1246 |
| 3594 | JEL 266 | Bristol K5G | 78.059 | L27/28R | 2/50 | Hants & Dorset, Bournemouth (HA) 1247 |
| 3595 | JEL 267 | Bristol K5G | 78.060 | L27/28R | 3/50 | Hants & Dorset, Bournemouth (HA) 1248 |
| 3596 | JEL 268 | Bristol K5G | 78.062 | L27/28R | 3/50 | Hants & Dorset, Bournemouth (HA) 1249 |
| 3597 | JEL 269 | Bristol K5G | 78.063 | L27/28R | 3/50 | Hants & Dorset, Bournemouth (HA) 1250 |

| | | | | | | | |
|---|---|---|---|---|---|---|---|
| 3598 | JEL 270 | Bristol K5G | 78.061 | L27/28R | 4/50 | Hants & Dorset, Bournemouth (HA) | 1251 |
| 3599 | JEL 271 | Bristol K5G | 78.123 | L27/28R | 4/50 | Hants & Dorset, Bournemouth (HA) | 1252 |
| 3600 | JEL 272 | Bristol K5G | 78.124 | L27/28R | 4/50 | Hants & Dorset, Bournemouth (HA) | 1253 |
| 3601 | JEL 273 | Bristol K5G | 78.125 | L27/28R | 4/50 | Hants & Dorset, Bournemouth (HA) | 1254 |
| 3602 | JEL 274 | Bristol K5G | 78.133 | L27/28R | 4/50 | Hants & Dorset, Bournemouth (HA) | 1255 |
| 3603 | JEL 275 | Bristol K5G | 78.115 | L27/28R | 4/50 | Hants & Dorset, Bournemouth (HA) | 1256 |
| 3604 | KUO 977 | Bristol K5G | 74.192 | L27/28R | 10/49 | Southern National, Exeter (DN) | 964 |
| 3605 | KUO 978 | Bristol K5G | 74.193 | L27/28R | 10/49 | Southern National, Exeter (DN) | 965 |
| 3606 | KUO 979 | Bristol K5G | 76.033 | L27/28R | 10/49 | Southern National, Exeter (DN) | 966 |
| 3607 | KUO 980 | Bristol K5G | 76.034 | L27/28R | 10/49 | Southern National, Exeter (DN) | 967 |
| 3608 | KUO 981 | Bristol K5G | 76.035 | L27/28R | 12/49 | Southern National, Exeter (DN) | 968 |
| 3609 | KUO 982 | Bristol K6B | 76.058 | L27/28R | 10/49 | Southern National, Exeter (DN) | 969 |
| 3610 | KUO 983 | Bristol K6B | 76.057 | L27/28R | 12/49 | Southern National, Exeter (DN) | 970 |
| 3611 | KUO 984 | Bristol K6B | 76.059 | L27/28R | 12/49 | Southern National, Exeter (DN) | 971 |
| 3612 | KUO 985 | Bristol K5G | 76.117 | L27/28R | 12/49 | Southern National, Exeter (DN) | 972 |
| 3613 | KUO 986 | Bristol K5G | 76.118 | L27/28R | 12/49 | Southern National, Exeter (DN) | 973 |
| 3614 | KUO 987 | Bristol K5G | 76.119 | L27/28R | 1/50 | Southern National, Exeter (DN) | 974 |
| 3615 | KUO 988 | Bristol K5G | 76.111 | L27/28R | 1/50 | Southern National, Exeter (DN) | 975 |
| 3616 | KUO 989 | Bristol K5G | 76.112 | L27/28R | 2/50 | Southern National, Exeter (DN) | 976 |
| 3617 | KUO 991 | Bristol K5G | 76.113 | L27/28R | 2/50 | Southern National, Exeter (DN) | 978 |
| 3618 | KUO 990 | Bristol K6B | 76.120 | L27/28R | 2/50 | Southern National, Exeter (DN) | 977 |
| 3619 | KUO 992 | Bristol K6B | 76.121 | L27/28R | 2/50 | Southern National, Exeter (DN) | 949 |
| 3620 | KUO 993 | Bristol K6B | 76.122 | L27/28R | 2/50 | Southern National, Exeter (DN) | 980 |
| 3621 | KUO 994 | Bristol K5G | 76.195 | L27/28R | 3/50 | Southern National, Exeter (DN) | 981 |
| 3622 | KUO 995 | Bristol K5G | 78.079 | L27/28R | 3/50 | Southern National, Exeter (DN) | 982 |
| 3623 | KUO 996 | Bristol K5G | 78.080 | L27/28R | 5/50 | Southern National, Exeter (DN) | 983 |
| 3624 | KUO 997 | Bristol K5G | 78.131 | L27/28R | 5/50 | Southern National, Exeter (DN) | 984 |
| 3625 | KUO 999 | Bristol K6B | 80.025 | L27/28R | 7/50 | Southern National, Exeter (DN) | 986 |
| 3626 | KUO 998 | Bristol K6B | 80.024 | L27/28R | 7/50 | Southern National, Exeter (DN) | 985 |
| 3627 | FDL 983 | Bristol K5G | 76.014 | L27/28R | 11/49 | Southern Vectis, Newport (IW) | 731 |
| 3628 | FDL 984 | Bristol K5G | 76.015 | L27/28R | 1/50 | Southern Vectis, Newport (IW) | 732 |
| 3629 | FDL 987 | Bristol K5G | 78.102 | L27/28R | 1/50 | Southern Vectis, Newport (IW) | 735 |
| 3630 | FDL 985 | Bristol K5G | 78.032 | L27/28R | 1/50 | Southern Vectis, Newport (IW) | 733 |
| 3631 | FDL 986 | Bristol K5G | 78.033 | L27/28R | 2/50 | Southern Vectis, Newport (IW) | 734 |
| 3632 | FBL 26 | Bristol K6B | 76.166 | L27/28R | 11/49 | Thames Valley, Reading (BE) | 524 |
| 3633 | FBL 27 | Bristol K6B | 76.167 | L27/28R | 12/49 | Thames Valley, Reading (BE) | 525 |
| 3634 | FBL 28 | Bristol K6B | 78.050 | L27/28R | 1/50 | Thames Valley, Reading (BE) | 526 |
| 3635 | FBL 29 | Bristol K6B | 78.051 | L27/28R | 2/50 | Thames Valley, Reading (BE) | 527 |
| 3636 | FBL 30 | Bristol K6B | 78.052 | L27/28R | 2/50 | Thames Valley, Reading (BE) | 528 |
| 3637 | FBL 31 | Bristol K6B | 78.105 | L27/28R | 3/50 | Thames Valley, Reading (BE) | 529 |
| 3638 | FBL 32 | Bristol K6B | 78.106 | L27/28R | 4/50 | Thames Valley, Reading (BE) | 530 |
| 3639 | FBL 33 | Bristol K6B | 78.126 | L27/28R | 4/50 | Thames Valley, Reading (BE) | 531 |
| 3640 | FMO 7 | Bristol K6B | 78.127 | L27/28R | 4/50 | Thames Valley, Reading (BE) | 532 |
| 3641 | FMO 8 | Bristol K6B | 78.128 | L27/28R | 4/50 | Thames Valley, Reading (BE) | 533 |
| 3642 | LHN 913 | Bristol K6B | 74.173 | L27/28R | 11/49 | United AS, Darlington (DM) | BDO113 |
| 3643 | LHN 914 | Bristol K6B | 74.174 | L27/28R | 11/49 | United AS, Darlington (DM) | BDO114 |
| 3644 | LHN 915 | Bristol K6B | 74.176 | L27/28R | 11/49 | United AS, Darlington (DM) | BDO115 |
| 3645 | LHN 916 | Bristol K6B | 74.175 | L27/28R | 12/49 | United AS, Darlington (DM) | BDO116 |
| 3646 | LHN 917 | Bristol K6B | 74.172 | L27/28R | 12/49 | United AS, Darlington (DM) | BDO117 |
| 3647 | LHN 918 | Bristol K6B | 76.021 | L27/28R | 1/50 | United AS, Darlington (DM) | BDO118 |
| 3648 | LHN 919 | Bristol K6B | 76.022 | L27/28R | 1/50 | United AS, Darlington (DM) | BDO119 |
| 3649 | LHN 920 | Bristol K6B | 76.023 | L27/28R | 2/50 | United AS, Darlington (DM) | BDO120 |
| 3650 | LHN 921 | Bristol K6B | 76.104 | L27/28R | 2/50 | United AS, Darlington (DM) | BDO121 |
| 3651 | LHN 922 | Bristol K6B | 76.105 | L27/28R | 2/50 | United AS, Darlington (DM) | BDO122 |
| 3652 | LHN 923 | Bristol K6B | 78.038 | L27/28R | 3/50 | United AS, Darlington (DM) | BDO123 |
| 3653 | LHN 924 | Bristol K6B | 78.040 | L27/28R | 3/50 | United AS, Darlington (DM) | BDO124 |
| 3654 | LHN 925 | Bristol K6B | 78.039 | L27/28R | 3/50 | United AS, Darlington (DM) | BDO125 |
| 3655 | LHN 926 | Bristol K6B | 78.041 | L27/28R | 3/50 | United AS, Darlington (DM) | BDO126 |
| 3656 | LHN 927 | Bristol K6B | 78.037 | L27/28R | 3/50 | United AS, Darlington (DM) | BDO127 |
| 3657 | LHN 928 | Bristol K6B | 78.107 | L27/28R | 3/50 | United AS, Darlington (DM) | BDO128 |
| 3658 | LHN 929 | Bristol K6B | 78.108 | L27/28R | 5/50 | United AS, Darlington (DM) | BDO129 |
| 3659 | LHN 930 | Bristol K6B | 78.109 | L27/28R | 5/50 | United AS, Darlington (DM) | BDO130 |
| 3660 | LHN 931 | Bristol K6B | 78.156 | L27/28R | 6/50 | United AS, Darlington (DM) | BDO131 |
| 3661 | LHN 932 | Bristol K6B | 78.157 | L27/28R | 6/50 | United AS, Darlington (DM) | BDO132 |

| | | | | | | | |
|---|---|---|---|---|---|---|---|
| 3662 | LHN 933 | Bristol K6B | 78.159 | L27/28R | 6/50 | United AS, Darlington (DM) BDO133 |
| 3663 | LHN 934 | Bristol K6B | 78.155 | L27/28R | 6/50 | United AS, Darlington (DM) BDO134 |
| 3664 | LHN 935 | Bristol K6B | 78.158 | L27/28R | 6/50 | United AS, Darlington (DM) BDO135 |
| 3665 | LHN 936 | Bristol K6B | 80.016 | L27/28R | 7/50 | United AS, Darlington (DM) BDO136 |
| 3666 | LHN 937 | Bristol K6B | 80.017 | L27/28R | 7/50 | United AS, Darlington (DM) BDO137 |
| 3667 | ERP 605 | Bristol K5G | 76.078 | L27/28R | 10/49 | United Counties, Northampton (NO) 665 |
| 3668 | ERP 606 | Bristol K5G | 76.077 | L27/28R | 11/49 | United Counties, Northampton (NO) 666 |
| 3669 | ERP 607 | Bristol K5G | 76.084 | L27/28R | 11/49 | United Counties, Northampton (NO) 667 |
| 3670 | ERP 608 | Bristol K6B | 78.023 | L27/28R | 12/49 | United Counties, Northampton (NO) 668 |
| 3671 | ERP 609 | Bristol K6B | 78.024 | L27/28R | 12/49 | United Counties, Northampton (NO) 669 |
| 3672 | ERP 610 | Bristol K6B | 78.025 | L27/28R | 12/49 | United Counties, Northampton (NO) 670 |
| 3673 | ERP 611 | Bristol K6B | 78.026 | L27/28R | 1/50 | United Counties, Northampton (NO) 671 |
| 3674 | ERP 612 | Bristol K6B | 78.027 | L27/28R | 1/50 | United Counties, Northampton (NO) 672 |
| 3675 | ERP 613 | Bristol K5G | 78.088 | L27/28R | 2/50 | United Counties, Northampton (NO) 673 |
| 3676 | ERP 614 | Bristol K5G | 78.089 | L27/28R | 2/50 | United Counties, Northampton (NO) 674 |
| 3677 | ERP 615 | Bristol K6B | 78.090 | L27/28R | 3/50 | United Counties, Northampton (NO) 675 |
| 3678 | ERP 616 | Bristol K6B | 78.091 | L27/28R | 3/50 | United Counties, Northampton (NO) 676 |
| 3679 | ERP 617 | Bristol K5G | 78.119 | L27/28R | 4/50 | United Counties, Northampton (NO) 677 |
| 3680 | ERP 618 | Bristol K5G | 78.120 | L27/28R | 4/50 | United Counties, Northampton (NO) 678 |
| 3681 | ERP 619 | Bristol K5G | 78.178 | L27/28R | 6/50 | United Counties, Northampton (NO) 679 |
| 3682 | ERP 620 | Bristol K5G | 78.179 | L27/28R | 6/50 | United Counties, Northampton (NO) 680 |
| 3683 | ERP 621 | Bristol K5G | 78.180 | L27/28R | 6/50 | United Counties, Northampton (NO) 681 |
| 3684 | ERP 623 | Bristol K5G | 78.184 | L27/28R | 6/50 | United Counties, Northampton (NO) 683 |
| 3685 | ERP 622 | Bristol K5G | 78.183 | L27/28R | 6/50 | United Counties, Northampton (NO) 682 |
| 3686 | DHJ 607 | Bristol K5G | 76.016 | L27/28R | 11/49 | Westcliff-on-Sea MS (EX) |
| 3687 | DHJ 608 | Bristol K5G | 76.017 | L27/28R | 11/49 | Westcliff-on-Sea MS (EX) |
| 3688 | DHJ 609 | Bristol K5G | 76.133 | L27/28R | 12/49 | Westcliff-on-Sea MS (EX) |
| 3689 | DHJ 610 | Bristol K6B | 76.024 | L27/28R | 1/50 | Westcliff-on-Sea MS (EX) |
| 3690 | DHJ 611 | Bristol K6B | 76.085 | L27/28R | 3/50 | Westcliff-on-Sea MS (EX) |
| 3691 | DHJ 612 | Bristol K6B | 76.025 | L27/28R | 3/50 | Westcliff-on-Sea MS (EX) |
| 3692 | KUO 927 | Bristol K5G | 74.188 | L27/28R | 9/49 | Western National, Exeter (DN) 914 |
| 3693 | KUO 929 | Bristol K5G | 74.187 | L27/28R | 9/49 | Western National, Exeter (DN) 916 |
| 3694 | KUO 928 | Bristol K5G | 74.189 | L27/28R | 9/49 | Western National, Exeter (DN) 915 |
| 3695 | KUO 930 | Bristol K5G | 74.190 | L27/28R | 9/49 | Western National, Exeter (DN) 917 |
| 3696 | KUO 931 | Bristol K5G | 74.191 | L27/28R | 9/49 | Western National, Exeter (DN) 918 |
| 3697 | KUO 932 | Bristol K5G | 76.030 | L27/28R | 10/49 | Western National, Exeter (DN) 919 |
| 3698 | KUO 933 | Bristol K5G | 76.031 | L27/28R | 10/49 | Western National, Exeter (DN) 920 |
| 3699 | KUO 934 | Bristol K5G | 76.032 | L27/28R | 10/49 | Western National, Exeter (DN) 921 |
| 3700 | KUO 935 | Bristol K5G | 76.044 | L27/28R | 10/49 | Western National, Exeter (DN) 922 |
| 3701 | KUO 936 | Bristol K5G | 76.054 | L27/28R | 11/49 | Western National, Exeter (DN) 923 |
| 3702 | KUO 937 | Bristol K5G | 76.055 | L27/28R | 11/49 | Western National, Exeter (DN) 924 |
| 3703 | KUO 938 | Bristol K5G | 76.135 | L27/28R | 12/49 | Western National, Exeter (DN) 925 |
| 3704 | KUO 939 | Bristol K5G | 76.045 | L27/28R | 12/49 | Western National, Exeter (DN) 923 |
| 3705 | KUO 940 | Bristol K5G | 76.056 | L27/28R | 12/49 | Western National, Exeter (DN) 927 |
| 3706 | KUO 941 | Bristol K6B | 76.079 | L27/28R | 12/49 | Western National, Exeter (DN) 928 |
| 3707 | KUO 942 | Bristol K6B | 76.082 | L27/28R | 12/49 | Western National, Exeter (DN) 929 |
| 3708 | KUO 943 | Bristol K5G | 76.134 | L27/28R | 12/49 | Western National, Exeter (DN) 930 |
| 3709 | KUO 944 | Bristol K6B | 76.080 | L27/28R | 12/49 | Western National, Exeter (DN) 931 |
| 3710 | KUO 945 | Bristol K6B | 76.081 | L27/28R | 12/49 | Western National, Exeter (DN) 932 |
| 3711 | KUO 946 | Bristol K6B | 76.083 | L27/28R | 12/49 | Western National, Exeter (DN) 933 |
| 3712 | KUO 947 | Bristol K5G | 76.151 | L27/28R | 12/49 | Western National, Exeter (DN) 934 |
| 3713 | KUO 948 | Bristol K5G | 76.152 | L27/28R | 12/49 | Western National, Exeter (DN) 935 |
| 3714 | KUO 949 | Bristol K5G | 76.153 | L27/28R | 12/49 | Western National, Exeter (DN) 936 |
| 3715 | KUO 950 | Bristol K5G | 76.154 | L27/28R | 12/49 | Western National, Exeter (DN) 937 |
| 3716 | KUO 951 | Bristol K5G | 76.155 | L27/28R | 12/49 | Western National, Exeter (DN) 938 |
| 3717 | KUO 952 | Bristol K5G | 76.165 | L27/28R | 1/50 | Western National, Exeter (DN) 939 |
| 3718 | KUO 953 | Bristol K5G | 76.164 | L27/28R | 12/49 | Western National, Exeter (DN) 940 |
| 3719 | KUO 954 | Bristol K5G | 76.090 | L27/28R | 2/50 | Western National, Exeter (DN) 941 |
| 3720 | KUO 955 | Bristol K5G | 76.106 | L27/28R | 2/50 | Western National, Exeter (DN) 942 |
| 3721 | KUO 956 | Bristol K5G | 76.107 | L27/28R | 2/50 | Western National, Exeter (DN) 943 |
| 3722 | KUO 957 | Bristol K5G | 76.168 | L27/28R | 2/50 | Western National, Exeter (DN) 944 |
| 3723 | KUO 958 | Bristol K5G | 76.169 | L27/28R | 2/50 | Western National, Exeter (DN) 945 |
| 3724 | KUO 960 | Bristol K6B | 76.189 | L27/28R | 3/50 | Western National, Exeter (DN) 947 |
| 3725 | KUO 959 | Bristol K6B | 76.188 | L27/28R | 3/50 | Western National, Exeter (DN) 946 |

| | | | | | | |
|---|---|---|---|---|---|---|
| 3726 | KUO 961 | Bristol K6B | 76.190 | L27/28R | 3/50 | Western National, Exeter (DN) 948 |
| 3727 | KUO 963 | Bristol K6B | 76.192 | L27/28R | 3/50 | Western National, Exeter (DN) 950 |
| 3728 | KUO 962 | Bristol K6B | 76.191 | L27/28R | 3/50 | Western National, Exeter (DN) 949 |
| 3729 | KUO 964 | Bristol K6B | 78.068 | L27/28R | 3/50 | Western National, Exeter (DN) 951 |
| 3730 | KUO 965 | Bristol K6B | 78.065 | L27/28R | 3/50 | Western National, Exeter (DN) 952 |
| 3731 | KUO 966 | Bristol K6B | 78.066 | L27/28R | 5/50 | Western National, Exeter (DN) 953 |
| 3732 | KUO 967 | Bristol K6B | 78.067 | L27/28R | 3/50 | Western National, Exeter (DN) 954 |
| 3733 | KUO 968 | Bristol K6B | 78.069 | L27/28R | 6/50 | Western National, Exeter (DN) 955 |
| 3734 | KUO 969 | Bristol K5G | 78.151 | L27/28R | 5/50 | Western National, Exeter (DN) 956 |
| 3735 | KUO 970 | Bristol K5G | 78.152 | L27/28R | 5/50 | Western National, Exeter (DN) 957 |
| 3736 | KUO 971 | Bristol K5G | 78.153 | L27/28R | 6/50 | Western National, Exeter (DN) 958 |
| 3737 | KUO 973 | Bristol K6B | 80.019 | L27/28R | 7/50 | Western National, Exeter (DN) 960 |
| 3738 | KUO 972 | Bristol K6B | 80.018 | L27/28R | 7/50 | Western National, Exeter (DN) 959 |
| 3739 | KUO 974 | Bristol K6B | 80.020 | L27/28R | 3/50 | Southern National, Exeter (DN) 961 |
| 3740 | KUO 975 | Bristol K6B | 80.021 | L27/28R | 3/50 | Southern National, Exeter (DN) 962 |
| 3741 | KUO 976 | Bristol K6B | 80.022 | L27/28R | 3/50 | Southern National, Exeter (DN) 963 |
| 3742 | HWW 864 | Bristol K6B | 74.183 | L27/28R | 11/49 | West Yorkshire RCC, Harrogate (WR) 775 |
| 3743 | HWW 865 | Bristol K6B | 74.184 | L27/28R | 12/49 | West Yorkshire RCC, Harrogate (WR) 776 |
| 3744 | HWW 866 | Bristol K6B | 74.185 | L27/28R | 12/49 | West Yorkshire RCC, Harrogate (WR) 777 |
| 3745 | HWW 863 | Bristol K6B | 74.182 | L27/28R | 1/50 | West Yorkshire RCC, Harrogate (WR) 774 |
| 3746 | HWW 867 | Bristol K6B | 74.186 | L27/28R | 3/50 | West Yorkshire RCC, Harrogate (WR) 778 |
| 3747 | HWW 868 | Bristol K6B | 78.075 | L27/28R | 3/50 | West Yorkshire RCC, Harrogate (WR) 779 |
| 3748 | HWW 869 | Bristol K6B | 78.076 | L27/28R | 3/50 | West Yorkshire RCC, Harrogate (WR) 780 |
| 3749 | HWW 870 | Bristol K6B | 78.077 | L27/28R | 3/50 | West Yorkshire RCC, Harrogate (WR) 781 |
| 3750 | HWW 871 | Bristol K6B | 78.078 | L27/28R | 3/50 | West Yorkshire RCC, Harrogate (WR) 782 |
| 3751 | HWW 872 | Bristol K6B | 78.129 | L27/28R | 3/50 | West Yorkshire RCC, Harrogate (WR) 783 |
| 3752 | HWW 873 | Bristol K6B | 78.130 | L27/28R | 3/50 | West Yorkshire RCC, Harrogate (WR) 784 |
| 3753 | HWW 874 | Bristol K6B | 80.008 | L27/28R | 6/50 | West Yorkshire RCC, Harrogate (WR) 785 |
| 3754 | HWW 875 | Bristol K6B | 80.009 | L27/28R | 7/50 | West Yorkshire RCC, Harrogate (WR) 786 |
| 3755 | HWW 876 | Bristol K6B | 80.010 | L27/28R | 6/50 | West Yorkshire RCC, Harrogate (WR) 787 |
| 3756 | HWW 878 | Bristol K6B | 80.012 | L27/28R | 7/50 | West Yorkshire RCC, Harrogate (WR) 789 |
| 3757 | HWW 879 | Bristol K6B | 80.013 | L27/28R | 7/50 | West Yorkshire RCC, Harrogate (WR) 790 |
| 3758 | HWW 877 | Bristol K6B | 80.011 | L27/28R | 7/50 | West Yorkshire RCC, Harrogate (WR) 788 |
| 3759 | HWW 880 | Bristol K6B | 80.023 | L27/28R | 7/50 | West Yorkshire RCC, Harrogate (WR) 791 |
| 3760 | HWW 881 | Bristol K6B | 76.087 | L27/28R | 11/49 | Keighley-West Yorkshire, Harrogate (WR) K792 |
| 3761 | HWW 882 | Bristol K6B | 76.088 | L27/28R | 1/50 | Keighley-West Yorkshire, Harrogate (WR) K793 |
| 3762 | HWW 883 | Bristol K6B | 78.137 | L27/28R | 5/50 | Keighley-West Yorkshire, Harrogate (WR) K794 |
| 3763 | HWW 884 | Bristol K6B | 78.138 | L27/28R | 5/50 | Keighley-West Yorkshire, Harrogate (WR) K795 |
| 3764 | GAM 10 | Bristol K5G | 76.046 | L27/28R | 12/49 | Wilts & Dorset, Salisbury (WI) 293 |
| 3765 | GAM 11 | Bristol K5G | 76.047 | L27/28R | 2/50 | Wilts & Dorset, Salisbury (WI) 294 |
| 3766 | GHR 199 | Bristol K5G | 78.121 | L27/28R | 2/50 | Wilts & Dorset, Salisbury (WI) 298 |
| 3767 | GHR 200 | Bristol K5G | 78.122 | L27/28R | 2/50 | Wilts & Dorset, Salisbury (WI) 299 |
| 3768 | GHR 364 | Bristol K5G | 78.140 | L27/28R | 4/50 | Wilts & Dorset, Salisbury (WI) 300 |
| 3769 | GHR 365 | Bristol K5G | 78.141 | L27/28R | 4/50 | Wilts & Dorset, Salisbury (WI) 301 |
| 3770 | GHR 366 | Bristol K5G | 78.142 | L27/28R | 5/50 | Wilts & Dorset, Salisbury (WI) 302 |
| 3771 | GHR 367 | Bristol K5G | 78.143 | L27/28R | 5/50 | Wilts & Dorset, Salisbury (WI) 303 |
| 3772 | GHR 368 | Bristol K5G | 78.144 | L27/28R | 5/50 | Wilts & Dorset, Salisbury (WI) 304 |
| 3773 | GMR 26 | Bristol K5G | 78.194 | L27/28R | 7/50 | Wilts & Dorset, Salisbury (WI) 311 |
| 3774 | GMR 27 | Bristol K5G | 78.195 | L27/28R | 7/50 | Wilts & Dorset, Salisbury (WI) 312 |
| 3775 | GMR 28 | Bristol K5G | 78.196 | L27/28R | 7/50 | Wilts & Dorset, Salisbury (WI) 313 |
| 3776 * | EPM 1 | Bristol K5G | 74.164 | H30/26R | 5/49 | Brighton, Hove & District (ES) 6404 |
| 3777 * | EPM 2 | Bristol K5G | 74.165 | H30/26R | 5/49 | Brighton, Hove & District (ES) 6405 |
| 3778 * | EPM 3 | Bristol K5G | 74.166 | H30/26R | 5/49 | Brighton, Hove & District (ES) 6406 |
| 3779 * | EPM 4 | Bristol K5G | 76.006 | H30/26R | 11/49 | Brighton, Hove & District (ES) 6407 |
| 3780 | EPM 5 | Bristol K5G | 76.007 | H30/26R | 11/49 | Brighton, Hove & District (ES) 6408 |
| 3781 | EPM 6 | Bristol K5G | 76.008 | H30/26R | 11/49 | Brighton, Hove & District (ES) 6409 |
| 3782 | EPM 7 | Bristol K5G | 76.009 | H30/26R | 11/49 | Brighton, Hove & District (ES) 6410 |
| 3783 | EPM 8 | Bristol K5G | 78.093 | H30/26R | 2/50 | Brighton, Hove & District (ES) 6411 |
| 3784 | EPM 9 | Bristol K5G | 78.094 | H30/26R | 3/50 | Brighton, Hove & District (ES) 6412 |
| 3785 | EPM 10 | Bristol K5G | 78.095 | H30/26R | 3/50 | Brighton, Hove & District (ES) 6413 |
| 3786 | EPM 11 | Bristol K5G | 78.161 | H30/26R | 5/50 | Brighton, Hove & District (ES) 6414 |
| 3787 | EPM 12 | Bristol K5G | 78.162 | H30/26R | 6/50 | Brighton, Hove & District (ES) 6415 |
| 3788 | EPM 13 | Bristol K5G | 78.163 | H30/26R | 6/50 | Brighton, Hove & District (ES) 6416 |
| 3789 | EPM 14 | Bristol K5G | 78.181 | H30/26R | 7/50 | Brighton, Hove & District (ES) 6417 |

| | | | | | | | |
|---|---|---|---|---|---|---|---|
| 3790 | EPM 15 | Bristol K5G | 78.182 | H30/26R | 7/50 | Brighton, Hove & District (ES) 6418 | |
| 3791 | KNG 152 | Bristol K5G | 76.180 | H30/26R | 11/49 | Eastern Counties, Norwich (NK) LKH152 | |
| 3792 | KNG 153 | Bristol K5G | 76.183 | H30/26R | 11/49 | Eastern Counties, Norwich (NK) LKH153 | |
| 3793 | KNG 154 | Bristol K5G | 76.184 | H30/26R | 11/49 | Eastern Counties, Norwich (NK) LKH154 | |
| 3794 | KNG 155 | Bristol K5G | 76.181 | H30/26R | 11/49 | Eastern Counties, Norwich (NK) LKH155 | |
| 3795 | KNG 156 | Bristol K5G | 76.182 | H30/26R | 11/49 | Eastern Counties, Norwich (NK) LKH156 | |
| 3796 | KNG 157 | Bristol K5G | 76.186 | H30/26R | 2/50 | Eastern Counties, Norwich (NK) LKH157 | |
| 3797 | KNG 158 | Bristol K5G | 76.185 | H30/26R | 1/50 | Eastern Counties, Norwich (NK) LKH158 | |
| 3798 | KNG 159 | Bristol K5G | 76.187 | H30/26R | 2/50 | Eastern Counties, Norwich (NK) LKH159 | |
| 3799 | KNG 160 | Bristol K5G | 76.193 | H30/26R | 2/50 | Eastern Counties, Norwich (NK) LKH160 | |
| 3800 | KNG 161 | Bristol K5G | 76.194 | H30/26R | 2/50 | Eastern Counties, Norwich (NK) LKH161 | |
| 3801 | KNG 162 | Bristol K5G | 76.196 | H30/26R | 3/50 | Eastern Counties, Norwich (NK) LKH162 | |
| 3802 | KNG 163 | Bristol K5G | 76.197 | H30/26R | 2/50 | Eastern Counties, Norwich (NK) LKH163 | |
| 3803 | KNG 164 | Bristol K5G | 76.200 | H30/26R | 3/50 | Eastern Counties, Norwich (NK) LKH164 | |
| 3804 | KNG 165 | Bristol K5G | 78.070 | H30/26R | 3/50 | Eastern Counties, Norwich (NK) LKH165 | |
| 3805 | KNG 250 | Bristol K5G | 78.071 | H30/26R | 3/50 | Eastern Counties, Norwich (NK) LKH250 | |
| 3806 | KNG 251 | Bristol K5G | 78.099 | H30/26R | 3/50 | Eastern Counties, Norwich (NK) LKH251 | |
| 3807 | KNG 252 | Bristol K5G | 78.100 | H30/26R | 5/50 | Eastern Counties, Norwich (NK) LKH252 | |
| 3808 | KNG 253 | Bristol K5G | 78.169 | H30/26R | 6/50 | Eastern Counties, Norwich (NK) LKH253 | |
| 3809 | KNG 254 | Bristol K5G | 78.170 | H30/26R | 6/50 | Eastern Counties, Norwich (NK) LKH254 | |
| 3810 | KNG 255 | Bristol K5G | 78.171 | H30/26R | 6/50 | Eastern Counties, Norwich (NK) LKH255 | |
| 3811 | KNG 256 | Bristol K5G | 78.172 | H30/26R | 6/50 | Eastern Counties, Norwich (NK) LKH256 | |
| 3812 | KNG 257 | Bristol K5G | 78.187 | H30/26R | 7/50 | Eastern Counties, Norwich (NK) LKH257 | |
| 3813 | KNG 258 | Bristol K5G | 78.185 | H30/26R | 7/50 | Eastern Counties, Norwich (NK) LKH258 | |
| 3814 | KNG 259 | Bristol K5G | 78.186 | H30/26R | 7/50 | Eastern Counties, Norwich (NK) LKH259 | |
| 3815 | KNG 260 | Bristol K5G | 78.188 | H30/26R | 7/50 | Eastern Counties, Norwich (NK) LKH260 | |
| 3816 | GBE 839 | Bristol K6B | 78.134 | H30/26R | 2/50 | Lincolnshire RCC, Bracebridge Heath (KN) 752 | |
| 3817 | GBE 840 | Bristol K6B | 78.135 | H30/26R | 5/50 | Lincolnshire RCC, Bracebridge Heath (KN) 753 | |
| 3818 | GBE 841 | Bristol K6B | 78.136 | H30/26R | 7/50 | Lincolnshire RCC, Bracebridge Heath (KN) 754 | |
| 3819 | HWW 885 | Bristol K6B | 76.004 | H30/26R | 11/49 | York-West Yorkshire, Harrogate (WR) Y796 | |
| 3820 | HWW 886 | Bristol K6B | 76.005 | H30/26R | 11/49 | York-West Yorkshire, Harrogate (WR) Y797 | |
| 3821 | HWW 887 | Bristol K6B | 78.058 | H30/26R | 2/50 | York-West Yorkshire, Harrogate (WR) Y798 | |
| 3822 | HWW 888 | Bristol K6B | 78.064 | H30/26R | 5/50 | York-West Yorkshire, Harrogate (WR) Y799 | |
| 3823 | HWW 889 | Bristol K6B | 80.005 | H30/26R | 7/50 | York-West Yorkshire, Harrogate (WR) Y800 | |
| 3824 | HWW 890 | Bristol K6B | 80.006 | H30/26R | 7/50 | York-West Yorkshire, Harrogate (WR) Y801 | |
| 3825 | HWW 891 | Bristol K6B | 78.160 | H30/26R | 7/50 | York-West Yorkshire, Harrogate (WR) Y802 | |
| 3826 | HWW 892 | Bristol K6B | 80.007 | H30/26R | 7/50 | York-West Yorkshire, Harrogate (WR) Y803 | |
| 3827 * | LHY 925 | Bristol K6B | 76.175 | H30/26R | 9/49 | Bristol Tramways (GL) C3436 | |
| 3828 | LHY 926 | Bristol K6B | 76.176 | H31/28R | 11/49 | Bristol Tramways (GL) C3437 | |
| 3829 | LHY 927 | Bristol K6B | 76.177 | H31/28R | 11/49 | Bristol Tramways (GL) C3438 | |
| 3830 | LHY 928 | Bristol K6B | 76.178 | H31/28R | 11/49 | Bristol Tramways (GL) C3439 | |
| 3831 | LHY 929 | Bristol K6B | 76.179 | H31/28R | 11/49 | Bristol Tramways (GL) C3440 | |
| 3832 | LHY 930 | Bristol K6B | 78.028 | H31/28R | 2/50 | Bristol Tramways (GL) C3441 | |
| 3833 | LHY 931 | Bristol K6B | 78.029 | H31/28R | 2/50 | Bristol Tramways (GL) C3442 | |
| 3834 | LHY 932 | Bristol K6B | 78.030 | H31/28R | 7/50 | Bristol Tramways (GL) C3443 | |
| 3835 | LHY 933 | Bristol K6B | 78.031 | H31/28R | 7/50 | Bristol Tramways (GL) C3444 | |
| 3836 | LHY 934 | Bristol K6B | 78.081 | H31/28R | 7/50 | Bristol Tramways (GL) C3445 | |
| 3837 | LHY 935 | Bristol K6B | 78.082 | H31/28R | 7/50 | Bristol Tramways (GL) C3446 | |
| 3838 | LHY 936 | Bristol K6B | 78.083 | H31/28R | 4/50 | Bristol Tramways (GL) 3773 | |
| 3839 | LHY 937 | Bristol K6B | 78.084 | H31/28R | 4/50 | Bristol Tramways (GL) 3774 | |
| 3840 | LHY 938 | Bristol K6B | 78.085 | H31/28R | 4/50 | Bristol Tramways (GL) 3775 | |
| 3841 | LHY 939 | Bristol K6B | 78.110 | H31/28R | 4/50 | Bristol Tramways (GL) 3776 | |
| 3842 | LHY 940 | Bristol K6B | 78.111 | H31/28R | 3/50 | Bristol Tramways (GL) C3451 | |
| 3843 | LHY 941 | Bristol K6B | 78.112 | H31/28R | 4/50 | Bristol Tramways (GL) 3777 | |
| 3844 | LHY 942 | Bristol K6B | 78.113 | H31/28R | 5/50 | Bristol Tramways (GL) 3778 | |
| 3845 | LHY 943 | Bristol K6B | 78.114 | H31/28R | 5/50 | Bristol Tramways (GL) 3779 | |
| 3846 | LHY 944 | Bristol K6B | 78.145 | H31/28R | 5/50 | Bristol Tramways (GL) 3780 | |
| 3847 | LHY 946 | Bristol K6B | 78.147 | H31/28R | 5/50 | Bristol Tramways (GL) 3781 | |
| 3848 | LHY 945 | Bristol K6B | 78.146 | H31/28R | 7/50 | Bristol Tramways (GL) C3453 | |
| 3849 | LHY 947 | Bristol K6B | 80.014 | H31/28R | 7/50 | Bristol Tramways (GL) C3454 | |
| 3850 | LHY 948 | Bristol K6B | 80.015 | H31/28R | 7/50 | Bristol Tramways (GL) C3455 | |
| 3851 | | | | | | Not Built | |
| 3852 | LHY 949 | Bristol LDX6B | LDX.001 | H35/23R | 9/49 | Bristol Tramways (GL) C5000 | |
| 3853 | JWT 712 | Bristol LDX6B | LDX.002 | H33/25R | 4/50 | West Yorkshire RCC, Harrogate (WR) 822 | |

| | | | | | | | |
|---|---|---|---|---|---|---|---|
| 3854 | AXG 669 | Guy Arab III | FD70325 | H30/26R | 6/50 | Middlesbrough Corporation (NR) 69 |
| 3855 | AXG 670 | Guy Arab III | FD70358 | H30/26R | 6/50 | Middlesbrough Corporation (NR) 70 |
| 3856 | AXG 671 | Guy Arab III | FD70170 | H30/26R | 6/50 | Middlesbrough Corporation (NR) 71 |
| 3857 | AXG 672 | Guy Arab III | FD70360 | H30/26R | 6/50 | Middlesbrough Corporation (NR) 72 |
| 3858 | AXG 673 | Guy Arab III | FD70169 | H30/26R | 6/50 | Middlesbrough Corporation (NR) 73 |
| 3859 | AXG 674 | Guy Arab III | FD70389 | H30/26R | 6/50 | Middlesbrough Corporation (NR) 74 |
| 3860 | AXG 675 | Guy Arab III | FD70400 | H30/26R | 6/50 | Middlesbrough Corporation (NR) 75 |
| 3861 | AXG 676 | Guy Arab III | FD70424 | H30/26R | 7/50 | Middlesbrough Corporation (NR) 76 |
| 3862 | AXG 677 | Guy Arab III | FD70430 | H30/26R | 7/50 | Middlesbrough Corporation (NR) 77 |
| 3863 | AXG 678 | Guy Arab III | FD70443 | H30/26R | 7/50 | Middlesbrough Corporation (NR) 78 |
| 3864 | AXG 679 | Guy Arab III | FD70474 | H30/26R | 7/50 | Middlesbrough Corporation (NR) 79 |
| 3865 | AXG 680 | Guy Arab III | FD70479 | H30/26R | 8/50 | Middlesbrough Corporation (NR) 80 |
| 3866 | AXG 681 | Guy Arab III | FD70471 | H30/26R | 8/50 | Middlesbrough Corporation (NR) 81 |
| 3867 | AXG 682 | Guy Arab III | FD70484 | H30/26R | 8/50 | Middlesbrough Corporation (NR) 82 |
| 3868 | AXG 683 | Guy Arab III | FD70487 | H30/26R | 9/50 | Middlesbrough Corporation (NR) 83 |
| 3869 | AXG 684 | Guy Arab III | FD70490 | H30/26R | 9/50 | Middlesbrough Corporation (NR) 84 |
| 3870 * | FM 8153 | Leyland TD3 | 4260 | L27/28R | 12/49 | Crosville MS, Chester (CH) M6 |
| 3871 * | FM 8150 | Leyland TD3 | 4257 | L27/28R | 12/49 | Crosville MS, Chester (CH) M3 |
| 3872 * | FM 8149 | Leyland TD3 | 4256 | L27/28R | 1/50 | Crosville MS, Chester (CH) M2 |
| 3873 * | FM 8155 | Leyland TD3 | 4262 | L27/28R | 1/50 | Crosville MS, Chester (CH) M8 |
| 3874 * | FM 8151 | Leyland TD3 | 4258 | L27/28R | 2/50 | Crosville MS, Chester (CH) M4 |
| 3875 * | FM 8152 | Leyland TD3 | 4259 | L27/28R | 3/50 | Crosville MS, Chester (CH) M5 |
| 3876 * | FM 8156 | Leyland TD3 | 4263 | L27/28R | 3/50 | Crosville MS, Chester (CH) M9 |
| 3877 * | FM 9056 | Leyland TD4c | 5948 | L27/28R | 12/49 | Crosville MS, Chester (CH) M20 |
| 3878 * | AFM 496 | Leyland TD4 | 10144 | L27/28R | 12/49 | Crosville MS, Chester (CH) M42 |
| 3879 * | FM 9057 | Leyland TD4c | 5949 | L27/28R | 1/50 | Crosville MS, Chester (CH) M21 |
| 3880 * | FM 9049 | Leyland TD4 | 5941 | L27/28R | 1/50 | Crosville MS, Chester (CH) M13 |
| 3881 * | FM 9051 | Leyland TD4 | 5943 | L27/28R | 2/50 | Crosville MS, Chester (CH) M15 |
| 3882 * | FM 9052 | Leyland TD4 | 5944 | L27/28R | 2/50 | Crosville MS, Chester (CH) M16 |
| 3883 * | AFM 501 | Leyland TD4 | 10148 | L27/28R | 2/50 | Crosville MS, Chester (CH) M46 |
| 3884 * | FM 9053 | Leyland TD4 | 5945 | L27/28R | 3/50 | Crosville MS, Chester (CH) M17 |
| 3885 * | FM 9054 | Leyland TD4 | 5946 | L27/28R | 3/50 | Crosville MS, Chester (CH) M18 |
| 3886 * | FM 9055 | Leyland TD4c | 5947 | L27/28R | 4/50 | Crosville MS, Chester (CH) M19 |
| 3887 * | AFM 495 | Leyland TD4 | 10143 | L27/28R | 4/50 | Crosville MS, Chester (CH) M41 |
| 3888 * | AFM 497 | Leyland TD4 | 10145 | L27/28R | 4/50 | Crosville MS, Chester (CH) M43 |
| 3889 * | AFM 499 | Leyland TD4 | 10147 | L27/28R | 4/50 | Crosville MS, Chester (CH) M45 |
| 3890 * | BAO 772 | Leyland TD4 | 10015 | L27/28R | 1/50 | Cumberland MS, Whitehaven (CU) 287 |
| 3891 * | DAO 49 | Leyland TD5 | 17799 | L27/28R | 2/50 | Cumberland MS, Whitehaven (CU) 292 |
| 3892 * | BAO 774 | Leyland TD4 | 10017 | L27/28R | 3/50 | Cumberland MS, Whitehaven (CU) 288 |
| 3893 * | DAO 50 | Leyland TD5 | 17800 | L27/28R | 4/50 | Cumberland MS, Whitehaven (CU) 293 |
| 3894 * | BRM 594 | Leyland TD4 | 11397 | L27/28R | 5/50 | Cumberland MS, Whitehaven (CU) 286 |
| 3895 * | DAO 51 | Leyland TD5 | 17801 | L27/28R | 6/50 | Cumberland MS, Whitehaven (CU) 294 |
| 3896 * | BAO 775 | Leyland TD4 | 10018 | L27/28R | 7/50 | Cumberland MS, Whitehaven (CU) 289 |
| 3897 * | BRM 595 | Leyland TD4 | 11398 | L27/28R | 8/50 | Cumberland MS, Whitehaven (CU) 290 |
| 3898 * | BRM 596 | Leyland TD4 | 11399 | L27/28R | 9/50 | Cumberland MS, Whitehaven (CU) 291 |
| 3899 * | NG 3864 | Leyland TD2 | 2350 | L27/26R | 10/49 | Eastern Counties, Norwich (NK) A203 |
| 3900 * | NG 2729 | Leyland TD2 | 1416 | L27/26R | 10/49 | Eastern Counties, Norwich (NK) A194 |
| 3901 * | NG 5402 | Leyland TD2 | 3515 | L27/26R | 10/49 | Eastern Counties, Norwich (NK) A211 |
| 3902 * | VG 4819 | Leyland TD2 | 1907 | L27/26R | 10/49 | Eastern Counties, Norwich (NK) A221 |
| 3903 * | VG 4823 | Leyland TD2 | 1911 | L27/26R | 10/49 | Eastern Counties, Norwich (NK) A225 |
| 3904 * | NG 2723 | Leyland TD2 | 1410 | L27/26R | 10/49 | Eastern Counties, Norwich (NK) A188 |
| 3905 * | VG 4824 | Leyland TD2 | 1912 | L27/26R | 10/49 | Eastern Counties, Norwich (NK) A226 |
| 3906 * | NG 3867 | Leyland TD2 | 2353 | L27/26R | 10/49 | Eastern Counties, Norwich (NK) A206 |
| 3907 * | NG 2732 | Leyland TD2 | 1441 | L27/26R | 12/49 | Eastern Counties, Norwich (NK) A197 |
| 3908 * | VG 4821 | Leyland TD2 | 1909 | L27/26R | 12/49 | Eastern Counties, Norwich (NK) A223 |
| 3909 * | NG 3868 | Leyland TD2 | 2354 | L27/26R | 12/49 | Eastern Counties, Norwich (NK) A207 |
| 3910 * | VG 4820 | Leyland TD2 | 1908 | L27/26R | 12/49 | Eastern Counties, Norwich (NK) A222 |
| 3911 * | CAE 861 | Bristol G.JW | G133 | H31/28R | 8/49 | Bristol Tramways (GL) C3016 |
| 3912 * | DHT 942 | Bristol GO5G | GO5G.165 | H31/28R | 8/49 | Bristol Tramways (GL) C3063 |
| 3913 * | CAE 863 | Bristol G.JW | G135 | H31/28R | 8/49 | Bristol Tramways (GL) C3018 |
| 3914 * | DHT 938 | Bristol GO5G | GO5G.170 | H31/28R | 8/49 | Bristol Tramways (GL) C3068 |
| 3915 * | CHU 707 | Bristol GO5G | GO5G.86 | H31/28R | 9/49 | Bristol Tramways (GL) C3030 |
| 3916 * | DHT 940 | Bristol GO5G | GO5G.167 | H31/28R | 9/49 | Bristol Tramways (GL) C3065 |
| 3917 * | BHW 639 | Bristol GO5G | GO5G.30 | H31/28R | 9/49 | Bristol Tramways (GL) C3024 |

| | | | | | | | |
|---|---|---|---|---|---|---|---|
| 3918 * | BHT 532 | Bristol G.JW | G107 | H31/28R | 9/49 | Bristol Tramways (GL) | C3009 |
| 3919 * | CHW 44 | Bristol GO5G | GO5G.87 | H31/28R | 9/49 | Bristol Tramways (GL) | C3033 |
| 3920 * | EAE 286 | Bristol GO5G | GO5G.210 | H31/28R | 9/49 | Bristol Tramways (GL) | C3077 |
| 3921 * | DAE 371 | Bristol GO5G | GO5G.135 | H31/28R | 10/49 | Bristol Tramways (GL) | C3056 |
| 3922 * | CHU 177 | Bristol GO5G | GO5G.62 | H31/28R | 10/49 | Bristol Tramways (GL) | C3025 |
| 3923 * | CAE 865 | Bristol G.JW | G137 | H31/28R | 10/49 | Bristol Tramways (GL) | C3020 |
| 3924 * | DHU 352 | Bristol GO5G | GO5G.161 | H31/28R | 10/49 | Bristol Tramways (GL) | C3059 |
| 3925 * | CHU 175 | Bristol GO5G | GO5G.115 | H31/28R | 10/49 | Bristol Tramways (GL) | C3027 |
| 3926 * | CHU 706 | Bristol GO5G | GO5G.85 | H31/28R | 10/49 | Bristol Tramways (GL) | C3029 |
| 3927 * | CHY 114 | Bristol GO6L | GO6L.1 | H31/28R | 10/49 | Bristol Tramways (GL) | C3044 |
| 3928 * | CHU 176 | Bristol GO5G | GO5G.63 | H31/28R | 10/49 | Bristol Tramways (GL) | C3026 |
| 3929 * | CHY 443 | Bristol GO5G | GO5G.127 | H31/28R | 11/49 | Bristol Tramways (GL) | C3048 |
| 3930 * | DAE 370 | Bristol GO5G | GO5G.136 | H31/28R | 11/49 | Bristol Tramways (GL) | C3057 |
| 3931 * | AHY 417 | Bristol GO6G | GO6G.3 | H31/28R | 11/49 | Bristol Tramways (GL) | C3022 |
| 3932 * | DHT 939 | Bristol GO5G | GO5G.169 | H31/28R | 11/49 | Bristol Tramways (GL) | C3067 |
| 3933 * | DAE 378 | Bristol GO5G | GO5G.128 | H31/28R | 11/49 | Bristol Tramways (GL) | C3049 |
| 3934 * | DHT 941 | Bristol GO5G | GO5G.166 | H31/28R | 11/49 | Bristol Tramways (GL) | C3064 |
| 3935 * | CAE 864 | Bristol G.JW | G136 | H31/28R | 11/49 | Bristol Tramways (GL) | C3019 |
| 3936 * | CHW 42 | Bristol GO5G | GO5G.82 | H31/28R | 12/49 | Bristol Tramways (GL) | C3031 |
| 3937 * | CAE 866 | Bristol G.JW | G138 | H31/28R | 12/49 | Bristol Tramways (GL) | C3021 |
| 3938 * | CAE 862 | Bristol G.JW | G134 | H31/28R | 12/49 | Bristol Tramways (GL) | C3017 |
| 3939 * | EAE 597 | Bristol GO5G | GO5G.209 | H31/28R | 12/49 | Bristol Tramways (GL) | C3076 |
| 3940 * | CHU 705 | Bristol GO5G | GO5G.84 | H31/28R | 12/49 | Bristol Tramways (GL) | C3028 |
| 3941 * | DKN 44 | Bristol GO5G | GO5G.144 | H31/28R | 12/49 | Bath Electric Tramways (SO) | 3827 |
| 3942 * | DKN 41 | Bristol GO5G | GO5G.153 | H31/28R | 12/49 | Bath Electric Tramways (SO) | 3824 |
| 3943 * | DKN 46 | Bristol GO5G | GO5G.146 | H31/28R | 1/50 | Bath Electric Tramways (SO) | 3829 |
| 3944 * | DKN 35 | Bristol GO5G | GO5G.142 | H31/28R | 1/50 | Bath Electric Tramways (SO) | 3818 |
| 3945 * | DKN 31 | Bristol GO5G | GO5G.138 | H31/28R | 1/50 | Bath Electric Tramways (SO) | 3814 |
| 3946 * | VG 4822 | Leyland TD2 | 1910 | H30/26R | 2/50 | Eastern Counties, Norwich (NK) | AH224 |
| 3947 * | NG 3863 | Leyland TD2 | 2349 | H30/26R | 2/50 | Eastern Counties, Norwich (NK) | AH202 |
| 3948 * | NG 3866 | Leyland TD2 | 2352 | H30/26R | 2/50 | Eastern Counties, Norwich (NK) | AH205 |
| 3949 * | NG 5405 | Leyland TD2 | 3518 | H30/26R | 2/50 | Eastern Counties, Norwich (NK) | AH214 |
| 3950 * | NG 2734 | Leyland TD2 | 1573 | H30/26R | 3/50 | Eastern Counties, Norwich (NK) | AH199 |
| 3951 * | NG 3870 | Leyland TD2 | 2356 | H30/26R | 3/50 | Eastern Counties, Norwich (NK) | AH209 |
| 3952 * | NG 5403 | Leyland TD2 | 3516 | H30/26R | 3/50 | Eastern Counties, Norwich (NK) | AH212 |
| 3953 * | NG 3865 | Leyland TD2 | 2351 | H30/26R | 4/50 | Eastern Counties, Norwich (NK) | AH204 |
| 3954 * | NG 5401 | Leyland TD2 | 3514 | H30/26R | 5/50 | Eastern Counties, Norwich (NK) | AH210 |
| 3955 * | NG 5406 | Leyland TD2 | 3519 | H30/26R | 5/50 | Eastern Counties, Norwich (NK) | AH215 |
| 3956 * | NG 2730 | Leyland TD2 | 1439 | H30/26R | 5/50 | Eastern Counties, Norwich (NK) | AH195 |
| 3957 * | NG 3869 | Leyland TD2 | 2355 | H30/26R | 5/50 | Eastern Counties, Norwich (NK) | AH208 |
| 3958 * | NG 3861 | Leyland TD2 | 2347 | H30/26R | 6/50 | Eastern Counties, Norwich (NK) | AH200 |
| 3959 * | NG 3862 | Leyland TD2 | 2348 | H30/26R | 6/50 | Eastern Counties, Norwich (NK) | AH201 |
| 3960 * | LHY 950 | Bristol L5G | 71.091 | B35R | 8/49 | Bristol Tramways (GL) | 2430 |
| 3961 * | LHY 951 | Bristol L5G | 71.092 | B35R | 9/49 | Bristol Tramways (GL) | 2431 |
| 3962 * | LHY 952 | Bristol L5G | 71.093 | B35R | 9/49 | Bristol Tramways (GL) | 2432 |
| 3963 * | LHY 953 | Bristol L5G | 71.094 | B35R | 9/49 | Bristol Tramways (GL) | 2433 |
| 3964 * | LHY 954 | Bristol L5G | 71.095 | B35R | 10/49 | Bristol Tramways (GL) | 2434 |
| 3965 * | LHY 955 | Bristol L5G | 71.096 | B35R | 10/49 | Bristol Tramways (GL) | 2435 |
| 3966 * | LHY 956 | Bristol L5G | 71.128 | B35R | 10/49 | Bristol Tramways (GL) | 2436 |
| 3967 * | LHY 957 | Bristol L5G | 71.129 | B35R | 10/49 | Bristol Tramways (GL) | 2437 |
| 3968 * | LHY 958 | Bristol L5G | 71.130 | B35R | 10/49 | Bristol Tramways (GL) | 2438 |
| 3969 * | LHY 959 | Bristol L5G | 71.131 | B35R | 10/49 | Bristol Tramways (GL) | 2439 |
| 3970 * | LHY 960 | Bristol L5G | 71.143 | B35R | 10/49 | Bristol Tramways (GL) | 2440 |
| 3971 * | LHY 961 | Bristol L5G | 71.144 | B35R | 10/49 | Bristol Tramways (GL) | 2441 |
| 3972 * | LHY 962 | Bristol L5G | 71.145 | B35R | 11/49 | Bristol Tramways (GL) | 2446 |
| 3973 * | LHY 963 | Bristol L5G | 71.146 | B35R | 10/49 | Bath Tramways Motor Co (SO) | 2289 |
| 3974 * | LHY 964 | Bristol L5G | 71.147 | B35R | 10/49 | Bath Tramways Motor Co (SO) | 2290 |
| 3975 * | LHY 965 | Bristol L5G | 71.148 | B35R | 10/49 | Bath Tramways Motor Co (SO) | 2291 |
| 3976 * | LHY 966 | Bristol L5G | 71.149 | B35R | 10/49 | Bath Tramways Motor Co (SO) | 2292 |
| 3977 * | LHY 967 | Bristol L5G | 71.150 | B35R | 10/49 | Bath Tramways Motor Co (SO) | 2293 |
| 3978 * | LHY 968 | Bristol L5G | 71.169 | B35R | 10/49 | Bath Tramways Motor Co (SO) | 2294 |
| 3979 * | LHY 969 | Bristol L5G | 71.170 | B35R | 10/49 | Bath Electric Tramways (SO) | 2295 |
| 3980 * | LHY 970 | Bristol L5G | 71.171 | B35R | 10/49 | Bath Tramways Motor Co (SO) | 2300 |
| 3981 * | LHY 971 | Bristol L5G | 71.172 | B35R | 10/49 | Bath Tramways Motor Co (SO) | 2301 |

| | | | | | | |
|---|---|---|---|---|---|---|
| 3982 | LHY 990 | Bristol L6B | 73.010 | B35R | 10/49 | Bristol Tramways (GL) 2442 |
| 3983 | LHY 991 | Bristol L6B | 73.015 | B35R | 10/49 | Bristol Tramways (GL) 2443 |
| 3984 | LHY 992 | Bristol L6B | 73.016 | B35R | 10/49 | Bristol Tramways (GL) 2444 |
| 3985 | LHY 993 | Bristol L6B | 73.017 | B35R | 10/49 | Bristol Tramways (GL) 2445 |
| 3986 | LHY 994 | Bristol L5G | 73.018 | B35R | 11/49 | Bristol Tramways (GL) 2447 |
| 3987 | LHY 995 | Bristol L5G | 73.019 | B35R | 11/49 | Bristol Tramways (GL) 2448 |
| 3988 | LHY 996 | Bristol L5G | 73.020 | B35R | 11/49 | Bristol Tramways (GL) 2449 |
| 3989 | LHY 997 | Bristol L5G | 73.021 | B35R | 11/49 | Bristol Tramways (GL) 2450 |
| 3990 | LHY 998 | Bristol L6B | 71.186 | B35R | 11/49 | Bristol Tramways (GL) 2451 |
| 3991 | LHY 999 | Bristol L6B | 73.014 | B35R | 5/50 | Bristol Tramways (GL) 2452 |
| 3992 * | MHW 988 | Bristol L5G | 79.086 | B35R | 4/50 | Bristol Tramways (GL) 2453 |
| 3993 * | MHW 989 | Bristol L5G | 79.087 | B35R | 4/50 | Bristol Tramways (GL) 2454 |
| 3994 * | MHW 990 | Bristol L5G | 79.088 | B35R | 5/50 | Bristol Tramways (GL) 2455 |
| 3995 * | MHW 991 | Bristol L5G | 79.091 | B35R | 5/50 | Bristol Tramways (GL) 2456 |
| 3996 * | MHW 992 | Bristol L5G | 79.104 | B35R | 5/50 | Bristol Tramways (GL) 2457 |
| 3997 * | MHW 993 | Bristol L5G | 79.105 | B35R | 5/50 | Bristol Tramways (GL) 2458 |
| 3998 * | MHW 994 | Bristol L5G | 79.106 | B35R | 5/50 | Bristol Tramways (GL) 2459 |
| 3999 * | MHW 995 | Bristol L5G | 79.107 | B35R | 5/50 | Bristol Tramways (GL) 2460 |
| 4000 * | MHW 998 | Bristol L6B | 79.110 | B35R | 5/50 | Bristol Tramways (GL) 2463 |
| 4001 * | MHW 996 | Bristol L5G | 79.108 | B35R | 5/50 | Bristol Tramways (GL) 2461 |
| 4002 * | MHW 997 | Bristol L6B | 79.109 | B35R | 5/50 | Bristol Tramways (GL) 2462 |
| 4003 * | MHW 999 | Bristol L5G | 79.127 | B35R | 5/50 | Bristol Tramways (GL) 2464 |
| 4004 * | JFM 140 | Bristol L5G | 71.182 | B35R | 11/49 | Crosville MS, Chester (CH) KG111 |
| 4005 * | JFM 141 | Bristol L5G | 73.074 | B35R | 11/49 | Crosville MS, Chester (CH) KG112 |
| 4006 * | JFM 142 | Bristol L5G | 73.075 | B35R | 1/50 | Crosville MS, Chester (CH) KG113 |
| 4007 | FNV 117 | Bristol L5G | 73.076 | B35R | 3/50 | United Counties, Northampton (NO) 817 |
| 4008 * | FNV 118 | Bristol L5G | 79.128 | B35R | 5/50 | United Counties, Northampton (NO) 818 |
| 4009 * | FNV 119 | Bristol L5G | 79.129 | B35R | 6/50 | United Counties, Northampton (NO) 819 |
| 4010 * | JFM 127 | Bristol L6A | 71.155 | B35R | 7/49 | Crosville MS, Chester (CH) KB98 |
| 4011 * | JFM 128 | Bristol L6A | 71.156 | B35R | 7/49 | Crosville MS, Chester (CH) KB99 |
| 4012 * | JFM 129 | Bristol L6A | 71.157 | B35R | 7/49 | Crosville MS, Chester (CH) KB100 |
| 4013 * | JFM 130 | Bristol L6A | 71.158 | B35R | 7/49 | Crosville MS, Chester (CH) KB101 |
| 4014 * | JFM 131 | Bristol L6A | 73.048 | B35R | 8/49 | Crosville MS, Chester (CH) KB102 |
| 4015 * | JFM 132 | Bristol L6A | 73.049 | B35R | 8/49 | Crosville MS, Chester (CH) KB103 |
| 4016 * | JFM 133 | Bristol L6A | 73.050 | B35R | 8/49 | Crosville MS, Chester (CH) KB104 |
| 4017 | JFM 134 | Bristol L6A | 73.052 | B35R | 11/49 | Crosville MS, Chester (CH) KB105 |
| 4018 | JFM 135 | Bristol L6A | 73.053 | B35R | 11/49 | Crosville MS, Chester (CH) KB106 |
| 4019 | JFM 136 | Bristol L6B | 73.054 | B35R | 11/49 | Crosville MS, Chester (CH) KW107 |
| 4020 | JFM 137 | Bristol L6B | 73.055 | B35R | 11/49 | Crosville MS, Chester (CH) KW108 |
| 4021 | JFM 138 | Bristol L6B | 73.064 | B35R | 11/49 | Crosville MS, Chester (CH) KW109 |
| 4022 | JFM 139 | Bristol L6B | 73.089 | B35R | 11/49 | Crosville MS, Chester (CH) KW110 |
| 4023 | KFM 763 | Bristol L6B | 73.088 | B35R | 1/50 | Crosville MS, Chester (CH) KW114 |
| 4024 | KFM 764 | Bristol L5G | 79.015 | B35R | 1/50 | Crosville MS, Chester (CH) KG115 |
| 4025 | KFM 765 | Bristol L5G | 79.016 | B35R | 1/50 | Crosville MS, Chester (CH) KG116 |
| 4026 | KFM 766 | Bristol L5G | 79.066 | B35R | 5/50 | Crosville MS, Chester (CH) KG117 |
| 4027 | KFM 767 | Bristol L5G | 79.093 | B35R | 3/50 | Crosville MS, Chester (CH) KG118 |
| 4028 | KFM 768 | Bristol L5G | 79.092 | B35R | 5/50 | Crosville MS, Chester (CH) KG119 |
| 4029 | KFM 769 | Bristol L5G | 79.111 | B35R | 5/50 | Crosville MS, Chester (CH) KG120 |
| 4030 | KFM 770 | Bristol L5G | 79.112 | B35R | 5/50 | Crosville MS, Chester (CH) KG121 |
| 4031 | KFM 771 | Bristol L5G | 79.113 | B35R | 6/50 | Crosville MS, Chester (CH) KG122 |
| 4032 | KFM 773 | Bristol L5G | 79.115 | B35R | 6/50 | Crosville MS, Chester (CH) KG124 |
| 4033 * | KFM 772 | Bristol L5G | 79.114 | B35R | 6/50 | Crosville MS, Chester (CH) KG123 |
| 4034 * | KFM 774 | Bristol L5G | 79.130 | B35R | 6/50 | Crosville MS, Chester (CH) KG125 |
| 4035 * | KFM 775 | Bristol L5G | 79.138 | B35R | 6/50 | Crosville MS, Chester (CH) KG126 |
| 4036 * | KFM 776 | Bristol L5G | 79.139 | B35R | 6/50 | Crosville MS, Chester (CH) KG127 |
| 4037 * | KFM 777 | Bristol L5G | 79.140 | B35R | 6/50 | Crosville MS, Chester (CH) KG128 |
| 4038 * | KFM 778 | Bristol L5G | 79.150 | B35R | 6/50 | Crosville MS, Chester (CH) KG129 |
| 4039 * | KFM 892 | Bristol L5G | 79.151 | B35R | 6/50 | Crosville MS, Chester (CH) KG130 |
| 4040 * | KFM 893 | Bristol L5G | 79.152 | B35R | 6/50 | Crosville MS, Chester (CH) KG131 |
| 4041 * | KFM 894 | Bristol L5G | 79.153 | B35R | 6/50 | Crosville MS, Chester (CH) KG132 |
| 4042 | ONO 41 | Bristol L5G | 73.034 | B35R | 10/49 | Eastern National, Chelmsford (EX) 4020 |
| 4043 | ONO 42 | Bristol L5G | 73.035 | B35R | 10/49 | Eastern National, Chelmsford (EX) 4021 |
| 4044 | ONO 43 | Bristol L5G | 73.038 | B35R | 11/49 | Eastern National, Chelmsford (EX) 4022 |
| 4045 | ONO 44 | Bristol L5G | 73.046 | B35R | 11/49 | Eastern National, Chelmsford (EX) 4023 |

| | | | | | | |
|---|---|---|---|---|---|---|
| 4046 | ONO 45 | Bristol L5G | 73.047 | B35R | 12/49 | Eastern National, Chelmsford (EX) 4024 |
| 4047 | ONO 46 | Bristol L5G | 73.065 | B35R | 12/49 | Eastern National, Chelmsford (EX) 4025 |
| 4048 | ONO 47 | Bristol L5G | 73.066 | B35R | 1/50 | Eastern National, Chelmsford (EX) 4026 |
| 4049 | ONO 48 | Bristol L5G | 73.067 | B35R | 2/50 | Eastern National, Chelmsford (EX) 4027 |
| 4050 | ONO 49 | Bristol L5G | 79.028 | B35R | 2/50 | Eastern National, Chelmsford (EX) 4028 |
| 4051 | ONO 50 | Bristol L5G | 79.029 | B35R | 3/50 | Eastern National, Chelmsford (EX) 4029 |
| 4052 | ONO 81 | Bristol L5G | 79.051 | B35R | 3/50 | Eastern National, Chelmsford (EX) 4060 |
| 4053 | ONO 82 | Bristol L5G | 79.052 | B35R | 3/50 | Eastern National, Chelmsford (EX) 4061 |
| 4054 | ONO 83 | Bristol L5G | 79.067 | B35R | 5/50 | Eastern National, Chelmsford (EX) 4062 |
| 4055 | ONO 988 | Bristol L5G | 79.068 | B35R | 5/50 | Eastern National, Chelmsford (EX) 4074 |
| 4056 | ONO 989 | Bristol L5G | 79.094 | B35R | 4/50 | Eastern National, Chelmsford (EX) 4075 |
| 4057 | ONO 990 | Bristol L5G | 79.095 | B35R | 4/50 | Eastern National, Chelmsford (EX) 4076 |
| 4058 * | ONO 991 | Bristol L5G | 79.096 | B35R | 6/50 | Eastern National, Chelmsford (EX) 4077 |
| 4059 * | ONO 992 | Bristol L5G | 79.146 | B35R | 7/50 | Eastern National, Chelmsford (EX) 4078 |
| 4060 * | ONO 993 | Bristol L5G | 79.154 | B35R | 7/50 | Eastern National, Chelmsford (EX) 4079 |
| 4061 * | ONO 994 | Bristol L5G | 79.155 | B35R | 7/50 | Eastern National, Chelmsford (EX) 4080 |
| 4062 | PTW 101 | Bristol L6B | 79.141 | FC26F | 6/50 | Eastern National, Chelmsford (EX) 4098 |
| 4063 | PTW 102 | Bristol L6B | 79.142 | FC31F | 6/50 | Eastern National, Chelmsford (EX) 4099 |
| 4064 | PTW 103 | Bristol L6B | 79.143 | FC31F | 6/50 | Eastern National, Chelmsford (EX) 4100 |
| 4065 | PTW 104 | Bristol L6B | 81.110 | FC31F | 9/50 | Eastern National, Chelmsford (EX) 4101 |
| 4066 | PTW 105 | Bristol L6B | 81.112 | FC31F | 9/50 | Eastern National, Chelmsford (EX) 4102 |
| 4067 | FFW 825 | Bristol L6B | 73.068 | B35R | 11/49 | Lincolnshire RCC, Bracebridge Heath (KN) 744 |
| 4068 | FFW 826 | Bristol L6B | 73.069 | B35R | 11/49 | Lincolnshire RCC, Bracebridge Heath (KN) 745 |
| 4069 | FFW 827 | Bristol L6B | 73.077 | B35R | 1/50 | Lincolnshire RCC, Bracebridge Heath (KN) 746 |
| 4070 | FFW 828 | Bristol L6B | 73.078 | B35R | 1/50 | Lincolnshire RCC, Bracebridge Heath (KN) 747 |
| 4071 | FFW 829 | Bristol L6B | 73.081 | B35R | 2/50 | Lincolnshire RCC, Bracebridge Heath (KN) 748 |
| 4072 | FFW 830 | Bristol L5G | 79.097 | B35R | 5/50 | Lincolnshire RCC, Bracebridge Heath (KN) 749 |
| 4073 | FFW 831 | Bristol L5G | 79.098 | B35R | 5/50 | Lincolnshire RCC, Bracebridge Heath (KN) 750 |
| 4074 | GBE 842 | Bristol K5G | 78.139 | H30/26R | 5/50 | Lincolnshire RCC, Bracebridge Heath (KN) 755 |
| 4075 | GBE 843 | Bristol K5G | 78.154 | H30/26R | 7/50 | Lincolnshire RCC, Bracebridge Heath (KN) 756 |
| 4076 | GBE 844 | Bristol K5G | 78.166 | H30/26R | 7/50 | Lincolnshire RCC, Bracebridge Heath (KN) 757 |
| 4077 | GBE 845 | Bristol K5G | 78.167 | H30/26R | 7/50 | Lincolnshire RCC, Bracebridge Heath (KN) 758 |
| 4078 | GBE 846 | Bristol K5G | 78.168 | H30/26R | 7/50 | Lincolnshire RCC, Bracebridge Heath (KN) 759 |
| 4079 | LKT 984 | Bristol L6A | 73.011 | B35R | 12/49 | Maidstone & District (KT) SO36 |
| 4080 | LKT 986 | Bristol L6A | 73.013 | B35R | 12/49 | Maidstone & District (KT) SO38 |
| 4081 | LKT 985 | Bristol L6A | 73.012 | B35R | 12/49 | Maidstone & District (KT) SO37 |
| 4082 | LKT 988 | Bristol L6A | 79.002 | B35R | 1/50 | Maidstone & District (KT) SO40 |
| 4083 | LKT 987 | Bristol L6A | 79.001 | B35R | 2/50 | Maidstone & District (KT) SO39 |
| 4084 | LKT 989 | Bristol L6A | 79.014 | B35R | 2/50 | Maidstone & District (KT) SO41 |
| 4085 | LKT 990 | Bristol L6A | 79.023 | B35R | 2/50 | Maidstone & District (KT) SO42 |
| 4086 | LKT 991 | Bristol L6A | 79.024 | B35R | 3/50 | Maidstone & District (KT) SO43 |
| 4087 | LKT 992 | Bristol L6A | 79.025 | B35R | 3/50 | Maidstone & District (KT) SO44 |
| 4088 | LKT 993 | Bristol L6A | 79.026 | B35R | 4/50 | Maidstone & District (KT) SO45 |
| 4089 | LKT 994 | Bristol L6A | 79.035 | B35R | 4/50 | Maidstone & District (KT) SO46 |
| 4090 | LKT 995 | Bristol L6A | 79.036 | B35R | 4/50 | Maidstone & District (KT) SO47 |
| 4091 | LKT 996 | Bristol L6A | 79.053 | B35R | 5/50 | Maidstone & District (KT) SO48 |
| 4092 | LKT 997 | Bristol L6A | 79.054 | B35R | 6/50 | Maidstone & District (KT) SO49 |
| 4093 | LKT 998 | Bristol L6A | 79.055 | B35R | 6/50 | Maidstone & District (KT) SO50 |
| 4094 | LKT 999 | Bristol L6A | 79.056 | B35R | 6/50 | Maidstone & District (KT) SO51 |
| 4095 | FBL 23 | Bristol L6B | 73.037 | B35R | 10/49 | Thames Valley, Reading (BE) 521 |
| 4096 | FBL 24 | Bristol L6B | 73.036 | B35R | 11/49 | Thames Valley, Reading (BE) 522 |
| 4097 | FBL 25 | Bristol L6B | 73.058 | B35R | 11/49 | Thames Valley, Reading (BE) 523 |
| 4098 | FMO 9 | Bristol L6B | 73.059 | B35R | 12/49 | Thames Valley, Reading (BE) 534 |
| 4099 | FMO 10 | Bristol L6B | 73.092 | B35R | 1/50 | Thames Valley, Reading (BE) 535 |
| 4100 | FMO 11 | Bristol L6B | 73.093 | B35R | 2/50 | Thames Valley, Reading (BE) 536 |
| 4101 | FMO 13 | Bristol L6B | 79.027 | B35R | 3/50 | Thames Valley, Reading (BE) 538 |
| 4102 | FMO 12 | Bristol L6B | 73.113 | B35R | 3/50 | Thames Valley, Reading (BE) 537 |
| 4103 | FMO 14 | Bristol L6B | 79.057 | B35R | 3/50 | Thames Valley, Reading (BE) 539 |
| 4104 | FMO 16 | Bristol L6B | 73119 | B35R | 5/50 | Thames Valley, Reading (BE) 541 |
| 4105 | FMO 15 | Bristol L6B | 73118 | B35R | 5/50 | Thames Valley, Reading (BE) 540 |
| 4106 | FMO 17 | Bristol L6B | 79.147 | B35R | 5/50 | Thames Valley, Reading (BE) 542 |
| 4107 | FMO 18 | Bristol L6B | 79.148 | B35R | 5/50 | Thames Valley, Reading (BE) 543 |
| 4108 * | FMO 19 | Bristol L6B | 79.149 | B35R | 6/50 | Thames Valley, Reading (BE) 544 |
| 4109 * | LHN 802 | Bristol L5G | 71.097 | B35R | 9/49 | United AS, Darlington (DM) BLO402 |

| | | | | | | | |
|---|---|---|---|---|---|---|---|
| 4110 * | LHN 803 | Bristol L5G | 71.123 | B35R | 9/49 | United AS, Darlington (DM) | BLO403 |
| 4111 * | LHN 804 | Bristol L5G | 71.124 | B35R | 9/49 | United AS, Darlington (DM) | BLO404 |
| 4112 * | LHN 811 | Bristol L5G | 71.125 | B35R | 9/49 | United AS, Darlington (DM) | BLO411 |
| 4113 * | LHN 805 | Bristol L5G | 71.126 | B35R | 10/49 | United AS, Darlington (DM) | BLO405 |
| 4114 * | LHN 806 | Bristol L5G | 71.127 | B35R | 10/49 | United AS, Darlington (DM) | BLO406 |
| 4115 * | LHN 807 | Bristol L5G | 71.132 | B35R | 10/49 | United AS, Darlington (DM) | BLO407 |
| 4116 * | LHN 808 | Bristol L5G | 71.133 | B35R | 11/49 | United AS, Darlington (DM) | BLO408 |
| 4117 * | LHN 809 | Bristol L5G | 71.134 | B35R | 11/49 | United AS, Darlington (DM) | BLO409 |
| 4118 * | LHN 810 | Bristol L5G | 71.135 | B35R | 3/50 | United AS, Darlington (DM) | BLO410 |
| 4119 * | LHN 812 | Bristol L5G | 71.174 | B35R | 6/50 | United AS, Darlington (DM) | BLO412 |
| 4120 * | LHN 813 | Bristol L5G | 71.175 | B35R | 6/50 | United AS, Darlington (DM) | BLO413 |
| 4121 * | LHN 814 | Bristol L5G | 71.176 | B35R | 6/50 | United AS, Darlington (DM) | BLO414 |
| 4122 * | LHN 815 | Bristol L5G | 71.177 | B35R | 6/50 | United AS, Darlington (DM) | BLO415 |
| 4123 * | LHN 816 | Bristol L5G | 71.178 | B35R | 6/50 | United AS, Darlington (DM) | BLO416 |
| 4124 * | LHN 817 | Bristol L5G | 71.179 | B35R | 6/50 | United AS, Darlington (DM) | BLO417 |
| 4125 * | LHN 818 | Bristol L5G | 71.183 | B35R | 6/50 | United AS, Darlington (DM) | BLO418 |
| 4126 * | LHN 819 | Bristol L5G | 73.009 | B35R | 6/50 | United AS, Darlington (DM) | BLO419 |
| 4127 * | LHN 820 | Bristol L5G | 73.008 | B35R | 6/50 | United AS, Darlington (DM) | BLO420 |
| 4128 * | LHN 821 | Bristol L5G | 73.006 | B35R | 6/50 | United AS, Darlington (DM) | BLO421 |
| 4129 * | LHN 822 | Bristol L5G | 73.007 | B35R | 7/50 | United AS, Darlington (DM) | BLO422 |
| 4130 * | LHN 823 | Bristol L5G | 73.025 | B35R | 7/50 | United AS, Darlington (DM) | BLO423 |
| 4131 * | LHN 824 | Bristol L5G | 73.026 | B35R | 7/50 | United AS, Darlington (DM) | BLO424 |
| 4132 * | LHN 825 | Bristol L5G | 73.027 | B35R | 7/50 | United AS, Darlington (DM) | BLO425 |
| 4133 * | LHN 826 | Bristol L5G | 73.028 | B35R | 7/50 | United AS, Darlington (DM) | BLO426 |
| 4134 * | LHN 827 | Bristol L5G | 73.070 | B35R | 7/50 | United AS, Darlington (DM) | BLO427 |
| 4135 * | LHN 829 | Bristol L5G | 73.072 | B35R | 7/50 | United AS, Darlington (DM) | BLO429 |
| 4136 * | LHN 828 | Bristol L5G | 73.071 | B35R | 7/50 | United AS, Darlington (DM) | BLO428 |
| 4137 * | LHN 830 | Bristol L5G | 73.082 | B35R | 7/50 | United AS, Darlington (DM) | BLO430 |
| 4138 * | LHN 831 | Bristol L5G | 73.083 | B35R | 7/50 | United AS, Darlington (DM) | BLO431 |
| 4139 * | LHN 832 | Bristol L5G | 73.094 | B35R | 7/50 | United AS, Darlington (DM) | BLO432 |
| 4140 * | LHN 833 | Bristol L5G | 73.095 | B35R | 7/50 | United AS, Darlington (DM) | BLO433 |
| 4141 * | LHN 835 | Bristol L5G | 73.097 | B35R | 7/50 | United AS, Darlington (DM) | BLO435 |
| 4142 * | LHN 837 | Bristol L5G | 73.099 | B35R | -/49 | United AS, Darlington (DM) | BLO437 |
| 4143 * | LHN 834 | Bristol L5G | 73.096 | B35R | 7/50 | United AS, Darlington (DM) | BLO434 |
| 4144 * | LHN 836 | Bristol L5G | 73.098 | B35R | 7/50 | United AS, Darlington (DM) | BLO436 |
| 4145 * | LHN 838 | Bristol L5G | 73.100 | B35R | 7/50 | United AS, Darlington (DM) | BLO438 |
| 4146 * | LHN 839 | Bristol L5G | 73.103 | B35R | 7/50 | United AS, Darlington (DM) | BLO439 |
| 4147 * | LHN 840 | Bristol L5G | 73.104 | B35R | 7/50 | United AS, Darlington (DM) | BLO440 |
| 4148 * | LHN 841 | Bristol L5G | 73.105 | B35R | 7/50 | United AS, Darlington (DM) | BLO441 |
| 4149 * | LHN 842 | Bristol L5G | 73.106 | B35R | 7/50 | United AS, Darlington (DM) | BLO442 |
| 4150 * | LHN 843 | Bristol L5G | 73.107 | B35R | 7/50 | United AS, Darlington (DM) | BLO443 |
| 4151 * | LHN 844 | Bristol L5G | 79.003 | B35R | 7/50 | United AS, Darlington (DM) | BLO444 |
| 4152 * | LHN 845 | Bristol L5G | 79.004 | B35R | 7/50 | United AS, Darlington (DM) | BLO445 |
| 4153 * | LHN 846 | Bristol L5G | 79.006 | B35R | 7/50 | United AS, Darlington (DM) | BLO446 |
| 4154 * | LHN 847 | Bristol L5G | 79.030 | B35R | 7/50 | United AS, Darlington (DM) | BLO447 |
| 4155 * | LHN 848 | Bristol L5G | 79.031 | B35R | 7/50 | United AS, Darlington (DM) | BLO448 |
| 4156 * | LHN 849 | Bristol L5G | 79.037 | B35R | 7/50 | United AS, Darlington (DM) | BLO449 |
| 4157 * | LHN 850 | Bristol L5G | 79.038 | B35R | 7/50 | United AS, Darlington (DM) | BLO450 |
| 4158 * | LHN 851 | Bristol L5G | 79.039 | B35R | 7/50 | United AS, Darlington (DM) | BLO451 |
| 4159 * | LHN 852 | Bristol L5G | 79.040 | B35R | 7/50 | United AS, Darlington (DM) | BLO452 |
| 4160 * | LHN 853 | Bristol L6B | 79.041 | B35R | 8/50 | United AS, Darlington (DM) | BLO453 |
| 4161 * | LHN 854 | Bristol L6B | 79.044 | B35R | 8/50 | United AS, Darlington (DM) | BLO454 |
| 4162 * | LHN 855 | Bristol L6B | 79.042 | B35R | 8/50 | United AS, Darlington (DM) | BLO455 |
| 4163 * | LHN 856 | Bristol L6B | 79.043 | B35R | 8/50 | United AS, Darlington (DM) | BLO456 |
| 4164 * | LHN 857 | Bristol L6B | 79.045 | B35R | 8/50 | United AS, Darlington (DM) | BLO457 |
| 4165 * | LHN 858 | Bristol L5G | 79.059 | B35R | 7/50 | United AS, Darlington (DM) | BLO458 |
| 4166 * | LHN 859 | Bristol L5G | 79.069 | B35R | 7/50 | United AS, Darlington (DM) | BLO459 |
| 4167 * | LHN 860 | Bristol L5G | 79.070 | B35R | 7/50 | United AS, Darlington (DM) | BLO460 |
| 4168 * | LHN 861 | Bristol L5G | 79.071 | B35R | 7/50 | United AS, Darlington (DM) | BLO461 |
| 4169 * | LHN 862 | Bristol L5G | 79.072 | B35R | 7/50 | United AS, Darlington (DM) | BLO462 |
| 4170 * | LHN 863 | Bristol L5G | 79.073 | B35R | 8/50 | United AS, Darlington (DM) | BLO463 |
| 4171 * | LHN 864 | Bristol L5G | 79.120 | B35R | 8/50 | United AS, Darlington (DM) | BLO464 |
| 4172 * | LHN 865 | Bristol L5G | 79.121 | B35R | 8/50 | United AS, Darlington (DM) | BLO465 |
| 4173 * | LHN 866 | Bristol L5G | 79.122 | B35R | 9/50 | United AS, Darlington (DM) | BLO466 |

| 4174 * | LHN 867 | Bristol L5G | 79.125 | B35R | 9/50 | United AS, Darlington (DM) BLO467 |
|---|---|---|---|---|---|---|
| 4175 * | LHN 868 | Bristol L5G | 79.123 | B35R | 9/50 | United AS, Darlington (DM) BLO468 |
| 4176 * | LHN 869 | Bristol L5G | 79.124 | B35R | 9/50 | United AS, Darlington (DM) BLO469 |
| 4177 * | NHN 82 | Bristol L6B | 79.136 | B35R | 6/51 | United AS, Darlington (DM) BLO482 |
| 4178 * | NHN 83 | Bristol L6B | 79.137 | B35R | 6/51 | United AS, Darlington (DM) BLO483 |
| 4179 * | NHN 84 | Bristol L5G | 79.156 | B35R | 6/51 | United AS, Darlington (DM) BLO484 |
| 4180 * | NHN 87 | Bristol L5G | 79.159 | B35R | 6/51 | United AS, Darlington (DM) BLO487 |
| 4181 * | NHN 85 | Bristol L5G | 79.157 | B35R | 6/51 | United AS, Darlington (DM) BLO485 |
| 4182 * | NHN 86 | Bristol L5G | 79.158 | B35R | 6/51 | United AS, Darlington (DM) BLO486 |
| 4183 * | NHN 88 | Bristol L5G | 79.160 | B35R | 6/51 | United AS, Darlington (DM) BLO488 |
| 4184 * | NHN 90 | Bristol L5G | 79.162 | B35R | 6/51 | United AS, Darlington (DM) BLO490 |
| 4185 * | NHN 91 | Bristol L5G | 79.163 | B35R | 6/51 | United AS, Darlington (DM) BLO491 |
| 4186 * | NHN 92 | Bristol L5G | 79.164 | B35R | 6/51 | United AS, Darlington (DM) BLO492 |
| 4187 * | NHN 93 | Bristol L5G | 79.165 | B35R | 6/51 | United AS, Darlington (DM) BLO493 |
| 4188 * | NHN 89 | Bristol L5G | 79.161 | B35R | 6/51 | United AS, Darlington (DM) BLO489 |
| 4189 * | NHN 94 | Bristol L6B | 79.166 | B35R | 6/51 | United AS, Darlington (DM) BLO494 |
| 4190 * | NHN 95 | Bristol L6B | 79.167 | B35R | 6/51 | United AS, Darlington (DM) BLO495 |
| 4191 * | NHN 96 | Bristol L6B | 79.168 | B35R | 6/51 | United AS, Darlington (DM) BLO496 |
| 4192 * | NHN 97 | Bristol L5G | 79.169 | B35R | 6/51 | United AS, Darlington (DM) BLO497 |
| 4193 * | NHN 98 | Bristol L5G | 79.170 | B35R | 6/51 | United AS, Darlington (DM) BLO498 |
| 4194 * | NHN 99 | Bristol L5G | 79.171 | B35R | 6/51 | United AS, Darlington (DM) BLO499 |
| 4195 | EBD 236 | Bristol L6B | 73.039 | FC31F | 5/50 | United Counties, Northampton (NO) 809 |
| 4196 | EBD 237 | Bristol L6B | 73.042 | FC31F | 5/50 | United Counties, Northampton (NO) 810 |
| 4197 * | JWT 283 | Bristol L5G | 71.168 | B35R | 1/50 | West Yorkshire RCC, Harrogate (WR) 255 |
| 4198 * | JWT 284 | Bristol L5G | 79.005 | B35R | 1/50 | West Yorkshire RCC, Harrogate (WR) 256 |
| 4199 * | JWT 285 | Bristol L5G | 79.007 | B35R | 2/50 | West Yorkshire RCC, Harrogate (WR) 257 |
| 4200 * | JWT 286 | Bristol L5G | 79.008 | B35R | 3/50 | West Yorkshire RCC, Harrogate (WR) 258 |
| 4201 * | JWT 288 | Bristol L5G | 79.010 | B35R | 3/50 | West Yorkshire RCC, Harrogate (WR) 260 |
| 4202 * | JWT 289 | Bristol L5G | 79.011 | B35R | 3/50 | West Yorkshire RCC, Harrogate (WR) 261 |
| 4203 * | JWT 290 | Bristol L5G | 79.012 | B35R | 3/50 | West Yorkshire RCC, Harrogate (WR) 262 |
| 4204 * | JWT 287 | Bristol L5G | 79.009 | B35R | 3/50 | West Yorkshire RCC, Harrogate (WR) 259 |
| 4205 * | JWT 291 | Bristol L5G | 79.074 | B35R | 3/50 | West Yorkshire RCC, Harrogate (WR) 263 |
| 4206 * | JWT 292 | Bristol L5G | 79.077 | B35R | 3/50 | West Yorkshire RCC, Harrogate (WR) 264 |
| 4207 * | JWT 293 | Bristol L5G | 79.078 | B35R | 3/50 | West Yorkshire RCC, Harrogate (WR) 265 |
| 4208 * | JWT 294 | Bristol L5G | 79.079 | B35R | 5/50 | West Yorkshire RCC, Harrogate (WR) 266 |
| 4209 * | JWT 295 | Bristol L5G | 79.080 | B35R | 5/50 | West Yorkshire RCC, Harrogate (WR) 267 |
| 4210 * | JWT 381 | Bristol L5G | 79.081 | B35R | 5/50 | West Yorkshire RCC, Harrogate (WR) 268 |
| 4211 * | JWT 382 | Bristol L5G | 79.126 | B35R | 6/50 | West Yorkshire RCC, Harrogate (WR) 269 |
| 4212 | LHY 972 | Bristol L5G | 71.154 | B33D | 12/49 | Bristol Tramways (GL) C2732 |
| 4213 | LHY 973 | Bristol L5G | 71.159 | B33D | 12/49 | Bristol Tramways (GL) C2733 |
| 4214 | LHY 974 | Bristol L5G | 71.161 | B33D | 12/49 | Bristol Tramways (GL) C2734 |
| 4215 | LHY 975 | Bristol L5G | 71.162 | B33D | 12/49 | Bristol Tramways (GL) C2735 |
| 4216 | LHY 976 | Bristol L5G | 71.173 | B33D | 12/49 | Bristol Tramways (GL) C2736 |
| 4217 | LHY 977 | Bristol L6B | 71.184 | B33D | 12/49 | Bristol Tramways (GL) C2737 |
| 4218 | LHY 978 | Bristol L6B | 71.185 | B33D | 12/49 | Bristol Tramways (GL) C2738 |
| 4219 | LHY 979 | Bristol L6B | 71.188 | B33D | 12/49 | Bristol Tramways (GL) C2739 |
| 4220 | LHY 980 | Bristol L6B | 71.189 | B33D | 12/49 | Bristol Tramways (GL) C2740 |
| 4221 | LHY 981 | Bristol L6B | 71.190 | B33D | 12/49 | Bristol Tramways (GL) C2741 |
| 4222 | LHY 982 | Bristol L6B | 71.187 | B33D | 12/49 | Bristol Tramways (GL) C2742 |
| 4223 | LHY 983 | Bristol L6B | 73.022 | B33D | 12/49 | Bristol Tramways (GL) C2743 |
| 4224 | LHY 984 | Bristol L6B | 73.023 | B33D | 2/50 | Bristol Tramways (GL) C2744 |
| 4225 | LHY 985 | Bristol L5G | 79.032 | B33D | 3/50 | Bristol Tramways (GL) C2745 |
| 4226 | LHY 986 | Bristol L5G | 79.033 | B33D | 3/50 | Bristol Tramways (GL) C2746 |
| 4227 | LHY 987 | Bristol L5G | 79.034 | B33D | 3/50 | Bristol Tramways (GL) C2747 |
| 4228 | LHY 988 | Bristol L5G | 79.046 | B33D | 6/50 | Bristol Tramways (GL) C2748 |
| 4229 | LHY 989 | Bristol L5G | 79.047 | B33D | 6/50 | Bristol Tramways (GL) C2749 |
| 4230 | MHW 977 | Bristol L6B | 79.048 | B33D | 6/50 | Bristol Tramways (GL) C2750 |
| 4231 | MHW 978 | Bristol L6B | 79.049 | B33D | 6/50 | Bristol Tramways (GL) C2751 |
| 4232 | MHW 979 | Bristol L6B | 79.050 | B33D | 6/50 | Bristol Tramways (GL) C2752 |
| 4233 | MHW 980 | Bristol L5G | 79.062 | B33D | 6/50 | Bristol Tramways (GL) C2753 |
| 4234 | MHW 981 | Bristol L5G | 79.063 | B33D | 6/50 | Bristol Tramways (GL) C2754 |
| 4235 | MHW 982 | Bristol L5G | 79.075 | B33D | 6/50 | Bristol Tramways (GL) C2755 |
| 4236 | MHW 983 | Bristol L5G | 79.076 | B33D | 6/50 | Bristol Tramways (GL) C2756 |
| 4237 | MHW 984 | Bristol L5G | 79.082 | B33D | 9/50 | Bristol Tramways (GL) C2757 |

1001 - Crosville   MB 251   FFM 432 - The first examples of the standard design of double deck lowbridge body were a batch of eight delivered to Crosville in early 1946. Illustrated here is the first of the batch with the square cornered sliding vents which gave the body a rather utilitarian look. (Maurice Doggett collection)

1043 - Lincolnshire   2116   DBE 188 - Originally numbered 662 in the Lincolnshire fleet, this example was included in the first batch of 25 highbridge bodies with the square cornered window vents. However, the bus was subsequently rebuilt with the later design produced from 1947 onwards. (Maurice Doggett collection)

1281 - Merthyr Tydfil   1   HB 6260 – Several Welsh operators had been customers of ECW prewar. One of the first Welsh operators to place a postwar order was Merthyr Tydfil Corporation for three standard single bodies on Bristol L5G chassis, seen here having been rebuilt with only two sliding vents on each side. (Maurice Doggett collection)

1551 - Western Welsh   856   CUH 856 – Western Welsh took delivery of a large batch of standard design single deck bodies on Leyland Tiger PS1 chassis in 1946 and 1947. The first examples had the square cornered sliding vents, but the rest had the ECW designed vents with rounded upper corners. (Maurice Doggett collection)

1649 - Southdown  1232  GUF 732 – A coach seated version of the standard single deck body was supplied to Southdown, who took delivery of 25 examples on Leyland Tiger PS1/1 chassis in the first half of 1947. After being fitted initially with the standard sliding window vents, all 25 received half-depth drop windows as shown. (Maurice Doggett collection)

1971 - Eastern Counties  LL673  GPW 673 – The standard single deck body on Bristol L type chassis was produced up to 1950. Eastern Counties took delivery of a batch of 40 examples (GPW 657-696), the last fourteen being built at Irthlingborough, identified by the front number plate being placed slightly higher than the bodies built at Lowestoft. (Maurice Doggett)

2207 - Aberdare  73  GTG 865 – Originally delivered as Aberdare's number 1, GTG 865 (73) is one of five Bristol K6A chassis delivered to this South Wales municipal operator. Aberdare's use of a predominantly pale coloured livery was unusual, whilst their destination box style was unique. (Roy Marshall)

2308 - Hants & Dorset  1146  GLJ 958 – 100 lowbridge bodies on Leyland PD1A chassis were shared between seven different Tilling Group operators, with another 10 being supplied to North Western. The main difference from the bodies mounted on Bristol K chassis was the sloping drivers' windscreen and only four bays on the upper deck being fitted with sliding vents. (Roy Marshall)

2354 - Isle of Man Road Services    57    HMN 789 – A 'one-off' customer for ECW was Isle of Man Road Services, who received four single deck bodies on Leyland Tiger PS1/1 chassis, not unlike those delivered to Western Welsh. The first of the batch (HMN 787) is now preserved and based on the island. (John May, via Mike Eyre)

2359 - Lough Swilly    56    IH 6245 – Another 'one-off' customer was the Londonderry and Lough Swilly Railway Company who also received four standard single deck bus bodies, but this time on AEC Regal III chassis. However, the buses were fitted with a roof-mounted luggage rack after delivery, common on buses operated in both Ulster and Eire. (Maurice Doggett collection)

2409 - Municipality of Benoni 2 TA 8212 – Bristol, following earlier successes on the export market, commissioned ECW to supply a batch of 50 single deck bodies on LWL model chassis, based on the standard outline, but modified for South African conditions. Eight operators received examples and the bus illustrated was exhibited at the 1948 Commercial Motor Show. (ECW, Maurice Doggett collection)

2453 - Ribble 1792 RN 8176 – A further 25 bodies, similar to those for East Kent, were supplied to Ribble on existing Titan TD5 chassis, but these, more typically of such bodies, had only four sliding vents, although the first bay window was seemingly of the same width as the others. (G Mead)

2464 - East Yorkshire   374   GAT 60 – East Yorkshire were also supplied with 15 new bodies on refurbished Leyland TD5 chassis, but these were of highbridge layout, incorporating the 'Beverley Bar' roofline, necessary to enable the vehicles to pass safely under the arch of that name. (John S Cockshott archive)

2982 - United Welsh   944   FCY 405 – Eight ECW lowbridge bodies were supplied on Albion CX19 chassis to United Welsh, as illustrated here, as part of a batch of 25, the remainder being delivered to Red & White. The lower half of the drivers' windscreen was somewhat shallower to accommodate the higher Albion radiator. (Maurice Doggett collection)

3011 - Middlesbrough  58  ADC 658 – The first ECW bodies built to 8 feet width for the home market were a batch of 16 highbridge bodies supplied to Middlesbrough Corporation on Leyland Titan PD1/3 chassis in 1949. These bodies had the usual features associated with double deck bodies on postwar Titan chassis. (G Mead)

3084 - Crosville  M515  HL 5339 – Most Leyland Titan TD1 and TD2 chassis which were rebodied with lowbridge double deck bodies received Covrad radiator conversions at the same time. However, Crosville's M515 was an exception, retaining the original radiator fitted when new to West Riding. This rather spoilt the effect of trying to modernise the bus. (AB Cross)

3107 - Crosville   JA14   FM 8984 –A number of Crosville's LT7 Lions were selected to receive new ECW bodies of the standard pattern in 1949. At the same time new Gardner or Leyland oil engines were fitted to some of them and the existing Lion radiator was retained, fitted flush with the front dash. (Maurice Doggett collection)

3127 - Western SMT    856    SM 9502 – Western SMT inherited this Leyland Lion LT5 with the Caledonian fleet on 1st January 1950. Caledonian had had the chassis fitted with a new ECW body in February 1949, when a Covrad radiator was also fitted. Note the narrower width window fitted in the first bay. (The Omnibus Society, Norris collection)

3136 - Eastern National 1249 ENO 931 – A number of Bristol G type double deckers from fleets of Tilling Group operators were selected to receive new ECW bodies in 1949 and 1950, Eastern National having 9 of the type so treated. Typically the drivers' windscreen was square in shape and the radiator fitted was a PV2 style replacement. (Maurice Doggett collection)

3224 - Bristol Tramways C3001 HY 3629 – Bristol Tramways had a large fleet of Bristol G types with highbridge bodies built by the operator. Most of them were considered suitable for further service by being rebodied in 1949 and 1950 by ECW and a total of 93 were involved in three batches. (Maurice Doggett collection)

3398 - Eastern Counties   CD843   HPW 828 – Sixteen of these useful buses were constructed by ECW, incorporating the running units of the Company's Dennis Ace fleet into new lightweight, integral construction vehicles. They formed the CD class and operated in the mainly flat western area of the Company's territory.  (The Omnibus Society, Roy Marshall collection)

3512 - Eastern Counties   LK366   KNG 366 – This Eastern Counties bus, LK366, was unique in being fitted with extra high windows in the lower saloon on the nearside, to allow standing passengers to view the surrounding countryside, mainly the Norfolk Broads, without having to stoop. (ECW, Maurice Doggett collection)

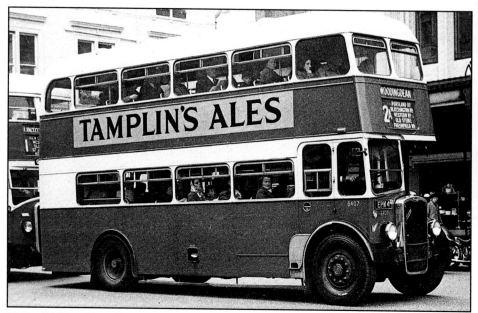

3779 - Brighton, Hove & District   6407   EPM 4 – Twelve examples of a modified version of the standard double deck highbridge body were built on Bristol K chassis where only four bays were provided. Brighton, Hove & District, Bristol Omnibus and West Yorkshire received one each, whilst the balance of 9 went to Eastern Counties. (AB Cross)

852 - Bristol Tramways   C5000   LHY 949 – A significant developments in bus design appeared in September 1949 when the first prototype Bristol Lodekka was delivered. The design featured a highbridge seating arrangement on the upper deck in a body of normal lowbridge body height. (The Omnibus Society, Roy Marshall collection)

3950 - Eastern Counties   AH199   NG 2734 – The only highbridge version of the standard double deck body to be mounted on refurbished Leyland Titan TD2 chassis were supplied to Eastern Counties in 1950. One noticeable feature was the provision of larger front mudguards, which gave the vehicles a slightly 'sit-up-and-beg' look. (Maurice Doggett collection)

4212 - Bristol Tramways   C2732   LHY 972 – Bristol Tramways took delivery of two batches of the dual-door version of the standard single deck body, for services within the City of Bristol, the bodies of which seated 33 passengers as opposed to the normal 35 in the single rear door version of the body. (Unknown photographer)

4255 - Eastern Counties  LL744  MAH 744 – Another new design of bus, produced jointly by Bristol and ECW, was the Bristol LS (Light Saloon) single deck with an underfloor engine. Again two prototypes were built, the first seen here in June1951 for the Eastern Counties fleet with its curved lower edge to the windscreen. (Maurice Doggett)

4325 - Hants & Dorset  1270  KEL 713 – The Bristol KS type double deck chassis was introduced in the second half of 1950, being built to the newly permitted length of 27 feet. A revised version of the standard body was designed to fit the chassis and featured only four bays. (Roy Marshall)

4456 - Brighton, Hove & District  428  FNJ 110 – The body designed to fit the Bristol KSW chassis was similar to that for the KS type, but was 8 feet in width, again newly permitted in 1950. However, some KS chassis were fitted with the 8 foot wide body, noticeable by the wheels being inset. (Unknown photographer)

4863 - Maidstone & District  SO57  MKN 206 – Having received a fleet of 16 bodies on Bristol L6A chassis between October 1949 and May 1950, the 15 bodies on the longer LL5G chassis for Maidstone & District appeared later in 1950. Being a BET company, M&D would no longer receive Bristol chassis, nor ECW bodies.  (Maurice Doggett collection)

4906 - Bristol Tramways 2466 NAE 2 – The first proper coach body produced by ECW after the war was an attractive curvaceous design. The first few built were of the shorter, narrower dimensions of the Bristol L6B chassis, complete with exposed radiators. The body design was given the nickname of 'Queen Mary'. (Maurice Doggett collection)

4988 - Southern Vectis 301 HDL 183 – The larger version of the 'Queen Mary' coach featured a concealed radiator and was built to the maximum dimensions on the Bristol LWL6B chassis, although some bodies had been constructed on the narrower LL6B chassis. The Bristol AVW engine provided the greater power required for coach work. (Maurice Doggett collection)

| | | | | | | |
|---|---|---|---|---|---|---|
| 4238 | MHW 985 | Bristol L5G | 79.083 | B33D | 9/50 | Bristol Tramways (GL) C2758 |
| 4239 | MHW 986 | Bristol L5G | 79.084 | B33D | 9/50 | Bristol Tramways (GL) C2759 |
| 4240 | MHW 987 | Bristol L5G | 79.085 | B33D | 9/50 | Bristol Tramways (GL) C2760 |
| 4241 * | FSM 381 | Bristol L5G | 56.005 | B35R | 6/49 | Caledonian OC, Dumfries (DF) 357 |
| 4242 * | ESM 537 | Bristol L5G | 50.070 | B35R | 6/49 | Caledonian OC, Dumfries (DF) 354 |
| 4243 * | ESM 538 | Bristol L5G | 50.071 | B35R | 6/49 | Caledonian OC, Dumfries (DF) 355 |
| 4244 * | FSM 380 | Bristol L5G | 56.004 | B35R | 6/49 | Caledonian OC, Dumfries (DF) 356 |
| 4245 * | FM 8986 | Leyland LT7 | 5902 | B35R | 8/49 | Crosville MS, Chester (CH) JG16 |
| 4246 * | FM 8974 | Leyland LT7 | 5890 | B35R | 8/49 | Crosville MS, Chester (CH) JG4 |
| 4247 * | FM 8980 | Leyland LT7 | 5896 | B35R | 8/49 | Crosville MS, Chester (CH) JG10 |
| 4248 * | FM 8981 | Leyland LT7 | 5897 | B35R | 9/49 | Crosville MS, Chester (CH) JG11 |
| 4249 * | FM 8982 | Leyland LT7 | 5898 | B35R | 9/49 | Crosville MS, Chester (CH) JG12 |
| 4250 * | FM 8987 | Leyland LT7 | 6139 | B35R | 9/49 | Crosville MS, Chester (CH) JG17 |
| 4251 * | FM 8990 | Leyland LT7 | 6142 | B35R | 9/49 | Crosville MS, Chester (CH) JG20 |
| 4252 * | FM 8989 | Leyland LT7 | 6141 | B35R | 9/49 | Crosville MS, Chester (CH) JG19 |
| 4253 * | FM 8995 | Leyland LT7 | 5904 | B35R | 9/49 | Crosville MS, Chester (CH) JG25 |
| 4254 * | FM 8992 | Leyland LT7 | 6144 | B35R | 9/49 | Crosville MS, Chester (CH) JG22 |
| 4255 | MAH 744 | Bristol LSX4G | LSX.002 | B42F | 6/51 | Eastern Counties, Norwich (NK) LL744 |
| 4256 * | KNG 697 | Bristol L5G | 71.180 | DP31R | 8/49 | Eastern Counties, Norwich (NK) LE697 |
| 4257 * | KNG 698 | Bristol L5G | 71.181 | DP31R | 8/49 | Eastern Counties, Norwich (NK) LE698 |
| 4258 | KNG 699 | Bristol L5G | 79.131 | DP31R | 7/50 | Eastern Counties, Norwich (NK) LE699 |
| 4259 | KNG 700 | Bristol L5G | 79.132 | DP31R | 7/50 | Eastern Counties, Norwich (NK) LE700 |
| 4260 | KNG 701 | Bristol L5G | 79.133 | DP31R | 7/50 | Eastern Counties, Norwich (NK) LE701 |
| 4261 | KNG 702 | Bristol L5G | 79.134 | DP31R | 5/50 | Eastern Counties, Norwich (NK) LE702 |
| 4262 | KNG 703 | Bristol L5G | 79.135 | DP31R | 4/50 | Eastern Counties, Norwich (NK) LE703 |
| 4263 | FFW 190 | Bristol L6A | 71.160 | DP31R | 8/49 | Lincolnshire RCC, Bracebridge Heath (KN) 736 |
| 4264 | FFW 191 | Bristol L6A | 71.163 | DP31R | 8/49 | Lincolnshire RCC, Bracebridge Heath (KN) 737 |
| 4265 | FFW 192 | Bristol L6A | 71.164 | DP31R | 8/49 | Lincolnshire RCC, Bracebridge Heath (KN) 738 |
| 4266 | FFW 193 | Bristol L6A | 71.195 | DP31R | 9/49 | Lincolnshire RCC, Bracebridge Heath (KN) 739 |
| 4267 | FFW 194 | Bristol L6A | 71.196 | DP31R | 8/49 | Lincolnshire RCC, Bracebridge Heath (KN) 740 |
| 4268 | FFW 195 | Bristol L6A | 71.197 | DP31R | 9/49 | Lincolnshire RCC, Bracebridge Heath (KN) 741 |
| 4269 | FFW 196 | Bristol L6A | 79.013 | DP31R | 5/50 | Lincolnshire RCC, Bracebridge Heath (KN) 742 |
| 4270 | FFW 197 | Bristol L6A | 79.022 | DP31R | 5/50 | Lincolnshire RCC, Bracebridge Heath (KN) 743 |
| 4271 | EBD 238 | Bristol L6B | 73.051 | FC31F | 5/50 | United Counties, Northampton (NO) 811 |
| 4272 | EBD 239 | Bristol L6B | 73.073 | FC31F | 6/50 | United Counties, Northampton (NO) 812 |
| 4273 | EBD 240 | Bristol L6B | 79.060 | FC31F | 6/50 | United Counties, Northampton (NO) 813 |
| 4274 | EBD 241 | Bristol L6B | 79.061 | FC31F | 6/50 | United Counties, Northampton (NO) 814 |
| 4275 | GWX 134 | Bristol L5G | 71.142 | DP31R | 6/49 | West Yorkshire RCC, Harrogate (WR) 249 |
| 4276 | GWX 135 | Bristol L5G | 71.141 | DP31R | 6/49 | West Yorkshire RCC, Harrogate (WR) 250 |
| 4277 | GWX 136 | Bristol L5G | 71.151 | DP31R | 6/49 | West Yorkshire RCC, Harrogate (WR) 251 |
| 4278 | GWX 137 | Bristol L5G | 71.165 | DP31R | 6/49 | West Yorkshire RCC, Harrogate (WR) 252 |
| 4279 | GWX 138 | Bristol L5G | 71.166 | DP31R | 6/49 | West Yorkshire RCC, Harrogate (WR) 253 |
| 4280 | GWX 139 | Bristol L5G | 71.167 | DP31R | 6/49 | West Yorkshire RCC, Harrogate (WR) 254 |
| 4281 | LNG 276 | Bristol K5G | 80.032 | L27/28R | 8/50 | Eastern Counties, Norwich (NK) LK276 |
| 4282 | LNG 277 | Bristol K5G | 80.033 | L27/28R | 8/50 | Eastern Counties, Norwich (NK) LK277 |
| 4283 | LNG 278 | Bristol K5G | 80.034 | L27/28R | 8/50 | Eastern Counties, Norwich (NK) LK278 |
| 4284 | LNG 279 | Bristol K5G | 80.035 | L27/28R | 8/50 | Eastern Counties, Norwich (NK) LK279 |
| 4285 | LNG 280 | Bristol KS5G | 80.067 | L27/28R | 9/50 | Eastern Counties, Norwich (NK) LK280 |
| 4286 | LNG 281 | Bristol KS5G | 80.066 | L27/28R | 9/50 | Eastern Counties, Norwich (NK) LK281 |
| 4287 | LNG 282 | Bristol KS5G | 80.068 | L27/28R | 10/50 | Eastern Counties, Norwich (NK) LK282 |
| 4288 | LNG 283 | Bristol KS5G | 80.069 | L27/28R | 10/50 | Eastern Counties, Norwich (NK) LK283 |
| 4289 | LNG 284 | Bristol KS5G | 80.127 | L27/28R | 10/50 | Eastern Counties, Norwich (NK) LK284 |
| 4290 | LNG 285 | Bristol KS5G | 80.128 | L27/28R | 10/50 | Eastern Counties, Norwich (NK) LK285 |
| 4291 | LNG 286 | Bristol KS5G | 80.129 | L27/28R | 10/50 | Eastern Counties, Norwich (NK) LK286 |
| 4292 | LNG 287 | Bristol KS5G | 80.130 | L27/28R | 10/50 | Eastern Counties, Norwich (NK) LK287 |
| 4293 | LNG 288 | Bristol KS5G | 80.163 | L27/28R | 12/50 | Eastern Counties, Norwich (NK) LK288 |
| 4294 | LNG 289 | Bristol KS5G | 80.164 | L27/28R | 12/50 | Eastern Counties, Norwich (NK) LK289 |
| 4295 | LNG 290 | Bristol KS5G | 80.165 | L27/28R | 12/50 | Eastern Counties, Norwich (NK) LK290 |
| 4296 | LNG 291 | Bristol KS5G | 80.166 | L27/28R | 12/50 | Eastern Counties, Norwich (NK) LK291 |
| 4297 | LNG 292 | Bristol KS5G | 80.171 | L27/28R | 1/51 | Eastern Counties, Norwich (NK) LK292 |
| 4298 | LNG 293 | Bristol KS5G | 80.172 | L27/28R | 1/51 | Eastern Counties, Norwich (NK) LK293 |
| 4299 | LNG 294 | Bristol KS5G | 80.175 | L27/28R | 12/50 | Eastern Counties, Norwich (NK) LK294 |
| 4300 * | LNG 295 | Bristol KS5G | 80.189 | L27/28R | 2/51 | Eastern Counties, Norwich (NK) LK295 |
| 4301 * | LNG 296 | Bristol KS5G | 80.190 | L27/28R | 2/51 | Eastern Counties, Norwich (NK) LK296 |

| | | | | | | |
|---|---|---|---|---|---|---|
| 4302 * | LNG 297 | Bristol KS5G | 80.191 | L27/28R | 3/51 | Eastern Counties, Norwich (NK) LK297 |
| 4303 * | LNG 298 | Bristol KS5G | 80.192 | L27/28R | 2/51 | Eastern Counties, Norwich (NK) LK298 |
| 4304 * | LNG 299 | Bristol KS5G | 80.194 | L27/28R | 3/51 | Eastern Counties, Norwich (NK) LK299 |
| 4305 * | LNG 300 | Bristol KS5G | 80.195 | L27/28R | 3/51 | Eastern Counties, Norwich (NK) LK300 |
| 4306 | RPU 521 | Bristol KS5G | 80.148 | L27/28R | 11/50 | Eastern National, Chelmsford (EX) 4111 |
| 4307 | RPU 522 | Bristol KS5G | 80.149 | L27/28R | 11/50 | Eastern National, Chelmsford (EX) 4112 |
| 4308 | RPU 523 | Bristol KS5G | 80.150 | L27/28R | 11/50 | Eastern National, Chelmsford (EX) 4113 |
| 4309 | RPU 524 | Bristol KS5G | 80.151 | L27/28R | 11/50 | Eastern National, Chelmsford (EX) 4114 |
| 4310 | RPU 525 | Bristol KS5G | 80.178 | L27/28R | 12/50 | Eastern National, Chelmsford (EX) 4115 |
| 4311 | RPU 526 | Bristol KS5G | 80.179 | L27/28R | 12/50 | Eastern National, Chelmsford (EX) 4116 |
| 4312 | RPU 527 | Bristol KS5G | 80.180 | L27/28R | 12/50 | Eastern National, Chelmsford (EX) 4117 |
| 4313 | KEL 700 | Bristol K6B | 78.193 | L27/28R | 7/50 | Hants & Dorset, Bournemouth (HA) 1257 |
| 4314 | KEL 703 | Bristol K6B | 78.199 | L27/28R | 7/50 | Hants & Dorset, Bournemouth (HA) 1260 |
| 4315 | KEL 704 | Bristol K6B | 78.200 | L27/28R | 7/50 | Hants & Dorset, Bournemouth (HA) 1261 |
| 4316 | KEL 701 | Bristol K6B | 78.197 | L27/28R | 7/50 | Hants & Dorset, Bournemouth (HA) 1258 |
| 4317 | KEL 702 | Bristol K6B | 78.198 | L27/28R | 7/50 | Hants & Dorset, Bournemouth (HA) 1259 |
| 4318 | KEL 705 | Bristol K6B | 80.036 | L27/28R | 8/50 | Hants & Dorset, Bournemouth (HA) 1262 |
| 4319 | KEL 706 | Bristol K6B | 80.037 | L27/28R | 8/50 | Hants & Dorset, Bournemouth (HA) 1263 |
| 4320 | KEL 707 | Bristol K6B | 80.038 | L27/28R | 8/50 | Hants & Dorset, Bournemouth (HA) 1264 |
| 4321 * | KEL 708 | Bristol K6B | 80.039 | L27/28R | 8/50 | Hants & Dorset, Bournemouth (HA) 1265 |
| 4322 | KEL 709 | Bristol K6B | 80.040 | L27/28R | 8/50 | Hants & Dorset, Bournemouth (HA) 1266 |
| 4323 | KEL 710 | Bristol K6B | 80.041 | L27/28R | 8/50 | Hants & Dorset, Bournemouth (HA) 1267 |
| 4324 | KEL 712 | Bristol KS6B | 80.093 | L27/28R | 9/50 | Hants & Dorset, Bournemouth (HA) 1269 |
| 4325 | KEL 713 | Bristol KS6B | 80.094 | L27/28R | 9/50 | Hants & Dorset, Bournemouth (HA) 1270 |
| 4326 | KEL 711 | Bristol KS6B | 80.092 | L27/28R | 9/50 | Hants & Dorset, Bournemouth (HA) 1268 |
| 4327 | KEL 714 | Bristol KS6B | 80.095 | L27/28R | 9/50 | Hants & Dorset, Bournemouth (HA) 1271 |
| 4328 | KEL 715 | Bristol KS6B | 80.096 | L27/28R | 9/50 | Hants & Dorset, Bournemouth (HA) 1272 |
| 4329 | KEL 716 | Bristol KS6B | 80.139 | L27/28R | 10/50 | Hants & Dorset, Bournemouth (HA) 1273 |
| 4330 | KEL 717 | Bristol KS6B | 80.140 | L27/28R | 10/50 | Hants & Dorset, Bournemouth (HA) 1274 |
| 4331 | KEL 718 | Bristol KS6B | 82.004 | L27/28R | 10/50 | Hants & Dorset, Bournemouth (HA) 1275 |
| 4332 | KEL 719 | Bristol KS6B | 82.005 | L27/28R | 10/50 | Hants & Dorset, Bournemouth (HA) 1276 |
| 4333 | KEL 720 | Bristol KS6B | 82.032 | L27/28R | 11/50 | Hants & Dorset, Bournemouth (HA) 1277 |
| 4334 | KEL 721 | Bristol KS6B | 82.033 | L27/28R | 11/50 | Hants & Dorset, Bournemouth (HA) 1278 |
| 4335 | KEL 722 | Bristol KSW6B | 82.058 | L27/28R | 2/51 | Hants & Dorset, Bournemouth (HA) 1279 |
| 4336 | KEL 723 | Bristol KSW6B | 82.059 | L27/28R | 2/51 | Hants & Dorset, Bournemouth (HA) 1280 |
| 4337 | KEL 724 | Bristol KSW6B | 82.060 | L27/28R | 2/51 | Hants & Dorset, Bournemouth (HA) 1281 |
| 4338 | KEL 725 | Bristol KSW6B | 82.070 | L27/28R | 2/51 | Hants & Dorset, Bournemouth (HA) 1282 |
| 4339 | KEL 726 | Bristol KSW6B | 82.071 | L27/28R | 2/51 | Hants & Dorset, Bournemouth (HA) 1283 |
| 4340 | KEL 727 | Bristol KSW6B | 82.072 | L27/28R | 2/51 | Hants & Dorset, Bournemouth (HA) 1284 |
| 4341 | KEL 728 | Bristol KSW6B | 82.089 | L27/28R | 3/51 | Hants & Dorset, Bournemouth (HA) 1285 |
| 4342 | KEL 729 | Bristol KSW6B | 82.090 | L27/28R | 3/51 | Hants & Dorset, Bournemouth (HA) 1286 |
| 4343 | KEL 730 | Bristol KSW6B | 82.091 | L27/28R | 3/51 | Hants & Dorset, Bournemouth (HA) 1287 |
| 4344 | LTA 937 | Bristol KS5G | 80.058 | L27/28R | 11/50 | Western National, Exeter (DN) 1827 |
| 4345 | LTA 938 | Bristol KS5G | 80.059 | L27/28R | 11/50 | Western National, Exeter (DN) 1828 |
| 4346 | LTA 936 | Bristol KS5G | 80.057 | L27/28R | 11/50 | Western National, Exeter (DN) 1826 |
| 4347 | LTA 939 | Bristol KS5G | 80.133 | L27/28R | 11/50 | Southern National, Exeter (DN) 1829 |
| 4348 | LTA 940 | Bristol KS5G | 80.134 | L27/28R | 11/50 | Southern National, Exeter (DN) 1830 |
| 4349 | LTA 941 | Bristol KS5G | 80.135 | L27/28R | 11/50 | Southern National, Exeter (DN) 1831 |
| 4350 | LTA 944 | Bristol KS5G | 80.161 | L27/28R | 12/50 | Southern National, Exeter (DN) 1834 |
| 4351 | LTA 945 | Bristol KS5G | 80.162 | L27/28R | 12/50 | Southern National, Exeter (DN) 1835 |
| 4352 | LTA 946 | Bristol KS6B | 82.025 | L27/28R | 12/50 | Southern National, Exeter (DN) 1836 |
| 4353 | LTA 947 | Bristol KS5G | 80.168 | L27/28R | 12/50 | Southern National, Exeter (DN) 1837 |
| 4354 | LTA 948 | Bristol KS5G | 80.169 | L27/28R | 12/50 | Southern National, Exeter (DN) 1838 |
| 4355 | LTA 949 | Bristol KS5G | 80.170 | L27/28R | 1/51 | Southern National, Exeter (DN) 1839 |
| 4356 | LTA 950 | Bristol KS5G | 80.198 | L27/28R | 3/51 | Southern National, Exeter (DN) 1840 |
| 4357 | LTA 951 | Bristol KS5G | 80.199 | L27/28R | 5/51 | Southern National, Exeter (DN) 1841 |
| 4358 | LTA 952 | Bristol KS5G | 80.200 | L27/28R | 5/51 | Southern National, Exeter (DN) 1842 |
| 4359 * | LTA 953 | Bristol KS5G | 82.073 | L27/28R | 6/51 | Southern National, Exeter (DN) 1843 |
| 4360 | LTA 942 | Bristol KSW6B | 80.107 | L27/28R | 1/51 | Southern National, Exeter (DN) 1832 |
| 4361 | LTA 943 | Bristol KSW6B | 80.108 | L27/28R | 1/51 | Southern National, Exeter (DN) 1833 |
| 4362 | GDL 711 | Bristol K5G | 80.046 | L27/28R | 4/50 | Southern Vectis, Newport (IW) 738 |
| 4363 | GDL 712 | Bristol K5G | 80.047 | L27/28R | 4/50 | Southern Vectis, Newport (IW) 739 |
| 4364 | GDL 713 | Bristol KS5G | 80.131 | L27/28R | 11/50 | Southern Vectis, Newport (IW) 740 |
| 4365 | GDL 714 | Bristol KS5G | 80.132 | L27/28R | 11/50 | Southern Vectis, Newport (IW) 741 |

| | | | | | | | |
|---|---|---|---|---|---|---|---|
| 4366 | GDL 715 | Bristol KS5G | 80.152 | L27/28R | 11/50 | Southern Vectis, Newport (IW) 742 |
| 4367 | FMO 968 | Bristol KS6B | 80.085 | L27/28R | 8/50 | Thames Valley, Reading (BE) 586 |
| 4368 | FMO 969 | Bristol KS6B | 80.086 | L27/28R | 9/50 | Thames Valley, Reading (BE) 587 |
| 4369 | FMO 970 | Bristol KS6B | 80.087 | L27/28R | 9/50 | Thames Valley, Reading (BE) 588 |
| 4370 | FMO 971 | Bristol KS6B | 82.009 | L27/28R | 11/50 | Thames Valley, Reading (BE) 589 |
| 4371 | FMO 972 | Bristol KS6B | 82.012 | L27/28R | 11/50 | Thames Valley, Reading (BE) 590 |
| 4372 | FMO 973 | Bristol KS6B | 82.013 | L27/28R | 11/50 | Thames Valley, Reading (BE) 591 |
| 4373 | FMO 974 | Bristol KS6B | 82.014 | L27/28R | 11/50 | Thames Valley, Reading (BE) 592 |
| 4374 | FMO 975 | Bristol KS6B | 82.021 | L27/28R | 11/50 | Thames Valley, Reading (BE) 593 |
| 4375 | FMO 976 | Bristol KS6B | 82.022 | L27/28R | 11/50 | Thames Valley, Reading (BE) 594 |
| 4376 | FMO 977 | Bristol KS6B | 82.023 | CL27/26RD1/51 | | Thames Valley, Reading (BE) 595 |
| 4377 | FMO 978 | Bristol KS6B | 82.024 | CL27/26RD1/51 | | Thames Valley, Reading (BE) 596 |
| 4378 | FMO 979 | Bristol KS6B | 82.038 | CL27/26RD1/51 | | Thames Valley, Reading (BE) 597 |
| 4379 | FMO 980 | Bristol KS6B | 82.039 | CL27/26RD1/51 | | Thames Valley, Reading (BE) 598 |
| 4380 | FMO 981 | Bristol KS6B | 82.040 | CL27/26RD1/51 | | Thames Valley, Reading (BE) 599 |
| 4381 | FMO 982 | Bristol KS6B | 82.041 | CL27/26RD1/51 | | Thames Valley, Reading (BE) 600 |
| 4382 | FMO 983 | Bristol KSW6B | 80.117 | L27/28R | 12/50 | Thames Valley, Reading (BE) 601 |
| 4383 | FMO 984 | Bristol KSW6B | 80.118 | L27/28R | 12/50 | Thames Valley, Reading (BE) 602 |
| 4384 | FMO 985 | Bristol KSW6B | 80.119 | L27/28R | 12/50 | Thames Valley, Reading (BE) 603 |
| 4385 | FRP 685 | Bristol KS6B | 80.098 | L27/28R | 9/50 | United Counties, Northampton (NO) 685 |
| 4386 | FRP 684 | Bristol KS6B | 80.097 | L27/28R | 9/50 | United Counties, Northampton (NO) 684 |
| 4387 | FRP 686 | Bristol KS5G | 80.153 | L27/28R | 10/50 | United Counties, Northampton (NO) 686 |
| 4388 | FRP 687 | Bristol KS5G | 80.154 | L27/28R | 10/50 | United Counties, Northampton (NO) 687 |
| 4389 | FRP 688 | Bristol KS5G | 80.155 | L27/28R | 10/50 | United Counties, Northampton (NO) 688 |
| 4390 | FRP 689 | Bristol KS5G | 80.156 | L27/28R | 10/50 | United Counties, Northampton (NO) 689 |
| 4391 | FRP 690 | Bristol KS5G | 80.176 | L27/28R | 11/50 | United Counties, Northampton (NO) 690 |
| 4392 | FRP 691 | Bristol KS5G | 80.177 | L27/28R | 11/50 | United Counties, Northampton (NO) 691 |
| 4393 | FRP 692 | Bristol KS5G | 80.181 | L27/28R | 12/50 | United Counties, Northampton (NO) 692 |
| 4394 | FRP 693 | Bristol KS5G | 80.182 | L27/28R | 11/50 | United Counties, Northampton (NO) 693 |
| 4395 * | FRP 694 | Bristol KS6B | 82.064 | L27/28R | 2/51 | United Counties, Northampton (NO) 694 |
| 4396 * | FRP 695 | Bristol KS5G | 80.196 | L27/28R | 3/51 | United Counties, Northampton (NO) 695 |
| 4397 * | FRP 696 | Bristol KS5G | 80.197 | L27/28R | 3/51 | United Counties, Northampton (NO) 696 |
| 4398 * | FRP 697 | Bristol KS5G | 82.080 | L27/28R | 3/51 | United Counties, Northampton (NO) 697 |
| 4399 | JWY 222 | Bristol KS6B | 82.010 | L27/28R | 11/50 | West Yorkshire RCC, Harrogate (WR) 804 |
| 4400 | JWY 223 | Bristol KS6B | 82.011 | L27/28R | 11/50 | West Yorkshire RCC, Harrogate (WR) 805 |
| 4401 | JWY 228 | Bristol KS6B | 82.043 | L27/28R | 12/50 | West Yorkshire RCC, Harrogate (WR) 810 |
| 4402 | JWY 229 | Bristol KS6B | 82.044 | L27/28R | 12/50 | West Yorkshire RCC, Harrogate (WR) 811 |
| 4403 | JWY 230 | Bristol KS6B | 82.045 | L27/28R | 12/50 | West Yorkshire RCC, Harrogate (WR) 812 |
| 4404 | JWY 231 | Bristol KS6B | 82.046 | L27/28R | 12/50 | West Yorkshire RCC, Harrogate (WR) 813 |
| 4405 | JWY 224 | Bristol KSW6B | 80.120 | L27/28R | 1/51 | West Yorkshire RCC, Harrogate (WR) 806 |
| 4406 | JWY 225 | Bristol KSW6B | 80.121 | L27/28R | 1/51 | West Yorkshire RCC, Harrogate (WR) 807 |
| 4407 | JWY 226 | Bristol KSW6B | 80.122 | L27/28R | 1/51 | West Yorkshire RCC, Harrogate (WR) 808 |
| 4408 | JWY 227 | Bristol KSW6B | 80.123 | L27/28R | 1/51 | West Yorkshire RCC, Harrogate (WR) 809 |
| 4409 | DJN 554 | Bristol KS5G | 80.063 | L27/28R | 9/50 | Westcliff-on-Sea MS (EX) |
| 4410 | DJN 556 | Bristol KS5G | 80.064 | L27/28R | 11/49 | Westcliff-on-Sea MS (EX) |
| 4411 | DJN 557 | Bristol KS5G | 80.065 | L27/28R | 9/50 | Westcliff-on-Sea MS (EX) |
| 4412 | DJN 558 | Bristol KS6B | 80.136 | L27/28R | 11/50 | Westcliff-on-Sea MS (EX) |
| 4413 | DJN 559 | Bristol KS6B | 82.042 | L27/28R | 12/50 | Westcliff-on-Sea MS (EX) |
| 4414 | LTA 808 | Bristol K5G | 80.042 | L27/28R | 8/50 | Western National, Exeter (DN) 989 |
| 4415 | LTA 809 | Bristol K5G | 80.043 | L27/28R | 8/50 | Western National, Exeter (DN) 990 |
| 4416 | LTA 811 | Bristol K5G | 80.045 | L27/28R | 8/50 | Western National, Exeter (DN) 992 |
| 4417 | LTA 810 | Bristol K5G | 80.044 | L27/28R | 8/50 | Western National, Exeter (DN) 991 |
| 4418 | LTA 812 | Bristol KS5G | 80.054 | L27/28R | 9/50 | Western National, Exeter (DN) 993 |
| 4419 | LTA 813 | Bristol KS5G | 80.055 | L27/28R | 9/50 | Western National, Exeter (DN) 994 |
| 4420 | LTA 815 | Bristol KS5G | 80.091 | L27/28R | 9/50 | Western National, Exeter (DN) 996 |
| 4421 | LTA 814 | Bristol KS5G | 80.088 | L27/28R | 9/50 | Western National, Exeter (DN) 995 |
| 4422 | LTA 816 | Bristol KS5G | 80.089 | L27/28R | 9/50 | Western National, Exeter (DN) 997 |
| 4423 | LTA 817 | Bristol KS5G | 80.090 | L27/28R | 9/50 | Western National, Exeter (DN) 998 |
| 4424 | LTA 818 | Bristol KS5G | 80.141 | L27/28R | 10/50 | Western National, Exeter (DN) 999 |
| 4425 | LTA 819 | Bristol KS5G | 80.142 | L27/28R | 11/50 | Western National, Exeter (DN) 1800 |
| 4426 | LTA 822 | Bristol KS5G | 80.157 | L27/28R | 12/50 | Western National, Exeter (DN) 1803 |
| 4427 | LTA 823 | Bristol KS5G | 80.158 | L27/28R | 12/50 | Western National, Exeter (DN) 1804 |
| 4428 | LTA 824 | Bristol KS5G | 80.159 | L27/28R | 12/50 | Western National, Exeter (DN) 1805 |
| 4429 | LTA 825 | Bristol KS5G | 80.160 | L27/28R | 12/50 | Western National, Exeter (DN) 1806 |

| | | | | | | | |
|---|---|---|---|---|---|---|---|
| 4430 | LTA 826 | Bristol KS5G | 80.167 | L27/28R | 12/50 | Western National, Exeter (DN) | 1807 |
| 4431 | LTA 827 | Bristol KS5G | 80.183 | L27/28R | 1/51 | Western National, Exeter (DN) | 1808 |
| 4432 | LTA 828 | Bristol KS5G | 80.184 | L27/28R | 1/51 | Western National, Exeter (DN) | 1809 |
| 4433 | LTA 830 | Bristol KSW6B | 82.054 | L27/28R | 2/51 | Western National, Exeter (DN) | 1811 |
| 4434 | LTA 829 | Bristol KSW6B | 82.055 | L27/28R | 2/51 | Western National, Exeter (DN) | 1810 |
| 4435 | LTA 831 | Bristol KSW6B | 82.056 | L27/28R | 3/51 | Western National, Exeter (DN) | 1812 |
| 4436 * | LTA 832 | Bristol KS5G | 82.081 | L27/28R | 3/51 | Western National, Exeter (DN) | 1813 |
| 4437 | LTA 820 | Bristol KSW6B | 80.124 | L27/28R | 1/51 | Western National, Exeter (DN) | 1801 |
| 4438 | LTA 821 | Bristol KSW6B | 80.125 | L27/28R | 1/51 | Western National, Exeter (DN) | 1802 |
| 4439 | GMR 893 | Bristol KS6B | 80.137 | L27/28R | 10/50 | Wilts & Dorset, Salisbury (WI) | 314 |
| 4440 | GMR 894 | Bristol KS6B | 80.138 | L27/28R | 10/50 | Wilts & Dorset, Salisbury (WI) | 315 |
| 4441 | GMW 194 | Bristol KS6B | 82.006 | L27/28R | 10/50 | Wilts & Dorset, Salisbury (WI) | 316 |
| 4442 | GMW 195 | Bristol KS6B | 82.007 | L27/28R | 11/50 | Wilts & Dorset, Salisbury (WI) | 317 |
| 4443 | GMW 196 | Bristol KS6B | 82.008 | L27/28R | 11/50 | Wilts & Dorset, Salisbury (WI) | 318 |
| 4444 | GMW 850 | Bristol KS5G | 80.173 | L27/28R | 12/50 | Wilts & Dorset, Salisbury (WI) | 319 |
| 4445 | GMW 851 | Bristol KS5G | 80.174 | L27/28R | 12/50 | Wilts & Dorset, Salisbury (WI) | 320 |
| 4446 | GWV 305 | Bristol KSW5G | 80.193 | L27/28R | 2/51 | Wilts & Dorset, Salisbury (WI) | 324 |
| 4447 | FNJ 101 | Bristol KS5G | 80.185 | H32/28R | 2/51 | Brighton, Hove & District (ES) | 6419 |
| 4448 | FNJ 102 | Bristol KS5G | 80.186 | H32/28R | 2/51 | Brighton, Hove & District (ES) | 6420 |
| 4449 | FNJ 103 | Bristol KS5G | 80.187 | H32/28R | 2/51 | Brighton, Hove & District (ES) | 6421 |
| 4450 | FNJ 104 | Bristol KS5G | 80.188 | H32/28R | 2/51 | Brighton, Hove & District (ES) | 6422 |
| 4451 * | FNJ 105 | Bristol KS5G | 82.082 | H32/28R | 3/51 | Brighton, Hove & District (ES) | 6423 |
| 4452 * | FNJ 106 | Bristol KS5G | 82.083 | H32/28R | 3/51 | Brighton, Hove & District (ES) | 6424 |
| 4453 * | FNJ 107 | Bristol KS5G | 82.084 | H32/28R | 5/51 | Brighton, Hove & District (ES) | 6425 |
| 4454 * | FNJ 108 | Bristol KS5G | 84.001 | H32/28R | 5/51 | Brighton, Hove & District (ES) | 6426 |
| 4455 | FNJ 109 | Bristol KSW6B | 80.109 | H32/28R | 1/51 | Brighton, Hove & District (ES) | 6427 |
| 4456 | FNJ 110 | Bristol KSW6B | 80.110 | H32/28R | 1/51 | Brighton, Hove & District (ES) | 6428 |
| 4457 | FNJ 111 | Bristol KSW6B | 80.111 | H32/28R | 1/51 | Brighton, Hove & District (ES) | 6429 |
| 4458 | NAE 11 | Bristol KS6B | 80.074 | H32/28R | 10/50 | Bristol Tramways (GL) | C3456 |
| 4459 | NAE 12 | Bristol KS6B | 80.077 | H32/28R | 10/50 | Bristol Tramways (GL) | C3457 |
| 4460 | NAE 13 | Bristol KS6B | 80.100 | H32/28R | 10/50 | Bristol Tramways (GL) | C3458 |
| 4461 | NAE 14 | Bristol KS6B | 80.073 | H32/28R | 10/50 | Bristol Tramways (GL) | C3459 |
| 4462 | NAE 15 | Bristol KS6B | 80.075 | H32/28R | 11/50 | Bristol Tramways (GL) | C3460 |
| 4463 | NAE 16 | Bristol KS6B | 80.076 | H32/28R | 11/50 | Bristol Tramways (GL) | C3461 |
| 4464 | NAE 17 | Bristol KS6B | 80.078 | H32/28R | 11/50 | Bristol Tramways (GL) | C3462 |
| 4465 | NAE 18 | Bristol KS6B | 80.079 | H32/28R | 11/50 | Bristol Tramways (GL) | C3463 |
| 4466 | NAE 19 | Bristol KS6B | 80.099 | H32/28R | 11/50 | Bristol Tramways (GL) | C3464 |
| 4467 | NAE 20 | Bristol KS6B | 80.126 | H32/28R | 3/51 | Bristol Tramways (GL) | C3465 |
| 4468 | NAE 21 | Bristol KS6B | 80.143 | H32/28R | 3/51 | Bristol Tramways (GL) | C3466 |
| 4469 | NAE 22 | Bristol KS6B | 80.144 | H32/28R | 3/51 | Bristol Tramways (GL) | C3467 |
| 4470 | NAE 23 | Bristol KS6B | 80.145 | H32/28R | 3/51 | Bristol Tramways (GL) | C3468 |
| 4471 | NAE 24 | Bristol KS6B | 80.146 | H32/28R | 3/51 | Bristol Tramways (GL) | C3469 |
| 4472 | NAE 25 | Bristol KS6B | 80.147 | H32/28R | 3/51 | Bristol Tramways (GL) | C3470 |
| 4473 | NAE 26 | Bristol KS6B | 82.001 | H32/28R | 3/51 | Bristol Tramways (GL) | C3471 |
| 4474 | NAE 27 | Bristol KS6B | 82.002 | H32/28R | 3/51 | Bristol Tramways (GL) | C3472 |
| 4475 | NAE 28 | Bristol KS6B | 82.003 | H32/28R | 3/51 | Bristol Tramways (GL) | C3473 |
| 4476 | NAE 29 | Bristol KS6B | 82.015 | H32/28R | 3/51 | Bristol Tramways (GL) | C3474 |
| 4477 | NAE 30 | Bristol KS6B | 82.016 | H32/28R | 3/51 | Bristol Tramways (GL) | C3475 |
| 4478 | NAE 31 | Bristol KS6B | 82.017 | H32/28R | 3/51 | Bristol Tramways (GL) | C3476 |
| 4479 | NAE 32 | Bristol KS6B | 82.018 | H32/28R | 3/51 | Bristol Tramways (GL) | C3477 |
| 4480 | NAE 33 | Bristol KS6B | 82.019 | H32/28R | 12/50 | Bristol Tramways (GL) | 3784 |
| 4481 | NAE 34 | Bristol KS6B | 82.020 | H32/28R | 1/51 | Bristol Tramways (GL) | 1521 |
| 4482 | NAE 35 | Bristol KS6B | 82.026 | H32/28R | 1/51 | Bristol Tramways (GL) | 1522 |
| 4483 | NAE 36 | Bristol KS6B | 82.027 | H32/28R | 1/51 | Bristol Tramways (GL) | 1523 |
| 4484 | NAE 37 | Bristol KS6B | 82.028 | H32/28R | 1/51 | Bristol Tramways (GL) | 1524 |
| 4485 | NAE 38 | Bristol KS6B | 82.029 | H32/28R | 1/51 | Bristol Tramways (GL) | 1525 |
| 4486 | NAE 39 | Bristol KS6B | 82.030 | H32/28R | 1/51 | Bristol Tramways (GL) | 1526 |
| 4487 * | NAE 40 | Bristol KS6B | 82.031 | H32/28R | 2/51 | Bristol Tramways (GL) | 8008 |
| 4488 * | NAE 41 | Bristol KS6B | 82.034 | H32/28R | 2/51 | Bristol Tramways (GL) | 8009 |
| 4489 | NAE 42 | Bristol KS6B | 82.050 | H32/28R | 2/51 | Bristol Tramways (GL) | 8010 |
| 4490 | NAE 43 | Bristol KS6B | 82.051 | H32/28R | 2/51 | Bristol Tramways (GL) | 8011 |
| 4491 | NAE 44 | Bristol KS6B | 82.052 | H32/28R | 2/51 | Bristol Tramways (GL) | 8012 |
| 4492 | NAE 45 | Bristol KS6B | 82.053 | H32/28R | 2/51 | Bristol Tramways (GL) | 8013 |
| 4493 | NAE 46 | Bristol KS6B | 82.057 | H32/28R | 2/51 | Bristol Tramways (GL) | 8014 |

| | | | | | | | |
|---|---|---|---|---|---|---|---|
| 4494 | NAE 47 | Bristol KS6B | 82.061 | H32/28R | 2/51 | Bath Electric Tramways (SO) 8015 |
| 4495 | NAE 48 | Bristol KS6B | 82.062 | H32/28R | 2/51 | Bath Tramways Motor Co (SO) 8016 |
| 4496 | NAE 49 | Bristol KS6B | 82.063 | H32/28R | 2/51 | Bath Tramways Motor Co (SO) 8017 |
| 4497 * | NAE 50 | Bristol KS6B | 82.074 | H32/28R | 3/51 | Bath Tramways Motor Co (SO) 8018 |
| 4498 * | NAE 51 | Bristol KS6B | 82.075 | H32/28R | 3/51 | Bath Tramways Motor Co (SO) 8019 |
| 4499 * | NAE 52 | Bristol KS6B | 82.076 | H32/28R | 3/51 | Bath Tramways Motor Co (SO) 8020 |
| 4500 * | NAE 53 | Bristol KS6B | 82.077 | H32/28R | 6/51 | Bristol Tramways (GL) 8021 |
| 4501 * | NAE 54 | Bristol KS6B | 82.078 | H32/28R | 6/51 | Bristol Tramways (GL) 8022 |
| 4502 * | NAE 55 | Bristol KS6B | 82.079 | H32/28R | 5/51 | Bristol Tramways (GL) 8023 |
| 4503 * | NAE 56 | Bristol KS5G | 82.085 | H32/28R | 5/51 | Bristol Tramways (GL) 8024 |
| 4504 * | NAE 57 | Bristol KS6B | 82.086 | H32/28R | 5/51 | Bristol Tramways (GL) 8025 |
| 4505 | NAE 58 | Bristol KSW6B | 82.087 | H32/28R | 6/51 | Bristol Tramways (GL) 8026 |
| 4506 | NAE 59 | Bristol KSW6B | 82.088 | H32/28R | 6/51 | Bristol Tramways (GL) 8027 |
| 4507 | NAE 60 | Bristol KSW6B | 80.101 | H32/28R | 1/51 | Bristol Tramways (GL) 8000 |
| 4508 | NAE 61 | Bristol KSW6B | 80.102 | H32/28R | 1/51 | Bristol Tramways (GL) 8001 |
| 4509 | NAE 62 | Bristol KSW6B | 80.103 | H32/28R | 1/51 | Bristol Tramways (GL) 8002 |
| 4510 | NAE 63 | Bristol KSW6B | 80.112 | H32/28R | 1/51 | Bristol Tramways (GL) 8003 |
| 4511 | NAE 64 | Bristol KSW6B | 80.113 | H32/28R | 1/51 | Bristol Tramways (GL) 8004 |
| 4512 | NAE 65 | Bristol KSW6B | 80.114 | H32/28R | 2/51 | Bristol Tramways (GL) 8005 |
| 4513 | NAE 66 | Bristol KSW6B | 80.115 | H32/28R | 2/51 | Bristol Tramways (GL) 8006 |
| 4514 | NAE 67 | Bristol KSW6B | 80.116 | H32/28R | 2/51 | Bristol Tramways (GL) 8007 |
| 4515 * | LNG 261 | Bristol KS6B | 82.065 | H32/28R | 1/51 | Eastern Counties, Norwich (NK) LKH261 |
| 4516 * | LNG 262 | Bristol KS6B | 82.066 | H32/28R | 1/51 | Eastern Counties, Norwich (NK) LKH262 |
| 4517 * | LNG 263 | Bristol KS6B | 82.067 | H32/28R | 1/51 | Eastern Counties, Norwich (NK) LKH263 |
| 4518 * | LNG 264 | Bristol KS6B | 82.068 | H32/28R | 3/51 | Eastern Counties, Norwich (NK) LKH264 |
| 4519 * | LNG 265 | Bristol KS6B | 82.069 | H32/28R | 3/51 | Eastern Counties, Norwich (NK) LKH265 |
| 4520 | GFW 278 | Bristol KS6B | 80.071 | H32/28R | 5/51 | Lincolnshire RCC, Bracebridge Heath (KN) 777 |
| 4521 | GFW 277 | Bristol KS6B | 80.070 | H32/28R | 5/51 | Lincolnshire RCC, Bracebridge Heath (KN) 776 |
| 4522 | GFW 279 | Bristol KS6B | 80.072 | H32/28R | 5/51 | Lincolnshire RCC, Bracebridge Heath (KN) 778 |
| 4523 | NHN 901 | Bristol K6B | 80.026 | H30/26R | 10/50 | United AS, Darlington (DM) BBH1 |
| 4524 | NHN 902 | Bristol K6B | 80.027 | H30/26R | 10/50 | United AS, Darlington (DM) BBH2 |
| 4525 | NHN 903 | Bristol K6B | 80.028 | H30/26R | 10/50 | United AS, Darlington (DM) BBH3 |
| 4526 | NHN 904 | Bristol K6B | 80.029 | H30/26R | 10/50 | United AS, Darlington (DM) BBH4 |
| 4527 | NHN 905 | Bristol K6B | 80.030 | H30/26R | 10/50 | United AS, Darlington (DM) BBH5 |
| 4528 | NHN 906 | Bristol K6B | 80.031 | H30/26R | 10/50 | United AS, Darlington (DM) BBH6 |
| 4529 | NHN 908 | Bristol K6B | 80.049 | H30/26R | 10/50 | United AS, Darlington (DM) BBH8 |
| 4530 | NHN 909 | Bristol K6B | 80.050 | H30/26R | 5/51 | United AS, Darlington (DM) BBH9 |
| 4531 | NHN 910 | Bristol K6B | 80.048 | H30/26R | 6/51 | United AS, Darlington (DM) BBH10 |
| 4532 | NHN 907 | Bristol KS6B | 80.056 | H32/28R | 5/51 | United AS, Darlington (DM) BBH7 |
| 4533 | NHN 911 | Bristol KS6B | 80.080 | H32/28R | 6/51 | United AS, Darlington (DM) BBH11 |
| 4534 | NHN 912 | Bristol KS6B | 80.081 | H32/28R | 6/51 | United AS, Darlington (DM) BBH12 |
| 4535 | NHN 914 | Bristol KSW6B | 80.104 | H32/28R | 7/51 | United AS, Darlington (DM) BBH21 |
| 4536 | NHN 913 | Bristol KSW6B | 80.105 | H32/28R | 7/51 | United AS, Darlington (DM) BBH20 |
| 4537 | NHN 915 | Bristol KSW6B | 80.106 | H32/28R | 7/51 | United AS, Darlington (DM) BBH22 |
| 4538 * | BHY 692 | Bristol G.JW | G129 | H31/28R | 6/50 | Bristol Tramways (GL) C3012 |
| 4539 * | BHY 695 | Bristol G.JW | G132 | H31/28R | 6/50 | Bristol Tramways (GL) C3015 |
| 4540 * | EAE 598 | Bristol GO5G | GO5G.214 | H31/28R | 5/50 | Bristol Tramways (GL) C3081 |
| 4541 * | CHW 48 | Bristol GO5G | GO5G.91 | H31/28R | 6/50 | Bristol Tramways (GL) C3037 |
| 4542 * | DAE 373 | Bristol GO5G | GO5G.133 | H31/28R | 6/50 | Bristol Tramways (GL) C3054 |
| 4543 * | CHW 835 | Bristol GO5G | GO5G.100 | H31/28R | 6/50 | Bristol Tramways (GL) C3069 |
| 4544 * | HY 3630 | Bristol G.JW | G101 | H31/28R | 7/50 | Bristol Tramways (GL) C3000 |
| 4545 * | HY 6896 | Bristol G.JW | G116 | H31/28R | 7/50 | Bristol Tramways (GL) C3004 |
| 4546 * | HY 6503 | Bristol G.JW | G117 | H31/28R | 7/50 | Bristol Tramways (GL) C3005 |
| 4547 * | HY 6198 | Bristol G.JW | G119 | H31/28R | 7/50 | Bristol Tramways (GL) C3002 |
| 4548 * | CWX 661 | Bristol K5G | 47.24 | H30/26R | 5/51 | York-West Yorkshire, Harrogate (WR) Y373 |
| 4549 * | CWX 663 | Bristol K5G | 47.27 | H30/26R | 5/51 | York-West Yorkshire, Harrogate (WR) Y375 |
| 4550 * | CWX 657 | Bristol K5G | 47.12 | H30/26R | 5/51 | York-West Yorkshire, Harrogate (WR) Y369 |
| 4551 * | CWX 666 | Bristol K5G | 47.31 | H30/26R | 5/51 | York-West Yorkshire, Harrogate (WR) Y378 |
| 4552 * | CWX 659 | Bristol K5G | 47.20 | H30/26R | 5/51 | York-West Yorkshire, Harrogate (WR) Y371 |
| 4553 * | CWX 660 | Bristol K5G | 47.21 | H30/26R | 5/51 | York-West Yorkshire, Harrogate (WR) Y372 |
| 4554 * | CWX 658 | Bristol K5G | 47.13 | H30/26R | 6/51 | York-West Yorkshire, Harrogate (WR) Y370 |
| 4555 * | CWX 664 | Bristol K5G | 47.28 | H30/26R | 6/51 | York-West Yorkshire, Harrogate (WR) Y376 |
| 4556 * | CWX 665 | Bristol K5G | 47.29 | H30/26R | 6/51 | York-West Yorkshire, Harrogate (WR) Y377 |
| 4557 * | CWX 656 | Bristol K5G | 47.11 | H30/26R | 10/51 | York-West Yorkshire, Harrogate (WR) Y368 |

| 4558 * | CWX 662 | Bristol K5G | 47.26 | H30/26R | 10/51 | York-West Yorkshire, Harrogate (WR) Y374 |
|---|---|---|---|---|---|---|
| 4559 | LFM 714 | Bristol L5G | 79.175 | B35R | 7/50 | Crosville MS, Chester (CH) KG133 |
| 4560 | LFM 715 | Bristol L5G | 79.173 | B35R | 7/50 | Crosville MS, Chester (CH) KG134 |
| 4561 | LFM 716 | Bristol L5G | 79.174 | B35R | 7/50 | Crosville MS, Chester (CH) KG135 |
| 4562 | LFM 717 | Bristol L5G | 79.172 | B35R | 7/50 | Crosville MS, Chester (CH) KG136 |
| 4563 | LFM 718 | Bristol L5G | 79.176 | B35R | 7/50 | Crosville MS, Chester (CH) KG137 |
| 4564 | LFM 719 | Bristol L5G | 79.177 | B35R | 7/50 | Crosville MS, Chester (CH) KG138 |
| 4565 | LFM 720 | Bristol L5G | 79.178 | B35R | 7/50 | Crosville MS, Chester (CH) KG139 |
| 4566 | LFM 721 | Bristol L5G | 81.001 | B35R | 7/50 | Crosville MS, Chester (CH) KG140 |
| 4567 | LFM 722 | Bristol L5G | 81.002 | B35R | 7/50 | Crosville MS, Chester (CH) KG141 |
| 4568 | LFM 723 | Bristol L5G | 81.033 | B35R | 7/50 | Crosville MS, Chester (CH) KG142 |
| 4569 | LFM 724 | Bristol L5G | 81.035 | B35R | 7/50 | Crosville MS, Chester (CH) KG143 |
| 4570 | LFM 725 | Bristol L5G | 81.031 | B35R | 7/50 | Crosville MS, Chester (CH) KG144 |
| 4571 | LFM 726 | Bristol L5G | 81.034 | B35R | 7/50 | Crosville MS, Chester (CH) KG145 |
| 4572 | LFM 727 | Bristol L5G | 81.037 | B35R | 7/50 | Crosville MS, Chester (CH) KG146 |
| 4573 | LFM 728 | Bristol L5G | 81.036 | B35R | 7/50 | Crosville MS, Chester (CH) KG147 |
| 4574 | LFM 729 | Bristol L5G | 81.032 | B35R | 7/50 | Crosville MS, Chester (CH) KG148 |
| 4575 | LFM 730 | Bristol L5G | 81.080 | B35R | 8/50 | Crosville MS, Chester (CH) KG149 |
| 4576 | LFM 733 | Bristol LL5G | 81.084 | B39R | 8/50 | Crosville MS, Chester (CH) KG152 |
| 4577 | LFM 731 | Bristol LL5G | 81.082 | B39R | 8/50 | Crosville MS, Chester (CH) KG150 |
| 4578 | LFM 732 | Bristol LL5G | 81.083 | B39R | 8/50 | Crosville MS, Chester (CH) KG151 |
| 4579 | LFM 734 | Bristol LL5G | 81.085 | B39R | 8/50 | Crosville MS, Chester (CH) KG153 |
| 4580 | LFM 735 | Bristol LL5G | 81.086 | B39R | 8/50 | Crosville MS, Chester (CH) KG154 |
| 4581 | LFM 736 | Bristol LL5G | 81.081 | B39R | 8/50 | Crosville MS, Chester (CH) KG155 |
| 4582 | LFM 756 | Bristol LL6B | 81.165 | B39R | 10/50 | Crosville MS, Chester (CH) KW175 |
| 4583 | LFM 757 | Bristol LL6B | 83.001 | B39R | 10/50 | Crosville MS, Chester (CH) KW176 |
| 4584 | LFM 737 | Bristol LL5G | 81.173 | B39R | 10/50 | Crosville MS, Chester (CH) KW156 |
| 4585 | LFM 738 | Bristol LL5G | 81.174 | B39R | 10/50 | Crosville MS, Chester (CH) KW157 |
| 4586 | LFM 758 | Bristol LL6B | 83.004 | B39R | 10/50 | Crosville MS, Chester (CH) KW177 |
| 4587 | LFM 759 | Bristol LL6B | 83.005 | B39R | 10/50 | Crosville MS, Chester (CH) KW178 |
| 4588 | LFM 760 | Bristol LL6B | 83.006 | B39R | 10/50 | Crosville MS, Chester (CH) KW179 |
| 4589 | LFM 740 | Bristol LL5G | 81.198 | B39R | 10/50 | Crosville MS, Chester (CH) KG159 |
| 4590 | LFM 739 | Bristol LL5G | 81.199 | B39R | 10/50 | Crosville MS, Chester (CH) KG158 |
| 4591 | LFM 761 | Bristol LL6B | 83.026 | B39R | 10/50 | Crosville MS, Chester (CH) KW180 |
| 4592 | LFM 762 | Bristol LL6B | 83.027 | B39R | 10/50 | Crosville MS, Chester (CH) KW181 |
| 4593 | LFM 763 | Bristol LL6B | 83.028 | B39R | 10/50 | Crosville MS, Chester (CH) KW182 |
| 4594 | LFM 764 | Bristol LL6B | 83.029 | B39R | 11/50 | Crosville MS, Chester (CH) KW183 |
| 4595 | LFM 766 | Bristol LL6B | 83.030 | B39R | 10/50 | Crosville MS, Chester (CH) KW185 |
| 4596 | LFM 768 | Bristol LL6B | 83.052 | B39R | 11/50 | Crosville MS, Chester (CH) KW187 |
| 4597 | LFM 767 | Bristol LL6B | 83.053 | B39R | 11/50 | Crosville MS, Chester (CH) KW186 |
| 4598 | LFM 765 | Bristol LL6B | 83.054 | B39R | 11/50 | Crosville MS, Chester (CH) KW184 |
| 4599 | LFM 741 | Bristol LL5G | 83.073 | B39R | 10/50 | Crosville MS, Chester (CH) KG160 |
| 4600 | LFM 745 | Bristol LL5G | 83.074 | B39R | 10/50 | Crosville MS, Chester (CH) KG164 |
| 4601 | LFM 742 | Bristol LL5G | 83.075 | B39R | 10/50 | Crosville MS, Chester (CH) KG161 |
| 4602 | LFM 743 | Bristol LL5G | 83.076 | B39R | 10/50 | Crosville MS, Chester (CH) KG162 |
| 4603 | LFM 744 | Bristol LL5G | 83.077 | B39R | 10/50 | Crosville MS, Chester (CH) KG163 |
| 4604 | LFM 769 | Bristol LL5G | 83.110 | B39R | 11/50 | Crosville MS, Chester (CH) KG188 |
| 4605 | LFM 770 | Bristol LL5G | 83.111 | B39R | 11/50 | Crosville MS, Chester (CH) KG189 |
| 4606 | LFM 771 | Bristol LL5G | 83.118 | B39R | 11/50 | Crosville MS, Chester (CH) KG190 |
| 4607 | LFM 772 | Bristol LL5G | 83.119 | B39R | 11/50 | Crosville MS, Chester (CH) KG191 |
| 4608 | LFM 773 | Bristol LL5G | 83.120 | B39R | 11/50 | Crosville MS, Chester (CH) KG192 |
| 4609 * | LFM 774 | Bristol LL5G | 83.137 | B39R | 5/51 | Crosville MS, Chester (CH) KG193 |
| 4610 * | LFM 775 | Bristol LL5G | 83.138 | B39R | 5/51 | Crosville MS, Chester (CH) KG194 |
| 4611 * | LFM 777 | Bristol LL5G | 83.139 | B39R | 5/51 | Crosville MS, Chester (CH) KG196 |
| 4612 * | LFM 778 | Bristol LL5G | 83.140 | B39R | 5/51 | Crosville MS, Chester (CH) KG197 |
| 4613 * | LFM 776 | Bristol LL5G | 83.141 | B39R | 5/51 | Crosville MS, Chester (CH) KG195 |
| 4614 * | LFM 779 | Bristol LL5G | 83.186 | B39R | 5/51 | Crosville MS, Chester (CH) KG198 |
| 4615 * | LFM 780 | Bristol LL5G | 83.187 | B39R | 7/51 | Crosville MS, Chester (CH) KG199 |
| 4616 * | LFM 781 | Bristol LL5G | 83.188 | B39R | 7/51 | Crosville MS, Chester (CH) KG200 |
| 4617 * | LFM 782 | Bristol LL5G | 83.195 | B39R | 7/51 | Crosville MS, Chester (CH) KG201 |
| 4618 * | LFM 784 | Bristol LL5G | 83.196 | B39R | 7/51 | Crosville MS, Chester (CH) KG203 |
| 4619 * | LFM 783 | Bristol LL5G | 83.197 | B39R | 7/51 | Crosville MS, Chester (CH) KG202 |
| 4620 * | LFM 785 | Bristol LWL5G | 83.260 | B39R | 7/51 | Crosville MS, Chester (CH) KG204 |
| 4621 * | LFM 786 | Bristol LWL5G | 83.261 | B39R | 7/51 | Crosville MS, Chester (CH) KG205 |

| | | | | | | | |
|---|---|---|---|---|---|---|---|
| 4622 * | LFM 787 | Bristol LWL5G | 83.262 | B39R | 7/51 | Crosville MS, Chester (CH) | KG206 |
| 4623 * | LFM 788 | Bristol LWL5G | 83.263 | B39R | 7/51 | Crosville MS, Chester (CH) | KG207 |
| 4624 * | LFM 789 | Bristol LWL5G | 83.264 | B39R | 7/51 | Crosville MS, Chester (CH) | KG208 |
| 4625 * | LFM 790 | Bristol LWL5G | 83.265 | B39R | 7/51 | Crosville MS, Chester (CH) | KG209 |
| 4626 | MFM 665 | Bristol LL6B | 83.221 | FC35F | 3/51 | Crosville MS, Chester (CH) | KW234 |
| 4627 | MFM 666 | Bristol LL6B | 83.222 | FC35F | 3/51 | Crosville MS, Chester (CH) | KW235 |
| 4628 | MFM 667 | Bristol LL6B | 83.223 | FC35F | 3/51 | Crosville MS, Chester (CH) | KW236 |
| 4629 | MFM 668 | Bristol LL6B | 83.224 | FC35F | 5/51 | Crosville MS, Chester (CH) | KW237 |
| 4630 | MFM 669 | Bristol LL6B | 83.230 | FC35F | 5/51 | Crosville MS, Chester (CH) | KW238 |
| 4631 | MFM 670 | Bristol LL6B | 83.231 | FC35F | 3/51 | Crosville MS, Chester (CH) | KW239 |
| 4632 | MFM 671 | Bristol LL6B | 83.232 | FC35F | 5/51 | Crosville MS, Chester (CH) | KW240 |
| 4633 | MFM 672 | Bristol LL6B | 83.233 | FC35F | 5/51 | Crosville MS, Chester (CH) | KW241 |
| 4634 | MFM 673 | Bristol LL6B | 83.234 | FC35F | 5/51 | Crosville MS, Chester (CH) | KW242 |
| 4635 | MFM 674 | Bristol LL6B | 83.235 | FC35F | 5/51 | Crosville MS, Chester (CH) | KW243 |
| 4636 | MFM 675 | Bristol LL6B | 83.236 | FC35F | 5/51 | Crosville MS, Chester (CH) | KW244 |
| 4637 | MFM 676 | Bristol LWL6B | 83.266 | FC35F | 5/51 | Crosville MS, Chester (CH) | KW245 |
| 4638 | MFM 677 | Bristol LWL6B | 83.282 | FC35F | 5/51 | Crosville MS, Chester (CH) | KW246 |
| 4639 | MFM 678 | Bristol LWL6B | 83.296 | FC35F | 5/51 | Crosville MS, Chester (CH) | KW247 |
| 4640 | MFM 679 | Bristol LWL6B | 83.297 | FC35F | 5/51 | Crosville MS, Chester (CH) | KW248 |
| 4641 | MFM 680 | Bristol LWL6B | 83.298 | FC35F | 5/51 | Crosville MS, Chester (CH) | KW249 |
| 4642 | MFM 681 | Bristol LWL6B | 83.299 | FC35F | 5/51 | Crosville MS, Chester (CH) | KW250 |
| 4643 | MFM 682 | Bristol LWL6B | 83.300 | FC35F | 5/51 | Crosville MS, Chester (CH) | KW251 |
| 4644 | MFM 683 | Bristol LWL6B | 83.301 | FC35F | 5/51 | Crosville MS, Chester (CH) | KW252 |
| 4645 | MFM 684 | Bristol LWL6B | 83.313 | FC35F | 5/51 | Crosville MS, Chester (CH) | KW253 |
| 4646 | MFM 685 | Bristol LWL6B | 83.314 | FC35F | 5/51 | Crosville MS, Chester (CH) | KW254 |
| 4647 | KNG 709 | Bristol L5G | 81.008 | B35R | 7/50 | Eastern Counties, Norwich (NK) | LL709 |
| 4648 | KNG 710 | Bristol L5G | 81.009 | B35R | 7/50 | Eastern Counties, Norwich (NK) | LL710 |
| 4649 | KNG 711 | Bristol L5G | 81.010 | B35R | 7/50 | Eastern Counties, Norwich (NK) | LL711 |
| 4650 | KNG 712 | Bristol L5G | 81.011 | B35R | 7/50 | Eastern Counties, Norwich (NK) | LL712 |
| 4651 | KNG 713 | Bristol LL5G | 81.102 | B39R | 9/50 | Eastern Counties, Norwich (NK) | LL713 |
| 4652 | KNG 714 | Bristol LL5G | 81.103 | B39R | 9/50 | Eastern Counties, Norwich (NK) | LL714 |
| 4653 | KNG 715 | Bristol LL5G | 81.104 | B39R | 9/50 | Eastern Counties, Norwich (NK) | LL715 |
| 4654 | KNG 716 | Bristol LL5G | 81.105 | B39R | 9/50 | Eastern Counties, Norwich (NK) | LL716 |
| 4655 | KNG 717 | Bristol LL5G | 81.175 | B39R | 10/50 | Eastern Counties, Norwich (NK) | LL717 |
| 4656 | KNG 718 | Bristol LL5G | 81.176 | B39R | 10/50 | Eastern Counties, Norwich (NK) | LL718 |
| 4657 | KNG 719 | Bristol LL5G | 81.177 | B39R | 10/50 | Eastern Counties, Norwich (NK) | LL719 |
| 4658 | KNG 720 | Bristol LL5G | 83.031 | B39R | 10/50 | Eastern Counties, Norwich (NK) | LL720 |
| 4659 | KNG 721 | Bristol LL5G | 83.032 | B39R | 11/50 | Eastern Counties, Norwich (NK) | LL721 |
| 4660 | KNG 722 | Bristol LL5G | 83.033 | B39R | 11/50 | Eastern Counties, Norwich (NK) | LL722 |
| 4661 | KNG 723 | Bristol LL5G | 83.034 | B39R | 11/50 | Eastern Counties, Norwich (NK) | LL723 |
| 4662 | LNG 724 | Bristol LL5G | 83.035 | B39R | 11/50 | Eastern Counties, Norwich (NK) | LL724 |
| 4663 | LNG 725 | Bristol LL5G | 83.145 | B39R | 1/51 | Eastern Counties, Norwich (NK) | LL725 |
| 4664 | LNG 726 | Bristol LL5G | 83.146 | B39R | 1/51 | Eastern Counties, Norwich (NK) | LL726 |
| 4665 | LNG 727 | Bristol LL5G | 83.152 | B39R | 1/51 | Eastern Counties, Norwich (NK) | LL727 |
| 4666 | LNG 728 | Bristol LL5G | 83.153 | B39R | 1/51 | Eastern Counties, Norwich (NK) | LL728 |
| 4667 * | LNG 729 | Bristol LL5G | 83.237 | B39R | 5/51 | Eastern Counties, Norwich (NK) | LL729 |
| 4668 * | LNG 730 | Bristol LL5G | 83.238 | B39R | 5/51 | Eastern Counties, Norwich (NK) | LL730 |
| 4669 * | LNG 731 | Bristol LL5G | 83.239 | B39R | 6/51 | Eastern Counties, Norwich (NK) | LL731 |
| 4670 | ONO 995 | Bristol LL5G | 81.134 | B39R | 9/50 | Eastern National, Chelmsford (EX) | 4081 |
| 4671 | ONO 996 | Bristol LL5G | 81.135 | B39R | 9/50 | Eastern National, Chelmsford (EX) | 4082 |
| 4672 | ONO 997 | Bristol LL5G | 81.136 | B39R | 9/50 | Eastern National, Chelmsford (EX) | 4083 |
| 4673 | ONO 998 | Bristol LL5G | 81.193 | B39R | 10/51 | Eastern National, Chelmsford (EX) | 4084 |
| 4674 | ONO 999 | Bristol LL5G | 81.194 | B39R | 10/51 | Eastern National, Chelmsford (EX) | 4085 |
| 4675 | RHK 121 | Bristol LL5G | 81.195 | B39R | 10/51 | Eastern National, Chelmsford (EX) | 4086 |
| 4676 | RHK 122 | Bristol LL5G | 83.117 | B39R | 12/50 | Eastern National, Chelmsford (EX) | 4087 |
| 4677 | RHK 123 | Bristol LL5G | 83.154 | B39R | 12/50 | Eastern National, Chelmsford (EX) | 4088 |
| 4678 | RHK 124 | Bristol LL5G | 83.155 | B39R | 1/51 | Eastern National, Chelmsford (EX) | 4089 |
| 4679 | RHK 125 | Bristol LL5G | 83.156 | B39R | 1/51 | Eastern National, Chelmsford (EX) | 4090 |
| 4680 | RHK 126 | Bristol LL5G | 83.157 | B39R | 1/51 | Eastern National, Chelmsford (EX) | 4091 |
| 4681 | RHK 127 | Bristol LWL5G | 83.206 | B39R | 3/51 | Eastern National, Chelmsford (EX) | 4092 |
| 4682 | RHK 128 | Bristol LWL5G | 83.207 | B39R | 3/51 | Eastern National, Chelmsford (EX) | 4093 |
| 4683 | RHK 129 | Bristol LWL5G | 83.208 | B39R | 3/51 | Eastern National, Chelmsford (EX) | 4094 |
| 4684 | RHK 130 | Bristol LWL5G | 83.209 | B39R | 3/51 | Eastern National, Chelmsford (EX) | 4095 |
| 4685 * | RHK 131 | Bristol LL5G | 83.240 | B39R | 4/51 | Eastern National, Chelmsford (EX) | 4096 |

| | | | | | | |
|---|---|---|---|---|---|---|
| 4686 * | RHK 132 | Bristol LL5G | 83.241 | B39R | 4/51 | Eastern National, Chelmsford (EX) 4097 |
| 4687 * | RHK 133 | Bristol LL5G | 83.242 | B39R | 4/51 | Eastern National, Chelmsford (EX) 4121 |
| 4688 | RHK 134 | Bristol LWL5G | 83.302 | B39R | 4/51 | Eastern National, Chelmsford (EX) 4122 |
| 4689 | RHK 135 | Bristol LWL5G | 83.303 | B39R | 4/51 | Eastern National, Chelmsford (EX) 4123 |
| 4690 | RHK 136 | Bristol LWL5G | 83.304 | B39R | 4/51 | Eastern National, Chelmsford (EX) 4124 |
| 4691 | GFW 280 | Bristol LL5G | 81.148 | B39R | 9/50 | Lincolnshire RCC, Bracebridge Heath (KN) 779 |
| 4692 | GFW 281 | Bristol LL5G | 81.149 | B39R | 9/50 | Lincolnshire RCC, Bracebridge Heath (KN) 780 |
| 4693 | GFW 282 | Bristol LL5G | 81.150 | B39R | 9/50 | Lincolnshire RCC, Bracebridge Heath (KN) 781 |
| 4694 | GFW 283 | Bristol LL5G | 81.188 | B39R | 10/50 | Lincolnshire RCC, Bracebridge Heath (KN) 782 |
| 4695 | GFW 284 | Bristol LL5G | 81.189 | B39R | 10/50 | Lincolnshire RCC, Bracebridge Heath (KN) 783 |
| 4696 | GFW 285 | Bristol LL5G | 81.190 | B39R | 11/50 | Lincolnshire RCC, Bracebridge Heath (KN) 784 |
| 4697 | GFW 846 | Bristol LL5G | 83.036 | B39R | 11/50 | Lincolnshire RCC, Bracebridge Heath (KN) 785 |
| 4698 | GFW 847 | Bristol LL5G | 83.037 | B39R | 11/50 | Lincolnshire RCC, Bracebridge Heath (KN) 786 |
| 4699 | GFW 848 | Bristol LL5G | 83.038 | B39R | 11/50 | Lincolnshire RCC, Bracebridge Heath (KN) 787 |
| 4700 | GFW 849 | Bristol LL5G | 83.091 | B39R | 12/50 | Lincolnshire RCC, Bracebridge Heath (KN) 788 |
| 4701 | GFW 850 | Bristol LL5G | 83.092 | B39R | 12/50 | Lincolnshire RCC, Bracebridge Heath (KN) 789 |
| 4702 | GFW 851 | Bristol LL5G | 83.112 | B39R | 12/50 | Lincolnshire RCC, Bracebridge Heath (KN) 790 |
| 4703 | GFW 852 | Bristol LL5G | 83.121 | B39R | 1/51 | Lincolnshire RCC, Bracebridge Heath (KN) 791 |
| 4704 | GFW 853 | Bristol LL5G | 83.122 | B39R | 1/51 | Lincolnshire RCC, Bracebridge Heath (KN) 792 |
| 4705 | GFW 854 | Bristol LL6B | 83.171 | B39R | 5/51 | Lincolnshire RCC, Bracebridge Heath (KN) 793 |
| 4706 | GFW 855 | Bristol LL6B | 83.172 | B39R | 5/51 | Lincolnshire RCC, Bracebridge Heath (KN) 794 |
| 4707 | GFW 856 | Bristol LL5G | 83.189 | B39R | 5/51 | Lincolnshire RCC, Bracebridge Heath (KN) 795 |
| 4708 | GDL 716 | Bristol LL5G | 81.171 | B39R | 9/50 | Southern Vectis, Newport (IW) 832 |
| 4709 | GDL 717 | Bristol LL5G | 81.172 | B39R | 10/50 | Southern Vectis, Newport (IW) 833 |
| 4710 | GDL 718 | Bristol LL5G | 83.078 | B39R | 11/50 | Southern Vectis, Newport (IW) 834 |
| 4711 | FMO 938 | Bristol LL6B | 81.121 | B39R | 8/50 | Thames Valley, Reading (BE) 556 |
| 4712 | FMO 939 | Bristol LL6B | 81.122 | B39R | 8/50 | Thames Valley, Reading (BE) 557 |
| 4713 | FMO 940 | Bristol LL6B | 81.123 | B39R | 8/50 | Thames Valley, Reading (BE) 558 |
| 4714 | FMO 941 | Bristol LL6B | 81.124 | B39R | 8/50 | Thames Valley, Reading (BE) 559 |
| 4715 | FMO 942 | Bristol LL6B | 83.093 | B39R | 11/50 | Thames Valley, Reading (BE) 560 |
| 4716 | FMO 943 | Bristol LL6B | 83.094 | B39R | 11/50 | Thames Valley, Reading (BE) 561 |
| 4717 | FMO 944 | Bristol LL6B | 83.095 | B39R | 11/50 | Thames Valley, Reading (BE) 562 |
| 4718 | FMO 945 | Bristol LL6B | 83.096 | B39R | 11/50 | Thames Valley, Reading (BE) 563 |
| 4719 | FMO 946 | Bristol LL6B | 83.097 | B39R | 11/50 | Thames Valley, Reading (BE) 564 |
| 4720 | FMO 947 | Bristol LL6B | 83.128 | B39R | 12/50 | Thames Valley, Reading (BE) 565 |
| 4721 | FMO 948 | Bristol LL6B | 83.129 | B39R | 12/50 | Thames Valley, Reading (BE) 566 |
| 4722 | FMO 949 | Bristol LL6B | 83.130 | B39R | 12/50 | Thames Valley, Reading (BE) 567 |
| 4723 | FMO 950 | Bristol LL6B | 83.173 | B39R | 12/50 | Thames Valley, Reading (BE) 568 |
| 4724 | FMO 951 | Bristol LL6B | 83.174 | B39R | 12/50 | Thames Valley, Reading (BE) 569 |
| 4725 | FMO 952 | Bristol LL6B | 83.175 | B39R | 1/51 | Thames Valley, Reading (BE) 570 |
| 4726 | FMO 953 | Bristol LL6B | 83.176 | B39R | 1/51 | Thames Valley, Reading (BE) 571 |
| 4727 | FMO 954 | Bristol LL6B | 83.177 | B39R | 2/51 | Thames Valley, Reading (BE) 572 |
| 4728 | FMO 955 | Bristol LL6B | 83.190 | B39R | 1/51 | Thames Valley, Reading (BE) 573 |
| 4729 | FMO 956 | Bristol LL6B | 83.191 | B39R | 1/51 | Thames Valley, Reading (BE) 574 |
| 4730 | FMO 957 | Bristol LL6B | 83.192 | B39R | 1/51 | Thames Valley, Reading (BE) 575 |
| 4731 | FMO 958 | Bristol LL6B | 83.193 | B39R | 2/51 | Thames Valley, Reading (BE) 576 |
| 4732 | FMO 959 | Bristol LWL6B | 83.272 | B39R | 3/51 | Thames Valley, Reading (BE) 577 |
| 4733 | FMO 960 | Bristol LWL6B | 83.273 | B39R | 3/51 | Thames Valley, Reading (BE) 578 |
| 4734 | FMO 961 | Bristol LWL6B | 83.274 | B39R | 3/51 | Thames Valley, Reading (BE) 579 |
| 4735 | FMO 962 | Bristol LWL6B | 85.014 | B39R | 3/51 | Thames Valley, Reading (BE) 580 |
| 4736 | FMO 963 | Bristol LWL6B | 85.015 | B39R | 3/51 | Thames Valley, Reading (BE) 581 |
| 4737 | FMO 964 | Bristol LWL6B | 85.016 | B39R | 3/51 | Thames Valley, Reading (BE) 582 |
| 4738 | FMO 965 | Bristol LWL6B | 85.017 | B39R | 3/51 | Thames Valley, Reading (BE) 583 |
| 4739 | FMO 966 | Bristol LWL6B | 85.018 | B39R | 3/51 | Thames Valley, Reading (BE) 584 |
| 4740 | FMO 967 | Bristol LWL6B | 85.019 | B39R | 3/51 | Thames Valley, Reading (BE) 585 |
| 4741 * | NHN 100 | Bristol L5G | 81.025 | B35R | 6/51 | United AS, Darlington (DM) BLO500 |
| 4742 * | NHN 101 | Bristol L5G | 81.043 | B35R | 7/51 | United AS, Darlington (DM) BLO501 |
| 4743 * | NHN 102 | Bristol L5G | 81.044 | B35R | 7/51 | United AS, Darlington (DM) BLO502 |
| 4744 * | NHN 103 | Bristol L5G | 81.045 | B35R | 7/51 | United AS, Darlington (DM) BLO503 |
| 4745 * | NHN 104 | Bristol L5G | 81.046 | B35R | 7/51 | United AS, Darlington (DM) BLO504 |
| 4746 * | NHN 105 | Bristol L5G | 81.047 | B35R | 7/51 | United AS, Darlington (DM) BLO505 |
| 4747 * | NHN 106 | Bristol L5G | 81.048 | B35R | 7/51 | United AS, Darlington (DM) BLO506 |
| 4748 * | NHN 107 | Bristol L5G | 81.049 | B35R | 7/51 | United AS, Darlington (DM) BLO507 |
| 4749 * | NHN 108 | Bristol L5G | 81.090 | B35R | 7/51 | United AS, Darlington (DM) BLO508 |

| | | | | | | |
|---|---|---|---|---|---|---|
| 4750 * | NHN 109 | Bristol L5G | 81.095 | B35R | 7/51 | United AS, Darlington (DM) BLO509 |
| 4751 * | NHN 120 | Bristol LL5G | 81.089 | B39R | 9/50 | United AS, Darlington (DM) BG452 |
| 4752 * | NHN 121 | Bristol LL5G | 81.091 | B39R | 9/50 | United AS, Darlington (DM) BG453 |
| 4753 * | NHN 122 | Bristol LL5G | 81.096 | B39R | 9/50 | United AS, Darlington (DM) BG454 |
| 4754 * | NHN 123 | Bristol LL5G | 81.130 | B39R | 9/50 | United AS, Darlington (DM) BG455 |
| 4755 * | NHN 124 | Bristol LL5G | 81.131 | B39R | 9/50 | United AS, Darlington (DM) BG456 |
| 4756 * | NHN 125 | Bristol LL5G | 81.132 | B39R | 9/50 | United AS, Darlington (DM) BG457 |
| 4757 * | NHN 126 | Bristol LL5G | 81.133 | B39R | 6/51 | United AS, Darlington (DM) BG458 |
| 4758 * | NHN 127 | Bristol LL5G | 81.153 | B39R | 6/51 | United AS, Darlington (DM) BG459 |
| 4759 * | NHN 128 | Bristol LL5G | 81.154 | B39R | 6/51 | United AS, Darlington (DM) BG460 |
| 4760 * | NHN 129 | Bristol LL5G | 81.155 | B39R | 6/51 | United AS, Darlington (DM) BG461 |
| 4761 * | NHN 130 | Bristol LL5G | 81.156 | B39R | 7/51 | United AS, Darlington (DM) BG462 |
| 4762 * | NHN 131 | Bristol LL5G | 81.157 | B39R | 7/51 | United AS, Darlington (DM) BG463 |
| 4763 * | NHN 132 | Bristol LL5G | 81.179 | B39R | 7/51 | United AS, Darlington (DM) BG464 |
| 4764 * | NHN 133 | Bristol LL5G | 81.180 | B39R | 7/51 | United AS, Darlington (DM) BG465 |
| 4765 * | NHN 134 | Bristol LL5G | 81.181 | B39R | 7/51 | United AS, Darlington (DM) BG466 |
| 4766 * | NHN 135 | Bristol LL5G | 81.182 | B39R | 7/51 | United AS, Darlington (DM) BG467 |
| 4767 * | NHN 136 | Bristol LL5G | 81.183 | B39R | 7/51 | United AS, Darlington (DM) BG468 |
| 4768 * | NHN 137 | Bristol LL5G | 81.184 | B39R | 7/51 | United AS, Darlington (DM) BG469 |
| 4769 * | NHN 138 | Bristol LL5G | 81.185 | B39R | 7/51 | United AS, Darlington (DM) BG470 |
| 4770 * | NHN 139 | Bristol LL5G | 81.186 | B39R | 7/51 | United AS, Darlington (DM) BG471 |
| 4771 * | NHN 140 | Bristol LL5G | 81.191 | B39R | 7/51 | United AS, Darlington (DM) BG472 |
| 4772 * | NHN 141 | Bristol LL5G | 81.192 | B39R | 7/51 | United AS, Darlington (DM) BG473 |
| 4773 * | NHN 142 | Bristol LL5G | 81.200 | B39R | 7/51 | United AS, Darlington (DM) BG474 |
| 4774 * | NHN 143 | Bristol LL5G | 83.022 | B39R | 7/51 | United AS, Darlington (DM) BG475 |
| 4775 * | NHN 144 | Bristol LL5G | 83.023 | B39R | 7/51 | United AS, Darlington (DM) BG476 |
| 4776 * | NHN 145 | Bristol LL5G | 83.024 | B39R | 7/51 | United AS, Darlington (DM) BG477 |
| 4777 * | NHN 146 | Bristol LL5G | 83.025 | B39R | 7/51 | United AS, Darlington (DM) BG478 |
| 4778 * | NHN 147 | Bristol LL5G | 83.046 | B39R | 7/51 | United AS, Darlington (DM) BG479 |
| 4779 * | NHN 148 | Bristol LL5G | 83.047 | B39R | 7/51 | United AS, Darlington (DM) BG480 |
| 4780 * | NHN 149 | Bristol LL5G | 83.048 | B39R | 7/51 | United AS, Darlington (DM) BG481 |
| 4781 * | NHN 150 | Bristol LL5G | 83.049 | B39R | 7/51 | United AS, Darlington (DM) BG482 |
| 4782 * | NHN 151 | Bristol LL5G | 83.050 | B39R | 7/51 | United AS, Darlington (DM) BG483 |
| 4783 * | NHN 152 | Bristol LL5G | 83.051 | B39R | 7/51 | United AS, Darlington (DM) BG484 |
| 4784 * | NHN 153 | Bristol LL5G | 83.055 | B39R | 7/51 | United AS, Darlington (DM) BG485 |
| 4785 * | NHN 154 | Bristol LL5G | 83.056 | B39R | 7/51 | United AS, Darlington (DM) BG486 |
| 4786 * | NHN 155 | Bristol LL5G | 83.079 | B39R | 7/51 | United AS, Darlington (DM) BG487 |
| 4787 * | NHN 156 | Bristol LL5G | 83.080 | B39R | 7/51 | United AS, Darlington (DM) BG488 |
| 4788 * | NHN 157 | Bristol LL5G | 83.081 | B39R | 7/51 | United AS, Darlington (DM) BG489 |
| 4789 * | NHN 158 | Bristol LL5G | 83.082 | B39R | 7/51 | United AS, Darlington (DM) BG490 |
| 4790 * | NHN 159 | Bristol LL5G | 83.083 | B39R | 7/51 | United AS, Darlington (DM) BG491 |
| 4791 * | NHN 160 | Bristol LL5G | 83.131 | B39R | 7/51 | United AS, Darlington (DM) BG492 |
| 4792 * | NHN 161 | Bristol LL5G | 83.132 | B39R | 7/51 | United AS, Darlington (DM) BG493 |
| 4793 * | NHN 162 | Bristol LL5G | 83.133 | B39R | 7/51 | United AS, Darlington (DM) BG494 |
| 4794 * | NHN 163 | Bristol LL5G | 83.134 | B39R | 7/51 | United AS, Darlington (DM) BG495 |
| 4795 * | NHN 164 | Bristol LL5G | 83.158 | B39R | 7/51 | United AS, Darlington (DM) BG496 |
| 4796 * | NHN 165 | Bristol LL5G | 83.159 | B39R | 8/51 | United AS, Darlington (DM) BG497 |
| 4797 * | NHN 166 | Bristol LL5G | 83.160 | B39R | 1/52 | United AS, Darlington (DM) BG498 |
| 4798 * | NHN 167 | Bristol LL5G | 83.161 | B39R | 6/52 | United AS, Darlington (DM) BG499 |
| 4799 * | NHN 168 | Bristol LL5G | 83.162 | B39R | 6/52 | United AS, Darlington (DM) BG500 |
| 4800 * | NHN 169 | Bristol LL5G | 83.163 | B39R | 6/52 | United AS, Darlington (DM) BG501 |
| 4801 * | NHN 170 | Bristol LL5G | 83.178 | B39R | 6/52 | United AS, Darlington (DM) BG502 |
| 4802 * | NHN 171 | Bristol LL5G | 83.179 | B39R | 6/52 | United AS, Darlington (DM) BG503 |
| 4803 | FRP 820 | Bristol L5G | 81.119 | B35R | 7/50 | United Counties, Northampton (NO) 820 |
| 4804 | FRP 821 | Bristol L5G | 81.088 | B35R | 7/50 | United Counties, Northampton (NO) 821 |
| 4805 | FRP 822 | Bristol LL5G | 81.158 | B39R | 9/50 | United Counties, Northampton (NO) 822 |
| 4806 | FRP 823 | Bristol LL5G | 81.159 | B39R | 9/50 | United Counties, Northampton (NO) 823 |
| 4807 | FRP 824 | Bristol LL5G | 81.160 | B39R | 9/50 | United Counties, Northampton (NO) 824 |
| 4808 | FRP 825 | Bristol LL5G | 81.187 | B39R | 9/50 | United Counties, Northampton (NO) 825 |
| 4809 | FRP 826 | Bristol LL6B | 83.149 | B39R | 11/50 | United Counties, Northampton (NO) 826 |
| 4810 | FRP 827 | Bristol LL6B | 83.150 | B39R | 11/50 | United Counties, Northampton (NO) 827 |
| 4811 | JWU 869 | Bristol L5G | 81.073 | B35R | 7/50 | West Yorkshire RCC, Harrogate (WR) 270 |
| 4812 | JWU 870 | Bristol L5G | 81.074 | B35R | 7/50 | West Yorkshire RCC, Harrogate (WR) 271 |
| 4813 | JWU 872 | Bristol LL5G | 81.098 | B39R | 8/50 | West Yorkshire RCC, Harrogate (WR) 273 |

| 4814 | JWU 871 | Bristol LL5G | 81.097 | B39R | 8/50 | West Yorkshire RCC, Harrogate (WR) 272 |
|------|---------|--------------|--------|------|------|----------------------------------------|
| 4815 | JWU 873 | Bristol LL5G | 83.086 | B39R | 12/50 | West Yorkshire RCC, Harrogate (WR) 403 |
| 4816 | JWU 874 | Bristol LL5G | 83.088 | B39R | 12/50 | West Yorkshire RCC, Harrogate (WR) 404 |
| 4817 | JWU 875 | Bristol LL5G | 83.089 | B39R | 3/51 | West Yorkshire RCC, Harrogate (WR) 405 |
| 4818 | JWU 876 | Bristol LL5G | 83.090 | B39R | 3/51 | West Yorkshire RCC, Harrogate (WR) 406 |
| 4819 | JWU 877 | Bristol LL5G | 83.098 | B39R | 5/51 | West Yorkshire RCC, Harrogate (WR) 407 |
| 4820 | JWU 878 | Bristol LL5G | 83.099 | B39R | 5/51 | West Yorkshire RCC, Harrogate (WR) 408 |
| 4821 | JWU 879 | Bristol LL5G | 83.100 | B39R | 5/51 | West Yorkshire RCC, Harrogate (WR) 409 |
| 4822 | JWU 880 | Bristol LL5G | 83.101 | B39R | 5/51 | West Yorkshire RCC, Harrogate (WR) 410 |
| 4823 | JWU 881 | Bristol LL5G | 83.180 | B39R | 5/51 | West Yorkshire RCC, Harrogate (WR) 411 |
| 4824 | JWU 882 | Bristol LL5G | 83.181 | B39R | 5/51 | West Yorkshire RCC, Harrogate (WR) 412 |
| 4825 | JWU 883 | Bristol LL5G | 83.182 | B39R | 5/51 | West Yorkshire RCC, Harrogate (WR) 413 |
| 4826 | JWU 884 | Bristol LL5G | 83.183 | B39R | 5/51 | West Yorkshire RCC, Harrogate (WR) 414 |
| 4827 | JWU 885 | Bristol LL5G | 83.184 | B39R | 5/51 | West Yorkshire RCC, Harrogate (WR) 415 |
| 4828 | JWU 886 | Bristol LL5G | 83.185 | B39R | 5/51 | West Yorkshire RCC, Harrogate (WR) 416 |
| 4829 | JWU 887 | Bristol LL5G | 83.198 | B39R | 5/51 | West Yorkshire RCC, Harrogate (WR) 417 |
| 4830 | JWU 888 | Bristol LL5G | 83.199 | B39R | 5/51 | West Yorkshire RCC, Harrogate (WR) 418 |
| 4831 | JYG 717 | Bristol LL5G | 83.200 | B39R | 5/51 | West Yorkshire RCC, Harrogate (WR) 423 |
| 4832 | JYG 718 | Bristol LL5G | 83.201 | B39R | 5/51 | West Yorkshire RCC, Harrogate (WR) 424 |
| 4833 | JYG 719 | Bristol LL5G | 83.202 | B39R | 5/51 | West Yorkshire RCC, Harrogate (WR) 425 |
| 4834 | JYG 720 | Bristol LL5G | 83.225 | B39R | 5/51 | West Yorkshire RCC, Harrogate (WR) 426 |
| 4835 | JYG 721 | Bristol LL5G | 83.226 | B39R | 5/51 | West Yorkshire RCC, Harrogate (WR) 427 |
| 4836 | JYG 722 | Bristol LL5G | 83.227 | B39R | 5/51 | West Yorkshire RCC, Harrogate (WR) 428 |
| 4837 | JYG 723 | Bristol LL5G | 83.228 | B39R | 6/51 | West Yorkshire RCC, Harrogate (WR) 429 |
| 4838 | JYG 724 | Bristol LWL6B | 83.309 | B39R | 6/51 | West Yorkshire RCC, Harrogate (WR) 430 |
| 4839 | JYG 725 | Bristol LWL6B | 83.310 | B39R | 6/51 | West Yorkshire RCC, Harrogate (WR) 431 |
| 4840 | JYG 726 | Bristol LWL6B | 85.020 | B39R | 6/51 | West Yorkshire RCC, Harrogate (WR) 432 |
| 4841 | JYG 727 | Bristol LWL6B | 85.021 | B39R | 6/51 | West Yorkshire RCC, Harrogate (WR) 433 |
| 4842 | JYG 728 | Bristol LWL6B | 85.022 | B39R | 6/51 | West Yorkshire RCC, Harrogate (WR) 434 |
| 4843 | JYG 729 | Bristol LWL6B | 85.023 | B39R | 7/51 | West Yorkshire RCC, Harrogate (WR) 435 |
| 4844 | JWU 895 | Bristol LL5G | 83.114 | B39R | 3/51 | Keighley-West Yorkshire, Harrogate (WR) K419 |
| 4845 | JWU 896 | Bristol LL5G | 83.115 | B39R | 3/51 | Keighley-West Yorkshire, Harrogate (WR) K420 |
| 4846 | JWU 897 | Bristol LL5G | 83.116 | B39R | 5/51 | Keighley-West Yorkshire, Harrogate (WR) K421 |
| 4847 | JWU 898 | Bristol LL5G | 83.168 | B39R | 5/51 | Keighley-West Yorkshire, Harrogate (WR) K423 |
| 4848 | JYG 742 | Bristol LL5G | 83.169 | B39R | 5/51 | Keighley-West Yorkshire, Harrogate (WR) K442 |
| 4849 | JYG 743 | Bristol LL5G | 83.170 | B39R | 5/51 | Keighley-West Yorkshire, Harrogate (WR) K443 |
| 4850 | LTA 767 | Bristol LWL5G | 83.283 | B39R | 3/51 | Western National, Exeter (DN) 1608 |
| 4851 | LTA 768 | Bristol LWL5G | 83.284 | B39R | 3/51 | Western National, Exeter (DN) 1609 |
| 4852 | LTA 769 | Bristol LWL5G | 83.285 | B39R | 3/51 | Western National, Exeter (DN) 1610 |
| 4853 | LTA 770 | Bristol LWL5G | 83.312 | B39R | 3/51 | Western National, Exeter (DN) 1611 |
| 4854 | GHR 866 | Bristol L6B | 81.028 | B35R | 6/50 | Wilts & Dorset, Salisbury (WI) 305 |
| 4855 | GHR 867 | Bristol L6B | 81.029 | B35R | 6/50 | Wilts & Dorset, Salisbury (WI) 306 |
| 4856 | GHR 868 | Bristol L6B | 81.030 | B35R | 6/50 | Wilts & Dorset, Salisbury (WI) 307 |
| 4857 | GMR 30 | Bristol L6B | 81.061 | B35R | 7/50 | Wilts & Dorset, Salisbury (WI) 309 |
| 4858 | GMR 29 | Bristol L6B | 81.060 | B35R | 7/50 | Wilts & Dorset, Salisbury (WI) 308 |
| 4859 | GMR 31 | Bristol L6B | 81.062 | B35R | 7/50 | Wilts & Dorset, Salisbury (WI) 310 |
| 4860 | GMW 911 | Bristol LL6B | 83.142 | B39R | 1/51 | Wilts & Dorset, Salisbury (WI) 321 |
| 4861 | GMW 912 | Bristol LL6B | 83.143 | B39R | 12/50 | Wilts & Dorset, Salisbury (WI) 322 |
| 4862 | GMW 913 | Bristol LL6B | 83.144 | B39R | 12/50 | Wilts & Dorset, Salisbury (WI) 323 |
| 4863 | MKN 206 | Bristol LL5G | 83.057 | B39R | 9/50 | Maidstone & District (KT) SO57 |
| 4864 | MKN 202 | Bristol LL5G | 83.018 | B39R | 9/50 | Maidstone & District (KT) SO53 |
| 4865 | MKN 203 | Bristol LL5G | 83.019 | B39R | 12/50 | Maidstone & District (KT) SO54 |
| 4866 | MKN 204 | Bristol LL5G | 83.020 | B39R | 12/50 | Maidstone & District (KT) SO55 |
| 4867 | MKN 205 | Bristol LL5G | 83.021 | B39R | 12/50 | Maidstone & District (KT) SO56 |
| 4868 | MKN 201 | Bristol LL6A | 83.017 | B39R | 10/50 | Maidstone & District (KT) SO52 |
| 4869 | MKN 207 | Bristol LL5G | 83.058 | B39R | 10/50 | Maidstone & District (KT) SO58 |
| 4870 | MKN 208 | Bristol LL5G | 83.059 | B39R | 10/50 | Maidstone & District (KT) SO59 |
| 4871 | MKN 209 | Bristol LL5G | 83.060 | B39R | 10/50 | Maidstone & District (KT) SO60 |
| 4872 | MKN 210 | Bristol LL5G | 83.061 | B39R | 10/50 | Maidstone & District (KT) SO61 |
| 4873 | MKN 211 | Bristol LL5G | 83.123 | B39R | 11/50 | Maidstone & District (KT) SO62 |
| 4874 | MKN 212 | Bristol LL5G | 83.124 | B39R | 11/50 | Maidstone & District (KT) SO63 |
| 4875 | MKN 213 | Bristol LL5G | 83.125 | B39R | 11/50 | Maidstone & District (KT) SO64 |
| 4876 | MKN 214 | Bristol LL5G | 83.126 | B39R | 12/50 | Maidstone & District (KT) SO65 |
| 4877 | MKN 215 | Bristol LL5G | 83.127 | B39R | 12/50 | Maidstone & District (KT) SO66 |

| | | | | | | | |
|---|---|---|---|---|---|---|---|
| 4878 | LFM 747 | Bristol L6B | 81.142 | DP31R | 6/50 | Crosville MS, Chester (CH) KW166 |
| 4879 | LFM 749 | Bristol L6B | 81.144 | DP31R | 6/50 | Crosville MS, Chester (CH) KW168 |
| 4880 | LFM 750 | Bristol L6B | 81.145 | DP31R | 6/50 | Crosville MS, Chester (CH) KW169 |
| 4881 | LFM 751 | Bristol L6B | 81.146 | DP31R | 6/50 | Crosville MS, Chester (CH) KW170 |
| 4882 | LFM 748 | Bristol L6B | 81.143 | DP31R | 6/50 | Crosville MS, Chester (CH) KW167 |
| 4883 | LFM 746 | Bristol L6B | 81.087 | DP31R | 8/50 | Crosville MS, Chester (CH) KW165 |
| 4884 | LFM 753 | Bristol L6B | 81.162 | DP31R | 7/50 | Crosville MS, Chester (CH) KW172 |
| 4885 | LFM 754 | Bristol L6B | 81.163 | DP31R | 7/50 | Crosville MS, Chester (CH) KW173 |
| 4886 | LFM 755 | Bristol L6B | 81.164 | DP31R | 7/50 | Crosville MS, Chester (CH) KW174 |
| 4887 | LFM 752 | Bristol L6B | 81.147 | DP31R | 7/50 | Crosville MS, Chester (CH) KW171 |
| 4888 | KNG 704 | Bristol LWL6B | 83.277 | FC31F | 3/51 | Eastern Counties, Norwich (NK) LS704 |
| 4889 | KNG 705 | Bristol LWL6B | 83.278 | FC35F | 5/51 | Eastern Counties, Norwich (NK) LS705 |
| 4890 | KNG 706 | Bristol LWL6B | 83.279 | FC35F | 6/51 | Eastern Counties, Norwich (NK) LS706 |
| 4891 | KNG 707 | Bristol LWL6B | 83.280 | FC35F | 6/51 | Eastern Counties, Norwich (NK) LS707 |
| 4892 | KNG 708 | Bristol LWL6B | 83.281 | FC35F | 6/51 | Eastern Counties, Norwich (NK) LS708 |
| 4893 * | HBE 505 | Bristol LL6B | 83.268 | FC35F | 3/51 | Lincolnshire RCC, Bracebridge Heath (KN) 951 |
| 4894 * | HBE 506 | Bristol LL6B | 83.269 | FC35F | 5/51 | Lincolnshire RCC, Bracebridge Heath (KN) 952 |
| 4895 * | HBE 507 | Bristol LL6B | 83.270 | FC35F | 5/51 | Lincolnshire RCC, Bracebridge Heath (KN) 953 |
| 4896 * | HBE 508 | Bristol LL6B | 83.271 | FC35F | 5/51 | Lincolnshire RCC, Bracebridge Heath (KN) 954 |
| 4897 | HBE 509 | Bristol LWL6B | 85.005 | FC35F | 6/51 | Lincolnshire RCC, Bracebridge Heath (KN) 955 |
| 4898 | HBE 510 | Bristol LWL6B | 85.006 | FC35F | 6/51 | Lincolnshire RCC, Bracebridge Heath (KN) 956 |
| 4899 * | HBE 756 | Bristol LL6B | 83.267 | B39R | 6/51 | Lincolnshire RCC, Bracebridge Heath (KN) 796 |
| 4900 | HBE 757 | Bristol LWL5G | 83.335 | B39R | 7/51 | Lincolnshire RCC, Bracebridge Heath (KN) 797 |
| 4901 | HBE 758 | Bristol LWL5G | 83.336 | B39R | 8/51 | Lincolnshire RCC, Bracebridge Heath (KN) 798 |
| 4902 | HBE 759 | Bristol LWL5G | 85.034 | B39R | 9/51 | Lincolnshire RCC, Bracebridge Heath (KN) 799 |
| 4903 | JYG 744 | Bristol LWL6B | 83.275 | FC35F | 3/51 | West Yorkshire RCC, Harrogate (WR) 666 |
| 4904 | JYG 745 | Bristol LWL6B | 83.276 | FC35F | 3/51 | West Yorkshire RCC, Harrogate (WR) 667 |
| 4905 | NAE 1 | Bristol L6B | 81.075 | FC31F | 8/50 | Bristol Tramways (GL) 2465 |
| 4906 | NAE 2 | Bristol L6B | 81.076 | FC31F | 8/50 | Bristol Tramways (GL) 2466 |
| 4907 | NAE 3 | Bristol L6B | 81.077 | FC31F | 9/50 | Bristol Tramways (GL) 2467 |
| 4908 | NAE 4 | Bristol LL6B | 81.078 | FC35F | 3/51 | Bristol Tramways (GL) 2801 |
| 4909 | NAE 5 | Bristol LL6B | 81.079 | FC35F | 3/51 | Bristol Tramways (GL) 2802 |
| 4910 | NAE 6 | Bristol LL6B | 83.002 | FC35F | 3/51 | Bristol Tramways (GL) 2803 |
| 4911 | NAE 7 | Bristol LL6B | 83.003 | FC35F | 3/51 | Bristol Tramways (GL) 2804 |
| 4912 | NAE 8 | Bristol LL6B | 83.007 | FC35F | 3/51 | Bristol Tramways (GL) 2805 |
| 4913 | NAE 9 | Bristol LL6B | 83.008 | FC35F | 3/51 | Bristol Tramways (GL) 2806 |
| 4914 | NAE 10 | Bristol LL6B | 83.039 | FC35F | 3/51 | Bristol Tramways (GL) 2807 |
| 4915 | PTW 106 | Bristol L6B | 81.137 | FC31F | 9/50 | Eastern National, Chelmsford (EX) 4103 |
| 4916 | PTW 107 | Bristol L6B | 81.138 | FC31F | 9/50 | Eastern National, Chelmsford (EX) 4104 |
| 4917 | PTW 108 | Bristol L6B | 81.140 | FC31F | 10/50 | Eastern National, Chelmsford (EX) 4105 |
| 4918 | PTW 109 | Bristol L6B | 81.141 | FC31F | 10/50 | Eastern National, Chelmsford (EX) 4106 |
| 4919 | PTW 110 | Bristol L6B | 81.139 | FC31F | 5/51 | Eastern National, Chelmsford (EX) 4107 |
| 4920 | NHN 110 | Bristol L6B | 81.016 | FC31F | 6/50 | United AS, Darlington (DM) BLO510 |
| 4921 | NHN 111 | Bristol L6B | 81.017 | FC31F | 6/50 | United AS, Darlington (DM) BLO511 |
| 4922 | NHN 112 | Bristol L6B | 79.065 | FC31F | 7/50 | United AS, Darlington (DM) BLO512 |
| 4923 | NHN 113 | Bristol L6B | 81.015 | FC31F | 7/50 | United AS, Darlington (DM) BLO513 |
| 4924 | NHN 114 | Bristol L6B | 81.018 | FC31F | 7/50 | United AS, Darlington (DM) BLO514 |
| 4925 | NHN 115 | Bristol L6B | 81.026 | FC31F | 7/50 | United AS, Darlington (DM) BLO515 |
| 4926 | NHN 116 | Bristol L6B | 81.027 | FC31F | 7/50 | United AS, Darlington (DM) BLO516 |
| 4927 | NHN 117 | Bristol L6B | 81.092 | FC31F | 7/50 | United AS, Darlington (DM) BLO517 |
| 4928 | NHN 118 | Bristol L6B | 81.094 | FC31F | 7/50 | United AS, Darlington (DM) BLO518 |
| 4929 | NHN 119 | Bristol L6B | 81.093 | FC31F | 7/50 | United AS, Darlington (DM) BLO519 |
| 4930 * | FRP 832 | Bristol LL6B | 83.012 | FC37F | 2/51 | United Counties, Northampton (NO) 832 |
| 4931 * | FRP 833 | Bristol LL6B | 83.013 | FC37F | 2/51 | United Counties, Northampton (NO) 833 |
| 4932 * | FRP 834 | Bristol LL6B | 83.068 | FC37F | 2/51 | United Counties, Northampton (NO) 834 |
| 4933 * | FRP 835 | Bristol LL6B | 83.069 | FC37F | 2/51 | United Counties, Northampton (NO) 835 |
| 4934 * | FRP 836 | Bristol LL6B | 83.070 | FC37F | 2/51 | United Counties, Northampton (NO) 836 |
| 4935 * | FRP 837 | Bristol LL6B | 83.071 | FC37F | 2/51 | United Counties, Northampton (NO) 837 |
| 4936 * | FRP 838 | Bristol LL6B | 83.072 | FC37F | 3/51 | United Counties, Northampton (NO) 838 |
| 4937 | JWU 889 | Bristol L6B | 81.152 | FC31F | 7/50 | West Yorkshire RCC, Harrogate (WR) 660 |
| 4938 | JWU 890 | Bristol L6B | 81.161 | FC31F | 7/50 | West Yorkshire RCC, Harrogate (WR) 661 |
| 4939 | JWU 891 | Bristol L6B | 81.151 | FC31F | 7/50 | West Yorkshire RCC, Harrogate (WR) 662 |
| 4940 | JWU 892 | Bristol L6B | 83.014 | FC31F | 8/50 | West Yorkshire RCC, Harrogate (WR) 663 |
| 4941 | JWU 893 | Bristol L6B | 83.015 | FC31F | 8/50 | West Yorkshire RCC, Harrogate (WR) 664 |

| | | | | | | |
|---|---|---|---|---|---|---|
| 4942 | JWU 894 | Bristol L6B | 83.016 | FC31F | 8/50 | West Yorkshire RCC, Harrogate (WR) 665 |
| 4943 | EHJ 27 | Bristol L6B | 79.144 | FC31F | 5/50 | Westcliff-on-Sea MS (EX) |
| 4944 | EHJ 28 | Bristol L6B | 79.145 | FC31F | 5/50 | Westcliff-on-Sea MS (EX) |
| 4945 | EHJ 29 | Bristol L6B | 81.109 | FC31F | 6/51 | Westcliff-on-Sea MS (EX) |
| 4946 * | FRP 839 | Bristol LL6B | 83.084 | FC37F | 2/51 | United Counties, Northampton (NO) 839 |
| 4947 * | FRP 840 | Bristol LL6B | 83.085 | FC37F | 3/51 | United Counties, Northampton (NO) 840 |
| 4948 * | FRP 841 | Bristol LL6B | 83.087 | FC37F | 2/51 | United Counties, Northampton (NO) 841 |
| 4949 * | FRP 842 | Bristol LL6B | 83.113 | FC37F | 2/51 | United Counties, Northampton (NO) 842 |
| 4950 * | FRP 843 | Bristol LL6B | 83.147 | FC37F | 2/51 | United Counties, Northampton (NO) 843 |
| 4951 * | FRP 844 | Bristol LL6B | 83.148 | FC37F | 2/51 | United Counties, Northampton (NO) 844 |
| 4952 | FRP 828 | Bristol LL6B | 83.151 | B39R | 12/50 | United Counties, Northampton (NO) 828 |
| 4953 | FRP 829 | Bristol LWL6B | 83.305 | B39R | 3/51 | United Counties, Northampton (NO) 829 |
| 4954 | FRP 830 | Bristol LWL6B | 83.306 | B39R | 4/51 | United Counties, Northampton (NO) 830 |
| 4955 | FRP 831 | Bristol LWL6B | 83.307 | B39R | 4/51 | United Counties, Northampton (NO) 831 |
| 4956 * | KEL 731 | Bristol LL6B | 83.210 | FC35F | 2/51 | Hants & Dorset, Bournemouth (HA) 688 |
| 4957 * | KEL 732 | Bristol LL6B | 83.211 | FC35F | 2/51 | Hants & Dorset, Bournemouth (HA) 689 |
| 4958 * | KEL 733 | Bristol LL6B | 83.212 | FC35F | 2/51 | Hants & Dorset, Bournemouth (HA) 690 |
| 4959 * | KEL 734 | Bristol LL6B | 83.248 | FC35F | 3/51 | Hants & Dorset, Bournemouth (HA) 691 |
| 4960 * | KEL 735 | Bristol LL6B | 83.249 | FC35F | 3/51 | Hants & Dorset, Bournemouth (HA) 692 |
| 4961 | KEL 736 | Bristol LL6B | 85.004 | FC35F | 4/51 | Hants & Dorset, Bournemouth (HA) 693 |
| 4962 * | NV 9651 | Bristol JO5G | JO5G.557 | B35R | 3/51 | United Counties, Northampton (NO) 470 |
| 4963 * | VV 5697 | Bristol JO5G | JO5G.390 | B35R | 4/51 | United Counties, Northampton (NO) 451 |
| 4964 * | NV 9648 | Bristol JO5G | JO5G.555 | B35R | 4/51 | United Counties, Northampton (NO) 468 |
| 4965 * | NV 9650 | Bristol JO5G | JO5G.556 | B35R | 4/51 | United Counties, Northampton (NO) 469 |
| 4966 * | VV 6259 | Bristol JO5G | JO5G.548 | B35R | 4/51 | United Counties, Northampton (NO) 461 |
| 4967 * | NV 9646 | Bristol JO5G | JO5G.553 | B35R | 4/51 | United Counties, Northampton (NO) 466 |
| 4968 * | NV 9644 | Bristol JO5G | JO5G.551 | B35R | 4/51 | United Counties, Northampton (NO) 464 |
| 4969 * | NV 9643 | Bristol JO5G | JO5G.550 | B35R | 4/51 | United Counties, Northampton (NO) 463 |
| 4970 * | NV 9645 | Bristol JO5G | JO5G.552 | B35R | 4/51 | United Counties, Northampton (NO) 465 |
| 4971 * | NV 9647 | Bristol JO5G | JO5G.554 | B35R | 4/51 | United Counties, Northampton (NO) 467 |
| 4972 * | NV 6639 | Bristol JO5G | JO5G.135 | DP31R | 4/51 | United Counties, Northampton (NO) 471 |
| 4973 * | NV 9652 | Bristol JO5G | JO5G.558 | DP31R | 4/51 | United Counties, Northampton (NO) 472 |
| 4974 | HBE 511 | Bristol LWL6B | 85.007 | FC35F | 6/51 | Lincolnshire RCC, Bracebridge Heath (KN) 957 |
| 4975 | HBE 512 | Bristol LWL6B | 85.008 | FC35F | 5/51 | Lincolnshire RCC, Bracebridge Heath (KN) 958 |
| 4976 | HBE 513 | Bristol LWL6B | 85.009 | FC35F | 5/51 | Lincolnshire RCC, Bracebridge Heath (KN) 959 |
| 4977 | HBE 514 | Bristol LWL6B | 85.010 | FC35F | 6/51 | Lincolnshire RCC, Bracebridge Heath (KN) 960 |
| 4978 | NHU 2 | Bristol LSX6B | LSX.001 | B42D | 12/50 | Bristol Tramways (GL) 2800 |
| 4979 * | LFM 811 | Bristol LL6B | 83.203 | FC35F | 2/51 | Crosville MS, Chester (CH) KW230 |
| 4980 * | MFM 662 | Bristol LL6B | 83.204 | FC35F | 2/51 | Crosville MS, Chester (CH) KW231 |
| 4981 * | MFM 663 | Bristol LL6B | 83.205 | FC35F | 2/51 | Crosville MS, Chester (CH) KW232 |
| 4982 * | MFM 664 | Bristol LL6B | 83.220 | FC35F | 2/51 | Crosville MS, Chester (CH) KW233 |
| 4983 | JYG 746 | Bristol LWL6B | 83.308 | FC35F | 3/51 | West Yorkshire RCC, Harrogate (WR) 668 |
| 4984 | JYG 747 | Bristol LWL6B | 83.311 | FC35F | 4/51 | West Yorkshire RCC, Harrogate (WR) 669 |
| 4985 | JYG 748 | Bristol LWL6B | 83.320 | FC35F | 4/51 | West Yorkshire RCC, Harrogate (WR) 670 |
| 4986 | JYG 749 | Bristol LWL6B | 85.001 | FC35F | 5/51 | West Yorkshire RCC, Harrogate (WR) 671 |
| 4987 | HDL 182 | Bristol LWL6B | 85.011 | FC37F | 6/51 | Southern Vectis, Newport (IW) 300 |
| 4988 | HDL 183 | Bristol LWL6B | 85.012 | FC37F | 5/51 | Southern Vectis, Newport (IW) 301 |
| 4989 | HDL 184 | Bristol LWL6B | 85.013 | FC37F | 6/51 | Southern Vectis, Newport (IW) 302 |
| 4990 | LTA 859 | Bristol LWL6B | 83.253 | FC37F | 10/51 | Western National, Exeter (DN) 1310 |
| 4991 | LTA 860 | Bristol LWL6B | 83.254 | FC37F | 10/51 | Western National, Exeter (DN) 1311 |
| 4992 | LTA 861 | Bristol LWL6B | 83.255 | FC37F | 10/51 | Western National, Exeter (DN) 1312 |
| 4993 | LTA 862 | Bristol LWL6B | 83.256 | FC37F | 10/51 | Western National, Exeter (DN) 1313 |
| 4994 | LTA 863 | Bristol LWL6B | 83.257 | FC37F | 10/51 | Western National, Exeter (DN) 1314 |
| 4995 | LTA 960 | Bristol LWL6B | 83.258 | FC37F | 5/51 | Southern National, Exeter (DN) 1326 |
| 4996 | LTA 961 | Bristol LWL6B | 83.259 | FC37F | 5/51 | Southern National, Exeter (DN) 1327 |
| 4997 | LTA 927 | Bristol LWL6B | 83.293 | FC37F | 1/51 | Southern National, Exeter (DN) 1332 |
| 4998 | LTA 928 | Bristol LWL6B | 83.294 | FC37F | 1/51 | Southern National, Exeter (DN) 1333 |
| 4999 | LTA 929 | Bristol LWL6B | 83.295 | FC37F | 1/51 | Southern National, Exeter (DN) 1334 |
| 5000 | LTA 962 | Bristol LWL6B | 85.031 | FC37F | 5/51 | Southern National, Exeter (DN) 1328 |

**Notes:**

Bristol Tramways vehicles with a C prefix to their fleet numbers were operated in the Bristol Joint Services fleet and those with 15xx fleet numbers in the Gloucester City fleet.

1075 (FPW 501): Was fitted with experimental perspex windows when new, but these were later replaced by standard toughened glass.
1122 (FRU 827): Received a new ECW (6787) L27/26R body in 3/56; body 1122 was transferred to Bristol K5G GLJ 967 in 5/56.
1140 (FRU 828): Quoted as K6B in PK781/82, believed to be an error.
1240 (EDL 14): Received a new ECW (12775) FB35F body in 4/61.
1241 (EDL 15): Received a new ECW (12776) FB35F body in 4/61.
1242 (EDL 16): Received a new ECW (12840) FB35F body in 4/62.
1286 (GHN 997): Body built at Irthlingborough.
1298-99 (GHN 998-99): Bodies built at Irthlingborough.
1300 (HHN 200): Body built at Irthlingborough.
1310 (HHN 201): Body built at Irthlingborough.
1311 (HHN 205): Body built at Irthlingborough.
1318 (GHN 963): Body built at Irthlingborough.
1322 (GHN 964): Body built at Irthlingborough.
1323-24 (GHN 969-70): Bodies built at Irthlingborough.
1332 (GHN 971): Body built at Irthlingborough.
1333 (HHN 206): Body built at Irthlingborough.
1337 (HHN 207): Body built at Irthlingborough.
1338 (HHN 210): Body built at Irthlingborough.
1339 (HHN 202): Body built at Irthlingborough.
1345-46 (HHN 203-04): Bodies built at Irthlingborough.
1347 (HHN 215): Body built at Irthlingborough.
1348-49 (HHN 208-09): Bodies built at Irthlingborough.
1361-62 (HHN 211-12): Bodies built at Irthlingborough.
1371-72 (HHN 213-14): Bodies built at Irthlingborough.
1373-74 (HHN 216-17): Bodies built at Irthlingborough.
1378-82 (HHN 218-22): Bodies built at Irthlingborough.
1436-38 (GHN 966-68): Bodies built at Irthlingborough.
1439-63 (GHN 972-96): Bodies built at Irthlingborough.
1573 (HUW 780): Received a new Windover (6941) C33F body in -/49; its ECW body was transferred to HE 6329 (Birch Bros K34).
1574 (HUW 781): Received a new Windover (6942) C33F body in -/49; its ECW body was transferred to BLO 978 (Birch Bros K45).
1575 (HUW 782): Received a new Windover (6943) C33F body in -/49; its ECW body was transferred to CLA 102 (Birch Bros K46).
1576 (HUW 783): Received a new Windover (6944) C33F body in -/49; its ECW body was transferred to CLA 103 (Birch Bros K47).
1577 (HUW 784): Received a new Windover (6945) C33F body in -/49; its ECW body was transferred to CLA 104 (Birch Bros K48).
1578 (HUW 785): Received a new Windover (6946) C33F body in -/49; its ECW body was transferred to CLA 105 (Birch Bros K49).
1737 (JHN 464): Body transferred to Bristol K5G HHN 56 ?-/60?.
1915 (GFM 852): Body built at Irthlingborough.
1916 (GFM 851): Body built at Irthlingborough.
1917-23 (GFM 853-59): Bodies built at Irthlingborough.
1949-54 (GFM 885-90): Bodies built at Irthlingborough.
1981-94 (GPW 683-96): Bodies built at Irthlingborough.
2016-46 (JHN 324-54): Bodies built at Irthlingborough.
2047-48 (JHN 356-57): Bodies built at Irthlingborough.
2049 (JHN 359): Body built at Irthlingborough.
2050 (JHN 363): Body built at Irthlingborough.
2051 (JHN 366): Body built at Irthlingborough.
2052 (JHN 355): Body built at Irthlingborough.
2053 (JHN 358): Body built at Irthlingborough.
2054-56 (JHN 360-62): Bodies built at Irthlingborough.
2057-58 (JHN 364-65): Bodies built at Irthlingborough.
2059-115 (JHN 367-423): Bodies built at Irthlingborough.
2098 (JHN 406): Body transferred to Bristol L6B LHN 336 -/50 and new body number 3306 fitted (q.v.)
2099 (JHN 407): Body transferred to Bristol L6B LHN 337 -/50 and new body number 3307 fitted (q.v.)
2100 (JHN 408): Body transferred to Bristol L6B LHN 338 -/50 and new body number 3308 fitted (q.v.)
2101 (JHN 409): Body transferred to Bristol L6B LHN 339 -/50 and new body number 3309 fitted (q.v.)
2105 (JHN 413): Body transferred to Bristol L6B LHN 340 -/50 and new body number 3310 fitted (q.v.)
2106 (JHN 414): Body transferred to Bristol L6B LHN 341 -/50 and new body number 3311 fitted (q.v.)

2107 (JHN 415): Body transferred to Bristol L6B LHN 342 -/50 and new body number 3312 fitted (q.v.)
2109 (JHN 417): Body transferred to Bristol L6B LHN 343 -/50 and new body number 3313 fitted (q.v.)
2114 (JHN 422): Body transferred to Bristol L6B NHN 95 -/50 and body 4190 from NHN 95 fitted in exchange.
2115 (JHN 423): Body transferred to Bristol L6B NHN 96 -/50 and body 4191 from NHN 96 fitted in exchange.
2176-89 (LHT 902-15): Bodies built at Irthlingborough.
2204 (DOD 505): Chassis new 7/40 with an ECW (6801) L30/26R body.
2205-09 (GTG 863-67): Body rebuilt by Longwell Green at an unknown date.
2360-2409: Chassis and bodies ordered by Trucks & Transport Equipment, Johannesburg and sold to the operators shown.
2410 (JG 7017): Chassis new 4/36 with a Brush L27/26R body.
2411 (JG 8202): Chassis new 11/36 with a Park Royal (4422) L27/26R body.
2412 (JG 9917): Chassis new 3/38 with a Park Royal (4947) L27/26R body.
2413 (JG 9928): Chassis new 4/38 with a Brush L27/26R body.
2414 (JG 9922): Chassis new 4/38 with a Brush L27/26R body.
2415 (JG 9929): Chassis new 4/38 with a Brush L27/26R body.
2416 (JG 7015): Chassis new 4/36 with a Brush L27/26R body.
2417 (JG 7022): Chassis new 4/36 with a Brush L27/26R body.
2418 (JG 8204): Chassis new 11/36 with a Park Royal (4424) L27/26R body.
2419 (JG 8229): Chassis new 1/37 with a Park Royal (4449) L27/26R body.
2420 (JG 8231): Chassis new 12/36 with a Park Royal (4451) L27/26R body.
2421 (JG 8243): Chassis new 2/37 with a Park Royal (4470) L27/26R body.
2422 (JG 8230): Chassis new 1/37 with a Park Royal (4450) L27/26R body.
2423 (JG 8244): Chassis new 3/37 with a Park Royal (4471) L27/26R body.
2424 (JG 8248): Chassis new 3/37 with a Park Royal (4475) L27/26R body.
2425 (JG 7018): Chassis new 4/36 with a Brush L27/26R body.
2426 (JG 8201): Chassis new 11/36 with a Park Royal (4421) L27/26R body.
2427 (JG 8240): Chassis new 2/37 with a Park Royal (4460) L27/26R body.
2428 (JG 7011): Chassis new 3/36 with a Brush L27/26R body.
2429 (JG 7024): Chassis new 5/36 with a Brush L27/26R body.
2430 (JG 8226): Chassis new 12/36 with a Park Royal (4446) L27/26R body.
2431 (JG 8228): Chassis new 12/36 with a Park Royal (4448) L27/26R body.
2432 (JG 8238): Chassis new 2/37 with a Park Royal (4458) L27/26R body.
2433 (JG 8227): Chassis new 12/36 with a Park Royal (4447) L27/26R body.
2434 (RN 8186): Chassis new 1/38 with a Brush L27/26R body.
2435 (RN 8187): Chassis new 2/38 with a Brush L27/26R body.
2436 (RN 8177): Chassis new 12/37 with a Brush L27/26R body.
2437 (RN 8314): Chassis new 3/38 with a Brush L27/26R body.
2438 (RN 8183): Chassis new 12/37 with a Brush L27/26R body.
2439 (RN 8174): Chassis new 12/37 with a Brush L27/26R body.
2440 (RN 8181): Chassis new 12/37 with a Brush L27/26R body.
2441 (RN 8165): Chassis new 2/38 with a Burlingham L27/26R body.
2442 (RN 8322): Chassis new 3/38 with a Brush L27/26R body.
2443 (RN 8156): Chassis new 2/38 with a Burlingham L27/26R body.
2444 (RN 8297): Chassis new 3/38 with a Burlingham L27/26R body.
2445 (RN 8182): Chassis new 12/37 with a Brush L27/26R body.
2446 (RN 8157): Chassis new 12/37 with a Burlingham L27/26R body.
2447 (RN 8311): Chassis new 1/38 with a Brush L27/26R body.
2448 (RN 8306): Chassis new 3/38 with a Burlingham L27/26R body.
2449 (RN 8189): Chassis new 2/38 with a Brush L27/26R body.
2450 (RN 8319): Chassis new 3/38 with a Brush L27/26R body.
2451 (RN 8313): Chassis new 3/38 with a Brush L27/26R body.
2452 (RN 8317): Chassis new 3/38 with a Brush L27/26R body.
2453 (RN 8176): Chassis new 12/37 with a Brush L27/26R body.
2454 (RN 8190): Chassis new 3/38 with a Brush L27/26R body.
2455 (RN 8301): Chassis new 5/38 with a Burlingham L27/26R body.
2456 (RN 8184): Chassis new 1/38 with a Brush L27/26R body.
2457 (RN 8188): Chassis new 1/38 with a Brush L27/26R body.
2458 (RN 8316): Chassis new 3/38 with a Brush L27/26R body.
2459 (DKH 466): Chassis new 12/37 with a Brush H26/26R body.
2460 (ERH 359): Chassis new 12/38 with a ECW (5911) H26/26R body.
2461 (ERH 362): Chassis new 12/38 with a ECW (5914) H26/26R body.
2462 (ERH 360): Chassis new 12/38 with a ECW (5912) H26/26R body.

2463 (ERH 366): Chassis new 12/38 with a ECW (5918) H26/26R body.
2464 (GAT 60): Chassis new 11/39 with a ECW (6488) H26/26R body.
2465 (GAT 62): Chassis new 11/39 with a ECW (6491) H26/26R body.
2466 (GAT 61): Chassis new 11/39 with a ECW (6490) H26/26R body.
2467 (GAT 66): Chassis new 12/39 with a ECW (6494) H26/26R body.
2468 (GAT 63): Chassis new 11/39 with a ECW (6489) H26/26R body.
2469 (GAT 69): Chassis new 12/39 with a ECW (6497) H26/26R body.
2470 (GAT 64): Chassis new 11/39 with a ECW (6492) H26/26R body.
2471 (GAT 70): Chassis new 12/39 with a ECW (6498) H26/26R body.
2472 (GAT 67): Chassis new 12/39 with a ECW (6495) H26/26R body.
2473 (GAT 68): Chassis new 12/39 with a ECW (6496) H26/26R body.
2474 (GR 5075): Chassis new 5/38 with a Weymann (M1456) H28/24F body.
2475 (GR 5077): Chassis new 4/38 with a Weymann (M1458) H28/24F body.
2476 (GR 5078): Chassis new 4/38 with a Weymann (M1459) H28/24F body.
2477 (GR 5076): Chassis new 4/38 with a Weymann (M1457) H28/24F body.
2478 (GR 5079): Chassis new 4/38 with a Weymann (M1460) H28/24F body.
2490 (HSM 644): On loan to London Transport from new until 12/49.
2491 (HSM 645): On loan to London Transport from new until 3/50.
2513 (JFM 72): On loan to London Transport from new until 3/50.
2515 (JFM 74): On loan to London Transport from new until 3/50.
2517-26 (JFM 76-85): On loan to London Transport from new until 4/50.
2527-28 (JFM 86-87): On loan to London Transport from new until 5/50.
2529-30 (JFM 88-89): On loan to London Transport from new until 4/50.
2531-34 (JFM 90-93): On loan to London Transport from new until 5/50.
2535-51 (JFM 94-110): Scheduled to be loaned to London Transport from new, but did not go on loan.
2559-64 (NNO 100-05): On loan to London Transport from new until 11/49.
2565-66 (NNO 106-07): On loan to London Transport from new until 3/50.
2577 (HLJ 25): On loan to London Transport from new until 3/50.
2578 (HLJ 27): On loan to London Transport from new until 3/50.
2579 (HLJ 26): On loan to London Transport from new until 3/50.
2580-96 (HLJ 28-44): On loan to London Transport from new until 3/50.
2597-602 (HRU 844-49): On loan to London Transport from new until 3/50.
2603-15 (HRU 850-62): On loan to London Transport from new until 4/50.
2628-30 (HOD 90-92): On loan to London Transport from new until 12/49.
2631-35 (HOD 93-97): On loan to London Transport from new until 3/50.
2641-42 (FDL 297-98): On loan to London Transport from new until 11/49.
2692 (KHN 392): On loan to London Transport from new until 3/50.
2693 (KHN 493): On loan to London Transport from new until 5/50.
2694 (KHN 494): On loan to London Transport from new until 3/50.
2695-99 (KHN 495-99): On loan to London Transport from new until 5/50.
2700 (KHN 500): On loan to London Transport from new until 3/50.
2701-04 (LHN 101-04): On loan to London Transport from new until 5/50.
2705-09 (LHN 305-09): On loan to London Transport from new until 5/50.
2717-21 (EBD 220-24): On loan to London Transport from new until 12/49.
2722 (EBD 225): On loan to London Transport from new until 1/50.
2723-24 (EBD 226-27): On loan to London Transport from new until 2/50.
2755-59 (HOD 5-9): On loan to London Transport from new until 12/49.
2760 (HOD 10): On loan to London Transport from new until 1/50.
2761-68 (HOD 11-18): On loan to London Transport from new until 2/50.
2769 (HOD 19): On loan to London Transport from new until 2/50.
2770 (HOD 20): On loan to London Transport from new until 2/50.
2771-74 (HOD 21-24): On loan to London Transport from new until 3/50.
2775-76 (HOD 25-26): On loan to London Transport from new until 4/50.
2781 (CJN 324): On loan to London Transport from new until 1/50.
2782 (CJN 325): On loan to London Transport from new until 2/50.
2783 (CJN 326): On loan to London Transport from new until 3/50.
2834 (EAP 8): On loan to London Transport from new until 4/50.
2835 (EAP 9): On loan to London Transport from new until 4/50.
2836 (EAP 10): On loan to London Transport from new until 4/50.
2837 (EAP 11): On loan to London Transport from new until 5/50.
2857 (HPW 94): On loan to London Transport from new until 1/50.
2858 (HPW 95): On loan to London Transport from new until 2/50.
2859-62 (HPW 96-99): On loan to London Transport from new until 1/50.
2865-69 (HPW 102-06): Had 4-bay bodies.

2870-71 (HPW 107-08): On loan to London Transport from new until 1/50.
2872 (HPW 109): On loan to London Transport from new until 2/50.
2873 (HPW 110): On loan to London Transport from new until 1/50.
2874-78 (HPW 111-15): On loan to London Transport from new until 2/50.
2879-84 (HPW 116-21): On loan to London Transport from new until 3/50.
2885-92 (HPW 122-29): On loan to London Transport from new until 4/50.
2893-99 (HPW 131-36): On loan to London Transport from new until 5/50.
2900-01 (HPW 137-38): On loan to London Transport from new until 6/50.
2902-05 (HPW 139-42): Had 4-bay bodies.
2918 (GWX 120): Had a 4-bay body.
2919-23 (LHT 916-20): Bodies built at Irthlingborough.
2924-27 (LHU 501-04): Bodies built at Irthlingborough.
2928-29 (LHW 902-03): Bodies built at Irthlingborough.
2930 (LHW 905): Body built at Irthlingborough.
2931 (LHW 917): Body built at Irthlingborough.
2932 (LHW 920): Body built at Irthlingborough.
2933 (LHW 922): Body built at Irthlingborough.
2939-41 (JFM 116-18): Bodies built at Irthlingborough.
2942-44 (NNO 108-10): Bodies built at Irthlingborough.
2948 (HLJ 48): Body built at Irthlingborough.
2949-50 (FBE 324-25): Bodies built at Irthlingborough.
2951-61 (KHN 424-34): Bodies built at Irthlingborough.
2962 (KHN 435): 1948 Commercial Motor Show exhibit on the Bristol stand.
2965 (GWX 131): Body built at Irthlingborough.
2966 (GWX 133): Body built at Irthlingborough.
2967 (GWX 132): Body built at Irthlingborough.
2968-69 (HRU 32-33): Bodies built at Irthlingborough.
2973 (FT 4497): Chassis new -/38 with a Weymann (M1373) H28/27F body.
2974 (FT 4500): Chassis new -/38 with a Weymann (M1376) H28/27F body.
2975 (FT 4498): Chassis new -/38 with a Weymann (M1374) H28/27F body.
2976 (FT 4502): Chassis new -/38 with a Weymann (M1378) H28/27F body.
2977 (FT 4499): Chassis new -/38 with a Weymann (M1375) H28/27F body.
2978 (FT 4496): Chassis new -/38 with a Weymann (M1372) H28/27F body.
2979 (FT 4501): Chassis new -/38 with a Weymann (M1377) H28/27F body.
2980 (FT 4503): Chassis new -/38 with a Weymann (M1379) H28/27F body.
3022 (JXT 490): was converted to full-front ?FC31R? by Park Royal at an unknown date.
3023 (JXT 492): was converted to full-front ?FC31R? by Park Royal at an unknown date.
3024 (JXT 493): was converted to full-front ?FC31R? by Park Royal at an unknown date.
3025 (JXT 491): was converted to full-front ?FC31R? by Park Royal at an unknown date.
3026 (JXT 494): was converted to full-front ?FC31R? by Park Royal at an unknown date.
3027 (JXT 495): was converted to full-front ?FC31R? by Park Royal at an unknown date.
3028 (BHN 269): Body built at Irthlingborough on a chassis new 6/36 with an ECOC (4084) B36R body.
3029 (AHN 431): Body built at Irthlingborough on a chassis new 6/35 with an ECOC (3574) B36R body.
3030 (BHN 263): Body built at Irthlingborough on a chassis new -/35 with a Burlingham C30R body.
3031 (BHN 276): Body built at Irthlingborough on a chassis new 3/36 with an ECOC (4091) B36R body.
3032 (AHN 385): Body built at Irthlingborough on a chassis new -/35 with a Burlingham C30R body.
3033 (BHN 271): Body built at Irthlingborough on a chassis new 3/36 with an ECOC (4086) B36R body.
3034 (BHN 278): Body built at Irthlingborough on a chassis new 3/36 with an ECOC (4093) B36R body.
3035 (AHN 814): Body built at Irthlingborough on a chassis new -/35 with a Burlingham C30R body.
3036 (BHN 261): Body built at Irthlingborough on a chassis new -/35 with a Burlingham C30R body.
3037 (BHN 279): Body built at Irthlingborough on a chassis new 3/36 with an ECOC (4094) B36R body.
3038 (AHN 812): Body built at Irthlingborough on a chassis new -/35 with a Burlingham C30R body.
3039 (BHN 268): Body built at Irthlingborough on a chassis new 3/36 with an ECOC (4083) B36R body.
3040 (BHN 272): Body built at Irthlingborough on a chassis new 3/36 with an ECOC (4087) B36R body.
3041 (AHN 433): Body built at Irthlingborough on a chassis new 6/35 with an ECOC (3576) B36R body.
3042 (AHN 434): Body built at Irthlingborough on a chassis new 6/35 with an ECOC (3577) B36R body.
3043 (AHN 435): Body built at Irthlingborough on a chassis new 6/35 with an ECOC (3578) B36R body.
3044 (BHN 265): Body built at Irthlingborough on a chassis new -/35 with a Burlingham C30R body.
3045 (BHN 270): Body built at Irthlingborough on a chassis new 2/36 with an ECOC (4085) B36R body.
3046 (AHN 432): Body built at Irthlingborough on a chassis new 6/35 with an ECOC (3575) B36R body.
3047 (AHN 811): Body built at Irthlingborough on a chassis new -/35 with a Burlingham C30R body.
3048 (BHN 262): Body built at Irthlingborough on a chassis new -/35 with a Burlingham C30R body.
3049 (BHN 275): Body built at Irthlingborough on a chassis new 3/36 with an ECOC (4090) B36R body.
3050 (BHN 273): Body built at Irthlingborough on a chassis new 3/36 with an ECOC (4088) B36R body.

3051 (AHN 813): Body built at Irthlingborough on a chassis new -/35 with a Burlingham C30R body.
3052 (BHN 266): Body built at Irthlingborough on a chassis new 3/36 with an ECOC (4081) B36R body.
3053 (BHN 267): Body built at Irthlingborough on a chassis new 3/36 with an ECOC (4082) B36R body.
3054 (BHN 277): Body built at Irthlingborough on a chassis new 3/36 with an ECOC (4092) B36R body.
3055 (BHN 280): Body built at Irthlingborough on a chassis new 3/36 with an ECOC (4095) B36R body.
3056 (BHN 274): Body built at Irthlingborough on a chassis new 3/36 with an ECOC (4089) B36R body.
3057 (BHN 264): Body built at Irthlingborough on a chassis new -/35 with a Burlingham C30R body.
3058 (VV 6255): Body built at Irthlingborough on a chassis new 9/37 with an ECW (4938) C31R body.
3059 (NV 6638): Body built at Irthlingborough on a chassis new 3/36 with a Burlingham B35R body.
3060 (VV 4564): Body built at Irthlingborough on a chassis new 3/36 with a Burlingham B35R body.
3061 (VV 5041): Body built at Irthlingborough on a chassis new 7/36 with an ECW (4328) B36R body.
3062 (VV 5042): Body built at Irthlingborough on a chassis new 7/36 with an ECW (4329) B36R body.
3063 (NV 7496): Body built at Irthlingborough on a chassis new 7/36 with an ECW (4330) B36R body.
3064 (VV 5693): Body built at Irthlingborough on a chassis new 3/37 with an ECW (4825) B32R body.
3065 (NV 7497): Body built at Irthlingborough on a chassis new 7/36 with an ECW (4331) B36R body.
3066 (NV 8666): Body built at Irthlingborough on a chassis new 3/37 with an ECW (4823) B32R body.
3067 (NV 8667): Body built at Irthlingborough on a chassis new 3/37 with an ECW (4824) B32R body.
3068 (VV 5694): Body built at Irthlingborough on a chassis new 3/37 with an ECW (4826) B32R body.
3069 (VV 5695): Body built at Irthlingborough on a chassis new 3/37 with an ECW (4827) B32R body.
3070 (VV 6257): Body built at Irthlingborough on a chassis new 8/37 with an ECW (4922) B35R body.
3071 (VV 6258): Body built at Irthlingborough on a chassis new 8/37 with an ECW (4923) B35R body.
3072 (VV 5696): Body built at Irthlingborough on a chassis new 3/37 with an ECW (4828) B32R body.
3073 (VV 6260): Body built at Irthlingborough on a chassis new 8/37 with an ECW (4925) B35R body.
3074 (WX 2111): Chassis new -/30 with a Leyland L27/24R body; body transferred to Bristol K5G (with an
    AEC A202 engine) FXT 412 2/56.
3075 (FM 6415): Chassis new 5/31 with a Leyland L27/24R body; body transferred to Leyland TD4 BWA
    409 11/51.
3076 (CK 4418): Chassis new -/30 with a Leyland L24/24R body; body transferred to Leyland PD1A CTH
    471 7/55.
3077 (FM 6416): Chassis new 5/31 with a Leyland L27/24R body; body transferred to Bristol K5G (with an
    AEC A202 engine) FXT 420 5/56.
3078 (UF 5644): Chassis new -/30 with a Leyland L24/24R body; body transferred to Bristol K5G (with an
    AEC A202 engine) FXT 422 2/56.
3079 (CK 4405): Chassis new -/30 with a Leyland L24/24R body; body transferred to Leyland TD4 CWB
    985 12/50.
3080 (CK 4403): Chassis new -/30 with a Leyland L24/24R body; body transferred to Bristol K5G (with an
    AEC A202 engine) FXT 427 4/56.
3081 (EK 8106): Chassis new -/30 with a NCME L24/24R body; body transferred to Leyland TD4 BWE  35
    11/50; then to Bristol K6B FFM 542 2/58.
3082 (CK 4411): Chassis new -/30 with a Leyland L24/24R body; body transferred to Leyland TD4 CWB
    479 1/51; then to Bristol K6A GFM 892 5/58.
3083 (CK 4406): Chassis new -/30 with a Leyland L24/24R body; body transferred to Bristol K5G (with an
    AEC A202 engine) FXT 424 4/56.
3084 (HL 5339): Chassis new -/32 with a Roe (GO2116) H24/24C body; body transferred to Bristol K6A
    FFM 454 1/57.
3085 (HL 5318): Chassis new -/32 with a Roe (GO2031) H24/24C body; body transferred to Bristol K6A
    FFM 455 1/57.
3086 (KG 1148): Chassis new -/32 with a NCME L24/24R body; body transferred to Leyland PD1A GFM
    922 7/56.
3087 (KG 1151): Chassis new -/32 with a NCME L24/24R body; body transferred to Leyland PD1A HFM
    70 7/56.
3088 (FM 7467): Chassis new -/31 with a Leyland L27/24R body; body transferred to Bristol K6B GFM 894
    1/57.
3089 (FM 7763): Chassis new 5/33 with a Leyland L24/24R body; body transferred to Bristol K6B GFM 895
    1/57.
3090 (FM 7234): Chassis new 6/32 with a Leyland L24/24R body; body transferred to Bristol K6A FFM 452
    11/56.
3091 (AG 8246): Chassis new -/32 with a Leyland H24/24R body; body transferred to Bristol K6A FFM 437
    7/56.
3092 (FM 6918): Chassis new -/32 with a Leyland L27/24R body; body transferred to Leyland PD1A HFM
    71 10/56.
3093 (FM 7462): Chassis new -/31 with a Leyland L27/24R body; body transferred to Bristol K6A FFM 435
    2/56.

3094 (AG 8258): Chassis new -/32 with a Leyland H24/24R body; body transferred to Bristol K6A FFM 445 10/56.

3095 (FM 7461): Chassis new -/31 with a Leyland L27/24R body; body transferred to Bristol K5G (with an AEC A202 engine) FXT 426 2/56.

3096 (FM 6919): Chassis new -/31 with a Leyland L27/24R body; body transferred to Bristol K6A GFM 891 1/57.

3097 (FM 7466): Chassis new -/31 with a Leyland L27/24R body; body transferred to Bristol K6A HGC 252 4/56.

3098 (FM 7463): Chassis new -/31 with a Leyland L27/24R body; body transferred to Bristol K6A FFM 440 7/56.

3099 (FM 6920): Chassis new -/31 with a Leyland L27/24R body; body transferred to Bristol K6A FFM 449 6/56.

3100 (FM 6276): Chassis new 10/33 with an ECOC (3025) L26/26R body; body transferred to Leyland PD1A GFM 909 3/56.

3101 (GP 6231): Chassis new -/31 with a Tilling (5521) H27/25RO body; body transferred to Bristol K6A HGC 241 2/54.

3102 (GP 6238): Chassis new -/31 with a Tilling (5528) H27/25RO body; body transferred to Bristol K6A HGC 237 11/54.

3103 (GP 6242): Chassis new -/31 with a Tilling (5532) H27/25RO body; body transferred to Bristol K6A HGC 242 2/54.

3104 (GN 6206): Chassis new -/31 with a Dodson H27/25RO body; body transferred to Bristol K5G (with an AEC A202 engine) FXT 419 11/54.

3105 (GW 6255): Chassis new -/32 with a Tilling (5565) H27/25RO body; body transferred to Bristol K6A HGC 248 11/54.

3106 (GW 6288): Chassis new -/32 with a Tilling (5598) H27/25RO body; body transferred to Bristol K5G (with an AEC A202 engine) FXT 425 11/54.

3107 (FM 8984): Chassis new -/35 with an ECOC (3683) B32F body.
3108 (FM 8979): Chassis new -/35 with an ECOC (3676) B32F body.
3109 (FM 8988): Chassis new -/35 with an ECOC (3668) B32F body.
3110 (FM 8993): Chassis new -/35 with an ECOC (3681) B34F body.
3111 (FM 8977): Chassis new -/35 with an ECOC (3675) B32F body.
3112 (FM 8996): Chassis new -/35 with an ECOC (3689) B34F body.
3113 (FM 8983): Chassis new -/35 with an ECOC (3682) B32F body.
3114 (FM 8998): Chassis new -/35 with an ECOC (3691) B34F body.
3115 (FM 8994): Chassis new -/35 with an ECOC (3686) B34F body.
3116 (FM 8975): Chassis new -/35 with an ECOC (3680) B32F body.
3117 (FM 8976): Chassis new -/35 with an ECOC (3671) B32F body.
3118 (FM 8985): Chassis new -/35 with an ECOC (3684) B32F body.
3119 (FM 8997): Chassis new -/35 with an ECOC (3690) B34F body.
3120 (FM 8991): Chassis new -/35 with an ECOC (3678) B34F body.
3121 (FM 8978): Chassis new -/35 with an ECOC (3672) B32F body.
3122 (FM 7482): Chassis new 6/33 with an ECOC (2795) B32F body.
3123 (SM 8851): Chassis new -/31 with a Leyland B26F body.
3124 (SM 8852): Chassis new -/31 with a Leyland B26F body.
3125 (SM 8853): Chassis new -/31 with a Leyland B26F body.
3126 (SM 8854): Chassis new -/31 with a Leyland B26F body.
3127 (SM 9502): Chassis new -/32 with an ECOC (2766) B32- body.
3128 (SM 9501): Chassis new -/32 with an ECOC (2765) B32- body.
3129 (BSM 826): Chassis new -/36 with a Weymann (C5047) B32F body.
3130 (DSM 453): Chassis new -/38 with a Brush B32F body.
3131 (ENO 932): Chassis new 6/37 with an ECW (4821) L24/24R body.
3132 (ENO 933): Chassis new 6/37 with an ECW (4822) L24/24R body.
3133 (DEV 479): Chassis new 7/36 with a Brush L27/26R body.
3134 (DEV 478): Chassis new 7/36 with a Brush L27/26R body.
3135 (DEV 477): Chassis new 8/36 with a Brush L27/26R body.
3136 (ENO 931): Chassis new 6/37 with an ECW (4820) L24/24R body.
3137 (DEV 480): Chassis new 8/36 with a Brush L27/26R body.
3138 (DEV 470): Chassis new 7/36 with a Brush L27/26R body.
3139 (DEV 476): Chassis new 7/36 with a Brush L27/26R body.
3140 (BTW 498): Chassis new 4/35 with an ECOC (3583) L28/28R body.
3141 (ENO 937): Chassis new 3/37 with an ECW (4816) L24/24R body.
3142 (ENO 936): Chassis new 3/37 with an ECW (4815) L24/24R body.
3143 (ENO 935): Chassis new 3/37 with an ECW (4814) L24/24R body.
3144 (ENO 939): Chassis new 5/37 with an ECW (4818) L24/24R body.

3145 (FEV 179): Chassis new 8/37 with a Brush L28/28R body.
3146 (FEV 176): Chassis new 7/37 with a Brush L28/28R body.
3147 (FEV 180): Chassis new 7/37 with a Brush L28/28R body.
3148 (FEV 178): Chassis new 7/37 with a Brush L28/28R body.
3149 (FEV 177): Chassis new 7/37 with a Brush L28/28R body.
3150 (FEV 182): Chassis new 8/37 with a Brush L28/28R body.
3151 (FEV 175): Chassis new 7/37 with a Brush L28/28R body.
3152 (FEV 181): Chassis new 8/37 with a Brush L28/28R body.
3153 (UH 7175): Chassis new -/29 with a Leyland L27/24R body. It was new to Cardiff Corporation, being acquired by Southern Vectis 6/45.
3154 (TF 6821): Chassis new -/31 with a Leyland L27/24R body. It was originally a Leyland demonstrator before passing to Cardiff Corporation, being acquired by Southern Vectis 6/45.
3155 (CHN 101): Chassis new 10/36 with an ECOC (4516) L27/28R body; body transferred to Bristol K5G GHN 187 11/55; then transferred to Bristol K6B JHN 462 12/59.
3156 (CHN 103): Chassis new 10/36 with an ECOC (4518) L27/28R body; body transferred to Bristol K6A (with a Gardner 5LW engine) GHN 636 5/55; then transferred to Bristol K6B JHN 466 1959.
3157 (CHN 104): Chassis new 10/36 with an ECOC (4519) L27/28R body; body transferred to Bristol K6A GHN 839 3/55; then transferred to Bristol K6B JHN 460 (1959?).
3158 (CHN 106): Chassis new 10/36 with an ECOC (4521) L27/28R body; body transferred to Bristol K6A GHN 631 10/55.
3159 (CHN 102): Chassis new 10/36 with an ECOC (4517) L27/28R body; body transferred to Bristol K6A GHN 841 1/55; then transferred to Bristol K5G HHN 56 11/58; then transferred to Bristol K6B JHN 464 (1960?).
3160 (CHN 105): Chassis new 10/36 with an ECOC (4520) L27/28R body; body transferred to Bristol K6A GHN 838 10/55.
3161 (HN 9012): Chassis new 6/33 with an ECOC (2915) H28/26R body; body transferred to Bristol K5G FHN 925 11/53; then transferred to Bristol K6B JHN 458 3/59.
3162 (HN 9013): Chassis new 6/33 with an ECOC (2916) H28/26R body; body transferred to Bristol K5G GHN 189 1954.
3163 (TF 7211): Chassis new 12/31 with a Leyland H24/24R body; body transferred to Bristol K5G FHN 924 10/53; then transferred to Bristol K6B JHN 461 10/59.
3164 (TF 9947): Chassis new 10/32 with a Leyland H24/24R body; body transferred to Bristol K6A GHN 633 2/54; then transferred to Bristol K6B JHN 459 4/58.
3165 (HN 9007): Chassis new 5/33 with an ECOC (2910) H28/26R body; body transferred to Bristol K6A GHN 837 11/54.
3166 (HN 9010): Chassis new 6/33 with an ECOC (2913) H28/26R body; body transferred to Bristol K6A GHN 635 1954.
3167 (HN 9014): Chassis new 6/33 with an ECOC (2917) H28/26R body; body transferred to Bristol K5G GHN 340 1954; then transferred to Bristol K5G HHN 42 7/58; then transferred to Bristol K6B JHN 465 12/59.
3168 (HN 9011): Chassis new 6/33 with an ECOC (2914) H28/26R body; body transferred to Bristol K5G FHN 922 11/53; then transferred to Bristol K6A GHN 632 7/58; then transferred to Bristol K6B JHN 463 10/60.
3169 (HN 9008): Chassis new 5/33 with an ECOC (2911) H28/26R body; body transferred to Bristol K5G GHN 188 1954; then transferred to Bristol K6B JHN 467 12/59.
3170 (HN 9009): Chassis new 5/33 with an ECOC (2912) H28/26R body; body transferred to Bristol K6A GHN 840 10/55.
3171 (NV 2276): Chassis new 3/33 with an ECOC (2889) L26/26R body.
3172 (NV 2270): Chassis new 3/33 with an ECOC (2883) L26/26R body.
3173 (NV 2277): Chassis new 3/33 with an ECOC (2890) L26/26R body.
3174 (NV 2280): Chassis new 4/33 with an ECOC (2893) L26/26R body.
3175 (NV 2272): Chassis new 3/33 with an ECOC (2885) L26/26R body.
3176 (NV 2268): Chassis new 3/33 with an ECOC (2882) L26/26R body.
3177 (NV 2271): Chassis new 3/33 with an ECOC (2884) L26/26R body.
3178 (NV 2278): Chassis new 4/33 with an ECOC (2891) L26/26R body.
3179 (BWY 984): Chassis new 10/37 with an ECW (5017) L27/26R body.
3180 (BWY 988): Chassis new 11/37 with an ECW (5022) L27/26R body.
3181 (BWY 982): Chassis new 10/37 with an ECW (5015) L27/26R body.
3182 (BWY 987): Chassis new 10/37 with an ECW (5021) L27/26R body.
3183 (BWY 981): Chassis new 10/37 with an ECW (5014) L27/26R body.
3184 (BWY 992): Chassis new 11/37 with an ECW (5026) L27/26R body.
3185 (BWY 990): Chassis new 11/37 with an ECW (5024) L27/26R body.
3186 (BWY 991): Chassis new 11/37 with an ECW (5025) L27/26R body.
3187 (BWY 983): Chassis new 10/37 with an ECW (5016) L27/26R body.

3188 (BWY 986): Chassis new 10/37 with an ECW (5019) L27/26R body.
3189 (BWY 985): Chassis new 10/37 with an ECW (5018) L27/26R body.
3190 (BWY 979): Chassis new 11/37 with an ECW (5020) L27/26R body.
3191 (BWY 989): Chassis new 11/37 with an ECW (5023) L27/26R body.
3192 (BWY 993): Chassis new 11/37 with an ECW (5027) L27/26R body.
3193 (BWY 980): Chassis new 10/37 with an ECW (5013) L27/26R body.
3194 (BWY 996): Chassis new 11/37 with an ECW (5030) L27/26R body.
3195 (CWX 667): Chassis new 10/38 with an ECW (6119) L27/26R body.
3196 (BWY 997): Chassis new 11/37 with an ECW (5031) L27/26R body.
3197 (BWY 999): Chassis new 11/37 with an ECW (5033) L27/26R body.
3198 (BWY 995): Chassis new 11/37 with an ECW (5029) L27/26R body.
3199 (CWX 668): Chassis new 11/38 with an ECW (6120) L27/26R body.
3200 (JN 4745): Chassis new 10/34 with a Weymann (M226) L24/24R body.
3201 (JN 4294): Chassis new 5/34 with a Weymann (M191) L26/26R body.
3202 (JN 6892): Chassis new -/36 with a Brush L27/26R body.
3203 (JN 6893): Chassis new -/36 with a Brush L27/26R body.
3204 (JN 6896): Chassis new -/36 with a Brush L27/26R body.
3205 (JN 6894): Chassis new -/36 with a Brush L27/26R body.
3206 (BFJ 158): Chassis new 8/35 with a Bristol H24/24R body; body transferred to Bristol K6A HHY 595
after chassis was fitted with a PV2 radiator 11/55.
3207 (AHW 953): Chassis new 8/34 with a Weymann (M205) H26/22R body; body transferred to Bristol
K5G JHT 122 5/56.
3208 (BFJ 156): Chassis new 8/35 with a Bristol H24/24R body; body transferred to Bristol K6A HHY 589
after chassis was fitted with a PV2 radiator 2/55.
3209 (BFJ 157): Chassis new 8/35 with a Bristol H24/24R body; body transferred to Bristol K6A JHT 117
9/54.
3210 (DKN  45): Chassis new 1/37 with a Bristol H30/26R body; body transferred to Bristol K6A JHT 114
9/55.
3211 (DKN  42): Chassis new 12/36 with a Bristol H30/26R body; body transferred to Bristol K6B KHY 741
in 11/56.
3212 (BFJ 155): Chassis new 8/35 with a Bristol H24/24R body; body transferred to Bristol K5G JHT 121
10/55.
3213 (DHT 943): Chassis new 1/37 with a Bristol H26/26R body; body transferred to Bristol K6A JAE 126
after chassis was fitted with a PV2 radiator 12/54.
3214 (EAE 281): Chassis new 6/37 with a Bristol H28/26R body; body transferred to Bristol K6A HHY 599
after chassis was fitted with a PV2 radiator 1/56.
3215 (EAE 596): Chassis new 8/37 with a Bristol H28/26R body; body transferred to Bristol K5G JHT 123
3/56.
3216 (BHT 530): Chassis new -/35 with a Bristol H24/24R body; body transferred to Bristol K5G JHT 810
7/57.
3217 (DKN  40): Chassis new 12/36 with a Bristol H30/26R body; body transferred to Bristol K6A KHU 620
in 3/58.
3218 (BHT 531): Chassis new -/35 with a Bristol H24/24R body; body transferred to Bristol K6A JAE 252
after chassis was fitted with a PV2 radiator 10/56.
3219 (DKN  32): Chassis new 12/36 with a Bristol H30/26R body; body transferred to Bristol K6B KHT 512
in 10/56.
3220 (DHU 349): Chassis new 2/37 with a Bristol H26/26R body; body transferred to Bristol K6A JHT  23
10/56.
3221 (CHW  45): Chassis new -/36 with a Bristol H28/24R body; body transferred to Bristol K6A HHY 587
after chassis was fitted with a PV2 radiator 6/55.
3222 (EAE 285): Chassis new 6/37 with a Bristol H28/26R body; body transferred to Bristol K5G JHT 129
5/56.
3223 (DHU 350): Chassis new 2/37 with a Bristol H26/26R body; body transferred to Bristol K6A JAE 762
after chassis was fitted with a PV2 radiator 2/56.
3224 (HY 3629): Chassis new 12/31 with a Brush H24/24R body; body transferred to Bristol K6A JHT  21
9/55.
3225 (CHY 116): Chassis new -/36 with a Bristol H28/24R body; body transferred to Bristol K6A HHY 598
after chassis was fitted with a PV2 radiator 5/55.
3226 (EAE 288): Chassis new 6/37 with a Bristol H28/26R body; body transferred to Bristol K5G JHT 126
5/56.
3227 (EAE 289): Chassis new 6/37 with a Bristol H28/26R body; body transferred to Bristol K6B KHT 516
in 9/57.
3228 (AHW  74): Chassis new -/34 with a Bristol H24/24R body; body transferred to Bristol K6A JAE 259
after chassis was fitted with a PV2 radiator 8/55.

3229 (BHT 533): Chassis new -/35 with a Bristol H24/24R body; body transferred to Bristol K6A JHT 20 10/56.

3230 (DKN 37): Chassis new 12/36 with a Bristol H30/26R body; body transferred to Bristol K6A JHT 112 2/56.

3231 (BHY 694): Chassis new -/35 with a Bristol H28/24R body;.

3232 (DKN 38): Chassis new 12/36 with a Bristol H30/26R body; body transferred to Bristol K6A KHU 617 in 1/58.

3233 (CHY 119): Chassis new -/36 with a Bristol H28/24R body; body transferred to Bristol K6A HHY 586 after chassis was fitted with a PV2 radiator 4/55.

3234 (EAE 282): Chassis new 6/37 with a Bristol H28/26R body; body transferred to Bristol K5G JHT 127 3/56.

3235 (EAE 283): Chassis new 6/37 with a Bristol H28/26R body; body transferred to Bristol K5G JHT 124 4/56.

3236 (EAE 287): Chassis new 6/37 with a Bristol H28/26R body; body transferred to Bristol K6A HHY 596 after chassis was fitted with a PV2 radiator 7/55.

3237 (DKN 33): Chassis new 12/36 with a Bristol H30/26R body; body transferred to Bristol K6A JHT 113 3/55.

3238 (DKN 34): Chassis new 12/36 with a Bristol H30/26R body; body transferred to Bristol K6A JHT 115 11/55.

3239 (BHT 534): Chassis new -/35 with a Bristol H24/24R body; body transferred to Bristol K6A JAE 251 after chassis was fitted with a PV2 radiator 10/56.

3240 (DKN 43): Chassis new 1/37 with a Bristol H30/26R body; body transferred to Bristol K6B JHT 821 in 5/58.

3241 (DKN 39): Chassis new 12/36 with a Bristol H30/26R body; body transferred to Bristol K5G KHU 613 in 12/56.

3242 (CHW 47): Chassis new -/36 with a Bristol H28/24R body; body transferred to Bristol K5G JHT 120 7/56.

3243 (DKN 36): Chassis new 12/36 with a Bristol H30/26R body; body transferred to Bristol K6A KHU 618 in 5/58.

3244 (DAE 374): Chassis new -/36 with a Bristol H26/28R body; body transferred to Bristol K6A JHT 22 6/56.

3245 (CHW 46): Chassis new -/36 with a Bristol H28/24R body; body transferred to Bristol K6A JAE 253 after chassis was fitted with a PV2 radiator 6/56.

3246 (DAE 369): Chassis new -/36 with a Bristol H26/28R body; body transferred to Bristol K6B KHT 513 in 1/57.

3247 (BHU 975): Chassis new -/35 with a Bristol H28/24R body; body transferred to Bristol K6A JAE 129 after chassis was fitted with a PV2 radiator 9/56.

3248 (BHY 693): Chassis new -/35 with a Bristol H28/24R body; body transferred to Bristol K5G JHT 808 1/57.

3249 (DAE 377): Chassis new -/36 with a Bristol H26/28R body; body transferred to Bristol K6A JAE 263 after chassis was fitted with a PV2 radiator 6/56.

3250 (CHY 118): Chassis new -/36 with a Bristol H28/24R body; body transferred to Bristol K6A HHY 593 after chassis was fitted with a PV2 radiator 6/55.

3251 (EAE 284): Chassis new -/36 with a Bristol H28/26R body; body transferred to Bristol K6A JHT 118 9/56.

3252 (CHY 120): Chassis new -/36 with a Bristol H28/24R body; body transferred to Bristol K5G JHT 125 11/56.

3253 (CHW 43): Chassis new -/36 with a Bristol H28/24R body; body transferred to Bristol K5G JHT 802 4/57.

3263-65 (LHW 907-09): Bodies built at Irthlingborough.
3266 (LHW 906): Body built at Irthlingborough.
3267-70 (LHW 910-13): Bodies built at Irthlingborough.
3272 (LHW 916): Body built at Irthlingborough.
3273 (LHW 914): Body built at Irthlingborough.
3275 (LHW 919): Body built at Irthlingborough.
3276 (LHW 921): Body built at Irthlingborough.
3277 (LHW 924): Body built at Irthlingborough.
3278 (LHW 923): Body built at Irthlingborough.
3279 (LHW 925): Body built at Irthlingborough.
3280 (LHW 927): Body built at Irthlingborough.
3281 (LHW 926): Body built at Irthlingborough.
3282-84 (LHW 929-31): Bodies built at Irthlingborough.
3285 (LHW 928): Body built at Irthlingborough.
3291-93 (JFM 124-26): Bodies built at Irthlingborough.

3294-95 (LHN 346-47): Bodies built at Irthlingborough.
3296-97 (LHN 344-45): Bodies built at Irthlingborough.
3298-305 (LHH 348-55): Bodies built at Irthlingborough.
3306-13 (JHN 406-09/13-15/17): New Bristol L6B chassis were sent direct to Darlington and were fitted
    with the DP31R bodies from JHN 406-09/13-15/17) and they were registered LHN 336-43. The
    Bristol L5G chassis were then sent to ECW and fitted with new B35R bodies as shown above.
3314 (ERU 514): Chassis new 3/39 with a Beadle (758) B34F body.
3315 (EEL 806): Chassis new 8/38 with a Beadle (686) B31F body.
3316 (ERU 516): Chassis new 2/39 with a Beadle (760) B34F body.
3317 (LJ 7095): Chassis new 4/33 with a Brush L26/26R body.
3318 (LJ 7097): Chassis new 4/33 with a Brush L26/26R body.
3319 (LJ 7091): Chassis new 4/33 with a Brush L26/26R body.
3320 (LJ 7092): Chassis new 4/33 with a Brush L26/26R body.
3321 (TK 8915): Chassis new 4/33 with a Brush L26/26R body.
3322 (LJ 7094): Chassis new 4/33 with a Brush L26/26R body.
3323 (TK 8916): Chassis new 4/33 with a Brush L26/26R body; body transferred to Guy Arab II FOP 447
    as Dodds (AA), Troon (AR) DT14 1/54.
3324 (LJ 7096): Chassis new 4/33 with a Brush L26/26R body.
3325 (FM 6917): Chassis new -/32 with a Leyland L27/24R body; body transferred to Bristol K6B FFM 540
    6/56.
3326 (FM 7464): Chassis new -/31 with a Leyland L27/24R body; body transferred to Bristol K6A HGC 249
    1/56.
3327 (CHT 337): Chassis new -/36 with a Bristol B34D body.
3328 (AHT 972): Chassis new -/36 with a Bristol B34D body; body transferred to Bristol L5G HY 2396 in
    12/54.
3329 (BHW 431): Chassis new -/35 with a Bristol B32F body.
3330 (CHU 563): Chassis new -/36 with a Bristol B34D body; body transferred to Bristol L5G HW 8369 in
    12/54.
3331 (CHU 567): Chassis new -/36 with a Bristol B34D body; body transferred to Bristol L5G HW 9059 in
    5/55.
3332 (CHU 564): Chassis new -/36 with a Bristol B34D body; body transferred to Bristol L5G HW 9493 in
    12/54.
3333 (CHU 565): Chassis new -/36 with a Bristol B34D body; body transferred to Bristol L5G HY 2394 in
    11/54.
3334 (EHT 548): Chassis new 10/37 with a Bristol B34D body.
3335 (BHU 981): Chassis new -/35 with a Bristol B34D body.
3336 (DHY 666): Chassis new 8/37 with a Bristol B34D body; body transferred to Bristol L5G LHW 920 in
    2/59.
3337 (CHT 332): Chassis new -/36 with a Bristol B34D body.
3338 (BHU 969): Chassis new -/35 with a Bristol B34D body.
3339 (BHW 432): Chassis new -/35 with a Bristol B32F body.
3340 (CHW 49): Chassis new -/36 with a Bristol B34D body; body transferred to Bristol L6A JHT 835 in
    11/57.
3341 (CHT 334): Chassis new -/36 with a Bristol B34D body.
3342 (CHT 336): Chassis new -/36 with a Bristol B34D body.
3343 (BHU 637): Chassis new -/35 with a Bristol C32R body; body transferred to Bristol L5G HW 8370 in
    5/55.
3344 (EHT 541): Chassis new 10/37 with a Bristol B34D body.
3345 (AHW 536): Chassis new -/34 with a Bristol C32F body.
3346 (CHU 569): Chassis new -/36 with a Bristol B34D body; body transferred to Bristol L6B LHT 906 in
    11/58.
3347 (CHT 333): Chassis new -/36 with a Bristol B34D body.
3348 (BHU 978): Chassis new -/35 with a Bristol B34D body.
3349 (CHY 821): Chassis new -/36 with a Bristol B34F body; body transferred to Bristol L5G DG 1432 in
    2/55.
3350 (BHY 691): Chassis new -/35 with a Bristol B34D body; body transferred to Bristol L5G HW 9499 in
    12/54.
3351 (CHU 413): Chassis new -/36 with a Bristol B32F body.
3352 (CHU 571): Chassis new -/36 with a Bristol B34D body.
3353 (BHU 979): Chassis new -/35 with a Bristol B34D body; body transferred to Bristol L6B LHT 904 in
    3/59.
3354 (BHW 430): Chassis new -/35 with a Bristol B32F body.
3387-401/42 (HPW 817-32): Were chassisless vehicles built by ECW incorporating Gardner 4LK oil
    engines, Dennis gearbox and other components from withdrawn Dennis Ace vehicles.

3412 (BTR 312): Chassis new 5/38 with a Brush L28/26R body.
3413 (BTR 308): Chassis new 4/38 with a Brush L28/26R body.
3414 (BTR 311): Chassis new 7/38 with a Brush L28/26R body.
3415 (JT 9355): Chassis new 7/38 with a Brush L28/26R body.
3416 (JT 9354): Chassis new 5/38 with a Brush L28/26R body.
3417 (JT 9357): Chassis new 7/38 with a Brush L28/26R body.
3418 (BTR 306): Chassis new 4/38 with a Brush L28/26R body.
3419 (JT 9360): Chassis new 7/38 with a Brush L28/26R body.
3420 (BTR 304): Chassis new 4/38 with a Brush L28/26R body.
3421 (FLJ 429): Chassis new 2/40 with a Beadle (813) B34F body.
3422 (FLJ 433): Chassis new 5/40 with a Beadle (817) B34F body.
3423 (FLJ 435): Chassis new 5/40 with a Beadle (819) B34F body.
3424 (EEL 801): Chassis new 8/38 with a Beadle (682) B31F body.
3425 (FLJ 430): Chassis new 2/40 with a Beadle (814) B34F body.
3426 (FLJ 437): Chassis new 5/40 with a Beadle (821) B34F body.
3427 (BOW 165): Chassis new 7/38 with a Beadle (675) B31F body.
3428 (BOW 163): Chassis new 7/38 with a Beadle (673) B31F body.
3429 (LJ 7093): Chassis new 4/33 with a Brush L26/26R body.
3430 (TK 8914): Chassis new 4/33 with a Brush L26/26R body.
3431 (DTA 423): Chassis new -/37 with a Beadle (611) H30/26R body.
3432 (DTA 425): Chassis new -/37 with a Beadle (613) H30/26R body.
3433 (DTA 422): Chassis new -/37 with a Beadle (610) H30/26R body.
3434 (DTA 424): Chassis new -/37 with a Beadle (612) H30/26R body.
3435 (ETA 966): Chassis new -/37 with a Beadle (628) H30/26R body.
3436 (ETA 967): Chassis new -/37 with a Beadle (629) H30/26R body.
3437 (ETA 984): Chassis new -/37 with a Beadle (624) H30/26R body.
3438 (ETA 986): Chassis new -/37 with a Beadle (626) H30/26R body.
3439 (ETA 985): Chassis new -/37 with a Beadle (625) H30/26R body.
3440 (ETA 987): Chassis new -/37 with a Beadle (627) H30/26R body.
3441 (JC 1343): Body built at Irthlingborough on a chassis new 7/33 with a Massey (846) C32R body; body transferred to Bristol L6A FFM 482 2/58.
3443 (FM 7468): Chassis new 4/33 with a Leyland C32R body; body transferred to Bristol L6A FFM 478 1/58.
3444 (FM 7469): Chassis new 4/33 with a Leyland C32R body; body transferred to Bristol L6A FFM 475 1/58.
3445 (FM 7470): Chassis new 4/33 with a Leyland C32R body; body transferred to Bristol L6A FFM 474 1/58.
3446 (FM 7471): Chassis new 4/33 with a Leyland C32R body; body transferred to Bristol L6A FFM 477 1/58.
3447 (FM 7472): Chassis new 4/33 with a Leyland C32R body; body transferred to Bristol L6A FFM 481 2/58.
3448 (LTA 723): Body originally ordered by Caledonian.
3449 (LTA 887): Body originally ordered by Caledonian.
3452 (KFM 234): scheduled to be loaned to London Transport from new, but did not go on loan.
3453 (KFM 235): scheduled to be loaned to London Transport from new, but did not go on loan.
3454 (KFM 236): scheduled to be loaned to London Transport from new, but did not go on loan.
3463-72 (KFM 245-54): On loan to London Transport from new until 5/50.
3512 (KNG 366): Body fitted with 'standee' windows on the nearside lower deck.
3542 (ONO 51): On loan to London Transport from new until 4/50.
3543-45 (ONO 52-54): On loan to London Transport from new until 5/50.
3546 (ONO 55): On loan to London Transport from new until 6/50.
3776 (EPM 1): On loan to London Transport from new until 5/50.
3777 (EPM 2): On loan to London Transport from new until 5/50.
3778 (EPM 3): On loan to London Transport from new until 6/50.
3779 (EPM 4): had a 4-bay body
3827 (LHY 925): had a 4-bay body
3870 (FM 8153): Chassis new 5/34 with an ECOC (3136) L26/26R body; body transferred to Bristol K6A FFM 538 5/57.
3871 (FM 8150): Chassis new 10/34 with a Leyland L27/26R body; body transferred to Bristol K6A FFM 439 4/57.
3872 (FM 8149): Chassis new 10/34 with a Leyland L27/26R body; body transferred to Bristol K6A FFM 453 4/57.
3873 (FM 8155): Chassis new 5/34 with an ECOC (3138) L26/26R body; body transferred to Bristol K6A FFM 536 4/57.

3874 (FM 8151): Chassis new 5/34 with an ECOC (3134) L26/26R body; body transferred to Bristol K6A FFM 442 4/57.

3875 (FM 8152): Chassis new 5/34 with an ECOC (3135) L26/26R body; body transferred to Bristol K6B FFM 541 6/57.

3876 (FM 8156): Chassis new 5/34 with an ECOC (3137) L26/26R body; body transferred to Bristol K6A FFM 450 5/57.

3877 (FM 9056): Chassis new 6/35 with a Leyland L26/26R body.

3878 (AFM 496): Chassis new 7/36 with an ECW (4323) L26/26R body; body transferred to Bristol K6B GFM 893 6/57.

3879 (FM 9057): Chassis new 6/35 with a Leyland L26/26R body.

3880 (FM 9049): Chassis new 6/35 with a Leyland L26/26R body; body transferred to Bristol K6A FFM 441 2/58.

3881 (FM 9051): Chassis new 6/35 with a Leyland L26/26R body; body transferred to Bristol K6A FFM 447 5/58.

3882 (FM 9052): Chassis new 6/35 with a Leyland L26/26R body; body transferred to Bristol K6A FFM 438 6/58.

3883 (AFM 501): Chassis new 7/36 with an ECW (4327) L26/26R body; body transferred to Bristol K6A FFM 451 5/58.

3884 (FM 9053): Chassis new 6/35 with a Leyland L26/26R body; body transferred to Bristol K6A FFM 443 4/58.

3885 (FM 9054): Chassis new 6/35 with a Leyland L26/26R body; body transferred to Bristol K6A FFM 446 3/58.

3886 (FM 9055): Chassis new 6/35 with a Leyland L26/26R body.

3887 (AFM 495): Chassis new 7/36 with an ECW (4322) L26/26R body.

3888 (AFM 497): Chassis new 7/36 with an ECW (4324) L26/26R body; body transferred to Bristol K6A FFM 448 5/58.

3889 (AFM 499): Chassis new 7/36 with an ECW (4326) L26/26R body.

3890 (BAO 772): Chassis new 4/36 with a Massey (933) L27/26R body.

3891 (DAO  49): Chassis new 6/38 with a Massey (1115) L27/26R body.

3892 (BAO 774): Chassis new 5/36 with a Massey (935) L27/26R body.

3893 (DAO  50): Chassis new 6/38 with a Massey (1116) L27/26R body.

3894 (BRM 594): Chassis new 10/36 with a Massey (982) L27/26R body.

3895 (DAO  51): Chassis new 6/38 with a Massey (1117) L27/26R body.

3896 (BAO 775): Chassis new 4/36 with a Massey (936) L27/26R body.

3897 (BRM 595): Chassis new 10/36 with a Massey (983) L27/26R body.

3898 (BRM 596): Chassis new 10/36 with a Massey (984) L27/26R body.

3899 (NG 3864): Chassis new 3/33 with an ECOC (2870) L30/26R body.

3900 (NG 2729): Chassis new 7/32 with an ECOC (2740) L30/26R body.

3901 (NG 5402): Chassis new 11/33 with an ECOC (3019) H30/26R body.

3902 (VG 4819): Chassis new 9/32 with a Leyland H24/24R body.

3903 (VG 4823): Chassis new 9/32 with a Leyland H24/24R body.

3904 (NG 2723): Chassis new 7/32 with an ECOC (2734) L30/26R body.

3905 (VG 4824): Chassis new 9/32 with a Leyland H24/24R body.

3906 (NG 3867): Chassis new 3/33 with an ECOC (2873) L30/26R body.

3907 (NG 2732): Chassis new 7/32 with an ECOC (2743) L30/26R body.

3908 (VG 4821): Chassis new 9/32 with a Leyland H24/24R body.

3909 (NG 3868): Chassis new 4/33 with an ECOC (2874) H30/26R body.

3910 (VG 4820): Chassis new 9/32 with a Leyland H24/24R body.

3911 (CAE 861): Chassis new -/36 with a Bristol H28/24R body; body transferred to Bristol K6A JAE 256 after chassis was fitted with a PV2 radiator 8/56.

3912 (DHT 942): Chassis new 1/37 with a Bristol H26/26R body; body transferred to Bristol K6B KHT 515 in 2/57.

3913 (CAE 863): Chassis new -/36 with a Bristol H28/24R body; body transferred to Bristol K6A HHY 594 after chassis was fitted with a PV2 radiator 10/55.

3914 (DHT 938): Chassis new 1/37 with a Bristol H26/26R body; body transferred to Bristol K6B KHT 514 in 1/57.

3915 (CHU 707): Chassis new -/36 with a Bristol H28/24R body; body transferred to Bristol K6B KHT 517 in 2/57.

3916 (DHT 940): Chassis new 1/37 with a Bristol H26/26R body; body transferred to Bristol K5G JHT 807 6/57.

3917 (BHW 639): Chassis new -/35 with a Bristol H28/24R body; body transferred to Bristol K6A JAE 764 after chassis was fitted with a PV2 radiator 11/55.

3918 (BHT 532): Chassis new -/35 with a Bristol H28/24R body; body transferred to Bristol K6A JAE 127 after chassis was fitted with a PV2 radiator 6/56.

3919 (CHW 44): Chassis new -/36 with a Bristol H28/24R body; body transferred to Bristol K6A JAE 262 after chassis was fitted with a PV2 radiator 11/56.

3920 (EAE 286): Chassis new 6/37 with a Bristol H28/26R body; body transferred to Bristol K6B KHT 518 in 10/57.

3921 (DAE 371): Chassis new -/36 with a Bristol H26/28R body; body transferred to Bristol K5G JHT 804 1/57.

3922 (CHU 177): Chassis new -/36 with a Bristol H28/24R body; body transferred to Bristol K5G JHT 812 7/57.

3923 (CAE 865): Chassis new -/36 with a Bristol H28/24R body; body transferred to Bristol K6A HHY 591 after chassis was fitted with a PV2 radiator 10/55.

3924 (DHU 352): Chassis new 2/37 with a Bristol H26/26R body; body transferred to Bristol K6A JHT 18 8/56.

3925 (CHU 175): Chassis new -/36 with a Bristol H28/24R body; body transferred to Bristol K6A JAE 130 after chassis was fitted with a PV2 radiator 7/56.

3926 (CHU 706): Chassis new -/36 with a Bristol H28/24R body; body transferred to Bristol K6A JAE 258 after chassis was fitted with a PV2 radiator 8/56.

3927 (CHY 114): Chassis new -/36 with a Bristol H28/24R body; body transferred to Bristol K5G JHT 128 10/56.

3928 (CHU 176): Chassis new -/36 with a Bristol H28/24R body; body transferred to Bristol K6A JAE 766 after chassis was fitted with a PV2 radiator 11/55.

3929 (CHY 443): Chassis new -/36 with a Bristol H28/24R body; body transferred to Bristol K6A HHY 590 after chassis was fitted with a PV2 radiator 7/55.

3930 (DAE 370): Chassis new -/36 with a Bristol H26/28R body; body transferred to Bristol K6A JAE 261 after chassis was fitted with a PV2 radiator 8/56.

3931 (AHY 417): Chassis new -/34 with a Bristol H28/26R body; body transferred to Bristol K6A JHT 19 12/55.

3932 (DHT 939): Chassis new 1/37 with a Bristol H26/26R body; body transferred to Bristol K6A JAE 765 after chassis was fitted with a PV2 radiator 1/56.

3933 (DAE 378): Chassis new -/36 with a Bristol H26/28R body; body transferred to Bristol K6A JAE 260 after chassis was fitted with a PV2 radiator 8/56.

3934 (DHT 941): Chassis new 1/37 with a Bristol H26/26R body; body transferred to Bristol K6A JAE 763 after chassis was fitted with a PV2 radiator 2/56.

3935 (CAE 864): Chassis new -/36 with a Bristol H28/24R body; body transferred to Bristol K6A HHY 592 after chassis was fitted with a PV2 radiator 7/55.

3936 (CHW 42): Chassis new -/36 with a Bristol H28/24R body; body transferred to Bristol K6A JAE 128 after chassis was fitted with a PV2 radiator 6/56.

3937 (CAE 866): Chassis new -/36 with a Bristol H28/24R body; body transferred to Bristol K6A HHY 597 after chassis was fitted with a PV2 radiator 12/55.

3938 (CAE 862): Chassis new -/36 with a Bristol H28/24R body; body transferred to Bristol K5G JHT 805 6/57.

3939 (EAE 597): Chassis new 8/37 with a Bristol H28/26R body; body transferred to Bristol K5G JHT 130 10/56.

3940 (CHU 705): Chassis new -/36 with a Bristol H28/24R body; body transferred to Bristol K6A JAE 264 after chassis was fitted with a PV2 radiator 1/55.

3941 (DKN 44): Chassis new 1/37 with a Bristol H30/26R body; body transferred to Bristol K6B JHT 819 in 3/58.

3942 (DKN 41): Chassis new 12/36 with a Bristol H30/26R body; body transferred to Bristol K6A JHT 116 11/55.

3943 (DKN 46): Chassis new 1/37 with a Bristol H30/26R body; body transferred to Bristol K6B KHY 389 in 1/58.

3944 (DKN 35): Chassis new 12/36 with a Bristol H30/26R body; body transferred to Bristol K6A KHU 619 in 8/56.

3945 (DKN 31): Chassis new 12/36 with a Bristol H30/26R body; body transferred to Bristol K6A JHT 111 11/55.

3946 (VG 4822): Chassis new 9/32 with a Leyland H24/24R body.

3947 (NG 3863): Chassis new 3/33 with an ECOC (2869) L30/26R body.

3948 (NG 3866): Chassis new 3/33 with an ECOC (2872) L30/26R body.

3949 (NG 5405): Chassis new 11/33 with an ECOC (3023) H30/26R body.

3950 (NG 2734): Chassis new 7/32 with an ECOC (2761) L30/26R body.

3951 (NG 3870): Chassis new 4/33 with an ECOC (2876) H30/26R body.

3952 (NG 5403): Chassis new 11/33 with an ECOC (3020) H30/26R body.

3953 (NG 3865): Chassis new 3/33 with an ECOC (2871) L30/26R body.

3954 (NG 5401): Chassis new 11/33 with an ECOC (3018) H30/26R body.

3955 (NG 5406): Chassis new 11/33 with an ECOC (3021) H30/26R body.

3956 (NG 2730): Chassis new 7/32 with an ECOC (2741) L30/26R body.
3957 (NG 3869): Chassis new 4/33 with an ECOC (2875) H30/26R body.
3958 (NG 3861): Chassis new 3/33 with an ECOC (2867) L30/26R body.
3959 (NG 3862): Chassis new 3/33 with an ECOC (2868) L30/26R body.
3960-81 (LHY 950-71): Bodies built at Irthlingborough.
3992-99 (MHW 988-95): Bodies built at Irthlingborough.
4000 (MHW 998): Body built at Irthlingborough.
4001-02 (MHW 996-97): Bodies built at Irthlingborough.
4003 (MHW 999): Body built at Irthlingborough.
4004-06 (JFM 140-42): Bodies originally ordered by Caledonian.
4008-09 (FNV 118-19): Bodies built at Irthlingborough.
4010-16 (JFM 127-33): Bodies built at Irthlingborough.
4033 (KFM 772): Body built at Irthlingborough.
4034-38 (KFM 774-78): Bodies built at Irthlingborough.
4039-41 (KFM 892-94): Bodies built at Irthlingborough.
4058-61 (ONO 991-94): Bodies built at Irthlingborough.
4108 (FMO 19): Body built at Irthlingborough.
4109-11 (LHN 802-04): Bodies built at Irthlingborough.
4112 (LHN 811): Body built at Irthlingborough.
4113-18 (LHN 805-10): Bodies built at Irthlingborough.
4119-34 (LHN 812-27): Bodies built at Irthlingborough.
4135 (LHN 829): Body built at Irthlingborough.
4136 (LHN 828): Body built at Irthlingborough.
4137-40 (LHN 830-33): Bodies built at Irthlingborough.
4141 (LHN 835): Body built at Irthlingborough.
4142 (LHN 837): Body built at Irthlingborough.
4143 (LHN 834): Body built at Irthlingborough.
4144 (LHN 836): Body built at Irthlingborough.
4145-76 (LHN 838-69): Bodies built at Irthlingborough.
4177-79 (NHN 82-84): Bodies built at Irthlingborough.
4180 (NHN 87): Body built at Irthlingborough.
4181-82 (NHN 85-86): Bodies built at Irthlingborough.
4183 (NHN 88): Body built at Irthlingborough.
4184-87 (NHN 90-93): Bodies built at Irthlingborough.
4188 (NHN 89): Body built at Irthlingborough.
4189-94 (NHN 94-99): Bodies built at Irthlingborough.
4190 (NHN 95): Body transferred to Bristol L5G JHN 422 -/50 and body 2114 from JHN 422 fitted in exchange.
4191 (NHN 96): Body transferred to Bristol L5G JHN 423 -/50 and body 2115 from JHN 423 fitted in exchange.
4197 (JWT 283): originally allocated registration number GWX 140.
4198 (JWT 284): originally allocated registration number GWX 141.
4199 (JWT 285): originally allocated registration number GWX 142.
4200 (JWT 286): originally allocated registration number GWX 143.
4201 (JWT 288): originally allocated registration number GWX 145.
4202 (JWT 289): originally allocated registration number GWX 146.
4203 (JWT 290): originally allocated registration number GWX 147.
4204 (JWT 287): originally allocated registration number GWX 144.
4205 (JWT 291): originally allocated registration number GWX 148.
4206 (JWT 292): originally allocated registration number GWX 149.
4207 (JWT 293): originally allocated registration number GWX 150.
4208 (JWT 294): originally allocated registration number GWX 151.
4209 (JWT 295): originally allocated registration number GWX 152.
4210 (JWT 381): Body built at Irthlingborough; originally allocated registration number GWX 152.
4211 (JWT 382): Body built at Irthlingborough.
4241 (FSM 381): Body built at Irthlingborough on a chassis new in -/42 with an East Lancs B35F body.
4242 (ESM 537): Body built at Irthlingborough on a chassis new in 7/39 with an ECW (6564) B35F body.
4243 (ESM 538): Body built at Irthlingborough on a chassis new in 7/39 with an ECW (6563) B35F body.
4244 (FSM 380): Body built at Irthlingborough on a chassis new in -/42 with an East Lancs B35F body.
4245 (FM 8986): Chassis new 6/35 with an ECOC (3685) B32F body.
4246 (FM 8974): Chassis new 6/35 with an ECOC (3679) B32F body.
4247 (FM 8980): Chassis new 6/35 with an ECOC (3673) B32F body.
4248 (FM 8981): Chassis new 6/35 with an ECOC (3677) B32F body.
4249 (FM 8982): Chassis new 6/35 with an ECOC (3687) B32F body.

4250 (FM 8987): Chassis new 6/35 with an ECOC (3667) B32F body.
4251 (FM 8990): Chassis new 6/35 with an ECOC (3670) B34F body.
4252 (FM 8989): Chassis new 6/35 with an ECOC (3669) B32F body.
4253 (FM 8995): Chassis new 6/35 with an ECOC (3688) B34F body.
4254 (FM 8992): Chassis new 6/35 with an ECOC (3674) B34F body.
4256-57 (KNG 697-98): Bodies originally ordered by Caledonian.
4300-05 (LNG 295-300): 8' 0" wide body constructed on a 7' 6" wide chassis.
4321 (KEL 708): Body destroyed by fire and replaced with ECW (6770 Series 1) L27/26R body from APR
    424 in 5/55.
4359 (LTA 953): 8' 0" wide body constructed on a 7' 6" wide chassis.
4395-98 (FRP 694-97): 8' 0" wide body constructed on a 7' 6" wide chassis.
4436 (LTA 832): 8' 0" wide body constructed on a 7' 6" wide chassis.
4451-54 (FNJ 105-08): 8' 0" wide body constructed on a 7' 6" wide chassis.
4487-88 (NAE 40-41): 8' 0" wide body constructed on a 7' 6" wide chassis.
4497-504 (NAE 50-57): 8' 0" wide body constructed on a 7' 6" wide chassis.
4515-19 (LNG 261-65): 8' 0" wide body constructed on a 7' 6" wide chassis.
4538 (BHY 692): Chassis new -/35 with a Bristol H28/24R body; body transferred to Bristol K6A JAE 255
    after chassis was fitted with a PV2 radiator 10/56.
4539 (BHY 695): Chassis new -/35 with a Bristol H28/24R body; body transferred to Bristol K5G JHT 801
    4/57.
4540 (EAE 598): Chassis new 8/37 with a Bristol H28/26R body; body transferred to Bristol K5G JHT 119
    6/56.
4541 (CHW 48): Chassis new -/36 with a Bristol H28/24R body; body transferred to Bristol K5G JHT 809
    9/57.
4542 (DAE 373): Chassis new -/36 with a Bristol H26/28R body; body transferred to Bristol K5G JHT 811
    3/57.
4543 (CHW 835): Chassis new 6/37 with an ECOC (4288) H28/26R body; body transferred to Bristol K5G
    JHT 806 4/57.
4544 (HY 3630): Chassis new 6/32 with a Bristol H24/26R body.
4545 (HY 6896): Chassis new -/32 with a Beadle (267) H26/26R body; body transferred to Bristol K6A JAE
    257 after chassis was fitted with a PV2 radiator 3/55.
4546 (HY 6503): Chassis new -/32 with a Beadle (268) H26/26R body; body transferred to Bristol K5G JHT
    803 1/57.
4547 (HY 6198): Chassis new 6/32 with a Beadle (269) H26/26R body; body transferred to Bristol K5G JAE
    265 after chassis was fitted with a PV2 radiator 3/55.
4548 (CWX 661): Chassis new 10/38 with an ECW (6108) H28/26R body.
4549 (CWX 663): Chassis new 10/38 with an ECW (6110) H28/26R body.
4550 (CWX 657): Chassis new 10/38 with an ECW (6112) H28/26R body.
4551 (CWX 666): Chassis new 11/38 with an ECW (6118) H28/26R body.
4552 (CWX 659): Chassis new 11/38 with an ECW (6115) H28/26R body.
4553 (CWX 660): Chassis new 11/38 with an ECW (6116) H28/26R body.
4554 (CWX 658): Chassis new 10/38 with an ECW (6114) H28/26R body.
4555 (CWX 664): Chassis new 10/38 with an ECW (6111) H28/26R body.
4556 (CWX 665): Chassis new 11/38 with an ECW (6117) H28/26R body.
4557 (CWX 656): Chassis new 11/38 with an ECW (6113) H28/26R body.
4558 (CWX 662): Chassis new 10/38 with an ECW (6109) H28/26R body.
4609-10 (LFM 774-75): 8' 0" wide body constructed on a 7' 6" wide chassis; body built at Irthlingborough.
4611-12 (LFM 777-78): 8' 0" wide body constructed on a 7' 6" wide chassis; body built at Irthlingborough.
4613 (LFM 776): 8' 0" wide body constructed on a 7' 6" wide chassis; body built at Irthlingborough.
4614-17 (LFM 779-82): 8' 0" wide body constructed on a 7' 6" wide chassis; body built at Irthlingborough.
4618 (LFM 784): 8' 0" wide body constructed on a 7' 6" wide chassis; body built at Irthlingborough.
4619 (LFM 783): 8' 0" wide body constructed on a 7' 6" wide chassis; body built at Irthlingborough.
4620-25 (LFM 785-90): Body built at Irthlingborough.
4626-36 (MFM 665-75): 8' 0" wide body constructed on a 7' 6" wide chassis.
4667-69 (LNG 729-31): 8' 0" wide body constructed on a 7' 6" wide chassis.
4685-87 (RHK 131-33): 8' 0" wide body constructed on a 7' 6" wide chassis.
4741-50 (NHN 100-09): Bodies built at Irthlingborough.
4751-802 (NHN 120-71): Bodies built at Irthlingborough.
4830 (JWU 888): 8' 0" wide body constructed on a 7' 6" wide chassis.
4831-37 (JYG 717-23): 8' 0" wide body constructed on a 7' 6" wide chassis.
4893-96 (HBE 505-08): 8' 0" wide body constructed on a 7' 6" wide chassis.
4899 (HBE 756): 8' 0" wide body constructed on a 7' 6" wide chassis.
4930-51 (FRP 832-44): 8' 0" wide body constructed on a 7' 6" wide chassis.
4956-60 (KEL 731-35): 8' 0" wide body constructed on a 7' 6" wide chassis.

4962 (NV 9651): Chassis new 9/37 with an ECW (4933) B35R.
4963 (VV 5697): Chassis new 3/37 with an ECW (4829) B32R.
4964 (NV 9648): Chassis new 8/37 with an ECW (4931) B35R.
4965 (NV 9650): Chassis new 9/37 with an ECW (4932) B35R.
4966 (VV 6259): Chassis new 8/37 with an ECW (4924) B35R.
4967 (NV 9646): Chassis new 8/37 with an ECW (4929) B35R.
4968 (NV 9644): Chassis new 8/37 with an ECW (4927) B35R.
4969 (NV 9643): Chassis new 8/37 with an ECW (4926) B35R.
4970 (NV 9645): Chassis new 8/37 with an ECW (4928) B35R.
4971 (NV 9647): Chassis new 8/37 with an ECW (4930) B35R.
4972 (NV 6639): Chassis new 3/36 with a Burlingham B35R.
4973 (VV 6251): Chassis new 9/37 with an ECW (4934) C31R.
4979 (LFM 811): 8' 0" wide body constructed on a 7' 6" wide chassis.
4980-82 (MFM 662-64): 8' 0" wide body constructed on a 7' 6" wide chassis.

# Delivery Dates

| No. | Date | No. | Date | No. | Date | No. | Date | No. | Date | No. | Date |
|---|---|---|---|---|---|---|---|---|---|---|---|
| 1001 | 22.2.46 | 1063 | 26.7.46 | 1125 | 4.6.46 | 1187 | 18.10.46 | 1249 | 5.11.46 | 1311 | 27.6.47 |
| 1002 | 1.3.46 | 1064 | 26.7.46 | 1126 | 23.5.46 | 1188 | 25.10.46 | 1250 | 11.10.46 | 1312 | 2.4.47 |
| 1003 | 22.2.46 | 1065 | 26.7.46 | 1127 | 31.5.46 | 1189 | 1.11.46 | 1251 | 12.11.46 | 1313 | 2.4.47 |
| 1004 | 22.2.46 | 1066 | 9.8.46 | 1128 | 10.5.46 | 1190 | 7.11.46 | 1252 | 12.11.46 | 1314 | 2.4.47 |
| 1005 | 1.3.46 | 1067 | 18.7.46 | 1129 | 25.5.46 | 1191 | 5.11.46 | 1253 | 15.11.46 | 1315 | 15.4.47 |
| 1006 | 1.3.46 | 1068 | 25.7.46 | 1130 | 25.5.46 | 1192 | 21.11.46 | 1254 | 15.11.46 | 1316 | 1.4.47 |
| 1007 | 1.3.46 | 1069 | 25.7.46 | 1131 | 25.5.46 | 1193 | 15.11.46 | 1255 | 15.11.46 | 1317 | 16.4.47 |
| 1008 | 8.3.46 | 1070 | 25.7.46 | 1132 | 1.6.46 | 1194 | 4.12.46 | 1256 | 15.11.46 | 1318 | 1.3.47 |
| 1009 | 8.3.46 | 1071 | 22.8.46 | 1133 | 14.6.46 | 1195 | 4.12.46 | 1257 | 19.11.46 | 1319 | 16.4.47 |
| 1010 | 8.3.46 | 1072 | 22.8.46 | 1134 | 21.6.46 | 1196 | 3.1.47 | 1258 | 20.11.46 | 1320 | 20.1.47 |
| 1011 | 12.3.46 | 1073 | 16.8.46 | 1135 | 21.6.46 | 1197 | 26.3.47 | 1259 | 23.11.46 | 1321 | 16.4.47 |
| 1012 | 12.3.46 | 1074 | 16.8.46 | 1136 | 21.6.46 | 1198 | 28.11.46 | 1260 | 26.11.46 | 1322 | 3.2.47 |
| 1013 | 15.3.46 | 1075 | 20.8.46 | 1137 | 16.7.46 | 1199 | 13.12.46 | 1261 | 29.1.46 | 1323 | 1.3.47 |
| 1014 | 15.3.46 | 1076 | 20.8.46 | 1138 | 30.5.46 | 1200 | 16.12.46 | 1262 | 4.12.46 | 1324 | 19.3.47 |
| 1015 | 15.3.46 | 1077 | 21.8.46 | 1139 | 3.7.46 | 1201 | 30.12.46 | 1263 | 13.12.46 | 1325 | 17.4.47 |
| 1016 | 28.3.46 | 1078 | 23.8.46 | 1140 | 14.6.46 | 1202 | 2.1.47 | 1264 | 6.12.46 | 1326 | 22.4.47 |
| 1017 | 27.3.46 | 1079 | 13.9.46 | 1141 | 18.12.46 | 1203 | 24.1.47 | 1265 | 4.12.46 | 1327 | 1.5.47 |
| 1018 | 29.3.46 | 1080 | 27.8.46 | 1142 | 14.3.47 | 1204 | 21.3.47 | 1266 | 7.12.46 | 1328 | 1.5.47 |
| 1019 | 29.3.46 | 1081 | 27.8.46 | 1143 | 30.8.46 | 1205 | 6.2.47 | 1267 | 14.12.46 | 1329 | 21.4.47 |
| 1020 | 29.3.46 | 1082 | 29.8.46 | 1144 | 27.8.46 | 1206 | 28.3.47 | 1268 | 7.12.46 | 1330 | 1.5.47 |
| 1021 | 29.3.46 | 1083 | 26.8.46 | 1145 | 21.8.46 | 1207 | 2.4.47 | 1269 | 16.12.46 | 1331 | 30.4.47 |
| 1022 | 29.3.46 | 1084 | 26.8.46 | 1146 | 11.10.46 | 1208 | 16.4.47 | 1270 | 16.12.46 | 1332 | 17.3.47 |
| 1023 | 3.4.46 | 1085 | 14.9.46 | 1147 | 11.10.46 | 1209 | 17.4.47 | 1271 | 20.12.46 | 1333 | 4.7.47 |
| 1024 | 3.4.46 | 1086 | 28.8.46 | 1148 | 24.10.46 | 1210 | 23.4.47 | 1272 | 20.12.46 | 1334 | 7.5.47 |
| 1025 | 8.4.46 | 1087 | 13.9.46 | 1149 | 15.11.46 | 1211 | 24.4.47 | 1273 | 3.1.47 | 1335 | 7.5.47 |
| 1026 | 2.7.46 | 1088 | 20.9.46 | 1150 | 15.11.46 | 1212 | 26.4.47 | 1274 | 19.12.46 | 1336 | 8.5.47 |
| 1027 | 10.7.46 | 1089 | 20.9.46 | 1151 | 26.11.46 | 1213 | 30.4.47 | 1275 | 19.12.46 | 1337 | 4.7.47 |
| 1028 | 10.7.46 | 1090 | 10.10.46 | 1152 | 13.12.46 | 1214 | 30.4.47 | 1276 | 20.12.46 | 1338 | 11.7.47 |
| 1029 | 12.7.46 | 1091 | 9.5.46 | 1153 | 19.12.46 | 1215 | 7.5.47 | 1277 | 3.1.47 | 1339 | 11.7.47 |
| 1030 | 12.7.46 | 1092 | 9.4.46 | 1154 | 24.3.47 | 1216 | 14.5.47 | 1278 | 3.1.47 | 1340 | 20.5.47 |
| 1031 | 12.7.46 | 1093 | 5.4.46 | 1155 | 21.3.47 | 1217 | 14.5.47 | 1279 | 3.1.47 | 1341 | 27.5.47 |
| 1032 | 18.7.46 | 1094 | 30.4.46 | 1156 | 27.3.47 | 1218 | 14.5.47 | 1280 | 8.1.47 | 1342 | 22.5.47 |
| 1033 | 18.7.46 | 1095 | 11.4.46 | 1157 | 27.3.47 | 1219 | 8.5.47 | 1281 | 5.1.47 | 1343 | 15.5.47 |
| 1034 | 2.7.46 | 1096 | 11.4.46 | 1158 | 27.3.47 | 1220 | 8.5.47 | 1282 | 5.1.47 | 1344 | 22.5.47 |
| 1035 | 27.6.46 | 1097 | 11.4.46 | 1159 | 14.3.47 | 1221 | 8.5.47 | 1283 | 5.1.47 | 1345 | 11.7.47 |
| 1036 | 5.7.46 | 1098 | 11.4.46 | 1160 | 20.3.47 | 1222 | 10.5.47 | 1284 | 24.1.47 | 1346 | 22.7.47 |
| 1037 | 28.6.46 | 1099 | 18.4.46 | 1161 | 18.3.47 | 1223 | 15.5.47 | 1285 | 12.6.47 | 1347 | 25.7.47 |
| 1038 | 3.7.46 | 1100 | 18.4.46 | 1162 | 17.4.47 | 1224 | 15.5.47 | 1286 | 13.6.47 | 1348 | 22.7.47 |
| 1039 | 5.7.46 | 1101 | 18.4.46 | 1163 | 17.4.47 | 1225 | 15.5.47 | 1287 | 13.1.47 | 1349 | 25.7.47 |
| 1040 | 16.7.46 | 1102 | 26.4.46 | 1164 | 17.4.47 | 1226 | 23.8.46 | 1288 | 9.1.47 | 1350 | 15.5.47 |
| 1041 | 16.7.46 | 1103 | 26.4.46 | 1165 | 22.4.47 | 1227 | 23.8.46 | 1289 | 13.1.47 | 1351 | 22.5.47 |
| 1042 | 12.7.46 | 1104 | 26.4.46 | 1166 | 22.4.47 | 1228 | 11.6.47 | 1290 | 11.1.47 | 1352 | 23.5.47 |
| 1043 | 12.7.46 | 1105 | 30.4.46 | 1167 | 30.4.47 | 1229 | 10.5.47 | 1291 | 18.1.47 | 1353 | 24.5.47 |
| 1044 | 24.7.46 | 1106 | 26.4.46 | 1168 | 28.8.46 | 1230 | 2.7.47 | 1292 | 21.1.47 | 1354 | 23.5.47 |
| 1045 | 19.7.46 | 1107 | 2.5.46 | 1169 | 28.8.46 | 1231 | 22.5.47 | 1293 | 24.1.47 | 1355 | 30.5.47 |
| 1046 | 25.7.46 | 1108 | 10.5.46 | 1170 | 6.9.46 | 1232 | 16.5.47 | 1294 | 1.4.47 | 1356 | 30.5.47 |
| 1047 | 25.7.46 | 1109 | 10.5.46 | 1171 | 6.9.46 | 1233 | 29.5.47 | 1295 | 6.2.47 | 1357 | 4.6.47 |
| 1048 | 13.8.46 | 1110 | 2.5.46 | 1172 | 6.9.46 | 1234 | 12.6.47 | 1296 | 6.2.47 | 1358 | 28.5.47 |
| 1049 | 9.8.46 | 1111 | 2.5.46 | 1173 | 11.9.46 | 1235 | 19.6.47 | 1297 | 27.2.47 | 1359 | 28.5.47 |
| 1050 | 9.8.46 | 1112 | 3.5.46 | 1174 | 6.9.46 | 1236 | 12.10.46 | 1298 | 13.6.47 | 1360 | 28.5.47 |
| 1051 | 12.7.46 | 1113 | 3.5.46 | 1175 | 13.9.46 | 1237 | 23.9.46 | 1299 | 20.6.47 | 1361 | 11.7.47 |
| 1052 | 12.7.46 | 1114 | 3.5.46 | 1176 | 13.9.46 | 1238 | 25.9.46 | 1300 | 20.6.47 | 1362 | 15.7.47 |
| 1053 | 5.7.46 | 1115 | 16.5.46 | 1177 | 13.9.46 | 1239 | 18.10.46 | 1301 | 17.3.47 | 1363 | 4.6.47 |
| 1054 | 5.7.46 | 1116 | 16.5.46 | 1178 | 13.9.46 | 1240 | 1.10.46 | 1302 | 17.3.47 | 1364 | 4.6.47 |
| 1055 | 20.7.46 | 1117 | 17.5.46 | 1179 | 13.9.46 | 1241 | 1.10.46 | 1303 | 14.3.47 | 1365 | 4.6.47 |
| 1056 | 29.6.46 | 1118 | 16.5.46 | 1180 | 17.9.46 | 1242 | 1.10.46 | 1304 | 14.3.47 | 1366 | 10.6.47 |
| 1057 | 18.7.46 | 1119 | 17.5.46 | 1181 | 26.9.46 | 1243 | 25.10.46 | 1305 | 21.3.47 | 1367 | 10.6.47 |
| 1058 | 26.7.46 | 1120 | 17.5.46 | 1182 | 26.9.46 | 1244 | 24.10.46 | 1306 | 28.3.47 | 1368 | 30.5.47 |
| 1059 | 29.6.46 | 1121 | 17.5.46 | 1183 | 26.9.46 | 1245 | 24.10.46 | 1307 | 21.3.47 | 1369 | 4.6.47 |
| 1060 | 20.7.46 | 1122 | 23.5.46 | 1184 | 20.9.46 | 1246 | 29.10.46 | 1308 | 28.3.47 | 1370 | 10.6.47 |
| 1061 | 22.7.46 | 1123 | 29.5.46 | 1185 | 1.10.46 | 1247 | 1.11.46 | 1309 | 1.4.47 | 1371 | 11.7.47 |
| 1062 | 26.7.46 | 1124 | 31.5.46 | 1186 | 18.10.46 | 1248 | 29.10.46 | 1310 | 27.6.47 | 1372 | 15.7.47 |

B1205/84

| No. | Date | No. | Date | No. | Date | No. | Date | No. | Date | No. | Date |
|---|---|---|---|---|---|---|---|---|---|---|---|
| 1373 | 15.7.47 | 1437 | 21.3.47 | 1501 | 2.11.46 | 1565 | 21.10.47 | 1629 | 25.3.48 | 1693 | 5.12.47 |
| 1374 | 15.7.47 | 1438 | 28.3.47 | 1502 | 26.10.46 | 1566 | 21.10.47 | 1630 | 21.5.48 | 1694 | 12.12.4 |
| 1375 | 4.6.47 | 1439 | 28.3.47 | 1503 | 12.11.46 | 1567 | 28.10.47 | 1631 | 21.5.48 | 1695 | 3.2.48 |
| 1376 | 4.6.47 | 1440 | 3.4.47 | 1504 | 23.11.46 | 1568 | 28.10.47 | 1632 | 28.5.48 | 1696 | 15.2.48 |
| 1377 | 12.6.47 | 1441 | 3.4.47 | 1505 | 12.11.46 | 1569 | 9.12.47 | 1633 | 7.6.48 | 1697 | 8.2.48 |
| 1378 | 11.7.47 | 1442 | 11.4.47 | 1506 | 23.11.46 | 1570 | 9.12.47 | 1634 | 11.6.48 | 1698 | 6.2.48 |
| 1379 | 17.7.47 | 1443 | 11.4.47 | 1507 | 7.12.46 | 1571 | 9.12.47 | 1635 | 23.7.48 | 1699 | 13.2.48 |
| 1380 | 17.7.47 | 1444 | 23.4.47 | 1508 | 30.11.46 | 1572 | 16.12.47 | 1636 | 4.2.47 | 1700 | 14.5.48 |
| 1381 | 17.7.47 | 1445 | 23.4.47 | 1509 | 14.12.46 | 1573 | 16.10.46 | 1637 | 4.2.47 | 1701 | 21.5.48 |
| 1382 | 17.7.47 | 1446 | 25.4.47 | 1510 | 7.12.46 | 1574 | 10.1.47 | 1638 | 4.2.47 | 1702 | 21.5.48 |
| 1383 | 5.6.47 | 1447 | 25.4.47 | 1511 | 10.1.47 | 1575 | 17.1.47 | 1639 | 4.3.47 | 1703 | 23.5.48 |
| 1384 | 11.6.47 | 1448 | 2.5.47 | 1512 | 10.1.47 | 1576 | 31.1.47 | 1640 | 12.3.47 | 1704 | 4.6.48 |
| 1385 | 17.6.47 | 1449 | 2.5.47 | 1513 | 10.1.47 | 1577 | 2.4.47 | 1641 | 4.3.47 | 1705 | 28.5.48 |
| 1386 | 11.6.47 | 1450 | 9.5.47 | 1514 | 18.1.47 | 1578 | 2.4.47 | 1642 | 4.3.47 | 1706 | 5.9.47 |
| 1387 | 11.6.47 | 1451 | 9.5.47 | 1515 | 10.1.47 | 1579 | 6.1.47 | 1643 | 12.3.47 | 1707 | 5.9.47 |
| 1388 | 2.7.47 | 1452 | 9.5.47 | 1516 | 18.1.47 | 1580 | 4.2.47 | 1644 | 12.3.47 | 1708 | 5.9.47 |
| 1389 | 11.6.47 | 1453 | 16.5.47 | 1517 | 25.1.47 | 1581 | 16.1.47 | 1645 | 12.3.47 | 1709 | 16.9.47 |
| 1390 | 18.6.47 | 1454 | 16.5.47 | 1518 | 25.1.47 | 1582 | 21.1.47 | 1646 | 24.3.47 | 1710 | 29.9.47 |
| 1391 | 17.6.47 | 1455 | 16.5.47 | 1519 | 8.2.47 | 1583 | 25.1.47 | 1647 | 24.3.47 | 1711 | 5.12.47 |
| 1392 | 17.6.47 | 1456 | 23.5.47 | 1520 | 8.2.47 | 1584 | 25.1.47 | 1648 | 24.3.47 | 1712 | 1.12.47 |
| 1393 | 18.6.47 | 1457 | 23.5.47 | 1521 | 13.3.47 | 1585 | 31.1.47 | 1649 | 24.3.47 | 1713 | 1.12.47 |
| 1394 | 20.6.47 | 1458 | 23.5.47 | 1522 | 13.3.47 | 1586 | 3.3.47 | 1650 | 1.4.47 | 1714 | 30.1.48 |
| 1395 | 20.6.47 | 1459 | 30.5.47 | 1523 | 18.3.47 | 1587 | 10.3.47 | 1651 | 1.4.47 | 1715 | 30.1.48 |
| 1396 | 20.6.47 | 1460 | 30.5.47 | 1524 | 26.3.47 | 1588 | 4.2.47 | 1652 | 2.4.47 | 1716 | 6.2.48 |
| 1397 | 25.6.47 | 1461 | 6.6.47 | 1525 | 26.3.47 | 1589 | 29.8.47 | 1653 | 2.4.47 | 1717 | 25.3.48 |
| 1398 | 26.6.47 | 1462 | 6.6.47 | 1526 | 1.4.47 | 1590 | 5.9.47 | 1654 | 21.4.47 | 1718 | 25.3.48 |
| 1399 | 2.7.47 | 1463 | 13.6.47 | 1527 | 15.4.47 | 1591 | 19.9.47 | 1655 | 21.4.47 | 1719 | 4.6.48 |
| 1400 | 25.6.47 | 1464 | 23.11.46 | 1528 | 3.4.47 | 1592 | 19.9.47 | 1656 | 21.4.47 | 1720 | 4.6.48 |
| 1401 | 26.6.47 | 1465 | 23.11.46 | 1529 | 15.4.47 | 1593 | 19.9.47 | 1657 | 21.4.47 | 1721 | 16.9.47 |
| 1402 | 3.7.47 | 1466 | 23.11.46 | 1530 | 29.4.47 | 1594 | 19.9.47 | 1658 | 1.5.47 | 1722 | 16.9.47 |
| 1403 | 26.6.47 | 1467 | 30.11.46 | 1531 | 29.4.47 | 1595 | 19.9.47 | 1659 | 1.5.47 | 1723 | 14.11.4 |
| 1404 | 1.7.47 | 1468 | 30.11.46 | 1532 | 29.4.47 | 1596 | 12.9.47 | 1660 | 5.5.47 | 1724 | 21.11.4 |
| 1405 | 30.6.47 | 1469 | 30.4.47 | 1533 | 6.5.47 | 1597 | 19.9.47 | 1661 | 18.8.47 | 1725 | 30.10.4 |
| 1406 | 2.7.47 | 1470 | 30.4.47 | 1534 | 6.5.47 | 1598 | 26.9.47 | 1662 | 18.8.47 | 1726 | 14.11.4 |
| 1407 | 2.7.47 | 1471 | 30.4.47 | 1535 | 11.6.47 | 1599 | 26.9.47 | 1663 | 12.12.47 | 1727 | 19.3.48 |
| 1408 | 2.7.47 | 1472 | 14.5.47 | 1536 | 11.6.47 | 1600 | 7.11.47 | 1664 | 30.10.47 | 1728 | 25.3.48 |
| 1409 | 19.2.47 | 1473 | 14.5.47 | 1537 | 1.7.47 | 1601 | 7.11.47 | 1665 | 15.12.47 | 1729 | 9.4.48 |
| 1410 | 20.3.47 | 1474 | 14.5.47 | 1538 | 17.6.47 | 1602 | 1.11.47 | 1666 | 12.12.47 | 1730 | 9.4.48 |
| 1411 | 27.3.47 | 1475 | 16.5.47 | 1539 | 24.6.47 | 1603 | 7.11.47 | 1667 | 12.12.47 | 1731 | 2.12.47 |
| 1412 | 20.5.47 | 1476 | 16.5.47 | 1540 | 15.7.47 | 1604 | 7.11.47 | 1668 | 13.2.48 | 1732 | 4.12.47 |
| 1413 | 20.5.47 | 1477 | 23.5.47 | 1541 | 22.7.47 | 1605 | 7.11.47 | 1669 | 13.2.48 | 1733 | 4.2.48 |
| 1414 | 23.5.47 | 1478 | 23.5.47 | 1542 | 22.7.47 | 1606 | 21.11.47 | 1670 | 24.3.48 | 1734 | 11.2.48 |
| 1415 | 23.5.47 | 1479 | 28.5.47 | 1543 | 15.7.47 | 1607 | 29.11.47 | 1671 | 24.3.48 | 1735 | 11.2.48 |
| 1416 | 14.6.47 | 1480 | 28.5.47 | 1544 | 26.7.47 | 1608 | 27.11.47 | 1672 | 24.3.48 | 1736 | 13.2.48 |
| 1417 | 2.7.47 | 1481 | 5.6.47 | 1545 | 26.7.47 | 1609 | 27.11.47 | 1673 | 2.4.48 | 1737 | 25.3.48 |
| 1418 | 2.7.47 | 1482 | 5.6.47 | 1546 | 28.7.47 | 1610 | 4.12.47 | 1674 | 25.3.48 | 1738 | 25.3.48 |
| 1419 | 2.7.47 | 1483 | 12.6.47 | 1547 | 15.8.47 | 1611 | 22.8.47 | 1675 | 2.4.48 | 1739 | 31.3.48 |
| 1420 | 8.7.47 | 1484 | 18.6.47 | 1548 | 28.7.47 | 1612 | 26.8.47 | 1676 | 25.8.47 | 1740 | 20.5.48 |
| 1421 | 2.7.47 | 1485 | 18.6.47 | 1549 | 19.8.47 | 1613 | 5.9.47 | 1677 | 29.8.47 | 1741 | 21.11.4 |
| 1422 | 3.7.47 | 1486 | 18.6.47 | 1550 | 26.8.47 | 1614 | 3.10.47 | 1678 | 5.9.47 | 1742 | 21.11.4 |
| 1423 | 3.7.47 | 1487 | 26.6.47 | 1551 | 19.8.47 | 1615 | 30.10.47 | 1679 | 5.9.47 | 1743 | 28.11.4 |
| 1424 | 8.7.47 | 1488 | 26.6.47 | 1552 | 28.8.47 | 1616 | 30.10.47 | 1680 | 12.9.47 | 1744 | 30.1.48 |
| 1425 | 10.7.47 | 1489 | 29.5.47 | 1553 | 2.9.47 | 1617 | 21.11.47 | 1681 | 3.10.47 | 1745 | 9.4.48 |
| 1426 | 2.7.47 | 1490 | 31.5.47 | 1554 | 16.9.47 | 1618 | 21.11.47 | 1682 | 3.10.47 | 1746 | 2.4.48 |
| 1427 | 3.7.47 | 1491 | 29.5.47 | 1555 | 2.9.47 | 1619 | 28.11.47 | 1683 | 7.11.47 | 1747 | 14.5.48 |
| 1428 | 10.7.47 | 1492 | 25.5.47 | 1556 | 16.9.47 | 1620 | 30.1.48 | 1684 | 7.11.47 | 1748 | 25.5.48 |
| 1429 | 10.7.47 | 1493 | 19.10.46 | 1557 | 23.9.47 | 1621 | 30.1.48 | 1685 | 14.11.47 | 1749 | 5.12.47 |
| 1430 | 8.7.47 | 1494 | 19.10.46 | 1558 | 23.9.47 | 1622 | 6.2.48 | 1686 | 14.11.47 | 1750 | 5.12.47 |
| 1431 | 12.7.47 | 1495 | 26.10.46 | 1559 | 25.9.47 | 1623 | 13.2.48 | 1687 | 16.11.47 | 1751 | 12.12.4 |
| 1432 | 10.7.47 | 1496 | 26.10.46 | 1560 | 25.9.47 | 1624 | 20.2.48 | 1688 | 16.11.47 | 1752 | 30.1.48 |
| 1433 | 10.7.47 | 1497 | 19.10.46 | 1561 | 30.9.47 | 1625 | 13.2.48 | 1689 | 21.11.47 | 1753 | 30.1.48 |
| 1434 | 10.7.47 | 1498 | 14.10.46 | 1562 | 30.9.47 | 1626 | 19.3.48 | 1690 | 28.11.47 | 1754 | 12.3.48 |
| 1435 | 12.7.47 | 1499 | 2.11.46 | 1563 | 2.10.47 | 1627 | 19.3.48 | 1691 | 30.11.47 | 1755 | 25.3.48 |
| 1436 | 19.3.47 | 1500 | 26.10.46 | 1564 | 2.10.47 | 1628 | 25.3.48 | 1692 | 2.12.47 | 1756 | 19.3.48 |

| | | | | | | | | | | | |
|---|---|---|---|---|---|---|---|---|---|---|---|
| 1757 | 25.3.48 | 1821 | 15.8.47 | 1885 | 8.7.48 | 1949 | 7.4.48 | 2013 | 19.3.48 | 2077 | 6.2.48 |
| 1758 | 14.5.48 | 1822 | 29.8.47 | 1886 | 9.7.48 | 1950 | 28.5.48 | 2014 | 2.4.48 | 2078 | 6.2.48 |
| 1759 | 14.5.48 | 1823 | 29.8.47 | 1887 | 9.7.48 | 1951 | 21.5.48 | 2015 | 7.5.48 | 2079 | 13.2.48 |
| 1760 | 14.5.48 | 1824 | 29.8.47 | 1888 | 16.7.48 | 1952 | 25.3.48 | 2016 | 8.8.47 | 2080 | 13.2.48 |
| 1761 | 17.6.48 | 1825 | 14.11.47 | 1889 | 16.7.48 | 1953 | 2.6.48 | 2017 | 8.8.47 | 2081 | 13.2.48 |
| 1762 | 4.6.48 | 1826 | 21.1.48 | 1890 | 24.7.48 | 1954 | 11.6.48 | 2018 | 15.8.47 | 2082 | 20.2.48 |
| 1763 | 17.6.48 | 1827 | 15.1.48 | 1891 | 1.9.48 | 1955 | 17.10.47 | 2019 | 15.8.47 | 2083 | 20.2.48 |
| 1764 | 11.6.48 | 1828 | 21.1.48 | 1892 | 17.9.48 | 1956 | 31.12.47 | 2020 | 22.8.47 | 2084 | 20.2.48 |
| 1765 | 15.8.47 | 1829 | 21.1.48 | 1893 | 16.7.48 | 1957 | 7.11.47 | 2021 | 22.8.47 | 2085 | 27.2.48 |
| 1766 | 22.8.47 | 1830 | 21.1.48 | 1894 | 24.7.48 | 1958 | 14.11.47 | 2022 | 29.8.47 | 2086 | 27.2.48 |
| 1767 | 22.8.47 | 1831 | 23.1.48 | 1895 | 24.7.48 | 1959 | 12.12.47 | 2023 | 5.9.47 | 2087 | 27.2.48 |
| 1768 | 29.8.47 | 1832 | 23.1.48 | 1896 | 19.12.47 | 1960 | 31.12.47 | 2024 | 5.9.47 | 2088 | 5.3.48 |
| 1769 | 15.9.47 | 1833 | 23.1.48 | 1897 | 19.12.47 | 1961 | 31.12.47 | 2025 | 12.9.47 | 2089 | 5.3.48 |
| 1770 | 15.9.47 | 1834 | 29.1.48 | 1898 | 12.12.47 | 1962 | 7.1.48 | 2026 | 12.9.47 | 2090 | 5.3.48 |
| 1771 | 19.9.47 | 1835 | 24.1.48 | 1899 | 20.2.48 | 1963 | 7.1.48 | 2027 | 19.9.47 | 2091 | 14.5.48 |
| 1772 | 19.9.47 | 1836 | 24.1.48 | 1900 | 20.2.48 | 1964 | 7.1.48 | 2028 | 19.9.47 | 2092 | 12.3.48 |
| 1773 | 29.9.47 | 1837 | 29.1.48 | 1901 | 1.9.47 | 1965 | 7.1.48 | 2029 | 3.10.47 | 2093 | 12.3.48 |
| 1774 | 29.9.47 | 1838 | 13.2.48 | 1902 | 21.8.47 | 1966 | 23.1.48 | 2030 | 26.9.47 | 2094 | 19.3.48 |
| 1775 | 5.12.47 | 1839 | 20.2.48 | 1903 | 3.11.47 | 1967 | 23.1.48 | 2031 | 3.10.47 | 2095 | 19.3.48 |
| 1776 | 20.11.47 | 1840 | 20.2.48 | 1904 | 23.1.48 | 1968 | 15.1.48 | 2032 | 14.10.47 | 2096 | 19.3.48 |
| 1777 | 5.12.47 | 1841 | 20.2.48 | 1905 | 7.5.48 | 1969 | 5.2.48 | 2033 | 14.10.47 | 2097 | 25.3.48 |
| 1778 | 5.12.47 | 1842 | 20.2.48 | 1906 | 14.5.48 | 1970 | 5.2.48 | 2034 | 23.10.47 | 2098 | 21.5.48 |
| 1779 | 30.1.48 | 1843 | 20.2.48 | 1907 | 14.5.48 | 1971 | 5.2.48 | 2035 | 17.10.47 | 2099 | 1.6.48 |
| 1780 | 30.1.48 | 1844 | 20.2.48 | 1908 | 7.5.48 | 1972 | 12.2.48 | 2036 | 23.10.47 | 2100 | 4.6.48 |
| 1781 | 6.2.48 | 1845 | 25.2.48 | 1909 | 14.5.48 | 1973 | 12.2.48 | 2037 | 31.10.47 | 2101 | 11.6.48 |
| 1782 | 6.2.48 | 1846 | 25.2.48 | 1910 | 14.5.48 | 1974 | 18.2.48 | 2038 | 31.10.47 | 2102 | 18.6.48 |
| 1783 | 6.2.48 | 1847 | 25.2.48 | 1911 | 26.9.47 | 1975 | 18.2.48 | 2039 | 7.11.47 | 2103 | 25.6.48 |
| 1784 | 6.2.48 | 1848 | 27.2.48 | 1912 | 10.10.47 | 1976 | 18.2.48 | 2040 | 7.11.47 | 2104 | 13.7.48 |
| 1785 | 13.2.48 | 1849 | 27.2.48 | 1913 | 21.11.47 | 1977 | 26.2.48 | 2041 | 7.11.47 | 2105 | 16.7.48 |
| 1786 | 2.4.48 | 1850 | 27.2.48 | 1914 | 14.11.47 | 1978 | 26.2.48 | 2042 | 14.11.47 | 2106 | 18.6.48 |
| 1787 | 2.4.48 | 1851 | 27.2.48 | 1915 | 12.9.47 | 1979 | 26.2.48 | 2043 | 14.11.47 | 2107 | 25.6.48 |
| 1788 | 11.6.48 | 1852 | 8.4.48 | 1916 | 2.9.47 | 1980 | 17.3.48 | 2044 | 14.11.47 | 2108 | 2.7.48 |
| 1789 | 11.6.48 | 1853 | 8.4.48 | 1917 | 25.9.47 | 1981 | 1.4.48 | 2045 | 21.11.47 | 2109 | 13.7.48 |
| 1790 | 16.7.48 | 1854 | 1.4.48 | 1918 | 25.9.47 | 1982 | 7.4.48 | 2046 | 21.11.47 | 2110 | 13.7.48 |
| 1791 | 16.7.48 | 1855 | 11.5.48 | 1919 | 14.10.47 | 1983 | 13.5.48 | 2047 | 21.11.47 | 2111 | 16.7.48 |
| 1792 | 14.11.47 | 1856 | 11.5.48 | 1920 | 14.10.47 | 1984 | 20.5.48 | 2048 | 28.11.47 | 2112 | 16.7.48 |
| 1793 | 7.11.47 | 1857 | 8.4.48 | 1921 | 14.10.47 | 1985 | 27.5.48 | 2049 | 28.11.47 | 2113 | 23.7.48 |
| 1794 | 5.12.47 | 1858 | 11.5.48 | 1922 | 28.10.47 | 1986 | 3.6.48 | 2050 | 28.11.47 | 2114 | 23.7.48 |
| 1795 | 5.12.47 | 1859 | 8.4.48 | 1923 | 28.10.47 | 1987 | 10.6.48 | 2051 | 5.12.47 | 2115 | 16.9.48 |
| 1796 | 25.3.48 | 1860 | 8.4.48 | 1924 | 10.10.47 | 1988 | 18.6.48 | 2052 | 5.12.47 | 2116 | 26.8.47 |
| 1797 | 28.5.48 | 1861 | 11.5.48 | 1925 | 17.10.47 | 1989 | 18.6.48 | 2053 | 5.12.47 | 2117 | 26.9.47 |
| 1798 | 11.6.48 | 1862 | 11.5.48 | 1926 | 30.10.47 | 1990 | 3.7.48 | 2054 | 12.12.47 | 2118 | 3.10.47 |
| 1799 | 21.11.47 | 1863 | 8.4.48 | 1927 | 7.11.47 | 1991 | 3.7.48 | 2055 | 12.12.47 | 2119 | 12.11.47 |
| 1800 | 28.11.47 | 1864 | 11.5.48 | 1928 | 17.12.47 | 1992 | 3.7.48 | 2056 | 12.12.47 | 2120 | 2.1.48 |
| 1801 | 16.12.47 | 1865 | 14.5.48 | 1929 | 15.12.47 | 1993 | 12.7.48 | 2057 | 19.12.47 | 2121 | 23.1.48 |
| 1802 | 16.12.47 | 1866 | 21.5.48 | 1930 | 15.12.47 | 1994 | 28.8.48 | 2058 | 19.12.47 | 2122 | 16.1.48 |
| 1803 | 22.3.48 | 1867 | 14.5.48 | 1931 | 22.12.47 | 1995 | 24.10.47 | 2059 | 19.12.47 | 2123 | 30.1.48 |
| 1804 | 24.3.48 | 1868 | 14.5.48 | 1932 | 22.12.47 | 1996 | 2.4.48 | 2060 | 23.12.47 | 2124 | 6.2.48 |
| 1805 | 11.6.47 | 1869 | 14.5.48 | 1933 | 17.12.47 | 1997 | 30.1.48 | 2061 | 6.1.48 | 2125 | 19.3.48 |
| 1806 | 18.7.47 | 1870 | 14.5.48 | 1934 | 17.12.47 | 1998 | 29.2.48 | 2062 | 6.1.48 | 2126 | 21.5.48 |
| 1807 | 18.7.47 | 1871 | 21.5.48 | 1935 | 23.1.48 | 1999 | 20.2.48 | 2063 | 6.1.48 | 2127 | 21.5.48 |
| 1808 | 24.7.47 | 1872 | 21.5.48 | 1936 | 23.1.48 | 2000 | 27.2.48 | 2064 | 9.1.48 | 2128 | 28.5.48 |
| 1809 | 1.8.47 | 1873 | 14.5.48 | 1937 | 30.1.48 | 2001 | 2.1.48 | 2065 | 9.1.48 | 2129 | 11.6.48 |
| 1810 | 24.7.47 | 1874 | 14.5.48 | 1938 | 30.1.48 | 2002 | 2.1.48 | 2066 | 9.1.48 | 2130 | 11.6.48 |
| 1811 | 24.7.47 | 1875 | 28.5.48 | 1939 | 6.2.48 | 2003 | 16.1.48 | 2067 | 16.1.48 | 2131 | 18.6.48 |
| 1812 | 24.7.47 | 1876 | 1.7.48 | 1940 | 6.2.48 | 2004 | 9.1.48 | 2068 | 16.1.48 | 2132 | 23.7.48 |
| 1813 | 1.8.47 | 1877 | 17.6.48 | 1941 | 8.3.48 | 2005 | 16.1.48 | 2069 | 16.1.48 | 2133 | 23.7.48 |
| 1814 | 1.8.47 | 1878 | 1.7.48 | 1942 | 8.3.48 | 2006 | 16.1.48 | 2070 | 23.1.48 | 2134 | 23.7.48 |
| 1815 | 1.8.47 | 1879 | 1.7.48 | 1943 | 10.3.48 | 2007 | 5.3.48 | 2071 | 23.1.48 | 2135 | 23.7.48 |
| 1816 | 1.8.47 | 1880 | 1.7.48 | 1944 | 8.3.48 | 2008 | 5.3.48 | 2072 | 23.1.48 | 2136 | 22.7.47 |
| 1817 | 1.8.47 | 1881 | 6.7.48 | 1945 | 19.3.48 | 2009 | 5.3.48 | 2073 | 30.1.48 | 2137 | 24.7.47 |
| 1818 | 15.8.47 | 1882 | 1.7.48 | 1946 | 25.3.48 | 2010 | 12.3.48 | 2074 | 30.1.48 | 2138 | 24.7.47 |
| 1819 | 15.8.47 | 1883 | 6.7.48 | 1947 | 25.3.48 | 2011 | 12.3.48 | 2075 | 30.1.48 | 2139 | 22.7.47 |
| 1820 | 15.8.47 | 1884 | 8.7.48 | 1948 | 2.4.48 | 2012 | 19.3.48 | 2076 | 6.2.48 | 2140 | 29.7.47 |

| | | | | | | | | | | | |
|---|---|---|---|---|---|---|---|---|---|---|---|
| 2141 | 29.7.47 | 2205 | 9.11.47 | 2269 | 17.10.47 | 2333 | 23.3.48 | 2397 | 19.10.48 | 2461 | 26.10.4 |
| 2142 | 29.7.47 | 2206 | 9.11.47 | 2270 | 24.10.47 | 2334 | 17.3.48 | 2398 | 15.11.48 | 2462 | 26.10.4 |
| 2143 | 13.8.47 | 2207 | 30.10.47 | 2271 | 9.1.48 | 2335 | ??.5.48 | 2399 | 15.11.48 | 2463 | 28.10.4 |
| 2144 | 19.8.47 | 2208 | 9.11.47 | 2272 | 9.1.48 | 2336 | 28.5.48 | 2400 | 19.11.48 | 2464 | 28.10.4 |
| 2145 | 19.8.47 | 2209 | 30.10.47 | 2273 | 9.1.48 | 2337 | 1.6.48 | 2401 | 19.11.48 | 2465 | 2.11.48 |
| 2146 | 22.8.47 | 2210 | 9.11.47 | 2274 | 19.12.47 | 2338 | 28.5.48 | 2402 | 19.11.48 | 2466 | 2.11.48 |
| 2147 | 2.9.47 | 2211 | 9.11.47 | 2275 | 19.12.47 | 2339 | 23.1.48 | 2403 | 19.11.48 | 2467 | 9.11.48 |
| 2148 | 5.9.47 | 2212 | 14.11.47 | 2276 | 19.12.47 | 2340 | 23.1.48 | 2404 | 15.11.48 | 2468 | 3.11.48 |
| 2149 | 5.9.47 | 2213 | 9.11.47 | 2277 | 22.12.47 | 2341 | 29.1.48 | 2405 | 19.11.48 | 2469 | 9.11.48 |
| 2150 | 5.9.47 | 2214 | 6.6.47 | 2278 | 22.12.47 | 2342 | 29.1.48 | 2406 | 19.11.48 | 2470 | 12.11.4 |
| 2151 | 18.9.47 | 2215 | 10.6.47 | 2279 | 22.12.47 | 2343 | 29.1.48 | 2407 | 19.11.48 | 2471 | 12.11.4 |
| 2152 | 3.10.47 | 2216 | 12.6.47 | 2280 | 5.3.48 | 2344 | 10.3.48 | 2408 | 19.10.48 | 2472 | 30.11.4 |
| 2153 | 1.10.47 | 2217 | 18.6.47 | 2281 | 5.3.48 | 2345 | 2.3.48 | 2409 | 25.5.48 | 2473 | 30.11.4 |
| 2154 | 3.10.47 | 2218 | 19.6.47 | 2282 | 5.3.48 | 2346 | 10.3.48 | 2410 | 25.5.48 | 2474 | 1.10.48 |
| 2155 | 8.10.47 | 2219 | 25.6.47 | 2283 | 5.3.48 | 2347 | 10.3.48 | 2411 | 1.6.48 | 2475 | 1.10.48 |
| 2156 | 1.10.47 | 2220 | 26.6.47 | 2284 | 8.3.48 | 2348 | 17.3.48 | 2412 | 25.5.48 | 2476 | 8.10.48 |
| 2157 | 8.10.47 | 2221 | 2.7.47 | 2285 | 5.3.48 | 2349 | 2.12.47 | 2413 | 25.5.48 | 2477 | 19.10.4 |
| 2158 | 8.10.47 | 2222 | 8.7.47 | 2286 | 10.3.48 | 2350 | 2.12.47 | 2414 | 1.6.48 | 2478 | 1.12.48 |
| 2159 | 15.10.47 | 2223 | 8.7.47 | 2287 | 12.3.48 | 2351 | 2.12.47 | 2415 | 1.6.48 | 2479 | 27.8.48 |
| 2160 | 26.11.47 | 2224 | 17.7.47 | 2288 | 12.3.48 | 2352 | 7.11.47 | 2416 | 1.6.48 | 2480 | 27.8.48 |
| 2161 | 26.11.47 | 2225 | 17.7.47 | 2289 | 1.1.48 | 2353 | 7.11.47 | 2417 | 1.6.48 | 2481 | 3.9.48 |
| 2162 | 28.11.47 | 2226 | 23.7.47 | 2290 | 31.12.47 | 2354 | 11.11.47 | 2418 | 1.6.48 | 2482 | 27.8.48 |
| 2163 | 28.11.47 | 2227 | 23.7.47 | 2291 | 1.1.48 | 2355 | 14.11.47 | 2419 | 8.6.48 | 2483 | 1.9.48 |
| 2164 | 3.12.47 | 2228 | 26.7.47 | 2292 | 1.1.48 | 2356 | 17.2.48 | 2420 | 8.6.48 | 2484 | 3.9.48 |
| 2165 | 10.12.47 | 2229 | 26.7.47 | 2293 | 1.1.48 | 2357 | 17.2.48 | 2421 | 8.6.48 | 2485 | 3.9.48 |
| 2166 | 10.12.47 | 2230 | 15.8.47 | 2294 | 2.1.48 | 2358 | 17.2.48 | 2422 | 15.6.48 | 2486 | 3.9.48 |
| 2167 | 17.12.47 | 2231 | 15.8.47 | 2295 | 2.1.48 | 2359 | 17.2.48 | 2423 | 15.6.48 | 2487 | 10.9.48 |
| 2168 | 24.10.47 | 2232 | 15.8.47 | 2296 | 2.1.48 | 2360 | 24.5.48 | 2424 | 15.6.48 | 2488 | 1.10.48 |
| 2169 | 30.10.47 | 2233 | 18.8.47 | 2297 | 2.1.48 | 2361 | 21.6.48 | 2425 | 22.6.48 | 2489 | 1.10.48 |
| 2170 | 30.10.47 | 2234 | 22.8.47 | 2298 | 2.1.48 | 2362 | 21.6.48 | 2426 | 22.6.48 | 2490 | 1.1.49 |
| 2171 | 30.10.47 | 2235 | 22.8.47 | 2299 | 3.10.47 | 2363 | 21.6.48 | 2427 | 22.6.48 | 2491 | 12.3.49 |
| 2172 | 30.10.47 | 2236 | 22.8.47 | 2300 | 6.10.47 | 2364 | 21.6.48 | 2428 | 22.6.48 | 2492 | 20.8.48 |
| 2173 | 14.11.47 | 2237 | 29.8.47 | 2301 | 3.10.47 | 2365 | 21.6.48 | 2429 | 22.6.48 | 2493 | 26.8.48 |
| 2174 | 14.11.47 | 2238 | 29.8.47 | 2302 | 2.1.48 | 2366 | 28.6.48 | 2430 | 22.6.48 | 2494 | 26.8.48 |
| 2175 | 14.11.47 | 2239 | 6.10.47 | 2303 | 20.1.48 | 2367 | 28.6.48 | 2431 | 15.6.48 | 2495 | 27.8.48 |
| 2176 | 29.6.48 | 2240 | 6.10.47 | 2304 | 9.1.48 | 2368 | 28.6.48 | 2432 | 22.6.48 | 2496 | 27.8.48 |
| 2177 | 1.7.48 | 2241 | 6.10.47 | 2305 | 16.1.48 | 2369 | 28.6.48 | 2433 | 22.6.48 | 2497 | 3.9.48 |
| 2178 | 1.7.48 | 2242 | 10.10.47 | 2306 | 22.1.48 | 2370 | 28.6.48 | 2434 | 5.6.48 | 2498 | 1.10.48 |
| 2179 | 8.7.48 | 2243 | 10.10.47 | 2307 | 11.1.48 | 2371 | 28.6.48 | 2435 | 5.6.48 | 2499 | 11.10.4 |
| 2180 | 8.7.48 | 2244 | 10.10.47 | 2308 | 11.1.48 | 2372 | 20.7.48 | 2436 | 5.6.48 | 2500 | 19.11.4 |
| 2181 | 8.7.48 | 2245 | 17.10.47 | 2309 | 9.1.48 | 2373 | 20.7.48 | 2437 | 15.6.48 | 2501 | 27.11.4 |
| 2182 | 13.8.48 | 2246 | 24.10.47 | 2310 | 16.1.48 | 2374 | 20.7.48 | 2438 | 5.6.48 | 2502 | 19.11.4 |
| 2183 | 13.8.48 | 2247 | 24.10.47 | 2311 | 9.1.48 | 2375 | 20.7.48 | 2439 | 15.6.48 | 2503 | 13.11.4 |
| 2184 | 27.8.48 | 2248 | 24.10.47 | 2312 | 19.3.48 | 2376 | 20.7.48 | 2440 | 29.6.48 | 2504 | 13.11.4 |
| 2185 | 28.8.48 | 2249 | 1.9.47 | 2313 | 12.3.48 | 2377 | 20.7.48 | 2441 | 21.6.48 | 2505 | 2.12.48 |
| 2186 | 18.9.48 | 2250 | 5.9.47 | 2314 | 9.10.47 | 2378 | 28.7.48 | 2442 | 21.6.48 | 2506 | 2.12.48 |
| 2187 | 24.9.48 | 2251 | 5.9.47 | 2315 | 9.10.47 | 2379 | 28.7.48 | 2443 | 29.6.48 | 2507 | 6.12.48 |
| 2188 | 24.9.48 | 2252 | 12.9.47 | 2316 | 17.10.47 | 2380 | 28.7.48 | 2444 | 29.6.48 | 2508 | 6.12.48 |
| 2189 | 1.10.48 | 2253 | 12.9.47 | 2317 | 17.10.47 | 2381 | 28.7.48 | 2445 | 29.6.48 | 2509 | 6.12.48 |
| 2190 | 10.10.47 | 2254 | 20.10.47 | 2318 | 23.12.47 | 2382 | 23.8.48 | 2446 | 6.7.48 | 2510 | 13.12.4 |
| 2191 | 10.10.47 | 2255 | 20.10.47 | 2319 | 23.12.47 | 2383 | 23.8.48 | 2447 | 29.6.48 | 2511 | 13.12.4 |
| 2192 | 17.10.47 | 2256 | 17.10.47 | 2320 | 23.12.47 | 2384 | 27.9.48 | 2448 | 6.7.48 | 2512 | 20.12.4 |
| 2193 | 17.10.47 | 2257 | 20.10.47 | 2321 | 1.1.48 | 2385 | 27.9.48 | 2449 | 6.7.48 | 2513 | 20.12.4 |
| 2194 | 27.10.47 | 2258 | 24.10.47 | 2322 | 3.3.48 | 2386 | 27.9.48 | 2450 | 6.7.48 | 2514 | 11.3.49 |
| 2195 | 9.1.48 | 2259 | 24.10.47 | 2323 | 28.2.48 | 2387 | 16.9.48 | 2451 | 13.7.48 | 2515 | 20.12.4 |
| 2196 | 2.1.48 | 2260 | 24.10.47 | 2324 | 28.2.48 | 2388 | 16.9.48 | 2452 | 13.7.48 | 2516 | 11.3.49 |
| 2197 | 2.1.48 | 2261 | 27.10.47 | 2325 | 28.2.48 | 2389 | 1.10.48 | 2453 | 6.7.48 | 2517 | 1.1.49 |
| 2198 | 9.1.48 | 2262 | 10.10.47 | 2326 | 10.3.48 | 2390 | 1.10.48 | 2454 | 13.7.48 | 2518 | 1.1.49 |
| 2199 | 14.5.48 | 2263 | 14.10.47 | 2327 | 10.3.48 | 2391 | 1.10.48 | 2455 | 13.7.48 | 2519 | 5.3.49 |
| 2200 | 5.9.47 | 2264 | 14.10.47 | 2328 | 10.3.48 | 2392 | 1.10.48 | 2456 | 13.7.48 | 2520 | 26.2.49 |
| 2201 | 7.11.47 | 2265 | 10.10.47 | 2329 | 17.3.48 | 2393 | 19.10.48 | 2457 | 13.7.48 | 2521 | 26.2.49 |
| 2202 | 19.11.47 | 2266 | 14.10.47 | 2330 | 17.3.48 | 2394 | 19.10.48 | 2458 | 13.7.48 | 2522 | 12.3.49 |
| 2203 | 25.11.47 | 2267 | 10.10.47 | 2331 | 17.3.48 | 2395 | 19.10.48 | 2459 | 16.10.48 | 2523 | 12.3.49 |
| 2204 | 23.5.47 | 2268 | 17.10.47 | 2332 | 23.3.48 | 2396 | 19.10.48 | 2460 | 26.10.48 | 2524 | 12.3.49 |

| | | | | | | | | | | | |
|---|---|---|---|---|---|---|---|---|---|---|---|
| 2525 | 12.3.49 | 2589 | 1.1.49 | 2653 | 21.12.48 | 2717 | 20.12.48 | 2781 | 12.2.49 | 2845 | 8.9.48 |
| 2526 | 5.3.49 | 2590 | 1.1.49 | 2654 | 21.12.48 | 2718 | 28.12.48 | 2782 | 26.2.49 | 2846 | 16.9.48 |
| 2527 | 30.4.49 | 2591 | 19.2.49 | 2655 | 31.12.48 | 2719 | 28.12.48 | 2783 | 5.3.49 | 2847 | 16.9.48 |
| 2528 | 25.4.49 | 2592 | 12.2.49 | 2656 | 4.1.49 | 2720 | 20.12.48 | 2784 | 8.7.49 | 2848 | 22.10.48 |
| 2529 | 9.4.49 | 2593 | 19.2.49 | 2657 | 4.1.49 | 2721 | 10.1.49 | 2785 | 8.7.49 | 2849 | 22.10.48 |
| 2530 | 9.4.49 | 2594 | 19.2.49 | 2658 | 22.7.49 | 2722 | 1.1.49 | 2786 | 14.12.48 | 2850 | 29.10.48 |
| 2531 | 9.4.49 | 2595 | 19.2.49 | 2659 | 22.7.49 | 2723 | 12.2.49 | 2787 | 18.12.48 | 2851 | 22.10.48 |
| 2532 | 9.4.49 | 2596 | 19.2.49 | 2660 | 26.7.49 | 2724 | 19.2.49 | 2788 | 16.12.48 | 2852 | 29.10.48 |
| 2533 | 19.4.49 | 2597 | 19.2.49 | 2661 | 26.7.49 | 2725 | 31.5.49 | 2789 | 9.9.49 | 2853 | 5.11.48 |
| 2534 | 19.4.49 | 2598 | 19.2.49 | 2662 | 5.8.49 | 2726 | 31.5.49 | 2790 | 7.9.49 | 2854 | 12.11.48 |
| 2535 | 14.4.49 | 2599 | 19.2.49 | 2663 | 5.8.49 | 2727 | 1.7.49 | 2791 | 5.9.49 | 2855 | 12.11.48 |
| 2536 | 14.4.49 | 2600 | 5.3.49 | 2664 | 5.8.49 | 2728 | 24.6.49 | 2792 | 28.9.48 | 2856 | 5.11.48 |
| 2537 | 21.4.49 | 2601 | 5.3.49 | 2665 | 5.8.49 | 2729 | 2.9.49 | 2793 | 29.9.48 | 2857 | 22.1.49 |
| 2538 | 14.4.49 | 2602 | 19.3.49 | 2666 | 5.8.49 | 2730 | 9.9.49 | 2794 | 29.9.48 | 2858 | 29.1.49 |
| 2539 | 21.4.49 | 2603 | 19.3.49 | 2667 | 12.8.49 | 2731 | 1.10.48 | 2795 | 1.10.48 | 2859 | 22.1.49 |
| 2540 | 14.4.49 | 2604 | 12.3.49 | 2668 | 1.9.48 | 2732 | 15.10.48 | 2796 | 1.10.48 | 2860 | 22.1.49 |
| 2541 | 21.4.49 | 2605 | 12.3.49 | 2669 | 1.9.48 | 2733 | 1.10.48 | 2797 | 6.10.48 | 2861 | 22.1.49 |
| 2542 | 21.4.49 | 2606 | 12.3.49 | 2670 | 24.9.48 | 2734 | 12.10.48 | 2798 | 6.10.48 | 2862 | 22.1.49 |
| 2543 | 25.4.49 | 2607 | 12.3.49 | 2671 | 24.9.48 | 2735 | 12.10.48 | 2799 | 6.10.48 | 2863 | 19.5.49 |
| 2544 | 25.4.49 | 2608 | 9.4.49 | 2672 | 8.10.48 | 2736 | 12.10.48 | 2800 | 6.10.48 | 2864 | 19.5.49 |
| 2545 | 25.4.49 | 2609 | 19.4.49 | 2673 | 12.10.48 | 2737 | 12.10.48 | 2801 | 6.10.48 | 2865 | 5.8.49 |
| 2546 | 25.4.49 | 2610 | 9.4.49 | 2674 | 8.10.48 | 2738 | 8.7.49 | 2802 | 6.10.48 | 2866 | 12.8.49 |
| 2547 | 25.4.49 | 2611 | 19.4.49 | 2675 | 15.10.48 | 2739 | 14.7.49 | 2803 | 21.10.48 | 2867 | 12.8.49 |
| 2548 | 29.4.49 | 2612 | 19.4.49 | 2676 | 15.10.48 | 2740 | 8.7.49 | 2804 | 21.10.48 | 2868 | 12.8.49 |
| 2549 | 6.5.49 | 2613 | 19.4.49 | 2677 | 20.10.48 | 2741 | 12.12.48 | 2805 | 21.10.48 | 2869 | 19.8.49 |
| 2550 | 1.6.49 | 2614 | 19.4.49 | 2678 | 15.10.48 | 2742 | 1.7.49 | 2806 | 24.10.48 | 2870 | 22.1.49 |
| 2551 | 3.6.49 | 2615 | 19.4.49 | 2679 | 16.11.48 | 2743 | 1.7.49 | 2807 | 24.10.48 | 2871 | 22.1.49 |
| 2552 | 8.10.48 | 2616 | 3.6.49 | 2680 | 19.11.48 | 2744 | 1.7.49 | 2808 | 31.10.48 | 2872 | 29.1.49 |
| 2553 | 26.10.48 | 2617 | 9.6.49 | 2681 | 25.11.48 | 2745 | 1.7.49 | 2809 | 26.10.48 | 2873 | 22.1.49 |
| 2554 | 12.11.48 | 2618 | 11.6.49 | 2682 | 16.11.48 | 2746 | 8.7.49 | 2810 | 31.10.48 | 2874 | 29.1.49 |
| 2555 | 12.11.48 | 2619 | 11.6.49 | 2683 | 28.6.49 | 2747 | 1.7.49 | 2811 | 3.11.48 | 2875 | 29.1.49 |
| 2556 | 19.11.48 | 2620 | 9.6.49 | 2684 | 1.7.49 | 2748 | 7.9.49 | 2812 | 3.11.48 | 2876 | 29.1.49 |
| 2557 | 26.11.48 | 2621 | 18.6.49 | 2685 | 7.7.49 | 2749 | 7.9.49 | 2813 | 3.11.48 | 2877 | 29.1.49 |
| 2558 | 29.11.48 | 2622 | 12.10.48 | 2686 | 7.7.49 | 2750 | 7.9.49 | 2814 | 4.11.48 | 2878 | 7.2.49 |
| 2559 | 6.12.48 | 2623 | 12.10.48 | 2687 | 9.7.49 | 2751 | 15.10.48 | 2815 | 7.11.48 | 2879 | 7.2.49 |
| 2560 | 6.12.48 | 2624 | 19.11.48 | 2688 | 14.7.49 | 2752 | 11.10.48 | 2816 | 7.11.48 | 2880 | 7.2.49 |
| 2561 | 6.12.48 | 2625 | 26.11.48 | 2689 | 14.7.49 | 2753 | 19.10.48 | 2817 | 16.1.49 | 2881 | 7.2.49 |
| 2562 | 19.3.49 | 2626 | 26.11.48 | 2690 | 16.7.49 | 2754 | 22.10.48 | 2818 | 16.1.49 | 2882 | 19.2.49 |
| 2563 | 19.3.49 | 2627 | 26.11.48 | 2691 | 20.7.49 | 2755 | 6.12.48 | 2819 | 21.1.49 | 2883 | 19.2.49 |
| 2564 | 19.3.49 | 2628 | 1.1.49 | 2692 | 25.4.49 | 2756 | 6.12.48 | 2820 | 27.5.49 | 2884 | 26.2.49 |
| 2565 | 19.3.49 | 2629 | 1.1.49 | 2693 | 30.4.49 | 2757 | 13.12.48 | 2821 | 20.5.49 | 2885 | 26.2.49 |
| 2566 | 19.3.49 | 2630 | 1.1.49 | 2694 | 25.4.49 | 2758 | 20.12.48 | 2822 | 27.5.49 | 2886 | 26.2.49 |
| 2567 | 3.9.48 | 2631 | 5.3.49 | 2695 | 30.4.49 | 2759 | 1.1.49 | 2823 | 27.5.49 | 2887 | 6.5.49 |
| 2568 | 16.9.48 | 2632 | 5.3.49 | 2696 | 6.5.49 | 2760 | 10.1.49 | 2824 | 27.5.49 | 2888 | 6.5.49 |
| 2569 | 10.9.48 | 2633 | 12.3.49 | 2697 | 30.4.49 | 2761 | 12.2.49 | 2825 | 30.5.49 | 2889 | 14.5.49 |
| 2570 | 3.9.48 | 2634 | 9.4.49 | 2698 | 30.4.49 | 2762 | 12.2.49 | 2826 | 27.5.49 | 2890 | 14.5.49 |
| 2571 | 1.10.48 | 2635 | 9.4.49 | 2699 | 30.4.49 | 2763 | 12.2.49 | 2827 | 30.5.49 | 2891 | 14.5.49 |
| 2572 | 22.10.48 | 2636 | 20.8.48 | 2700 | 30.4.49 | 2764 | 12.2.49 | 2828 | 27.7.48 | 2892 | 14.5.49 |
| 2573 | 7.11.48 | 2637 | 20.8.48 | 2701 | 30.4.49 | 2765 | 12.2.49 | 2829 | 2.7.48 | 2893 | 14.5.49 |
| 2574 | 12.11.48 | 2638 | 27.8.48 | 2702 | 30.4.49 | 2766 | 12.2.49 | 2830 | 10.9.48 | 2894 | 14.5.49 |
| 2575 | 5.11.48 | 2639 | 27.8.48 | 2703 | 6.5.49 | 2767 | 26.2.49 | 2831 | 10.9.48 | 2895 | 14.5.49 |
| 2576 | 5.11.48 | 2640 | 27.8.48 | 2704 | 6.5.49 | 2768 | 26.2.49 | 2832 | 5.11.48 | 2896 | 14.5.49 |
| 2577 | 14.12.48 | 2641 | 10.1.49 | 2705 | 6.5.49 | 2769 | 5.3.49 | 2833 | 12.11.48 | 2897 | 14.5.49 |
| 2578 | 13.12.48 | 2642 | 12.3.49 | 2706 | 6.5.49 | 2770 | 26.2.49 | 2834 | 17.1.49 | 2898 | 23.5.49 |
| 2579 | 13.12.48 | 2643 | 12.11.48 | 2707 | 6.5.49 | 2771 | 5.3.49 | 2835 | 17.1.49 | 2899 | 23.5.49 |
| 2580 | 13.12.48 | 2644 | 19.11.48 | 2708 | 6.5.49 | 2772 | 19.3.49 | 2836 | 10.1.49 | 2900 | 23.5.49 |
| 2581 | 28.12.48 | 2645 | 19.11.48 | 2709 | 7.6.49 | 2773 | 9.4.49 | 2837 | 17.1.49 | 2901 | 23.5.49 |
| 2582 | 28.12.48 | 2646 | 19.11.48 | 2710 | 16.7.49 | 2774 | 9.4.49 | 2838 | 8.9.48 | 2902 | 19.8.49 |
| 2583 | 28.12.48 | 2647 | 19.11.48 | 2711 | 20.7.49 | 2775 | 9.4.49 | 2839 | 8.9.48 | 2903 | 1.9.49 |
| 2584 | 1.1.49 | 2648 | 17.12.48 | 2712 | 22.7.49 | 2776 | 9.4.49 | 2840 | 8.9.48 | 2904 | 26.8.49 |
| 2585 | 1.1.49 | 2649 | 17.12.48 | 2713 | 20.8.49 | 2777 | 5.11.48 | 2841 | 16.9.48 | 2905 | 1.9.49 |
| 2586 | 1.1.49 | 2650 | 10.12.48 | 2714 | 20.8.49 | 2778 | 5.11.48 | 2842 | 8.9.48 | 2906 | 10.9.48 |
| 2587 | 1.1.49 | 2651 | 17.12.48 | 2715 | 24.8.48 | 2779 | 5.11.48 | 2843 | 16.9.48 | 2907 | 15.9.48 |
| 2588 | 1.1.49 | 2652 | 21.12.48 | 2716 | 24.8.48 | 2780 | 1.7.49 | 2844 | 16.9.48 | 2908 | 20.10.48 |

| | | | | | | | | | |
|---|---|---|---|---|---|---|---|---|---|
| 2909 | 24.9.48 | 2973 | 1.10.48 | 3037 | 10.12.48 | 3101 | 27.11.48 | 3165 | 21.4.49 | 3229 | 5.2.49 |
| 2910 | 24.9.48 | 2974 | 1.10.48 | 3038 | 17.12.48 | 3102 | 1.12.48 | 3166 | 21.4.49 | 3230 | 22.2.49 |
| 2911 | 4.11.48 | 2975 | 3.10.48 | 3039 | 29.12.48 | 3103 | 1.12.48 | 3167 | 19.3.49 | 3231 | 22.2.49 |
| 2912 | 5.11.48 | 2976 | 19.10.48 | 3040 | 17.12.48 | 3104 | 13.12.48 | 3168 | 25.3.49 | 3232 | 22.2.49 |
| 2913 | 12.11.48 | 2977 | 1.12.48 | 3041 | 29.12.48 | 3105 | 15.12.48 | 3169 | 19.3.49 | 3233 | 24.2.49 |
| 2914 | 18.11.48 | 2978 | 8.12.48 | 3042 | 7.1.49 | 3106 | 15.12.48 | 3170 | 23.3.49 | 3234 | 8.3.49 |
| 2915 | 5.11.48 | 2979 | 8.12.48 | 3043 | 7.1.49 | 3107 | 5.5.49 | 3171 | 18.1.49 | 3235 | 9.3.49 |
| 2916 | 3.6.49 | 2980 | 8.12.48 | 3044 | 7.1.49 | 3108 | 4.5.49 | 3172 | 14.1.49 | 3236 | 17.3.49 |
| 2917 | 27.5.49 | 2981 | 2.7.48 | 3045 | 14.1.49 | 3109 | 5.5.49 | 3173 | 18.1.49 | 3237 | 23.3.49 |
| 2918 | 26.8.49 | 2982 | 9.7.48 | 3046 | 14.1.49 | 3110 | 5.5.49 | 3174 | 8.1.49 | 3238 | 23.3.49 |
| 2919 | 15.10.48 | 2983 | 16.7.48 | 3047 | 28.1.49 | 3111 | 10.5.49 | 3175 | 14.1.49 | 3239 | 25.3.49 |
| 2920 | 15.10.48 | 2984 | 16.7.48 | 3048 | 4.2.49 | 3112 | 10.5.49 | 3176 | 1.4.49 | 3240 | 1.4.49 |
| 2921 | 15.10.48 | 2985 | 16.7.48 | 3049 | 4.2.49 | 3113 | 10.5.49 | 3177 | 5.8.49 | 3241 | 1.4.49 |
| 2922 | 15.10.48 | 2986 | 25.7.48 | 3050 | 4.2.49 | 3114 | 17.5.49 | 3178 | 5.8.49 | 3242 | 23.6.49 |
| 2923 | 22.10.48 | 2987 | 25.7.48 | 3051 | 15.2.49 | 3115 | 24.5.49 | 3179 | 8.2.49 | 3243 | 23.6.49 |
| 2924 | 22.10.48 | 2988 | 25.7.48 | 3052 | 18.2.49 | 3116 | 17.5.49 | 3180 | 8.2.49 | 3244 | 8.7.49 |
| 2925 | 30.10.48 | 2989 | 25.7.48 | 3053 | 18.2.49 | 3117 | 17.5.49 | 3181 | 8.2.49 | 3245 | 4.7.49 |
| 2926 | 30.10.48 | 2990 | 25.7.48 | 3054 | 25.2.49 | 3118 | 25.5.49 | 3182 | 1.3.49 | 3246 | 14.7.49 |
| 2927 | 6.11.48 | 2991 | 25.7.48 | 3055 | 19.3.49 | 3119 | 30.5.49 | 3183 | 1.3.49 | 3247 | 17.7.49 |
| 2928 | 25.11.48 | 2992 | 13.8.48 | 3056 | 4.3.49 | 3120 | 24.5.49 | 3184 | 1.3.49 | 3248 | 3.8.49 |
| 2929 | 25.11.48 | 2993 | 13.8.48 | 3057 | 11.3.49 | 3121 | 30.5.49 | 3185 | 29.3.49 | 3249 | 22.7.49 |
| 2930 | 30.11.48 | 2994 | 13.8.48 | 3058 | 30.12.48 | 3122 | 2.3.49 | 3186 | 25.5.49 | 3250 | 5.8.49 |
| 2931 | 23.12.48 | 2995 | 13.8.48 | 3059 | 21.1.49 | 3123 | 15.2.49 | 3187 | 18.5.49 | 3251 | 9.8.49 |
| 2932 | 7.1.49 | 2996 | 13.8.48 | 3060 | 3.1.49 | 3124 | 15.2.49 | 3188 | 24.6.49 | 3252 | 10.8.49 |
| 2933 | 7.1.49 | 2997 | 13.8.48 | 3061 | 13.1.49 | 3125 | 22.2.49 | 3189 | 28.6.49 | 3253 | 24.8.49 |
| 2934 | 28.5.48 | 2998 | 13.8.48 | 3062 | 21.1.49 | 3126 | 22.2.49 | 3190 | 7.7.49 | 3254 | 14.10.4 |
| 2935 | 3.6.48 | 2999 | 13.8.48 | 3063 | 28.1.49 | 3127 | 22.2.49 | 3191 | 12.7.49 | 3255 | 21.10.4 |
| 2936 | 3.6.48 | 3000 | 13.8.48 | 3064 | 28.1.49 | 3128 | 2.3.49 | 3192 | 12.7.49 | 3256 | 3.11.48 |
| 2937 | 10.6.48 | 3001 | 13.8.48 | 3065 | 14.2.49 | 3129 | 3.3.49 | 3193 | 5.8.49 | 3257 | 21.10.4 |
| 2938 | 10.6.48 | 3002 | 20.8.48 | 3066 | 18.2.49 | 3130 | 3.3.49 | 3194 | 28.3.49 | 3258 | 3.11.48 |
| 2939 | 27.8.48 | 3003 | 20.8.48 | 3067 | 17.3.49 | 3131 | 22.1.49 | 3195 | 30.3.49 | 3259 | 14.11.4 |
| 2940 | 3.9.48 | 3004 | 20.8.48 | 3068 | 18.3.49 | 3132 | 28.1.49 | 3196 | 19.5.49 | 3260 | 25.11.4 |
| 2941 | 10.9.48 | 3005 | 20.8.48 | 3069 | 25.3.49 | 3133 | 29.1.49 | 3197 | 24.6.49 | 3261 | 25.11.4 |
| 2942 | 9.8.48 | 3006 | 18.3.49 | 3070 | 8.4.49 | 3134 | 28.1.49 | 3198 | 19.7.49 | 3262 | 25.11.4 |
| 2943 | 17.8.48 | 3007 | 6.5.49 | 3071 | 8.4.49 | 3135 | 4.2.49 | 3199 | 14.7.49 | 3263 | 9.5.49 |
| 2944 | 23.8.48 | 3008 | 12.5.49 | 3072 | 29.4.49 | 3136 | 4.2.49 | 3200 | 22.7.49 | 3264 | 20.5.49 |
| 2945 | 18.6.48 | 3009 | 30.5.49 | 3073 | 29.4.49 | 3137 | 12.2.49 | 3201 | 30.9.49 | 3265 | 13.5.49 |
| 2946 | 16.7.48 | 3010 | 30.5.49 | 3074 | 14.1.49 | 3138 | 12.2.49 | 3202 | 28.1.49 | 3266 | 26.5.49 |
| 2947 | 23.7.48 | 3011 | 2.6.49 | 3075 | 14.1.49 | 3139 | 25.2.49 | 3203 | 28.1.49 | 3267 | 27.5.49 |
| 2948 | 30.8.48 | 3012 | 2.6.49 | 3076 | 21.1.49 | 3140 | 8.7.49 | 3204 | 4.2.49 | 3268 | 27.5.49 |
| 2949 | 12.8.48 | 3013 | 9.6.49 | 3077 | 1.2.49 | 3141 | 17.6.49 | 3205 | 6.5.49 | 3269 | 27.5.49 |
| 2950 | 20.8.48 | 3014 | 30.6.49 | 3078 | 10.8.49 | 3142 | 2.6.49 | 3206 | 14.11.48 | 3270 | 3.6.49 |
| 2951 | 23.9.48 | 3015 | 30.6.49 | 3079 | 4.8.49 | 3143 | 1.7.49 | 3207 | 21.11.48 | 3271 | 10.6.49 |
| 2952 | 1.10.48 | 3016 | 30.6.49 | 3080 | 4.8.49 | 3144 | 21.2.50 | 3208 | 21.11.48 | 3272 | 3.6.49 |
| 2953 | 1.10.48 | 3017 | 7.7.49 | 3081 | 10.8.49 | 3145 | 13.5.49 | 3209 | 26.11.48 | 3273 | 10.6.49 |
| 2954 | 8.10.48 | 3018 | 14.7.49 | 3082 | 10.8.49 | 3146 | 24.6.49 | 3210 | 26.11.48 | 3274 | 17.6.49 |
| 2955 | 15.10.48 | 3019 | 20.7.49 | 3083 | 10.8.49 | 3147 | 20.8.49 | 3211 | 5.12.48 | 3275 | 17.6.49 |
| 2956 | 22.10.48 | 3020 | 25.8.49 | 3084 | 30.12.48 | 3148 | 16.9.49 | 3212 | 21.11.48 | 3276 | 1.7.49 |
| 2957 | 29.10.48 | 3021 | 1.9.49 | 3085 | 6.1.49 | 3149 | 21.10.49 | 3213 | 28.11.48 | 3277 | 1.7.49 |
| 2958 | 10.11.48 | 3022 | 17.9.49 | 3086 | 6.1.49 | 3150 | 15.12.49 | 3214 | 28.11.48 | 3278 | 1.7.49 |
| 2959 | 10.11.48 | 3023 | 24.9.49 | 3087 | 30.12.48 | 3151 | 23.12.49 | 3215 | 5.12.48 | 3279 | 8.7.49 |
| 2960 | 10.11.48 | 3024 | 1.10.49 | 3088 | 21.1.49 | 3152 | 27.1.50 | 3216 | 13.12.48 | 3280 | 8.7.49 |
| 2961 | 19.11.48 | 3025 | 1.10.49 | 3089 | 14.1.49 | 3153 | 25.1.49 | 3217 | 13.12.48 | 3281 | 8.7.49 |
| 2962 | 30.11.48 | 3026 | 1.10.49 | 3090 | 20.1.49 | 3154 | 25.1.49 | 3218 | 18.2.49 | 3282 | 15.7.49 |
| 2963 | 27.8.48 | 3027 | 8.10.48 | 3091 | 20.1.49 | 3155 | 21.6.49 | 3219 | 18.12.49 | 3283 | 15.7.49 |
| 2964 | 2.9.48 | 3028 | 19.11.48 | 3092 | 22.3.49 | 3156 | 21.6.49 | 3220 | 20.12.49 | 3284 | 15.7.49 |
| 2965 | 17.9.48 | 3029 | 26.11.48 | 3093 | 25.3.49 | 3157 | 21.6.49 | 3221 | 3.1.49 | 3285 | 22.7.49 |
| 2966 | 17.9.48 | 3030 | 26.11.48 | 3094 | 29.3.49 | 3158 | 21.6.49 | 3222 | 18.1.49 | 3286 | 1.2.49 |
| 2967 | 24.9.48 | 3031 | 26.11.48 | 3095 | 29.3.49 | 3159 | 21.6.49 | 3223 | 3.1.49 | 3287 | 12.49 |
| 2968 | 3.9.48 | 3032 | 3.12.48 | 3096 | 25.3.49 | 3160 | 24.6.49 | 3224 | 9.1.49 | 3288 | 4.2.49 |
| 2969 | 10.9.48 | 3033 | 3.12.48 | 3097 | 31.3.49 | 3161 | 14.1.49 | 3225 | 9.1.49 | 3289 | 1.2.49 |
| 2970 | | 3034 | 3.12.48 | 3098 | 10.8.49 | 3162 | 14.1.49 | 3226 | 31.1.49 | 3290 | 4.2.49 |
| 2971 | | 3035 | 10.12.48 | 3099 | 18.8.49 | 3163 | 14.1.49 | 3227 | 31.9.49 | 3291 | 11.2.49 |
| 2972 | | 3036 | 10.12.48 | 3100 | 22.8.49 | 3164 | 21.4.49 | 3228 | 11.2.49 | 3292 | 25.2.49 |

| | | | | | | | | | | | |
|---|---|---|---|---|---|---|---|---|---|---|---|
| 3293 | 25.2.49 | 3357 | 31.3.49 | 3421 | 27.3.49 | 3485 | 23.12.49 | 3549 | 20.10.49 | 3613 | 2.12.49 |
| 3294 | 15.3.49 | 3358 | 31.3.49 | 3422 | 27.3.49 | 3486 | 30.12.49 | 3550 | 20.10.49 | 3614 | 16.12.49 |
| 3295 | 17.3.49 | 3359 | 31.3.49 | 3423 | 8.4.49 | 3487 | 21.1.50 | 3551 | 9.12.49 | 3615 | 16.12.49 |
| 3296 | 22.3.49 | 3360 | 6.4.49 | 3424 | 16.4.49 | 3488 | 21.1.50 | 3552 | 16.12.49 | 3616 | 27.1.50 |
| 3297 | 22.3.49 | 3361 | 14.4.49 | 3425 | 14.4.49 | 3489 | 21.1.50 | 3553 | 30.12.49 | 3617 | 27.1.50 |
| 3298 | 22.3.49 | 3362 | 14.4.49 | 3426 | 6.5.49 | 3490 | 10.2.50 | 3554 | 3.1.50 | 3618 | 27.1.50 |
| 3299 | 25.3.49 | 3363 | 21.4.49 | 3427 | 20.5.49 | 3491 | 15.2.50 | 3555 | 3.2.50 | 3619 | 16.2.50 |
| 3300 | 1.4.49 | 3364 | 29.4.49 | 3428 | 27.5.49 | 3492 | 15.2.50 | 3556 | 3.2.50 | 3620 | 16.2.50 |
| 3301 | 1.4.49 | 3365 | 21.4.49 | 3429 | 24.3.49 | 3493 | 15.2.50 | 3557 | 27.1.50 | 3621 | 10.3.50 |
| 3302 | 14.4.49 | 3366 | 2.6.49 | 3430 | 25.3.49 | 3494 | 29.2.50 | 3558 | 16.2.50 | 3622 | 17.3.50 |
| 3303 | 14.4.49 | 3367 | 2.6.49 | 3431 | 25.3.49 | 3495 | 3.3.50 | 3559 | 20.2.50 | 3623 | 4.4.50 |
| 3304 | 26.4.49 | 3368 | 9.6.49 | 3432 | 1.4.49 | 3496 | 23.2.50 | 3560 | 20.2.50 | 3624 | 14.4.50 |
| 3305 | 26.4.49 | 3369 | 9.6.49 | 3433 | 1.4.49 | 3497 | 3.3.50 | 3561 | 13.3.50 | 3625 | 14.7.50 |
| 3306 | 26.4.49 | 3370 | 13.6.49 | 3434 | 20.5.49 | 3498 | 3.3.50 | 3562 | 24.3.50 | 3626 | 7.7.50 |
| 3307 | 29.4.49 | 3371 | 11.6.49 | 3435 | 27.5.49 | 3499 | 10.3.50 | 3563 | 21.3.50 | 3627 | 18.11.49 |
| 3308 | 29.4.49 | 3372 | 13.6.49 | 3436 | 2.9.49 | 3500 | 17.3.50 | 3564 | 2.6.50 | 3628 | 23.12.49 |
| 3309 | 6.5.49 | 3373 | 11.6.49 | 3437 | 1.4.49 | 3501 | 10.3.50 | 3565 | 9.6.50 | 3629 | 3.1.50 |
| 3310 | 21.5.49 | 3374 | 21.6.49 | 3438 | 1.4.49 | 3502 | 17.3.50 | 3566 | 9.6.50 | 3630 | 6.1.50 |
| 3311 | 14.5.49 | 3375 | 16.6.49 | 3439 | 3.6.49 | 3503 | 23.3.50 | 3567 | 12.6.50 | 3631 | 27.1.50 |
| 3312 | 14.5.49 | 3376 | 16.6.49 | 3440 | 26.8.49 | 3504 | 31.3.50 | 3568 | 7.7.50 | 3632 | 18.11.49 |
| 3313 | 3.6.49 | 3377 | 24.6.49 | 3441 | 10.6.49 | 3505 | 31.3.50 | 3569 | 1.7.50 | 3633 | 2.12.49 |
| 3314 | 18.3.49 | 3378 | 1.7.49 | 3442 | 10.11.50 | 3506 | 20.4.50 | 3570 | 14.7.50 | 3634 | 3.1.50 |
| 3315 | 18.3.49 | 3379 | 18.8.49 | 3443 | 28.4.49 | 3507 | 4.5.50 | 3571 | 14.7.50 | 3635 | 3.2.50 |
| 3316 | 8.4.49 | 3380 | 18.8.49 | 3444 | 28.4.49 | 3508 | 20.4.50 | 3572 | 16.9.49 | 3636 | 3.2.50 |
| 3317 | 4.2.49 | 3381 | 23.8.49 | 3445 | 6.7.49 | 3509 | 20.4.50 | 3573 | 17.9.49 | 3637 | 31.3.50 |
| 3318 | 4.2.49 | 3382 | 23.8.49 | 3446 | 6.7.49 | 3510 | 25.5.49 | 3574 | 16.9.49 | 3638 | 6.4.50 |
| 3319 | 5.2.49 | 3383 | 25.8.49 | 3447 | 12.7.49 | 3511 | 19.5.50 | 3575 | 30.9.49 | 3639 | 6.4.50 |
| 3320 | 11.3.49 | 3384 | 26.8.49 | 3448 | 4.11.49 | 3512 | 1.9.49 | 3576 | 2.10.49 | 3640 | 14.4.50 |
| 3321 | 20.3.49 | 3385 | 25.8.49 | 3449 | 9.12.49 | 3513 | 23.9.49 | 3577 | 30.9.49 | 3641 | 14.4.50 |
| 3322 | 20.3.49 | 3386 | 14.9.49 | 3450 | 23.12.49 | 3514 | 23.9.49 | 3578 | 2.10.49 | 3642 | 1.10.49 |
| 3323 | 22.3.49 | 3387 | 5.4.50 | 3451 | 3.2.50 | 3515 | 23.9.49 | 3579 | 11.11.49 | 3643 | 15.10.49 |
| 3324 | 22.3.49 | 3388 | 21.4.50 | 3452 | 3.6.49 | 3516 | 23.9.49 | 3580 | 18.11.49 | 3644 | 15.10.49 |
| 3325 | 16.8.49 | 3389 | 1.5.50 | 3453 | 3.6.49 | 3517 | 23.9.49 | 3581 | 11.11.49 | 3645 | 11.11.49 |
| 3326 | 22.3.49 | 3390 | 5.5.50 | 3454 | 3.6.49 | 3518 | 29.9.49 | 3582 | 25.11.49 | 3646 | 22.11.49 |
| 3327 | 12.7.49 | 3391 | 19.5.50 | 3455 | 15.9.49 | 3519 | 10.11.49 | 3583 | 18.11.49 | 3647 | 15.12.49 |
| 3328 | 12.7.49 | 3392 | 12.6.50 | 3456 | 15.9.49 | 3520 | 10.11.49 | 3584 | 16.12.49 | 3648 | 22.12.49 |
| 3329 | 14.7.49 | 3393 | 26.6.50 | 3457 | 7.7.49 | 3521 | 11.11.49 | 3585 | 9.12.49 | 3649 | 8.1.50 |
| 3330 | 14.7.49 | 3394 | 14.7.50 | 3458 | 15.9.49 | 3522 | 11.11.49 | 3586 | 9.12.49 | 3650 | 8.1.50 |
| 3331 | 15.7.49 | 3395 | 21.7.50 | 3459 | 16.9.49 | 3523 | 11.11.49 | 3587 | 23.12.49 | 3651 | 9.1.50 |
| 3332 | 15.7.49 | 3396 | 11.8.50 | 3460 | 16.9.49 | 3524 | 11.11.49 | 3588 | 30.12.49 | 3652 | 9.2.50 |
| 3333 | 19.7.49 | 3397 | 18.8.50 | 3461 | 21.9.49 | 3525 | 11.11.49 | 3589 | 20.1.50 | 3653 | 9.2.50 |
| 3334 | 20.7.49 | 3398 | 8.7.50 | 3462 | 21.9.49 | 3526 | 27.12.49 | 3590 | 27.1.50 | 3654 | 9.2.50 |
| 3335 | 15.9.49 | 3399 | 8.7.50 | 3463 | 23.9.49 | 3527 | 16.12.49 | 3591 | 3.2.50 | 3655 | 10.3.50 |
| 3336 | 14.9.49 | 3400 | 6.10.50 | 3464 | 23.9.49 | 3528 | 28.12.49 | 3592 | 3.2.50 | 3656 | 7.3.50 |
| 3337 | 12.9.49 | 3401 | 27.10.50 | 3465 | 23.9.49 | 3529 | 30.12.49 | 3593 | 10.2.50 | 3657 | 24.3.50 |
| 3338 | 19.9.49 | 3402 | 29.6.49 | 3466 | 25.9.49 | 3530 | 6.1.50 | 3594 | 10.2.50 | 3658 | 31.3.50 |
| 3339 | 4.10.49 | 3403 | 6.7.49 | 3467 | 5.11.49 | 3531 | 6.1.50 | 3595 | 3.3.50 | 3659 | 5.4.50 |
| 3340 | 7.10.49 | 3404 | 6.7.49 | 3468 | 5.11.49 | 3532 | 3.2.50 | 3596 | 3.3.50 | 3660 | 2.5.50 |
| 3341 | 4.10.49 | 3405 | 6.7.49 | 3469 | 5.11.49 | 3533 | 13.2.50 | 3597 | 24.3.50 | 3661 | 3.5.50 |
| 3342 | 7.10.49 | 3406 | 6.7.49 | 3470 | 5.11.49 | 3534 | 3.2.50 | 3598 | 31.3.50 | 3662 | 2.5.50 |
| 3343 | 26.10.49 | 3407 | 22.7.49 | 3471 | 5.11.49 | 3535 | 3.2.50 | 3599 | 6.4.50 | 3663 | 5.5.50 |
| 3344 | 4.11.49 | 3408 | 22.7.49 | 3472 | 3.11.49 | 3536 | 27.2.50 | 3600 | 14.4.50 | 3664 | 9.5.50 |
| 3345 | 26.10.49 | 3409 | 22.7.49 | 3473 | 3.11.49 | 3537 | 10.3.50 | 3601 | 6.4.50 | 3665 | 16.6.50 |
| 3346 | 31.10.49 | 3410 | 19.8.49 | 3474 | 3.11.49 | 3538 | 10.3.50 | 3602 | 14.4.50 | 3666 | 23.6.50 |
| 3347 | 2.12.49 | 3411 | 19.8.49 | 3475 | 3.11.49 | 3539 | 20.3.50 | 3603 | 14.4.50 | 3667 | 7.10.49 |
| 3348 | 2.12.49 | 3412 | 11.6.49 | 3476 | 3.11.49 | 3540 | 24.3.50 | 3604 | 30.9.49 | 3668 | 25.11.49 |
| 3349 | 5.12.49 | 3413 | 16.6.49 | 3477 | 24.11.49 | 3541 | 31.3.49 | 3605 | 30.9.49 | 3669 | 18.11.49 |
| 3350 | 6.12.49 | 3414 | 11.6.49 | 3478 | 1.12.49 | 3542 | 7.6.49 | 3606 | 7.10.49 | 3670 | 2.12.49 |
| 3351 | 10.1.50 | 3415 | 15.6.49 | 3479 | 8.12.49 | 3543 | 7.6.49 | 3607 | 7.10.49 | 3671 | 23.12.49 |
| 3352 | 30.12.49 | 3416 | 16.6.49 | 3480 | 1.12.49 | 3544 | 13.6.49 | 3608 | 16.11.49 | 3672 | 23.12.49 |
| 3353 | 13.1.50 | 3417 | 19.6.49 | 3481 | 8.12.49 | 3545 | 13.6.49 | 3609 | 16.11.49 | 3673 | 13.1.50 |
| 3354 | 13.1.50 | 3418 | 19.8.49 | 3482 | 23.12.49 | 3546 | 13.6.49 | 3610 | 10.11.49 | 3674 | 20.1.50 |
| 3355 | 29.3.49 | 3419 | 19.8.49 | 3483 | 23.12.49 | 3547 | 30.9.49 | 3611 | 16.11.49 | 3675 | 10.2.50 |
| 3356 | 25.3.49 | 3420 | 26.8.49 | 3484 | 30.12.49 | 3548 | 30.9.49 | 3612 | 9.12.49 | 3676 | 10.2.50 |

| | | | | | | | | | | | |
|---|---|---|---|---|---|---|---|---|---|---|---|
| 3677 | 24.3.50 | 3741 | 30.6.50 | 3805 | 21.3.50 | 3869 | 4.9.50 | 3933 | 21.11.49 | 3997 | 12.5.50 |
| 3678 | 24.3.50 | 3742 | 21.10.49 | 3806 | 21.3.50 | 3870 | 13.12.49 | 3934 | 21.11.49 | 3998 | 19.5.50 |
| 3679 | 7.4.50 | 3743 | 2.12.49 | 3807 | 31.3.50 | 3871 | 16.12.49 | 3935 | 25.11.49 | 3999 | 19.5.50 |
| 3680 | 7.4.50 | 3744 | 10.12.49 | 3808 | 26.5.50 | 3872 | 4.1.50 | 3936 | 6.12.49 | 4000 | 19.5.50 |
| 3681 | 16.6.50 | 3745 | 30.12.49 | 3809 | 26.5.50 | 3873 | 5.1.50 | 3937 | 6.12.49 | 4001 | 26.5.50 |
| 3682 | 16.6.50 | 3746 | 14.2.50 | 3810 | 26.5.50 | 3874 | 13.2.50 | 3938 | 14.12.49 | 4002 | 26.5.50 |
| 3683 | 23.6.50 | 3747 | 21.2.50 | 3811 | 30.5.50 | 3875 | 9.3.50 | 3939 | 6.12.49 | 4003 | 2.6.50 |
| 3684 | 23.6.50 | 3748 | 21.2.50 | 3812 | 30.6.50 | 3876 | 17.3.50 | 3940 | 17.12.49 | 4004 | 6.10.49 |
| 3685 | 27.6.50 | 3749 | 3.3.50 | 3813 | 30.6.50 | 3877 | 16.12.49 | 3941 | 30.12.49 | 4005 | 3.11.49 |
| 3686 | 21.10.49 | 3750 | 17.3.50 | 3814 | 7.7.50 | 3878 | 13.12.49 | 3942 | 30.12.49 | 4006 | 16.12.4 |
| 3687 | 21.10.49 | 3751 | 24.3.50 | 3815 | 23.6.50 | 3879 | 6.1.50 | 3943 | 10.1.50 | 4007 | 17.3.5 |
| 3688 | 25.11.49 | 3752 | 31.3.50 | 3816 | 20.1.50 | 3880 | 12.1.50 | 3944 | 12.1.50 | 4008 | 26.5.5 |
| 3689 | 23.12.49 | 3753 | 9.6.50 | 3817 | 25.4.50 | 3881 | 13.2.50 | 3945 | 24.1.50 | 4009 | 1.6.50 |
| 3690 | 23.12.49 | 3754 | 16.6.50 | 3818 | 25.4.50 | 3882 | 13.2.50 | 3946 | 3.2.50 | 4010 | 21.7.4 |
| 3691 | 23.12.49 | 3755 | 9.6.50 | 3819 | 28.12.49 | 3883 | 15.2.50 | 3947 | 3.2.50 | 4011 | 21.7.4 |
| 3692 | 9.9.49 | 3756 | 16.6.50 | 3820 | 28.12.49 | 3884 | 10.3.50 | 3948 | 3.2.50 | 4012 | 5.8.49 |
| 3693 | 9.9.49 | 3757 | 27.6.50 | 3821 | 28.12.49 | 3885 | 21.3.50 | 3949 | 10.2.50 | 4013 | 5.8.49 |
| 3694 | 9.9.49 | 3758 | 30.6.50 | 3822 | 14.4.50 | 3886 | 5.4.50 | 3950 | 10.3.50 | 4014 | 12.8.4 |
| 3695 | 9.9.49 | 3759 | 7.7.50 | 3823 | 12.5.50 | 3887 | 5.4.50 | 3951 | 10.3.50 | 4015 | 19.8.4 |
| 3696 | 9.9.49 | 3760 | 28.10.49 | 3824 | 12.5.50 | 3888 | 11.4.50 | 3952 | 31.3.50 | 4016 | 26.8.4 |
| 3697 | 14.10.49 | 3761 | 30.12.49 | 3825 | 19.5.50 | 3889 | 5.4.50 | 3953 | 6.4.50 | 4017 | 14.10.4 |
| 3698 | 14.10.49 | 3762 | 14.4.50 | 3826 | 20.6.50 | 3890 | 6.1.50 | 3954 | 5.5.50 | 4018 | 14.10.4 |
| 3699 | 14.10.49 | 3763 | 14.4.50 | 3827 | 7.10.49 | 3891 | 8.2.50 | 3955 | 5.5.50 | 4019 | 14.10.4 |
| 3700 | 14.10.49 | 3764 | 2.12.49 | 3828 | 21.10.49 | 3892 | 10.3.50 | 3956 | 19.5.50 | 4020 | 27.10.4 |
| 3701 | 21.10.49 | 3765 | 13.2.50 | 3829 | 21.10.49 | 3893 | 5.4.50 | 3957 | 19.5.50 | 4021 | 7.11.4 |
| 3702 | 21.10.49 | 3766 | 8.2.50 | 3830 | 31.10.49 | 3894 | 17.5.50 | 3958 | 2.6.50 | 4022 | 7.11.4 |
| 3703 | 30.11.49 | 3767 | 15.2.50 | 3831 | 21.10.49 | 3895 | 12.6.50 | 3959 | 2.6.50 | 4023 | 16.12.4 |
| 3704 | 30.11.49 | 3768 | 21.4.50 | 3832 | 13.1.50 | 3896 | 13.7.50 | 3960 | 5.8.49 | 4024 | 30.12.4 |
| 3705 | 29.11.49 | 3769 | 28.4.50 | 3833 | 12.1.50 | 3897 | 16.8.50 | 3961 | 12.8.49 | 4025 | 26.1.50 |
| 3706 | 29.11.49 | 3770 | 2.5.50 | 3834 | 20.1.50 | 3898 | 25.9.50 | 3962 | 19.8.49 | 4026 | 9.2.50 |
| 3707 | 25.11.49 | 3771 | 4.5.50 | 3835 | 17.1.50 | 3899 | 6.10.49 | 3963 | 2.9.49 | 4027 | 9.2.50 |
| 3708 | 2.12.49 | 3772 | 9.5.50 | 3836 | 17.1.50 | 3900 | 6.10.49 | 3964 | 9.9.49 | 4028 | 14.4.50 |
| 3709 | 25.11.49 | 3773 | 7.7.50 | 3837 | 20.1.50 | 3901 | 7.10.49 | 3965 | 9.9.49 | 4029 | 28.4.50 |
| 3710 | 2.12.49 | 3774 | 7.7.50 | 3838 | 21.2.50 | 3902 | 7.10.49 | 3966 | 16.9.49 | 4030 | 11.5.50 |
| 3711 | 9.12.49 | 3775 | 7.7.50 | 3839 | 21.2.50 | 3903 | 7.10.49 | 3967 | 16.9.49 | 4031 | 11.5.50 |
| 3712 | 2.12.49 | 3776 | 14.5.49 | 3840 | 3.3.50 | 3904 | 14.10.49 | 3968 | 16.9.49 | 4032 | 11.5.50 |
| 3713 | 9.12.49 | 3777 | 23.5.49 | 3841 | 21.3.50 | 3905 | 14.10.49 | 3969 | 23.9.49 | 4033 | 11.5.50 |
| 3714 | 2.12.49 | 3778 | 23.5.49 | 3842 | 17.3.50 | 3906 | 14.10.49 | 3970 | 23.9.49 | 4034 | 2.6.50 |
| 3715 | 2.12.49 | 3779 | 22.10.49 | 3843 | 17.3.50 | 3907 | 9.12.49 | 3971 | 23.9.49 | 4035 | 9.6.50 |
| 3716 | 30.12.49 | 3780 | 21.10.49 | 3844 | 25.4.50 | 3908 | 16.12.49 | 3972 | 30.9.49 | 4036 | 9.6.50 |
| 3717 | 3.1.50 | 3781 | 28.10.49 | 3845 | 24.4.50 | 3909 | 9.12.49 | 3973 | 30.9.49 | 4037 | 9.6.50 |
| 3718 | 30.12.49 | 3782 | 28.10.49 | 3846 | 25.4.50 | 3910 | 9.12.49 | 3974 | 30.9.49 | 4038 | 16.6.50 |
| 3719 | 27.1.50 | 3783 | 28.1.50 | 3847 | 25.4.50 | 3911 | 24.8.49 | 3975 | 8.10.49 | 4039 | 22.6.50 |
| 3720 | 27.1.50 | 3784 | 24.2.50 | 3848 | 19.5.50 | 3912 | 24.8.49 | 3976 | 8.10.49 | 4040 | 22.6.50 |
| 3721 | 27.1.50 | 3785 | 3.3.50 | 3849 | 19.5.50 | 3913 | 26.8.49 | 3977 | 8.10.49 | 4041 | 22.6.50 |
| 3722 | 27.1.50 | 3786 | 31.3.50 | 3850 | 26.5.50 | 3914 | 25.8.49 | 3978 | 14.10.49 | 4042 | 23.9.49 |
| 3723 | 3.2.50 | 3787 | 19.5.50 | 3851 | - | 3915 | 9.9.49 | 3979 | 14.10.49 | 4043 | 23.9.49 |
| 3724 | 24.2.50 | 3788 | 19.5.50 | 3852 | 10.9.49 | 3916 | 9.9.49 | 3980 | 14.10.49 | 4044 | 14.10.4 |
| 3725 | 21.2.50 | 3789 | 16.6.50 | 3853 | 3.4.50 | 3917 | 9.9.49 | 3981 | 28.10.49 | 4045 | 21.10.4 |
| 3726 | 3.3.50 | 3790 | 16.6.50 | 3854 | 5.5.50 | 3918 | 9.9.49 | 3982 | 19.9.49 | 4046 | 11.11.4 |
| 3727 | 24.2.50 | 3791 | 21.10.49 | 3855 | 5.5.50 | 3919 | 12.9.49 | 3983 | 19.9.49 | 4047 | 4.11.4 |
| 3728 | 10.3.50 | 3792 | 27.10.49 | 3856 | 10.5.50 | 3920 | 20.9.49 | 3984 | 23.9.49 | 4048 | 23.12.4 |
| 3729 | 17.3.50 | 3793 | 27.10.49 | 3857 | 10.5.50 | 3921 | 4.10.49 | 3985 | 23.9.49 | 4049 | 10.1.50 |
| 3730 | 17.3.50 | 3794 | 29.10.49 | 3858 | 22.5.50 | 3922 | 7.10.49 | 3986 | 4.10.49 | 4050 | 25.1.50 |
| 3731 | 31.3.50 | 3795 | 29.10.49 | 3859 | 15.5.50 | 3923 | 10.10.49 | 3987 | 4.10.49 | 4051 | 3.2.50 |
| 3732 | 24.3.50 | 3796 | 6.1.50 | 3860 | 15.5.50 | 3924 | 10.10.49 | 3988 | 3.10.49 | 4052 | 16.2.50 |
| 3733 | 31.3.50 | 3797 | 13.1.50 | 3861 | 12.6.50 | 3925 | 14.10.49 | 3989 | 3.10.49 | 4053 | 16.2.50 |
| 3734 | 28.4.50 | 3798 | 20.1.50 | 3862 | 12.6.50 | 3926 | 14.10.49 | 3990 | 4.10.49 | 4054 | 13.3.50 |
| 3735 | 28.4.50 | 3799 | 20.1.50 | 3863 | 7.6.50 | 3927 | 13.10.49 | 3991 | 27.1.50 | 4055 | 17.3.50 |
| 3736 | 19.5.50 | 3800 | 20.1.50 | 3864 | 22.6.50 | 3928 | 21.10.49 | 3992 | 3.5.50 | 4056 | 14.4.50 |
| 3737 | 7.7.50 | 3801 | 27.1.50 | 3865 | 28.7.50 | 3929 | 4.11.49 | 3993 | 3.5.50 | 4057 | 21.4.50 |
| 3738 | 14.7.50 | 3802 | 20.1.50 | 3866 | 26.7.50 | 3930 | 4.11.49 | 3994 | 5.5.50 | 4058 | 11.5.50 |
| 3739 | 14.7.50 | 3803 | 8.3.50 | 3867 | 26.7.50 | 3931 | 7.11.49 | 3995 | 5.5.50 | 4059 | 16.6.50 |
| 3740 | 21.7.50 | 3804 | 21.3.50 | 3868 | 10.8.50 | 3932 | 14.11.49 | 3996 | 12.5.50 | 4060 | 30.6.50 |

| | | | | | | | | | | | |
|---|---|---|---|---|---|---|---|---|---|---|---|
| 4061 | 30.6.50 | 4125 | 11.11.49 | 4189 | 10.4.50 | 4253 | 7.9.49 | 4317 | 21.7.50 | 4381 | 23.1.51 |
| 4062 | 12.5.50 | 4126 | 11.11.49 | 4190 | 18.4.50 | 4254 | 9.9.49 | 4318 | 10.8.50 | 4382 | 15.12.50 |
| 4063 | 26.5.50 | 4127 | 18.11.49 | 4191 | 18.4.50 | 4255 | 26.6.51 | 4319 | 11.8.50 | 4383 | 15.12.50 |
| 4064 | 26.5.50 | 4128 | 18.11.49 | 4192 | 21.4.50 | 4256 | 22.7.49 | 4320 | 28.7.50 | 4384 | 15.12.50 |
| 4065 | 25.8.50 | 4129 | 18.11.49 | 4193 | 21.4.50 | 4257 | 22.7.49 | 4321 | 18.8.50 | 4385 | 22.9.50 |
| 4066 | 1.9.50 | 4130 | 29.11.49 | 4194 | 21.4.50 | 4258 | 20.3.50 | 4322 | 15.8.50 | 4386 | 22.9.50 |
| 4067 | 21.10.49 | 4131 | 29.11.49 | 4195 | 18.5.50 | 4259 | 20.3.50 | 4323 | 17.8.50 | 4387 | 27.10.50 |
| 4068 | 21.10.49 | 4132 | 29.11.49 | 4196 | 19.5.50 | 4260 | 25.3.50 | 4324 | 8.9.50 | 4388 | 31.10.50 |
| 4069 | 11.11.49 | 4133 | 6.12.49 | 4197 | 9.12.49 | 4261 | 25.3.50 | 4325 | 12.9.50 | 4389 | 27.10.50 |
| 4070 | 11.11.49 | 4134 | 6.12.49 | 4198 | 9.12.49 | 4262 | 5.4.50 | 4326 | 14.9.50 | 4390 | 31.10.50 |
| 4071 | 23.12.49 | 4135 | 6.12.49 | 4199 | 6.1.50 | 4263 | 5.8.49 | 4327 | 15.9.50 | 4391 | 30.11.50 |
| 4072 | 28.4.50 | 4136 | 9.12.49 | 4200 | 3.3.50 | 4264 | 12.8.49 | 4328 | 22.9.50 | 4392 | 30.11.50 |
| 4073 | 28.4.50 | 4137 | 9.12.49 | 4201 | 3.3.50 | 4265 | 12.8.49 | 4329 | 13.10.50 | 4393 | 8.12.50 |
| 4074 | 21.4.50 | 4138 | 9.12.49 | 4202 | 10.3.50 | 4266 | 19.8.49 | 4330 | 24.10.50 | 4394 | 30.11.50 |
| 4075 | 1.6.50 | 4139 | 16.12.49 | 4203 | 10.3.50 | 4267 | 12.9.49 | 4331 | 20.10.50 | 4395 | 9.2.51 |
| 4076 | 1.6.50 | 4140 | 16.12.49 | 4204 | 17.3.50 | 4268 | 19.2.50 | 4332 | 27.10.50 | 4396 | 2.3.51 |
| 4077 | 8.6.50 | 4141 | 16.12.49 | 4205 | 17.3.50 | 4269 | 10.2.50 | 4333 | 24.11.50 | 4397 | 2.3.51 |
| 4078 | 8.6.50 | 4142 | 23.12.49 | 4206 | 24.3.50 | 4270 | 16.2.50 | 4334 | 24.11.50 | 4398 | 16.3.51 |
| 4079 | 20.10.49 | 4143 | 23.12.49 | 4207 | 24.3.50 | 4271 | 12.5.50 | 4335 | 6.2.51 | 4399 | 3.11.50 |
| 4080 | 25.11.49 | 4144 | 23.12.49 | 4208 | 13.4.50 | 4272 | 29.6.50 | 4336 | 6.2.51 | 4400 | 10.11.50 |
| 4081 | 2.12.49 | 4145 | 30.12.49 | 4209 | 14.4.50 | 4273 | 29.6.50 | 4337 | 8.2.51 | 4401 | 24.11.50 |
| 4082 | 23.12.49 | 4146 | 30.12.49 | 4210 | 3.5.50 | 4274 | 29.6.50 | 4338 | 9.2.51 | 4402 | 1.12.50 |
| 4083 | 3.1.50 | 4147 | 6.1.50 | 4211 | 26.5.50 | 4275 | 13.6.49 | 4339 | 9.2.51 | 4403 | 1.12.50 |
| 4084 | 27.1.50 | 4148 | 6.1.50 | 4212 | 12.11.49 | 4276 | 17.6.49 | 4340 | 16.2.51 | 4404 | 8.12.50 |
| 4085 | 20.1.50 | 4149 | 6.1.50 | 4213 | 18.11.49 | 4277 | 17.6.49 | 4341 | 2.3.51 | 4405 | 28.12.50 |
| 4086 | 3.2.50 | 4150 | 13.1.50 | 4214 | 25.11.49 | 4278 | 23.6.49 | 4342 | 6.3.51 | 4406 | 28.12.50 |
| 4087 | 3.2.50 | 4151 | 14.1.50 | 4215 | 18.11.49 | 4279 | 23.6.49 | 4343 | 22.3.51 | 4407 | 28.12.50 |
| 4088 | 3.3.50 | 4152 | 13.1.50 | 4216 | 18.11.49 | 4280 | 23.6.49 | 4344 | 29.8.50 | 4408 | 28.12.50 |
| 4089 | 3.3.50 | 4153 | 20.1.50 | 4217 | 18.11.49 | 4281 | 21.7.50 | 4345 | 1.9.50 | 4409 | 25.8.50 |
| 4090 | 6.4.50 | 4154 | 20.1.50 | 4218 | 24.11.49 | 4282 | 21.7.50 | 4346 | 1.9.50 | 4410 | 1.9.50 |
| 4091 | 14.4.50 | 4155 | 20.1.50 | 4219 | 25.11.49 | 4283 | 28.7.50 | 4347 | 20.10.50 | 4411 | 1.9.50 |
| 4092 | 5.5.50 | 4156 | 7.2.50 | 4220 | 25.11.49 | 4284 | 28.7.50 | 4348 | 13.10.50 | 4412 | 20.10.50 |
| 4093 | 5.5.50 | 4157 | 7.2.50 | 4221 | 25.11.49 | 4285 | 31.8.50 | 4349 | 13.10.50 | 4413 | 30.11.50 |
| 4094 | 12.5.50 | 4158 | 7.2.50 | 4222 | 6.12.49 | 4286 | 31.8.50 | 4350 | 10.11.50 | 4414 | 18.8.50 |
| 4095 | 21.10.49 | 4159 | 16.2.50 | 4223 | 27.1.50 | 4287 | 3.9.50 | 4351 | 10.11.50 | 4415 | 11.8.50 |
| 4096 | 11.11.49 | 4160 | 16.2.50 | 4224 | 27.1.50 | 4288 | 6.9.50 | 4352 | 17.11.50 | 4416 | 11.8.50 |
| 4097 | 11.11.49 | 4161 | 16.2.50 | 4225 | 24.2.50 | 4289 | 14.9.50 | 4353 | 24.11.50 | 4417 | 11.8.50 |
| 4098 | 3.12.49 | 4162 | 16.2.50 | 4226 | 17.2.50 | 4290 | 15.9.50 | 4354 | 17.11.50 | 4418 | 1.9.50 |
| 4099 | 9.1.50 | 4163 | 22.2.50 | 4227 | 24.2.50 | 4291 | 22.9.50 | 4355 | 1.12.50 | 4419 | 29.8.50 |
| 4100 | 24.2.50 | 4164 | 22.2.50 | 4228 | 28.2.50 | 4292 | 15.9.50 | 4356 | 2.3.51 | 4420 | 15.9.50 |
| 4101 | 3.3.50 | 4165 | 22.2.50 | 4229 | 5.4.50 | 4293 | 17.11.50 | 4357 | 20.2.51 | 4421 | 15.9.50 |
| 4102 | 3.3.50 | 4166 | 22.2.50 | 4230 | 31.3.50 | 4294 | 17.11.50 | 4358 | 6.4.51 | 4422 | 15.9.50 |
| 4103 | 10.3.50 | 4167 | 24.2.50 | 4231 | 31.3.50 | 4295 | 17.11.50 | 4359 | 30.3.51 | 4423 | 15.9.50 |
| 4104 | 19.5.50 | 4168 | 24.2.50 | 4232 | 5.4.50 | 4296 | 17.11.50 | 4360 | 15.12.50 | 4424 | 20.10.50 |
| 4105 | 19.5.50 | 4169 | 24.2.50 | 4233 | 31.3.50 | 4297 | 24.11.50 | 4361 | 15.12.50 | 4425 | 28.10.50 |
| 4106 | 19.5.50 | 4170 | 24.2.50 | 4234 | 25.4.50 | 4298 | 24.11.50 | 4362 | 18.8.50 | 4426 | 10.11.50 |
| 4107 | 26.5.50 | 4171 | 3.3.50 | 4235 | 28.4.50 | 4299 | 1.12.50 | 4363 | 18.8.50 | 4427 | 11.11.50 |
| 4108 | 16.6.50 | 4172 | 3.3.50 | 4236 | 28.4.50 | 4300 | 23.1.51 | 4364 | 6.10.50 | 4428 | 10.11.50 |
| 4109 | 11.8.49 | 4173 | 3.3.50 | 4237 | 5.5.50 | 4301 | 23.1.51 | 4365 | 13.10.50 | 4429 | 17.11.50 |
| 4110 | 19.8.49 | 4174 | 10.3.50 | 4238 | 3.5.50 | 4302 | 6.2.51 | 4366 | 27.10.50 | 4430 | 10.11.50 |
| 4111 | 26.8.49 | 4175 | 10.3.50 | 4239 | 3.5.50 | 4303 | 23.1.51 | 4367 | 25.8.50 | 4431 | 8.12.50 |
| 4112 | 26.8.49 | 4176 | 10.3.50 | 4240 | 5.5.50 | 4304 | 9.2.51 | 4368 | 8.9.50 | 4432 | 8.12.50 |
| 4113 | 2.9.49 | 4177 | 17.3.50 | 4241 | 17.6.49 | 4305 | 9.2.51 | 4369 | 8.9.50 | 4433 | 26.1.51 |
| 4114 | 2.9.49 | 4178 | 17.3.50 | 4242 | 28.6.49 | 4306 | 20.10.50 | 4370 | 2.11.50 | 4434 | 26.5.51 |
| 4115 | 9.9.49 | 4179 | 17.3.50 | 4243 | 28.6.49 | 4307 | 20.10.50 | 4371 | 7.11.50 | 4435 | 6.2.51 |
| 4116 | 21.10.49 | 4180 | 24.3.50 | 4244 | 28.6.49 | 4308 | 23.10.50 | 4372 | 2.11.50 | 4436 | 2.3.51 |
| 4117 | 21.10.49 | 4181 | 24.3.50 | 4245 | 26.8.49 | 4309 | 23.10.50 | 4373 | 7.11.50 | 4437 | 29.12.50 |
| 4118 | 28.10.49 | 4182 | 24.3.50 | 4246 | 29.8.49 | 4310 | 11.12.50 | 4374 | 7.11.50 | 4438 | 29.12.50 |
| 4119 | 28.10.49 | 4183 | 31.3.50 | 4247 | 26.8.49 | 4311 | 8.12.50 | 4375 | 17.11.50 | 4439 | 13.10.50 |
| 4120 | 28.10.49 | 4184 | 31.3.50 | 4248 | 2.9.49 | 4312 | 8.12.50 | 4376 | 19.1.51 | 4440 | 24.10.50 |
| 4121 | 4.11.49 | 4185 | 31.3.50 | 4249 | 2.9.49 | 4313 | 7.7.50 | 4377 | 5.1.51 | 4441 | 27.10.50 |
| 4122 | 4.11.49 | 4186 | 6.4.50 | 4250 | 2.9.49 | 4314 | 26.7.50 | 4378 | 5.1.51 | 4442 | 3.11.50 |
| 4123 | 4.11.49 | 4187 | 6.4.50 | 4251 | 5.9.49 | 4315 | 13.7.50 | 4379 | 19.1.51 | 4443 | 10.11.50 |
| 4124 | 11.11.49 | 4188 | 6.4.50 | 4252 | 5.9.49 | 4316 | 14.7.50 | 4380 | 23.1.51 | 4444 | 1.12.50 |

| | | | | | | | | | | | |
|---|---|---|---|---|---|---|---|---|---|---|---|
| 4445 | 1.12.50 | 4509 | 19.12.50 | 4573 | 28.7.50 | 4637 | 19.4.51 | 4701 | 3.11.50 | 4765 | 15.9.50 |
| 4446 | 6.2.51 | 4510 | 20.12.50 | 4574 | 28.7.50 | 4638 | 19.4.51 | 4702 | 24.11.50 | 4766 | 15.9.50 |
| 4447 | 28.12.50 | 4511 | 19.12.50 | 4575 | 10.8.50 | 4639 | 20.4.51 | 4703 | 8.12.50 | 4767 | 22.9.50 |
| 4448 | 28.12.50 | 4512 | 21.12.50 | 4576 | 24.8.50 | 4640 | 20.4.51 | 4704 | 1.12.50 | 4768 | 22.9.50 |
| 4449 | 1.1.51 | 4513 | 22.12.50 | 4577 | 17.8.50 | 4641 | 27.4.51 | 4705 | 29.12.50 | 4769 | 22.9.50 |
| 4450 | 1.1.51 | 4514 | 21.12.50 | 4578 | 17.8.50 | 4642 | 3.5.51 | 4706 | 29.12.50 | 4770 | 22.9.50 |
| 4451 | 16.3.51 | 4515 | 8.12.50 | 4579 | 24.8.50 | 4643 | 20.4.51 | 4707 | 10.1.51 | 4771 | 22.9.50 |
| 4452 | 16.3.51 | 4516 | 19.12.50 | 4580 | 31.8.50 | 4644 | 3.5.51 | 4708 | 1.9.50 | 4772 | 29.9.50 |
| 4453 | 30.3.51 | 4517 | 8.12.50 | 4581 | 31.8.50 | 4645 | 27.4.51 | 4709 | 22.9.50 | 4773 | 29.9.50 |
| 4454 | 12.4.51 | 4518 | 19.2.51 | 4582 | 7.9.50 | 4646 | 5.5.51 | 4710 | 27.10.50 | 4774 | 29.9.50 |
| 4455 | 22.12.50 | 4519 | 9.2.51 | 4583 | 7.9.50 | 4647 | 2.6.50 | 4711 | 11.8.50 | 4775 | 6.10.50 |
| 4456 | 22.12.50 | 4520 | 3.10.50 | 4584 | 6.9.50 | 4648 | 2.6.50 | 4712 | 11.8.50 | 4776 | 13.10.50 |
| 4457 | 15.12.50 | 4521 | 29.9.50 | 4585 | 6.9.50 | 4649 | 12.6.50 | 4713 | 15.8.50 | 4777 | 6.10.50 |
| 4458 | 22.9.50 | 4522 | 3.10.50 | 4586 | 14.9.50 | 4650 | 16.6.50 | 4714 | 15.8.50 | 4778 | 13.10.5 |
| 4459 | 29.9.50 | 4523 | 19.7.50 | 4587 | 8.9.50 | 4651 | 18.8.50 | 4715 | 2.11.50 | 4779 | 20.10.5 |
| 4460 | 29.9.50 | 4524 | 25.7.50 | 4588 | 14.9.50 | 4652 | 18.8.50 | 4716 | 2.11.50 | 4780 | 20.10.5 |
| 4461 | 6.10.50 | 4525 | 14.7.50 | 4589 | 20.9.50 | 4653 | 18.8.50 | 4717 | 10.11.50 | 4781 | 20.10.5 |
| 4462 | 6.10.50 | 4526 | 27.7.50 | 4590 | 20.9.50 | 4654 | 25.8.50 | 4718 | 10.11.50 | 4782 | 27.10.5 |
| 4463 | 29.9.50 | 4527 | 25.7.50 | 4591 | 20.9.50 | 4655 | 15.9.50 | 4719 | 24.11.50 | 4783 | 27.10.5 |
| 4464 | 6.10.50 | 4528 | 25.7.50 | 4592 | 28.9.50 | 4656 | 15.9.50 | 4720 | 8.12.50 | 4784 | 10.11.5 |
| 4465 | 17.10.50 | 4529 | 23.8.50 | 4593 | 5.10.50 | 4657 | 15.9.50 | 4721 | 8.12.50 | 4785 | 3.11.50 |
| 4466 | 17.10.50 | 4530 | 23.8.50 | 4594 | 5.10.50 | 4658 | 28.9.50 | 4722 | 8.12.50 | 4786 | 10.11.5 |
| 4467 | 10.10.50 | 4531 | 23.8.50 | 4595 | 29.9.50 | 4659 | 6.10.50 | 4723 | 29.12.50 | 4787 | 17.11.5 |
| 4468 | 10.10.50 | 4532 | 29.9.50 | 4596 | 13.10.50 | 4660 | 13.10.50 | 4724 | 29.12.50 | 4788 | 17.11.5 |
| 4469 | 17.10.50 | 4533 | 5.10.50 | 4597 | 11.10.50 | 4661 | 13.10.50 | 4725 | 25.1.51 | 4789 | 21.11.5 |
| 4470 | 10.10.50 | 4534 | 6.10.50 | 4598 | 13.10.50 | 4662 | 13.10.50 | 4726 | 25.1.51 | 4790 | 24.11.5 |
| 4471 | 20.10.50 | 4535 | 3.7.51 | 4599 | 13.10.50 | 4663 | 8.12.50 | 4727 | 2.2.51 | 4791 | 24.11.5 |
| 4472 | 3.11.50 | 4536 | 3.7.51 | 4600 | 11.10.50 | 4664 | 19.12.50 | 4728 | 30.1.51 | 4792 | 24.11.5 |
| 4473 | 3.11.50 | 4537 | 3.7.51 | 4601 | 27.10.50 | 4665 | 19.12.50 | 4729 | 30.1.51 | 4793 | 28.11.5 |
| 4474 | 3.11.50 | 4538 | 2.6.50 | 4602 | 27.10.50 | 4666 | 22.12.50 | 4730 | 30.1.51 | 4794 | 28.11. |
| 4475 | 10.11.50 | 4539 | 2.6.50 | 4603 | 25.10.50 | 4667 | 27.4.51 | 4731 | 2.2.51 | 4795 | 14.1.51 |
| 4476 | 10.11.50 | 4540 | 31.5.50 | 4604 | 26.10.50 | 4668 | 27.4.51 | 4732 | 9.3.51 | 4796 | 14.1.51 |
| 4477 | 10.11.50 | 4541 | 6.6.50 | 4605 | 27.10.50 | 4669 | 4.5.51 | 4733 | 9.3.51 | 4797 | 15.1.51 |
| 4478 | 10.11.50 | 4542 | 16.6.50 | 4606 | 30.11.50 | 4670 | 28.8.50 | 4734 | 9.3.51 | 4798 | 15.1.51 |
| 4479 | 17.11.50 | 4543 | 9.6.50 | 4607 | 30.11.50 | 4671 | 25.8.50 | 4735 | 20.3.51 | 4799 | 9.1.51 |
| 4480 | 17.11.50 | 4544 | 19.7.50 | 4608 | 30.11.50 | 4672 | 28.8.50 | 4736 | 16.3.51 | 4800 | 9.1.51 |
| 4481 | 20.11.50 | 4545 | 21.7.50 | 4609 | 6.2.51 | 4673 | 22.9.50 | 4737 | 16.3.51 | 4801 | 16.1.51 |
| 4482 | 20.11.50 | 4546 | 19.7.50 | 4610 | 6.2.51 | 4674 | 22.9.50 | 4738 | 16.3.51 | 4802 | 16.1.51 |
| 4483 | 20.11.50 | 4547 | 21.7.50 | 4611 | 6.2.51 | 4675 | 25.9.50 | 4739 | 20.3.51 | 4803 | 1.7.50 |
| 4484 | 28.11.50 | 4548 | 17.4.51 | 4612 | 6.2.51 | 4676 | 1.12.50 | 4740 | 22.3.51 | 4804 | 28.7.50 |
| 4485 | 28.11.50 | 4549 | 17.4.51 | 4613 | 16.2.51 | 4677 | 11.12.50 | 4741 | 7.7.50 | 4805 | 1.9.50 |
| 4486 | 1.12.50 | 4550 | 17.4.51 | 4614 | 16.2.51 | 4678 | 22.12.50 | 4742 | 7.7.50 | 4806 | 8.9.50 |
| 4487 | 22.12.50 | 4551 | 27.4.51 | 4615 | 16.2.51 | 4679 | 22.12.50 | 4743 | 4.7.50 | 4807 | 1.9.50 |
| 4488 | 29.12.50 | 4552 | 27.4.51 | 4616 | 21.2.51 | 4680 | 22.12.50 | 4744 | 7.7.50 | 4808 | 26.9.50 |
| 4489 | 5.1.51 | 4553 | 4.5.51 | 4617 | 5.3.51 | 4681 | 9.2.51 | 4745 | 14.7.50 | 4809 | 17.11.5 |
| 4490 | 5.1.51 | 4554 | 25.5.51 | 4618 | 5.3.51 | 4682 | 23.2.51 | 4746 | 14.7.50 | 4810 | 24.11.5 |
| 4491 | 5.1.51 | 4555 | 25.5.51 | 4619 | 5.3.51 | 4683 | 2.3.51 | 4747 | 14.7.50 | 4811 | 14.7.50 |
| 4492 | 29.12.50 | 4556 | 25.5.51 | 4620 | 19.3.51 | 4684 | 23.2.51 | 4748 | 21.7.50 | 4812 | 14.7.50 |
| 4493 | 30.3.51 | 4557 | 21.9.51 | 4621 | 2.4.51 | 4685 | 2.3.51 | 4749 | 21.7.50 | 4813 | 28.7.50 |
| 4494 | 5.1.51 | 4558 | 21.9.51 | 4622 | 19.3.51 | 4686 | 9.3.51 | 4750 | 21.7.50 | 4814 | 11.8.50 |
| 4495 | 12.1.51 | 4559 | 28.6.50 | 4623 | 2.4.51 | 4687 | 9.3.51 | 4751 | 28.7.50 | 4815 | 3.11.50 |
| 4496 | 12.1.51 | 4560 | 28.6.50 | 4624 | 16.4.51 | 4688 | 22.3.51 | 4752 | 28.7.50 | 4816 | 3.11.50 |
| 4497 | 23.2.51 | 4561 | 6.7.50 | 4625 | 16.4.51 | 4689 | 30.3.51 | 4753 | 28.7.50 | 4817 | 3.11.50 |
| 4498 | 16.2.51 | 4562 | 14.7.50 | 4626 | 20.3.51 | 4690 | 30.3.51 | 4754 | 11.8.50 | 4818 | 3.11.50 |
| 4499 | 23.2.51 | 4563 | 6.7.50 | 4627 | 20.3.51 | 4691 | 25.8.50 | 4755 | 11.8.50 | 4819 | 10.11.5 |
| 4500 | 9.3.51 | 4564 | 14.7.50 | 4628 | 20.3.51 | 4692 | 29.8.50 | 4756 | 11.8.50 | 4820 | 17.11.5 |
| 4501 | 2.3.51 | 4565 | 14.7.50 | 4629 | 30.3.51 | 4693 | 29.8.50 | 4757 | 1.9.50 | 4821 | 10.11.5 |
| 4502 | 30.3.51 | 4566 | 17.7.50 | 4630 | 20.3.51 | 4694 | 22.9.50 | 4758 | 1.9.50 | 4822 | 17.11.5 |
| 4503 | 30.3.51 | 4567 | 20.7.50 | 4631 | 20.3.51 | 4695 | 26.9.50 | 4759 | 1.9.50 | 4823 | 9.1.51 |
| 4504 | 6.4.51 | 4568 | 17.7.50 | 4632 | 30.3.51 | 4696 | 29.9.50 | 4760 | 8.9.50 | 4824 | 12.1.5 |
| 4505 | 8.6.51 | 4569 | 20.7.50 | 4633 | 30.3.51 | 4697 | 6.10.50 | 4761 | 8.9.50 | 4825 | 12.1.5 |
| 4506 | 5.6.51 | 4570 | 20.7.50 | 4634 | 30.3.51 | 4698 | 6.10.50 | 4762 | 8.9.50 | 4826 | 12.1.5 |
| 4507 | 8.12.50 | 4571 | 20.7.50 | 4635 | 6.4.51 | 4699 | 20.10.50 | 4763 | 15.9.50 | 4827 | 19.1.5 |
| 4508 | 19.12.50 | 4572 | 28.7.50 | 4636 | 6.4.51 | 4700 | 27.10.50 | 4764 | 15.9.50 | 4828 | 12.1.5 |

| | | | | | | | | | | | |
|---|---|---|---|---|---|---|---|---|---|---|---|
| 4829 | 2.2.51 | 4858 | 13.7.50 | 4887 | 28.6.50 | 4916 | 8.9.50 | 4945 | 15.9.50 | 4974 | 17.4.50 |
| 4830 | 16.2.51 | 4859 | 21.7.50 | 4888 | 2.3.51 | 4917 | 18.9.50 | 4946 | 16.2.51 | 4975 | 17.4.50 |
| 4831 | 23.2.51 | 4860 | 12.1.51 | 4889 | 2.3.51 | 4918 | 25.9.50 | 4947 | 6.3.51 | 4976 | 19.4.50 |
| 4832 | 16.2.51 | 4861 | 15.12.50 | 4890 | 9.3.51 | 4919 | 8.11.50 | 4948 | 16.2.51 | 4977 | 20.4.50 |
| 4833 | 23.2.51 | 4862 | 15.12.50 | 4891 | 2.3.51 | 4920 | 25.5.50 | 4949 | 20.2.51 | 4978 | 12.12.50 |
| 4834 | 2.3.51 | 4863 | 29.9.50 | 4892 | 9.3.51 | 4921 | 30.5.50 | 4950 | 20.2.51 | 4979 | 29.1.51 |
| 4835 | 9.3.51 | 4864 | 29.9.50 | 4893 | 23.2.51 | 4922 | 6.6.50 | 4951 | 23.2.51 | 4980 | 29.1.51 |
| 4836 | 4.5.51 | 4865 | 6.10.50 | 4894 | 2.3.51 | 4923 | 6.6.50 | 4952 | 22.12.50 | 4981 | 2.2.51 |
| 4837 | 6.6.51 | 4866 | 6.10.50 | 4895 | 9.3.51 | 4924 | 16.6.50 | 4953 | 22.3.50 | 4982 | 2.2.51 |
| 4838 | 30.5.51 | 4867 | 13.10.50 | 4896 | 9.3.51 | 4925 | 16.6.50 | 4954 | 20.4.50 | 4983 | 16.3.51 |
| 4839 | 8.6.51 | 4868 | 20.10.50 | 4897 | 6.4.51 | 4926 | 20.6.50 | 4955 | 27.4.50 | 4984 | 16.3.51 |
| 4840 | 8.6.51 | 4869 | 20.10.50 | 4898 | 12.4.51 | 4927 | 23.6.50 | 4956 | 20.2.50 | 4985 | 16.3.51 |
| 4841 | 15.6.51 | 4870 | 20.10.50 | 4899 | 22.3.51 | 4928 | 30.6.50 | 4957 | 22.2.50 | 4986 | 22.3.51 |
| 4842 | 15.6.51 | 4871 | 20.10.50 | 4900 | 29.6.51 | 4929 | 7.7.50 | 4958 | 23.2.50 | 4987 | 5.6.51 |
| 4843 | 28.6.51 | 4872 | 23.10.50 | 4901 | 17.8.51 | 4930 | 13.2.51 | 4959 | 1.3.50 | 4988 | 18.5.51 |
| 4844 | 17.11.50 | 4873 | 17.11.50 | 4902 | 24.8.51 | 4931 | 9.2.51 | 4960 | 17.3.50 | 4989 | 5.6.51 |
| 4845 | 17.11.50 | 4874 | 24.11.50 | 4903 | 16.3.51 | 4932 | 9.2.51 | 4961 | 12.4.50 | 4990 | 10.5.51 |
| 4846 | 24.11.50 | 4875 | 24.11.50 | 4904 | 16.3.51 | 4933 | 13.2.51 | 4962 | 30.3.50 | 4991 | 10.5.51 |
| 4847 | 2.1.51 | 4876 | 1.12.50 | 4905 | 28.7.50 | 4934 | 13.2.51 | 4963 | 6.4.50 | 4992 | 10.5.51 |
| 4848 | 28.12.50 | 4877 | 1.12.50 | 4906 | 28.7.50 | 4935 | 20.2.51 | 4964 | 30.3.50 | 4993 | 18.5.51 |
| 4849 | 9.1.51 | 4878 | 1.6.50 | 4907 | 25.8.50 | 4936 | 6.3.51 | 4965 | 6.4.50 | 4994 | 8.6.51 |
| 4850 | 9.3.51 | 4879 | 1.6.50 | 4908 | 19.1.51 | 4937 | 23.6.50 | 4966 | 6.4.50 | 4995 | 23.5.51 |
| 4851 | 16.3.51 | 4880 | 2.6.50 | 4909 | 19.1.51 | 4938 | 23.6.50 | 4967 | 10.4.50 | 4996 | 23.5.51 |
| 4852 | 22.3.51 | 4881 | 9.6.50 | 4910 | 19.1.51 | 4939 | 27.6.50 | 4968 | 10.4.50 | 4997 | 1.6.51 |
| 4853 | 22.3.51 | 4882 | 9.6.50 | 4911 | 31.1.51 | 4940 | 28.7.50 | 4969 | 12.4.50 | 4998 | 8.6.51 |
| 4854 | 23.6.50 | 4883 | 16.6.50 | 4912 | 26.1.51 | 4941 | 29.7.50 | 4970 | 10.4.50 | 4999 | 8.6.51 |
| 4855 | 30.6.50 | 4884 | 23.6.50 | 4913 | 2.2.51 | 4942 | 18.8.50 | 4971 | 12.4.50 | 5000 | 6.7.51 |
| 4856 | 30.6.50 | 4885 | 23.6.50 | 4914 | 16.2.51 | 4943 | 17.5.50 | 4972 | 20.4.50 | | |
| 4857 | 11.7.50 | 4886 | 6.7.50 | 4915 | 1.9.50 | 4944 | 19.5.50 | 4973 | 20.4.50 | | |

# Cross Reference of Registrations to Body Numbers

| Reg | No | Reg | No | Reg | No | Reg | No | Reg | No | Reg | No |
|---|---|---|---|---|---|---|---|---|---|---|---|
| AG 8246 | 3091 | FM 9049 | 3880 | JG 8229 | 2419 | NV 7497 | 3065 | VV 6259 | 4966 | BHN 261 | 3036 |
| AG 8258 | 3094 | FM 9051 | 3881 | JG 8230 | 2422 | NV 8666 | 3066 | VV 6260 | 3073 | BHN 262 | 3048 |
| CK 4403 | 3080 | FM 9052 | 3882 | JG 8231 | 2420 | NV 8667 | 3067 | WX 2111 | 3074 | BHN 263 | 3030 |
| CK 4405 | 3079 | FM 9053 | 3884 | JG 8238 | 2432 | NV 9643 | 4969 | ADC 653 | 3007 | BHN 264 | 3057 |
| CK 4406 | 3083 | FM 9054 | 3885 | JG 8240 | 2427 | NV 9644 | 4968 | ADC 654 | 3006 | BHN 265 | 3044 |
| CK 4411 | 3082 | FM 9055 | 3886 | JG 8243 | 2421 | NV 9645 | 4970 | ADC 655 | 3008 | BHN 266 | 3052 |
| CK 4418 | 3076 | FM 9056 | 3877 | JG 8244 | 2423 | NV 9646 | 4967 | ADC 656 | 3009 | BHN 267 | 3053 |
| EK 8106 | 3081 | FM 9057 | 3879 | JG 8248 | 2424 | NV 9647 | 4971 | ADC 657 | 3010 | BHN 268 | 3039 |
| FM 541 | 1225 | FT 4496 | 2978 | JG 9917 | 2412 | NV 9648 | 4964 | ADC 658 | 3011 | BHN 269 | 3028 |
| FM 6276 | 3100 | FT 4497 | 2973 | JG 9922 | 2414 | NV 9650 | 4965 | ADC 659 | 3012 | BHN 270 | 3045 |
| FM 6415 | 3075 | FT 4498 | 2975 | JG 9928 | 2413 | NV 9651 | 4962 | ADC 660 | 3013 | BHN 271 | 3033 |
| FM 6416 | 3077 | FT 4499 | 2977 | JG 9929 | 2415 | RN 8156 | 2443 | ADC 661 | 3014 | BHN 272 | 3040 |
| FM 6917 | 3325 | FT 4500 | 2974 | JN 4294 | 3201 | RN 8157 | 2446 | ADC 662 | 3015 | BHN 273 | 3050 |
| FM 6918 | 3092 | FT 4501 | 2979 | JN 4745 | 3200 | RN 8165 | 2441 | ADC 663 | 3016 | BHN 274 | 3056 |
| FM 6919 | 3096 | FT 4502 | 2976 | JN 6892 | 3202 | RN 8174 | 2439 | ADC 664 | 3017 | BHN 275 | 3049 |
| FM 6920 | 3099 | FT 4503 | 2980 | JN 6893 | 3203 | RN 8176 | 2453 | ADC 665 | 3018 | BHN 276 | 3031 |
| FM 7234 | 3090 | GN 6206 | 3104 | JN 6894 | 3205 | RN 8177 | 2436 | ADC 666 | 3019 | BHN 277 | 3054 |
| FM 7461 | 3095 | GP 6231 | 3101 | JN 6896 | 3204 | RN 8181 | 2440 | ADC 667 | 3021 | BHN 278 | 3034 |
| FM 7462 | 3093 | GP 6238 | 3102 | JT 9354 | 3416 | RN 8182 | 2445 | ADC 668 | 3020 | BHN 279 | 3037 |
| FM 7463 | 3098 | GP 6242 | 3103 | JT 9355 | 3415 | RN 8183 | 2438 | AFM 495 | 3887 | BHN 280 | 3055 |
| FM 7464 | 3326 | GR 5075 | 2474 | JT 9357 | 3417 | RN 8184 | 2456 | AFM 496 | 3878 | BHT 530 | 3216 |
| FM 7466 | 3097 | GR 5076 | 2477 | JT 9360 | 3419 | RN 8186 | 2434 | AFM 497 | 3888 | BHT 531 | 3218 |
| FM 7467 | 3088 | GR 5077 | 2475 | KG 1148 | 3086 | RN 8187 | 2435 | AFM 499 | 3889 | BHT 532 | 3918 |
| FM 7468 | 3443 | GR 5078 | 2476 | KG 1151 | 3087 | RN 8188 | 2457 | AFM 501 | 3883 | BHT 533 | 3229 |
| FM 7469 | 3444 | GR 5079 | 2478 | LJ 7091 | 3319 | RN 8189 | 2449 | AHN 385 | 3032 | BHT 534 | 3239 |
| FM 7470 | 3445 | GW 6255 | 3105 | LJ 7092 | 3320 | RN 8190 | 2454 | AHN 431 | 3029 | BHU 637 | 3343 |
| FM 7471 | 3446 | GW 6288 | 3106 | LJ 7093 | 3429 | RN 8297 | 2444 | AHN 432 | 3046 | BHU 969 | 3338 |
| FM 7472 | 3447 | HB 6260 | 1281 | LJ 7094 | 3322 | RN 8301 | 2455 | AHN 433 | 3041 | BHU 975 | 3247 |
| FM 7482 | 3122 | HB 6261 | 1282 | LJ 7095 | 3317 | RN 8306 | 2448 | AHN 434 | 3042 | BHU 978 | 3348 |
| FM 7763 | 3089 | HB 6262 | 1283 | LJ 7096 | 3324 | RN 8311 | 2447 | AHN 435 | 3043 | BHU 979 | 3353 |
| FM 8149 | 3872 | HL 5318 | 3085 | LJ 7097 | 3318 | RN 8313 | 2451 | AHN 811 | 3047 | BHU 981 | 3335 |
| FM 8150 | 3871 | HL 5339 | 3084 | NG 2723 | 3904 | RN 8314 | 2437 | AHN 812 | 3038 | BHW 430 | 3354 |
| FM 8151 | 3874 | HN 9007 | 3165 | NG 2729 | 3900 | RN 8316 | 2458 | AHN 813 | 3051 | BHW 431 | 3329 |
| FM 8152 | 3875 | HN 9008 | 3169 | NG 2730 | 3956 | RN 8317 | 2452 | AHN 814 | 3035 | BHW 432 | 3339 |
| FM 8153 | 3870 | HN 9009 | 3170 | NG 2732 | 3907 | RN 8319 | 2450 | AHT 972 | 3328 | BHW 639 | 3917 |
| FM 8155 | 3873 | HN 9010 | 3166 | NG 2734 | 3950 | RN 8322 | 2442 | AHW 74 | 3228 | BHY 691 | 3350 |
| FM 8156 | 3876 | HN 9011 | 3168 | NG 3861 | 3958 | SM 8851 | 3123 | AHW 536 | 3345 | BHY 692 | 4538 |
| FM 8974 | 4246 | HN 9012 | 3161 | NG 3862 | 3959 | SM 8852 | 3124 | AHW 953 | 3207 | BHY 693 | 3248 |
| FM 8975 | 3116 | HN 9013 | 3162 | NG 3863 | 3947 | SM 8853 | 3125 | AHY 417 | 3931 | BHY 694 | 3231 |
| FM 8976 | 3117 | HN 9014 | 3167 | NG 3864 | 3899 | SM 8854 | 3126 | AXG 669 | 3854 | BHY 695 | 4539 |
| FM 8977 | 3111 | HY 3629 | 3224 | NG 3865 | 3953 | SM 9501 | 3128 | AXG 670 | 3855 | BJA 436 | 1464 |
| FM 8978 | 3121 | HY 3630 | 4544 | NG 3866 | 3948 | SM 9502 | 3127 | AXG 671 | 3856 | BJA 437 | 1465 |
| FM 8979 | 3108 | HY 6198 | 4547 | NG 3867 | 3906 | UF 5644 | 3078 | AXG 672 | 3857 | BJA 438 | 1466 |
| FM 8980 | 4247 | HY 6503 | 4546 | NG 3868 | 3909 | UH 7175 | 3153 | AXG 673 | 3858 | BJA 439 | 1467 |
| FM 8981 | 4248 | HY 6896 | 4545 | NG 3869 | 3957 | VG 4819 | 3902 | AXG 674 | 3859 | BJA 440 | 1468 |
| FM 8982 | 4249 | IH 6242 | 2356 | NG 3870 | 3951 | VG 4820 | 3910 | AXG 675 | 3860 | BJA 441 | 1469 |
| FM 8983 | 3113 | IH 6243 | 2357 | NG 5401 | 3954 | VG 4821 | 3908 | AXG 676 | 3861 | BJA 442 | 1470 |
| FM 8984 | 3107 | IH 6244 | 2358 | NG 5402 | 3901 | VG 4822 | 3946 | AXG 677 | 3862 | BJA 443 | 1471 |
| FM 8985 | 3118 | IH 6245 | 2359 | NG 5403 | 3952 | VG 4823 | 3903 | AXG 678 | 3863 | BJA 444 | 1472 |
| FM 8986 | 4245 | JC 1343 | 3441 | NG 5405 | 3949 | VG 4824 | 3905 | AXG 679 | 3864 | BJA 445 | 1473 |
| FM 8987 | 4250 | JG 7011 | 2428 | NG 5406 | 3955 | VV 4564 | 3060 | AXG 680 | 3865 | BJA 446 | 1474 |
| FM 8988 | 3109 | JG 7015 | 2416 | NV 2268 | 3176 | VV 5041 | 3061 | AXG 681 | 3866 | BJA 447 | 1481 |
| FM 8989 | 4252 | JG 7017 | 2410 | NV 2270 | 3172 | VV 5042 | 3062 | AXG 682 | 3867 | BJA 448 | 1482 |
| FM 8990 | 4251 | JG 7018 | 2425 | NV 2271 | 3177 | VV 5693 | 3064 | AXG 683 | 3868 | BJA 449 | 1475 |
| FM 8991 | 3120 | JG 7022 | 2417 | NV 2272 | 3175 | VV 5694 | 3068 | AXG 684 | 3869 | BJA 450 | 1476 |
| FM 8992 | 4254 | JG 7024 | 2429 | NV 2276 | 3171 | VV 5695 | 3069 | BAO 772 | 3890 | BJN 111 | 1115 |
| FM 8993 | 3110 | JG 8201 | 2426 | NV 2277 | 3173 | VV 5696 | 3072 | BAO 774 | 3892 | BJN 112 | 1117 |
| FM 8994 | 3115 | JG 8202 | 2411 | NV 2278 | 3178 | VV 5697 | 4963 | BAO 775 | 3896 | BJN 113 | 1116 |
| FM 8995 | 4253 | JG 8204 | 2418 | NV 2280 | 3174 | VV 6251 | 4973 | BFJ 155 | 3212 | BJN 114 | 1185 |
| FM 8996 | 3112 | JG 8226 | 2430 | NV 6638 | 3059 | VV 6255 | 3058 | BFJ 156 | 3208 | BOW 163 | 3428 |
| FM 8997 | 3119 | JG 8227 | 2433 | NV 6639 | 4972 | VV 6257 | 3070 | BFJ 157 | 3209 | BOW 165 | 3427 |
| FM 8998 | 3114 | JG 8228 | 2431 | NV 7496 | 3063 | VV 6258 | 3071 | BFJ 158 | 3206 | BRM 594 | 3894 |

| | | | | | | | | | | | |
|---|---|---|---|---|---|---|---|---|---|---|---|
| BRM 595 | 3897 | CDB 181 | 2156 | CHY 118 | 3250 | CUH 835 | 1530 | DAO 50 | 3893 | DHT 942 | 3912 |
| BRM 596 | 3898 | CDB 182 | 2157 | CHY 119 | 3233 | CUH 836 | 1531 | DAO 51 | 3895 | DHT 943 | 3213 |
| BSM 826 | 3129 | CDB 183 | 2158 | CHY 120 | 3252 | CUH 837 | 1532 | DBD 980 | 1741 | DHU 349 | 3220 |
| BTR 304 | 3420 | CDB 184 | 2159 | CHY 443 | 3929 | CUH 838 | 1534 | DBD 981 | 1742 | DHU 350 | 3223 |
| BTR 306 | 3418 | CDB 185 | 2160 | CHY 821 | 3349 | CUH 839 | 1533 | DBD 982 | 1743 | DHU 352 | 3924 |
| BTR 308 | 3413 | CDB 186 | 2161 | CJN 321 | 2778 | CUH 840 | 1535 | DBD 983 | 1744 | DHY 666 | 3336 |
| BTR 311 | 3414 | CDB 187 | 2162 | CJN 322 | 2779 | CUH 841 | 1536 | DBD 984 | 1746 | DJN 554 | 4409 |
| BTR 312 | 3412 | CDB 188 | 2163 | CJN 323 | 2780 | CUH 842 | 1537 | DBD 985 | 1745 | DJN 556 | 4410 |
| BTW 498 | 3140 | CDB 189 | 2164 | CJN 324 | 2781 | CUH 843 | 1538 | DBD 986 | 1747 | DJN 557 | 4411 |
| BWY 979 | 3190 | CDB 190 | 2165 | CJN 325 | 2782 | CUH 844 | 1539 | DBD 987 | 1748 | DJN 558 | 4412 |
| BWY 980 | 3193 | CDB 191 | 2166 | CJN 326 | 2783 | CUH 845 | 1540 | DBE 185 | 1040 | DJN 559 | 4413 |
| BWY 981 | 3183 | CDB 192 | 2167 | CJN 327 | 2784 | CUH 846 | 1541 | DBE 186 | 1041 | DKH 466 | 2459 |
| BWY 982 | 3181 | CDB 213 | 2339 | CJN 328 | 2785 | CUH 847 | 1542 | DBE 187 | 1042 | DKN 31 | 3945 |
| BWY 983 | 3187 | CDB 214 | 2340 | CPN 1 | 1037 | CUH 848 | 1543 | DBE 188 | 1043 | DKN 32 | 3219 |
| BWY 984 | 3179 | CDB 215 | 2342 | CPN 2 | 1038 | CUH 849 | 1544 | DBE 189 | 1044 | DKN 33 | 3237 |
| BWY 985 | 3189 | CDB 216 | 2341 | CPN 3 | 1039 | CUH 850 | 1545 | DBE 190 | 1045 | DKN 34 | 3238 |
| BWY 986 | 3188 | CDB 217 | 2344 | CPN 4 | 1143 | CUH 851 | 1546 | DBL 151 | 1168 | DKN 35 | 3944 |
| BWY 987 | 3182 | CDB 218 | 2343 | CPN 5 | 1144 | CUH 852 | 1547 | DBL 152 | 1172 | DKN 36 | 3243 |
| BWY 988 | 3180 | CDB 219 | 2348 | CPN 6 | 1145 | CUH 853 | 1548 | DBL 153 | 1173 | DKN 37 | 3230 |
| BWY 989 | 3191 | CDB 220 | 2345 | CPN 7 | 1159 | CUH 854 | 1549 | DBL 154 | 1180 | DKN 38 | 3232 |
| BWY 990 | 3185 | CDB 221 | 2347 | CPN 8 | 1160 | CUH 855 | 1550 | DBL 155 | 1181 | DKN 39 | 3241 |
| BWY 991 | 3186 | CDB 222 | 2346 | CPN 9 | 1161 | CUH 856 | 1551 | DBL 156 | 1186 | DKN 40 | 3217 |
| BWY 992 | 3184 | CHJ 250 | 1792 | CPN 10 | 1164 | CUH 857 | 1552 | DBL 157 | 1189 | DKN 41 | 3942 |
| BWY 993 | 3192 | CHJ 251 | 1793 | CRX 548 | 1111 | CUH 858 | 1553 | DBL 158 | 1190 | DKN 42 | 3211 |
| BWY 995 | 3198 | CHJ 252 | 1794 | CRX 549 | 1110 | CUH 859 | 1554 | DBL 159 | 1192 | DKN 43 | 3240 |
| BWY 996 | 3194 | CHJ 253 | 1795 | CRX 550 | 1127 | CUH 860 | 1556 | DBL 160 | 1193 | DKN 44 | 3941 |
| BWY 997 | 3196 | CHJ 254 | 1796 | CRX 551 | 1126 | CUH 861 | 1557 | DBL 161 | 1196 | DKN 45 | 3210 |
| CAE 861 | 3911 | CHJ 255 | 1797 | CUH 798 | 1493 | CUH 862 | 1558 | DBL 162 | 1197 | DKN 46 | 3943 |
| CAE 862 | 3938 | CHJ 256 | 1798 | CUH 799 | 1494 | CUH 863 | 1559 | DBL 163 | 1262 | DMO 670 | 1725 |
| CAE 863 | 3913 | CHN 101 | 3155 | CUH 800 | 1495 | CUH 864 | 1560 | DBL 164 | 1271 | DMO 671 | 1726 |
| CAE 864 | 3935 | CHN 102 | 3159 | CUH 801 | 1496 | CUH 865 | 1561 | DBL 165 | 1272 | DMO 672 | 1727 |
| CAE 865 | 3923 | CHN 103 | 3156 | CUH 802 | 1497 | CUH 866 | 1562 | DBL 166 | 1331 | DMO 673 | 1728 |
| CAE 866 | 3937 | CHN 104 | 3157 | CUH 803 | 1498 | CUH 867 | 1555 | DBL 167 | 1331 | DMO 674 | 1729 |
| CDB 151 | 1477 | CHN 105 | 3160 | CUH 804 | 1499 | CUH 868 | 1567 | DDL 985 | 1108 | DMO 675 | 1730 |
| CDB 152 | 1478 | CHN 106 | 3158 | CUH 805 | 1500 | CUH 869 | 1563 | DDL 986 | 1109 | DMO 676 | 2001 |
| CDB 153 | 1479 | CHT 332 | 3337 | CUH 806 | 1501 | CUH 870 | 1568 | DEV 470 | 3138 | DMO 677 | 2002 |
| CDB 154 | 1480 | CHT 333 | 3347 | CUH 807 | 1502 | CUH 871 | 1564 | DEV 476 | 3139 | DMO 678 | 2003 |
| CDB 155 | 1483 | CHT 334 | 3341 | CUH 808 | 1503 | CUH 872 | 1565 | DEV 477 | 3135 | DMO 679 | 2004 |
| CDB 156 | 1484 | CHT 336 | 3342 | CUH 809 | 1504 | CUH 873 | 1566 | DEV 478 | 3134 | DMO 680 | 2005 |
| CDB 157 | 1485 | CHT 337 | 3327 | CUH 810 | 1505 | CUH 874 | 1569 | DEV 479 | 3133 | DMO 681 | 2006 |
| CDB 158 | 1486 | CHU 175 | 3925 | CUH 811 | 1506 | CUH 875 | 1570 | DEV 480 | 3137 | DMO 682 | 2007 |
| CDB 159 | 1487 | CHU 176 | 3928 | CUH 812 | 1507 | CUH 876 | 1571 | DFW 353 | 1911 | DMO 683 | 2008 |
| CDB 160 | 1488 | CHU 177 | 3922 | CUH 813 | 1508 | CUH 877 | 1572 | DFW 354 | 1912 | DMO 684 | 2009 |
| CDB 161 | 2136 | CHU 413 | 3351 | CUH 814 | 1509 | CWX 656 | 4557 | DFW 355 | 1913 | DMO 685 | 2010 |
| CDB 162 | 2137 | CHU 563 | 3330 | CUH 815 | 1510 | CWX 657 | 4550 | DFW 356 | 1914 | DMO 686 | 2011 |
| CDB 163 | 2138 | CHU 564 | 3332 | CUH 816 | 1511 | CWX 658 | 4554 | DFW 357 | 2200 | DMO 687 | 2012 |
| CDB 164 | 2139 | CHU 565 | 3333 | CUH 817 | 1512 | CWX 659 | 4552 | DFW 358 | 2201 | DMO 688 | 2013 |
| CDB 165 | 2140 | CHU 567 | 3331 | CUH 818 | 1513 | CWX 660 | 4553 | DFW 359 | 2202 | DMO 689 | 2014 |
| CDB 166 | 2141 | CHU 569 | 3346 | CUH 819 | 1514 | CWX 661 | 4548 | DFW 360 | 2203 | DMO 690 | 2015 |
| CDB 167 | 2142 | CHU 571 | 3352 | CUH 820 | 1515 | CWX 662 | 4558 | DFW 566 | 2303 | DMR 836 | 1018 |
| CDB 168 | 2143 | CHU 705 | 3940 | CUH 821 | 1519 | CWX 663 | 4549 | DFW 567 | 2304 | DMR 837 | 1022 |
| CDB 169 | 2144 | CHU 706 | 3926 | CUH 822 | 1516 | CWX 664 | 4555 | DFW 568 | 2305 | DMR 838 | 1123 |
| CDB 170 | 2145 | CHU 707 | 3915 | CUH 823 | 1517 | CWX 665 | 4556 | DFW 569 | 2306 | DMR 839 | 1124 |
| CDB 171 | 2146 | CHW 42 | 3936 | CUH 824 | 1523 | CWX 666 | 4551 | DHJ 21 | 2777 | DMR 840 | 1125 |
| CDB 172 | 2147 | CHW 43 | 3253 | CUH 825 | 1521 | CWX 667 | 3195 | DHJ 607 | 3686 | DNJ 995 | 1896 |
| CDB 173 | 2148 | CHW 44 | 3919 | CUH 826 | 1522 | CWX 668 | 3199 | DHJ 608 | 3687 | DNJ 996 | 1897 |
| CDB 174 | 2149 | CHW 45 | 3221 | CUH 827 | 1525 | DAE 369 | 3246 | DHJ 609 | 3688 | DNJ 997 | 1898 |
| CDB 175 | 2150 | CHW 46 | 3245 | CUH 828 | 1520 | DAE 370 | 3930 | DHJ 610 | 3689 | DNJ 998 | 1899 |
| CDB 176 | 2151 | CHW 47 | 3242 | CUH 829 | 1524 | DAE 371 | 3921 | DHJ 611 | 3690 | DNJ 999 | 1900 |
| CDB 177 | 2152 | CHW 48 | 4541 | CUH 830 | 1518 | DAE 373 | 4542 | DHJ 612 | 3691 | DOD 505 | 2204 |
| CDB 178 | 2153 | CHW 49 | 3340 | CUH 831 | 1526 | DAE 374 | 3244 | DHT 938 | 3914 | DSM 453 | 3130 |
| CDB 179 | 2154 | CHW 835 | 4543 | CUH 832 | 1528 | DAE 377 | 3249 | DHT 939 | 3932 | DTA 422 | 3433 |
| CDB 180 | 2155 | CHY 114 | 3927 | CUH 833 | 1527 | DAE 378 | 3933 | DHT 940 | 3916 | DTA 423 | 3431 |
| | | CHY 116 | 3225 | CUH 834 | 1529 | DAO 49 | 3891 | DHT 941 | 3934 | DTA 424 | 3434 |

| | | | | | | | | | | | |
|---|---|---|---|---|---|---|---|---|---|---|---|
| DTA 425 | 3432 | EDL 658 | 1723 | ERH 362 | 2461 | EWY 434 | 1389 | FFM 446 | 1103 | FFW 197 | 4270 |
| EAE 281 | 3214 | EDL 659 | 1724 | ERH 366 | 2463 | EWY 435 | 1403 | FFM 447 | 1104 | FFW 825 | 4067 |
| EAE 282 | 3234 | EEL 801 | 3424 | ERP 605 | 3667 | EWY 436 | 1404 | FFM 448 | 1106 | FFW 826 | 4068 |
| EAE 283 | 3235 | EEL 806 | 3315 | ERP 606 | 3668 | FAM 4 | 2786 | FFM 449 | 1107 | FFW 827 | 4069 |
| EAE 284 | 3251 | EHJ 27 | 4943 | ERP 607 | 3669 | FAM 5 | 2787 | FFM 450 | 1129 | FFW 828 | 4070 |
| EAE 285 | 3222 | EHJ 28 | 4944 | ERP 608 | 3670 | FAM 6 | 2788 | FFM 451 | 1130 | FFW 829 | 4071 |
| EAE 286 | 3920 | EHJ 29 | 4945 | ERP 609 | 3671 | FBE 321 | 2906 | FFM 452 | 1131 | FFW 830 | 4072 |
| EAE 287 | 3236 | EHT 541 | 3344 | ERP 610 | 3672 | FBE 322 | 2907 | FFM 453 | 1132 | FFW 831 | 4073 |
| EAE 288 | 3226 | EHT 548 | 3334 | ERP 611 | 3673 | FBE 323 | 2908 | FFM 454 | 1133 | FLJ 429 | 3421 |
| EAE 289 | 3227 | EJB 214 | 2643 | ERP 612 | 3674 | FBE 324 | 2949 | FFM 455 | 1139 | FLJ 430 | 3425 |
| EAE 596 | 3215 | EJB 215 | 2644 | ERP 613 | 3675 | FBE 325 | 2950 | FFM 470 | 1051 | FLJ 433 | 3422 |
| EAE 597 | 3939 | EJB 216 | 2645 | ERP 614 | 3676 | FBL 23 | 4095 | FFM 471 | 1052 | FLJ 435 | 3423 |
| EAE 598 | 4540 | EJB 217 | 2646 | ERP 615 | 3677 | FBL 24 | 4096 | FFM 472 | 1073 | FLJ 437 | 3426 |
| EAM 612 | 1212 | EJB 218 | 2647 | ERP 616 | 3678 | FBL 25 | 4097 | FFM 473 | 1074 | FMO 7 | 3640 |
| EAM 613 | 1211 | EJB 219 | 2648 | ERP 617 | 3679 | FBL 26 | 3632 | FFM 474 | 1077 | FMO 8 | 3641 |
| EAM 614 | 1228 | EJB 220 | 2649 | ERP 618 | 3680 | FBL 27 | 3633 | FFM 475 | 1078 | FMO 9 | 4098 |
| EAP 2 | 2828 | EJB 221 | 2650 | ERP 619 | 3681 | FBL 28 | 3634 | FFM 476 | 1079 | FMO 10 | 4099 |
| EAP 3 | 2829 | EJB 222 | 2651 | ERP 620 | 3682 | FBL 29 | 3635 | FFM 477 | 1090 | FMO 11 | 4100 |
| EAP 4 | 2830 | EJB 223 | 2652 | ERP 621 | 3683 | FBL 30 | 3636 | FFM 478 | 1236 | FMO 12 | 4102 |
| EAP 5 | 2831 | EJB 224 | 2653 | ERP 622 | 3685 | FBL 31 | 3637 | FFM 479 | 1246 | FMO 13 | 4101 |
| EAP 6 | 2832 | EJB 225 | 2654 | ERP 623 | 3684 | FBL 32 | 3638 | FFM 480 | 1248 | FMO 14 | 4103 |
| EAP 7 | 2833 | EJB 226 | 2655 | ERU 514 | 3314 | FBL 33 | 3639 | FFM 481 | 1249 | FMO 15 | 4105 |
| EAP 8 | 2834 | EJB 227 | 2656 | ERU 516 | 3316 | FCY 405 | 2982 | FFM 482 | 1255 | FMO 16 | 4104 |
| EAP 9 | 2835 | EJB 228 | 2657 | ESM 537 | 4242 | FCY 406 | 2984 | FFM 483 | 1256 | FMO 17 | 4106 |
| EAP 10 | 2836 | EJB 229 | 2658 | ESM 538 | 4243 | FCY 407 | 2986 | FFM 484 | 1274 | FMO 18 | 4107 |
| EAP 11 | 2837 | EJB 230 | 2659 | ETA 966 | 3435 | FCY 408 | 2988 | FFM 485 | 1275 | FMO 19 | 4108 |
| EBD 216 | 2713 | EJB 231 | 2660 | ETA 967 | 3436 | FCY 409 | 2990 | FFM 512 | 1278 | FMO 938 | 4711 |
| EBD 217 | 2714 | EJB 235 | 2661 | ETA 984 | 3437 | FCY 410 | 2996 | FFM 513 | 1292 | FMO 939 | 4712 |
| EBD 218 | 2715 | EJB 236 | 2662 | ETA 985 | 3439 | FCY 411 | 2998 | FFM 514 | 1293 | FMO 940 | 4713 |
| EBD 219 | 2716 | EJB 237 | 2663 | ETA 986 | 3438 | FCY 412 | 2994 | FFM 515 | 1294 | FMO 941 | 4714 |
| EBD 220 | 2717 | EJB 238 | 2665 | ETA 987 | 3440 | FDL 292 | 2636 | FFM 516 | 1312 | FMO 942 | 4715 |
| EBD 221 | 2718 | EJB 239 | 2664 | EWY 401 | 1019 | FDL 293 | 2637 | FFM 517 | 1313 | FMO 943 | 4716 |
| EBD 222 | 2719 | EJB 240 | 2666 | EWY 402 | 1020 | FDL 294 | 2638 | FFM 518 | 1314 | FMO 944 | 4717 |
| EBD 223 | 2720 | EJB 241 | 2667 | EWY 403 | 1021 | FDL 295 | 2639 | FFM 519 | 1342 | FMO 945 | 4718 |
| EBD 225 | 2722 | EMW 181 | 1799 | EWY 404 | 1221 | FDL 296 | 2640 | FFM 520 | 1343 | FMO 946 | 4719 |
| EBD 226 | 2723 | EMW 182 | 1800 | EWY 405 | 1231 | FDL 297 | 2641 | FFM 521 | 1344 | FMO 947 | 4720 |
| EBD 227 | 2724 | EMW 285 | 1801 | EWY 406 | 1095 | FDL 298 | 2642 | FFM 522 | 1355 | FMO 948 | 4721 |
| EBD 228 | 2725 | EMW 286 | 1802 | EWY 407 | 1096 | FDL 983 | 3627 | FFM 523 | 1356 | FMO 949 | 4722 |
| EBD 229 | 2726 | EMW 287 | 1803 | EWY 408 | 1097 | FDL 984 | 3628 | FFM 524 | 1357 | FMO 950 | 4723 |
| EBD 230 | 2727 | EMW 288 | 1804 | EWY 409 | 1204 | FDL 985 | 3630 | FFM 525 | 1364 | FMO 951 | 4724 |
| EBD 231 | 2728 | ENO 931 | 3136 | EWY 410 | 1219 | FDL 986 | 3631 | FFM 526 | 1365 | FMO 952 | 4725 |
| EBD 232 | 2729 | ENO 932 | 3131 | EWY 411 | 1220 | FDL 987 | 3629 | FFM 527 | 1368 | FMO 953 | 4726 |
| EBD 233 | 2730 | ENO 933 | 3132 | EWY 412 | 1034 | FEV 175 | 3151 | FFM 528 | 1377 | FMO 954 | 4727 |
| EBD 234 | 2963 | ENO 935 | 3143 | EWY 413 | 1035 | FEV 176 | 3146 | FFM 529 | 1395 | FMO 955 | 4728 |
| EBD 235 | 2964 | ENO 936 | 3142 | EWY 414 | 1036 | FEV 177 | 3149 | FFM 530 | 1396 | FMO 956 | 4729 |
| EBD 236 | 4195 | ENO 937 | 3141 | EWY 415 | 1155 | FEV 178 | 3148 | FFM 531 | 1397 | FMO 957 | 4730 |
| EBD 237 | 4196 | ENO 939 | 3144 | EWY 416 | 1156 | FEV 179 | 3145 | FFM 532 | 1398 | FMO 958 | 4731 |
| EBD 238 | 4271 | EPM 1 | 3776 | EWY 417 | 1080 | FEV 180 | 3147 | FFM 533 | 1399 | FMO 959 | 4732 |
| EBD 239 | 4272 | EPM 2 | 3777 | EWY 418 | 1081 | FEV 181 | 3152 | FFM 534 | 1400 | FMO 960 | 4733 |
| EBD 240 | 4273 | EPM 3 | 3778 | EWY 419 | 1263 | FEV 182 | 3150 | FFM 535 | 1401 | FMO 961 | 4734 |
| EBD 241 | 4274 | EPM 4 | 3779 | EWY 420 | 1264 | FFM 432 | 1001 | FFM 536 | 1182 | FMO 962 | 4735 |
| EBD 244 | 2721 | EPM 5 | 3780 | EWY 421 | 1265 | FFM 433 | 1002 | FFM 537 | 1191 | FMO 963 | 4736 |
| EDL 14 | 1240 | EPM 6 | 3781 | EWY 422 | 1276 | FFM 434 | 1003 | FFM 538 | 1203 | FMO 964 | 4737 |
| EDL 15 | 1241 | EPM 7 | 3782 | EWY 423 | 1277 | FFM 435 | 1004 | FFM 539 | 1214 | FMO 965 | 4738 |
| EDL 16 | 1242 | EPM 8 | 3783 | EWY 424 | 1305 | FFM 436 | 1005 | FFM 540 | 1224 | FMO 966 | 4739 |
| EDL 17 | 1409 | EPM 9 | 3784 | EWY 425 | 1306 | FFM 437 | 1006 | FFM 542 | 1234 | FMO 967 | 4740 |
| EDL 18 | 1410 | EPM 10 | 3785 | EWY 426 | 1307 | FFM 438 | 1007 | FFM 543 | 1235 | FMO 968 | 4367 |
| EDL 19 | 1411 | EPM 11 | 3786 | EWY 427 | 1336 | FFM 439 | 1008 | FFW 190 | 4263 | FMO 969 | 4368 |
| EDL 20 | 1412 | EPM 12 | 3787 | EWY 428 | 1350 | FFM 440 | 1128 | FFW 191 | 4264 | FMO 970 | 4369 |
| EDL 21 | 1413 | EPM 13 | 3788 | EWY 429 | 1351 | FFM 441 | 1092 | FFW 192 | 4265 | FMO 971 | 4370 |
| EDL 22 | 1414 | EPM 14 | 3789 | EWY 430 | 1363 | FFM 442 | 1099 | FFW 193 | 4266 | FMO 972 | 4371 |
| EDL 23 | 1415 | EPM 15 | 3790 | EWY 431 | 1375 | FFM 443 | 1100 | FFW 194 | 4267 | FMO 973 | 4372 |
| EDL 656 | 1721 | ERH 359 | 2460 | EWY 432 | 1383 | FFM 444 | 1101 | FFW 195 | 4268 | FMO 974 | 4373 |
| EDL 657 | 1722 | ERH 360 | 2462 | EWY 433 | 1384 | FFM 445 | 1102 | FFW 196 | 4269 | FMO 975 | 4374 |

| | | | | | | | | | | | |
|---|---|---|---|---|---|---|---|---|---|---|---|
| FMO 976 | 4375 | FPW 522 | 1388 | FWX 810 | 2135 | GDL 716 | 4708 | GFM 912 | 2220 | GHN 973 | 1440 |
| FMO 977 | 4376 | FPW 523 | 1394 | FWX 811 | 2116 | GDL 717 | 4709 | GFM 913 | 2221 | GHN 974 | 1441 |
| FMO 978 | 4377 | FPW 524 | 1405 | FWX 812 | 2117 | GDL 718 | 4710 | GFM 914 | 2222 | GHN 975 | 1442 |
| FMO 979 | 4378 | FPW 525 | 1406 | FWX 813 | 2118 | GFM 851 | 1916 | GFM 915 | 2223 | GHN 976 | 1443 |
| FMO 980 | 4379 | FPW 526 | 1407 | FWX 814 | 2119 | GFM 852 | 1915 | GFM 916 | 2224 | GHN 977 | 1444 |
| FMO 981 | 4380 | FPW 527 | 1408 | FWX 815 | 2120 | GFM 853 | 1917 | GFM 917 | 2225 | GHN 978 | 1445 |
| FMO 982 | 4381 | FRP 684 | 4386 | FWX 816 | 2121 | GFM 854 | 1918 | GFM 918 | 2226 | GHN 979 | 1446 |
| FMO 983 | 4382 | FRP 685 | 4385 | FWX 817 | 2122 | GFM 855 | 1919 | GFM 919 | 2227 | GHN 980 | 1447 |
| FMO 984 | 4383 | FRP 686 | 4387 | FWX 818 | 2123 | GFM 856 | 1920 | GFM 920 | 2228 | GHN 981 | 1448 |
| FMO 985 | 4384 | FRP 687 | 4388 | FWX 819 | 2124 | GFM 857 | 1921 | GFM 921 | 2229 | GHN 982 | 1449 |
| FMW 652 | 2789 | FRP 688 | 4389 | FWX 820 | 2125 | GFM 858 | 1922 | GFM 922 | 2230 | GHN 983 | 1450 |
| FMW 653 | 2790 | FRP 689 | 4390 | FWX 821 | 1755 | GFM 859 | 1923 | GFM 923 | 2231 | GHN 984 | 1451 |
| FMW 827 | 2791 | FRP 690 | 4391 | FWX 822 | 1756 | GFM 860 | 1924 | GFM 924 | 2232 | GHN 985 | 1452 |
| FNG 810 | 1011 | FRP 691 | 4392 | FWX 823 | 1757 | GFM 861 | 1925 | GFM 925 | 2233 | GHN 986 | 1453 |
| FNG 811 | 1012 | FRP 692 | 4393 | FWX 824 | 1758 | GFM 862 | 1926 | GFW 277 | 4521 | GHN 987 | 1454 |
| FNG 812 | 1023 | FRP 693 | 4394 | FWX 825 | 1759 | GFM 863 | 1927 | GFW 278 | 4520 | GHN 988 | 1455 |
| FNG 813 | 1024 | FRP 694 | 4395 | FWX 826 | 1760 | GFM 864 | 1928 | GFW 279 | 4522 | GHN 989 | 1456 |
| FNG 814 | 1093 | FRP 695 | 4396 | FWX 827 | 1761 | GFM 865 | 1929 | GFW 280 | 4691 | GHN 990 | 1457 |
| FNG 815 | 1226 | FRP 696 | 4397 | FWX 828 | 1762 | GFM 866 | 1930 | GFW 281 | 4692 | GHN 991 | 1458 |
| FNG 816 | 1227 | FRP 697 | 4398 | FWX 829 | 1763 | GFM 867 | 1931 | GFW 282 | 4693 | GHN 992 | 1459 |
| FNG 817 | 1229 | FRP 820 | 4803 | FWX 830 | 1764 | GFM 868 | 1932 | GFW 283 | 4694 | GHN 993 | 1460 |
| FNG 819 | 1046 | FRP 821 | 4804 | FWX 831 | 1749 | GFM 869 | 1933 | GFW 284 | 4695 | GHN 994 | 1461 |
| FNG 820 | 1047 | FRP 822 | 4805 | FWX 832 | 1750 | GFM 870 | 1934 | GFW 285 | 4696 | GHN 995 | 1462 |
| FNG 821 | 1048 | FRP 823 | 4806 | FWX 833 | 1751 | GFM 871 | 1935 | GFW 846 | 4697 | GHN 996 | 1463 |
| FNG 823 | 1142 | FRP 824 | 4807 | FWX 834 | 1752 | GFM 872 | 1936 | GFW 847 | 4698 | GHN 997 | 1286 |
| FNG 824 | 1154 | FRP 825 | 4808 | FWX 835 | 1753 | GFM 873 | 1937 | GFW 848 | 4699 | GHN 998 | 1298 |
| FNG 825 | 1157 | FRP 826 | 4809 | FWX 836 | 1754 | GFM 874 | 1938 | GFW 849 | 4700 | GHN 999 | 1299 |
| FNG 826 | 1158 | FRP 827 | 4810 | FWX 906 | 2131 | GFM 875 | 1939 | GFW 850 | 4701 | GHR 199 | 3766 |
| FNH 822 | 1141 | FRP 828 | 4952 | GAM 10 | 3764 | GFM 876 | 1940 | GFW 851 | 4702 | GHR 200 | 3767 |
| FNJ 101 | 4447 | FRP 829 | 4953 | GAM 11 | 3765 | GFM 877 | 1941 | GFW 852 | 4703 | GHR 364 | 3768 |
| FNJ 102 | 4448 | FRP 830 | 4954 | GAT 60 | 2464 | GFM 878 | 1942 | GFW 853 | 4704 | GHR 365 | 3769 |
| FNJ 104 | 4450 | FRP 831 | 4955 | GAT 61 | 2466 | GFM 879 | 1943 | GFW 854 | 4705 | GHR 366 | 3770 |
| FNJ 105 | 4451 | FRP 832 | 4930 | GAT 62 | 2465 | GFM 880 | 1944 | GFW 855 | 4706 | GHR 367 | 3771 |
| FNJ 106 | 4452 | FRP 833 | 4931 | GAT 63 | 2468 | GFM 881 | 1945 | GFW 856 | 4707 | GHR 368 | 3772 |
| FNJ 107 | 4453 | FRP 834 | 4932 | GAT 64 | 2470 | GFM 882 | 1946 | GHN 943 | 1053 | GHR 866 | 4854 |
| FNJ 108 | 4454 | FRP 835 | 4933 | GAT 66 | 2467 | GFM 883 | 1947 | GHN 944 | 1054 | GHR 867 | 4855 |
| FNJ 109 | 4455 | FRP 836 | 4934 | GAT 67 | 2472 | GFM 884 | 1948 | GHN 945 | 1068 | GHR 868 | 4856 |
| FNJ 110 | 4456 | FRP 837 | 4935 | GAT 68 | 2473 | GFM 885 | 1949 | GHN 946 | 1069 | GLJ 362 | 1200 |
| FNJ 111 | 4457 | FRP 838 | 4936 | GAT 69 | 2469 | GFM 886 | 1950 | GHN 947 | 1070 | GLJ 363 | 1201 |
| FNK 103 | 4449 | FRP 839 | 4946 | GAT 70 | 2471 | GFM 887 | 1951 | GHN 948 | 1071 | GLJ 364 | 1202 |
| FNV 117 | 4007 | FRP 840 | 4947 | GBE 839 | 3816 | GFM 888 | 1952 | GHN 949 | 1072 | GLJ 957 | 2307 |
| FNV 118 | 4008 | FRP 841 | 4948 | GBE 840 | 3817 | GFM 889 | 1953 | GHN 950 | 1087 | GLJ 958 | 2308 |
| FNV 119 | 4009 | FRP 842 | 4949 | GBE 841 | 3818 | GFM 890 | 1954 | GHN 951 | 1088 | GLJ 959 | 2309 |
| FPW 501 | 1075 | FRP 843 | 4950 | GBE 842 | 4074 | GFM 891 | 1661 | GHN 952 | 1089 | GLJ 960 | 2310 |
| FPW 502 | 1076 | FRP 844 | 4951 | GBE 843 | 4075 | GFM 892 | 1662 | GHN 953 | 1238 | GLJ 961 | 2311 |
| FPW 503 | 1237 | FRU 824 | 1025 | GBE 844 | 4076 | GFM 893 | 1664 | GHN 954 | 1239 | GLJ 962 | 2312 |
| FPW 504 | 1257 | FRU 825 | 1120 | GBE 845 | 4077 | GFM 894 | 1663 | GHN 955 | 1243 | GLJ 963 | 2313 |
| FPW 505 | 1258 | FRU 826 | 1121 | GBE 846 | 4078 | GFM 895 | 1665 | GHN 956 | 1251 | GLJ 964 | 1676 |
| FPW 506 | 1259 | FRU 827 | 1122 | GBJ 190 | 1579 | GFM 896 | 1666 | GHN 957 | 1252 | GLJ 965 | 1677 |
| FPW 507 | 1267 | FRU 828 | 1140 | GBJ 191 | 1580 | GFM 897 | 1667 | GHN 958 | 1253 | GLJ 966 | 1678 |
| FPW 508 | 1268 | FSM 380 | 4244 | GBJ 192 | 1581 | GFM 898 | 1668 | GHN 959 | 1254 | GLJ 967 | 1679 |
| FPW 509 | 1295 | FSM 381 | 4241 | GBJ 193 | 1582 | GFM 899 | 1669 | GHN 960 | 1285 | GLJ 968 | 1680 |
| FPW 510 | 1296 | FTX 476 | 1083 | GBJ 194 | 1583 | GFM 900 | 1670 | GHN 961 | 1273 | GLJ 969 | 1681 |
| FPW 511 | 1297 | FTX 477 | 1084 | GBJ 195 | 1584 | GFM 901 | 1671 | GHN 962 | 1280 | GLJ 970 | 1682 |
| FPW 512 | 1315 | FTX 478 | 1250 | GBJ 196 | 1585 | GFM 902 | 1672 | GHN 963 | 1318 | GLJ 971 | 1682 |
| FPW 513 | 1316 | FTX 479 | 1320 | GBJ 197 | 1586 | GFM 903 | 1673 | GHN 964 | 1322 | GLJ 972 | 1683 |
| FPW 514 | 1317 | FWX 801 | 2126 | GBJ 198 | 1587 | GFM 904 | 1674 | GHN 965 | 1284 | GLJ 973 | 1684 |
| FPW 515 | 1329 | FWX 802 | 2127 | GDL 434 | 3450 | GFM 905 | 1675 | GHN 966 | 1436 | GLJ 974 | 1686 |
| FPW 516 | 1330 | FWX 803 | 2128 | GDL 435 | 3451 | GFM 906 | 2214 | GHN 967 | 1437 | GLJ 975 | 1687 |
| FPW 517 | 1358 | FWX 804 | 2129 | GDL 711 | 4362 | GFM 907 | 2215 | GHN 968 | 1438 | GLJ 976 | 1688 |
| FPW 518 | 1359 | FWX 805 | 2130 | GDL 712 | 4363 | GFM 908 | 2216 | GHN 969 | 1323 | GLJ 977 | 1689 |
| FPW 519 | 1360 | FWX 807 | 2132 | GDL 713 | 4364 | GFM 909 | 2217 | GHN 970 | 1324 | GLJ 978 | 1690 |
| FPW 520 | 1386 | FWX 808 | 2133 | GDL 714 | 4365 | GFM 910 | 2218 | GHN 971 | 1332 | GLJ 979 | 1691 |
| FPW 521 | 1387 | FWX 809 | 2134 | GDL 715 | 4366 | GFM 911 | 2219 | GHN 972 | 1439 | GLJ 980 | 1692 |

| | | | | | | | | | | | |
|---|---|---|---|---|---|---|---|---|---|---|---|
| GLJ 981 | 1693 | GPW 666 | 1964 | GUF 741 | 1650 | GWX 131 | 2965 | HHN 200 | 1300 | HOD 3 | 2753 |
| GLJ 982 | 1694 | GPW 667 | 1965 | GUF 742 | 1651 | GWX 132 | 2967 | HHN 201 | 1310 | HOD 4 | 2754 |
| GLJ 983 | 1695 | GPW 668 | 1966 | GUF 743 | 1637 | GWX 133 | 2966 | HHN 202 | 1339 | HOD 5 | 2755 |
| GLJ 984 | 1697 | GPW 669 | 1967 | GUF 744 | 1638 | GWX 134 | 4275 | HHN 203 | 1345 | HOD 6 | 2756 |
| GLJ 985 | 1698 | GPW 670 | 1968 | GUF 745 | 1639 | GWX 135 | 4276 | HHN 204 | 1346 | HOD 7 | 2757 |
| GLJ 986 | 1696 | GPW 671 | 1969 | GUF 746 | 1640 | GWX 136 | 4277 | HHN 205 | 1311 | HOD 8 | 2758 |
| GLJ 987 | 1699 | GPW 672 | 1970 | GVF 65 | 1901 | GWX 137 | 4278 | HHN 206 | 1333 | HOD 9 | 2759 |
| GLJ 988 | 1700 | GPW 673 | 1971 | GVF 66 | 1902 | GWX 138 | 4279 | HHN 207 | 1337 | HOD 10 | 2760 |
| GLJ 989 | 1701 | GPW 674 | 1972 | GVF 67 | 1903 | GWX 139 | 4280 | HHN 208 | 1348 | HOD 11 | 2761 |
| GLJ 990 | 1702 | GPW 675 | 1973 | GVF 68 | 1904 | HAH 230 | 1230 | HHN 209 | 1349 | HOD 12 | 2762 |
| GLJ 991 | 1703 | GPW 676 | 1974 | GVF 69 | 1905 | HAL 841 | 1588 | HHN 210 | 1338 | HOD 13 | 2763 |
| GLJ 992 | 1704 | GPW 677 | 1975 | GVF 70 | 1906 | HBE 505 | 4893 | HHN 211 | 1361 | HOD 14 | 2764 |
| GLJ 993 | 1705 | GPW 678 | 1976 | GVF 71 | 1907 | HBE 506 | 4894 | HHN 212 | 1362 | HOD 15 | 2765 |
| GLJ 994 | 1995 | GPW 679 | 1977 | GVF 72 | 1908 | HBE 507 | 4895 | HHN 213 | 1371 | HOD 16 | 2766 |
| GLJ 995 | 1996 | GPW 680 | 1978 | GVF 73 | 1909 | HBE 508 | 4896 | HHN 214 | 1372 | HOD 17 | 2767 |
| GLJ 996 | 1997 | GPW 681 | 1979 | GVF 74 | 1910 | HBE 509 | 4897 | HHN 215 | 1347 | HOD 18 | 2768 |
| GLJ 997 | 1998 | GPW 682 | 1980 | GWO 882 | 2981 | HBE 510 | 4898 | HHN 216 | 1373 | HOD 19 | 2769 |
| GLJ 998 | 1999 | GPW 683 | 1981 | GWO 883 | 2983 | HBE 511 | 4974 | HHN 217 | 1374 | HOD 20 | 2770 |
| GLJ 999 | 2000 | GPW 684 | 1982 | GWO 884 | 2985 | HBE 512 | 4975 | HHN 218 | 1378 | HOD 21 | 2771 |
| GMR 26 | 3773 | GPW 685 | 1983 | GWO 885 | 2987 | HBE 513 | 4976 | HHN 219 | 1379 | HOD 22 | 2772 |
| GMR 27 | 3774 | GPW 686 | 1984 | GWO 886 | 2989 | HBE 514 | 4977 | HHN 220 | 1380 | HOD 23 | 2773 |
| GMR 28 | 3775 | GPW 687 | 1985 | GWO 887 | 2991 | HBE 756 | 4899 | HHN 221 | 1381 | HOD 24 | 2774 |
| GMR 29 | 4858 | GPW 688 | 1986 | GWO 888 | 2997 | HBE 757 | 4900 | HHN 222 | 1382 | HOD 25 | 2775 |
| GMR 30 | 4857 | GPW 689 | 1987 | GWO 916 | 2992 | HBE 759 | 4902 | HHW 886 | 3820 | HOD 26 | 2776 |
| GMR 31 | 4859 | GPW 690 | 1988 | GWO 917 | 2993 | HBR 758 | 4901 | HLJ 15 | 2567 | HOD 84 | 2622 |
| GMR 893 | 4439 | GPW 691 | 1989 | GWO 918 | 2995 | HCD 447 | 1642 | HLJ 16 | 2568 | HOD 85 | 2623 |
| GMR 894 | 4440 | GPW 692 | 1990 | GWO 919 | 3001 | HCD 448 | 1643 | HLJ 17 | 2569 | HOD 86 | 2624 |
| GMW 194 | 4441 | GPW 693 | 1991 | GWO 920 | 3002 | HCD 449 | 1644 | HLJ 18 | 2570 | HOD 87 | 2625 |
| GMW 195 | 4442 | GPW 694 | 1992 | GWO 921 | 2999 | HCD 450 | 1645 | HLJ 19 | 2571 | HOD 88 | 2626 |
| GMW 196 | 4443 | GPW 695 | 1993 | GWO 922 | 3003 | HCD 451 | 1646 | HLJ 20 | 2572 | HOD 89 | 2627 |
| GMW 850 | 4444 | GPW 696 | 1994 | GWO 923 | 3004 | HDL 182 | 4987 | HLJ 21 | 2573 | HOD 90 | 2628 |
| GMW 851 | 4445 | GSM 120 | 1307 | GWO 924 | 3005 | HDL 183 | 4988 | HLJ 22 | 2574 | HOD 91 | 2629 |
| GMW 911 | 4860 | GSM 121 | 1308 | GWO 925 | 3000 | HDL 184 | 4989 | HLJ 23 | 2575 | HOD 92 | 2630 |
| GMW 912 | 4861 | GSM 122 | 1309 | GWV 305 | 4446 | HFM 63 | 2274 | HLJ 24 | 2576 | HOD 93 | 2631 |
| GMW 913 | 4862 | GSM 123 | 1327 | GWX 101 | 2731 | HFM 64 | 2275 | HLJ 25 | 2577 | HOD 94 | 2632 |
| GPW 346 | 2238 | GSM 124 | 1328 | GWX 102 | 2732 | HFM 65 | 2276 | HLJ 26 | 2579 | HOD 95 | 2633 |
| GPW 347 | 2234 | GSM 125 | 1340 | GWX 103 | 2733 | HFM 66 | 2277 | HLJ 27 | 2578 | HOD 96 | 2634 |
| GPW 348 | 2235 | GSM 126 | 1341 | GWX 104 | 2734 | HFM 67 | 2278 | HLJ 28 | 2580 | HOD 97 | 2635 |
| GPW 349 | 2236 | GSM 127 | 1366 | GWX 105 | 2735 | HFM 68 | 2279 | HLJ 29 | 2581 | HPW 75 | 2838 |
| GPW 350 | 2237 | GSM 128 | 1367 | GWX 106 | 2736 | HFM 69 | 2280 | HLJ 30 | 2582 | HPW 76 | 2839 |
| GPW 351 | 2239 | GSM 129 | 1385 | GWX 107 | 2737 | HFM 70 | 2282 | HLJ 31 | 2583 | HPW 77 | 2840 |
| GPW 352 | 2240 | GTG 863 | 2205 | GWX 108 | 2738 | HFM 71 | 2281 | HLJ 32 | 2584 | HPW 78 | 2841 |
| GPW 353 | 2241 | GTG 864 | 2206 | GWX 109 | 2739 | HFM 72 | 2283 | HLJ 33 | 2585 | HPW 79 | 2842 |
| GPW 354 | 2242 | GTG 865 | 2207 | GWX 110 | 2740 | HFM 73 | 2284 | HLJ 34 | 2586 | HPW 80 | 2843 |
| GPW 355 | 2243 | GTG 866 | 2208 | GWX 111 | 2909 | HFM 74 | 2285 | HLJ 35 | 2587 | HPW 81 | 2844 |
| GPW 356 | 2244 | GTG 867 | 2209 | GWX 112 | 2910 | HFM 75 | 2286 | HLJ 36 | 2588 | HPW 82 | 2845 |
| GPW 357 | 2245 | GTG 868 | 2210 | GWX 113 | 2913 | HFM 76 | 2287 | HLJ 37 | 2589 | HPW 83 | 2846 |
| GPW 358 | 2246 | GTG 869 | 2211 | GWX 114 | 2911 | HFM 77 | 2288 | HLJ 38 | 2590 | HPW 84 | 2847 |
| GPW 359 | 2247 | GTG 870 | 2212 | GWX 115 | 2914 | HHN 42 | 1013 | HLJ 39 | 2591 | HPW 85 | 2848 |
| GPW 360 | 2248 | GTG 871 | 2213 | GWX 116 | 2912 | HHN 43 | 1014 | HLJ 40 | 2592 | HPW 86 | 2849 |
| GPW 361 | 2289 | GUF 727 | 1654 | GWX 117 | 2915 | HHN 44 | 1015 | HLJ 41 | 2593 | HPW 87 | 2850 |
| GPW 362 | 2290 | GUF 728 | 1655 | GWX 118 | 2916 | HHN 45 | 1112 | HLJ 42 | 2594 | HPW 88 | 2851 |
| GPW 363 | 2291 | GUF 729 | 1656 | GWX 119 | 2917 | HHN 46 | 1113 | HLJ 43 | 2595 | HPW 89 | 2852 |
| GPW 364 | 2292 | GUF 730 | 1652 | GWX 120 | 2918 | HHN 47 | 1098 | HLJ 44 | 2596 | HPW 90 | 2853 |
| GPW 365 | 2293 | GUF 731 | 1647 | GWX 121 | 2741 | HHN 48 | 1114 | HLJ 45 | 2945 | HPW 91 | 2854 |
| GPW 657 | 1955 | GUF 732 | 1649 | GWX 122 | 2742 | HHN 49 | 1091 | HLJ 46 | 2946 | HPW 92 | 2855 |
| GPW 658 | 1956 | GUF 733 | 1659 | GWX 123 | 2743 | HHN 50 | 1187 | HLJ 47 | 2947 | HPW 93 | 2856 |
| GPW 659 | 1957 | GUF 734 | 1658 | GWX 124 | 2744 | HHN 51 | 1188 | HLJ 48 | 2948 | HPW 94 | 2857 |
| GPW 660 | 1958 | GUF 735 | 1641 | GWX 125 | 2745 | HHN 52 | 1194 | HMN 787 | 2352 | HPW 95 | 2858 |
| GPW 661 | 1959 | GUF 736 | 1657 | GWX 126 | 2746 | HHN 53 | 1195 | HMN 788 | 2353 | HPW 96 | 2859 |
| GPW 662 | 1960 | GUF 737 | 1653 | GWX 127 | 2747 | HHN 54 | 1215 | HMN 789 | 2354 | HPW 97 | 2860 |
| GPW 663 | 1961 | GUF 738 | 1636 | GWX 128 | 2748 | HHN 55 | 1216 | HMN 790 | 2355 | HPW 98 | 2861 |
| GPW 664 | 1962 | GUF 739 | 1660 | GWX 129 | 2749 | HHN 56 | 1217 | HOD 1 | 2752 | HPW 99 | 2862 |
| GPW 665 | 1963 | GUF 740 | 1648 | GWX 130 | 2750 | HHN 57 | 1218 | HOD 2 | 2751 | HPW 100 | 2863 |

| | | | | | |
|---|---|---|---|---|---|
| HPW 101 2864 | HRU 848 2601 | HWW 866 3744 | JFM 54 2495 | JFM 118 2941 | JHN 364 2057 |
| HPW 102 2865 | HRU 849 2602 | HWW 867 3746 | JFM 55 2496 | JFM 119 3286 | JHN 365 2058 |
| HPW 103 2866 | HRU 850 2603 | HWW 868 3747 | JFM 56 2497 | JFM 120 3287 | JHN 366 2051 |
| HPW 104 2867 | HRU 851 2604 | HWW 869 3748 | JFM 57 2498 | JFM 121 3288 | JHN 367 2059 |
| HPW 105 2868 | HRU 852 2605 | HWW 870 3749 | JFM 58 2499 | JFM 122 3289 | JHN 368 2060 |
| HPW 106 2869 | HRU 853 2606 | HWW 871 3750 | JFM 59 2500 | JFM 123 3290 | JHN 369 2061 |
| HPW 107 2870 | HRU 854 2607 | HWW 872 3751 | JFM 60 2501 | JFM 124 3291 | JHN 370 2062 |
| HPW 108 2871 | HRU 855 2608 | HWW 873 3752 | JFM 61 2502 | JFM 125 3292 | JHN 371 2063 |
| HPW 109 2872 | HRU 856 2609 | HWW 874 3753 | JFM 62 2503 | JFM 126 3293 | JHN 372 2064 |
| HPW 110 2873 | HRU 857 2610 | HWW 875 3754 | JFM 63 2504 | JFM 127 4010 | JHN 373 2065 |
| HPW 111 2874 | HRU 858 2611 | HWW 876 3755 | JFM 64 2505 | JFM 128 4011 | JHN 374 2066 |
| HPW 112 2875 | HRU 859 2612 | HWW 877 3758 | JFM 65 2506 | JFM 129 4012 | JHN 375 2067 |
| HPW 113 2876 | HRU 860 2613 | HWW 878 3756 | JFM 66 2507 | JFM 130 4013 | JHN 376 2068 |
| HPW 114 2877 | HRU 861 2614 | HWW 879 3757 | JFM 67 2508 | JFM 131 4014 | JHN 377 2069 |
| HPW 115 2878 | HRU 862 2615 | HWW 880 3759 | JFM 68 2509 | JFM 132 4015 | JHN 378 2070 |
| HPW 116 2879 | HRU 863 2616 | HWW 881 3760 | JFM 69 2510 | JFM 133 4016 | JHN 379 2071 |
| HPW 117 2880 | HRU 864 2617 | HWW 882 3761 | JFM 70 2511 | JFM 134 4017 | JHN 380 2072 |
| HPW 118 2881 | HRU 865 2618 | HWW 883 3762 | JFM 71 2512 | JFM 135 4018 | JHN 381 2073 |
| HPW 119 2882 | HRU 866 2619 | HWW 884 3763 | JFM 72 2513 | JFM 136 4019 | JHN 382 2074 |
| HPW 120 2883 | HRU 867 2620 | HWW 885 3819 | JFM 73 2514 | JFM 137 4020 | JHN 383 2075 |
| HPW 121 2884 | HRU 868 2621 | HWW 887 3821 | JFM 74 2515 | JFM 138 4021 | JHN 384 2076 |
| HPW 122 2885 | HSM 642 2488 | HWW 888 3822 | JFM 75 2516 | JFM 139 4022 | JHN 385 2077 |
| HPW 123 2886 | HSM 643 2489 | HWW 889 3823 | JFM 76 2517 | JFM 140 4004 | JHN 386 2078 |
| HPW 124 2887 | HSM 644 2490 | HWW 890 3824 | JFM 77 2518 | JFM 141 4005 | JHN 387 2079 |
| HPW 125 2888 | HSM 645 2491 | HWW 891 3825 | JFM 78 2519 | JFM 142 4006 | JHN 388 2080 |
| HPW 126 2889 | HTT 970 1016 | HWW 892 3826 | JFM 79 2520 | JHN 324 2016 | JHN 389 2081 |
| HPW 127 2890 | HTT 971 1017 | JAT 618 2349 | JFM 80 2521 | JHN 325 2017 | JHN 390 2082 |
| HPW 128 2891 | HTT 972 1105 | JAT 619 2351 | JFM 81 2522 | JHN 326 2018 | JHN 391 2083 |
| HPW 129 2892 | HTT 973 1138 | JAT 620 2350 | JFM 82 2523 | JHN 327 2019 | JHN 392 2084 |
| HPW 130 2894 | HTT 974 1137 | JEL 244 3572 | JFM 83 2524 | JHN 328 2020 | JHN 393 2085 |
| HPW 131 2893 | HTT 975 1171 | JEL 245 3573 | JFM 84 2525 | JHN 329 2021 | JHN 394 2086 |
| HPW 132 2895 | HTT 976 1169 | JEL 246 3575 | JFM 85 2526 | JHN 330 2022 | JHN 395 2087 |
| HPW 133 2896 | HTT 977 1174 | JEL 247 3574 | JFM 86 2527 | JHN 331 2023 | JHN 396 2088 |
| HPW 134 2897 | HTT 978 1175 | JEL 248 3576 | JFM 87 2528 | JHN 332 2024 | JHN 397 2089 |
| HPW 135 2898 | HTT 979 1176 | JEL 249 3577 | JFM 88 2529 | JHN 333 2025 | JHN 398 2090 |
| HPW 136 2899 | HTT 980 1183 | JEL 250 3578 | JFM 89 2530 | JHN 334 2026 | JHN 399 2091 |
| HPW 137 2900 | HTT 981 1184 | JEL 251 3579 | JFM 90 2531 | JHN 335 2027 | JHN 400 2092 |
| HPW 138 2901 | HTT 982 1198 | JEL 252 3580 | JFM 91 2532 | JHN 336 2028 | JHN 401 2093 |
| HPW 139 2902 | HTT 983 1199 | JEL 253 3581 | JFM 92 2533 | JHN 337 2029 | JHN 402 2094 |
| HPW 140 2903 | HTT 984 1205 | JEL 254 3582 | JFM 93 2534 | JHN 338 2030 | JHN 403 2095 |
| HPW 141 2904 | HTT 985 1206 | JEL 255 3583 | JFM 94 2535 | JHN 339 2031 | JHN 404 2096 |
| HPW 142 2905 | HTT 986 1207 | JEL 256 3584 | JFM 95 2536 | JHN 340 2032 | JHN 406 2098 |
| HPW 817 3387 | HTT 987 1208 | JEL 257 3585 | JFM 96 2537 | JHN 341 2033 | JHN 407 2099 |
| HPW 818 3388 | HTT 988 1222 | JEL 258 3586 | JFM 97 2538 | JHN 342 2034 | JHN 408 2100 |
| HPW 819 3389 | HTT 989 1223 | JEL 259 3587 | JFM 98 2539 | JHN 343 2035 | JHN 409 2101 |
| HPW 820 3390 | HTT 990 1232 | JEL 260 3588 | JFM 99 2540 | JHN 344 2036 | JHN 410 2102 |
| HPW 821 3391 | HTT 991 1492 | JEL 261 3589 | JFM 100 2541 | JHN 346 2038 | JHN 411 2103 |
| HPW 822 3392 | HTT 992 1094 | JEL 262 3590 | JFM 101 2542 | JHN 347 2039 | JHN 412 2104 |
| HPW 823 3393 | HTT 993 1136 | JEL 263 3591 | JFM 102 2543 | JHN 348 2040 | JHN 413 2105 |
| HPW 824 3394 | HTT 994 1134 | JEL 264 3592 | JFM 103 2544 | JHN 349 2041 | JHN 414 2106 |
| HPW 825 3395 | HTT 995 1135 | JEL 265 3593 | JFM 104 2545 | JHN 350 2042 | JHN 415 2107 |
| HPW 826 3396 | HTT 996 1170 | JEL 266 3594 | JFM 105 2546 | JHN 351 2043 | JHN 416 2108 |
| HPW 827 3397 | HTT 997 1209 | JEL 267 3595 | JFM 106 2547 | JHN 352 2044 | JHN 417 2109 |
| HPW 828 3398 | HTT 998 1210 | JEL 268 3596 | JFM 107 2548 | JHN 353 2045 | JHN 418 2110 |
| HPW 829 3399 | HTT 999 1213 | JEL 269 3597 | JFM 108 2549 | JHN 354 2046 | JHN 419 2111 |
| HPW 830 3400 | HUW 780 1573 | JEL 270 3598 | JFM 109 2550 | JHN 355 2052 | JHN 420 2112 |
| HPW 831 3401 | HUW 781 1574 | JEL 271 3599 | JFM 110 2551 | JHN 356 2047 | JHN 421 2113 |
| HPW 832 3442 | HUW 782 1575 | JEL 272 3600 | JFM 111 2937 | JHN 357 2048 | JHN 422 2114 |
| HRU 32 2968 | HUW 783 1576 | JEL 273 3601 | JFM 112 2934 | JHN 358 2053 | JHN 423 2115 |
| HRU 33 2969 | HUW 784 1577 | JEL 274 3602 | JFM 113 2936 | JHN 359 2049 | JHN 458 1731 |
| HRU 844 2597 | HUW 785 1578 | JEL 275 3603 | JFM 114 2935 | JHN 360 2054 | JHN 459 1732 |
| HRU 845 2598 | HWW 863 3745 | JFM 51 2492 | JFM 115 2938 | JHN 361 2055 | JHN 460 1733 |
| HRU 846 2599 | HWW 864 3742 | JFM 52 2493 | JFM 116 2939 | JHN 362 2056 | JHN 461 1734 |
| HRU 847 2600 | HWW 865 3743 | JFM 53 2494 | JFM 117 2940 | JHN 363 2050 | JHN 462 1735 |

| | | | | | | | | | | | | | |
|---|---|---|---|---|---|---|---|---|---|---|---|---|---|
| JHN 463 | 1736 | JHT 860 | 1430 | JUO 970 | 1713 | JWY 228 | 4401 | KEL 723 | 4336 | KFM 284 | 3502 | | |
| JHN 464 | 1737 | JHT 861 | 1431 | JUO 971 | 1714 | JWY 229 | 4402 | KEL 724 | 4337 | KFM 285 | 3503 | | |
| JHN 465 | 1738 | JHT 862 | 1432 | JUO 972 | 1715 | JWY 230 | 4403 | KEL 725 | 4338 | KFM 286 | 3504 | | |
| JHN 466 | 1739 | JHT 863 | 1433 | JUO 973 | 1716 | JWY 231 | 4404 | KEL 726 | 4339 | KFM 287 | 3505 | | |
| JHN 467 | 1740 | JHT 864 | 1434 | JUO 974 | 1717 | JXT 490 | 3022 | KEL 727 | 4340 | KFM 288 | 3506 | | |
| JHT 801 | 1026 | JHT 865 | 1435 | JUO 975 | 1718 | JXT 491 | 3025 | KEL 728 | 4341 | KFM 289 | 3507 | | |
| JHT 802 | 1027 | JNH 406 | 3306 | JUO 976 | 1719 | JXT 492 | 3023 | KEL 729 | 4342 | KFM 290 | 3508 | | |
| JHT 803 | 1028 | JNH 407 | 3307 | JUO 977 | 1720 | JXT 493 | 3024 | KEL 730 | 4343 | KFM 291 | 3509 | | |
| JHT 804 | 1029 | JNH 408 | 3308 | JUO 990 | 2299 | JXT 494 | 3026 | KEL 731 | 4956 | KFM 292 | 3510 | | |
| JHT 805 | 1030 | JNH 409 | 3309 | JUO 991 | 2300 | JXT 495 | 3027 | KEL 732 | 4957 | KFM 293 | 3511 | | |
| JHT 806 | 1031 | JNH 413 | 3310 | JUO 992 | 2301 | JYG 717 | 4831 | KEL 733 | 4958 | KFM 763 | 4023 | | |
| JHT 807 | 1032 | JNH 414 | 3311 | JUO 993 | 2302 | JYG 718 | 4832 | KEL 734 | 4959 | KFM 764 | 4024 | | |
| JHT 808 | 1033 | JNH 415 | 3312 | JWT 283 | 4197 | JYG 719 | 4833 | KEL 735 | 4960 | KFM 765 | 4025 | | |
| JHT 809 | 1049 | JNH 417 | 3313 | JWT 284 | 4198 | JYG 720 | 4834 | KEL 736 | 4961 | KFM 766 | 4026 | | |
| JHT 810 | 1050 | JTT 996 | 1233 | JWT 285 | 4199 | JYG 721 | 4835 | KFM 234 | 3452 | KFM 767 | 4027 | | |
| JHT 811 | 1146 | JTT 997 | 1489 | JWT 286 | 4200 | JYG 722 | 4836 | KFM 235 | 3453 | KFM 768 | 4028 | | |
| JHT 812 | 1147 | JTT 998 | 1490 | JWT 287 | 4204 | JYG 723 | 4837 | KFM 236 | 3454 | KFM 769 | 4029 | | |
| JHT 813 | 1148 | JTT 999 | 1491 | JWT 288 | 4201 | JYG 724 | 4838 | KFM 237 | 3455 | KFM 770 | 4030 | | |
| JHT 814 | 1149 | JUO 905 | 1765 | JWT 289 | 4202 | JYG 725 | 4839 | KFM 238 | 3456 | KFM 771 | 4031 | | |
| JHT 815 | 1150 | JUO 906 | 1766 | JWT 290 | 4203 | JYG 726 | 4840 | KFM 239 | 3457 | KFM 772 | 4033 | | |
| JHT 816 | 1151 | JUO 907 | 1768 | JWT 291 | 4205 | JYG 727 | 4841 | KFM 240 | 3458 | KFM 773 | 4032 | | |
| JHT 817 | 1152 | JUO 908 | 1767 | JWT 292 | 4206 | JYG 728 | 4842 | KFM 241 | 3459 | KFM 774 | 4034 | | |
| JHT 818 | 1153 | JUO 909 | 1769 | JWT 293 | 4207 | JYG 729 | 4843 | KFM 242 | 3460 | KFM 775 | 4035 | | |
| JHT 819 | 1166 | JUO 910 | 1770 | JWT 294 | 4208 | JYG 742 | 4848 | KFM 243 | 3461 | KFM 776 | 4036 | | |
| JHT 820 | 1162 | JUO 911 | 1771 | JWT 295 | 4209 | JYG 743 | 4849 | KFM 244 | 3462 | KFM 777 | 4037 | | |
| JHT 821 | 1167 | JUO 912 | 1772 | JWT 381 | 4210 | JYG 744 | 4903 | KFM 245 | 3463 | KFM 778 | 4038 | | |
| JHT 822 | 1163 | JUO 913 | 1773 | JWT 382 | 4211 | JYG 745 | 4904 | KFM 246 | 3464 | KFM 892 | 4039 | | |
| JHT 823 | 1165 | JUO 914 | 1774 | JWT 712 | 3853 | JYG 746 | 4983 | KFM 247 | 3465 | KFM 893 | 4040 | | |
| JHT 824 | 1057 | JUO 915 | 1775 | JWU 869 | 4811 | JYG 747 | 4984 | KFM 248 | 3466 | KFM 894 | 4041 | | |
| JHT 825 | 1058 | JUO 916 | 1776 | JWU 870 | 4812 | JYG 748 | 4985 | KFM 249 | 3467 | KHK 513 | 1009 | | |
| JHT 826 | 1065 | JUO 917 | 1777 | JWU 871 | 4814 | JYG 749 | 4986 | KFM 250 | 3468 | KHK 514 | 1010 | | |
| JHT 827 | 1066 | JUO 918 | 1778 | JWU 872 | 4813 | KAH 401 | 3402 | KFM 251 | 3469 | KHM 345 | 2037 | | |
| JHT 828 | 1067 | JUO 919 | 1779 | JWU 873 | 4815 | KAH 402 | 3403 | KFM 252 | 3470 | KHN 368 | 2668 | | |
| JHT 829 | 1085 | JUO 920 | 1780 | JWU 874 | 4816 | KAH 403 | 3404 | KFM 253 | 3471 | KHN 369 | 2669 | | |
| JHT 830 | 1244 | JUO 921 | 1781 | JWU 875 | 4817 | KAH 404 | 3405 | KFM 254 | 3472 | KHN 370 | 2670 | | |
| JHT 831 | 1245 | JUO 922 | 1782 | JWU 876 | 4818 | KAH 405 | 3406 | KFM 255 | 3473 | KHN 371 | 2671 | | |
| JHT 832 | 1247 | JUO 923 | 1783 | JWU 877 | 4819 | KAH 406 | 3410 | KFM 256 | 3474 | KHN 372 | 2672 | | |
| JHT 833 | 1266 | JUO 924 | 1784 | JWU 878 | 4820 | KAH 407 | 3407 | KFM 257 | 3475 | KHN 373 | 2673 | | |
| JHT 834 | 1287 | JUO 925 | 1785 | JWU 879 | 4821 | KAH 408 | 3411 | KFM 258 | 3476 | KHN 374 | 2674 | | |
| JHT 835 | 1288 | JUO 926 | 1786 | JWU 880 | 4822 | KAH 409 | 3408 | KFM 259 | 3477 | KHN 375 | 2675 | | |
| JHT 836 | 1289 | JUO 927 | 1787 | JWU 881 | 4823 | KAH 410 | 3409 | KFM 260 | 3478 | KHN 376 | 2676 | | |
| JHT 837 | 1301 | JUO 928 | 1788 | JWU 882 | 4824 | KEL 700 | 4313 | KFM 261 | 3479 | KHN 377 | 2677 | | |
| JHT 838 | 1302 | JUO 929 | 1789 | JWU 883 | 4825 | KEL 701 | 4316 | KFM 262 | 3480 | KHN 379 | 2679 | | |
| JHT 839 | 1325 | JUO 930 | 1790 | JWU 884 | 4826 | KEL 702 | 4317 | KFM 263 | 3481 | KHN 380 | 2680 | | |
| JHT 840 | 1326 | JUO 931 | 1791 | JWU 885 | 4827 | KEL 703 | 4314 | KFM 264 | 3482 | KHN 381 | 2681 | | |
| JHT 841 | 1334 | JUO 945 | 2262 | JWU 886 | 4828 | KEL 704 | 4315 | KFM 265 | 3483 | KHN 382 | 2682 | | |
| JHT 842 | 1335 | JUO 946 | 2263 | JWU 887 | 4829 | KEL 705 | 4318 | KFM 266 | 3484 | KHN 383 | 2683 | | |
| JHT 843 | 1352 | JUO 947 | 2264 | JWU 888 | 4830 | KEL 706 | 4319 | KFM 267 | 3485 | KHN 384 | 2684 | | |
| JHT 844 | 1353 | JUO 948 | 2265 | JWU 889 | 4937 | KEL 707 | 4320 | KFM 268 | 3489 | KHN 385 | 2685 | | |
| JHT 845 | 1354 | JUO 949 | 2266 | JWU 890 | 4938 | KEL 708 | 4321 | KFM 269 | 3490 | KHN 386 | 2686 | | |
| JHT 846 | 1416 | JUO 950 | 2267 | JWU 891 | 4939 | KEL 709 | 4322 | KFM 270 | 3486 | KHN 387 | 2687 | | |
| JHT 847 | 1417 | JUO 951 | 2268 | JWU 892 | 4940 | KEL 710 | 4323 | KFM 271 | 3487 | KHN 388 | 2688 | | |
| JHT 848 | 1422 | JUO 952 | 2269 | JWU 893 | 4941 | KEL 711 | 4326 | KFM 272 | 3488 | KHN 389 | 2689 | | |
| JHT 849 | 1423 | JUO 953 | 2270 | JWU 894 | 4942 | KEL 712 | 4324 | KFM 273 | 3491 | KHN 390 | 2690 | | |
| JHT 850 | 1424 | JUO 954 | 2271 | JWU 895 | 4844 | KEL 713 | 4325 | KFM 274 | 3492 | KHN 391 | 2691 | | |
| JHT 851 | 1425 | JUO 955 | 2272 | JWU 896 | 4845 | KEL 714 | 4327 | KFM 275 | 3493 | KHN 392 | 2692 | | |
| JHT 852 | 1418 | JUO 956 | 2273 | JWU 897 | 4846 | KEL 715 | 4328 | KFM 276 | 3494 | KHN 405 | 2097 | | |
| JHT 853 | 1419 | JUO 963 | 1706 | JWU 898 | 4847 | KEL 716 | 4329 | KFM 277 | 3495 | KHN 424 | 2951 | | |
| JHT 854 | 1420 | JUO 964 | 1707 | JWY 222 | 4399 | KEL 717 | 4330 | KFM 278 | 3496 | KHN 425 | 2952 | | |
| JHT 855 | 1426 | JUO 965 | 1708 | JWY 223 | 4400 | KEL 718 | 4331 | KFM 279 | 3497 | KHN 426 | 2953 | | |
| JHT 856 | 1421 | JUO 966 | 1709 | JWY 224 | 4405 | KEL 719 | 4332 | KFM 280 | 3499 | KHN 427 | 2954 | | |
| JHT 857 | 1427 | JUO 967 | 1710 | JWY 225 | 4406 | KEL 720 | 4333 | KFM 281 | 3498 | KHN 428 | 2955 | | |
| JHT 858 | 1428 | JUO 968 | 1711 | JWY 226 | 4407 | KEL 721 | 4334 | KFM 282 | 3500 | KHN 429 | 2956 | | |
| JHT 859 | 1429 | JUO 969 | 1712 | JWY 227 | 4408 | KEL 722 | 4335 | KFM 283 | 3501 | KHN 430 | 2957 | | |

| | | | | | | | | | | | |
|---|---|---|---|---|---|---|---|---|---|---|---|
| KHN 431 | 2958 | KHW 638 | 1609 | KNG 376 | 3522 | KNO 611 | 1270 | KUO 976 | 3741 | LAE 316 | 1875 |
| KHN 432 | 2959 | KHW 639 | 1610 | KNG 377 | 3523 | KNO 612 | 1290 | KUO 977 | 3604 | LAE 317 | 1876 |
| KHN 433 | 2960 | KHW 640 | 2168 | KNG 378 | 3524 | KNO 613 | 1291 | KUO 978 | 3605 | LAE 318 | 1878 |
| KHN 434 | 2961 | KHW 641 | 2169 | KNG 379 | 3525 | KNO 614 | 1303 | KUO 979 | 3606 | LAE 319 | 1870 |
| KHN 435 | 2962 | KHW 642 | 2170 | KNG 380 | 3526 | KNO 615 | 1304 | KUO 980 | 3607 | LAE 320 | 1871 |
| KHN 493 | 2693 | KHW 643 | 2171 | KNG 381 | 3527 | KNO 616 | 1319 | KUO 981 | 3608 | LAE 701 | 1877 |
| KHN 494 | 2694 | KHW 644 | 2172 | KNG 382 | 3528 | KNO 617 | 1321 | KUO 982 | 3609 | LAE 702 | 1872 |
| KHN 495 | 2695 | KHY 381 | 2173 | KNG 383 | 3529 | KNO 618 | 1369 | KUO 983 | 3610 | LAE 703 | 1873 |
| KHN 496 | 2696 | KHY 382 | 2174 | KNG 384 | 3530 | KNO 619 | 1370 | KUO 984 | 3611 | LAE 704 | 1874 |
| KHN 497 | 2697 | KHY 383 | 2175 | KNG 385 | 3531 | KNO 620 | 1376 | KUO 985 | 3612 | LAE 705 | 1879 |
| KHN 498 | 2698 | KHY 384 | 1826 | KNG 386 | 3532 | KNO 621 | 1390 | KUO 986 | 3613 | LAE 706 | 1880 |
| KHN 499 | 2699 | KHY 385 | 1827 | KNG 387 | 3533 | KNO 622 | 1391 | KUO 987 | 3614 | LAE 707 | 1881 |
| KHN 500 | 2700 | KHY 386 | 1828 | KNG 388 | 3534 | KNO 623 | 1392 | KUO 988 | 3615 | LAE 708 | 1882 |
| KHT 511 | 1818 | KHY 387 | 1829 | KNG 389 | 3535 | KNO 624 | 1393 | KUO 989 | 3616 | LAE 709 | 1883 |
| KHT 512 | 1816 | KHY 388 | 1830 | KNG 390 | 3536 | KNO 625 | 1402 | KUO 990 | 3618 | LAE 710 | 1890 |
| KHT 513 | 1813 | KHY 389 | 1831 | KNG 391 | 3537 | KUO 927 | 3692 | KUO 991 | 3617 | LAE 711 | 1891 |
| KHT 514 | 1814 | KHY 390 | 1832 | KNG 392 | 3538 | KUO 928 | 3694 | KUO 992 | 3619 | LAE 712 | 1884 |
| KHT 515 | 1815 | KHY 395 | 2324 | KNG 393 | 3539 | KUO 929 | 3693 | KUO 993 | 3620 | LAE 713 | 1885 |
| KHT 516 | 1819 | KHY 399 | 2336 | KNG 394 | 3540 | KUO 930 | 3695 | KUO 994 | 3621 | LAE 714 | 1886 |
| KHT 517 | 1817 | KHY 741 | 1833 | KNG 395 | 3541 | KUO 931 | 3696 | KUO 995 | 3622 | LAE 715 | 1887 |
| KHT 518 | 1820 | KHY 742 | 1834 | KNG 697 | 4256 | KUO 932 | 3697 | KUO 996 | 3623 | LAE 716 | 1888 |
| KHT 519 | 1805 | KHY 743 | 1835 | KNG 698 | 4257 | KUO 933 | 3698 | KUO 997 | 3624 | LAE 717 | 1889 |
| KHT 520 | 1806 | KHY 744 | 1836 | KNG 699 | 4258 | KUO 934 | 3699 | KUO 998 | 3626 | LAE 718 | 1892 |
| KHT 521 | 1807 | KHY 745 | 1837 | KNG 700 | 4259 | KUO 935 | 3700 | KUO 999 | 3625 | LAE 719 | 1893 |
| KHT 522 | 1808 | KHY 746 | 1838 | KNG 701 | 4260 | KUO 936 | 3701 | LAE 1 | 2337 | LAE 720 | 1894 |
| KHU 601 | 1597 | KHY 747 | 1839 | KNG 702 | 4261 | KUO 937 | 3702 | LAE 3 | 2338 | LFM 714 | 4559 |
| KHU 602 | 1596 | KHY 748 | 1840 | KNG 703 | 4262 | KUO 938 | 3703 | LAE 4 | 2333 | LFM 715 | 4560 |
| KHU 603 | 1598 | KHY 749 | 1841 | KNG 704 | 4888 | KUO 939 | 3704 | LAE 5 | 2326 | LFM 716 | 4561 |
| KHU 604 | 1599 | KHY 750 | 1842 | KNG 705 | 4889 | KUO 940 | 3705 | LAE 6 | 2327 | LFM 717 | 4562 |
| KHU 605 | 1593 | KNG 152 | 3791 | KNG 706 | 4890 | KUO 941 | 3706 | LAE 7 | 2325 | LFM 718 | 4563 |
| KHU 606 | 1594 | KNG 153 | 3792 | KNG 707 | 4891 | KUO 942 | 3707 | LAE 8 | 2330 | LFM 719 | 4564 |
| KHU 607 | 1595 | KNG 154 | 3793 | KNG 708 | 4892 | KUO 943 | 3708 | LAE 11 | 2328 | LFM 720 | 4565 |
| KHU 608 | 1600 | KNG 155 | 3794 | KNG 709 | 4647 | KUO 944 | 3709 | LAE 12 | 2334 | LFM 721 | 4566 |
| KHU 609 | 1601 | KNG 156 | 3795 | KNG 710 | 4648 | KUO 945 | 3710 | LAE 13 | 2331 | LFM 722 | 4567 |
| KHU 610 | 1602 | KNG 157 | 3796 | KNG 711 | 4649 | KUO 946 | 3711 | LAE 14 | 2332 | LFM 723 | 4568 |
| KHU 611 | 1603 | KNG 158 | 3797 | KNG 712 | 4650 | KUO 947 | 3712 | LAE 15 | 2329 | LFM 724 | 4569 |
| KHU 612 | 1604 | KNG 159 | 3798 | KNG 713 | 4651 | KUO 948 | 3713 | LAE 18 | 2335 | LFM 725 | 4570 |
| KHU 613 | 1809 | KNG 160 | 3799 | KNG 714 | 4652 | KUO 949 | 3714 | LAE 19 | 1843 | LFM 726 | 4571 |
| KHU 614 | 1810 | KNG 161 | 3800 | KNG 715 | 4653 | KUO 950 | 3715 | LAE 20 | 1844 | LFM 727 | 4572 |
| KHU 615 | 1811 | KNG 162 | 3801 | KNG 716 | 4654 | KUO 951 | 3716 | LAE 21 | 1845 | LFM 728 | 4573 |
| KHU 616 | 1812 | KNG 163 | 3802 | KNG 717 | 4655 | KUO 952 | 3717 | LAE 22 | 1846 | LFM 729 | 4574 |
| KHU 617 | 1821 | KNG 164 | 3803 | KNG 718 | 4656 | KUO 953 | 3718 | LAE 23 | 1850 | LFM 730 | 4575 |
| KHU 618 | 1822 | KNG 165 | 3804 | KNG 719 | 4657 | KUO 954 | 3719 | LAE 24 | 1847 | LFM 731 | 4577 |
| KHU 619 | 1823 | KNG 250 | 3805 | KNG 720 | 4658 | KUO 955 | 3720 | LAE 25 | 1851 | LFM 732 | 4578 |
| KHU 620 | 1824 | KNG 251 | 3806 | KNG 721 | 4659 | KUO 956 | 3721 | LAE 26 | 1852 | LFM 733 | 4576 |
| KHU 621 | 1589 | KNG 252 | 3807 | KNG 722 | 4660 | KUO 957 | 3722 | LAE 27 | 1848 | LFM 734 | 4579 |
| KHU 622 | 1592 | KNG 253 | 3808 | KNG 723 | 4661 | KUO 958 | 3723 | LAE 28 | 1849 | LFM 735 | 4580 |
| KHU 623 | 1590 | KNG 254 | 3809 | KNO 442 | 1118 | KUO 959 | 3725 | LAE 29 | 1853 | LFM 736 | 4581 |
| KHU 624 | 1591 | KNG 255 | 3810 | KNO 443 | 1119 | KUO 960 | 3724 | LAE 30 | 1854 | LFM 737 | 4584 |
| KHW 623 | 2314 | KNG 256 | 3811 | KNO 596 | 1177 | KUO 961 | 3726 | LAE 301 | 1856 | LFM 738 | 4585 |
| KHW 624 | 2318 | KNG 257 | 3812 | KNO 597 | 1178 | KUO 962 | 3728 | LAE 302 | 1857 | LFM 739 | 4590 |
| KHW 625 | 2319 | KNG 258 | 3813 | KNO 598 | 1179 | KUO 963 | 3727 | LAE 303 | 1855 | LFM 740 | 4589 |
| KHW 626 | 2317 | KNG 259 | 3814 | KNO 599 | 1055 | KUO 964 | 3729 | LAE 304 | 1858 | LFM 741 | 4599 |
| KHW 627 | 2315 | KNG 260 | 3815 | KNO 600 | 1058 | KUO 965 | 3730 | LAE 305 | 1859 | LFM 742 | 4601 |
| KHW 628 | 2316 | KNG 366 | 3512 | KNO 601 | 1059 | KUO 966 | 3731 | LAE 306 | 1860 | LFM 744 | 4603 |
| KHW 629 | 2321 | KNG 367 | 3513 | KNO 602 | 1060 | KUO 967 | 3732 | LAE 307 | 1861 | LFM 745 | 4600 |
| KHW 630 | 2320 | KNG 368 | 3514 | KNO 603 | 1061 | KUO 968 | 3733 | LAE 308 | 1862 | LFM 746 | 4883 |
| KHW 631 | 2322 | KNG 369 | 3516 | KNO 604 | 1062 | KUO 969 | 3734 | LAE 309 | 1863 | LFM 747 | 4878 |
| KHW 632 | 2323 | KNG 370 | 3515 | KNO 605 | 1063 | KUO 970 | 3735 | LAE 310 | 1864 | LFM 748 | 4882 |
| KHW 633 | 1605 | KNG 371 | 3517 | KNO 606 | 1064 | KUO 971 | 3736 | LAE 311 | 1867 | LFM 749 | 4879 |
| KHW 634 | 1825 | KNG 372 | 3518 | KNO 607 | 1086 | KUO 972 | 3738 | LAE 312 | 1865 | LFM 750 | 4880 |
| KHW 635 | 1606 | KNG 373 | 3519 | KNO 608 | 1260 | KUO 973 | 3737 | LAE 313 | 1866 | LFM 751 | 4881 |
| KHW 636 | 1607 | KNG 374 | 3520 | KNO 609 | 1261 | KUO 974 | 3739 | LAE 314 | 1868 | LFM 752 | 4887 |
| KHW 637 | 1608 | KNG 375 | 3521 | KNO 610 | 1269 | KUO 975 | 3740 | LAE 315 | 1869 | LFM 753 | 4884 |

| | | | | | | | | | | | |
|---|---|---|---|---|---|---|---|---|---|---|---|
| LFM 754 | 4885 | LHN 369 | 3368 | LHN 834 | 4143 | LHT 904 | 2178 | LHU 987 | 2820 | LHY 949 | 3852 |
| LFM 755 | 4886 | LHN 370 | 3369 | LHN 835 | 4141 | LHT 905 | 2179 | LHU 988 | 2821 | LHY 950 | 3960 |
| LFM 756 | 4582 | LHN 371 | 3370 | LHN 836 | 4144 | LHT 906 | 2180 | LHU 989 | 2822 | LHY 951 | 3961 |
| LFM 757 | 4583 | LHN 372 | 3371 | LHN 837 | 4142 | LHT 907 | 2181 | LHU 990 | 2823 | LHY 952 | 3962 |
| LFM 758 | 4586 | LHN 373 | 3372 | LHN 838 | 4145 | LHT 908 | 2182 | LHU 991 | 2824 | LHY 953 | 3963 |
| LFM 759 | 4587 | LHN 374 | 3373 | LHN 839 | 4146 | LHT 909 | 2183 | LHU 992 | 2825 | LHY 954 | 3964 |
| LFM 760 | 4588 | LHN 375 | 3374 | LHN 840 | 4147 | LHT 910 | 2184 | LHU 993 | 2826 | LHY 955 | 3965 |
| LFM 761 | 4591 | LHN 376 | 3375 | LHN 841 | 4148 | LHT 911 | 2185 | LHU 994 | 2827 | LHY 956 | 3966 |
| LFM 762 | 4592 | LHN 377 | 3376 | LHN 842 | 4149 | LHT 912 | 2186 | LHU 995 | 3260 | LHY 957 | 3967 |
| LFM 763 | 4593 | LHN 378 | 2678 | LHN 843 | 4150 | LHT 913 | 2187 | LHW 901 | 3261 | LHY 958 | 3968 |
| LFM 764 | 4594 | LHN 556 | 3355 | LHN 844 | 4151 | LHT 914 | 2188 | LHW 902 | 2928 | LHY 959 | 3969 |
| LFM 765 | 4598 | LHN 557 | 3356 | LHN 845 | 4152 | LHT 915 | 2189 | LHW 903 | 2929 | LHY 960 | 3970 |
| LFM 766 | 4595 | LHN 558 | 3357 | LHN 846 | 4153 | LHT 916 | 2919 | LHW 904 | 3262 | LHY 961 | 3971 |
| LFM 767 | 4597 | LHN 559 | 3358 | LHN 847 | 4154 | LHT 917 | 2920 | LHW 905 | 2930 | LHY 962 | 3972 |
| LFM 768 | 4596 | LHN 560 | 3359 | LHN 848 | 4155 | LHT 918 | 2921 | LHW 906 | 3266 | LHY 963 | 3973 |
| LFM 769 | 4604 | LHN 561 | 3360 | LHN 849 | 4156 | LHT 919 | 2922 | LHW 907 | 3263 | LHY 964 | 3974 |
| LFM 770 | 4605 | LHN 562 | 3361 | LHN 850 | 4157 | LHT 920 | 2923 | LHW 908 | 3264 | LHY 965 | 3975 |
| LFM 771 | 4606 | LHN 563 | 3364 | LHN 851 | 4158 | LHU 501 | 2924 | LHW 909 | 3265 | LHY 966 | 3976 |
| LFM 772 | 4607 | LHN 564 | 3363 | LHN 852 | 4159 | LHU 502 | 2925 | LHW 910 | 3267 | LHY 967 | 3977 |
| LFM 773 | 4608 | LHN 565 | 3362 | LHN 853 | 4160 | LHU 503 | 2926 | LHW 911 | 3268 | LHY 968 | 3978 |
| LFM 774 | 4609 | LHN 566 | 3365 | LHN 854 | 4161 | LHU 504 | 2927 | LHW 912 | 3269 | LHY 969 | 3979 |
| LFM 775 | 4610 | LHN 567 | 3366 | LHN 855 | 4162 | LHU 505 | 3259 | LHW 913 | 3270 | LHY 970 | 3980 |
| LFM 776 | 4613 | LHN 578 | 3377 | LHN 856 | 4163 | LHU 506 | 3258 | LHW 914 | 3273 | LHY 971 | 3981 |
| LFM 777 | 4611 | LHN 579 | 3378 | LHN 857 | 4164 | LHU 507 | 3257 | LHW 915 | 3271 | LHY 972 | 4212 |
| LFM 778 | 4612 | LHN 580 | 3381 | LHN 858 | 4165 | LHU 508 | 3256 | LHW 916 | 3272 | LHY 973 | 4213 |
| LFM 779 | 4614 | LHN 581 | 3379 | LHN 859 | 4166 | LHU 509 | 3255 | LHW 917 | 2931 | LHY 974 | 4214 |
| LFM 780 | 4616 | LHN 582 | 3380 | LHN 860 | 4167 | LHU 510 | 3254 | LHW 918 | 3274 | LHY 975 | 4215 |
| LFM 781 | 4616 | LHN 583 | 3383 | LHN 861 | 4168 | LHU 511 | 2479 | LHW 919 | 3275 | LHY 976 | 4216 |
| LFM 782 | 4617 | LHN 584 | 3382 | LHN 862 | 4169 | LHU 512 | 2480 | LHW 920 | 2932 | LHY 977 | 4217 |
| LFM 783 | 4619 | LHN 585 | 3384 | LHN 863 | 4170 | LHU 513 | 2485 | LHW 921 | 3276 | LHY 978 | 4218 |
| LFM 784 | 4618 | LHN 586 | 3385 | LHN 864 | 4171 | LHU 514 | 2486 | LHW 922 | 2933 | LHY 979 | 4219 |
| LFM 785 | 4620 | LHN 587 | 3386 | LHN 865 | 4172 | LHU 515 | 2481 | LHW 923 | 3278 | LHY 980 | 4220 |
| LFM 786 | 4621 | LHN 802 | 4109 | LHN 866 | 4173 | LHU 516 | 2482 | LHW 924 | 3277 | LHY 981 | 4221 |
| LFM 787 | 4622 | LHN 803 | 4110 | LHN 867 | 4174 | LHU 517 | 2483 | LHW 925 | 3279 | LHY 982 | 4222 |
| LFM 788 | 4623 | LHN 804 | 4111 | LHN 868 | 4175 | LHU 518 | 2484 | LHW 926 | 3281 | LHY 983 | 4223 |
| LFM 789 | 4624 | LHN 805 | 4113 | LHN 869 | 4176 | LHU 519 | 2487 | LHW 927 | 3280 | LHY 984 | 4224 |
| LFM 790 | 4625 | LHN 806 | 4114 | LHN 913 | 3642 | LHU 520 | 2798 | LHW 928 | 3285 | LHY 985 | 4225 |
| LFM 811 | 4979 | LHN 807 | 4115 | LHN 914 | 3643 | LHU 521 | 2792 | LHW 929 | 3282 | LHY 986 | 4226 |
| LFN 743 | 4602 | LHN 808 | 4116 | LHN 915 | 3644 | LHU 522 | 2793 | LHW 930 | 3283 | LHY 987 | 4227 |
| LHN 101 | 2701 | LHN 809 | 4117 | LHN 916 | 3645 | LHU 523 | 2799 | LHW 931 | 3284 | LHY 988 | 4228 |
| LHN 102 | 2702 | LHN 810 | 4118 | LHN 917 | 3646 | LHU 524 | 2794 | LHY 925 | 3827 | LHY 989 | 4229 |
| LHN 103 | 2703 | LHN 811 | 4112 | LHN 918 | 3647 | LHU 525 | 2795 | LHY 926 | 3828 | LHY 990 | 3982 |
| LHN 104 | 2704 | LHN 812 | 4119 | LHN 919 | 3648 | LHU 526 | 2800 | LHY 927 | 3829 | LHY 991 | 3983 |
| LHN 305 | 2705 | LHN 813 | 4120 | LHN 920 | 3649 | LHU 527 | 2801 | LHY 928 | 3830 | LHY 992 | 3984 |
| LHN 306 | 2706 | LHN 814 | 4121 | LHN 921 | 3650 | LHU 528 | 2796 | LHY 929 | 3831 | LHY 993 | 3985 |
| LHN 307 | 2707 | LHN 815 | 4122 | LHN 922 | 3651 | LHU 529 | 2797 | LHY 930 | 3832 | LHY 994 | 3986 |
| LHN 308 | 2708 | LHN 816 | 4123 | LHN 923 | 3652 | LHU 530 | 2802 | LHY 931 | 3833 | LHY 995 | 3987 |
| LHN 309 | 2709 | LHN 817 | 4124 | LHN 924 | 3653 | LHU 531 | 2803 | LHY 932 | 3834 | LHY 996 | 3988 |
| LHN 310 | 2710 | LHN 818 | 4125 | LHN 925 | 3654 | LHU 971 | 2810 | LHY 933 | 3835 | LHY 997 | 3989 |
| LHN 311 | 2711 | LHN 819 | 4126 | LHN 926 | 3655 | LHU 972 | 2804 | LHY 934 | 3836 | LHY 998 | 3990 |
| LHN 312 | 2712 | LHN 820 | 4127 | LHN 927 | 3656 | LHU 973 | 2807 | LHY 935 | 3837 | LHY 999 | 3991 |
| LHN 344 | 3296 | LHN 821 | 4128 | LHN 928 | 3657 | LHU 974 | 2805 | LHY 936 | 3838 | LKT 984 | 4079 |
| LHN 345 | 3297 | LHN 822 | 4129 | LHN 929 | 3658 | LHU 975 | 2806 | LHY 937 | 3839 | LKT 985 | 4081 |
| LHN 346 | 3294 | LHN 823 | 4130 | LHN 930 | 3659 | LHU 976 | 2808 | LHY 938 | 3840 | LKT 986 | 4080 |
| LHN 347 | 3295 | LHN 824 | 4131 | LHN 931 | 3660 | LHU 977 | 2809 | LHY 939 | 3841 | LKT 987 | 4083 |
| LHN 348 | 3298 | LHN 825 | 4132 | LHN 932 | 3661 | LHU 978 | 2811 | LHY 940 | 3842 | LKT 988 | 4082 |
| LHN 349 | 3299 | LHN 826 | 4133 | LHN 933 | 3662 | LHU 979 | 2812 | LHY 941 | 3843 | LKT 989 | 4084 |
| LHN 350 | 3300 | LHN 827 | 4134 | LHN 934 | 3663 | LHU 980 | 2813 | LHY 942 | 3844 | LKT 990 | 4085 |
| LHN 351 | 3301 | LHN 828 | 4136 | LHN 935 | 3664 | LHU 981 | 2814 | LHY 943 | 3845 | LKT 991 | 4086 |
| LHN 352 | 3302 | LHN 829 | 4135 | LHN 936 | 3665 | LHU 982 | 2815 | LHY 944 | 3846 | LKT 992 | 4087 |
| LHN 353 | 3303 | LHN 830 | 4137 | LHN 937 | 3666 | LHU 983 | 2816 | LHY 945 | 3848 | LKT 993 | 4088 |
| LHN 354 | 3304 | LHN 831 | 4138 | LHT 901 | 1895 | LHU 984 | 2817 | LHY 946 | 3847 | LKT 994 | 4089 |
| LHN 355 | 3305 | LHN 832 | 4139 | LHT 902 | 2176 | LHU 985 | 2818 | LHY 947 | 3849 | LKT 995 | 4090 |
| LHN 368 | 3367 | LHN 833 | 4140 | LHT 903 | 2177 | LHU 986 | 2819 | LHY 948 | 3850 | LKT 996 | 4091 |

| | | | | | | | | | | | | | |
|---|---|---|---|---|---|---|---|---|---|---|---|---|---|
| LKT 997 | 4092 | LTA 826 | 4430 | MHW 979 | 4232 | MPU 29 | 2193 | NAE 40 | 4487 | NHN 118 | 4928 | | |
| LKT 998 | 4093 | LTA 827 | 4431 | MHW 980 | 4233 | MPU 30 | 2194 | NAE 41 | 4488 | NHN 119 | 4929 | | |
| LKT 999 | 4094 | LTA 828 | 4432 | MHW 981 | 4234 | MPU 31 | 2195 | NAE 42 | 4489 | NHN 120 | 4751 | | |
| LNG 261 | 4515 | LTA 829 | 4434 | MHW 982 | 4235 | MPU 32 | 2196 | NAE 43 | 4490 | NHN 121 | 4752 | | |
| LNG 262 | 4516 | LTA 830 | 4433 | MHW 983 | 4236 | MPU 33 | 2197 | NAE 44 | 4491 | NHN 122 | 4753 | | |
| LNG 263 | 4517 | LTA 831 | 4436 | MHW 984 | 4237 | MPU 34 | 2198 | NAE 45 | 4492 | NHN123 | 4754 | | |
| LNG 264 | 4518 | LTA 832 | 4436 | MHW 985 | 4238 | MPU 35 | 2199 | NAE 46 | 4493 | NHN 124 | 4755 | | |
| LNG 265 | 4519 | LTA 859 | 4990 | MHW 986 | 4239 | MPU 36 | 2249 | NAE 47 | 4494 | NHN 125 | 4756 | | |
| LNG 276 | 4281 | LTA 860 | 4991 | MHW 987 | 4240 | MPU 37 | 2252 | NAE 48 | 4495 | NHN 126 | 4757 | | |
| LNG 277 | 4282 | LTA 861 | 4992 | MHW 988 | 3992 | MPU 38 | 2250 | NAE 49 | 4496 | NHN 127 | 4758 | | |
| LNG 278 | 4283 | LTA 862 | 4993 | MHW 989 | 3993 | MPU 39 | 2253 | NAE 50 | 4497 | NHN 128 | 4759 | | |
| LNG 279 | 4284 | LTA 863 | 4994 | MHW 990 | 3994 | MPU 40 | 2251 | NAE 51 | 4498 | NHN 129 | 4760 | | |
| LNG 280 | 4285 | LTA 887 | 3449 | MHW 991 | 3995 | MPU 41 | 2254 | NAE 52 | 4499 | NHN 130 | 4761 | | |
| LNG 281 | 4286 | LTA 927 | 4997 | MHW 992 | 3996 | MPU 42 | 2255 | NAE 53 | 4500 | NHN 131 | 4762 | | |
| LNG 282 | 4287 | LTA 928 | 4998 | MHW 993 | 3997 | MPU 43 | 2256 | NAE 54 | 4501 | NHN 132 | 4763 | | |
| LNG 283 | 4288 | LTA 929 | 4999 | MHW 994 | 3998 | MPU 44 | 2258 | NAE 55 | 4502 | NHN 133 | 4764 | | |
| LNG 284 | 4289 | LTA 936 | 4346 | MHW 995 | 3999 | MPU 45 | 2257 | NAE 56 | 4503 | NHN 134 | 4765 | | |
| LNG 285 | 4290 | LTA 937 | 4344 | MHW 996 | 4001 | MPU 46 | 2259 | NAE 57 | 4504 | NHN 135 | 4766 | | |
| LNG 286 | 4291 | LTA 938 | 4435 | MHW 997 | 4002 | MPU 47 | 2260 | NAE 58 | 4505 | NHN 136 | 4767 | | |
| LNG 287 | 4292 | LTA 939 | 4347 | MHW 998 | 4000 | MPU 48 | 2261 | NAE 59 | 4506 | NHN 137 | 4768 | | |
| LNG 288 | 4293 | LTA 940 | 4348 | MHW 999 | 4003 | MPU 49 | 2294 | NAE 60 | 4507 | NHN 138 | 4769 | | |
| LNG 289 | 4294 | LTA 941 | 4349 | MKN 201 | 4868 | MPU 50 | 2295 | NAE 61 | 4508 | NHN 139 | 4770 | | |
| LNG 290 | 4295 | LTA 942 | 4360 | MKN 202 | 4864 | MPU 51 | 2296 | NAE 62 | 4509 | NHN 140 | 4771 | | |
| LNG 291 | 4296 | LTA 943 | 4361 | MKN 203 | 4865 | MPU 52 | 2297 | NAE 63 | 4510 | NHN 141 | 4772 | | |
| LNG 292 | 4297 | LTA 944 | 4350 | MKN 204 | 4866 | MPU 53 | 2298 | NAE 64 | 4511 | NHN 142 | 4773 | | |
| LNG 293 | 4298 | LTA 945 | 4351 | MKN 205 | 4867 | NAE 1 | 4905 | NAE 65 | 4512 | NHN 143 | 4774 | | |
| LNG 294 | 4299 | LTA 946 | 4352 | MKN 206 | 4863 | NAE 2 | 4906 | NAE 66 | 4513 | NHN 144 | 4775 | | |
| LNG 295 | 4300 | LTA 947 | 4353 | MKN 207 | 4869 | NAE 3 | 4907 | NAE 67 | 4514 | NHN 145 | 4776 | | |
| LNG 296 | 4301 | LTA 948 | 4354 | MKN 208 | 4870 | NAE 4 | 4908 | NHN 82 | 4177 | NHN 146 | 4777 | | |
| LNG 297 | 4302 | LTA 949 | 4355 | MKN 209 | 4871 | NAE 5 | 4909 | NHN 83 | 4178 | NHN 147 | 4778 | | |
| LNG 298 | 4303 | LTA 950 | 4356 | MKN 210 | 4872 | NAE 6 | 4910 | NHN 84 | 4179 | NHN 148 | 4779 | | |
| LNG 299 | 4304 | LTA 951 | 4357 | MKN 211 | 4873 | NAE 7 | 4911 | NHN 85 | 4181 | NHN 149 | 4780 | | |
| LNG 300 | 4305 | LTA 952 | 4358 | MKN 212 | 4874 | NAE 8 | 4912 | NHN 86 | 4182 | NHN 150 | 4781 | | |
| LNG 724 | 4662 | LTA 953 | 4359 | MKN 213 | 4875 | NAE 9 | 4913 | NHN 87 | 4180 | NHN 151 | 4782 | | |
| LNG 725 | 4663 | LTA 960 | 4995 | MKN 214 | 4876 | NAE 10 | 4914 | NHN 88 | 4183 | NHN 152 | 4783 | | |
| LNG 726 | 4664 | LTA 961 | 4996 | MKN 215 | 4877 | NAE 11 | 4458 | NHN 89 | 4188 | NHN 153 | 4784 | | |
| LNG 727 | 4665 | LTA 962 | 5000 | MPU 1 | 1611 | NAE 12 | 4459 | NHN 90 | 4184 | NHN 154 | 4785 | | |
| LNG 728 | 4666 | MAH 744 | 4255 | MPU 2 | 1612 | NAE 13 | 4460 | NHN 91 | 4185 | NHN 155 | 4786 | | |
| LNG 729 | 4667 | MFM 662 | 4980 | MPU 3 | 1613 | NAE 14 | 4461 | NHN 92 | 4186 | NHN 156 | 4787 | | |
| LNG 730 | 4668 | MFM 663 | 4981 | MPU 4 | 1614 | NAE 15 | 4462 | NHN 93 | 4187 | NHN 157 | 4788 | | |
| LNG 731 | 4669 | MFM 664 | 4982 | MPU 5 | 1615 | NAE 16 | 4463 | NHN 94 | 4189 | NHN 158 | 4789 | | |
| LTA 723 | 3448 | MFM 665 | 4626 | MPU 6 | 1616 | NAE 17 | 4464 | NHN 95 | 4190 | NHN 159 | 4790 | | |
| LTA 767 | 4850 | MFM 666 | 4627 | MPU 7 | 1617 | NAE 18 | 4465 | NHN 96 | 4191 | NHN 160 | 4791 | | |
| LTA 768 | 4851 | MFM 667 | 4628 | MPU 8 | 1618 | NAE 19 | 4466 | NHN 97 | 4192 | NHN 161 | 4792 | | |
| LTA 769 | 4852 | MFM 668 | 4629 | MPU 9 | 1619 | NAE 20 | 4467 | NHN 98 | 4193 | NHN 162 | 4793 | | |
| LTA 770 | 4853 | MFM 669 | 4630 | MPU 10 | 1620 | NAE 21 | 4468 | NHN 99 | 4194 | NHN 163 | 4794 | | |
| LTA 808 | 4414 | MFM 670 | 4631 | MPU 11 | 1621 | NAE 22 | 4469 | NHN 100 | 4741 | NHN 164 | 4795 | | |
| LTA 809 | 4415 | MFM 671 | 4632 | MPU 12 | 1622 | NAE 23 | 4470 | NHN 101 | 4742 | NHN 165 | 4796 | | |
| LTA 810 | 4417 | MFM 672 | 4633 | MPU 13 | 1623 | NAE 24 | 4471 | NHN 102 | 4743 | NHN 166 | 4797 | | |
| LTA 811 | 4416 | MFM 673 | 4634 | MPU 14 | 1624 | NAE 25 | 4472 | NHN 103 | 4744 | NHN 167 | 4798 | | |
| LTA 812 | 4418 | MFM 674 | 4635 | MPU 15 | 1626 | NAE 26 | 4473 | NHN 104 | 4745 | NHN 168 | 4799 | | |
| LTA 813 | 4419 | MFM 675 | 4636 | MPU 16 | 1625 | NAE 27 | 4474 | NHN 105 | 4746 | NHN 169 | 4800 | | |
| LTA 814 | 4421 | MFM 676 | 4637 | MPU 17 | 1627 | NAE 28 | 4475 | NHN 106 | 4747 | NHN 170 | 4801 | | |
| LTA 815 | 4420 | MFM 677 | 4638 | MPU 18 | 1628 | NAE 29 | 4476 | NHN 107 | 4748 | NHN 171 | 4802 | | |
| LTA 816 | 4422 | MFM 678 | 4639 | MPU 19 | 1629 | NAE 30 | 4477 | NHN108 | 4749 | NHN 901 | 4523 | | |
| LTA 817 | 4423 | MFM 679 | 4640 | MPU 20 | 1630 | NAE 31 | 4478 | NHN 109 | 4750 | NHN 902 | 4524 | | |
| LTA 818 | 4424 | MFM 680 | 4641 | MPU 21 | 1631 | NAE 32 | 4479 | NHN 110 | 4920 | NHN 903 | 4525 | | |
| LTA 819 | 4425 | MFM 681 | 4642 | MPU 22 | 1632 | NAE 33 | 4480 | NHN 111 | 4921 | NHN 904 | 4526 | | |
| LTA 820 | 4437 | MFM 682 | 4643 | MPU 23 | 1633 | NAE 34 | 4481 | NHN 112 | 4922 | NHN 905 | 4527 | | |
| LTA 821 | 4438 | MFM 683 | 4644 | MPU 24 | 1634 | NAE 35 | 4482 | NHN 113 | 4923 | NHN 906 | 4528 | | |
| LTA 822 | 4426 | MFM 684 | 4645 | MPU 25 | 1635 | NAE 36 | 4483 | NHN 114 | 4924 | NHN 907 | 4532 | | |
| LTA 823 | 4427 | MFM 685 | 4646 | MPU 26 | 2190 | NAE 37 | 4484 | NHN 115 | 4925 | NHN 908 | 4529 | | |
| LTA 824 | 4428 | MHW 977 | 4230 | MPU 27 | 2191 | NAE 38 | 4485 | NHN 116 | 4926 | NHN 909 | 4530 | | |
| LTA 825 | 4429 | MHW 978 | 4231 | MPU 28 | 2192 | NAE 39 | 4486 | NHN 117 | 4927 | NHN 910 | 4531 | | |

| | | | | | | | | | |
|---|---|---|---|---|---|---|---|---|---|
| NHN 911 | 4533 | NNO 106 | 2565 | ONO 53 | 3544 | ONO 72 | 3563 | ONO 995 | 4670 | RHK 125 | 4679 |
| NHN 912 | 4534 | NNO 107 | 2566 | ONO 54 | 3545 | ONO 73 | 3564 | ONO 996 | 4671 | RHK 126 | 4680 |
| NHN 913 | 4536 | NNO 108 | 2942 | ONO 55 | 3546 | ONO 74 | 3565 | ONO 997 | 4672 | RHK 127 | 4681 |
| NHN 914 | 4535 | NNO 109 | 2943 | ONO 56 | 3547 | ONO 75 | 3566 | ONO 998 | 4673 | RHK 128 | 4682 |
| NHN 915 | 4537 | NNO 110 | 2944 | ONO 57 | 3548 | ONO 76 | 3567 | ONO 999 | 4674 | RHK 129 | 4683 |
| NHU 2 | 4978 | OJB 108 | 2396 | ONO 58 | 3549 | ONO 77 | 3568 | PTW 101 | 4062 | RHK 131 | 4685 |
| NNO 93 | 2554 | OKC 4464 | 2407 | ONO 59 | 3550 | ONO 78 | 3569 | PTW 102 | 4063 | RHK 132 | 4686 |
| NNO 94 | 2555 | ONO 41 | 4042 | ONO 60 | 3551 | ONO 79 | 3570 | PTW 103 | 4064 | RHK 133 | 4687 |
| NNO 95 | 2556 | ONO 42 | 4043 | ONO 61 | 3552 | ONO 80 | 3571 | PTW 104 | 4065 | RHK 134 | 4688 |
| NNO 96 | 2552 | ONO 43 | 4044 | ONO 62 | 3553 | ONO 81 | 4052 | PTW 105 | 4066 | RHK 135 | 4689 |
| NNO 97 | 2553 | ONO 44 | 4045 | ONO 63 | 3554 | ONO 82 | 4053 | PTW 106 | 4915 | RHK 136 | 4690 |
| NNO 98 | 2557 | ONO 45 | 4046 | ONO 64 | 3555 | ONO 83 | 4054 | PTW 107 | 4916 | RPU 521 | 4306 |
| NNO 99 | 2558 | ONO 46 | 4047 | ONO 65 | 3556 | ONO 988 | 4055 | PTW 108 | 4917 | RPU 522 | 4307 |
| NNO 100 | 2559 | ONO 47 | 4048 | ONO 66 | 3558 | ONO 989 | 4056 | PTW 109 | 4918 | RPU 523 | 4308 |
| NNO 101 | 2560 | ONO 48 | 4049 | ONO 67 | 3557 | ONO 990 | 4057 | PTW 110 | 4919 | RPU 524 | 4309 |
| NNO 102 | 2561 | ONO 49 | 4050 | ONO 68 | 3559 | ONO 991 | 4058 | RHK 121 | 4675 | RPU 525 | 4310 |
| NNO 103 | 2562 | ONO 50 | 4051 | ONO 69 | 3560 | ONO 992 | 4059 | RHK 122 | 4676 | RPU 526 | 4311 |
| NNO 104 | 2563 | ONO 51 | 3542 | ONO 70 | 3561 | ONO 993 | 4060 | RHK 123 | 4677 | RPU 527 | 4312 |
| NNO 105 | 2564 | ONO 52 | 3543 | ONO 71 | 3562 | ONO 994 | 4061 | RHK 124 | 4678 | | |

# HISTORICAL COUNTY CODES

GOV      Government Department

| Code | County | Code | County |
|---|---|---|---|
| AD | Aberdeenshire | KK | Kirkcudbrightshire |
| AH | Armagh | KN | Kesteven division of Lincolnshire |
| AL | Argyllshire | KS | Kinross-shire |
| AM | Antrim | KT | Kent |
| AR | Ayrshire | LA | Lancashire |
| AS | Angus | LC | Lincoln (City) |
| AY | Isle of Anglesey | LE | Leicestershire |
| BC | Brecknockshire | LI | Lindsey division of Lincolnshire |
| BD | Bedfordshire | LK | Lanarkshire |
| BE | Berkshire | LN | London Postal area |
| BF | Banffshire | LY | Londonderry |
| BK | Buckinghamshire | ME | Merionethshire |
| BU | Buteshire | MH | Monmouthshire |
| BW | Berwickshire | MN | Midlothian |
| CG | Cardiganshire | MO | Montgomeryshire |
| CH | Cheshire | MR | Morayshire |
| CI | Channel Islands | MX | Middlesex |
| CK | Clackmannanshire | ND | Northumberland |
| CM | Cambridgeshire | NG | Nottinghamshire |
| CN | Caernarvonshire | NK | Norfolk |
| CO | Cornwall | NN | Nairnshire |
| CR | Carmarthenshire | NO | Northamptonshire |
| CS | Caithness | NR | North Riding of Yorkshire |
| CU | Cumberland | OK | Orkney Islands |
| DB | Dunbartonshire | OX | Oxfordshire |
| DE | Derbyshire | PB | Peebles-shire |
| DF | Dumfries-shire | PE | Pembrokeshire |
| DH | Denbighshire | PH | Perthshire |
| DM | County Durham | RD | Rutland |
| DN | Devon | RH | Roxburghshire |
| DO | Down | RR | Radnorshire |
| DT | Dorset | RW | Renfrewshire |
| EI | Eire | RY | Ross-shire & Cromarty |
| EK | East Suffolk | SD | Shetland Islands |
| EL | East Lothian | SH | Shropshire |
| ER | East Riding of Yorkshire | SI | Selkirkshire |
| ES | East Sussex | SN | Stirlingshire |
| EX | Essex | SO | Somerset |
| EY | Isle of Ely | SP | Soke of Peterborough |
| FE | Fife | SR | Surrey |
| FH | Fermanagh | ST | Staffordshire |
| FT | Flintshire | SU | Sutherland |
| GG | Glamorgan | TY | Tyrone |
| GL | Gloucestershire | WF | West Suffolk |
| HA | Hampshire | WI | Wiltshire |
| HD | Holland division of Lincolnshire | WK | Warwickshire |
| HN | Huntingdonshire | WL | West Lothian |
| HR | Herefordshire | WN | Wigtownshire |
| HT | Hertfordshire | WO | Worcestershire |
| IM | Isle of Man | WR | West Riding of Yorkshire |
| IV | Inverness | WS | West Sussex |
| IW | Isle of Wight | WT | Westmorland |
| KE | Kincardineshire | YK | York (City) |

Note: A 'G' prefix (eg GLA) indicates the vehicle had been converted to goods (eg lorry or van) and the operator was a goods operator (in this case, in Lancashire).